Dervla Murphy was born in Ireland in 1931, to a family involved in the Irish Republican movement. She was educated at the Ursuline Convent in Waterford until she was fourteen, when she left to keep house for her father and to nurse her mother who had been invalided by arthritis. Dervla did this for sixteen years with occasional breaks bicycling across Europe. Her mother's death left her free to go farther afield and in 1963 she cycled to India. Here she worked with Tibetan refugee children before returning home after a year to write her first two books. Dervla's first book, *Full Tilt: Ireland to India with a Bicycle*, was published in 1965. Over twenty other titles have followed. Dervla has won worldwide praise for her writing and has been described as a 'travel legend' and 'the first lady of Irish cycling'. Now in her eighties, she continues to travel around the world and remains passionate about politics, conservation, bicycling and beer.

Praise for *Full Tilt*

'She avoided wolves (animal and human), floods, robbery, had three ribs broken in a brawl in an Afghan bus; waded across an ice torrent, hugging a cow…suffered extremes of heat and cold, ate everything, liked almost everybody.'

—*Homes and Gardens*

'This vivid journal…would have delighted Cervantes with its almost incredible surprises: a valley full of birds the size of butterflies and butterflies as big as robins; a village where the cattle eat apricots and the villagers eat clover… Somewhere between Kabul and Jalalabad, she thought she was dreaming when she awoke from a roadside nap to find that nomads had raised a tent over her to shield her from the sun.'

—*The New Yorker*

'I don't know when I've enjoyed the account of a journey more. A great part of the enchantment of her book is that it is so good humoured and so funny. I laughed…and learned a good deal…one follows her with pleasure…a brave, intelligent, rare and amusing human being.'

—Margaret Lane

'A journey fraught with incalculable hardships and perils. It is unexpected, but then everything Dervla Murphy does is unexpected…an enchantment that holds the reader as engrossed as would an exciting thriller.'

—*Irish Independent*

'Warmly described, and with a lack of self-regard that immediately endears her to the reader.'

—*Sunday Times*

'Punctures, broken ribs, hornets and scorpions notwithstanding, it was a high old time between Miss Murphy and her Islamic hosts… her book is sensible, warm-hearted, unfinicky.'

—*The Observer*

Full Tilt

Ireland to India with a Bicycle

DERVLA
MURPHY

SPEAKING
TIGER

SPEAKING TIGER PUBLISHING PVT. LTD
4281/4 Ansari Road, Daryaganj,
New Delhi – 110002, India

First published in England by John Murray (Publishers) Ltd 1965
Published by Eland Publishing Limited 2010

First published in India in paperback by Speaking Tiger 2018

ISBN: 978-93-87693-16-6
eISBN: 978-93-87693-17-3

For sale in South Asia only

10 9 8 7 6 5 4 3 2 1

Printed at: Printworks, Delhi-92

To the peoples of
Afghanistan and Pakistan,
with gratitude for their hospitality,
with admiration for their principles
and with affection for those who befriended me

Contents

Foreword

On my tenth birthday a bicycle and an atlas coincided as presents and a few days later I decided to cycle to India. I've never forgotten the exact spot on a hill near my home at Lismore, County Waterford, where the decision was made and it seemed to me then, as it still seems to me now, a logical decision, based on the discoveries that cycling was a most satisfactory method of transport and that (excluding the USSR for political reasons) the way to India offered fewer watery obstacles than any other destination at a similar distance.

However, I was a cunning child so I kept my ambition to myself, thus avoiding the tolerant amusement it would have provoked among my elders. I did not want to be soothingly assured that this was a passing whim because I was quite confident that one day I *would* cycle to India.

That was at the beginning of December 1941, and on 14 January 1963, I started to cycle from Dunkirk towards Delhi.

The preparations had been simple; one of the advantages of cycling is that it automatically prevents a journey from becoming an Expedition. I already possessed an admirable Armstrong Cadet man's bicycle named Rozinante, but always known as 'Roz'. By a coincidence I had bought her on 14 January 1961, so our journey started on her second birthday. This was ideal; we were by then a happy team, having already covered thousands of miles together, yet she was young enough to be dependable. The only preparation Roz needed was the removal of her three-speed derailleur gear, which I reckoned would be too sensitive to survive Asian roads. Apart from the normal accessories – saddle-bag, bell, lamp and pump – she carried only pannier-bag holders on either side of the back wheel. Unloaded she weighs thirty-seven pounds and at the start of the journey she was taking twenty-eight pounds of kit while I carried another six pounds in a small knapsack. (A list of kit is given on page 231.) Before leaving Ireland, four spare tyres had been posted ahead to various British Embassies, Consulates and High Commissions en route; Roz takes 27½" x 1¼" tyres, which are not a standard measurement abroad.

In London, at the end of November 1962, I obtained without difficulty visas for Yugoslavia and Bulgaria; I planned to get my visas for Persia in Istanbul and for Afghanistan in Teheran. During the same visit to London I endured vaccinations and inoculations for smallpox, cholera, typhoid and yellow-fever – the latter in case I decided to return from India via Africa.

Most of the following month was spent bending over maps bought through the AA in Dublin, working out the distances between towns which had intoxicatingly improbable names. I calculated that it was 4,445 miles from Dunkirk to Peshawar, and by New Year's Eve I could have told you without hesitation where I planned to be on any given date between 14 January and 14 May, when I hoped to arrive in Peshawar. The object of this exercise was to ensure that my mail – sent care of the British Council offices en route – would not miss me; nor did it, despite many inevitable changes in my original plans.

In the intervals between mapping I took myself off to remote areas in the mountains around Lismore and practised firing and reloading my ·25, the purchase of which had recently been achieved with the full and rather awe-struck co-operation of the local police. My friends regarded this purchase as so much adolescent melodrama on my part but fortunately I ignored their criticisms and stuck to my gun, though its presence in the right-hand pocket of my slacks – where I habitually carried it to accustom myself to the presence of a loaded weapon – frightened me considerably more than it did anyone else. Yet within a month of leaving home the seemingly childish game of whipping it out of my pocket and flicking up the safety catch was fully justified.

I arrived in Delhi on 18 July 1963, almost six months after leaving Ireland. People with mathematical brains are always anxious to know exactly how many miles I had cycled by then and what my daily average was. Unfortunately gadgets for measuring mileage do not function on Asian roads, so I can only estimate vaguely that Roz and I covered about three thousand miles, including our detours to Murree and Gilgit. From this the mathematically inclined can easily calculate our average daily mileage, but their findings would be slightly misleading, because there were so many days when we did not cover even a mile together. Our shortest run was, I think, nineteen miles, and our longest 118 miles, but I reckon that our average on a normal cycling day was between seventy and eighty miles.

This is perhaps the moment to contradict the popular fallacy that a solitary woman who undertakes this sort of journey must be 'very courageous'. Epictetus put it in a nutshell when he said, 'For it is not death or hardship that is a fearful thing, but the fear of death and hardship.' And because in general the possibility of physical danger does not frighten me, courage is not required; when a man tries to rob or assault me or when I find myself, as darkness is falling, utterly exhausted and waist-deep in snow halfway up a mountain pass, then I *am* afraid – but in such circumstances it is the instinct of self-preservation, rather than courage, that takes over.

For the first two months of the trip I struggled hard to keep my four closest friends informed of my progress through letters but the effort was too much; so from Teheran onwards I adopted the diary-keeping method used by most travellers and sent instalments home whenever a reliable-looking post office appeared en route. My friends circulated these instalments amongst themselves, the last on the circuit line storing the manuscript away for future reference. This book is the 'Future Reference'.

Apart from burnishing the spelling and syntax, which are apt to suffer when one makes nightly entries whether half asleep or not, I have left the diary virtually unchanged. A few very personal or very topical comments or allusions have been excised, but the temptation to make myself sound more learned than I am, by gleaning facts and figures from an encyclopaedia and inserting them in appropriate places, has been resisted. For this reason the narrative which follows will be seen to suffer from statistic-deficiency; it only contains such information as any traveller might happen to pick up from day to day along my route.

After arriving in Delhi I worked for six months with the Tibetan refugees in northern India and then enjoyed a few more treks with Roz in the Himalayas and in south-west Nepal, before submitting to the degradation of flying home on 23 February 1964, with a dismantled Roz by my side as 'personal effects'.

My thanks go in many directions: to the British and American consular officials in those countries where Ireland is not diplomatically represented, who adopted and cared for me as though I were their own; to the scores of individuals and families in every country on my route whose boundless hospitality taught me that for all the horrible chaos of the contemporary political scene this world is full of kindness; to the chance friends I made in odd places, whose names I never knew or have forgotten but whose companionship made a sometimes lonely journey much more pleasant; and last, but certainly not least, to Daphne Pearce, who suggested the title and gave invaluable help in editing the manuscript; to Patricia Truell, who compiled the index and guided me through the ordeal of correcting my first proofs; and to my other friends in Ireland, who loyally and patiently read over 200,000 words in an execrable hand and whose interest in my experiences was both the inspiration and the reward of keeping this diary.

For my part I travel not to go anywhere, but to go. I travel for travel's sake. The great affair is to move, to feel the needs and hitches of our life more nearly, to come down off the feather-bed of civilization and find the globe granite underfoot and strewn with cutting flints.

ROBERT LOUIS STEVENSON

FRO
OSLO
DUBLIN
Lismore
LONDON
Dunkirk
BERLIN
WARSAW
MOSCOW
PARIS
PRAGUE
VIENNA
Budapest
Grenoble
Turin
Venice
Ljubljana
Nova Gorizia
Zagreb
BUCHAREST
BELGRADE
Cuprija
Pirot
SOFIA
LISBON
ROME
CAI
SCALE
0
250
500
750
1000 Miles
0
400
800
1200
1600 Kilometres

RELAND TO
INDIA
Gilgit
Rawalpindi
Peshawar
Lahore
Sirhind
DELHI
Bulola
KABUL
Ghazni
Meshed
Nishapur
Herat
Kalat-i-Gilzai
Sabzevar
Ghurion
Khandahar
Shahrud
Dogubayzit
Tabriz
Ardebil
TEHERAN
Deh-Namak
BAGHDAD

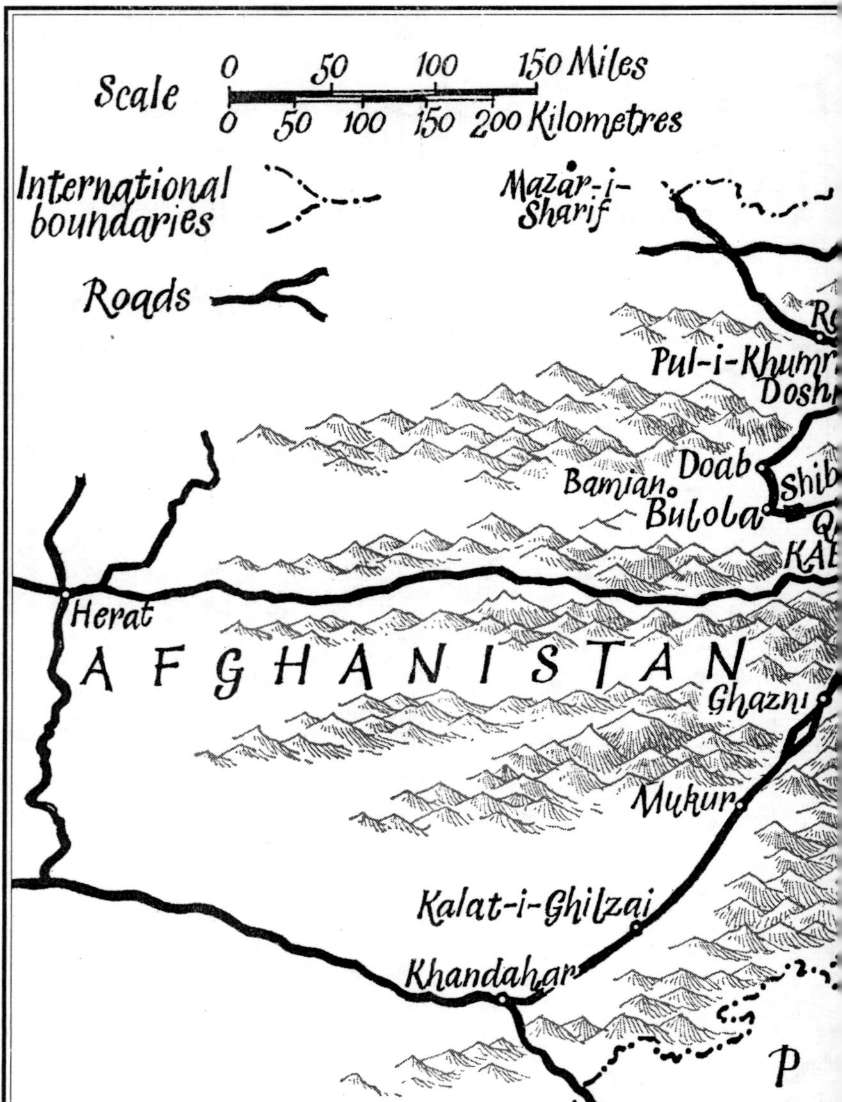

Scale
0 50 100 150 Miles
0 50 100 150 200 Kilometres
International boundaries
Roads
Mazar-i-Sharif
Doab
Bamian
Bulola
Herat
AFGHANISTAN
Ghazni
Mukur
Kalat-i-Ghilzai
Khandahar

Rakaposhi
Gupis
Gakuch
Sher Quila
Gilgit
Chitral
Chilas
Babusar
Nanga Parbat
Saidu Shariff
Kagan
Malakand Pass
Muzafferabad
Landi Khotal
Mardan
Abbottabad
Nowshera
Murree
KASHMIR
Tangi Sharo Gorge
Peshawar
Wah
Rawalpindi
Amritsar
Lahore
ISTAN
INDIA

Introduction to the Journey

DUNKIRK TO TEHERAN

I had planned a route to India through France, Italy, Yugoslavia, Bulgaria, Turkey, Persia, Afghanistan and Pakistan. Departure Day was to have been 7 January 1963, but by then the freak weather of that year had reached even Ireland and I postponed 'D-Day' for a week, innocently supposing that these conditions 'could not go on'. But of course they did go on, and in my impatience to be off I decided that to postpone departure from week to week would not be practical – though in retrospect I realised that it would have been a lot more practical than heading for Central Europe during the coldest winter in eighty years.

I shall never forget that dark ice-bound morning when I began to cycle east from Dunkirk; to have the fulfilment of a twenty-one-year-old ambition apparently within one's grasp can be quite disconcerting. This was a moment I had thought about so often that when I actually found myself living through it I felt as though some favourite scene from a novel had come, incredibly, to life. However, within a few weeks my journey had degenerated from a happy-go-lucky cycle trek to a grim struggle for progress by *any* means along roads long lost beneath snow and ice.

At first my disappointment was acute, but I had set out to enjoy myself by seeing the world, not to make or break any record, so I soon became adjusted to these conditions, which led to quite a few interesting adventures. Also, I was aware of 'seeing the world' in circumstances unique to my generation. Should I survive to the end of this century it will be impressive to recall that I crossed the breadth of Europe in the winter of 1963, when every humdrum detail of daily life was made tensely dramatic by the weather and going shopping became a scaled-down Expedition to the Antarctic. It was neat hell at the time – I cycled up to the Rouen Youth Hostel with a quarter-inch icicle firmly attached to my nose and more than once the agony of frozen fingers made me weep rather uncharacteristically – yet it seemed a reasonably good exchange for the satisfaction of cycling all the way to India.

I give full marks to Italy for the superb efficiency with which her main northern roads were kept clear during that January. Having been compelled to take a train from Grenoble to Turin, across the Alps, I found myself able to cycle, and enjoy it, almost all the way to Nova Gorizia, through a deserted and impeccably beautiful Venice.

At this bisected frontier town of Nova Gorizia the formalities for being admitted into Yugoslavia seemed diabolically complicated. Repeatedly I was shuttled back and forth through the darkness from Police to Customs Officers; then, while innumerable forms were being completed in triplicate, I stood shivering outside warm offices, trying to explain why I was so improbably entering Yugoslavia with a bicycle on 28 January. And every time I took off a glove to sign yet another document the bitter wind seared my hand like caustic acid.

Suddenly a policeman shouted to someone in another room and a tall, rugged-featured woman, wearing Customs Officer's uniform, appeared beside me. I stared at her in horror, only then remembering that my automatic lay in the right-hand pocket of my slacks, where the most casual search would at once detect a sinister hard object. In the stress and strain of searching Gorizia for the open frontier post (there were four in all, but three were closed to tourists) I had quite forgotten my ingenious scheme for concealing the weapon. So now I foresaw myself being hurled into the nearest dungeon, from which I would eventually emerge, emaciated and broken in spirit, after years of negotiations between two governments who are not, diplomatically, on speaking terms. But alarm was unnecessary. The formidable female took one quick look at my intricately laden bicycle, my knapsack with its protruding loaf of bread and my scruffy self. Then she burst into good-humoured laughter – of which one would not have believed her capable – slapped me on the back and waved me towards the frontier. It was 6.15 p.m. when I passed under the railway bridge with 'Jugoslavija' painted across it in huge letters.

Two miles from the frontier, having cycled along an unlighted road that leads away from Italy and then curves back, I came to Nova Gorica, the Yugoslav half of the town. Here, beneath the weak glow of a street lamp, a solitary figure was walking ahead of me. Overtaking it I saw a good-looking girl who, in reply to my questions, said, 'Yes' she spoke German, but 'No' there wasn't a cheap inn available, only the Tourist Hotel, which was very expensive. Even in the dim light my look of dismay must have been apparent, because she immediately added an invitation to come home with her for the night. As this was within my first hour of entering Slovenia I was astonished; but soon I learnt that such kindness is common form in that region.

While we walked between high blocks of workers' flats, Romana told me that she shared a room with two other typists employed in a local factory at £3 per week, but as one was away in hospital there would be plenty of space for me.

The little room, at the top of three flights of stairs, was clean and adequately furnished, though the only means of cooking was an electric ring, and the bathroom and lavatory were shared with three families living, in one room each, on the same floor. Arita, Romana's room-mate, gave me a most enthusiastic welcome and we settled down to a meal of very curious soup, concocted out of some anaemic meat broth, in which lightly whipped eggs were cooked, followed by my bread and cheese (imported from Italy) and coffee (imported from Ireland).

I found these youngsters delightful company – vivacious, perfectly mannered and intelligent. They were simply dressed and it was pleasant to see their clear-skinned faces, innocent of any make-up, and their well-groomed heads of unpermed sanely-cut hair. I noted too the impressive row of books in the little shelf by the stove – among them translations of *Dubliners, The Heart of the Matter, The Coiners, Black and Red* and *The Leopard.*

Anticipating a tough mountain ride on the following day I was relieved to find that 9.30 p.m. was bedtime, as these girls rise at 5.30 a.m. to catch the factory bus and be at work by seven o'clock.

It was a deceptively fine morning when I left Nova Gorica. The second-class but well-kept road to Ljubljana wound through a range of fissured mountains, whose lower slopes were studded with tiny villages of brown-roofed, ramshackle farmhouses, and whose upper slopes, of perpendicular bare rock, gave the valley an odd appearance, as though it had been artificially walled in from the rest of the world. Then, towards midday, as I was revelling in the still, crisp air and brilliant sunshine, a violent wind arose. Whether because of the peculiar configuration of the mountains here, or because it was one more manifestation of freakish weather, this wind blew with a force such as I had never previously encountered. Before I could adjust myself on the saddle to do battle with my new enemy it had lifted me right off Roz and deposited me on a heap of gravel by the wayside. None the worse, I remounted, but ten minutes later, despite my efforts to hold Roz on the road and myself on Roz, we were again separated, and this time I went rolling down a fifteen-foot sloping ditch, unable to get a grip on the icy bank to check my fall. I ended up on a stream which happily was frozen so solid that my impact produced not a crack in the ice. After crawling cautiously along the stream for some twenty yards, to find a way up to the road and Roz, I decided that from now on walking was the only logical means of progress.

At the valley's end my road started to climb the mountains, sweeping up and up and again up, in a series of hairpin bends that each revealed a view more wild and splendid than the last. At one such bend I was actually frightened by the power of the gale; I couldn't walk against it, and for some four or five minutes I simply stood, bent over Roz, my body braced with all its strength in the effort to hold us both on the road.

Near the top of the pass, seven miles from the valley floor, things were further complicated by the reappearance of my old enemies – packed snow and black ice underfoot. On the west side of this mountain range there had been strangely little snow (although everything that could freeze had frozen) but now, going over the pass, I was abruptly back to the too-familiar vision of a landscape completely white, each contour and angle rounded and disguised. Then yet another blizzard started, the flakes whirling round me like a host of malicious little white demons.

By now I was exhausted from the struggle uphill against the gale and the agony of frost-bitten hands and feet. My hands were too numb for me to consult the map, which in any case would probably have been ripped away by the wind or rendered illegible by the snow. Crawling along over the ice, I told myself that this was an advantage, because if no village was marked I would probably curl up by the wayside in despair.

In fact there was a tiny village, called Hr̂usevje, less than two miles ahead, and on arriving there I thanked my guardian angel, as I blundered about among piles of snow stacked four and five feet high on either side of the road, searching for something that looked like an inn. At last I saw two old men emerging from a doorway, wiping their moustaches with the backs of their hands. This looked hopeful, so I dragged Roz over a pile of snow, propped her against the wall, and entered the two-storeyed stone house.

Obviously the primary need was brandy, yet my face was so numb that I couldn't articulate one word. I merely pointed to the relevant bottle, and stood by the stove to thaw out, while a group of card-playing men stared at me with a trace of that hostility shown by all peasants in remote places to unexpected strangers. Then an old man came rushing in to inform the company that I had arrived with a bicycle – and, as I soon recovered the power of speech, friendly relations were easily established.

I now broached the subject of accommodation for the night and the landlady at once broke into excited discussions with her customers. In the middle of this the door opened again and a young woman entered. She was hailed with great relief all round, and turning to me introduced herself in English as a local social worker. She explained that tourists are not allowed to stay in any but Tourist Hotels – which meant yet another disruption of my plans, for I had intended, on crossing the frontier from expensive Italy, to settle down in some village such as Hr̂usevje and wait there, living cheaply, until weather conditions again permitted cycling.

However, *pace* Government regulations, it was obvious that this particular tourist could not now be accommodated anywhere but at the village inn. The next step was to contact the local policeman, so that he might give his blessing to the irregularity. This formality completed, I was shown up to my large room, which contained one small bed in a corner and nothing else whatever.

When I came down to eat some bread and cheese by the stove in the pub I found a young girl waiting for me – one who was to prove a true friend and who provided me with the most congenial companionship during the following days. A daughter of the local postman and postwoman, Irena was a student of psychology at Ljubljana University, and was now home for the winter vacation, that is to say, the month of January. She was due to return to Ljubljana on 31 January, and she advised me to wait at Hȓusevje until then, as the road down to the plain would be impassable after such a blizzard. She added that she would smuggle me into her room at the University Students' Hostel, where one of the five beds was vacant, thus saving me the expense of the Tourist Hotel.

For the next two days my landlady mothered me so successfully that I settled down to write as happily as though I were in my own home. Indeed, I was enthusiastically adopted by the whole locality; the men reported my arrival to their womenfolk who paid a special call at the inn to shake me by the hand, slap me on the back, tell me that I was welcome to Slovenia, and, as often as not, invite me to come and stay in their homes indefinitely.

On the 31st Roz and I left for Ljubljana in a snow-chained truck and that drive was one of the worst frustrations of the expedition. The road swept down for thirty miles through magnificent mountains and valleys and pine forests, all glittering in the sunshine as though covered in diamond-dust, yet here was I being ignominiously transported by truck. However, I could not complain of having no time to admire my surroundings, for the ice was so treacherous that it took us three hours to cover forty-five miles.

The university hostel, converted from an old convent, was such a vast building that there was little difficulty in smuggling me to Irena's room. Personally I was of the opinion that the Authorities, who had given me a warm welcome when I arrived in search of Irena, were perfectly well aware of the situation and quite happy about it, but my room-mates were obviously enjoying the conspiracy so I entered into the spirit of the thing with as much enthusiasm as my more advanced years allowed.

On the following morning Roz and I left Irena and her companions in Ljubljana, equipped with a bundle of introductions from them to Slovenes living all along our route, but after cycling about twenty miles we were again forced to get a lift by truck to Zagreb.

After a stay of four days in Zagreb I arrived in Belgrade, following a nightmarish journey by truck over the 250 miles of frozen plain which stretched with relentless white anonymity from Zagreb to the capital. During our thirty-nine hours on the road we saw not one other vehicle – fortunately for me this truck was carrying some vital, mysterious military load – and the only traffic was an occasional pony-sleigh travelling between villages. Three times the engine broke down and once, in the middle of the night, repairs took so long that by the time we were ready to start again an impassable snowdrift had formed in front of us. But the two drivers and I agreed afterwards that this was a blessing, because by the time we had dug ourselves out with spades carried for the purpose we were almost warm.

Apart from these breakdowns we never stopped, so our average speed over the ridged surface of rock-hard snow was about eight miles per hour. I remember these two Serbs with a special affection, so gruelling were the hardships which we shared and so brave was the gaiety with which they faced them.

By now I felt that I had lost my rôle of 'traveller' and become no more than a demoralised fugitive from the weather and I retain only confused, unreal impressions of Zagreb and Belgrade.

However, on the morning of my third day in Belgrade, there came a rise in temperature that not merely eased the body but relaxed the nerves. Never shall I forget the joy of standing bareheaded in my host's front garden, watching tenuous, milky clouds drifting across the blue sky; only then did I appreciate the peculiar tension imposed by the savageness of the past weeks. Yet the thaw held its own dangers. That day thick, six-foot icicles came crashing from eaves to pavements, killing at least two pedestrians in Belgrade; the streets became uncontrollable torrents, as the ten-foot walls of dirty snow which lined them gradually dwindled.

On the following morning, with the optimism of impatience, I started to cycle towards Nîs; but it had frozen again during the night and though the cold was no longer intolerable I had to admit defeat by black ice once more.

Before midday a Montenegrin driver had taken Roz and me up ten miles outside Belgrade, but at dusk we were still trying, by one road or another, to reach Nîs. In despair my companion finally decided to try a détour via a third-class mountain road of which he knew nothing. So, as darkness gathered in the deep valleys, and spread upwards to cover the wooded mountains, we slowly ascended a twisting track, its ridged surface made all the more dangerous by the beginnings of the thaw. My companion had been driving all through the night from Zagreb, his mate having been taken ill there, so I felt the greatest sympathy for him, and I attribute our next misfortune to his extreme fatigue.

At one of the bends, before I could realise what was happening, the truck had skidded off the road and was leaning at a slight angle against a sturdy and very fortunately placed tree, which probably saved us from death at the foot of the precipice.

Having reassured each other that we had received no more than minor injuries, we got out the map, which told us that a village lay about two miles away through the forest on our left. It seemed unlikely that any other traffic would appear and my companion was obviously too exhausted, and too shaken by the crash, to undertake the walk himself, so I suggested that he should write a note for me to deliver to the village policeman, explaining the situation.

It was soon after 6 p.m. when, leaving Roz on the truck, I set off along a convenient cart-track through the trees, where the snow had been packed down by sleighs collecting fire-wood. It was some fifteen minutes later when a heavy weight hurled itself at me without warning.

I stumbled, dropping the torch that I had been carrying, then recovered my balance, and found one animal hanging by its teeth from the left shoulder of my wind-cheater, another worrying at the trousers around my right ankle, and a third standing about two yards away, looking on, only its eyes visible in the starlight.

Ironically enough, I had always thought that there was something faintly comical in the idea of being devoured by wolves. It had seemed to me the sort of thing that doesn't *really* happen . . . So now, as I braced my body against the hanging weight, slipped off my glove, pulled my ·25 out of my pocket, flicked up the safety-catch and shot the first animal through the skull, I was possessed by the curious conviction that none of this was true, while at the same time all my actions were governed by sheer panic.

At the sound of the report, and as the first animal dropped to the ground, the second one released my ankle and was about to make off when I fired at him. Meanwhile the third member of the pack (if three can be said to constitute a pack) had tactfully disappeared. Retrieving the torch, I found that one bullet had got the second animal in the ribs – a fantastic fluke shot. Both animals (some authorities think they may have been wild dogs) were males, hardly as big as the average Irish sheep-dog, with dreadfully emaciated bodies.

It was when I had left the scene that the reaction set in. Also, forgetting that there was another mile and a half between me and the village, I had lavishly, and quite unnecessarily, emptied my gun, so that every real or imaginary sound made me tremble with apprehension. Walking rapidly, I dwelt with morbid fascination on the part that luck had played in my escape, and the longer I thought about this the more terrified I became, until at last the conviction that I must have gone astray prompted me to take out my compass to confirm the fact that I was still going towards the village.

When I arrived there, the policeman and his wife were having their supper of cold garlic sausage and pickled cucumbers. While the policeman was driving by sleigh to the truck his wife bathed the scalp-wound I had suffered in the crash and gave me hot rum. I slept soundly that night; only during the following week did I start having nightmares about wolves . . .

The next morning was overcast and very much milder so, reunited with Roz, I set off at 8 a.m. to walk the twelve miles to the low-lying main road, where the thaw might be sufficiently advanced to permit cycling.

There was a strange feeling in the air that day. It was warm enough for me to leave my wind-cheater open as I pushed Roz uphill, yet there were no visible signs of the thaw at this height. All around me the mountains, valleys and forests lay white and lifeless under a low, grey sky, in the profound stillness of a landscape where no breeze stirred, there was neither house nor bird to be seen and the streams were silent under their covering of ice. I stopped often to look around me, and savour the uncanny sensation of being the only living, moving thing in the midst of this hushed desolation, where my own breathing sounded loud.

Then, on the other side of the pass, the spell was broken. Villages appeared, huddled improbably on the steep mountain-sides, and I joined a group of friendly peasants, sitting on their sleigh behind two ambling, cream-coloured oxen. One of the men spoke German, and told me that down on the plains flooding was already extensive.

At midday I reached the main road, but found the icy patches still too frequent for cycling, though the surface was streaming with water. So I thumbed the next truck, and was taken twenty-five miles to Svetozarevo.

Here, at last, I saw a road completely free of ice and snow. After weeks of using Roz as a hand-cart for pushing luggage my exhilaration at being able to cycle again made up for my lack of training and I sped joyously towards Nîs, too pleased with myself to heed the ominous fact that in every direction flood-waters covered the flat fields.

I did not speed for long. After five or six miles the road dipped slightly, and now the floods were right across it, some twelve inches deep, so that at each revolution of the pedals my feet were alternately submerged. As it would not have helped to dismount, I cycled slowly on, passing anxious-looking groups of people in bullock- and pony-carts, watching men in little boats punting over the fields to rescue families from farmhouses which had been suddenly isolated by the rapidly rising waters.

Leaving these scenes behind me I saw that the Morava River was now flowing on my left, parallel to and level with the road. From the near distance came a dull, booming sound, as soldiers blew up the gigantic accumulations of rock-hard snow which, unless artificially loosened, would have dammed the river and sent its overflow rushing through the nearby town of Cuprija.

It was awe-inspiring to see the wide, angry Morava swiftly sweeping its tremendous burden of ice and snow-chunks through the vast wilderness of sullen, brown flood-waters, and my awe was soon justified when a massive wave came crashing across the road, swept me off Roz and rolled me over and over, choking as I swallowed the muddy water and gasping as its iciness penetrated my clothes. Next a branch of a little roadside tree appeared above me and pulling myself up by it I found that the water, though still flowing strongly, was now no more than three feet deep. I looked for Roz and, during one appalling moment, thought that she had disappeared. Then I saw a yellow handlebar grip in a ditch, and hurried to rescue her. Fortunately my kit had been wrapped in waterproof coverings, to avoid the danger of melting snow seeping through the bags when we entered warm buildings at night, so most of it remained undamaged.

Cuprija was less than half a mile away, but as I was semi-paralysed by my sodden clothes, had to half-carry Roz to keep the pannier-bags clear of the water, and was in constant danger of being again swept off-balance by the strength of the current, this half-mile seemed one of the longest that I have ever travelled.

Reaching the safety of the bridge outside Cuprija I saw hundreds of people standing watching the threatening river in an atmosphere of tense excitement. My appearance proved almost too much for them in their already overwrought state and I was accorded a singularly undeserved Hero's Welcome, when I should have been presented with a Dunce's Cap.

At Pirot, fifteen miles north of Bulgaria, the mutual antagonism of Yugoslavia and her southern neighbour becomes irritatingly obvious. So contemptuous are the Yugoslavs of their Communist cousins that they simply ignore Sofia's existence, thereby failing to maintain the high standard of sign-posting found throughout the rest of the country. They have also, with what can only be malice aforethought, so efficiently neglected the road to the frontier town of Dimitrovgrad that its surface would deter any sane traveller from attempting to enter Bulgaria.

This road, part of one of the world's most important intercontinental highways, was marked first-class on my map. As I stood outside Pirot, looking from the map to the unglorified goat-track ahead of me, which I had been repeatedly assured by the locals really was the road to Sofia, I felt a sense of betrayal. However illustrious it might have been in past history, or might still be in theory, it should now be described by map-makers, in realistic terms, as a tenth-class track, negotiable only by those with no respect either for their persons or their mode of conveyance. Admittedly I cycled along it under very trying conditions, but in summer it would be just as bad.

All through the previous night it had been snowing – a fall of quickly melting snow, typical of this thawing period – and now the track was covered in slush, between deep broad craters brimful of yellow-brown water. At first I attempted to weave acrobatically around these miniature lakes, through the slush, but as they occupied at least seventy per cent of the surface area I soon decided to pedal on regardless, plunging and bouncing in and out of the water. It was 'cycling with a difference', as one never knew just how deep the next crater would be, and there was always the stimulating possibility that it would be deep enough to unseat one . . .

Pirot and Dimitrovgrad lie at opposite ends of an oval shaped, level valley some eight miles wide, and completely enclosed by low mountains with a sparse covering of trees on their stony slopes. Through the centre of this valley, which was now a dismal expanse of mud and water, runs the 'road' and the railway line connecting Europe and Asia. Apart from trains, of which there were a prodigious number, both passenger and goods (though the carriages and wagons were almost always empty), I saw no traffic whatever, a fact which could have been explained by the general wisdom of mankind, or by the flood which had swept away the wooden bridge over the Nisava about five miles from Dimitrovgrad.

At first I was appalled by this catastrophe. It had taken me two hours to cycle the ten miles from Pirot and there was nothing I wanted to do less than return there. Then I saw the concrete and steel railway bridge on my left and waded towards it through a flooded field. First I made sure that there were no trains coming (a precaution easily taken, as Yugoslav trains emit volcanic clouds of smoke, and are constantly whistling excited variations on an unidentifiable theme) before climbing with Roz on to the line, and crossing the bridge, to join the road again through a field three feet deep in water. By this time worrying about pneumonia seemed futile; for days I had been living in a state of permanent saturation from the waist down, so that the only sensible reaction was lots of rum and no fuss.

While cycling the two miles from Dimitrovgrad to the Bulgarian frontier my attention was equally divided between the odd things that craters in the road can do to one's lunch and the excitement of approaching for the first time the sinister Iron Curtain. At each bend I looked eagerly for tangled masses of barbed wire, watch-towers manned by vigilant soldiers armed with machine-guns and binoculars, and alert policemen keenly observing every movement for miles around. But not one of these thrilling phenomena appeared and it was only when I saw a locked, five-foot high gate across the road that I realised I had arrived at the significant point.

Looking around, I saw a neat little bungalow beside the road which, though it didn't actually say so, was obviously the Police-cum-Customs post. I knocked loudly on the open hall-door, got no reply, entered and knocked on each of the doors leading out of the hall, with no more success, and finally opened one of them, yelling and whistling hopefully; stamps on my passport are the only souvenirs that I can afford to collect, and I didn't want to be cheated of this one. Still nothing happened, and I stood in the doorway viewing the desk and reflecting that if I wanted to enter the spy business here was my chance to make away with a fine collection of vitally important seals. Finally I left the building, to investigate the possibilities of getting into Bulgaria unaided.

If one looked hard enough, a half-hearted barbed-wire fence was visible stretching away from the road in either direction, marking the frontier. It was so like the kind of ineffectual barrier that some Irish farmers put up to prevent their sheep from straying that I felt quite home-sick. I had no difficulty in dragging Roz through one of the many gaps made by the local peasants and then, returning to the main road, I entered the insignificant little house which is Bulgaria's Northern Frontier Fortress. Again my knock remained unanswered, but this time, when I opened a door leading out of the hall, I found a policeman happily dozing by the stove, with a cat and two kittens on his lap. I immediately diagnosed that he was a *nice* policeman, and when I had gently roused him, and he had recovered from the shock of being required to function officially, I had my diagnosis confirmed.

In December, the Bulgarian Embassy in London had issued me with a visa valid for only four days. Now this genial policeman, who spoke fluent English, took one look at the card, said that it was ridiculous, and issued me with a new visa entitling me to stay in Bulgaria as long as I wished! After which we sat by the stove and amiably discussed our two countries over glasses of brandy.

On leaving the Bulgarian frontier-post, I propped Roz against a tree and returned to Yugoslavia, in another attempt to obtain my souvenir passport-stamp. By now a pathetically bored-looking young man was sitting at the desk, listlessly attempting to solve a crossword puzzle. I explained how it was that my passport had received a Bulgarian entry stamp before it had had a Yugoslav exit one, and he said wearily that he had gone into Dimitrovgrad for a hot lunch. Obviously, at both frontier-posts, the attitude was that not even spies, much less tourists, would operate in the prevailing weather.

I had entered my first orthodox Communist country as a 'neutral' equally suspicious of both pro- and anti-Communist propaganda, but after a week in Bulgaria I left it as an admirer of the limited good that Communism can achieve within less than two decades.

Everywhere I was received with spontaneous friendliness and if any Secret Police had me under surveillance they were very discreet indeed. My movements remained completely unrestricted and I spent two nights as a guest in the households of a factory-worker and a collective farmer, where the standard of living was comparable with that of present-day Irish workers. On my last night I stayed at the home of a regional Party leader and was interested to observe that his standard of living was almost on a par with that of the ordinary workers. Nowhere did I see any evidence of extreme poverty and the average citizen – a cheerful, singularly unoppressed-looking individual – appeared to be adequately clothed, housed and fed.

Admittedly, this spectacular improvement in Bulgaria's standard of living has been gained at the cost of religious and intellectual freedom, though judging by some conversations I had with the younger generation it will not be long before the phoenix of the individual human spirit rises again from its ashes.

Personally I recoil at once from regimentation and I am far too reactionary to regard 'backward peasants' as being *ipso facto* in need of modernisation; yet in fairness I must give my personal impression of that side of the Communist coin which is not popular among Western propagandists.

I was able to cycle almost all the way from Cuprija to Istanbul, through Bulgaria and Turkey-in-Europe, but the Turkish highlands were still under snow so here again we became dependent on buses and trucks – when such vehicles could operate between blizzards. Mercifully the temperature was not quite as low as it had been in Europe, but the quantity of snow was far in excess of anything I had yet experienced; it was common to see fifty-foot high drifts, shaped so exquisitely by the wind that I still catch my breath at the memory.

En route to Erzurum our bus barely escaped being entombed in snow. We were stuck in a drift on a narrow mountain road and the gallant snowplough which had come to rescue us skidded over a precipice, killing both men on board. Another snowplough then set out from the opposite direction but its progress was understandably slow and meanwhile the blizzard began again. As we waited the snow piled higher and higher around us, its silent softness contrasting eerily with the whine of the gale through the pass.

It is on occasions such as these that I thank God for my sanguine temperament, which refuses to allow me to believe in disaster until it is finally manifest, and I noticed that my comrades in distress were equally well fortified against panic by their fatalistic acceptance of Allah's Will. Yet perhaps we were all more apprehensive than we had allowed ourselves to recognise, for we cheered very loudly when the second snowplough eventually appeared.

An ancient Jewish legend says that the Kurds are descended from four hundred virgins who were deflowered by devils while on their way to King Solomon's court and my own experiences in both Turkish and Persian Azerbaijan prompt me to accept this genealogy as an historic fact.

At Dogubayzit, the last little town en route to the Persian frontier-post, I stayed in the local doss-house, where my bedroom was a tiny box leading off the wide loft which accommodated the majority of the 'Otel's' patrons. This room had a flimsy door, without any fastening, and there was no movable piece of furniture which could have been placed against it as a security measure. The squalid bedding was inhabited by a host of energetic fleas, but their attentions were wasted on me and within minutes of retiring I was sound asleep.

Some hours later I awoke to find myself bereft of bedding and to see a six-foot, scantily-clad Kurd bending over me in the moonlight. My gun was beneath the pillow and one shot fired at the ceiling concluded the matter. I felt afterwards that my suitor had showed up rather badly; a more ardent admirer, of his physique, could probably have disarmed me without much difficulty.

As a result of the loud report and my visitor's rapid retreat there was a stirring of many bodies on the floor outside my room and a few sleepy mutterings – then quiet. Obviously gunshots in the small hours are not regarded locally as signs of an emergency.

By now I had finally escaped from snow and ice and on the following morning came one of the most glorious experiences of the entire journey – a fifteen-mile cycle-run in perfect weather around the base of Mount Ararat. This extraordinary mountain, which inspires the most complex emotions in the least imaginative traveller, affected me so deeply that I have thought of it ever since as a personality encountered, rather than a landscape observed.

Then came the Persian frontier – the most closely guarded we had yet crossed – and now Roz and I were really in our stride, cycling day after day beneath a sky of intense blue, through wild mountains whose solitude and beauty surpassed anything I had been able to imagine during my day-dreams about this journey. Particularly I remember the unique purity of the light, which gave to every variation of every colour an individual vitality and which lucidly emphasised every line, curve and angle. Here, for the first time, I became fully aware of light as something positive, rather than as a taken-for-granted aid to perceiving objects.

Between Tabriz and the Caspian coast the terrain becomes fiercely wild and the few inhabitants match it. One midday when I was sitting eating my lunch at the edge of the track, near a hairpin bend overlooking a deep valley, three elderly men came round the bend, carrying spades on their shoulders. As a little farming village lay some two miles back this seemed to me a most natural sight, but then, as I was about to salute the group, two of them seized Roz, who was leaning against the cliff a few yards away, and made off down the track with her, while the third advanced towards me, his spade raised threateningly. I fired over his head and quickly backed along the edge of the track, ready to fire again, but the amateur bandits had had enough and bolted like rabbits, mercifully abandoning Roz.

Many experienced travellers have since advised me that it is wiser to go unarmed in such areas, where a gun can provoke more trouble than it averts. Obviously, this would be true if one became involved with genuine armed bandits – yet a ·25 does have its uses.

However, my next misadventure was such that I judged it best not to produce the pistol. Passing through Adabile at lunchtime on a cold day (we had now risen to a considerable altitude) I paused to treat myself to a hot meal in an eating-house. As usual Roz and I attracted a curious crowd and soon a young police officer, gorgeously uniformed and braided, approached me to say that as this was a Restricted Area, because of Russia's proximity, I must accompany him to the police-barracks to fill in some forms. My inbred trust in police had not yet been undermined so, having finished my lunch, I innocently followed him through a maze of alleyways between mud houses. At last he turned into a little compound with a well in the centre, ushered me through a doorway, locked the door and put the key in his trouser pocket. Only then did I realise that we were alone in an obviously empty private house.

At first my captor was ingratiatingly amiable. But soon, having discovered that European women are not as obliging as he had supposed them to be, he lost all control, and the ensuing scene was too sordid for repetition. As my adversary was armed with a revolver I kept my gun in my pocket and used unprintable tactics to reduce him to a state of temporary agony. During this respite I grabbed his trousers, which by then were lying on the floor, fled to the hallway, found the key, unlocked the door just as my victim appeared behind me, and raced back through the alleyways to the centre of the town.

It is perhaps understandable that, of all the regions I travelled through, Azerbaijan is the only one I would not wish to revisit alone.

Roz and I arrived in Teheran on 20 March, the eve of the Shiah Muslims' New Year of 1342, and the Now Ruz Festival involved me in a delay of five days. Before continuing my journey I had to get a visa for Afghanistan, collect a spare tyre from the Customs and change a travellers' cheque into Afghan currency – none of which transactions would be possible until the conclusion of the Now Ruz celebrations.

I

The Elusive Visa

TEHERAN

TEHERAN, 26 MARCH

Today a deep depression has moved over Dervla; I presented myself to the Afghan Embassy at 9 a.m. this morning, only to be told that under no circumstances whatever would they grant a visa to a woman who intended cycling alone through Afghanistan. But if this is true, why wasn't I told of the ruling at the Afghan Embassy in London? Apparently about six years ago a lone Swedish woman motorist was carved up into small pieces, since when solitary female travellers have been banned – or so they say here. Probably I could easily get a visa in New Delhi, as official decisions rarely confirm each other in this part of the world: but that's not much consolation at the moment. Of course everyone at the Embassy was very sorry to frustrate me thus and they offered to provide free transport from here to Kabul and looked bewildered when I patiently pointed out that I wanted to cycle because I liked cycling, not because of economic distress. I also pointed out that women get murdered in Europe with monotonous regularity and that the hazards of travelling alone through their country were probably no greater than the hazards of doing likewise in Britain or France. But they refused to be swayed by my eloquence, so this evening it looks as though I'm beaten. However, since leaving the Embassy I've incubated a few nefarious schemes to be tried out tomorrow.

This afternoon, having expensively cut through interminable lengths of red tape, I extricated my tyre from the Customs. Those who know assure me that I'm very lucky to have received a parcel posted from Dublin on only 8 January. Yesterday one of my hosts received a letter sent from Brussels by airmail on 18 November, and letters posted in Teheran to Teheran addresses often spend a week en route.

The temperature has been around 72° F. for the past few days but this evening a cool wind rose suddenly and we've had a heavy, homelike shower.

TEHERAN, 27 MARCH

The Afghans have the most kindly way of trying to thwart one. On arrival at the Embassy this morning, I was received like an old friend and informed that all arrangements had been made for my safe transport to Kabul. Two German motorists – a writer and a painter – were enlisted for the purpose and had very kindly agreed to take on Roz and myself, without even seeing how presentable or otherwise either of us might be. The idea was that I'd be entered like a camera or a radio on their passports, so that they'd have to produce me to the police in Kabul and I couldn't get away on Roz once we're over the frontier without *them* being involved in trouble. Being thus reduced to the status of a piece of luggage naturally did no good to my *amour propre*, but with everyone being so pleasantly insistent on my reaching India alive I couldn't decently lose my temper. This lightning move – as it was by local standards – kiboshed one of my nefarious schemes, so having profusely thanked all concerned, I said that I had an important appointment in half an hour and that I would be back later to fill in and sign the countless relevant documents. Then I sped off by taxi to the Embassy of a 'Friendly Power' where I set about implementing the second nefarious scheme.

Having pleaded my way into the office of a sufficiently senior man, I outlined my miserable predicament and begged for a letter written on his government's behalf requesting the Afghan Government to grant bearer a visa for a month's travelling by cycle through Afghanistan at her own risk. I added that no one need worry about the consequences if I vanished, as none of my relatives are close enough to 'create'. Fortunately, the victim of my machinations was an upholder of Free Enterprise and the Liberty of the Individual. He looked at me in silence for a moment, then said, 'Well, I suppose if visas had been required in

1492, the New World would not have been discovered. All right – I'll play ball. But remember that all this is very unofficial and unbecoming to my position and I'm depending on you to come out alive at the other end, for my sake – which I somehow think you will do.' Then he proceeded to devise a most impressive document, all red ribbons and massive seals and flourishing signatures, in which concoction he took a fatherly pride. So now I simply *cannot* allow myself to be murdered in Afghanistan!

Half an hour later I was back in the Afghan Embassy, waving the Ruritanian-looking scroll with ill-concealed triumph. Not surprisingly, it worked. No one was happy at the thought of me being granted a visa, but since another state had nobly elected to hold the baby they gloomily agreed – against their better judgement, underlined – to give the lunatic her head. However, Kabul has to be contacted so I won't have everything signed, sealed and delivered until the 30th; but I'm too elated tonight to fuss about another few days' delay.

TEHERAN, 28 MARCH

At a party yesterday evening I met three Pakistani officers – a general, a brigadier and a colonel – who are here on a three-months' military mission and who immediately took me under their collective wing. They are all Pathans and are the first people I've met who do *not* expect me to be murdered in Afghanistan. For this, among other reasons, I find their company singularly congenial; being generally regarded as something next door to a corpse becomes tedious after a while. Acting on their cheerfully original assumption that I will eventually cross the Khyber Pass in one piece, they have advised me on which parts of Pakistan are most worth seeing and have given me a list of addresses of their friends and relatives all along my route. Colonel Jahan Zeb went to enormous trouble to plan an itinerary for me, which included a detour to the Tribal Territory of Gilgit, so now all is set fair for Pakistan and I'm assured I'll have the Army behind me there – which is quite something in a country now run by the Army!

TEHERAN, 29 MARCH

On leaving Constantinople, where one spends a small fortune on beggars, I had resolved to give nothing to anyone during the rest of the journey lest I end up with a begging-bowl myself. But of course Persia has undermined that resolution: the pathetic wretches seen here simply can't be ignored. (Many of them in the towns and villages are lepers diagnosed too late for treatment – even if treatment were available in their area, which it often isn't – and left to die slowly at home.) So now I've got the problem worked out systematically. I reckon that by being a guest at my friend's house I'm saving £1 a day, which I distribute as baksheesh. This obviously is an oblique form of selfishness; one couldn't come home after a walk through Teheran and settle down to enjoy the luxuries of Capitalism if one hadn't done something, however trivial, to alleviate the surrounding misery. Yet it's well to remember that this misery is not as total or as neglected as it appears to be. One of the religious duties of Muslims – as of Christians – is to give alms to the needy and the vast majority of Muslims of every sect regularly fulfil this duty in proportion to their means. In effect the citizens of these countries provide for their deprived brothers as generously as do the tax-paying citizens of a Welfare State and the disparity between the circumstances of the disabled of Persia and the disabled of Britain is no greater than that between the circumstances of the working men of the two countries: in fact it may well be less, though the distribution of funds is more haphazard. Also the Muslim method of providing 'Social Services' has the important virtue of maintaining a natural and humane link between individuals. It is obviously more desirable to have citizens giving to beggars voluntarily, out of compassion, rather than to have them grumblingly paying taxes to an impersonal government which dispenses what is left, after its civil servants have been paid, to unknown sufferers who are mere names in a filing cabinet.

Similarly, the bribery which is so rife here, is another, though much less desirable form of indirect taxation; everyone is paid so inadequately that they simply augment their official income as best they can from day to day – a situation accepted by all with much the same brand of resentful resignation as we show towards tax-paying. House-owners pay the local police a regular monthly sum to ensure that their homes and cars will be properly guarded – and if some newcomer refuses to pay on principle his home will be the inevitable target for the next burglary. I've asked several responsible Persians why an orthodox tax isn't imposed and their answer was that you can't do that sort of thing with a mainly illiterate population and that the people who can afford property which needs protection can also afford to subsidise the police. But of course this is only one example and bribery is the determining factor in every sphere of activity from the university professor's correction of exam papers down to the dustman's collection of garbage. I must admit that it's difficult to get adjusted to such a fetid atmosphere, in which one is always conscious of the power of money over integrity.

TEHERAN, 30 MARCH

Today I've been receiving Good Advice in bulk from various Responsible Persons. H.I.M. the Shah was to have gone to Meshed this morning but the papers announced that his trip has been cancelled because of 'bad weather'; as the weather at the moment is perfection (74°F. and cloudless sky) everyone thinks the government a bit dim for not inventing a better excuse. The fact is that the Mullahs are now stirring up serious trouble there about Land Redistribution and Women's Emancipation and as they still have a very strong grip in that area, and are capable of working certain sections of the people into an anti-Shah frenzy, it was judged wiser for H.I.M. to avoid the Holy City just now. (Since I left Tabriz, two women have been killed there in Mullah-provoked anti-Women's Emancipation riots.) As Meshed is the next – and last – Persian city on my route I am being warned repeatedly that I must do my best to look like a man in that area. Also I'm to be very careful about using my camera between here and there as, if I were accidentally to include even a distant mosque in a picture and the crowd happened to be in the mood, I could be stoned and possibly seriously injured, as recently happened to two over-keen French photographers.

I've also been advised that hotel bedrooms without locks call for empty bottles balanced on top of the door to ensure that one is not taken altogether by surprise should wandering lechers have designs on one's virtue. (As creating empty bottles is one of the few things I'm good at, this is an appropriate suggestion.) However, I intend staying as often as possible in gendarmerie barracks between here and Afghanistan, as the Persian gendarmerie is a force existing primarily to protect travellers and is reputedly more dependable than other branches of the national police – how much more dependable remains to be seen.

Tonight I enjoyed a farewell hooley with my Pakistani friends – though hooley is hardly the *mot juste* as they drink only water. I suppose, if one will mix with good Muslims, it's only to be expected that they'll open for themselves another bottle of Pure Water (guaranteed) every time they refill your glass. And certainly Colonel Zeb needs no alcohol to stimulate his brain or improve his masterly skill in the use of the English language: quite apart from the considerable interest of what he has to say on an incredibly wide variety of topics, it's a joy to merely hear him *saying* it. I haven't enjoyed such a good evening's discussion for a long time: the five of us started talking at 6 p.m. and got so involved on so many fascinating points that no one wanted to break it up and we didn't have dinner till 10.40 p.m.! It's now 2.10 a.m. so, as I'm planning an early start, some sleep might not be a bad idea.

2

Hospitality of the Police

TEHERAN TO THE AFGHAN FRONTIER

DEH-NAMAK, 31 MARCH

Roz and I left Teheran at 6.30 a.m. and arrived here soon after 6 p.m. having covered 108 miles because of a strong following wind.

The road remained reasonable by Persian standards, though if I had met it at home I would have taken one horrified look and gone the other way round; it's amazing how quickly one becomes conditioned. It was such glorious cycling weather that I seemed to have boundless energy and did the last ten miles feeling positively fresh.

This really is a beautiful country and every mile from Teheran was pure joy – as much the joy of space and silence as of visual loveliness. These extravagantly sweeping lines of plain and mountain are intoxicating to an islander and the blending of shades on the barren hillsides is a symphony of colour. Yet that's only one aspect of the region; as a background to daily life it's cruel and contemptuous country where cultivation is a fight all the way, with victory not worth much.

The main crop is wheat and to come on a few little fields of it, looking so fresh and green, is a physical rest for the eyes after twenty or thirty miles of harsh, grey-brown desert, shuddering in the midday heat-haze. The mud villages of this area are much better designed than those of western Persia, where the houses are as primitive as you could find anywhere. Here they are most attractive, with domed roofs and miniature 'Gothic' windows and endless variations between one house and another. I longed to take a few photographs but Muslims being so sensitive on the subject it seemed wiser not to risk spoiling the good relations I'd achieved with the locals.

Twice I left the road to explore villages formerly belonging to the Shah and now handed over to the peasants. These people are totally different to the Azerbaijan toughs: I found them friendly and polite and there were no 'hands-out-for-baksheesh' though they went to endless trouble showing me round the farms. It may sound silly, but I maintain that I know instinctively the temper of a place, after being five minutes with the inhabitants. So today I hadn't the slightest qualm about abandoning Roz and my kit in the centre of the villages, and though on my return I found her surrounded by at least a hundred filthy, ragged children, nothing had been touched. In my experience this is the prevailing standard of honesty in Turkey and Persia at least towards guests and Azerbaijan was the unhappy exception.

On one of these farms I saw my very first tractor since entering Persia – it was the common property of a village. Elsewhere oxen are still pulling the most primitive form of all-wooden plough. There are very few camels in this area, oddly enough, nor are there many horses or cattle. Hundreds of sturdy little donkeys provide transportation for both people and goods and a few herds of sheep and goats are grazed by each village.

It was a most moving experience to see the pride and joy of those men and boys at *owning* their land. Some of the youths spoke a little English and repeatedly I heard the phrases 'This is *our* land', '*We* own this', 'This belongs to *us*', as they all beamed with fond pride at their pathetic few fertile acres in the midst of hundreds of square miles of desert. Obviously they can't quite believe it yet. Many of them carry photographs of the Shah in their pockets (I had to admire about thirty-five of these individually) and pictures of His Imperial Majesty and the Empress and the Crown Prince are in almost every home. They genuinely love their Shah – and would you blame them! Political commentators may question the motives behind his Land Reform but the effect for the peasants remains wholly good. When I think of those wretched Mullahs who try to persuade the villagers that it's immoral and against the Koran for the masses to *own* land – just because they themselves own so much of it . . . ! I suppose the nearest analogy in Christendom is the Spanish Church, even if its tactics were slightly more subtle. It's disconcerting how the men in the religious saddle repeatedly abuse their spiritual authority for personal gain.

Eighty per cent of the land here is useless for anything, yet when you observe how the irrigated patches flourish it becomes clear that a few hundred more dams are the answer, as the cultivated land is basically the same as the rest. When I first saw the whitened surface of the plain today I thought it had been snowing a little, even though that seemed wildly unlikely. Then I stopped and tasted the concentrated salt which forms a light film over everything; we're now just north of the Great Salt Desert.

On arriving at this little village I went straight to the gendarmerie barracks, left Roz there and walked beyond the sun-gold huddle of mud houses to attempt to get some pictures of the goat and sheep herds being penned for the night. I was followed by scores of children, all obviously regarding me as a sort of circus; they didn't beg but just wanted to be with me. I had to tell the gendarmerie to let them come as their tendency was literally to beat the infants back lest the visitor be annoyed. Actually it did me good to be able to provide so much innocent amusement by merely arriving in the village and soon my photography expedition degenerated into games for all, with me pretending to be a sheep-dog and the children convulsed by giggles and then me being a donkey (not difficult!) crawling around the sand on all fours, braying loudly, with two or three toddlers on my back.

This barrack where I'm staying the night is a huge old fort, built entirely of mud but very impressively proportioned. I'm half-blind now from writing by a feeble oil-lamp – you'd think they'd have enough oil here in Persia!

GOOSHEH, 1 APRIL

It's very funny – around here the idea of a woman travelling alone is so completely outside the experience and beyond the imagination of everyone that it's universally assumed I'm a man. This convenient illusion is fostered by the very short haircut I deliberately got in Teheran, and by a contour-obliterating shirt presented to me at Adabile by the US Army in the Middle East, who also donated a wonderful pair of boots – the most comfortable footwear I've ever had and ideal for tramping these stony roads. The result of the locals' little error of judgement is that last night and tonight I was shown to my bed in the gendarmerie dormitory. These beds consist of wooden planks with padded sleeping-bags laid on them and I have the bed of one of those on night-patrol. There are no problems involved as 'getting ready for bed' consists of removing boots, gun and belt and sliding into a flea-bag so I simply do likewise and that's that! Incidentally, these barracks are kept spotlessly clean: as much as an accidental crumb or cigarette ash isn't allowed on the mud floor and everything is neat and tidy. I bring in my own food and get hot water for coffee from the lads. I'm now sitting on the edge of my bed writing by a little oil-lamp while six gendarmes sleep soundly around me.

We left Deh-Namak at 5.30 a.m. when the sun was just up and the air pleasantly cool. Though the road was much worse than yesterday we covered eighty-two miles, arriving here at 6.40 p.m. I stopped for lunch at 12.30 p.m. and slept for an hour in blazing sun; apart from sunburn (there was no shade available) this is perfectly safe, as in the wide open spaces between villages there are no men, beasts, insects or reptiles to molest one, but I suspect I'm in for trouble with sunburnt arms as I was using my wind-cheater to cover Roz's tyres while I slept. Actually it is only when stationary that one is aware of the sun's power, whilst moving there's no sensation of it being 'too hot'. I believe it'll be the same in Afghanistan, before becoming intolerably hot in Pakistan and India. (I feel I've earned a few months of perfect weather!)

Soon after lunch I abandoned the road for over ten miles and cycled along a dried-up river-bed where the baked mud was firm and smooth and the boulders en route seemed a mere triviality as compared with the excruciating, sharp-edged gravel on a road with an inexorably corrugated surface. When I found the river-bed veering too much to the south I reluctantly left it and walked over a mile or so of desert back to the road. The last thirty miles were through another magnificent mountain range with a very stiff climb up to this village. I passed the scene of a ghastly smash-up reported a few days ago in the

English-language Teheran paper. A truck and bus were in a head-on collision on a V-bend – both went into a ravine and fifty-one were killed. Something similar happens almost every day somewhere in Persia and the drivers are always blamed. Watching Persian buses on mountain roads makes me feel quite ill; when I see the dust-cloud that heralds one I dismount and remove myself to a safe distance. During ten days in Teheran I witnessed seven bad traffic accidents, four of them involving the deaths of nine people.

This is a tiny village of some twenty domed mud huts, a tea-house and the barracks. There should be a level road tomorrow as the map shows no passes – but probably we'll have a worse surface each day.

SHAHRUD, 2 APRIL

How right can you be! We only covered sixty-six miles today (5.45 a.m.–6.50 p.m.) and I had to walk over twenty-five of them, not because of hills, but because no one with any regard for their cycle would ride it over this sort of infernal track. I haven't seen one private car or one lorry since leaving Teheran, though many buses pass, packed with people and overloaded on the roofs with rolls of carpet, bicycles, crates of hens, lambs and kids (alive and kicking – literally!) and diverse bundles containing God knows what. These buses unload for lunch (between 12 and 3) at village eating-houses, which have streams running beside them and a few green trees shading the carpet-covered 'tables' on which everyone sits cross-legged eating their bread and chives and hard-boiled eggs and minced-meat balls and *mast* (the Persian yoghourt). Before the meal all babies present have their napkins changed and these are washed in the stream (as are the chives and everybody's teeth after eating) and spread out to dry before the resumption of the journey. Today I joined one of these parties (obviously a pilgrimage returning from Meshed) and though I was addressed as 'Monsieur' the mere fact that I was from a Christian country provoked hostility. I didn't dare use the camera, though I would have valued a few shots of those fanatical-looking chaps in filthy rags and tatters. Many of them were adolescents, so it's going to take H.I.M. a long, long time to tame this lot. The children were terrified of me and wouldn't come for the sweets I offered and the whole atmosphere was so unpleasant that I removed myself sooner than I would have otherwise and took my siesta in the safety of the desert a few miles away.

A phenomenon that intrigues me is the number of Catholic religious oleographs in all these eating-houses and tea-houses – Christ as a baby in the manger or working in the carpenter's shop, the Immaculate Heart of Mary picture, highly coloured, Our Lady of Perpetual Succour, Our Lady of Good Counsel, cheap prints of the Raphael Madonna, and St Joseph. These are in addition, of course, to the Shah, the Empress and baby Prince in various stages of growth, not to mention luscious semi-nude females advertising Pepsi-Cola and aspirin. But how all these Christian pictures got here baffles me; granted the Muslims are devoted to Christ as a Prophet and to Our Lady, but I wouldn't have thought their devotion would go so far.

When I arrived on the outskirts of this town a car overtook me and the driver (manager of a local sugar factory and reader of the daily paper) stopped and said, 'Dervla going to India, yes?' I blushed with becoming modesty at this proof of fame and replied that I was indeed Dervla going to India, so he invited me to spend the night at his home, where I now am, having had a shower and a huge supper. It's quite impossible to retain one's youthful curves in these countries: to refuse food is an insult so one merely unbuttons one's slacks in a surreptitious way and goes on and on eating. Before the meal everyone consumes a vast amount of biscuits, oranges, pastries, figs stuffed with almonds, toffees and bon-bons of all descriptions, pistachio nuts and endless glasses of tea. Then you're expected to welcome with a glad smile a mound of rice you can hardly see over and masses of meat and vegetables.

This is a big town (8,000 population) with electricity, no less! My host's house is full of mod cons, including a telephone, fridge and washing-machine. But inevitably there's no bath because of the Islamic law about washing in running water – the bathroom is a marble-floored outfit with a shower. (In fact every room in every Persian house is marble- or mud-floored because of the shortage of wood.) My host's wife is away in Teheran on a Now Ruz visit to her family and will be home tomorrow. This is the last day of the Now Ruz festival but my route today was so gloriously desolate that I saw little evidence of the traditional picnicking in the open. The four children here are delightful – two boys, two girls – and are tickled to bits by my arrival, having read about me in the Teheran paper. We were joined for supper by a twenty-year-old nephew of my host, with his sixteen-year-old wife – a made match that was clearly not working very well.

I'm in for torture with sunburn on my right arm – not, I now realise, the result of lying in the sun, but the result of cycling every day due east so that this arm is continuously exposed; and though I don't feel it when cycling it is a fierce sun. There's nothing like carrying six tubes of sunburn lotion across two continents and then forgetting to use it in time!

ABBAS-ABAD, 3 APRIL

We covered eighty-three miles today, but that meant breaking my 'not-after-dark' rule and cycling till 9.30 p.m. However, in such uninhabited country I don't think there's any danger and bright moonlight showed the way; it was indescribably beautiful on the huge sand-dunes, which look like mountains. I'm at last getting used to the uncanny silence of desert landscape and to the odd experience of seeing things that disappear as you approach them. Also I've discovered that what looks like a village two miles ahead is actually a village twenty miles ahead, and I've got acclimatised to fine dust permeating every crevice of self and kit. In short, I'm broken in!

There was an amusing interlude today when an American engineer going back by jeep to his work in Afghanistan pulled up to investigate me and the following conversation took place:

American: 'What the hell are you doing on this goddam road?'

Me: (having taken an instant dislike to him) 'Cycling.'

American: 'I can see that – but what the hell for?'

Me: 'For fun.'

American: 'Are you a nut-case or what? Gimme that bike and I'll stick it on behind and you get in here and we'll get out of this goddam frying-pan as fast as we can. This track isn't fit for a camel!'

Me: 'When you're on a cycle instead of in a jeep it doesn't feel like a frying-pan. Moreover, if you look around you you'll notice that the landscape compensates for the admittedly deplorable state of the road. In fact I *enjoy* cycling through this sort of country – but thank you for the kind offer. Goodbye.'

As I rode on he passed me and yelled: 'You *are* a goddam nut-case!'

I regard this sort of life, with just Roz and me and the sky and the earth, as sheer bliss. My one worry at the moment is Roz's complete disintegration. So far the rear-lamp, the rear mudguard and half the front mudguard have fallen off; the straps tying saddle-bag to saddle have both broken; the left pannier-bag holder has come apart and the right pedal has loosened. Everything is being held together by a system of rope and wire more complicated than you'd believe possible, but fortunately none of these disabilities is serious. The trouble will start when wheels or frame crack up. It's astonishing that I haven't had a puncture since leaving Teheran – a tribute to the extreme care with which I'm cycling. But obviously my claim that cycling is the best way to *see* a country just isn't valid in this region. I daren't take my eyes off the road for one second and my 'seeing' is confined to the walking intervals and to the frequent stops I make just to look around me.

This village is the most primitive place I've hit so far, with not even a gendarmerie barracks. It's a collection of the usual mud huts, very roughly constructed, and in the tea-house everything is of mud – the 'counter', the seats all around the walls and the steps leading up to an attic where men are smoking opium. I went up there to investigate sleeping accommodation and found five braves all in a trance with their pipes – that's what comes of having no gendarmerie in a place! (My right arm is so stiff tonight that I can't bend it and the pain is *intense* – but better that than frost-bite.) The three men now drinking tea here seem to be neutral towards me: they show no friendliness, but no apparent hostility either. I feel it's just as well I arrived late: the fewer people who know about my presence the better. I'll sleep on one of the long mud seats with Roz tied to me and my knapsack under my head with its straps round my neck – though it's not clear how me being strangled by my own straps will help the situation if someone tries to rob me!

BAGH-JAR, 4 APRIL

I survived last night without incident but despite tiredness slept badly as the sunburn agony woke me every time I moved. We set out at 5.30 a.m. and the whole of today's eighty-five-mile ride was through the Great Salt Desert with flat sand on either side to the horizon and only one town (Salzevar) en route. This seemed an interesting place but was full of Mullahs and turbaned youths who stoned me and cut my sunburned arm five minutes after I'd arrived, so I departed hastily before a riot started. Salzevar is in the heart of the Mullah-dominated country, where the police are afraid of the clergy and simply don't appear if there's trouble, so discretion was most emphatically the better part of valour. I'm now safe with the gendarmerie in a little village, sitting up in my bunk and feeling rotten. My right arm is half the size again of my left and tomorrow all the blisters will burst. I can't think why it's swelled so much; that didn't happen in Spain, where I also had very bad sunburn. Anyway, it's entirely my own fault.

The road was slightly improved today, except where so much sand had blown over it that one couldn't cycle without skidding. I feel quite feverish this evening; possibly it's slight heat-stroke though I didn't feel over-heated to any great degree.

NISHAPUR, 5 APRIL

I woke up feeling much better, though my arm has not burst yet. We only did fifty-five miles today as this is Omar Khayyám's town and I've stopped here to pay homage. Besides, I think I've been pushing myself too hard, so an easy day was not a bad idea.

On leaving Bagh-Jar I had a twelve-mile walk through the mountains on a ghastly road but surrounded by tremendously exciting scenery. Then we suffered more desert until reaching here.

I find the Persian fauna very un-exotic. Bird life round the villages consists of crows, magpies, willy-wagtails, swallows and sparrows. The only unfamiliar birds are little crested chaps rather like thrushes and an occasional fierce, enormous hawk; I've also heard a few nightjars. Animal life is almost nil, though today I saw four roebuck crossing the road. Insect life consists to date of houseflies (very few) and black beetles as in Ireland.

This is a very lovely town; I notice that the towns of Persia tend to be much more attractive than the cities, especially now when the gardens are so beautiful with their smooth lawns, pale green cascades of weeping willow and brilliant beds of carnations, roses, pansies and geraniums. The main streets are always wide and the sun-soaked mud walls look golden under the violet blue of the Persian sky. Almost all the traffic consists of pony-phaeton taxis and innumerable laden donkeys and bicycles. The inevitable *jube* (a channel of water flowing between footpath and road) runs everywhere but on the whole the streets are quite clean and I've come to the conclusion that Persian water is safe if you make it clear you want to *drink* it, not wash with it. Anyway I've been drinking it uninhibitedly with no ill effects.

We arrived here at 3.15 p.m. and I was immediately captured by a twenty-year-old boy who secured me as his guest for the night against terrific competition from his class-mates; the local students have to pay fifty *reals* for a thirty minutes' English lesson, so an English-speaking guest for the night is considered precious. Three days ago Khayyám's new tomb was opened to the public by the Shah (pity I missed that) and a bevy of youths, laden with dictionaries, grammars and simplified versions of *Jane Eyre*, took me there this afternoon, all bombarding me en route with their particular problems of pronunciation, sentence construction and spelling. The keenness of Persian youths to learn English is positively fanatical but their opportunities remain very limited as few competent teachers are available outside Teheran.

The new tomb represents modern architecture at its grotesque worst; I almost wept to see it over the body of such a man as Omar Khayyám. I also saw the old tomb which is very simple, dignified and appropriate. Why tens of thousands of *reals* had to be spent on this new contraption when the country is swarming with undernourished children I do not know.

The family with whom I'm staying consists of the mother (aged thirty-five), three sons aged twenty, eighteen and twelve, and four girls aged sixteen, fourteen, nine and six. The father works as a draper's assistant in Teheran and the household is obviously very poor. This being Friday (the Muslim Sunday) twelve relatives were rounded up to come and meet me at supper time, but even though the men were close relatives the mother and daughters, including the six-year-old, veiled themselves the moment the visitors appeared. Islam is so rigid around here that *no* man, except father, husband and sons, is allowed to glimpse a woman's face; no wonder the boys can't take their eyes off my poor mug – at least it's a change from mother and sisters!

I ate with the women and was relieved to get lentils instead of rice. We also had a savoury omelette and salad – which I declined, having seen it washed in the *jube* and been warned by everyone to avoid *jube*-washed salad at all costs. There were no chairs or tables or beds in the house and no cutlery – you use the flat pieces of bread to dig your share out of the communal dish. *Mast* with sugar was served as dessert and I found the whole meal very appetising.

Everyone is most concerned about my arm, which certainly looks alarming, though it feels better tonight.

After the meal grandmother and mother took turns smoking the hookah, while one girl played on a timbrel and the rest danced – the traditional Friday evening pastime. I've got to appreciate Arabic music to the point where I have my favourite tunes and I could watch Persian dancing for hours; it's marvellously graceful, particularly in the use of arms and hands. The six-year-old gave a magnificent performance and a two-year-old already had the general idea!

SANG BAST, 6 APRIL

There was quite a change in the landscape today, though none in the road surface. We covered seventy-two miles, some of them between wonderful mountains, and most through what, for this area, is fertile land – i.e. a village, surrounded by little irrigated fields, every twenty miles or so, and in between huge flocks of sheep and goats grazing on some invisible herbage. There are hundreds of tiny lambs and kids with the flocks now and they look absolutely adorable; the lambs have thick fleeces and enormous floppy ears like spaniels, and the kids are very dainty and frisky. I stopped to have lunch with a fierce-looking but actually very amiable shepherd and admired his flocks while eating: we solemnly exchanged bread and salt so are friends forever, according to local custom.

As if Persia wanted to show me what it could do in the way of fauna I saw seven more deer today and one big dog fox of a horrid yellow-grey colour. I also met a tortoise, two scorpions, a hamster and an eagle and along much of the way I was accompanied by lark-song, which made me feel quite homesick.

This village is at the junction of the Teheran–Meshed–Afghanistan road, so I'll be returning to it tomorrow evening after a detour to see the sights of Meshed and to collect my mail. The local gendarmerie are exceptionally nice and sufficiently sophisticated to diagnose my sex so a flea-bag has been put on the office floor for me.

There was a strong east wind against us today – very wearing combined with the atrocious surface. It got quite cloudy too – there might be a nice bit of rain tomorrow, but that's not likely, though last week they did have their first inch for four years in South Persia.

One of the things that most intrigues Persians about me is the fact that I have no brothers and sisters: obviously only children are quite unknown here and they have the greatest sympathy for me. They're certainly a very family-minded people: brothers and sisters show tremendous mutual affection and in times of family trouble do all they can to help each other.

This was the first evening my expired visa was spotted, as a Lieutenant is in charge here; usually there's only an NCO as illiterate as his men. But the Lieutenant is a nice young man who winked and took twenty American cigarettes and said I could be fined over £50 for having American cigarettes in Persia.

SANG BAST, 7 APRIL

We arrived outside the British Council office in Meshed at 7.50 a.m. – ten long minutes to wait for mail! It was a perfect metalled road for the twenty-five miles and I met with no hostility from the locals, who were friendlier than in many other places; but I had to avoid going to the shrine area alone, though I would have given a lot to explore it. Meshed is by far the nicest of the four Persian cities I've seen and it *did* rain this morning so all along the fine wide boulevards, which are lined with birches as big as our oaks, the new green leaves were freshly sparkling. A car was kindly laid on to take me round the city yet it was most frustrating just to glimpse the out-of-bounds beauties of the mosques and shrine and museum and library. That quarter was teeming with Mullahs; I saw three in green turbans, which means they are descended from the Prophet. An American girl who took herself off there two days ago against advice was badly hurt by stones when trying to get colour-shots of the domes and minarets.

One is told the most blood-curdling tales at each stop. Here the *pièce de résistance* is about three Americans who, when motoring from Meshed to the Afghan frontier, stopped for a picnic and were all shot dead by bandits, who then escaped into Afghanistan but were hunted, by the Afghan police, back into Persia, where they were captured by the Army and publicly hanged in the main square of Teheran. Mr Jones of the British Council said there's no question of me going to Kabul via Mazar-i-Sharif as that area has lots of Communist-inspired trouble. The Russians are really trying hard at the moment to take over the whole of Afghanistan and there's a terrific tug-of-war going on between them and the Americans.

I left the British Council at 2.45 p.m. after lunch with the Joneses. (Very nice – both lunch and Joneses – and the British Council premises, which used to be the Consulate quarters when Britain had a Consul in Meshed, are really magnificent, with gardens and grounds that seem like Paradise when one comes to them from the desert.) I had decided that Roz would have to go to hospital before tackling Afghanistan so I took her to the city's biggest cycle shop where a few jobs which should have taken half an hour took two and a half hours so that we didn't get out of Meshed till 5.30 p.m. This sounds incredible but everyone who has lived here knows it's true: Persians will *not* use a screwdriver – instead they *hammer* every screw into place, and all other repairs and readjustments are done with corresponding brutality. You can't imagine what I suffered, sitting on a stool beside the patient, chain-smoking and drinking my emergency supply of Courvoisier through sheer nerves, while they attacked that unfortunate, long-suffering cycle with hammer and chisel. Eventually we left, having abandoned the back mudguard. I am now anticipating the worst, as no machine could survive an assault like that without dire repercussions.

It was dark, though with a bright moon from 6. p.m., and I would have enjoyed the ride through the cool evening but for being badly scared by five men (plus a rifle) in a car who kept stopping and trying to persuade me to go with them to Sang Bast. Maybe they meant well but twelve miles from anywhere after dark I didn't relish their attentions and they disappeared with what looked like guilty haste when two gendarmes on horseback came patrolling up the road. I'm now safely back with my friends in the barracks here, who are all very worried about my arm (which at this stage looks a lot worse than it feels) and have just given me a soothing cream to apply – what they use for 'Marchers' Feet'. I notice it's Swiss-made.

TIEABAD, 8 APRIL

This morning my flat length of breakfast bread (called *none*) was covered with snail-tracks – much to my astonishment, as I wouldn't have thought snails to be a feature of such a dry country. This seemed slightly off-putting at first but then I reminded myself that some people are *outré* enough to *eat* snails and as there can't be much chemical difference between a snail and a snail-track I went on from there. It was rather disillusioning to discover that a gendarme – it couldn't have been anyone else – stole sixty American cigarettes out of my saddle-bag last evening, but I suppose this is not really astonishing in a country where the C-in-C of the Army is at present on trial at the Teheran High Court, for large-scale corruption. Anyway it was entirely my own fault: I know by now that American cigarettes are much coveted here (if you had smoked Persian ones you'd realise why!) and I should have kept them in my knapsack. On the whole, apart from a few incidents, I've found the gendarmerie a very decent, kind and reliable lot of boys; they are the Shah's special interest and he does all he can to keep up the standard of the corps.

We left Sang Bast at 5.15 a.m. and had covered just over forty-five miles when, at 11 a.m., the inevitable happened and the back wheel came off; fortunately we were going very slowly up an incline at the time, so I wasn't injured myself. Investigating the situation I discovered that the thread of the relevant screw had been ruined, which seemed a natural enough consequence to it having been hammered into place. At this point I was twenty-five miles from the last town and twenty miles from the next and Roz couldn't be wheeled so I ate my lunch and went to sleep till such time as something might come to rescue me. (Since leaving Ireland I've acquired the habit of sleeping whenever I want to, which is very convenient.)

Only two trucks had passed all morning, taking petrol to Herat from the oil refinery at Meshed, and it was nearly 2 p.m. before the next one woke me as it came rattling along the execrable road. The driver was a barefooted Afghan with a flowing turban and as you can't put a bicycle on top of an oil-tanker he nonchalantly roped Roz to the engine; the fact that she completely obscured his view of the road was quite irrelevant since Asian drivers never look where they're going. As I was getting into the cab he noticed my sunburn and was appalled. Before I could try to explain that if not touched it didn't hurt he had coated my arm with Premium Pure Motor Oil, applied on a filthy piece of cotton wool out of his own First Aid box. He was so gentle that the treatment didn't pain me in the least but it remains to be seen whether Premium Pure Motor Oil on raw sunburn is a cure or the beginning of a lingering, fatal illness!

The cab of this truck had no doors and no windscreen glass and no seats but an upturned box for the driver; it seemed to be entirely home-made and the petrol engine stank so strongly that, despite all the fresh air, I was feeling violently ill in less than half an hour. Only the fact that we had three breakdowns in less than a hundred miles saved me: I was able to get out then and recover. The driver told me that there was no bicycle shop before the frontier town of Tieabad so here I am a day ahead of schedule; actually the road was so bad for the last sixty miles that even if Roz hadn't succumbed I would probably have given up the unequal struggle and hitched a ride over that stretch for both our sakes: the only alternative would have been to walk every yard of the way.

The first thirty miles today was through quite prosperous country with an unusual number of cattle and many acres of wheat, well up. The people, who are supposed to be even more unreliable than those of Azerbaijan, were very nice to me at both the villages where I stopped for tea and water. A minority of them are Mongolians, which is quite thrilling – a proof I'm nearing Central Asia! One point that intrigued me was that there do not appear to be any half-breeds: one sees either pure Aryan features or pure Mongolian, so there must be no intermarrying, which seems odd, as they're all Muslims.

I had a second lunch at 2.30 with the driver at a tiny village eating-house. The mutton soup was delicious (if you like your soup twenty-five per cent grease with lumps of fat floating in it, as I do) and was followed by perfectly cooked and beautifully flavoured mutton stew with beans, bread, raw onion and Pepsi-Cola (Persia's national drink!). I find the style of building evolved to suit mud very attractive; there are no corners or angles; everything is rounded and arched and curved. I've now got used to the Eastern way of sitting silently doing nothing whatever for an indefinite period. These people don't indulge in conversation as a pastime: they have occasional fierce arguments about some particular point and the rest is silence. I found it very pleasant today, just sitting cross-legged on my carpet (a posture which is no longer agonising as my joints are in training) looking out through the arched doorway at the blue sky and the few green trees growing beside the stream and the pale gold landscape and the donkey-traffic – little boys galloping by, old men walking their steeds sedately, and young men leading donkeys which were almost hidden under enormous leather pannier-bags filled with earth for some new building. The stream (which is also the local fridge) was flowing eloquently over boxes of bottles of Pepsi and the water was bubbling companionably in the men's hookahs all around me. I couldn't help wondering what all these millions of people think about during all these countless hours spent silently sitting – they have so few mental stimulants that it's difficult to believe they think at all. My Afghan driver was much more alert than the average Persian; he's an awfully nice bloke, giving a good first impression of the 'savages' of Afghanistan.

On arriving here I took Roz to the cycle shop and after infinite trouble found a screw to fit, seized it by force from the proprietor and personally did the job with my own screwdriver. In future, if anything goes wrong I, myself, am coping – or dying in the attempt.

I seem to have lost the thread of my narrative somewhere – I was going to say that after thirty miles the rest of today's journey was through sand desert, with only a few tiny villages. This town is a pleasant little place, where I am staying at the hotel, having been through the Customs and got an exit stamp on my passport, so that I'm all set for Afghanistan first thing in the morning. Not one word was said about the expired visa, which shows what you can get away with if you try – thirty-two days on a fifteen-day visa!

I'm quite sorry to be leaving Persia. Beneath all the physical dirt and moral corruption there is an elegance and dignity about life here which you can't appreciate at first, while suffering under the impact of the more obvious and disagreeable national characteristics. The graciousness with which peasants greet each other and the effortless art with which a few beautiful rags and pieces of silver are made to furnish and decorate a whole house – in these and many other details Persia can still teach the West. I suppose it's all a question of seeing one of the oldest and richest civilisations in the world long past its zenith. But I've decided that the Persians, though it's impossible for me to *like* them as I do the Turks, are more to be pitied than censured. Hundreds of years of in-breeding and malnutrition have undermined the race and it is only when you approach them from that angle and treat them with the necessary patience that you can come to terms with them.

I've gone completely native myself and now wash face, hands, teeth and clothes in the *jube*, though I remember being shocked five weeks ago at the sight of the Persians doing just that. However, I've now realised that the dreadful colour of the water is partly due to soil erosion, one of the chief national problems; there's no such thing as a clear stream here. But I do draw the line at drinking the *jube* water!

At the moment I'm sitting in the hotel courtyard, writing by the light of a full moon, beside a nimble, sparkling fountain, with richly scented shrubs all around me and the mountains of Afghanistan jagged against a royal blue sky on the eastern horizon. The air feels like silk as a little breeze moves among the birch trees that enclose two sides of the courtyard. The town's electricity supply has broken down and the tall pillars of the verandah look very lovely by moonlight.

Actually I shouldn't be here – on arrival the proprietor told me that no women are allowed outside the Women's Quarter. I meekly went off to same but it consisted of a tiny room with six beds and just enough space to walk between them. One bed was mine; the other five were occupied by women who possessed a minimum of two infants apiece – all being fed and changed at the time of my appearance. Both window and door were tightly sealed and the stink was appalling, so I got hold of an Indian, also staying here, and used him as interpreter to tell the proprietor that (*a*) The Shah condemned the segregation of women, (*b*) The Government was trying to encourage tourism and (*c*) I was prepared to respect religious conventions within reason but was *not* prepared to lock myself up for hours in a room like that when I could be sitting in a courtyard like this. The proprietor said, 'Very well, if you don't mind being stared at', to which I irritably replied that I'd been getting stared at by every man I met for thirty-two days and that if they had nothing better to do I didn't really mind.

GHURION, AFGHANISTAN, 9 APRIL

We left Tieabad at 6 a.m. with nineteen miles to go to the Afghan Customs, though the actual frontier is only ten miles away. The road ran through more sand desert, and lots of sand had been blown over it, which was an advantage in a way on such a rough surface. We crossed the frontier at 7.45 a.m. and whoever said the weather in Afghanistan would be ideal for cycling was wrong because even at this hour it was almost too hot. Those 150 miles I came south yesterday have made an extraordinary difference to the temperature. However, last winter remains so vivid in my mind that I am still grateful for too much sun.

The only indication of the Persian-Afghan frontier is a seven-foot stone pillar, conspicuous from far across the desert, which lucidly announces 'Afghanistan'. Here I stopped to photograph Roz. Three miles further on a long branch served as Customs barrier and beside it lay a very young soldier in a very ragged uniform, sound asleep with one hand on his rifle. I quietly raised the barrier for myself and continued towards the Customs and Passport Office two hundred yards ahead.

There, no one took the slightest notice of either my kit or my passport, no uniformed officials appeared and no series of dingy, uncomfortable offices had to be visited. Instead, I was ushered into a cool, dim, carpeted room and entertained by three men who, though ignorant of any European language, made me feel welcome and at home. They all wore baggy cotton trousers and loose, cleverly embroidered shirts hanging below the knees and turbans piled high above broad, smooth brows. As we sat cross-legged, performing the ritual of tea-drinking, I felt myself being happily weaned from the twentieth century by their reposefulness.

I was two hours at the Customs and might have been sitting there yet if another petrol truck hadn't arrived en route from Meshed. The driver wanted to take me to Herat but after yesterday's experience I know that the one thing more deleterious than being fried on a cycle in a desert is being rattled through a desert by truck. However, I asked the driver to take two petrol cans of water and leave them fifteen and thirty miles away on the roadside, as I couldn't possibly carry enough water on Roz to replace the gallons of sweat lost.

The village near the Customs – Islam Qu'ala – which I had expected to look like an East Persian village, didn't look like anything but an Afghan village: every house was a miniature fortress, with special apertures for firing at your neighbour when there's a feud on. At a little distance from the houses was an encampment of black goat-hair tents similar to one I had passed on the outskirts of Meshed, with a few camels lying chewing the cud beside it; it would have been good for a photo but I decided I'd like to get the 'feel' of the country before drawing unnecessary attention to the fact that I was about to cross forty miles of uninhabited desert.

We arrived here at 6.30 p.m. after a most gruelling struggle; I thought nothing could be worse than Persian roads but of course Afghan roads are much, much worse. Poor Roz – how long will she survive?

Ghurion is off the 'main' road so I decided to spend the night in a little tea-house at the junction, which is run by a delightful old man. I'm still working on the principle that the fewer people who know I'm around the better. (Despite myself all the fuss about the dangers of Afghanistan is having its effect on my nerves: probably a few days among the Afghans will soothe me down.)

The tea here comes by the tea-pot, instead of by the glass as in Turkey and Persia. You get about a pint of it and a little china bowl half filled with sugar into which you pour the tea and by the time you've had four bowlfuls the sugar is all gone. Having seen nothing of Afghanistan but a Customs House, a desert and a tea-house, there's no more to report till I get to Herat tomorrow morning.

3

Compulsory Bus Rides

HERAT TO KABUL

HERAT, 10 APRIL

I slept very well last night in my roadside tea-house, curled up in a corner of the one-roomed building, with moonlight streaming through the doorway that had no door and the 'proprietor' curled up under his camel-hair rug in another corner, rifle and turban to hand. He was a dear old boy, who seemed quite shocked when I attempted to pay him before leaving at 5.30 a.m.

It took me four and a half hours to cover the thirty miles to Herat but I enjoyed the wide silence of the desert in the cool of the morning.

This is a city of absolute enchantment in the literal sense of the word. It loosens all the bonds binding the traveller to his own age and sets him free to live in a past that is vital and crude but never ugly. Herat is as old as history and as moving as a great epic poem – if Afghanistan had nothing else it would have been worth coming to experience this. Even the loss of my wallet containing over £12 hasn't been able to depress me today. (It was not stolen but just slipped out of my pocket somehow, as I was exploring.) Of course I'd feel worse about such a loss in Europe; the fact that every Afghan I've seen so far obviously needs £12 even more than I do is quite a consolation. During a long trek some disaster of the sort is inevitable.

The Afghans impress me as a people with very clear-cut personalities, in contrast to the rather characterless Persians. Everyone I've met so far stands out as an individual; for example, the three servants at this hotel. One is an elderly man, very slim and sad-looking and withdrawn from the world. When not working (and that means most of the time) he sits in odd corners sipping tea or stands at strategic points of the stairs and corridors looking through everyone who passes and giving the impression of being in a mystical trance. When I arrived he came to my room with the book to sign and the whole scene was like some solemn religious ritual. The door curtain was pushed aside to admit this individual, wearing a long, pale pink muslin turban and bearing the book open at the relevant page. He bowed very low and glided across the floor in bare feet, laid it on the table before me, bowed again and glided backwards towards the door where he stood erect with arms folded looking into the far distance while I filled in details. Then he glided back to collect the book, bowed, backed to the door, gave a final and most profound bow and disappeared soundlessly – the whole performance without attempting to utter a word and, despite all the bowing, there was not a trace of servility.

The waiter is equally fascinating in a different way. Aged about twenty and very handsome, with pale, clear white skin, luminous brown eyes and wonderfully clear-cut features, he has a princely bearing and paces slowly round the dining-room; he is extremely efficient, in a quiet way, and looks as though he has some special private joy which makes him supremely happy. The little 'boots' is a character too; aged about twelve, he has a round Mongolian face, a big permanent grin and a bouncing friendly manner. Watching me washing my teeth is for him an entertainment beyond compare – he positively holds his breath at the sheer excitement of the spectacle!

This is a 'Grade A' hotel: i.e. it has an Eastern lavatory but with flush attached (when I pulled the string the whole apparatus collapsed and I was drenched in rusty water – but perhaps I used immodest vigour!) and there is also a holder for lavatory paper on the wall which makes one feel that if one stayed here long enough it might have paper too some day. The establishment sports electrical fittings as well – but the supply failed an hour ago and I am now writing by oil-lamp – and my room has a door with a padlock and a window that opens, and clean though very threadbare sheets and blankets on the bed. Other amenities include a bathroom on this first-floor landing; the cold water is contained in a zinc barrel with tap attached and, as you wash, it drains away through a hole in the wall down into the yard. For all these luxuries one pays 6*s.* 2*d.* per night.

Afghan 'fashions' for men look marvellously dignified, even when in tatters. The most common garment is one piece of cloth (usually cotton) which is worn so that it provides both a shirt and loose trousers to halfway down the calves. (Is this the 'seamless' garment of the Gospels?) Waist-length turbans, to protect the spinal cord against the sun, often have beautiful fringes and come in pastel shades of blue or pink or yellow. But there is no uniformity about dress – some wear sleeveless leather jackets inlaid with gold and silver, some fabulous brocade knee-length shirts, some heavy brocade coats, thrown over the shoulders in this weather, some brown homespun cloaks and others the flowing white robes which I have always associated with Arab countries. About fifty per cent go barefooted, even on horses and cycles – the latter being almost the only evidence of the twentieth century in Herat. The men, if Aryan, are considerably taller than Turks or Persians and are very handsome indeed. The women I simply haven't seen; very few appear on the streets and those few are completely veiled – not in the *chador* of east Turkey and Persia, which leaves eyes and nose just visible, but in the *burkah*, a garment like a tent with a piece of lace at eye-level. This lace is of such fine mesh that you have to be right beside them to distinguish it from the rest of the material and seeing the wearer standing still you don't know which is back or front: they look like people dressed up as ghosts. This afternoon I saw two women riding splendid ponies and asked their husband if I might photograph them, but he very vigorously refused permission. The only female face I've seen in the city was that of a Mongolian tribeswoman down from the mountains, bringing cloth to sell in the bazaar; she was galloping along the main street, astride and bareheaded with a baby tied to her back and its father galloping along behind on his silver-grey pony stallion.

I notice that most of the phaeton ponies are stallions who dash spiritedly around, their vehicles taking the corners on one wheel. This is all right if the mares are kept in purdah too – and evidently they are! It's a joy to see these ponies after the miserable specimens in Persian cities; they are well groomed and well fed here and their coats ripple with reflected sunlight. Oddly enough, they're the only clean looking objects, animate or inanimate, to be seen in the streets. Another point of contrast with Persia is that I haven't seen any beggars here, except for a few cripples in the immediate vicinity of the mosque.

The Afghan has not yet learned that tourists were invented to be fleeced and twice today my money was refused when I attempted to pay for tea. I am a guest of the country, so it pleases Allah when someone provides me with free refreshment . . .

During one of these pauses in a tea-house a man, whom I had never seen before and will never see again, silently approached, laid a packet of cigarettes beside me and vanished before I even had time to thank him; I couldn't help thinking then of my kind European friends who had warned me so often of the dangers of being a woman and a Christian in Muslim countries.

Strolling through the bazaar I was delightedly conscious of the fact that when Alexander's soldiers passed this way they must have witnessed scenes almost identical to those now surrounding me – bakers cooking flat bread in underground ovens, having spread the dough on leather cushions stuffed with straw and damped with filthy water; blindfolded camels walking round and round churning *mast* in stinking little dens behind their owners' stalls; butchers skinning and disembowelling a sheep and throwing scraps to the yellow, crop-eared dogs who have been waiting all morning for this happy event; tanners curing hides, weavers at their looms, potters skilfully firing pitchers of considerable beauty, cobblers making the curly-toed, exquisitely inlaid regional shoes and tailors cutting out the long, fleece-padded coats which when thrown over the shoulders of an Afghan makes him look like a fairy-story king.

On my way back to the hotel I observed hens importantly leading their excited broods to unrevealed destinations, tiny boys sitting cross-legged on the pavement meticulously cleaning oil-lamps, diminutive, anxious, furry donkey-foals who had temporarily lost their mothers, and youths squatting in doorways preparing hookahs for the men to smoke. It's unlikely that the other Afghan cities will be equally attractive; Herat is now so cut off from everywhere on every side that it's just gone jogging along happily while the rest of the country is being modernised by the US and the USSR.

The 'traffic' police here take my fancy particularly; obviously they're trained in the French system and they stand on little platforms with batons, wearing caps to prove they're police but otherwise keeping to the national costume. The joke is that you see them making a quick sweeping movement with one hand and a 'stop' movement with the other and in answer to the 'come on' signal, with its flourish of the baton that should herald the rush past of a stream of high-powered cars, twelve camels appear, heavily laden and chained together, and pace solemnly by the police-box taking about ten minutes to clear the junction. Meanwhile the 'stop' signal has briefly halted a horseman who pulls up his steed on its hind legs, looks from the camels to the policeman with a curl of the lip and then proceeds to canter round the caravan and gallop away up the main street. Occasionally a truck appears from Persia (because of the Pakistan blockade, everything now has to come from the outside world via Russia or Persia), and then there is real commotion which the police are helpless to control; donkeys, horsemen, camels, phaetons and flocks of sheep and goats all flee in the wrong direction at the wrong moment, the camels looking outraged at having to amble faster than usual.

This morning I went to the outskirts of the town just to wander among the green woods and sit on green grass beside a little stream in a beautifully kept public park. Many of the streets are lined with enormous pine trees and a glorious garden of lawns and lavishly blooming rose bushes stretches in front of the mosque. There were no restrictions about me visiting this mosque (without a camera) and it is so very beautiful that I felt it compensated for the Meshed frustration. I sat on the shady side of the enormous courtyard for almost an hour, enjoying the mosaics and the gold of the brickwork glowing against the blue sky. It was very peaceful there with no sound or movement except for a myriad twittering martins swooping in and out of the cool, dim passages between the hundreds of pillared archways. Meshed is probably as beautiful but it would be difficult to surpass this. The predominant colour here is blue of all shades, with yellow, black, pink, brown, green and orange tiles blended so skilfully that from a certain distance a façade or minaret looks as though made of some magic precious metal for the colour of which there is no name. Also, quite apart from its colouring, the proportions of the whole vast series of buildings are superb.

ROBAT, 11 APRIL

There was so much to say yesterday that I failed to mention the big route problem. My original intention was to go to Kabul via the northern road as this is by far the most beautiful and interesting, but that plan has been ruled out because of the current tricky situation with Russia. Therefore, when I reported to the police in Herat yesterday I told them I wished to go by the central route, which is the next most interesting – but the Commander said, 'No!' Apparently this road is closed to all traffic because it is too infested with bandits to be adequately policed. Even if I had wanted to have fun and games with the authorities, as in Persia, I realised that I couldn't as they're quite a different type here – clearly their 'No' means 'No'; so now I'm on the third, southern route, via Khandahar, and am lucky to have my permit to cycle confirmed by the police who took a very dim view of my ambitions and tried to get me aboard a bus. In fact I may have to give in at some stage on this road as it would be silly to risk more than fifty miles unbroken desert with Roz and there may be one eighty-mile stretch. I'll investigate the situation fully when we get to that point.

We left Herat at 4.45 a.m. because it will get hotter every day now, going due south. A glorious eight- or nine-mile oasis of green fields and woods surrounds the city and the wheat and barley are within a few weeks of harvesting. Then – about five miles out – the road became perfect! I nearly fell off with astonishment and joy and Roz really let herself go and whizzed along at an average of 15 m.p.h. Our unexpected bliss lasted all day – God bless Russia! There's an average of one truck and two buses a day on this route so the Russians certainly didn't build a flawless road here for the convenience of the Afghans; but at the moment I couldn't care less who built it or why – I only hope it lasts.

A double row of pines, alternating with a richly pink flowering shrub, lasted well beyond the green belt out into the desert. Then, just as it was getting hot enough to make me fret slightly about having no hat, the road began to climb through mountains that were great barren piles of grey, slaty rock, but, because of the good surface, we covered just over eighty miles today despite much walking. I used my chlorinated pills for the first time in some doubtful-looking water obtained during the afternoon from a nomad camp, where the people were very courteous and kind. They invited me to have a meal with them and served some sort of porridge mixed with cheese and camel's milk; I suppose I'll get used to it but at the moment I wouldn't actually say that camel's milk is my favourite beverage. Huge herds of camels were being grazed around the encampment; goats or sheep wouldn't survive this terrain. I asked if I might take photographs but though they didn't refuse they were obviously against the idea so it would have been an abuse of hospitality to insist.

We arrived here at 7.20 p.m., just after dark. This is a small town with some rather grim-looking characters around and I'm almost sorry I didn't stay for the night with my nomads, where I would have felt safer. But one can't judge yet; the Afghans seem very reserved and distant people and what I feel as 'grimness' may be merely aloofness.

From the map it looks like more lovely mountains tomorrow – if only the road keeps Russian! Early bed now.

KHANDAHAR, 12 AND 13 APRIL

For reasons that will soon become apparent I'd no opportunity to report on the day's activities last night, so I'm doing both dates now.

I was up at 4.30 a.m. yesterday morning, after a good sleep on carpets in a corner of a tea-house. I have decided that Afghans are much more 'comfortable' people to travel among than Persians, despite their unbending gravity – or perhaps because of it. A dense, curious throng surrounded us every time we stopped in Persia but though here our arrival must be equally a rarity, no one crowds us out – you'd think they were used to a continual flow of cycling women through their villages! They are very interested to know where one has come from and what route was taken to Afghanistan, but they ask no questions – just listen and look politely if you choose to explain by mime and a map. I find the contrast very intriguing; Afghanistan never attained the heights of civilisation that Persia did, nor has she ever descended to Persia's present depths. Is it that if a nation expends sufficient energy to get to a peak she hasn't enough left to maintain herself there and falls far, whereas if she remains at a certain restricted level a limited degree of national well-being can be maintained indefinitely? I suppose history proves that this is the pattern.

But to get back to 4.30 a.m., when I set off down the road and after fifty yards was held up by two police, this time wearing the jackets of their uniforms to emphasise the solemnity of the occasion. They said I'd have to go by autobus to Khandahar, and I said, 'What rot!' and showed my pass from the Commander in Herat. Then they pointed to a petrol-tanker and signed that it couldn't go on either, and to their own jeep containing two soldiers with machine-guns! (You never saw anything quite so unhappy as an Afghan soldier wearing Western uniform – the poor lads looked as though they were in a torture-chamber.) I began to wonder now whether (*a*) World War III had started or (*b*) a little local war with Russia was brewing. Anyway something was happening somewhere so I retired to the tea-house and went asleep again until 7 a.m., having been told that the bus was coming at 7.30. Eventually it came at 10 a.m. and all the passengers tumbled out for *chi* and hands and face washing in the *jube*, and lavatory work in an adjacent field; unlike Turkish and Persian tea-houses, Afghan tea-houses have no lavatories attached. Two women were travelling on the roof amidst everyone's goods and chattels – very symbolic! I simply can't imagine what torture it must have been for them. Of course they don't often travel at all and my horror was multiplied by ten when I discovered that these two were going to Kabul hospital because they were very *ill*; yet for 1,000 km they had to adhere to the top of a bouncing bus on an awful road through blazing sun and cold night air and choking dust.

The bus looked like something left on a municipal dump for a year and then retrieved during a National Emergency. It was almost entirely home-made with no cover on the engine and no doors or windows. You could read on the ceiling inside that it was constructed partly from wooden boxes in which something had been imported from the USSR. The wheels had belonged to a truck and were far too big for the body and the seats were planks across which you scrambled to get to your place as no space was wasted on an aisle down the middle. The bus had been so overcrowded on leaving Herat that my entry made no difference to the general misery (not that the Afghans seemed to regard it as misery) of being tightly wedged with nothing to lean on back or front and no chance to move an inch in any direction once you sat down. Eventually at 11 a.m. we set off and about ten miles from Robat the road petered out – not merely the good road, but any road at all. For the next two hours we bumped on over the hard rock and baked sand of the desert till the faintest trace of a track reappeared – which was worse than the desert. In the agony of the journey I'd forgotten to wonder why we were being compelled to travel in convoy but towards evening we passed a Land-Rover with its windshield shattered and its doors riddled by bullet-holes and two soldiers on guard.

I won't go into all the harrowing details, beyond saying that it took us twenty-two and a half hours to cover 420 miles. Apart from some eighty miles of sheer desert it would have been good cycling country with lots of mountains – not in the least as monotonous as I'd expected. But the road – or lack of road – would have made it very gruelling. With the seven days I estimate I've saved I'm planning to go up from Kabul to Mazar-i-Sharif via Bamian and return via Kunduz – I think it is permitted to go up from the east side.

The one compensation last night was the beauty of that wonderfully desolate landscape by moonlight, never to be forgotten. We stopped often as, apart from praying and eating sessions, the bus had two punctures and the truck three. Also the bus frequently threatened to come apart at the seams and then the driver leaped out with a mallet and went round giving it unmerciful bangs on the vital spots. Of course no one minded all these delays: people here have no concept of time as we understand it. The majority wear watches as ornaments and I was diverted to discover that they can't read the time and don't see why they should learn! Yesterday is over, today is something to be enjoyed without fuss, and tomorrow – well, it's sinful to plan anything for the future because that's Allah's department and humans have no business to meddle with it. This basic tenet of Islam is obviously one reason why Muslim countries are so materially undeveloped; after a thousand years of living by such a doctrine it is difficult to think ahead constructively.

The majority of Afghans practise their religion very seriously. Yesterday evening at about 6.30 the convoy suddenly put on terrific speed – I thought my whole unfortunate carcase would be disjointed – and after some ten miles pulled up before a tea-house beside a stream. Then the truck drivers, the soldiers and the bus passengers all rushed together to the water for ritual washing, before taking off their cloaks, which they use as prayer mats, and spreading them on the dusty ground. By sundown the whole surrounding desert was dotted with standing, bowing and kneeling men: no wonder they remain so supple in old age for this performance five times daily would keep anyone fit. They had been through it all before at 3.30 p.m. and were to repeat it at 4.10 a.m. today. Meanwhile those two unhappy women were cowering in their burkahs up on the roof among the crates and bales and Roz. They didn't even come down for meals though their husbands passed them up bread and tea occasionally.

When I first boarded the bus the men simply ignored me, but after a couple of hours they thawed out and became very pleasant companions. Of course they wouldn't allow me to pay for anything en route (it was poetic justice that I lost my £12 in this country) though they were not forthcoming with the conventions we're used to – opening doors, ladies first, and all that; in fact it was taken for granted that I should be served *last* at meals. We had a very good stew last night with mincemeat balls and deliciously prepared spinach and the ubiquitous rice. After one mouthful of the rice I admitted defeat – it tasted as though cooked in *jube*-water and most Afghan *jubes* are stagnant. So I concentrated on bread (probably mixed with *jube*-water) which is darker here than in Persia and much more palatable. Breakfast was a bowl of hot sheep's milk with bread in it and a tea-potful of very sweet cocoa made of milk and finally green tea. Having toured Khandahar today and studied the butchers and the flies and the 'sanitary' conveniences, I've reluctantly decided to avoid meat, good though it tastes, and concentrate on boiled eggs for protein – I haven't forgotten my last Spanish trip and what dysentery feels like. In Turkey and Persia it wasn't the fly season, but here everything is permanently black with the pests.

We arrived in Khandahar at 9.30 a.m. and I said goodbye to my buddies and wished them joy on the next 515 km to Kabul. The armed guard went off to get a few hours sleep before going back to Herat with another convoy made up of a bus, two trucks and two Australians motoring to England and wishing they weren't. I'm afraid I've very little patience with people who complain indignantly about places like Afghanistan being primitive. Why didn't they (*a*) find that out before coming here and then (*b*) fly from Lahore to London?

I came straight to the hotel, got my sore bones into bed and slept till 2 p.m. This hotel is a filthy building, but again my bed is clean and the only furniture in the room, apart from bed and chair, is a fine solid writing desk which compensates for a lot.

When I went off to explore at 2.30 p.m. it was overcast so not too hot. This is quite an attractive city but after Herat anything would be an anticlimax and it's disquieting to find the place teeming with Americans and their works. Obviously a terrific battle is going on to win over Afghanistan, but I hope neither side succeeds.

The Afghans smoke fewer cigarettes than the Persians. Not one passenger smoked in the bus but many chewed a green powdery stuff out of little tins kept in their pockets and the results were spat out incessantly on to the floor. No cigarettes are made here; Russian blends cost 9*d.* for twenty (pure poison) and English blends, specially ordered by the Afghan Government from England and labelled to that effect, cost 2*s.* for twenty. All the popular American blends are also 2*s.* a packet.

I've a bad sore throat this evening, which is not surprising, as last night it turned very cold from about 3 to 5 a.m., when we were crossing the mountains, and I was chilled through – I am still thinking of those two unfortunate women.

An hour ago a fierce southerly gale blew a sandstorm over the city; I felt very glad that Roz and I were not exposed to its horrors.

Undoubtedly (despite clean beds) the Afghans are, on balance, *much* dirtier in clothes, personal habits and dwellings than either the Turks or Persians. And I thought Persia bad enough when I got there! The light here goes out every ten or fifteen minutes for about five minutes, which is very right and proper; it would be too boring to travel all the way to Central Asia and then have an infallible electricity supply.

In many ways English influence is apparent here: most of the Afghans I met today spoke a little English and addressed me as 'Memsahib', which I find infuriating. Also a number of shop and public signs are in English as well as in Pushto or Pharsi; one sees some lovely spellings – 'CLOADS DRI CLEENED'! But nearly all the few Afghan-owned cars, jeeps and trucks seem to be Russian. I must write to Mr Khrushchev and tell him that a few buses would not be superfluous in the next consignment.

I hope to make Kabul in five or six days, depending on heat, roads and other contingencies such as mountain passes. Of course one never knows – we could be there under escort in forty-eight hours if the bandits move the scene of their activities.

KALAT-E-GHIZLOT, 14 APRIL

I woke this morning at 4 a.m. and leapt energetically out of bed, stark naked, to see a fine bearded warrior in each of the other two beds, which had been empty when I retired; happily they missed the fun, being sound asleep. This intrusion didn't really surprise me because I had already observed the craziness of the hotel key system. There was only *one* key to twenty rooms, and as all the rooms were occupied – which here means families of up to ten members in a room containing four single beds – with people coming and going and wanting their doors locked and unlocked and relocked, or their womenfolk incarcerated while they went out to town, the distraught lad in charge of the key had been kept in a state of perpetual motion on the previous evening.

Roz and I left Khandahar at 4.30 a.m. and the road was good for all of today's ninety miles – and will continue good for the first ten miles tomorrow. This time it's 'God bless the Americans' who within four years expect to have completed the 320 miles from Kabul to Khandahar. On the outskirts of Khandahar I passed various other evidences of American A.I.D. – little factories, a new school and an electricity power plant.

It was very hot today, with only two little villages en route. I would have been tormented by thirst but for milk obtained from various nomad camps (there were plenty of them) and now I'm quite muzzy in the head after so much sun. At 11 a.m. the heat compelled me to stop for four hours at a village; I slept for two hours and then wrote a sheaf of 'duty' letters to be posted in Kabul.

We arrived here at 7.15 p.m. This local hotel is inexplicably vast and I'm the only inhabitant; as food is not served I went to an eating-house in the village and gorged on bread and mutton-stew. (I felt too hungry to keep my good resolution about not eating meat!) The roof of the eating-house was so low that big six-footers in flowing robes had to bend their heads while walking to the carpet they had chosen to sit on. More wood than usual is in evidence in the buildings around here – though one sees few trees growing – and the ceiling and 'pillars' were of big, crudely-hewn trunks blackened by years of lamp and hookah smoke; but everything else, including the cooking stove, was of mud. I love the washing-ritual. Here, as in Persia, a special boy is employed for the purpose. Serious as an acolyte, he comes to each person with a brass or copper jug, round-bellied and long-spouted, containing very hot water, and with a basin shaped like a witch's hat turned upside-down. Having poured water over the hands into the basin he then presents a filthy towel and as cutlery is unknown here, this rite is repeated after the meal. It is fascinating to sit on the floor in a corner watching it all by the soft light of oil-lamps suspended on chains from the ceiling to about eighteen inches above floor level. This light reflects on the copper jugs, and glows in the quick dark eyes of the men, their faces strong-featured beneath high turbans. Huge shadows stir on the walls when someone arrives or departs, moving lithely in bare feet, and then the small room seems even smaller. The rapid trickling of the washing-water mingles with the meditative gurgle of the hookahs as they are passed from man to man, puffed at ceremoniously and then repacked and relit no less ceremoniously, with embers carried from the stove in lieu of matches. And always there's the other ritual of *chi*-drinking, so that when I left I had to pick my way carefully among a litter of little Japanese tea-pots and bowls. By now I'm in love with Afghanistan – with its simplicity, its courtesy and its leisureliness and with the underlying *sanity* of an area fortunate enough to have remained very backward indeed . . .

Despite the heat, today's was a glorious ride, across vast unpeopled widths of sand and barren sun-split clay. Lines of naked peaks, like broken swords, were just visible along the horizon and the only alleviation of the surrounding flatness was the deep, dead canyons which are waiting for the floods to revive them. When I came to the oasis at midday its green orchards and meadows seemed passionately fertile amidst the unproductive wastes and on entering its shade the temperature dropped by 15°. It is just as well I'm moving north because I couldn't stand much more of this – at 3.30 p.m. furnace blasts of hot air were ricocheting off the face of the desert and even my hair was soaked with sweat. I'm deadbeat now so early to bed.

MUKUR, 15 APRIL

We only covered sixty-eight miles today; the road was appalling once the American contribution to my comfort ended and we wouldn't have got even this far but for a deliciously cool northerly breeze which blew all day.

Prepare for shocks. At 10 a.m. Roz had a puncture and by 11.15 a.m. *I* had repaired it. Even more sensational – at 1.30 p.m. the chain broke and again I, myself (alone and unaided!), got out the spare links and after one and three-quarter hours of intense concentration figured how the thing operated and mended it! It is astonishing what latent talents are suddenly revealed by breakdowns in mid-desert.

The first half of today's ride was through comparatively fertile country with many streams and consequently many little villages surrounded by acres of wheat and lucerne and by groves of poplars. Then we were back to the desert and the nomad camps. One of these donated water for mending the puncture, which was jolly decent considering that they have to bring water-skins about ten miles on camels to the nearest well. At this camp I saw a pure white, new-born camel, whose mother was ill, being fed out of a leather bottle by an adorable nomad infant aged about four years. After the broken chain interlude came some dramatically beautiful gorges and extraordinary landscapes of fissured earth. Afghanistan is certainly living up to my expectations; it's a pity brainwashing tactics were used to dissuade me because I must admit that I'm now aware all the time of a slight underlying tension which mars what would otherwise be a completely enjoyable experience. I suppose *all* the people can't be wrong *all* the time and every Afghan I've met has said that he personally would *not* cycle alone through his own country.

We arrived here at 6.45 p.m. and I asked for the chief's house as there is no hotel or police barracks and I funked the tea-house after one quick look. A young man led me to the outskirts of the town and through a most beautiful orchard, where the trees were gay with bell-shaped, flame-coloured blossoms and a cool, deep carpet of lucerne lay beneath them. Then we came to an enormous mud compound, where the chief, his *five* wives, fourteen sons and uncounted daughters, thirty-eight grandchildren and sundry cousins all live in various apartments around a courtyard through which flows a swift stream with weeping willows and birches lining its banks.

Several of the chief's sons speak English and/or German, and I had a long conversation with one of them, aged nineteen, whose seventeen-year-old wife has borne him three children and who is about to acquire a second, fourteen-year-old wife. When I asked him what his wife thought about a second wife arriving on the scene, he said that Afghan women don't talk to their husbands and anyway it's none of her business *how* many wives he has! His father's fifth wife, aged eighteen, was acquired three years ago when the senior wife, now aged forty-eight, retired from stud. A total of 135 members of the family plus twenty-two servants live in the compound.

I'm writing this sitting by the stream waiting for supper (I suggested bread and boiled eggs but very much fear rice will come) and one of the servants has just glided up with a new lantern to give me more light: it's all deliciously like the Arabian Nights. Tonight I'll sleep in the maidens' (eleven- to fourteen-year-old girls) quarters and of course this has been my first chance to *see* any Afghan women. Physically they're very beautiful (the men being so tanned, one doesn't realise that Afghans are as white-skinned as we are) but the effect on their mental development of the purdah-system, as practised here, is horrifying. We should feel grateful for having been born 'free' and 'equal' – something we take completely for granted though the majority of the world's women do not yet enjoy this right.

Most Afghan village houses have no windows and the walls are lined with little alcoves which serve as cupboards. One misses the Persian carpets; coarse matting is more usual here. I can now see a servant coming with my supper on a tray; obviously I am considered not really fit company for the women of the family, so I must eat in solitude!

GHAZNI, 16 APRIL

I went to bed last night *dead drunk*. I was enjoying my 'Irish stew' of mutton, potatoes and onions when one of my host's sons arrived with a bottle and said he'd heard Christian women liked alcohol and would I have some wine? It is hardly necessary to record my reply. He then filled a tumbler ('Made in Czechoslovakia') with what looked like white wine and I, being thirsty and having eschewed the muddy water served with the meal, took a gulp of it in all innocence – and nearly collapsed! I don't pretend to know what it was, but it certainly was not wine as we know it. My gullet must be fairly leathery by now but I felt as if my mouth, throat and tummy were being cauterised. When I'd stopped choking the boy said, 'With water, yes, it is better?' and I nodded, feeling that however many lethal bacteria the water contained they would all die instantly on meeting this brew. So I finished it diluted and then, to my horror, found myself almost incapable of standing up and going to bed, and quite incapable of talking coherently. It comes to something when *one* drink can knock me out! I was in a besotted coma by 9.30 p.m. but up at 4 a.m. as usual – without a 'head', to my astonishment.

It was much cooler today and the road was slightly less agonising, so we covered the seventy miles from Mukur by 2.30 p.m. I was pushing myself to allow time to explore this city which I guessed would be congenial because of historical associations and no Americanisation; in fact it's a good second to Herat.

I tried to buy a film here, but none was available, which was very frustrating as the fine old fortifications, ruined mosques (which you may photograph), the river and camel-market make Ghazni even more photogenic than Herat. However, as things developed I was perhaps lucky to be without a film today.

Leaving Roz in the hotel, I went off to explore, still carrying my camera in hope of finding a film. For some time I strolled around the base of the old city – which looks like a more primitively constructed Avila – doing no harm to anyone and scarcely noticing the battalion of inconceivably scruffy soldiers who were marching past me, until suddenly two privates broke rank, seized my arms and hustled me about a hundred yards up the street to a military police barracks. There they asked for my passport, which I explained was in the hotel, so my camera was promptly confiscated and I was locked for fifty minutes in a cell which had been used as a lavatory by all its former occupants and never cleaned out. Then an officer appeared in a frenzied flurry of profuse apologies and said that it was all a mistake – the army was on manoeuvres in the locality and his men had been instructed to look out for 'hostile observers'. He saw by my passport that I was harmless and hoped I would forgive the incident and would now have vodka with him. I told him there was no offence taken but explained that unhappily I hadn't time for vodka as I wanted to see the old city of Ghazni and the Moghul tomb – so by way of atonement he laid on an army car to drive me there.

The tomb of Afghanistan's most famous poet, whose name no one could reasonably be expected to remember, is a very impressive marble affair in a little mosque all to itself on a hilltop outside the city. I walked up there at sunset and stood overlooking a rich spread of grain-fields, orchards dense with blossom, and groves of slim, graceful sinjit trees. The bird-song in these oases is continuous and very sweet; now, apart from swallows, the birds are all unfamiliar to me.

I've just been informed that the Americans are moving in here soon; I'm glad I saw it first. It's quite cold tonight, with snow on the hills to the east and the sky overcast – what a change!

KABUL, 17 APRIL

Today was a repeat of the Robat performance. I slept late, having had no siesta yesterday, and woke at 6.45 a.m. to find a tremendous thunderstorm in progress and *rain* (of all unlikely things!) coming down in buckets. I enjoyed a leisurely breakfast of omelette and bread as I had only intended covering forty-eight miles today (to Top, the village midway between Ghazni and Kabul) and when the rain stopped at 8 a.m. we left the hotel. But then, outside the town, came another road block, with what was by local standards a vast convoy of two buses, five trucks and a motorcyclist, all lined up outside a tea-house. I joined the queue and asked what it was this time. No one knew definitely; some said that a Danish engineer working for an American company had been shot at and wounded while others maintained that two Indians going to Europe had copped it yesterday evening twenty miles north of Ghazni. I wasn't surprised at this vagueness; the authorities here are extremely sensitive about such 'incidents' and cover them up as best they can. Anyway, whatever the cause, the effect was that Roz and I boarded one of the 'buses' at 9.30 a.m. and arrived here, having covered a distance of only ninety-three miles, at 10 p.m. A young army officer who sat beside me on the bus said that Pakistani tribesmen were behind all the trouble; he accused them of coming over the frontier and shooting up travellers (especially foreigners) to discredit Afghanistan in the eyes of the world. Maybe that's partly true, but it certainly wasn't Pakistanis who attacked the Land-Rover on the road between Robat and Farah.

I have just been told that Afghan time is one hour and ten minutes ahead of Persian time – a comical refinement in this land where ten hours or ten days more or less mean nothing whatever to the average citizen.

4

Misadventure with a Rifle-butt

KABUL TO BAMIAN

KABUL, 18 APRIL

I have just registered the fact that Easter happened four days ago – that's what comes of travelling in 'Eathen Lands! It gives me all I can do to cope with the date and I've long since given up the unequal struggle to distinguish one day of the week from another; when Friday is Sunday and Thursday is Saturday and Saturday is Monday it seems hardly worth the effort. But presumably I'll register the significance of 25 December when the time comes.

Kabul, though so much of it has been recently rebuilt, is an attractive little city. Many of the new buildings and public monuments are hideously *avant-garde* but their incongruity is so extreme in this country that the total effect is comic rather than offensive. The city streets were paved (by the Russians) only a few years ago and today I saw a traffic policeman abandoning his post to kneel on the footpath and say his prayers at the appointed hour.

This frank devotion is for me one of the most impressive features of Islamic culture. If we accept that it is more than a superstition then there is something very wonderful indeed about mixing one's daily deeds and one's daily prayers in such an unselfconscious fashion, instead of keeping each in an airtight compartment.

Kabul reminds me of Sofia in that the traffic is virtually nil by capital city standards; you can cycle happily around with only camel caravans, herds of pack-donkeys and droves of fellow-cyclists to impede the way. Among the injuries which Roz sustained in Meshed was a damaged back brake so I took her into a cycle shop today and she was efficiently cured in five minutes.

One sees a few women and quite a number of girls unveiled in the streets here and many men wear European suits, though happily these are still in the minority. I bought a first (and last) souvenir for myself this morning – one of the famous Afghan sheepskin coats. It's a second-hand (or more likely fifth-hand) model and looks and smells exactly like a dead sheep, which is logical enough, as the Afghans haven't a clue about curing skins. Anyway the main thing is that it cost only 28*s*., whereas a new one would have cost about £6. It still has years of wear in it, if the Irish public can bear the stink.

The weather here today is just like April at home – showery, warm sun, cool breeze – but with growth about two weeks ahead of us. This is the month when northern Afghanistan gets all its rainfall – heavy showers and thunderstorms nearly every day.

German seems to be more widely spoken than English among Afghans educated before the war. At that period the country was teeming with Germans – it is now beginning to teem with them again – and I am told that German is still the first foreign language of the ten per cent who go to school. Russian is widely understood too, even by the illiterate majority. In each city I noticed that the radio news from Russia was switched on regularly and listened to attentively. Russians seem to handle the propaganda tool of aid to backward countries much more intelligently than the Americans do. They achieve lots of *little* things – electricity for small towns, paving city streets, building silos and presenting superior seeds for crops – as well as launching big projects such as roads, whereas the Americans concentrate on enormous schemes – roads and dams that cost five times what the Russians spend but will take years to complete and make no impression whatever on the minds of simple people. The more I see of life in these 'undeveloped countries' and of the methods adopted to 'improve' them, the more depressed I become. It seems criminal that the backwardness of a country like Afghanistan should be used as an excuse for America and Russia to have a tug-of-war for possession. Having spoken to nine or ten young Afghans who have been exposed to Western influences, I notice an impatient feeling of contempt for their own country, an undiscriminating worship of everything American and a general restlessness, rootlessness and discontent. They repudiate their native culture yet cannot succeed in adopting an alien civilisation which they imagine is superior, though they don't understand the first thing about it. Give me the nomads' outlook every time – they haven't heard of America yet. I don't claim to know the right answer to the 'underdeveloped' problem but I feel most strongly that the Communist answer is less wrong than the Western; the Communists have much more imaginative understanding of different national temperaments, as two Russians I spoke to here today revealed very clearly. They want to impose Communism as a way of life, but with the minimum of damage to the traditional foundations of the country concerned, whereas Westerners have told me repeatedly that they want to bulldoze those foundations right away and start a nice, new, hygienic society from scratch – an ambition that seems to me almost too stupid to be true.

I have just discovered that the sale or consumption of alcohol in Afghanistan is strictly forbidden by law – a piece of information handed to me with a glass of Scotch by my hostess in the Diplomatic Enclave! Even tourists can't get permission to have it here as they can in the prohibition states of India.

My plans for the immediate future are in 'a state of chassis'; my host wants to drive me to Bamian tomorrow (a Friday, so the Embassy will be closed) and I, of course, want to cycle there and, if possible, on up to Mazar-i-Sharif. But no one seems to know whether the road beyond Bamian is free of snow or not.

I had to register with the police as a tourist this morning, which involved going to three separate offices and waiting hours in each. The head of the Tourist Department, Mr Tarzi, is a great buddy of our Mr Driscoll, this year's President of the International Tourist Board. I couldn't believe it when I met an Afghan who knew Dublin! He's an exceptionally nice man and is now trying to find out about the Mazar road before issuing me with my permits to move from Kabul. But everything is so slow here that, tomorrow being Friday, Saturday is the first day I can get my papers straightened out and make definite plans. Everyone agrees that the business of being a tourist in Kabul involves so much paperwork and waiting in offices that one has no time to see the sights. Not that there are many; apart from the magnificent museum, the city itself, with its lovely semicircle of mountains curving round it, is the chief 'sight'.

KABUL, 19 APRIL

If my arrival in Teheran was a sensation, it has been a riot here! The Tourist Office and Press photographers, complete with flashlights, were on my heels the whole day, and my 'Impressions of Afghanistan' will be in the *Kabul Times* tomorrow. 'Everyone' wants to meet me – not that I'm surprised or imagine that it's because I'm me. Kabul is wonderful from a visitor's point of view, but if one had to live here for two years, and if one were accustomed to cars (which only senior officials can have) and to TV, daily papers, mod. cons, pubs, cafés, cinemas and theatres, life without them must seem rather monotonous. This is rated a 'hardship post' by foreign services and everyone is paid a twenty-five per cent bonus to come to Kabul. It's funny to see the sedate Embassy staffs scooting round on bicycles or walking, but it does mean that for at least two years of their existence they lead healthy lives with daily exercise.

KABUL, 20 APRIL

Cheers! By signing a statement to say that I was cycling alone to Mazar entirely on my own responsibility I obtained the necessary police pass, so off we go first thing tomorrow. I spent eight and a quarter hours in four different offices getting the pass because forty-five Hajis were looking for permits to go on a pilgrimage to Mecca and I was at the end of their queue in every office.

I'm only taking the saddlebag with essential kit as there is no point in dragging my panniers and knapsack from here to Mazar and back again.

QU'LAH DOAB, 21 APRIL

I've decided that when I suspected the Afghans of a narrow hostility to emancipated women, I was being unfair. Many of them give the impression of being almost frightened by the spectacle of a lone woman roaming around their land – a phenomenon so startling to their simple minds that they are at a loss as to how they should react. Obviously this situation throws the onus on the more flexible-minded Westerner and, now that I've realised how much depends on my approach to them, relations are far easier to manage. I already love the country and the people and somehow language barriers don't matter when one feels such a degree of sympathy with a race which responds so graciously and kindly to a smile or a gesture of friendship.

We left Kabul at 7 a.m. in perfect cycling weather with a brilliant, warm sun, a cool breeze behind us and the air crisp and clear. Beyond a doubt today's run up the Ghorband valley was the most wonderful cycle-ride of my life. Surely this must have been the Garden of Eden – it's so beautiful that I was too excited to eat the lunch my hostess had packed for me and spent the day in a sort of enchanted trance. High hills look down on paddy-fields and vivid patches of young wheat and neat vineyards; on orchards of apricot, peach, almond, apple and cherry trees smothered in blossom, and on woods of willows, ash, birch and sinjit, their new leaves shivering and glistening in wind and sun. Lean, alert youths, their clothes all rags and their bearing all pride, guard herds of cattle and nervous, handsome horses and donkeys with woolly, delicately tripping foals, and fat-tailed sheep with hundreds of bounding lambs, and long-haired goats whose kids are among the most delightful of young animals. At intervals there are breaks in the walls of sheer rock on either side and then one sees the more distant peaks of the Hindu Kush rising to 18,000 feet, their snows so brilliant that they are like Light itself, miraculously solidified and immobilised. The little mud villages remain invisible until you reach them, so perfectly do they blend with their background, and the occasional huge, square, mud fortresses, straddling hilltops, recall the cruel valour of this region's past and have the same rigid, proud beauty as the men who built them. The 'road' – narrow and rough – alternately runs level with the flashing river and leaps up mountain-sides to give unimpeded views for miles and miles along the valley.

This is the part of Afghanistan I was most eager to see, but in my wildest imaginings I never thought any landscape could be so magnificent. If I *am* murdered en route it will have been well worth while! Not that I think there's much chance of that; the seventy-eight miles of my route today were patrolled by armed soldiers in pairs, apparently for my special protection as the last pair went off duty when they had led me, at dusk, to the home of the Provincial Governor in this village. I should think that if solitary travellers do get killed here it is because they've not told the police, as requested, where they are going and when. It seems to be beyond dispute that Afghanistan has slightly more than its share of bandits, yet almost everyone who travels through is favourably impressed by the treatment they receive and it's high time the silly nonsense about the extreme dangers of this land were 'exposed' as exaggeration.

The average Afghan is at once hard-working and easy-going and retains lots of things that industrial psychiatrists are now laboriously struggling to rediscover. He is good-humoured but not very talkative. He loves music and often sings quietly to himself for hours on end. He also loves bird-song and flowers, is very sensitive to natural beauty and on the whole treats animals well – not only his superb horses, but also his pack-donkeys, who are pushed in the required direction more often than beaten, his strings of cynical camels, who show few signs of returning affection, and his flocks of goats and sheep, one of whom is usually a special pet. Most of all, he loves his children, who may well number up to thirty if he can afford four wives. He is, of course, hot-tempered and uncontrollably ferocious when roused, but once a dispute is settled without loss of honour on either side he embraces his opponent and they sing a duet. (One must applaud Mohammed's common-sense in prohibiting alcohol among his followers; if they stopped at pubs as often as they do at tea-houses the populations of the Islamic countries would long since have exterminated each other.) He is indifferent to hardship, on which he has been nurtured, he endures acute pain without a moan and he is among the most fearless of soldiers. In short, he's a man after my own heart.

The latest hair-raiser I heard in Kabul concerned a four-man team of Western surveyors who were recently shot up by the tribesmen because the tribal chiefs don't want the Government to know how much land they own, since a new system of land taxes is soon to be levied. Obviously the tribesmen had been given orders not to kill, as the surveyors were only wounded, and no Afghan would miss a man-sized target. I've often seen them potting tiny birds from fantastic distances just for the hell of it, which sounds a horrid hobby but is no worse than shooting such a glorious thing as a cock-pheasant for its food value. By now I've got quite used to all the men around me carrying rifles as Irishmen carry umbrellas and I've learned to beware of falling over the stacked weapons when entering a dark, windowless tea-house from bright sunshine.

This house reveals what some might describe as the poverty of Afghanistan but what I prefer to call its simplicity, since poverty denotes a lack of necessities and simplicity a lack of needs. The Governor is the most important man in the district yet the poorest Irish peasant would have a more elaborate home, though when one examines it every essential comfort is here.

The family consists of Mohammad Musa – my thirty-one-year-old host – his elderly mother, his seventeen-year-old wife, their five-months-old first baby and four servants. They are natives of Kabul and Mohammad, who speaks fluent English, is extremely well educated. At first he was most uncomfortable about entertaining a Westerner in such a home but my very evident happiness here has reassured him. His is, of course, a 'made marriage' but it seems very successful, although the young wife, who attended a Kabul Secondary School, tends to rebel against wearing the veil and would like to meet her husband's friends – concessions which he will never allow.

Mohammad's mother is a tremendous character – one of those old people who make the young realise that old age is not something to be dreaded, when it can give such mellowness and balance and contentment to a human being. I would have readily forgiven her for being distant to someone who represented, according to her traditions, the complete negation of womanhood but, although she speaks no English, the warmth of her welcome has made me feel truly 'one of the family' this evening. Not for the first time, I am astonished and humbled by the tolerance of Muslims, who so easily accept the fact that my standards differ from theirs, yet give me no feeling of being regarded as inferior on that account. Even more remarkable, the liberty which they recognise as my inheritance does not deter them from treating me with a courtesy too rarely found in modern Europe; by this civilised fusion of our two cultures I have all the advantages and none of the disadvantages of their own womenfolk. I think it is fair to say that the modern Muslim, even if he is an uneducated peasant, shows less prejudice towards other religions than we Christians do, with our persistent tendency to brand any religion not our own as 'ignorant superstition'. This Muslim tolerance makes it all the sadder that politicians so often artificially stimulate religious differences for their own ends.

As I write, sitting in a corner on a rug on the floor, with a roll of bedding at my back and a dim oil-lamp beside me, prayer-time has come and the old lady has gone off to her room for private devotions. Mohammad is kneeling on his prayer-mat in another corner, just now touching the ground with his forehead, his wife is sitting near me, breast-feeding the baby, and a manservant is spreading a cloth on the floor in front of us for supper. When my host heard that I was coming he took one of his guns (five of them are stacked beside the door) and went out and shot a deer – the answer to unexpected guests in this region! So it's venison and rice for supper, cooked on a mud stove in the compound.

BAMIAN, 22 APRIL

Another day of incredible, unforgettable and indescribable beauty, plus our highest climb yet – 10,380 feet over the Shibar Pass; I felt like a fly going up a wall.

At breakfast this morning Mohammad tried to persuade me to go by truck as he simply didn't believe a cycle could be got over the Shibar but when I reached the foot of the pass I was very glad I hadn't agreed to his kind suggestion. At the moment there is heavy traffic on this route because Afghanistan and Pakistan are not on speaking terms and their frontier is closed, so that many of the goods which would normally be imported via Karachi and the Khyber Pass are coming from Russia via Mazar-i-Sharif. But this track was never meant to be a grand trunk road and the sight of grossly overloaded and mainly 'home-made' trucks negotiating these fantastic hairpin bends, with inches between the outer wheels and a 1,000-foot drop, made me sweat with vicarious terror – and thank God that it was only vicarious as I pushed Roz up, keeping close to the cliffside. In fact, the climb wasn't as stiff as I had anticipated, because the foot of the pass is itself about 7,000 feet above sea level; yet over the last thousand feet I did notice the effects of the altitude – shortness of breath and aching calf-muscles. But it was worth it all to rise gradually from that fertile, warm valley to the still, cold splendour of the snow-line, where the highest peaks of the Hindu Kush crowd the horizon in every direction and one begins to understand why some people believe that gods live on mountain tops.

There's an astounding change on this northern side of the range. Within a few miles the whole landscape has altered from early summer to late winter; trees are almost bare, grass and wheat are just beginning to show and the temperature is many degrees lower.

The downward gradient is much less severe and at one point the road goes through a glorious narrow gorge of red-brown cliffs; these are so close, so high and so sheer that standing between them, looking up, one has the sensation of being a midget dropped into some ruggedly built edifice with a slight crack in the roof.

It was at the end of this gorge that disaster hit Roz; she suffered two vicious rips in the back tyre and I doubt if they can be patched. The road is excruciating but personally I've got used to the feeling of being dislocated in every joint at one bump and relocated at the next. However, it's different for poor Roz and today's calamity was my fault; I let her go too fast down the pass. This was because of the back brake again giving trouble so that the alternative to cycling too fast was walking, and when you've walked up to 10,380 feet you don't feel much like walking down. At this stage it was 5.15 p.m. and we were some twenty miles from Bamian, near the junction of the Mazar–Bamian road where there is a tiny village called Bulola. I asked about a bus and one was pointed out as going to Bamian 'in a few minutes', so Roz was loaded up and I sat in. My other buses were luxurious compared with this one. The floor was covered in sheep and goat droppings and the steering-wheel was held together with sticking-plaster – a device not calculated to soothe one's nerves on a journey in this terrain. We finally set off at 6.20 p.m., by which time I was frozen stiff – it had been raining hard and there was no glass in the windows, as usual – after sitting patiently watching huge piles of hides being roped together and tied to the roof till the whole rickety contraption looked gruesomely top-heavy. And just before our departure nine men had climbed up and settled down on top of the hides, wrapping themselves in their huge rugs.

About two miles beyond Bulola the engine broke down; it was now dark and raining, and the repairs, during which the headlights were put out of order, took very nearly an hour. At 7.30 p.m. we resumed the journey up and over a 10,000-foot pass on a corkscrew 'road', barely wide enough for one vehicle, with sheer drops which I could imagine, but happily not see, as there was no light. Then quite soon there *was* light – lots of it – when the daily spring thunderstorm began. For several minutes lightning was continuous – not flashes as we know them, but glaring sheets of blue illumination, revealing gaunt peaks on one side and sickening ravines on the other; yet it was all so beautiful and awe-inspiring that one simply forgot to be afraid. The thunder reverberating in the mountains was deafening – peal after peal, the echoes of each being drowned in the crash of the next. With all this came gusts of gale-force wind carrying enormous hailstones which took the skin off my nose where they struck it as I sat next to the window-that-wasn't. There are limits even to Afghan toughness and when this demonstration started the bus stopped for the nine men on the roof to come below. As the 'inside' was already overcrowded beyond belief this meant that I had three children on my lap for the rest of the journey; I had only one two-year-old at the beginning. We waited for about fifteen minutes until the worst was over because to attempt to negotiate that winding track with the driver intermittently dazzled by lightning would have been suicidal. (To my mind the whole trip wasn't far short of suicidal anyway.) Yet what an experience to see a landscape, dramatic in itself, under such melodramatic conditions – like some inspired choreographer's setting for *Faust*.

Soon after we had restarted a melodrama of a different kind began. The system on these privately owned buses is that the owner-driver's assistant, usually an adolescent known as a *bacha*, collects the fares during the journey. The *bacha* now asked twelve *afghanis* from everyone and a number of passengers protested that ten had been agreed on before the start. Hell then broke loose and while I was bundling the children under the seat an infuriated tribesman, brandishing his rifle, climbed over me, trying to get at the driver; the *bacha* pushed him, and he fell backwards, striking me a frightful blow on the ribs with the rifle-butt. I looked round to see a terrifying forest of rifle-barrels behind me – terrifying because in a jolting bus I imagined them going off accidentally; but of course these men know exactly what they are doing with their triggers, if not with their butts, and nothing of the sort happened. The unarmed *bacha* continued his heroic defence of the driver, the bus stopped yet again, the driver got out and stood grasping *his* gun and refusing to go another yard until everyone had paid their twelve *afghanis* and I hastily produced mine, vaguely hoping to set a good example. But I was completely ignored while the verbal battle raged and everyone fingered his trigger menacingly as though it wouldn't be verbal much longer; the angry shouts of all concerned almost drowned both the thunder and the hiss of the hail slashing down. Finally one of the passengers threatened to smash the inside light with his rifle-butt. Then a compromise of eleven *afghanis* was accepted, whereupon the driver resumed his seat and off we went again. This time – rather to my astonishment – we kept on going, at some 15 m.p.h., until reaching Bamian, where Roz and I were decanted in total darkness and I was told that the hotel lay on my left. As I was switching on Roz's light a policeman appeared and almost wept with joy when he saw me – he'd been expecting me hours earlier. He had a storm-lantern and led me on a mile-long walk up a very steep hill to the hotel; we were halfway up when we encountered a car, stuck in deep, loose gravel and being pushed by two softly swearing men. Afghanistan's tourist trade is so flourishing that after a few weeks in the country most tourists are on christian name terms with each other, so I yelled 'Hi, what's wrong?' having recognised three very nice Indians I'd met in Kabul. They said that after the 140 miles from Kabul everything that could go wrong with a car was wrong and now they just wanted to get her as far as the hotel, to avoid leaving her unguarded all night. So Roz was dropped by the wayside and the policeman and I added our pushes, during which operation I began to suspect that my lowest right rib has been fractured by the rifle butt. When we eventually got the unfortunate machine over the crest of the hill the policeman said that he'd go back to the village as I had found friends and then, having retrieved Roz, I walked on with two of the Indians, who had stayed out of the car to save it extra weight. We were trotting along, numb with cold and exchanging our harrowing experiences of the road, when a blood-curdling yell halted us and we found ourselves looking down the barrel of a rifle held by a very young soldier. We gave a chorus of little yelps of terror and said 'Hotel! Hotel! Tourist's Hotel!' But the sentry wasn't at all sure that three strangers – one with a bicycle and two without luggage – coming suddenly out of the black, cold night, could be genuine tourists, so he kept us covered until another soldier had examined our passports. This second lad then led us to the hotel, some 200 yards away from what is apparently a military barracks.

It was depressing, if not altogether surprising, to discover that here there was (*a*) no food or drink of any description, (*b*) no light, (*c*) no water, (*d*) no heating and (*e*) only one thin blanket on each bed. As we were now 8,550 feet above sea level (*e*) was not funny. I had coffee and sugar and bread with me and the boys had some tinned sausages and pineapples so we scraped together a meal of sorts by the light of oil-lamps borrowed from the military, making coffee with the boys' emergency water supply. (The side-splitting part of this story is that Bamian Hotel is listed as Luxury, Grade A!) Then we raided a vast number of empty bedrooms and accumulated six blankets each; I am now sitting up in bed swathed in my six, with numb hands and feet and a howling gale blowing through the loose window-frame. But I suppose I should be grateful for glass in the windows . . .

BAMIAN, 23 APRIL

I woke this morning, looked through my window and almost fell out of bed with excitement. This hotel is built on a 1,000-foot cliff rising sheer from the valley floor and across the valley, distinct in the brilliant, early sunshine, I saw a 120-foot-high statue of the Lord Buddha standing, as it has stood for over 2,000 years, in a gigantic alcove in the golden sandstone mountain – both alcove and statue having been carved with extraordinary skill out of the rock. The whole face of this mountain is pitted with the caves of Buddhist monks and another, eighty-foot, statue stands about a quarter of a mile east of the giant one. Quite apart from this unique spectacle the valley itself is superbly beautiful; a depression in the centre of the mountains, fertile and neatly tilled, dotted with tiny villages and criss-crossed with lines of silver-barked sinjit trees, whose diminutive rosy buds were glowing softly in the early light. Even though I was mentally prepared for those Buddhas the impact was tremendous when I actually saw them presiding impassively over the valley.

After breakfast of two boiled eggs, dry bread and tea, I investigated Roz fully; there are five severe cuts in the back tyre and eleven punctures in that tube and three in the front tube. Definitely this is where I gracefully accept defeat, admit that Afghanistan is not a suitable country for cycle-touring and get on the next bus for Mazar. No one knows when another bus will come to Bamian but that aspect doesn't worry me – I could happily spend a month here. The spare tyre is in Kabul, yet even if it were here I'd hesitate to put it on as it would probably be in shreds before we got back to Kabul and the next spare is with the British High Commission in Peshawar. So a bus to Mazar and back is the obvious though acutely disappointing solution. From Kabul, where I'll put the new tyre on, much of the road to Peshawar via the Khyber Pass is metalled.

My experience to date of Afghan buses leads me to expect that the trip to Mazar will be (*a*) infinitely more dangerous than by cycle, (*b*) a thousand times more wearying and uncomfortable and (*c*) at least as long in travelling hours. It will also be fraught with frustration – so many places where I'll want to stop and be alone – but better to go by bus than not at all.

Having discovered the worst about Roz I went with the Indians to see the Buddhas and caves. This is one of Afghanistan's main tourist attractions (hence a 'luxury' hotel), but what a contrast to our idea of a tourist centre! Apart from the hotel the whole valley is completely unspoiled; nothing comes between the ancient past and the moment when you walk beneath the shadow of those immense monuments of an era when Bamian was the centre of the Buddhist religion. The statues, however, look far less impressive close-to than from the other side, or centre, of the valley. There the effect of so many centuries of weathering is not apparent, although, considering their great antiquity, the damage is very slight and much skilful restoring has recently been done; even the paintings executed on the arches of the alcoves and in the caves are still traceable. The monastery of caves is fabulous; one could spend days wandering (chiefly on one's tummy) through the maze of connecting passages between one cell and another. Similar caves, all blackened with the smoke of fires that burned so long ago, are located in other mountains around the valley and I hope to explore these tomorrow on my own; delightful as the Indians are, I prefer being alone in places like this.

After a lunch of tea and dry bread and two boiled eggs (the variety of the menu here is *fascinating*) I wandered off to a little village at the foot of the massive, snowy mountains that overhang this valley to the south. The fields were being ploughed by the most primitive methods, which involve tremendously hard work on the part of the men as well as the yokes of bullocks, and irrigation channels were rippling smoothly along between the cultivated patches. In the village, of well-fortified houses, the little children were so terrified at the sight of me that they fled like chickens before a fox. Yet to my extreme astonishment when a group of ten- to fourteen-year-olds gathered to investigate me and asked where I came from and when I replied 'Ireland' they immediately said 'Dublin!' in unison. They were dressed in the usual filthy rags, but instead of begging from the tourist they offered me revolting fly-blown sweets, nuts and raisins out of the (probably lousy) recesses of their garments. I didn't like refusing but one has to draw the line somewhere. They also organised a bird-fight for my entertainment; this is one of the most popular sports among the villagers. Two birds, about the size of hen-pheasants, but in build and plumage like doves, are released from their cages on the ground and go for each other; the fight lasts until one bird has the other pinned to the ground so that it can't get up. There's no bloodshed and no killing, only plenty of feathers flying, and since the tactics are quite beautiful to watch it was a lot more enjoyable than I had expected. Of course my last film had been used on the Buddhas; I've discovered that one of the chief griefs of a photographer's life is that the last film has always been used immediately before a 'special' picture presents itself.

After this I went off to explore the ruins of 'The City of Sighs', where the King of Bamian was successfully besieged by Genghis Khan in 1222. It stands on a hill isolated in the centre of the valley and the climb is so sheer that I was completely breathless by the time I got to the top, with its remains of two watch towers. The view of the valley would be well worth climbing Everest to see; I had deliberately chosen this time, to watch the sunset from here. Bamian valley runs from east to west and the hilltop is 900 feet above the valley floor. Looking down I could see right into the compounds of all those inscrutable blank-walled villages and watch tiny figures of unveiled, red-trousered women scuttling around at their household jobs. Across the fields men were moving home with their pairs of oxen and down from the hillsides came little shepherd boys driving their flocks of sheep and goats and frisking lambs and kids. I must digress here to expatiate on the loveableness of Afghan kids, so nimble and playful and alert of expression and beautiful to look at, with their short, glossy coats and upturned tails and almost snub-nosed faces and delicate bones. They come in jet-black, nigger-brown and an extraordinarily lovely shade of blue-grey. Their elders look very dignified before shearing, with coats sweeping the ground and horns curving handsomely back – quite a contrast to the comical fat-tailed sheep with that vast bundle (weighing from 100 to 140 pounds) swaying along behind them. Arab sheep are also fairly common, bred exclusively for their skins as the wool is of little value; these sheep are very lightly built and can be confused with short-haired goats at a distance. I haven't yet seen any of the breed from which comes genuine Persian Lamb – most unjustly misnamed. The cattle here are small and dainty; some remind me of Kerries but they're mostly like Jerseys.

North of this valley are the sandstone mountains of the statues and caves and to the east lie low hills like vast mounds of velvet dropped from the sky and delicately shaded in violet, brown, pink and beige. (Such formations are very common in Persia, too, where the colouring is usually brown or grey.) To the south, in complete contrast to these soft contours and tints, rears a craggy range of 14–18,000-foot peaks, covered in fiercely white snow which turned to radiant gold a few moments before the sun dropped behind the lower, bluish-tinged peaks at the far western end of the valley, leaving one splendid billowy cloud of bronze behind it.

The ruins among which I stood were equally moving in their way. Archaeologists reckon that 'The City of Sighs' must have had between seven and eight thousand inhabitants and as I climbed the silent laneways between those houses – some still in an excellent state of preservation, with many traces of paintings on the walls – a curious feeling of melancholy crept over me. Local techniques of building seem to have remained unchanged over all those centuries; the Afghans one sees building new houses today construct them in exactly the same manner with identical materials.

Climbing down in the rapidly fading light was almost eerie; the locals, who firmly believe in an endless variety of ghosts and spirits, wouldn't come near the place day or night. On reaching level ground I found two soldiers, complete with the usual armoury of revolver, rifle and sword, posted one on either side of the hill, and when they had escorted me back to the hotel the manager explained that some years ago a German boy was murdered among those ruins, so now tourists are always supervised there. Then I had supper of dry bread and two boiled eggs and tea (sorry for the monotony!) followed by a most interesting discussion with one of the Indian boys on Hinduism and Christianity.

BAMIAN, 24 APRIL

How stupid can one be? I woke this morning to find my rib markedly worse; then, as I was having breakfast (bet you can't guess the menu!) the Police Commander called and said that since there was no sign of a bus going from Bamian in the foreseeable future perhaps I'd like to spend the day riding up the valley? Commonsense prompted me to say, 'No, thanks; it's very kind of you but not with a cracked rib.' However, the temptation was too strong – a day on horseback in the Hindu Kush is the nearest thing I can think of to Heaven. But half an hour later, looking out of the window, my heart sank at the sight of a gleaming, rearing chestnut stallion on the gravel. I then proceeded to disprove the theory that if you go up in a plane – or whatever – immediately after an accident you won't lose your nerve. Last October I remounted an Aran Island demon of a mare three times after being thrown, yet the moment my steed appeared this morning I began to positively tremble with terror. But I needn't have worried; he was a darling and seemed to understand the situation perfectly as soon as he felt me shivering fearfully on his back. The Afghan saddle further demoralised me – no fancy leather, but solid wood and make the best of it. I did register a protest about the girth being too loose and the stirrups too long and had both adjusted; the Persians ride very short stirrups but the Afghans in this region go to the other extreme. After about twenty minutes I regained my nerve and from then on enjoyed myself thoroughly – *what* a day! I had my usual two guards who combined business with pleasure by shooting three deer and two foxes between them. It was tremendously exciting to sit watching them galloping along mountainsides in pursuit of deer and bringing them down with magnificent shots fired while going at full speed. (Not that I really approve of shooting deer, but one has to admire the skill and it *does* mean venison instead of boiled eggs for supper!) We went deep into that magnificent range of snowy peaks, through lush green ravines and across streams and up hillsides and through woods. Quite apart from my normal inability to convey the beauty of it all, I'm too exhausted tonight even to try. After nine and a half hours in the saddle I'd have been a stiff mass of agony tomorrow, however fit at the start, but with that rib it was just idiotic to ride. The day's beauty so excited me that I didn't heed the pain increasing every hour; time will tell what damage has been done.

5

The Oddities of Afghan Trucks

BAMIAN TO PUL-I-KHUMRI

DOAB, 25 APRIL

My body was suffering such universal torture when I dragged it out of bed this morning that I can't yet determine the precise extent of damage to my rib. At 7 a.m. the Police Commissioner appeared again to say that a bus was leaving for Bolola at 8 a.m., but I've been long enough in Afghanistan now to know what that means, so I crawled down to the village at 9.30 and sat in the sun, drinking tea and watching the Bazaar Day crowd, till the bus was ready to go at 12.15 p.m. In these parts no bus will start until double the number of passengers that it was designed to hold have been crammed into and on to it. If there's room for just *one* more, it'll wait hours for that one to turn up, with the *bacha* standing out in the middle of the road hoarsely yelling the bus's destination to attract the necessary extra passenger. As Afghans are so indifferent to time (the vast majority have no idea how old they are) it follows that every passenger comes when it suits him so that it can take up to six hours to fill a bus. Afghans are equally vague about distance: a truck-driver who goes from Kabul to Mazar once a week won't have the remotest idea how far it is; he just knows that if he keeps driving long enough, and if Allah is willing, he'll get there some day. Personally I find all this most endearing after a lifetime of being tyrannised by the clock.

Next to food, fuel is the scarcest thing in this region at this season and on Thursdays dozens of donkeys come in from the surrounding few hamlets laden with bushes of some herb which smells like incense and weighs so light that one donkey can carry a load twice the size of itself. Everyone lines up to bid for these loads and the owners of tea-houses, who need it most and can bid highest, go off with the bulk of what's available.

The winter is so cold round here that no potatoes or other vegetables will grow and the pasturage is so poor now that neither cows', sheep's nor goats' milk will make butter or cheese. Within a few weeks all that will be changed; even during the days I've been here the trees have turned from bareness to greenness and the grass and wheat have come up well. Meanwhile, the people live on tea and dry bread and eggs.

I got a very pleasant surprise when the bus stopped to take us on, having loaded up elsewhere; it was the bus which had brought us here and the driver promptly handed me the two water-bottles and the plastic mug I thought I'd lost for ever. Not bad in an alleged 'nation of robbers' – it hadn't even occurred to me to enquire about them.

One significant thing I notice in Afghanistan is that many men with severe physical disabilities are seen doing the same jobs (although more slowly and perhaps less efficiently) as their healthy brothers. In Persia, these men would be lying on the sidewalks begging.

Officially Mongolians are supposed to form less than fifteen per cent of the Afghan population, but anyone can see that this is nonsense – forty per cent would be more like it, and around this region sixty to seventy per cent. In the centuries following Ghenghis Khan's invasion the Mongolians were important and prosperous citizens; now they are all in the poorer class.

The first twenty miles today was back along the stretch we came over by the light of heaven the other night and seeing the road by the light of day I realised that our survival was a miracle. This road is marked third-class on maps and when one remembers that a first-class Afghan road would be marked as a track on any European map – well, you see what I mean! (A recent United Nations survey declared Afghan roads to be the worst in the whole wide world – a description which I now have no difficulty in accepting.) This goat-track crawls around mountains, overhanging a river the whole way, and in these twenty miles I saw the remains of two recently crashed buses: mercifully the lightning didn't reveal them the other night. In several places the river has eaten away so much of the track that one can only drive at

5 m.p.h. with inches to spare and it took us one and three-quarters hours to cover those twenty miles. Actually I was very glad, for this stretch is just about the most beautiful part of the Hindu Kush I have seen. The glory of those mountains makes one feel that it must all be a dream. Every peak and slope and outcrop is different in shape, texture and colour, the rock and shale and clay shaded purple, rose, green, ochre, black, pale grey, dark grey, brown, navy and off-white. Then, below those arid, soaring cliffs – so vertical that not even an Afghan goat attempts them – is this narrow vale of Bamian, all graceful with willows and poplars, and soft with new grass and filled with bird-song and the rush of the river. Towards the end of the vale, the mountains closed in ahead and we entered a permanently shadowed gorge no more than fifty feet wide, where the river was forced into a deep channel, half-filled with gigantic boulders through which it roared and foamed in a series of waterfalls. When the gorge ended we crossed a bridge built entirely of wood and mud.

A few miles further on, at the junction village, I transferred to a truck going to Mazar; this must be one of the easiest routes in the world for hitch-hiking because so many empty trucks go to Russia from Kabul to import essential supplies. Afghanistan's closing of her border with Pakistan was a classical example of biting off one's nose, etc.; the gesture hurt no one but Afghanistan and benefited no one but Russia, who now has almost a monopoly of trade with Afghanistan. (What makes me so sick in Afghan vehicles is the nauseating reek of Russian petrol, which is very inferior stuff; I'm told it ruins cars.) A lot of people thought that when the old pro-Russian Prime Minister 'resigned' (i.e. was dismissed by the Emir) the border would re-open, and perhaps it will soon. Its closure means that the prices of all imported goods in Kabul are almost as high as in Teheran.

Afghan trucks are unique. To make up for the absence of windows, wipers, mirrors, handbrakes and all the other refinements we take for granted, their exteriors are so brilliantly painted with a series of elaborate pictures that they look like circus caravans; also they have a railed-in compartment built on top of the cab which can carry extra goods or four humans – or both. I chose to ride up there, (*a*) so that I wouldn't miss anything of the scenery and (*b*) so that I wouldn't get sick. Of course it all depends upon what makes you sick – if you'd a bad head for heights those fantastic valleys and gullies and ravines and gorges, seen from the top of a truck crawling along with no margin of error, might make you feel sicker than any Russian petrol fumes could. The situation on this route is one that could only occur in a deliciously crazy land; during the two years since the border closed eighty per cent of Afghanistan's traffic has travelled on it, yet it's the country's worst road.

The *bacha* acts as rear-mirror, horn-blower (the horns are fabulous things like trumpets, eighteen inches long and audible miles away) and windscreen wiper if the truck is posh enough to have a windscreen. He also leaps down whenever the truck stops and inserts a huge wooden block to act as a brake beneath a back wheel. Every mile or so the road widens enough to let two trucks pass if one remains stationary and you can imagine the chaos involved. The really exciting part of the performance comes when you have to *back* down this track, overhanging a gorge for about a quarter of a mile, because your truck is the one nearest the passing point; that's when it's wiser to look up rather than down. For this manoeuvre the *bacha* is of course out on the road, walking backwards shouting instructions to the driver.

The average speed of forward progression is 15 m.p.h. and allowing for frequent reversings, and for one puncture or other breakdown every two hours, it takes four hours to cover forty miles – at this rate I'll be in Mazar for Christmas! But these Afghan drivers are really magnificent – good-humoured about their hardships, brilliantly resourceful when mechanical improvisations are required, and very sensible and cautious. The only thing that terrifies me is the appalling state of repair of the trucks; if a brake went or the steering column broke on this road the best drivers in the world couldn't avoid disaster. Fortunately, the beauty of the landscape leaves little time for these morbid broodings.

For about the first twenty of this afternoon's forty miles we were going through a narrow gorge overhung by mountains eroded to many grotesquely beautiful shapes – some were like the ruins of colossal

Gothic cathedrals, others had crags worn by wind and water into parodies of sculptured human faces and always there was that incredible display of colours. Then the valley widened slightly and we came to a region of devastation, a shattered wilderness where giant rocks, the size of cottages, lay strewn everywhere, and wide fissures in the mountains warned that at the next earth tremor – and they are frequent here – the whole appearance of the area would change. Before the border trouble this track was often blocked by rock-falls; now the Russians have teams of men camped at intervals to clear away the débris as soon as it crashes down.

I reckon that today's forty miles were only about ten miles as the crow flies, so tortuously did the road and river wind back and forth through the mountains. After such a jolting on top of the truck, added to yesterday's gallivanting, the rib is neat hell tonight and the rest of my ill-treated carcase feels not much better. 'Bed' in a tea-shop corner now.

DOSHI, 26 APRIL

It took us eleven hours to cover ninety miles today; we were afflicted by two punctures and three engine breakdowns. This obviously suited my purpose as, while the repairs were being done, I could wander off and absorb the beauty of a landscape no less spectacular than yesterday's. But I couldn't wander far or do anything energetic – merely climbing into the truck this morning was agony. Definitely I'm in for real trouble with this rib and I must take it to a Russian doctor in Mazar, if we ever get as far.

The valley was wider and more fertile and more populous today. Women in this region lead a very active life and lovely splashes of crimson against grey rocks or green pastures indicate that a shepherdess is on duty. Almost all the villagers here seem to be Mongolians, who are much less conservative than the Aryan Muslims. The women have elaborate patterns tattooed on their foreheads and chins, and girl-babies wear silver ornaments permanently embedded in their noses. Both men and women use massive silver bangles and ear-rings and their curly-toed shoes are inlaid with silver and gold. They all look sturdy, rosy-cheeked and healthy beneath the dirt of bodies that certainly do not know what water feels like.

This is the centre of the Afghan horse-breeding area, where herds of magnificent animals graze beneath the mountains on velvet pastures, with scores of frolicking foals, and to see them galloping away from the sound of the truck is a heart-stopping sight. Here too the famous sport of Buzkashi is most popular. This involves two teams, of up to a hundred horsemen each, who try to drop a sheep's carcase in a hole in the centre of a mile-long pitch; I hope to see it before leaving the region. This explains the wooden 'handle' on my saddle the other day – riders hang on to it with one hand while they bend down to spear a sheep off the ground with the other.

Tonight I'm again staying with a Provincial Governor, one who spent seven years in an American university and speaks perfect English. His house is so primitive that his wife prefers to remain in Kabul with their children; only one room is fit to sleep in and despite his foreign education he takes it for granted that I won't mind sharing it with him. As it happens he's quite right in this case, since by now I equate 'Afghan' with 'gentleman'. He's a very nice fellow who paid me one of the most valued compliments I've ever received when he said that he had never before met a foreigner who had become so completely adjusted to Afghan life in so brief a time. I replied that it isn't difficult to get adjusted when you love a country as much as I love this one. He had been warned by the other Governor to expect me, so there was quite a banquet for supper – fried chicken, spinach beautifully prepared, hard-boiled eggs, the usual flat wholemeal bread, sheep's butter, goat's and sheep's cheese and masses of sultanas; sultanas eaten with unsalted goat's cheese are quite a gastronomic experience and on that course I made a pig of myself. Then we had hot cow's milk with lots of sugar in it and finally green tea, and the more I filled my tummy the sorer my rib got – from expansion!

PUL-I-KHUMRI, 27 APRIL

I slept very little last night and couldn't stand up without help this morning; I was in too much pain to eat an elaborate breakfast. While drinking my tea I coughed involuntarily and at once fainted clean away because of the agony. When I had come to, my host and I held an emergency conference and he advised me to go to the German-built hospital in this town, fifty-five miles from Doshi. I'll skip details of the journey – I did *not* observe the landscape and fainted twice more: I'm getting quite expert at it. A young Afghan doctor said that three ribs are broken; he plastered them and ordered me to bed and banned cycling for a month.

This hospital is exactly what you would expect an Afghan hospital to be – even one built by Germans. A male nurse undressed me and two police officers and three other officials stood by as interested spectators while I stood naked from the waist up being plastered. There are a few women nurses here – elderly widows without sons or husbands or fathers to restrain them from leading such immoral lives! A bathroom-cum-lavatory leads off my room but the water supply has been broken down since the Germans left in 1945. However, this doesn't deter everyone from using the lavatory: it would be so much healthier to have an Eastern one outside instead of a Western one, minus water, inside. I can't see myself escaping from this dive without dysentery – the room is *dense* with flies. Fortunately it opens on to a verandah and the bed is beside a big window with a wide view of the heavenly garden which is like a miniature forest, full of chestnuts heavy with blossom and Scotch firs and many other big trees, unfamiliar to me, in early summer foliage. There are also blazing flower-beds, smooth lawns and a little bubbling stream. Possibly I'll survive; a Czech doctor is going to re-examine me tomorrow.

PUL-I-KHUMRI, 28 APRIL

A grim night, and now I know what it feels like to be a guinea-pig. The Czech doctor arrived at 7.30 a.m. (an odd chap, who has been here sixteen years; he might be a Graham Greene character), and having taken one look at my ribs he sent for the Afghan doctor. I was made to stand in the centre of the floor and told to turn round slowly while the Czech demonstrated that this was how *not* to strap broken ribs. Then the plaster was removed and the Czech doctor put on a new lot whilst the Afghan watched respectfully; my ribs feel much better now. The Czech said that I could probably cycle in about two weeks, as all the breaks seemed to be clean. I asked why they were so painful, as I always thought broken bones not such agony, but he said broken *ribs* are, because of nerves that run from the spine between them. He told me that I could return to Kabul by the next jeep going there, but not by truck as it would be too jolting. Mazar-i-Sharif has to be abandoned as it would involve another 300 miles on these roads, which might be unwise. It would be all right if I could fly there and back but the Mazar airport has been swept away by spring floods and won't reopen for three or four weeks. (It's swept away every spring with monotonous regularity.) When I get to Kabul I'm to rest until my two weeks are up, and longer if still painful, but my injuries always heal very quickly so I should be in working order by 12 May or so. I feel that Fate has dealt very kindly with me: if I had had to choose a country in which to be delayed I would certainly have chosen Afghanistan. I'm considering returning home this way to see the bits I've had to miss.

Not a dull moment today. By 10 a.m. my room was overflowing with roses, polyanthuses and geraniums, and a myriad visitors were in attendance.

This is one of Afghanistan's very few industrial centres – it has cement, sugar and textile factories, run by Russians and Czechs – so I don't feel too frustrated at not being able to explore the town. There is a big secondary school (co-educational) and the girls come streaming in after classes to look at me and beam. They go unveiled and are extraordinarily beautiful; unlike the Turkish and Persian girls, who rarely have any colour in their cheeks, these youngsters are all roses and cream, with glossy, wavy waist-length hair. When you see how good-looking they are it makes the veil seem either more iniquitous or more prudent. Undoubtedly the Afghans must be, by our standards, the best-looking people in the world. They have everything; height, proportions, carriage, features and complexion.

The food is atrocious here and even dirtier than usual, or perhaps it's just that there's more light to examine it by.

6

A Medical Break

PUL-I-KHUMRI TO JALALABAD

PUL-I-KHUMRI, 29 APRIL

Here in Afghanistan, the majority are Sunni Muslims, with a minority of Shias in certain areas and, as usual, no love is lost between the two sects. Sunnis consider Shias a pack of unwholesome fanatics and Shias consider Sunnis a gang of lukewarm no-goods – there's nothing like religion for spreading brotherly love!

I have at last, after ceaseless querying, got a definition of Afghanistan's government; it's a Theocracy, all laws being based on Islamic Law (Sunni interpretation) and the Emir's first duty is to defend Islam. For this reason I think it unlikely that Afghanistan will ever, in the foreseeable future, turn Communist, however many Russian helpers and however much Russian money she accepts.

One aspect of the Divorce Laws seems very odd: a husband has to return to his wife's family all the dowry cash, but he automatically retains custody of the children. However, if he can't return the cash, having spent it, he gives *half* the children instead (it's not clear what happens if there are nine or eleven children – another case for Solomon!). The manager of Bamian Hotel told me all this. He was married at eighteen to a fourteen-year-old wife and they have six children. Now he has just divorced her to marry the twenty-two-year-old daughter of an American posted to Afghanistan. The girl must be badly bitten if she's willing to take on six Afghan infants as well as an Afghan husband, who rather peevishly pointed out to me that he's losing a lot of money because of the tiresome American habit of having only one wife at a time. Normally he wouldn't dream of divorcing and forfeiting all that cash.

I had such a bad night and the pain was so grim this morning that the doctor said travelling today was out, though the police had a Russian jeep going to Kabul all lined up to take me. I feel better this evening so may get going the day after tomorrow in a Swede-driven UN jeep. Meanwhile I'm quite happy here.

PUL-I-KHUMRI, 30 APRIL

The ribs are much better today, *Deo gratias*, and the doctor said that I could go tomorrow if a jeep is available and if I sit in front. However, after today's developments I'm not all that keen on going tomorrow. The centre of life in this town is a textile company founded by Germans in the late 1930s and now run by Afghans. It owns the hospital and also the local hotel, built by the Germans as a club for themselves when they settled here. At 10 a.m. today the manager of the hotel arrived and invited me to stay there as a guest of the textile company till I could find transport to Kabul, so off I went with him in his jeep to this palatial outfit, built in a semicircle around a garden that is quite breath-taking, with a superb view of mountains in the near distance. I was shown over the whole building and in one of the vast lounges the manager said casually, 'That's a radiogram and there are some records in the cabinet.' I made a dive for the cabinet and the first thing I picked up was Schubert's Trout Quintet. Further investigation revealed four Beethoven symphonies, Mozart's Jupiter Symphony, Brahms' Violin and 2nd Piano Concertos, and a selection of opera – what *bliss*! They were, of course, the old 78s, but so are all my own at home. I had the Fifth on before 12 o'clock lunch and was edging back towards the relevant lounge when the factory manager collared me to come and tour the works. I could hardly refuse and found it quite interesting watching the whole process, from raw cotton leaving the growers' sacks to the finished product – some quite lovely fabrics – emerging at the other end. Two thousand are employed, including four hundred boys and girls in the ten to fourteen age group; for certain jobs their small fingers are best: pretty grim. As a result of the industrialisation of Pul-i-Khumri one sees more unveiled women here than in Kabul, and there are hundreds of neat little houses built by the Germans for their workers. The two electricity plants were also built by them and this is the only place in Afghanistan where you can depend on the electricity supply.

PUL-I-KHUMRI, 1 MAY

The ribs are very much better today but my big toe got bitten by a scorpion this morning, so I'm having serum treatment. It was a very traditional scorpion, lurking in my boot, and I've never seen anything quite so horrifying; the sooner the better I wake up to the fact that I'm now in Asia and act accordingly. I'd no idea the creatures were so enormous; my picture was of something about the size of a black beetle but this brute was as big as an adult mouse. I've decided that even the fattest and hairiest spider would be companionable in comparison. The morning was spent nursing my foot with Brahms to soothe the nerves.

DOAB, 2 MAY

Life is becoming dangerous! I was hardly out of bed this morning when a hornet stung me on the neck, but evidently the scorpion serum is still operating as there were no ill effects, apart from the immediate pain.

All the jeeps that might possibly have been going to Kabul today (two in number) were not going after all, so I was entrusted to a svelte Russian oil-tanker instead. With my infallible instinct for being in every country at the time of the national annual Big Feast (end of Ramadan in Turkey, Now Ruz in Persia) I find myself stranded this evening in central Afghanistan on the eve of their five-day Id holiday, when no trucks will be travelling. As other traffic is almost non-existent it's anybody's guess when I'll get to Kabul. The idea today was that I'd go all the way with the Russian tanker, but (*a*) I didn't want to travel in darkness through this lovely region and (*b*) the ribs, which seemed almost cured when I was sitting in Pul-i-Khumri, became acutely painful again on the road.

Today's journey taught me that despite the tribulations incidental to travelling by Afghan buses and trucks, they are in fact the vehicles best adapted to Afghan roads. On being helped into the Russian tanker this morning I felt as disconcerted as though I'd been transferred without warning from a local eating-house to Dublin's Shelbourne Hotel. Sinking back in the well-upholstered seat (with arm-rest) I stretched out my legs and put down the window (with glass) and watched the clean-shaven driver in his neat Western clothes hanging my wind-cheater from a hook. Definitely, I thought, this is the next best thing to the comfort of an ambulance. Then as soon as we started I realised that Comrade Ivan, lacking that native Afghan philosophy which alone makes such journeys tolerable, was in a *hurry*, which jarred me in every direction; mentally it was incongruous and physically it was hell. Holding my semi-knit ribs together with one hand and hanging on to the door with the other, I found myself being bounced off that excessively well-sprung seat every five minutes; I longed then for a vehicle with no springs and six passengers in a space meant for three, each keeping the other firmly wedged. We passed a total of eight happily broken-down Afghan trucks surrounded by little groups of ragged, barefooted, undismayed men; looking enviously at them I pondered the symbolism of luxury trucks being so uncomfortable on Afghan roads. Our smug engine had no breakdown though we did suffer four punctures, which even the best bred tanker could not avoid on such a surface, but each time the wheels were changed with disgusting speed, giving me no opportunity to see what lay beyond the nearest hill. Russians use a newfangled thing called a 'jack'; Afghans, on the other hand, dig a hole in the road beneath the relevant wheel . . .

Many changes have been taking place since I first travelled this way a week ago. Melting snow on the high peaks has transformed what were mere streams into wide, frenzied rivers, the colour of café-au-lait, which forcefully sweep giant boulders along their course. Several new rock-falls are keeping the Russians busy, the wheat is almost turning colour, blue and orange migrant birds flash splendidly across the sky and shrubs that were just coming into leaf are now feathery masses of pale green, like enormous ferns, showing a profusion of tiny, mauve blooms. Right over the tops of the rounded, earthy mountains (2,000 feet above the valley floor and over 10,000 feet above sea level) patches of cultivated land are visible in neat squares of green or brown. (Who's going to get up there with a tractor?) The few flat expanses where the valleys widen are covered by a thick, smooth carpet of dark golden moss. The tender rice shoots have sprung up, the blossoms have fallen from the fruit trees and, now that the lambs and kids are of grazing age, sheep and goats have bound udders to save milk for butter and cheese.

I saw an unusual sight in the middle of the road today – an eagle killing a snake about two and a half feet long. We stopped and watched him start to eat it, then, when the engine revved, he picked it up and swept off to the mountains to lunch in peace.

Tonight I've rejoined Roz at the home of my good friend the Provincial Governor, who has been cherishing her since I went to hospital. A few moments ago he announced that he himself is going to Kabul tomorrow, to be with the family for Id, but his jeep is so decrepit that he regretfully advised me against accompanying him; he thinks an ordinary truck, if such were available, would be better for the ribs. He has promised to bring Roz with him in the jeep – so now I have only myself to worry about.

. . . 3 MAY

I can't give an address, for God alone knows where we are; an hour ago we found ourselves stranded in the mountains miles from the nearest tea-shop, not to say village. This Afghan truck rolled up to Doab at 8 a.m., on a day when none was expected, because it had had nine engine breakdowns and four punctures en route from Russia yesterday. But now it's the road which has broken down – a rock-fall, estimated by the Russians who are blasting it away at 500 tons. There is no hope of the job being done before morning so we will sleep on the tyres that are our load: they should be comfortable enough. I'm writing this by the light of Roz's lamp, sitting on a rock by a crashing torrent under a sheer precipice in magically bright moonlight. I notice that the authorities seem to have given up trying to cope with the situation and have left me to my own devices. In the circumstances it's just as well I'm over my initial nervousness of Afghanistan. This is the only country I was ever in where not one single man of any type has made the slightest attempt to 'get off' with me, so I feel no qualms about a night at the mercy of my five companions. They all look as though murder was their favourite hobby (and maybe it is – among themselves) yet they're as gentle as lambs with me. The Russians wanted me to spend the night on a camp-bed in their tent but as all except the foreman are convicts I prefer to stick to my Noble Savages. We're all desperately hungry but there's nothing to be done about it; the Russians have so little food and are so isolated that we couldn't accept any from them.

KABUL, 4 AND 5 MAY

It cost me 7*s.* to post the last instalment of the diary on my arrival here at 4 p.m. yesterday and this was such a shock to the system that I couldn't bring myself to start writing it again last night.

I'm feeling rather miserable today, having left the Hindu Kush behind, yet the past weeks have given me something that I know will prove permanent. It may sound ridiculous, but I feel I've been privileged to see Man at this best – still in possession of the sort of liberty and dignity that we have exchanged for what it pleases us to call 'progress'. Even a brief glimpse of what we were is valuable to help to understand what we are. Living in the West, it's now impossible for most of us to envisage our own past by a mere exercise of the imagination, so we're rather like adults who have forgotten the childhood that shaped them. And that increases the unnaturalness of our lives. So to realise this past through contact with a people like the Afghans should help us to cope better with our present – though it also brings the sadness of knowing what we're missing. At times during these past weeks I felt so *whole* and so at peace that I was tempted seriously to consider settling in the Hindu Kush. Nothing is false there, for humans and animals and earth, intimately interdependent, partake together in the rhythmic cycle of nature. To lose one's petty, sophisticated complexities in that world would be heaven – but impossible, because of the fundamental falsity involved in attempting to abandon our own unhappy heritage. Yet the awareness that one cannot go back is a bitter pill to swallow.

KABUL, 6 MAY

Today I met a twenty-five-year-old American boy in the Museum who was typical of a certain category of youngster – European, Commonwealth and American – I've met all along the route. To them, travel is more a *going away from* rather than a *going towards*, and they seem empty and unhappy and bewildered and pathetically anxious for companionship, yet are afraid to commit themselves to any ideal or cause or other individual. I find something both terrifying and touching in young people without an aim, however foolish or even wrong it may be. This young man was pleasant and intelligent but wasting himself and resentfully conscious of the fact. He doesn't want to return home in the foreseeable future, yet, after two years of it, is weary of travelling, probably because he always holds himself aloof from the people he travels among – not through hostility or superiority but through a strange unconsciousness of the unity of mankind. Is this something else our age does – on the one hand make communication easier than ever before, while on the other hand widening the gulf between those who are 'developed' and those who are not?

KABUL, 7 MAY

Continuing the 'gulf' theme – what an artificial life is led by the foreign colonies in these Asian cities! The sense of their isolation from the world around them is quite stifling. At a dinner party tonight I met a European couple who have been in Kabul for eighteen months without once entering the home of an ordinary Afghan – and they are not exceptions. The attitude is that the 'natives' are people to be observed from a discreet distance and photographed as often as possible, but not lived among. The result is boredom and an obsessional longing for home leave. The collecting of souvenirs seems to be a substitute for the cheaper and richer experience of being temporarily integrated in the life of the country. Apparently if you can bring home to Malvern or Minneapolis or Munich a sufficiently overwhelming bulk of 'typical native products' this concrete evidence of your travels is enough.

This evening I also met a young Dutch couple who arrived in Kabul a fortnight ago, on their first assignment abroad, and who are still wondering what hit them. I must admit that I do see their point and am duly grateful that I approached Afghanistan gradually. Had I flown direct from Dublin and landed in Kabul as a wide-eyed, sensitive-nostrilled newcomer to the East, I too might well have been unable to appreciate the finer points of Afghan life and culture. As it is, during my two months' travelling from Istanbul to Meshed, the roads became daily less road-like, the mountains higher, the atmosphere rarer, the clothes stranger, the chairs scarcer, the Moslems more Islamic, the sanitary arrangements more alarming, the weather hotter, the stenches stronger, and the food dirtier. By the time I arrived at the Afghan frontier it seemed quite natural, before a meal, to scrape the dried mud off the bread, pick the hairs out of the cheese and remove the bugs from the sugar. I had also stopped registering the presence of fleas, the absence of cutlery, and the fact that I hadn't taken off my clothes or slept in a bed for ten days.

KABUL, 8 MAY

I had dinner this evening at the home of the Provincial Governor with whom I had stayed in Doab. His young nineteen-year-old brother came on a cycle to guide me to the house and I tried out my ribs by going the two or three miles on Roz – an experiment of which the ribs did *not* approve.

The party was by way of being an Id family reunion. However, since the ramifications of even the average Afghan family overtax my brain I didn't so much as attempt to grasp who was related to whom, or how, in this re-united family; but they were all equally hospitable and gracious and sincerely welcoming.

The large two-storey house was built – of mud, as usual – round three sides of a courtyard whose fourth side, facing the road, was a high secretive wall behind which the women could move about the garden unveiled. One small ground-floor room had been furnished in Western style and when I arrived everyone was dressed in Western clothes and sitting Western-fashion on the chairs, half of them with bouncing, gurgling, cherubic offspring on their knees (Afghans make very doting Daddies). They all spoke English or German with varying degrees of fluency – including the Governor's wife, who is a university graduate in economics – and conversation flowed easily. After about half an hour, by which time we had become the best of friends, first one and then another rose and disappeared for a few minutes, to return in Afghan dress and resettle themselves, comfortably cross-legged, on their chairs. They could have made no more eloquent gesture of acceptance than this tacit admission that it was unnecessary to impress me by affecting Western ways.

While the younger women were helping the servants to prepare dinner their elders and I sat listening to the family orchestra playing the sort of traditional music that gets into your blood. I loved every minute of it and one of the young men was a quite exceptionally talented musician who afterwards played several solos on an eight-stringed instrument.

Dinner was served at 9 p.m., the dishes being laid on an enormous cloth spread on the floor of a room completely bare of furniture. It was a banquet such as I have not had since leaving Turkey and I feel now that I won't need to eat again in the foreseeable future.

During the meal we discussed the 'progress' now being made by Afghanistan. The Government has recently produced a very fine book called *Afghanistan: Ancient Land with Modern Ways*, which, as the title implies, gives a rosy picture of the present situation – but that is understandable. What alarms me is that the general tone of the book reveals the Afghan Government's unquestioning acceptance of progress along Western lines as being something entirely good and desirable. This educated Afghan family held the same tragic belief in the superiority of our ways over their ways. It is frightening to belong to, and be in a fractional way responsible for, a civilisation that has such a hypnotic fascination for simple people everywhere – people whose very simplicity leaves them totally at our mercy. And so far we have shown little mercy, if that means anything more than the distribution of vaccines and the building of roads. With our mad lust for Uniformity and a Higher Standard of Living and Expanding Markets, we go to a country like Afghanistan and cruelly try to jerk her forward two thousand years in two decades, giving no thought to the profound shock this must be to her national psychology. The present state of our own national psychologies is a good enough advertisement for the need of a far more gradual change. I tried to point out to my friends that once they have created this terrible idol of the Modern State it will enslave them for ever and then it will be too late for them to see that 'the good old days' were best; they will be forced to continue worshipping their idol whatever the cost to their humanity. However, they thought I was mad to find more happiness and peace in an Afghan village than in a European industrial city.

One of my most pleasant memories of Kabul will be the walk home after dinner tonight, with the moon spilling silver over the mountains into the streets and the perfume of the acacia, in full bloom now, rich on the damp air, and not a mouse stirring from one side of the city to the other. I wonder is there any other capital city which one could cross at 10.30 p.m. without seeing a solitary person or a car or any sign of life.

KABUL, 9 MAY

This afternoon I changed £30-worth of travellers' cheques in the bazaar and got Rs 20 for each £1, which is one-third more than the official Bank Rate. Of course the whole thing is madly illegal and I'll have to smuggle the currency into both Pakistan and India, but it does mean only spending 1*s.* instead of 1*s.* 6*d.* every time I part with a rupee. In Teheran the money-changers work openly but here it's all frightfully hush-hush and melodramatic. You go down into a maze of smelly little alleys and walk along with your hands held in a certain position, indicating that you've been initiated by someone the changer already trusts. Then a little boy of about seven or eight appears, wearing an appropriately significant expression, and he looks at you and you look at him, after which he saunters casually off and you follow and enter a bakery and go behind the scenes where you sit sipping tea and haggling in a leisurely way about the rate of exchange; it's all wonderfully unlike the respectability of changing a cheque in the West.

When I set off for Jalalabad in the morning I'm leaving behind the two pannier-bags and knapsack and all kit that would be superfluous during the next few months; I'll collect it on the return journey. My friends here are paralysed with horror at the thought of anyone going on a five-month trip with only a saddlebag of luggage, but the fact is that the further you travel the less you find you need and I see no sense in frolicking around the Himalayas with a load of inessentials. So I'm down to two pens, writing-paper, Blake's poems, map, passport, camera, comb, toothbrush, one spare pair of nylon pants and nylon shirt – and there's plenty of room left over for food as required from day to day. It's a good life that teaches you how little you need to be healthy and happy, if not particularly clean!

JALALABAD, 10 MAY

I left Kabul at 6.30 a.m. and covered 115 miles today. The ribs are still uncomfortable but not actually painful and a strong east wind tempered the fierce sun while Roz and I were moving. The road was atrocious for forty miles, though excellent for the rest, and it was an odd sensation to be going gradually but steadily *down* over most of the way, just pedalling automatically – but think of the return journey! Kabul is at 7,000 feet and, though I don't know what the altitude here is, the air feels positively thick with oxygen after so long on the heights. Roz got one puncture in her new tyre this afternoon and a truck-driver stopped when he saw me struggling with it and did the job in less than ten minutes. Of course he would *not* accept the gift of a packet of American cigarettes.

We passed through some tremendous scenery and saw a most awe-inspiring engineering feat – the road through the Tangi Sharo Gorge. Here the mountains are almost sheer walls of solid grey rock and the road pirouettes its way down thousands of feet to river level. The surface has not been metalled yet so I walked, which was safer anyway with no back brake. From the top the Kabul river looks a mere thread of water, though in fact it's a torrent in a mad, foaming rush to join the Indus.

During the afternoon I had a most exciting bathe (not swim) in the Kabul. I picked a spot where the current would wash me up about a quarter of a mile downstream on a bank of gravel, and just went with it, enjoying the thrilling sensation of being swept along at such speed by the flood; I went down four times and watching Pathans obviously thought me too mad to be quite true! That was near here, where harvesting is in full swing, wheat being cut by hand with the most primitive sickles and carried home on men's backs. It is very lovely to see rows of trees in early dense fresh greenery standing amidst fields of pure gold corn, with low blue mountains behind and beyond them again the massive ranges of the southern Hindu Kush burning against the sky like a white fire. Orchards of (I think) pomegranate trees sometimes line the road and look like a new sort of Christmas tree with their profusion of scarlet, bell-shaped blossom. I can't attempt to describe the various exotic shrubs of the region; they line the streets of this city and their scent defeats even the stagnant *jubes* – which are equally remarkable in their own way.

I have left a dozen broken hearts behind me in Kabul, which is not as romantic as it sounds, since they are all in the Tourist Bureau! Obviously, *qua* tourist, I'm the answer to an Afghan's prayer – they admitted I was one of the few to enter their offices without a list of complaints from here to Eternity. Anyway I implored them, almost with tears in my eyes, not to pander to outsiders and defile Afghanistan with cafés on every mountain pass and juke-boxes in hotels and souvenir shops in Bamian. Tourists who want these extras can get them in practically every accessible country of the world.

The poor chaps at the Tourist Bureau were in misery about my accident on the bus, yet, as I pointed out, it could as easily have happened in Ireland, only there it wouldn't be a fight about fares but a drunken brawl going home from a hurling match and a hurley instead of a rifle-butt!

At midday I went asleep for about half an hour on a mountainside, having been up since 5.30 a.m., and woke to find myself in a *tent.* I had decided that I was still asleep and dreaming when a filthy old man of the Kochi (nomad) tribes appeared and explained by signs that they'd noticed me going to sleep with no shade, which they thought very bad, so he erected one of their goat-hair tents over me -- without loosening a pebble, they move so very stealthily. The moral here is that the basis of a successful psychological approach to Afghans is *not* to be afraid of them. Yet it's literally true that the same old man would think nothing of murdering his own daughter if she ran away and married into an enemy tribe. It does take a while to sort out the fact that such people don't want to murder *you*!

This city is full of Sikhs, who are undoubtedly the most forthcoming people on my route since Bulgaria. They told me that I could stay as long as I like in their Golden Temple at Amritsar, where a bed and three meals a day are given free to all travellers of every colour, class and creed – one of these religious 'things'. The complexity of Eastern religions is quite beyond me – when you think of how Sikhs and Muslims massacred each other in 1947–48! Yet it's absolutely true that once you leave Europe you could, if you were stingy enough, live entirely free on the generosity of people with about a twentieth of the average European income. The other day in a tea-house I made a casual remark to a total stranger about the postal rates here and he immediately offered to pay all my stamp bills – a man with no shoes to his feet! This is typical. Again, on my return from Pul-i-Khumri I found an envelope with 500 *afghanis* (£3 10*s*.) in my writing case, and no one could have put it there but the Afghan doctor. This anonymity is characteristic; they don't want to impress with their wealth or kindness, they just want to please Allah and obey Mohammed by 'helping strangers in the land'. I realised that this gift was made to me under false pretences as my destitution, judging by outward appearances, is now beyond all, with trousers, shirt and shoes in small shreds, just hanging together – I hope – till I get to Peshawar. (This is why I didn't give the ribs more time to recover; they could have been a good excuse to stay longer in Afghanistan.) I sent the money, equally anonymously, to the TB Centre, which is desperately short of funds.

One of the current scandals of the world -- I've been hearing about it from the Americans and British ever since I got to Asia – is the number of so-called Christians who take advantage of this Muslim doctrine to 'borrow' from the locals in these countries. The classic case concerns an Englishman and his wife driving home from Australia. They stayed with a doctor who befriended them in Tabriz, went to town on Persian rugs, 'borrowed' all the poor man's savings (over £300) to pay for their souvenirs – and that was that. Of course this sponging is usually on a smaller scale and is chiefly done by hitch-hikers. Personally, I haven't the slightest objection to accepting hospitality from *Westerners* – they can usually well afford it and their religion doesn't forbid them to accept farewell gifts – but it enrages me to think of 'our side' being let down by such scroungers.

7

Anticlimax

JALALABAD TO PESHAWAR

LANDI KOTAL, PAKISTAN, 11 MAY

As far as I'm concerned the Khyber Pass hasn't had a chance so far. It's quite beautiful, though not comparable to the Shibar Pass, but I simply wasn't in the mood to give it credit since for me it's the route out of my beloved Afghanistan. From the top you can see Kabul, 156 miles away, with all the intervening mountains in a wild jumble of peaks below you. Then you say goodbye to Afghanistan – a sad moment – and turn a corner round the mountainside and it's all Pakistan ahead, beautiful and friendly and primitive enough to satisfy anyone not newly parted from Afghanistan!

Now I'd better begin at the beginning. We left Jalalabad at 5.45 a.m. with fifty-six miles to go on a perfect road to reach the frontier. At first the level plain was wide and cultivated to the foot of distant, snow-crested mountains; then we came to rough brown hills overlooking the road and dotted with fortresses, in case we might forget that this is territory where trigger-happy tribesmen have been busy for centuries. By this stage, at about 10 a.m., the heat was so intense that I had to pack it up and retire to a nearby nomad camp where I slept till noon. I woke to find the sky full of lovely rain-clouds and Kochis grilling lamb for my lunch – a very classy menu in this camp. It was almost as though they knew how I felt about leaving their country, they were so kind to me.

There is little traffic on this road, because of the frontier being closed. I arrived at the Afghan Customs at 3 p.m. and at once I could feel the twentieth century ready to pounce on me. The Customs building here is positively contemporary compared with the one at the Persian frontier and the officers wear European clothes, speak a little English and smoke cigarettes . . . They said they hoped I had enjoyed my stay in Afghanistan and didn't I think Sarobi hydroelectric plant (which I passed yesterday and tried not to notice) was wonderful? I said I'd enjoyed myself more in Afghanistan than in any other country of the world but that the cycle run from Kabul to the frontier was the least enjoyable part, because here 'progress' is fastest. They stared at me as though I were a lunatic and then we parted.

On crossing the bridge which marks the Durand Line, the first thing I saw was a Pakistani bus, all spick and span and not in the least likely to break down or do anything unexpected within the next five years. Then there were *signposts* – a phenomenon unknown in Afghanistan – which gave distances in miles, and a 'Drive on the Left' sign, and a detachment of the Khyber Rifles, who looked quite the smartest soldiers I've ever seen anywhere; their uniform is distinctive and gay, and apparently newly issued from the Army stores every morning! Their drill is of course equally impeccable – shades of Sandhurst! Unmistakably I have entered a Commonwealth country. (Afghan privates literally have their behinds showing through their ragged pants – just like me now – and are paid 3*s*. 2*d*. per *month*.)

A great fuss was made of me in the Pakistani Customs' Rest House (complete with bathroom, armchairs and electric fans) but though I appreciated being given such a welcome and having a pot of tea served as at home – for the first time since leaving England – I couldn't adjust happily to the change, and haven't yet. The five-mile walk up took me one and a half hours and I didn't arrive till 5.30 p.m., an hour after curfew, but no one fussed. I saw my first railway since leaving Meshed (Afghanistan and Tibet are the only countries in the world without railways) and while going through the bazaar here met my first beggars since Persia and heard the old baksheesh whine. Landi Kotal's is a notorious bazaar where you can buy almost anything from any country in the world, presumably all smuggled, and it's rather startling to come on this exotic sort of supermarket in the middle of nowhere. By now it's to some extent a tourist attraction, yet I bought a very nice new watch-strap for 2*s*. which would probably have cost 5*s*. at home.

But then it's fairly obvious from my present attire that I'm not a tourist within the meaning of the act. I left my cigarette holder by mistake on the counter of the watch-stall and five minutes later a boy came rushing through the alleyway shouting for the Memsahib from Ireland and brandishing the holder; this makes one wonder if Landi Kotal's nickname, 'The Town of Ten Thousand Thieves', is quite fair.

Muslim hospitality is continuing unabated here and I have just had an excellently cooked, though simple, dinner in the home of a local official, where I'm invited to stay the night. It certainly makes travelling more interesting when one can converse freely with the average citizens of a country, but it also makes for embarrassments, as at dinner this evening when the conversation was all political – on the Kashmir and Pakhtoonistan problems. The former was easy for me as I'm with the Pakistanis on Kashmir, simply because I like things carried to logical conclusions, and if India had to be partitioned and the basis of partition was religious then Kashmir should be part of Pakistan. On the other issue, however, I was torn between loyalty to Afghanistan and politeness to my hosts, so I made a big effort and remained silent. Granted that the advisability of giving independence to Pakhtoonistan is debatable, in a world of tedious amalgamations I can't help favouring the idea. Here again, as at every frontier I've crossed, I notice that enmity between neighbouring nations which is one of the most depressing features of travel. Even the closest racial and religious ties don't tone it down – in fact they seem to heighten it in the present case. But I always blame the politicians for this. The man-in-the-bazaar is easily led and the virulent propaganda that emanates from all the National Radio Stations in this part of the world is proof of how grossly his leaders abuse their authority. To me this type of propaganda is so blatant as to appear childish but in an Asian context it's criminally clever.

Landi Kotal, being at the top of the pass, is deliciously cool and this evening it's raining steadily; my room is filled with the scent of huge mulberry trees on the lawn outside. Peshawar is thirty miles down the pass – I hope it's fine by morning. I'm now covered in funny things acquired in the nomad tent today; they look exactly like lice but hop like fleas when you try to catch them.

PESHAWAR, 12 MAY

I was awakened at 1 a.m. by thunder and was kept awake for two hours by its continuous crashing and by torrents of rain on the tin roof. It was still raining in an Irish sort of downpour when I rose at 6.30, and my host said that this would go on all day. Therefore (since sitting on top of the Khyber Pass unable to see your hand in front of your face is not my idea of fun) I decided temporarily to abandon Roz, come down here by bus for my mail to cheer myself up and return to collect Roz when the rain stops. Judging by the way the road drops to the Plain of Peshawar in a sort of convulsion of twists around mountains it must be a thrilling run, but I didn't *see* anything except what looked like mist imported from Connemara. It's still pouring here, which means there's no great heat yet, and it's just like a July day in Ireland. Everyone says it's fantastic weather; normally they have no rain in May and the present torrent has nothing to do with the monsoon due next month.

Peshawar is like an English city with a few water-buffaloes and vultures and lizards thrown in. I'm installed in a dak bungalow, which is the cheapest accommodation for tourists in Pakistan and India. These bungalows were originally built by the British for the comfort of their officials on tour and I'm told one finds them in even the remotests spots. My bearer here supports nine children on £2 10*s.* a month. His two-year-old son has seven fingers on one hand and he's so proud of this that he's bringing the infant for me to admire tomorrow.

PESHAWAR, 13 MAY

I'm getting over my mourning for Afghanistan today and settling down to make the best of this country. To be objective about the Indian subcontinent – discarding my inherited anti-colonialism, and a temperamental bias towards mediaeval Afghanistan – even two days in this one city make nonsense of the argument that Britain exploited the country without compensation. Of course she exploited her, but in what city between Constantinople and

Peshawar do you see good and plentiful schools, hospitals, homes for the blind, orphanages, clinics and Christian churches that are allowed to function? And where in the Middle East do you find efficient transport services, reliable communications, an army that *looks* like an army, well-trained civil servants, electricity plants that actually produce electricity and roads that *are* roads? Britain grew fat on Indian wealth, but enough was ploughed back to make the familiar picture of her as a heartless bandit look just plain silly.

Of course the social atmosphere of Afghanistan is much more congenial. There the poorest peasant looks you in the eyes, instead of cringing because you're a white memsahib, as the Punjabis here do. (My bearer is different; he's a Pathan and it wasn't hard to train him to sit down and talk sociably instead of squatting eternally outside the door ready to dart in and turn on the fan if I tried to do it myself.) Yet you can't blame the British for this servility either: if the Indians had had as much guts as the Afghans they'd never have been conquered – Afghanistan wasn't!

Yesterday was Sunday, which *is* Sunday here – very confusing after ten weeks of Friday being Sunday. I set off after lunch to buy something to cover my nakedness but the bazaar was shut, so I went on to see the Irish priests, with hordes of children running after me pointing to the unsewable split in the back of my slacks and enjoying the fun like mad. The good priests, dressed in unclerical garb, were themselves almost as decrepit. Going on to the Peshawar Club I found that Mr Beck from the British Embassy in Kabul had come down for a few days and he took me to dinner with Indian friends of his, which was very enjoyable. Afterwards we saw the sixteen city gates being shut for the night to keep the tribesmen out – and it's quite a ceremony.

Today is, if possible, even wetter than yesterday. I went off first thing to the bazaar and got a second-hand pair of men's trousers for 7*s*., plus my old ones in exchange. They're a bit long in the leg but I'm not planning to feature in any fashion show in the immediate future, so why worry! (I've had the most adorable lizard on my wall all day – he makes a very companionable sound as he scampers up and down industriously catching flies – so hygienic of him!) I was given tea and Marie biscuits – made in Karachi – by the second-hand clothes merchant, while he sent his peon off with my boots to be resoled. Thick new soles cost only 2*s.* and I got a second-hand khaki shirt for 3*s.* On arriving back here I was absolutely soaked; the rain has been coming down persistently all day.

Before returning to Landi Kotal for Roz I must get a permit to re-enter the Khyber area so I'll go round to the office now and be ready to leave early in the morning if it's fine. This Khyber set-up is a curious one; the region is politically in Pakistan but is legally independent and the road through is not *owned* by Pakistan but is leased from the tribes and maintained by Pakistan for the convenience of people going and coming via the pass. That's why the area is rated as dangerous: Tribal Laws only are in force.

Today I heard the sad story of two motoring tourists who were driving to Quetta when, east of Khandahar, a Kochi child ran in front of their car and was killed. They naturally, although in those special circumstances unwisely, stopped and the men of the tribe attacked the husband and knifed him in the lungs – he's now in Quetta hospital seriously ill and would have been killed if a bus-load of Afghans hadn't intervened; two men on the bus were injured during the fight.

Later. This really is a very pleasant city, with trees and flowering shrubs lining every street in the Cantonment area and acres of lush grass stretching in all directions. There was no trouble about getting my pass so I'm all set for the morning. One sees the funniest little taxis here – called rickshaws – with three tiny wheels and plastic awnings and motorbike handlebars and engines. These take three passengers and cost 6*d.* per mile. There's very little traffic in Peshawar and the standard of driving is quite good.

PESHAWAR, 14 MAY

At 6.30 a.m. it was not actually raining and looked as though the skies might clear, so I went to catch the 7.30 bus back to Landi Kotal, reaching the terminus at 7.28. The bus started at 7.29, which shook me badly; I'm not yet sufficiently reconditioned to be able to take this sort of thing in my stride!

The Khyber Pass is very fine, but, after the Hindu Kush, something of an anticlimax. Its fame is based on history rather than on scenery, and one has both in Afghanistan, though British travellers find the Khyber uniquely significant, with all its sad little graveyards on the mountainsides and the regimental plaques on the cliff-faces. I spoke to several Pathans who said that the British were the soldiers most worth a Pathan's ammunition!

I thought rifles common in Afghanistan but around the Khyber Pass every male over twelve years old carries one, and often a revolver as well, with as much ammunition slung across his chest as one human body can accommodate. Family blood feuds are still carried on, though not quite with the old fervour, and among the Afridis and Shinwalis wives are expected to be able to take over the defence of a compound in emergencies. I stopped at four villages on the way down and was told in three of them that I looked like a Pathan woman; this, naturally, is the highest compliment a Pathan man can think of! Today every one of these hardy warriors was solemnly holding an umbrella over his head – probably to keep his ammunition dry, for instead of improving, the day got damper hourly.

There are two roads through Khyber. The old one, which has been in use for the past 3,500 years, follows the river most of the way at the foot of the mountains, but the new one, built around the side of the mountains by the British, is considerably shorter. However, as it avoids the tribal villages the old one seemed more attractive so, having collected Roz, I followed it for much of the descent, enjoying many lengthy stops in teahouses, talking to the tribesmen, some of whom speak a little English. I'm invited to spend 'as long as I like' in one Afridi village on my way back in November – a date I hope to keep. One of the most impressive things about the pass is the railway – a stupendous piece of engineering which thrilled even me. I was lucky enough to see one of the very rare trains go up, with an engine in front pulling and another behind pushing, as the gradient is so steep. On almost every hilltop (and there are a good many hilltops) stands a fort, commanding the stretch of road to the next bend. These are not now manned but of course the big HQ fort of the Khyber Rifles – Jamrud – is still very much in use.

PESHAWAR, 15 MAY

Today the local British Council opened an exhibition of books on Afghanistan, so I spent most of the day browsing amongst these; they were very interesting though of course they didn't form as rare a collection as that in the British Embassy library in Kabul. At midday I stopped browsing for long enough to lunch with the family of a Pakistani Army colonel. They were delightful people, who of course all spoke flawless English, though my hostess and her eighteen-year-old daughter both observe purdah. The daughter was educated by Irish nuns at Murree (Pakistan's hill-station) and is anxious to study medicine but her father wishes her to marry now and be a good, traditional wife to the man of his choice. Her mother, who is only thirty-five, told me when we were alone before lunch that she fully supports her daughter's bid for liberty. I hardly knew what to say; obviously she expected me to agree with her completely, but I'm not yet long enough in this environment to have evolved definite personal opinions on the subject. At first glance this is, by our standards, a monstrous situation. Yet the colonel, far from being an unreasonable tyrant, is a most kindly and humorous man, truly cultured, tolerant without being indecisive and, I feel, *wise*. So what's the answer? Perhaps the mistake is to give daughters a glimpse of Western freedom by educating them at European-run schools, and then to expect them to revert unprotestingly to their own traditions. Of course one condemns without reservations that perversion of the Koran which leads to the subjection in which the majority of Afghan women are kept. But in this milieu things are very different, the women being treated with affection and respect and, on the deepest level, as equals, even though the father is so decidedly the ruler of the family when it comes to practical matters. Today I felt sympathy both towards the daughter who had acquired a taste for what we consider basic human rights, and towards the father who knows the value of Islamic traditions and the danger of exchanging them for ours.

After lunch a friend of my host called and the women of the family retired to purdah quarters before the visitor was shown into the sitting-room. During the conversation that followed it became very clear that the Colonel's apparently irrational conservatism was based on a sincere desire to protect his daughter from what he considered the worst evils of Western society – materialism, sexual promiscuity and general godlessness. I put the point that in our view youngsters have to be turned loose to take their chance in these matters and he quickly challenged me to deny that the results of such liberalism had proved disastrous, both for individual youngsters and for society as a whole. To this I could only reply that it's entirely a matter of one's inherited way of thinking. Clearly this stratum of Pakistani society is now the scene of a rather pathetic struggle to achieve an honourable compromise between old and new, and one hopes that the Muslims can preserve the most valuable elements in their traditions despite mounting pressure from the West. The Colonel argued that the worship of God and keeping the women by the hearth form a better basis for human happiness and stability than the worship of mammon and women in the professions. At this point I was tempted to ask how and where one drew the dividing line between God and mammon when human nature has a foot in both camps and our reactions in either direction can be so variously interpreted; but feeling that the Colonel might not relish this question I restrained myself. Perhaps it's because I am so conscious personally of the results of godlessness that I failed to follow my first instinct and argue wholeheartedly for his daughter's freedom.

PESHAWAR, 16 MAY

Today I called again on the Irish priests and on the convent of Irish Presentation nuns. The Catholics run two schools here, one a very expensive college for the sons of rich Muslims and the other a free primary school for poor Christians. I'm intrigued by the subtlety of making Muslims pay for Christians to be educated! The teaching of Christian doctrine is, of course, absolutely taboo at the Muslim college, which is packed to overflowing with all the local (and other) Big Men's sons avid for good teaching. Seemingly the standard of teaching at Pakistani-run schools, where the staffs are incredibly underpaid, is appalling.

I can't even begin to imagine what it must feel like to be a Christian missionary in a Muslim country where one daren't ever attempt to convert anybody, except by the vague method of 'example'. But then to me Christian missionaries in Muslim countries, however genuine their fervour, are at best unattractive manifestations of self-righteousness and at worst an impertinence. Yet that attitude is narrow too in its own way. If you are convinced of your duty to spread the gospel there is obviously a certain nobility in settling in a place like Peshawar, without hope of any material gain whatsoever, and in patiently leading a Christian life for the purpose of influencing those around you.

This evening I went to dine at the home of Mr Mohammad Ali, the Vice-Chancellor of Peshawar University, to whom I had an introduction. The new university is four miles outside the city, beautifully situated in the centre of a semicircle of mountains, with the snowy Central Asian range to the far north. A big, purring, chauffeur-driven Mercedes came to fetch me but the Vice-Chancellor's family is unassuming and homely and Mr Ali himself kindly took me around all the new buildings – the majority are very handsome indeed – in which he takes a fatherly pride. Like most men of outstanding intellectual abilities he is simple and easy to get on with and I felt very much at home in this family. They have invited me to stop with them on my return journey and if possible to come for their second son's wedding festivities in October. This son, who is a senior lecturer in English (BA Cantab.) at the university, earns £20 a month, and other salaries are in proportion, although prices of commodities here are *not* correspondingly low, as one would expect.

8

Welcome at the Waliahad

PESHAWAR TO SAIDU SHARIFF

BAGDADA, 17 MAY

This sounds as though I've somehow got to Iraq overnight and forgotten my spelling en route, but in fact it's a delightful frontier village forty-five miles north of Peshawar where I'm staying with the chief in a vast but primitive house. My spirits are completely restored now that I've escaped from Peshawar and its European luxuries. Suinabhayat Khan, my host, is a brother of Colonel Zeb, whom I met in Teheran, and is a son of the official who helped rescue Miss Molly Ellis from the Afridis. As I can still remember the day some twenty years ago, when I first read an account of this adventure, you can imagine the thrill I got out of being shown the handwritten report submitted by my hero on his return.

I've had a most enjoyable evening – back to eating with fingers off plates on the floor, surrounded by Pathans. My Colonel host from Peshawar also came up, by car, today, and looks much more handsome in his Pathan garb than in a European suit. (He is another brother: why they all have different surnames is one of the local mysteries I haven't got around to solving yet.) In the middle of supper we heard gunfire from the direction of the bazaar and the chief dashed off to investigate. He came back in fifteen minutes and reported that a policeman had been shot dead, while sitting in a tea-house, by a tribesman whom the police couldn't capture as the crowd were 'with him'. I'm sure you'll agree that though regrettable, this is the sort of thing that *should* happen during supper in the NWFP (North West Frontier Province), as everyone here still insists on calling the region.

A few days ago at a nearby court the magistrate awarded a case to A against B. B promptly stood up and shot A dead in front of the magistrate, who equally promptly and very wisely dived under a table. Perhaps, after all, Pakistan is not *quite* the same as England.

I learned a lot this evening about the habits of Pathans. These sons of Moghul Baz Khan don't wear guns when motoring with their wives and children because if they did so and were held up – as is quite likely around here – they would have no alternative, according to the code, but to shoot at the bandits, who would then shoot back, possibly injuring the wives and children. And however long any of these men may have been in English schools or universities or military colleges they still adhere most rigidly to the Pathan code. The inheritance laws are the same here as in Afghanistan – Islamic. When a man dies, his wife or wives get one-eighth of his property and sons get a portion each of the rest and daughters a half of what the sons get: Muslims disapprove violently of primogeniture. But as they often produce ten to twenty sons apiece this doesn't seem to make much sense. More than one wife is now illegal here, but I doubt if that will make any impression on anyone in the immediate future. My host told me that his twelve-year-old daughter, now at the Murree convent school, has insisted on putting herself into purdah although he has assured her that she needn't if she preferred to go unveiled. He also told me that when he took his wife to Europe last year he could not persuade her to take off her *burkah* in Paris, London or anywhere else. This contrast in the attitude of two brothers reveals the extent to which Islamic traditions are currently in the melting pot.

I left Peshawar at 7.30 a.m. today and the traffic on this road was the heaviest I've met since Italy. It's grim to see so many buffaloes and horses and dogs half-starved. The people en route were very friendly and I was frequently pursued by loud cheers. After the desolation of Afghanistan the density of population seems extraordinary. I cycled twenty-two miles looking for a 'quiet corner' and finally was driven to emulating the natives and not bothering about spectators – one gets adjusted, I suppose! The stinks are even worse than Afghanistan – obviously, since so many more are contributing to them per square mile. At one tea-house the stench was so overpowering that I simply couldn't sit there and drink tea; no wonder there's so much typhoid in the area. I collected more mail from Nowshera and here I must pause to record for posterity a word that definitely deserves its place in the *OED*. It is the property of one of my correspondents who in his last letter begged me not to become too 'Afghanatical'. The fact that I had become rabidly and irreparably 'Afghanatical' before the plea arrived is irrelevant.

The whole of today's cycling was over level, rather dull countryside that looked heavily wooded in comparison with Afghanistan. The road seemed very good to me although the locals complain bitterly about it. I whizzed along happily at 16 m.p.h. and was just congratulating myself on the perfection of the weather for cycling when a blue Morris Minor overtook me, slowed up and drove ahead for a few minutes, then stopped and decanted a worried-looking European woman who held me up and began a lecture on heat stroke being the consequence of anyone cycling at that speed in that heat. While moving I'd felt perfectly comfortable but the instant I stopped the sweat began to run off me as I stood in the sun. I said meekly that I hadn't felt hot and she said that that had nothing to do with it. Apparently heat stroke is a cumulative thing and you don't notice it happening till you drop like a stone. Then she noticed the sweat that was streaming down my face and neck and arms, non-stop, and said, 'Oh well, if you sweat like that I think you're safe enough and probably that's why you don't feel it so much.' Before proceeding on her way she kindly invited me to lunch at Mardan, and when I arrived there I found that she was the wife of the Danish Lutheran Bishop of NWFP. They are a very charming couple who have been forty years in this area and speak Pushto like Pathans. I was told this evening about their son's murder thirty-five years ago. Their Pathan gardener wanted to have their Christian Indian ayah as his second wife but the Bishop vetoed the marriage, so in revenge the Pathan shot the ayah and their seven-year-old son and then fled back to his Shinwali tribe and was never heard of again. The Bishop's wife very understandably wanted to go back to Denmark after that and leave the Pathans to stew in their own heretical juice, but the

Bishop said, 'No, let's turn the other cheek', and they've been turning it ever since.

I went round the local cane-sugar factory – the biggest in Asia – after my siesta. The men are paid £5 per month for an eight-hour six-day week. It's a very interesting process but would put you off sugar for life.

TAKHT-I-BAI, 18 MAY

Last night, in honour of some village wedding, a band played throbbingly outside my window until 2 a.m.: the wild, martial airs were not sleep-inducing but I was happy to lie on my charpoy enjoying the concert. I was wakened again at 5.45 a.m. by quite different sounds – fierce arguing in the courtyard. Looking out I saw my host sitting in the shade of an awning of rushes surrounded by villagers, two of whom were arguing like demons – and an angry Pathan-Afghan has to be seen to be believed, as I know to my cost. Later Sai Rab told me that this is a daily routine; from 5.30 to 8.30 a.m. people come with disputes for him to settle and he has such a tremendous personality and such authority over the local branch of the Afridis that they usually accept his decisions, which are based on Tribal Laws. This is all part of President Ayub's effort to re-introduce what is known here as 'Basic Democracy' and is in fact a reversion to things as they were before the British came. It works smoothly when men like Sai Rab Khan are available to take over; but men of his type are, unfortunately, rare in any country.

We only covered eight miles today because of three detours involving over twenty miles of walking and the climbing of three mountains to inspect some fascinating Buddhist ruins. It was a most enjoyable day although from 5 p.m. I was being saturated by another downpour of rain. An introduction to a Scots engineer at a sugar factory here led to my being invited to his home, where we've just been listening to a Communist broadcast in English accusing America of nuclear tests above the atmosphere which have completely upset the world's weather.

SAIDU SHARIFF, 19 MAY

What a deluge! I left Takht-i-Bai at 8 a.m. and it poured non-stop till I arrived here at 4 p.m. However, it's good training for India, where I'll have to endure something similar every day during the monsoon. I found the Malakand Pass baby-food after my efforts in the Hindu Kush: it wasn't necessary to dismount once although we climbed 5,000 feet in seven miles – but of course the road is beautifully surfaced and well graded. Unfortunately, I missed all the views because of mist and saw only enough of the renowned valley of Swat to make me recognise it as the nearest thing to Irish scenery met with since leaving home.

My arrival here was one of the classic episodes of the expedition. On the outskirts of Saidu I asked for Aurang Zeb's house [sic] and was directed to one end of the town. I went there and asked again. A policeman pointed down the street and I pedalled off in the indicated direction, noting en route a palatial-looking building complete with sentry-boxes. Not seeing any house that looked a 'likely' I returned to the crossroads and repeated my query. The policeman pointed again, rather impatiently, and I shook my head and repeated 'Aurang Zeb's house.' The policeman nodded and said, '*That's* his house.' I said, 'That's not a house – it's a ruddy great palace!' The policeman nodded yet again and said, 'Yes, Wali of Swat's Palace.' 'Blast it, I don't *want* Wali of Swat's palace – I want Aurang Zeb's house.' The policeman continued nodding and said 'Aurang Zeb is Wali's prince and lives in father's palace.' I said nothing for a moment after that, then murmured 'Thank you,' rather faintly, and wrung some water out of my hair in a vague way, to make myself look slightly more respectable before approaching one of the two sentry-boxes. The sentries immediately came to attention and another soldier appeared from within the gates and said, 'Are you the lady with the bicycle?' I replied, 'I'm afraid so,' apologetically, as he obviously only credited the bicycle clause, and he continued in an 'outraged Jeeves' voice, 'You are to be brought directly in.' A few moments later I was sitting on the verandah, where a very self-possessed peke promptly took over my lap, while the servant to whom I'd been delivered by the soldier went to announce my arrival. It seemed to me as I waited that Colonel Zeb, on giving me this introduction in Teheran, should have warned me that it involved walis, princes, palaces and sentries – all contingencies which I felt singularly ill-equipped to meet. But then Begum Naseem Aurang Zeb came walking down the verandah and I realised at a glance that the complications of the situation were more apparent than real. Naseem, President Ayub's eldest daughter, is Prince Aurang Zeb's wife and her physical beauty (striking even by Pathan standards) is equalled by true gentleness of nature, sincerity and simplicity of manner and warmth of heart. She told me not to stand up because of the peke and sat down and talked to me as though we were continuing an interrupted conversation rather than getting acquainted. Naseem accompanies her father on his State Visits abroad and Pakistan is fortunate indeed to have such a remarkable young woman to represent her in other countries. Characteristically, she told me first about her three oldest children's mumps and her fear that the six-weeks-old baby might get them. As a twenty-four-year-old girl whose eldest daughter is aged seven many of her Western contemporaries might pity her, but when you have been conditioned to regard the rôle of wife and mother as the most honourable one there is for a woman, the – to us slightly premature – responsibility of a growing family at twenty-four is a source of deep satisfaction. I couldn't help contrasting the basic contentment so evident in Naseem, and in most of the young Pakistani women I've met to date, with the uncertainty as to what *is* fulfilment shown by the young of the West. Yet these Pakistani girls, unlike the simple peasants of Afghanistan, live in luxurious Western-style homes, have been educated in Irish-run schools, speak English as fluently as Pushto and are in close cultural contact with the West. It will be interesting, and probably saddening, to observe the changes within the next quarter-century; it seems too much to hope that the present delicate balance between East and West – using the best of both worlds – can be maintained by future generations.

Naseem and I had been talking only a few minutes when Prince

Aurang Zeb and his younger brother arrived to welcome me. I don't quite know what it is about the Pathans (perhaps some profound racial affinity with the Irish) but I find them extraordinarily easy to get on with; ever since meeting those three officers in Teheran every contact with this race has been an unqualified success. I'm not exactly uncritical of my fellow-beings, but I haven't yet met one unlikable Pathan. Of course their educational ties with Ireland and consequent knowledge of my own little country – which most people have never heard of – undoubtedly has something to do with this, although there's obviously a lot more to it. Anyway, whatever the cause, I become assimilated into Pathan families with delightful ease and am now as happy in my present surroundings of unparalleled splendour as though I were in a nomad camp, which just shows that it's *people* who count and that the human qualities I found to admire in Afghanistan are still present here, despite the very different material environment.

SAIDU SHARIFF, 20 MAY

The happy-go-lucky informality of this establishment effectively counteracts the outward glory and the awe-inspiring fact that all sorts of VIPs, including Mr Khrushchev and Queen Elizabeth II, have occupied one's rooms in the past. Yesterday afternoon, when it became obvious that something must be done about clothing me while my shirt and pants dried, Aurang Zeb sent for a measuring tape and personally confirmed that his trousers would fit me, to the great amusement of the family, my fellow-guests and a semicircle of delightedly grinning servants, who have assuredly never before witnessed the arrival at the Waliahad of such an unlikely looking guest.

Incidentally, I notice that in Pakistan – and I believe it's the same in India – women never wear Western dress, though in Persia and Afghanistan the majority of middle- and upper-class women wear the latest European fashions under their *chadors* and *burkahs*.

I find it very interesting that Muslim families can carry suddenly acquired wealth and power so much more graciously than their European counterparts usually do. Aurang Zeb's grandfather was an illiterate tribal leader who by a combination of intelligence, ruthlessness and sheer personality secured control of Swat State in 1917 and Aurang Zeb himself hints with a chuckle that the ethics of the take-over left a lot to be desired. Yet in this case the end appears to have justified the means, as the little mountain state (area 4,000 sq. miles, population 600,000 in 1961) is now the most prosperous region of Pakistan, with the best roads – as I noticed yesterday on reaching the state boundary – and with a higher percentage of rural hospitals and primary schools than I've seen anywhere else in Asia. There is obviously a moral here to be pointed by someone better qualified than I am in such matters.

Again, Naseem's paternal grandfather was a peasant-boy recruited to the old Indian Army from his village near Abbottabad, but in his distinguished descendants there is neither any self-conscious defensive bragging about this background nor any wish to forget it. In fact, President Ayub's strongest psychological card in the political game is probably his genuinely felt link with the ordinary village people, and his understanding of them is no doubt one of the reasons why he doesn't repeat the fatally unrealistic mistake of trying to run Pakistan as thought it were a Western democracy. Islamic countries have their own traditional type of democracy which, as I mentioned a few days ago, President Ayub is now attempting to revive in Pakistan. Whether the flair for accepting a drastic change of status with such natural dignity is due to the democratic aspects of Muslim philosophy or to the sense and sensibility of the individuals concerned it is difficult to know, but this characteristic certainly makes for a very pleasant social atmosphere.

I woke to a cloudless sky this morning and from my verandah the view of the long, broad valley of Swat was very lovely indeed. Blue mountains enclose wide sweeps of pastoral land, the cornfields shining gold between clumps of trees, now heavily green, and the river swirling brilliantly through the valley centre. The little 'capital' town of Saidu Shariff (altitude 3,150 feet), with the Waliahad on a slight rise above it, looks north towards the snow peaks and gives me the same feeling of carefree isolation as Andorra out of the tourist season. It's a comparatively clean and very gay town where the people are all spontaneous friendliness and uninhibited, but not embarrassing, curiosity. Roz has been minutely examined more times today than at any previous stop. She also had her back brake mended again (free, of course) and while the operation was being performed I was invited to have tea with a young doctor from Lahore who has recently taken up practice here. His living conditions were on a par with those of an Irish farm-labourer, but that didn't worry him. His only complaint was of the lack of cultured people with whom to talk, and his motive for moving from Lahore was that his widowed mother wanted him to marry a girl of whom, for some undisclosed reason, he didn't approve. In this he was a rare exception as the majority of young Muslims are very content with their parent's choice. I suspect him of being one of those who lose more than they gain by a university education on the Western pattern.

Unfortunately, the most interesting corners of Swat are still snow-bound and won't be accessible for at least another month so I explored the nearby excavations of Buddhist remains at Butkara and Udezhan. The latter town, captured by Alexander and known to the Greeks as Ora, was interesting enough to make up for anything. This valley, once the centre of a very advanced Buddhist civilisation, is an archaeological treasure-trove; wherever you dig something exciting comes up. The arrangement is that the Rome Academy finances Professor Tucci's expeditions and in return gets half the movable finds, Swat retaining the other half. Some of the Gandhara bas-reliefs I saw today decorating the outside walls of stupas were exquisitely beautiful and made me very conscious of the relative youth of our civilisation – which seems to be about to die in early middle-age!

SAIDU SHARIFF, 21 MAY

Being entertained by oriental potentates is fine – among other luxuries I have a complete set of Beethoven Symphonies at my disposal, presented to President Ayub by Dr Adenauer! But the position also has snags, one of them being that it's considered very bad form for a house-guest of the ruler of a state to transport herself around the said state on a lowly cycle, as I did yesterday. So today I was gently but firmly organised and driven up the length of the valley by Hassan, Aurang Zeb's younger brother. We went much too fast for my liking, but it was worth it to get to Bahrain where the Swat River, coming from its source in the surrounding 20,000-foot mountains, leaps triumphantly over cliffs on its way down to the valley floor. We drove along a rough track up the narrowing valley, and then got out and climbed mountains through cool forests of pine and walnut and larch. It had been a hot, cloudless day when we left Saidu but here the air was invigoratingly fresh. At about 4 p.m. dark clouds began to gather around the peaks and within half an hour torrential rain had reduced visibility to a few yards, but by then we were back in the little village where we had left the car and where we ate a huge tea of *paratas* and roast chicken and syrupy pastries.

Almost the best part of every day here is the interval before 9 p.m. dinner when Naseem and Aurang Zeb and I sit talking for a few hours, sometimes joined by Hassan or by Aurang Zeb's youngest uncle, the Wali's 'kid brother', who is the same age (thirty-five) as Aurang Zeb. If any visitor calls, Naseem has to retire to the women's quarters because while in Swat she must keep strict purdah, her father-in-law being the religious as well as the civil Head of State. I feel that this is very hard on someone who is accustomed to complete freedom in Pindi and who has no other educated woman in the household with whom to converse. However, the main thing is that she and Aurang Zeb are very happy together, which makes all the restrictions of life in Saidu relatively unimportant to her.

SAIDU SHARIFF, 22 MAY

Professor Tucci's excavations have made Swat very conscious of its past as a centre of Buddhist civilisation, but the proud emphasis on an era that ended *c.* AD 800 seems faintly *non-sequitur* in view of the fact that the present population is descended from the Yusafzai tribe of Afghanistan who migrated *c.* AD 1500 and chased the then inhabitants across the Indus before settling down to enjoy the comparative ease of life in a fertile valley.

This evening Aurang Zeb told me that the first Wali's grandfather (the Akhund of Swat) was a warrior saint who led the Yusafzai tribe at the battle of Ambella in 1862 when the British forces were commanded by Neville Chamberlain's grandfather.

It was after the Akhund's death in 1877 that Swat became involved in a forty-year crisis of constant tribal warfare – mainly because the Akhund's two sons had predeceased him and there was no acceptable leader. Then, in 1917, Badshah Sahib got a grip on the situation and since then Swat has never looked back. In 1949, after thirty-two years of vigorous work for his people, Badshah Sahib abdicated in favour of his son and has since spent his time leading the life of an ascetic.

Swat's legal status is that of a princely state within Pakistan – it was the first state to accede to Pakistan after independence. The Wali runs all internal affairs and only on foreign policy does the Central Government intervene; justice is imparted according to custom and Islamic law and under the Wali's orders. An army of 8,000 men and a police force of 2,000 are maintained by the state, whose annual revenue is approximately three-quarters of a million pounds sterling. There is no income-tax but the emerald mines near here annually provide one million rupees.

Today we visited a leper colony in a valley hidden away in the depths of the Bruner Range. A special mosque has been built there for the lepers, who spend most of their time praying – not to be cured themselves, but that nobody else may ever get the disease. There were appalling sights as we walked around, some too gruesome for description, but the lepers were pathetically pleased to see their Wali's son and he was very kind and gentle with them, shaking hands without batting an eyelid even when there was hardly any hand left.

9

Sweating out of Swat

SAIDU SHARIFF TO RAWALPINDI

RUSTAM, 23 MAY

This was definitely my most enjoyable day's cycling since leaving Afghanistan. We covered seventy-eight miles, crossing three mountain passes – all babies of between 6 and 7,000 feet, but so steep that they involved walking a total of over fourteen miles which is not particularly relaxing when the temperature is 102° F in the shade and you have *no* shade. I passed only two vehicles and no town, had three swims in a deep river, ate nothing but four teaspoons of salt, drank twenty-four pints of water and must have lost about forty-eight pints of sweat. (Aurang Zeb had presented me with his old army water-bottle, which holds six pints, and I had no trouble refilling it en route from the river.)

Between the infrequent villages peasants were busily harvesting barley and a little wheat, which is mostly blackened by the unusual rains. Their threshing is completely biblical – throwing the grain up in the air for the breeze to blow away the chaff. The landscape, as throughout Swat, was very green and we passed through many pine woods where the aroma of resin mingled in the hot air with the scents of a multitude of flowering wild shrubs and herbs. Weeping willows lined some stretches of the road, granting a brief escape from the sun, 'Irish' bramble hedges and ditches induced homesickness, and on the slopes of the grey, round-topped mountains little green bushes like juniper grew thickly. Crossing the last pass before coming down again to the Plain of Peshawar I saw enormous slabs of grey rock that reminded me very much of Inishmaan although they weren't quite as big as those on the island. I also saw five of the lizards for which this locality is famous; when resting under a tree I noticed the first one and for a brief, crazy moment imagined it to be a baby dragon. They're between three and four feet long and are very fat and much respected by the locals who believe that they kill snakes, which seems to me a doubtful occupation for a lizard.

I passed hundreds of nomads today, trudging along beneath that brutal sun carrying all their possessions. Obviously they're much poorer than the Afghan nomads, most of whom own huge herds of camels, goats and sheep; these people just have a few donkeys and goats and no tents. The women carry huge wicker baskets on their heads containing kettles, tin mugs, frying-pans, a hen or two and a few clothes. The men carry the babies tied to their backs and the toddlers sit on their shoulders; sick goats and lame kids travel in their arms. At this season they come up from the plains to the mountains where they live mostly on wild fruit and nuts. They're not nearly as friendly as their Afghan cousins though the peasant people of these valleys are very kind and were really distressed at the sight of me pedalling along leaving a trail of sweat behind me in the dust. On two of the passes shepherd boys came leaping down from halfway up the mountainside to take over the job of pushing Roz to the top. And they weren't looking for baksheesh – just being 'Pathanical'!

The road we followed today is classified as a track but is fifty times better than Afghan main roads, though the last twelve miles (all downhill), after I'd passed the Swat frontier post, were very tricky; the Pakistan Government has covered the surface with about five inches of fine sand for the convenience of the camels and Roz did *not* like this. After she'd skidded twice near the edge of precipices I got off and walked. These mountains are north-east of the Plain of Peshawar and the descent reminded me of going down the Khyber Pass, though it is much more desolate and beautiful here. It's extraordinary how the mountains rise absolutely sheer from this plain, with no intervening foothills – the effect is quite wonderful.

RAWALPINDI, 24 MAY

It got dark last night before I could finish with a description of my bed in Rustam – a tiny village miles from everywhere. I arrived there at 7 p.m. and after a supper of fried eggs and dry bread (shades of Bamian!) I was given a charpoy outside a tea-house under an awning of cane-leaves and wrote till it got dark at 8 p.m., when I went to sleep with the entire male population of Rustam standing around in an awestruck circle. I woke at 4.30 a.m., as it was just beginning to get light, and we started out at 5 a.m.

We covered 118 miles today over a level metalled road, through pleasant but not exciting scenery. There was heavy traffic for the last sixty-six miles, once we joined the grand trunk road, where water-buffalo carts make cycling conditions almost as unpleasantly dangerous as in Teheran.

I've evolved a new technique of cycling in this sort of weather. Instead of taking a three-hour midday break I experimented yesterday and today with quarter-hour rests every twelve or fifteen miles and found this much more satisfactory. By 7.30 a.m. today it was uncomfortably hot and I find that fifteen miles is the limit at a stretch without a feeling of exhaustion setting in. Then just ten or fifteen minutes out of the sun, with hot, *very* sweet tea, restores one for the next lap. Perhaps this technique is quite wrong medically; I'm just going on instinct as to what best suits my physique. At 2 p.m. today an American AID man in a jeep pulled up to tell me that the temperature was 102° in the shade and that I was *mad*. I thanked him and explained my technique, but just standing still under that sun for a few minutes while talking to him made me feel quite dizzy. Roz will have to get rubber grips for her brakes as I burnt three fingers today on the over-heated metal. What's really worrying me is the effect this heat must be having on her tyres.

I am staying here with a Pakistani General's family. The General himself is in London now but his wife and elder daughter gave me a very warm welcome; their house resembles a military museum as the General collects ancient weapons and armour. My room is his library, which gives me a nice homey feeling – it's a long time since I slept in a book-lined room. This is the first completely Westernised Pakistani home I've been in and a very faint but always perceptible 'pseudoness' pervades the atmosphere, which is much more formal than in Saidu. But I don't mean to sound ungrateful; everyone here is very kind and sincerely hospitable and can't do enough for me so it's just a question of *my* limitations.

Last night I was bitten all over by mosquitoes while asleep on my charpoy and I'm tormented with itch this evening. Between that and the jackals who are howling like damned souls beyond the garden wall I see no prospect of sleep tonight: unfortunately all the drinking is done before dinner here, so that by bedtime one has sobered up.

I stopped six times for tea today and at none of these little tea-houses would they accept money from me; they usually pressed me to have a meal also, which I had to refuse, as the mere thought of food in that heat made my tummy turn over – though I realise it can't be good to cycle such distances without eating.

At dinner this evening while discussing my journey to Gilgit it was casually mentioned that all pilots on the Pindi–Gilgit air-route get a fifty per cent danger bonus because flying through the Himalayas is so dicey. Then and there I almost abandoned my ambition to see Gilgit, but as usual my Scots blood won the argument and I decided that since I'm going as Aurang Zeb's guest, I'd risk it. However, not being very brave about flying, even under the best conditions, I won't be sorry when we've landed safely. Of course Roz is coming too and by mid-June (with luck) the Babusar Pass will be open again and we'll come back at our leisure.

RAWALPINDI, 25 MAY

I spent much of today rapidly sorting out Pindi Society. The 'Smart Set' suffers in general from too much money and the depressing sort of snobbery that sometimes accompanies this affliction. The Orthodox Set, though no less exalted in military rank and social standing, is very much nicer. I called on a brother and sister of Colonel Zeb and found both homes very congenial. Begum Ghawas invited me to stop with them on my return from Gilgit, an invitation which I accepted with pleasure.

The basis of wealth in Pakistan now is either inherited money or profits from one of the new industries – not, as formerly, officers' pay, which has been drastically cut. The two households which I visited today (of a Brigadier and a Major-General) were quite dilapidated and barely 'keeping up appearances': but there was such a pleasantly genuine feeling that the 'no drinking or smoking' and 'women in purdah' rules were more than compensated for by the sense that one was being treated as a *person* rather than as a circus-act, which is the feeling some of the 'Smart Set' give me.

Today the National Assembly opened a new session and Aurang Zeb came down to represent Swat. He called for me at 9 a.m. and swept me off to the Distinguished (!) Visitors' Gallery, where I met myriads of genuine Big Shots, who obviously thought someone had made a hideous mistake by admitting such a battered-looking object to their corner of the House.

The intricacies of the political system here are slightly beyond me. President Ayub appoints ministers who are not members of the Assembly, but who appear before the House to answer criticisms and defend themselves. There is complete freedom of speech within the House; members can, and do, stand up and denounce everyone from the President down, and on the whole this régime is probably the best for Pakistan at the moment even if some rich citizens dislike it. Certainly it is *not* a totalitarian régime, as Pakistan's enemies would have us believe.

All the proceedings of the Assembly are in English, which is the only practical national language when the two wings of Pakistan speak so many different tongues. One motion concerned the movement for a separate nation which is now starting up in East Pakistan; apparently the feeling among many there is – 'We've got rid of the British, now let's get rid of the West Pakistanis.'

Ethnically of course the vast majority of East Pakistanis are Bengalis and the only tie between East and West Pakistan is religious. Also the poverty in the Eastern wing is much greater than in the Western, with 950 people to the square mile as against 150 here. In 1960 a census of agriculture was taken, and the report on East Pakistan has just come out. I give a few details below.

Average Farm 3·5 acres of which 3·1 acres are cultivated. The main crop is rice of different kinds

Owner Farms	61%
Owner-cum-Tenant	37%
Tenant Farms	2%
Fragmented Farms	90%
Manured Farms	45%
Farms with no work animals	35%
Milch Farms	38%
Farmers in debt	48%
Official loans	10%
Private loans	90%
Average Farm Family	6 people

The experiment of transplanting families from East to West Pakistan is being tried but naturally is not being very successful; you might as well expect Italians to be happy if semi-forcibly settled in Lapland. Bengali farmers just don't know *what* to make of the land around Karachi. Today there were heated arguments in the Assembly about this and when talking to a few experienced politicians I got the impression that it is possible to make a nation out of a country of which the two parts are separated without even overland communications.

RAWALPINDI, 26 MAY

This afternoon I went to visit the Presentation nuns here; there are thirty of them, all Irish. The Rev. Mother, who has been fifty years in India, had lots of interesting observations to make. She said that since Partition the only safe person in power from their Christian viewpoint was President Ayub, who is very liberal-minded. Of course all his daughters were at this school, and he knows where Pakistan would be without the Christian educationalists; also the best hospital in Pakistan is run by French nuns.

The temperature yesterday and today has remained around 110° and the strong breeze feels like a blast from the ovens of hell, even during the night.

Yesterday evening, while having dinner in the garden, we saw (at 8.40) the latest Russian satellite travelling at tremendous speed across the sky, looking just like a moving star.

I have decided that my old theory about extreme cold being better for cycling than extreme heat is now kiboshed. After all, minus 25° positively *stops* cycling whereas one can struggle on through 112° and live to tell the tale. But, In'she Allah, by this time tomorrow I'll be cooling off in Gilgit or lying in small pieces on a Himalayan peak and either alternative seems preferable to sitting in Pindi at this temperature. There was a frantic flap today about whether I could cycle back from Gilgit or not: no one knows the exact state of the pass because now all supplies and personnel go by air, but general opinion was that it wouldn't be open this year till mid-July, because of late snow.

The Muslims have a saying that 'a man's name is the sweetest sound in the language', and as a result they consider it good manners to use your name every time they speak to you – which is disastrous for me as I find their names so difficult to remember. Of course they find Dervla equally impossible, so all the way through since Turkey I've been known as D. Except in the most Westernised circles they don't use surnames – which explains why brothers have different names. What really intrigues me is the mixture of Urdu, English and Pushto spoken by all these Western-educated people; they habitually use the three languages, often in the same sentence, while speaking among themselves. A very curious phenomenon!

RAWALPINDI, 27 MAY

More chaos this morning. First my plane couldn't go as the cloud was too dense in the Himalayas; some of the peaks en route are 20–26,000 feet high, and as Dakotas can't fly *over* these they only take off when visibility is perfect for flying *between* them. Then my hostess, who really is being endlessly kind and helpful, started an elaborate series of phone calls in sixteen different directions and finally announced that the majority opinion of experts was that I *could* cycle back by the end of June. So the latest plan is that I fly up on 2 June and meanwhile go to Murree and what is known as 'Free Kashmir', starting tomorrow.

I went this morning for the inevitable interview with Radio Pakistan. It was very frustrating as I couldn't say I loved Afghanistan, took a very dim view of Persia, approved of Bulgaria and etc. Having to be non-committal irritates me more than anything else in the world.

It's quite cool today – only 96° in the shade. I've been told that my biggest risk cycling in this weather is pneumonia – of all unlikely things; but it's good to be warned.

MURREE, 28 MAY

Last night soon after I went out to dinner one of the dust storms, for which Pindi is famous, blew up so that within five minutes everything and everyone in the room was coated in dust; you could see it on the food and feel it in your mouth and smell it horribly. Then all the lights went out and, what was far more disastrous, the fans stopped and we all sat in lamplight, streaming sweat and grinding dust with our pilau.

You'd think that the people here would take this heat in their stride but the papers go to town on it with banner headlines – 'Eighty per cent of Lahore's cab-horses fainted . . . ', 'Pindi streets deserted as all flee from sun . . . ' and so on. Evidently being born to it doesn't make people immune. In summer factory-production goes down and the general efficiency level drops in the Civil Service, business, etc. Coming from sun-starved Ireland it takes time to adjust to the custom of avoiding the sun: it seems so *odd* to sit at lunch with curtains drawn and lights on.

We left Pindi at 7.30 a.m. today after what is here a 'late night' (bed at 11.15 p.m.) and covered forty-four miles, the last sixteen of which had to be walked as the road rose from 1,300 to 7,040 feet and the average gradient was one in fourteen. It fascinated me to watch the plain falling farther and farther away as we ascended and to notice the flora becoming more and more familiar until we were surrounded by daisies, dandelions, heavy blossomed chestnuts, stately pines, lavishly flowering white and pink dog-roses and many very lovely shrubs, my favourite being one with dark green leaves and flame-coloured flowers. Despite going up and up the heat remained intense. So, at 1 p.m., I abandoned

Roz in a tea-shop and retired to the depths of a silent pine wood where I slept for an hour before exploring the cool dimness of the forest. (Murree is Pakistan's only hill-station and the road was pretty busy all day as rich families in sleek cars sped up from the plains to their mountain residences. During summer the population of Murree rises from 15,000 to 50,000 so it's not exactly my sort of place . . .) At 5 p.m. I continued the sweaty crawl upwards, stopping at every tea-house to absorb sugar and salt and mango-juice, this being reputedly the best remedy of all for heat-exhaustion, from which I suspect I'm now permanently suffering; but the mangos must be *un*ripe and baked and the juice then squeezed out, so I carried a supply from Pindi.

The hour from 6.30 to 7.30 p.m. was unforgettable, with sunset colours tinting the snowy ridges of the Himalayan foothills, and long shadows stretching across the valley's steep slopes, which were terraced and irrigated in orderly patterns and dotted by tiny mud houses. Then the cool radiance of moonlight succeeded the brief dusk as I dragged myself up the last and steepest two miles to the PWD rest-house where I'm now half asleep as I write. There's a small snake in the corner of this room but he also seems to be half asleep and, as I'm too exhausted to face the fuss and flap-doodle if I report his presence to the authorities, I'll chance his company for the night: probably he's harmless anyway.

MUZAFFARABAD, 29 MAY

Now that I've forgiven Pakistan for not being Afghanistan I'm enjoying it like mad and have had a most blissful day today. I left Murree at 7.30, having called on the Irish Presentation nuns at the somewhat startling hour of 6.45 a.m. and got a terrific reception. They're always so pathetically pleased to see someone fresh from Ireland that it's worth the effort of answering all the usual questions for the umpteenth time. On the way out of Murree a carload of tourists stopped to ask was I the Irish woman? When I said 'yes' they asked if I was going to Madras, and I said 'perhaps', whereupon they gave me their address and told me I must stop with them. Then they drove on – just like that! I should be used to it by now, but I'm being repeatedly touched and astonished by the hospitality and kindness of *everyone* in this part of the world.

The first thirty miles today were all one continual sweep downhill – even finer scenery than yesterday and no traffic as this is the Prohibited Zone of Azad Kashmir. I saw my first monkeys and spent one and three-quarter hours stalking them through a dense forest with my camera – which is funny when you come to think of it. One wonders how I expected to photograph two monkeys, considering that I can't even get a moderately good picture of a mountain that stands still and waits to be photographed. Needless to say they effortlessly eluded me, but only when they had with deliberate malice led me almost to the top of a mountain so steep that I was terrified to look down and realised that I had to go back. For minutes I stayed hanging on to a shrub, gazing miserably down seeking inspiration as to how best to begin the descent, while those two sat hugging themselves with joy and positively giggling at my predicament. Then I suddenly remembered that Roz had been left unguarded by the roadside and this gave me such a fright that I just let go of the shrub and began the descent by falling six feet into a bramble bush – which doubtless rounded off the monkeys' joy – acquiring innumerable horrid scratches in the process. After that I carried the camera in my mouth and went down like a monkey myself, swinging from branch to branch of the pines and big shrubs.

I can't understand the birds here; they sing – very melodiously too – right through the midday heat, a thing no well brought up Irish bird would ever dream of doing. And such glorious colours. Some are only the size of our butterflies, and some of the equally beautiful butterflies are the size of our robins. There's masses of lovely heather too – white and an extraordinary red-gold colour, but no purple.

After thirty miles we were down to 2,000 feet and level with the river, now flooded by melting snows and tearing furiously along between high mountains. For the next thirty-five miles this road, more or less level, followed the river: a memorable cycle-ride though it was so hot that I could only cover about eight m.p.h. with countless stops to sit nude under waterfalls. I saw lots of logs going down from high up-river, being swept along at tremendous speed. There were no bridges after the one I crossed at the foot of the mountains; the locals use pulley ropes, suspended above the foaming, forty-foot deep, fifty-yard wide waters which they cross as nonchalantly as circus artistes, using only their hands. I notice the people in this region build their cottages of stones, just like the Aran Islanders, and roof them with a flat thatch of straw covered over by mud.

Here I'm still being entertained by the Army in a wonderfully primitive camp by the river-bank. This is being written sitting on a charpoy overlooking the noisy rush of water, glinting in the moonlight. Yet it's too hot even now because this is a narrow valley enclosed by rock mountains which retain and throw back the day's heat during the night and though there's a strong breeze it's hot too.

I stopped in the little town of Muzaffarabad for half an hour and talked to the locals about the Kashmir problem. On my Bartholomew's map this region is in India, but they tell me here it's in Pakistan – I give it up! Anyway, they've their own separate 'Government of Azad (Free) Kashmir' which is financed by the Pakistan Government. The people are in general the most moronic I've met since Persia, but they're friendly once over the initial shock of witnessing such an unusual arrival. I met two government officials and a local 'doctor' (who is not qualified but has a second-hand stethoscope and can give injections – so people think he's wonderful) and they all said that the only way to get Kashmir is to fight for it, an opinion shared by most Pakistanis of all types.

From the town to this camp is a two-mile walk on a dirt-track by the river, past one of Akbar's colossal forts – a splendid sight in the moonlight, overlooking a wide curve of the river and overlooked in turn by jagged mountains. It's very peaceful here with a little village near by where peasants are still sifting the grain by moonlight on their beaten mud threshing-floor. I'm going to sleep now under the stars.

ABBOTTABAD, 30 MAY

Another wonderful day. I slept from 9.30 p.m. to 4.30 and was wakened by pale light spreading over the mountains and slowly filling the valley. We were on the road by 5.15 a.m. and at the top of a tremendous pass, after a six-mile walk up, by 7 a.m. As usual, no film was left for the glorious sight of a river forming a semicircle round the base of a granite mountain thousands of feet directly below me. The mountain we were on was so sheer that I was able to drop a big stone into the water from that distance. Then came a ten-mile free-wheel down, overlooking another very different but equally lovely river valley. Next followed a very steep eight-mile climb through hushed, ancient pine woods, where massive Himalayan peaks, sharp and snow-covered, could be seen in the distance between the giant trees. After that we again free-wheeled down for five miles and the final twenty-five miles were through undulating country, with lots of trees and golden cornfields and reddish cliffs of clay and tiny mud villages. The heat is now extreme and is making me unusually irritable; if people are stupid on the road and nearly get knocked down by Roz I lose my temper and swear like a trooper at them – poor devils, it's probably just the heat softening their brains too!

Since leaving Swat I've seen very few cows, goats or sheep; it's mostly grain farming around here. One of the most appalling local sights is a cow in calf; they're so underfed that you can see plainly the whole shape of the calf in the womb. Only the poorest people use cows' milk; most prefer buffaloes' because buffaloes are immune to TB, whereas the cows are reeking with it, as are many of the human population. Buffalo milk is delicious – pure white and much richer than cows'.

The family with whom I'm staying tonight are delightful people. One daughter is a doctor now working in Lahore who previously ran the hospital here for two years single-handed, performing an average of twenty Caesarean operations per week without a single nurse or anaesthetist to help her. One of the results of malnutrition is that the mother's pelvic (and other) bones disintegrate during pregnancy, when the system's calcium is going to form the baby's bones, and as a result they can't give birth normally. Some time ago, having tried to push birth-control and failed, the Government in despair put a tax on every new-born baby, but that didn't work either and has now been dropped.

Yet eighty per cent of the girls still marry as soon as they reach puberty and produce ten or fifteen children, seventy per cent of whom are born diseased and, because epidemics are coming under control, the majority of these babies are fated to live on as semi-invalids.

WAH, 31 MAY

The temperature on the plains shot up to 112° today and your correspondent began to think that Yugoslavia in February '63 wasn't such a bad place after all! Pindi was my original destination for this evening, but I couldn't cover more than fifty-seven miles and even that felt like fifty-six too many. There can be no report on today's scenery because I was past observing it as I slogged along with my very lungs being blistered by the hot air. I only know that there were few trees and little greenery, a lack which always accentuates the heat. On every side stretched bare stubble fields and arid wastes of rock and stony soil – if you never hear from me again you'll know that I was thinking of you all as I lay expiring by the wayside! The very pleasant family I'm with tonight are friends of my Abbottabad host, as were the people I stopped with for the afternoon from 1 to 5.30. I reached here at 7.30 this evening in a state of collapse.

PINDI, 1 JUNE

When Roz and I left Wah at 8.30 a.m. there was such a strong headwind that we could only crawl at 5 m.p.h. despite the level road. The gale felt absolutely scorching, as if coming from an open furnace, and after about three hours I was suddenly overcome by headache, nausea and severe cramps in the leg muscles – the latter I believe due to salt deficiency, although I've eaten over three-quarters of a pound of solid salt in the last few days. Fortunately we were on the main Peshawar–Pindi road, where buses pass frequently, so I stopped one and was pulled on to it by a twinkling-eyed passenger who asked whether I was a mad dog or an Englishman? This immediately made me feel better, and I replied 'neither – an Irishwoman', and he said that that was obviously much the same thing. It was only five miles back to Pindi and after lying down in my air-conditioned room at the General's house, and absorbing eight pints of mango-juice and sour milk heavily salted, I had recovered by 2 p.m. – as much as anyone could recover in this infernal region.

This afternoon I had a date with one Father O'Leary at the Mission Hospital eight miles away. At 3 p.m. I put my head outside the door, felt as though my face was being burnt, retreated rapidly, rang the bell and ordered the air-conditioned Jaguar in a lordly way – poor Roz must have felt jilted!

I prefer to try to forget the sights I saw in hospital, particularly in the children's wards. Infants a month old weighing only a pound and a half, fitting on to the palm of my hand – *not* premature – and that was the least of it . . .

Father O'Leary told me that this is one of the few dioceses where Roman Catholics can get dispensations from the Bishop to marry Muslims. From the Islamic angle, if a Muslim girl marries a Christian *he* must become Muslim, but if a Muslim man marries a Christian girl, she can keep her own faith. (Christians and Jews are the only non-Muslims the sons of the Prophet may marry.)

Another fabulous dust-storm is performing now and all electricity has gone off again, so I'm writing by oil-lamp in a bath of sweat.

PINDI, 2 JUNE

I was up at 5.30 a.m. to see the sky overcast and feel the temperature down to a cool, delicious 85°. I then rang the airport to ask about flights to Gilgit but the weather is so cloudy in the Himalayas that none is going till Tuesday afternoon at the earliest: a disappointing development, yet in the relief of today's coolness nothing else seems to matter very much. Now it's 1 p.m. and the temperature is only 89° – I'm still dripping sweat but without that awful feeling of complete physical and mental exhaustion.

At breakfast we had an interesting discussion on the various Christian workers in Pakistan. I was understandably gratified to notice that everyone to whom I have spoken is very appreciative of the fact that no attempt at conversion is ever made by the Catholic teachers or medical workers. In the past thirty-five years, during which they have educated thousands of Muslim girls, the Presentation nuns haven't had *one* convert; I've spoken by now to over twenty of their past pupils and the nuns are universally loved and admired. On the other hand, all the Protestant Missions (educational and medical) stink in Muslim nostrils because their teaching and medical treatment is always accompanied by what the Muslims call 'insulting propaganda'. In their schools the children have to study the Bible and Christian doctrine and with their medicines they also dispense leaflets and pamphlets on the 'Good Path to God'. I know that this is true because I visited a Protestant Mission Hospital the other day and the matron showed me the 'literature' they distribute – awful sickly stuff that would put a Pope off Christianity for life. My host summed it up pretty well this morning when he said, 'The Protestants seem to come here because they hate Islam and the Catholics because they love God.' No doubt it's a matter of opinion which attitude is correct, but personally I'm entirely with the Catholics who have the good sense and good manners to admit in practice, if not in theory, that Islam is a different, but not necessarily inferior or wrong 'Path to God'. And, of course, the result is that in Pakistan a genuine good feeling exists between educated Muslims and Catholics, though here, as elsewhere, the semi-illiterate Mullahs hate any form of Christianity.

I suppose you've been reading and hearing about the cyclone disaster in East Pakistan. Many people I've met take the attitude that it's Allah's way of cutting down the population and there's no sense of a 'National Calamity' in the air, though the President has declared it to be such. What happens in East Pakistan is no more or less important to the average West Pakistani than what happens in Madras or Hyderabad. By now I've met very many Pakistanis who regard India as their home and who complain of not being able to go back to see their relatives there or of not being accepted by the *real* natives of this area, or of having lost all their property at the time of Partition, as well as most of their friends, who were either Hindu or Sikh. I asked several such people why they chose Pakistan when India is so much nearer and dearer to them and they said, 'for the sake of the children'. Apparently, although in ordinary Indian social life the various religions (at least among the cultured classes) meet and mingle without bigotry, *officially* the Muslim youth in the new India are discriminated against – or so they say here. I'll investigate that situation as best as I can when I get to India. What a tragic muddle it all is.

I spent the afternoon taking advantage of the coolness and the consequent return of my brain to (what I consider) normal to work on an article and after dinner went out to observe the scene in the streets. This is the end of the Shia's Muharram period, when they mourn the murder of one of the Prophet's followers by another and do penance most masochistically by lashing themselves with whips and sometimes cutting their own bodies with knives. It's supposed to be a dangerous time for women to go unprotected through the country, as the end-result of the penance is often an uncontrollable sexual frenzy, but of course there's no danger in a well-policed and (over-) civilised city like Pindi. I saw many coming from mosques carrying their whips and two men with blood actually seeping through their shirts. There are not many Shiahs in Pakistan and most of these are around Gilgit, where there's also one area populated by the Ismailis (followers of the Aga Khan). Tomorrow is a holiday in the Muslim world – their religious holidays are legion – and I've discovered that's why there's no flight to Gilgit. Anyway, the Himalayan forecast is bad; also the local forecast for tomorrow is bad – a rise in temperature! The weather here in summer is regarded as a National Emergency, with two-hourly broadcasts to tell the populace what the temperature is so that they can act accordingly and not die of heat-stroke. As far as discomfort goes there's very little difference between 100° and 110°, but from a health point of view 110° is lethal and one daren't take risks under such a sun; hence the broadcast warnings that now is the time to go in and stay in. Naturally enough, nothing much gets done at this season. There are five servants here but apart from providing meals they lie asleep on the marble floors all day and no one has the heart to point out that the whole house is coated with dust. I'm very impressed by the way Pakistani family servants are treated. In every household where I've stayed the relations between family and staff are a credit to all concerned. There's no insurance stamp nonsense and no need for it, because when a servant falls ill the family pays all expenses and some member visits them daily in hospital. When they are old and retired, and their places filled by their children and grandchildren, the servants continue to live in the household till they die and the younger members of the family love and respect them as though they were elderly relatives, and go to them with their various problems for advice and consolation. The average wage is £2 per month but they are clothed free and get the same food as the family. At first I found it very difficult to adjust myself to the business of ringing a bell when I wanted a drink or had forgotten to bring my cigarettes from another room, but now that I've got the feel of the set-up I don't mind. It outrages the staff's sense of propriety if Memsahib goes to fetch her own cigarettes, and I must admit that in this sort of weather Memsahib is damn glad to have someone else fetch them. (I've become addicted to chewing betel-nut and my teeth are being ruined – must really abandon the habit.)

One of the unsettling things about local customs is that servants never knock before entering a room. As I'm prone to nudity this weather, in what I regard as the privacy of my boudoir, the result is that all concerned are unnerved – me grabbing a bath towel at the sound of any footsteps and the bearers leaving my tea-tray outside the door in terror of what they might behold if they entered.

10

Scraping through the Himalayas

RAWALPINDI TO GULAPUR

GILGIT, 4 JUNE

Never, *never* again will I allow myself to be persuaded to leave Mother Earth, and bounce in a nightmarish way through the Himalayas. If I have to stay here in Gilgit until August, waiting for the pass to open, I am *not* going back in that unspeakable little plane over that monstrous route to Pindi. I had expected the flight to be fairly blood-curdling but it was beyond my worst imaginings.

I got to the airport at 1.30 p.m. and after the six-mile cycle run out from the city I needed to drink every drop in my six-pint water-bottle. Today was the hottest yet, with the sky an ugly colourless arc and the sun fiendishly scourging the city and its surrounding dust-suffocated plain.

There were only two other passengers waiting on the verandah – a couple of young men from Karachi named Mukhtar and Rifat, who thought the combination of a woman and a bicycle flying to Gilgit was the weirdest thing that had ever happened.

'But *why* are you going?' asked Mukhtar.

'To get away from all this,' I replied, watching the sweat trickle briskly down my arms and cascading off at the elbows on to my already saturated shorts.

They both considered this reply very witty indeed and chuckled with delight. Mukhtar said provokingly, 'You don't like our weather?'

I diverted a torrent of sweat from my eyes and answered savagely, 'I *hate* your weather,' adding, 'but it's the only thing in Pakistan I don't like, and no country can be perfect.'

Rifat then ordered a round of Coca-Colas and remarked, in a

friendly, reproving voice, 'You must know that Gilgit is a very interesting and historical place – it should be taken seriously.'

'Yes,' I agreed wearily, 'once upon a time I had lots of positively erudite reasons for wanting to visit Gilgit, but now I can only think of one moronic reason.'

Rifat sighed, 'I'm afraid you'll be disappointed,' he said, 'because Gilgit itself is quite hot.' (He was right, as I now know.)

At 2 p.m. a few figures moved lethargically across the tarmac, towards our plane, pushing a hand-cart loaded with supplies for Gilgit – plus Roz. By 2.20 p.m. I was inside the little Dakota which had been standing exposed to the sun for hours, and was so hot inside that I would have fainted if I hadn't been too afraid. Somehow it seemed even more likely that I'd be killed if I was not fully conscious when hurtling through the Himalayas in a contraption like this. As I tied my safety belt, one of the crew handed me a newspaper to distract me from my worries. On the front page I read 'Twenty-three killed in Indian Himalayan Air-crash'.

We took off punctually at 2.30 p.m., when the heat was rising up so frenziedly from the plain that we fell, rather than bumped, in and out of air-pockets, until I didn't know whether my tummy was in my head or my head in my tummy – but I thought I knew that the next time we fell, we'd fall all the way. Yet at that point I almost longed for the crash; at least my tummy would then remain *in situ*, or, if it didn't, the matter would be of no importance to me.

Soon the plain was left behind and we passed over the terrain I had cycled through on the Azad Kashmir detour. Then this region of brown, rounded foothills and deep green valleys was replaced by a landscape of naked rock peaks, giant glaciers and vast sweeps of loose shale. We were flying so low that it was, in a sense, the next best thing to trekking through this area, which even the hardiest tribes have never attempted to inhabit and which has been trodden by no more than a few of the bravest traders and mountaineers. Yet only in one sense was it the next best thing; when we passed the 26,000-foot Nanga Parbat, whose triple peak dominated the thousands of snow mountains which stretched to the horizon in every direction, I suddenly became acutely aware that this was the wrong approach to a noble range. One should *win* the privilege of looking down on such a scene, and because I had done nothing to earn a glimpse of these remote beauties I felt that I was cheating and that this nasty, noisy little impertinence, mechanically transporting me, was an insult to the mountains. You will probably accuse me of a tiresome outburst of romanticism – but I'm not sure you'll be right. The more I see of unmechanised places and people the more convinced I become that machines have done incalculable damage by unbalancing the relationship between Man and Nature. The mere fact that we think and talk as we do about Nature is symptomatic. For us to refer to Nature as a separate entity – something we admire or avoid or study or paint – shows how far we've removed ourselves from it. Marco Polo saw it as the background to human adventures and endeavours – a healthy reaction possible only when our lives are basically in harmony with it. (Granted that Roz is a machine and that to be logical I should have walked or ridden from Ireland, but at least one exerts oneself cycling and the speed is not too outrageous and one is constantly exposed to the elements.) I suppose all our scientific advances are a wonderful boost for the superior intellect of the human race but what those advances are doing to us seems to me quite literally tragic. After all, only a handful of people are concerned in the excitement and stimulation of discovering and developing, while millions lead feebler and more synthetic lives because of the achievements of that handful. When Sterne toured France and Italy he needed more guts and initiative than the contemporary traveller needs to tour the five continents; people now use less than half their potential forces because 'Progress' has deprived them of the incentive to live fully. All this has been brought to the surface of my mind by the general attitude to my conception of travelling, which I once took for granted as normal behaviour but which strikes most people as wild eccentricity, merely because it involves a certain amount of what is now regarded as hardship but was to all our ancestors a feature of everyday life – using physical energy to get from point A to point B. I don't know what the end result of all this 'progress' will be – something pretty dire, I should think. We remain *part of Nature*, however startling our scientific advances, and the more successfully we forget or ignore this fact, the less we can be proud of being men.

During the last fifteen minutes of the flight, however, I had no time for such quasi-philosophical speculations, for by then we had left behind the prosaic world of passenger transport and had entered the sphere of aerial acrobatics. Here the mountains are far too high for a Dakota to fly over them, so we were confined to a rock-strewn gorge which in my opinion is far too narrow for a Dakota to fly *through*. It is said that at this point even hardened air-travellers begin to think of alternative routes back to Pindi. The sensation of looking out to see rough rock-walls apparently within one and a quarter inches of the wing-tips is not a pleasant one. I am assured that there are twenty yards to spare on either side, but I stick to it that from the passenger's point of view this is, morally speaking, one and a quarter inches! When we came out over the valley we descended so abruptly that I got an excruciating pain in my right ear – it was so severe that I could think of nothing else and forgot to be afraid of the landing, which usually reduces me to a bundle of craven terror. Before I'd even registered the touchdown, Roz and I were being hurled out with the rest of the cargo and I found myself in the charge of a young lieutenant of the Gilgit Scouts who had been sent with a jeep to meet me. Ten minutes later I was being welcomed to the headquarters of the Scouts by Colonel Shah, who obviously thought he had a lunatic on his hands and immediately began to dissuade me from attempting to cross the Babusar Pass with Roz. But fortunately he is a perceptive man and he soon realised that every time he uttered 'impossible' my perverse determination hardened. So we changed the subject and discussed the Gilgit Agency from more impersonal angles.

My host told me that the first jeepable track from the Kagan Valley to Chilas was constructed about four years ago and is now frequently used during those three summer months when the Babusar Pass remains open. The arrival of the first jeep in Chilas was an historic occasion. Everyone turned out to see it and with characteristic thoughtfulness the peasants provided a large meal of freshly-cut grass for this strange new animal. They were then quite convinced that a jeep is the offspring of two of those curious creatures so often seen in the sky over the valleys and they assumed that it would be able to fly when mature. This, of course, is not an original story – all over the world primitive peoples react thus on first meeting machines. Nor, to my mind, is it a funny story, though it is so often told as a joke at the expense of 'ignorant peasants'.

Colonel Shah went on to inform me proudly that work is now in progress on an all-weather jeep road, which, within a few years, will greatly improve communications with the rest of Pakistan – always referred to as 'down-country' by the English-speaking residents of Gilgit. You can imagine how unenthusiastically I received this information. Granted something must be done to improve this area's economy – after even a few hours here I can see that for myself – but as usual I fear that the disimprovements will outweigh the improvements when the Twentieth Century comes bustling along the New Road. If only someone could think of a way to utilise Gilgit's natural resources – chiefly a superabundance of fruit – without destroying her individuality! After all, this region has only recently become impoverished and forgotten. Before international tensions made their terrible impact on the ordinary man's life Gilgit Town was an important trade centre on the Sinkiang–India route and was a thriving market for the sale and exchange of Central Asian, Chinese and Indian wares – a sad contrast to its present importance as a Military Centre.

It was very pleasant sitting on the smooth lawn of the officers' mess beneath plane trees so tall and graceful that it was impossible to associate them with their sooty London cousins. An orderly served us with frequent orange drinks to which everyone automatically added quantities of salt, because it *is* hot here, with an average June temperature of 94° in the shade – which I'd consider hellish if I hadn't come direct from Pindi. Behind us, almost overhanging the mess buildings, rose a 9,000-foot mountain wall of stark, grey rock which was repeated on the other side of the narrow valley; it's this confinement which keeps the temperature so high despite an altitude of nearly 5,000 feet. Down the valley snow-capped peaks of over 20,000 feet were sharply beautiful against the gentle evening sky and as the setting sun caught the valley walls they changed colour so that their pink and violet glow seemed to illuminate the whole scene.

While we were having dinner on the verandah a full moon rose and by the time the meal was over the valley looked so very lovely that I took myself off for a walk – to the unspoken disapproval of all those present! Having descended steeply for about half a mile my path turned west along the valley floor, leaving the shuttered stalls of the bazaar behind. Tall mulberry and apricot trees laid intricate shadows on the sandy path and the silence was broken only by the snow-enraged Gilgit River. The sky was a strange royal-blue with all but the brightest stars quenched, while on either side the mountains were transformed into silver barricades, as their quartz surfaces reflected the moonlight. I walked for over an hour and that walk alone made the horrors of the flight here seem well worth while.

My bed for tonight is a charpoy under a plane tree and I've written this by moonlight-cum-cycle-lamplight. Yesterday, as you may have noticed, there was no entry. I should have gone out to watch the Muharram procession at 10 a.m. but I simply hadn't the guts to leave my air-conditioned room – even within it I hadn't the energy to put pen to paper. However, atonement has now been made at the expense of my eyesight.

GILGIT, 5 JUNE

I set out at 6 a.m. to climb the mountain directly overlooking Gilgit Town from the south. The path went through a tiny farming hamlet which, if Gilgit were a city, might be described as its suburb, and filthy pot-bellied children collected in groups to stare at me. The Gilgitis are white-skinned (or would be if they washed themselves) though they are of different origins, none of which has been definitely established. Probably some have Pathan ancestors, as Afghan raiders periodically crossed the border in the past, and Afghan traders still bring their camel-caravans over the Babusar Pass during the summer months. A tradition which, as far as I am aware, has no supporting evidence, claims that the valleys were first populated by a detachment of Alexander's army which went astray in the course of his Indian campaign. Despite the lack of evidence there is, of course, nothing inherently ridiculous about this legend, and it is pleasingly romantic. Another theory refers to Arab ancestry – doubtless a lost detachment of the Arab army which invaded Afghanistan in the 9th century – but this theory is supported only by the fact that the Gilgitis carry all loads on their backs, not on their heads as in the neighbouring countries, and such tenuous support invites disagreement more than does the lack of any support for the Alexandrian theory.

I was told yesterday evening that many mutually incomprehensible languages are spoken throughout the Gilgit Agency, and most of them are unwritten. The majority of the people understand neither Pushto nor Urdu, and are of course illiterate, though every village of any size now has its school. However, throughout rural Pakistan the standard of intelligence of the average village schoolteacher is incredibly low and the children's help is needed by their farming parents – a combination of circumstances which makes it extremely difficult to cope with rural illiteracy. Many Western observers find this quite shocking, yet I must admit that it leaves me undisturbed; we have yet to prove that universal literacy as we know it advances the mass of the people in any worthwhile direction.

Walking slowly upwards through the hamlet and across the fertile strip of land at the base of the mountain I was again reminded of the Aran Islands. Here too the fields are 'made' and enclosed within high stone walls, grassy lane-ways run between the walls, little donkeys carry big loads, the sense of remoteness is strong and the tiny cottages are built of stone – though instead of thatch they have flat stone and mud roofs, laid on wooden beams. At one stage the similarity was so great that if I lowered my eyes from the mountains I could almost hear the music of the Atlantic on the shores of Inishere.

Less than two miles from Gilgit the cultivated land ends abruptly and the steepening slope is covered with large loose stones. Now all around me were jagged brown-grey rocks, and stretches of barren scree, and devastated dry water courses, revealing the savage velocity of melted snows. The only vegetation was a splendid shrub, about five feet high, which at intervals flared up spectacularly in the midst of a wide desolation of grey stones and was so laden with deep pink flowers that from a distance it looked like some mysterious bonfire burning untended.

It was quite a stiff climb to the top and at times I had to go very cautiously indeed. Once I was so 'trapped' that the only way up was through a waterfall, where the secure stones offered safer hand- and foot-holds than the loose scree on either side. It was a 'thin' waterfall, yet the power of even that comparatively low volume of water astonished me. (By this time the sun was so hot that my clothes were dry in half an hour.)

Just before this I found the corpse of a young man – dead eight or ten days I should think. His skull had been bashed in so I've officially 'forgotten' the discovery as I wish to remain on good terms with *all* the local factions while trekking here. My nose led me to the poor devil, who was pushed into a crevice between two big boulders. I notice that rifles are not carried in this part of the Agency but they evidently manage to liquidate each other without them. After investigating I was quite glad to immerse myself in the waterfall!

From the summit I had a magnificent view of a tumult of rough white peaks in every direction – including Nanga Parbat again, triumphantly conspicuous above the rest. On the way down I saw a couple of caveman types, with long, tangled hair and beards, carrying ice from the glaciers to Gilgit Town. By following them my return route was shorter – but much more hair-raising – and I got back at 5.20 p.m. utterly exhausted and ravenously hungry.

After a nameless but very satisfying meal I went for a stroll around the town. In some stalls of the bazaar goods from down-country – films, biscuits, toothpaste and the like – are on sale, but they all look excessively fly-blown and cost the earth because of air-freight charges. The townspeople strike me as a surly lot – not impolite or in any way unpleasant, but lacking the frank friendliness which so impressed me in Afghanistan and Pakistan proper. In fact, from the human society point of view it's rather like being back in Persia, except that these people are more uncouth than the Persians – and by uncouth I don't mean spitting on the street or squatting in public, but something deeper inside that governs a man's attitude to others. The actual town has nothing to distinguish it and but for its surroundings would be slightly depressing. Now (10 p.m.) I'm going to bed early in preparation for tomorrow's trek up the valley.

GULAPUR, 6 JUNE

My 'military advisers' had laughed at the idea of anyone cycling up the valley, but I couldn't bear the thought of abandoning Roz now so we left Gilgit at 4.45 a.m., soon after sunrise, to attempt the first stage of the trek together, and for a few miles it was possible to cycle – though at little more than walking pace, over a track covered with several inches of sand.

Already, taking advantage of the morning coolness, peasants were harvesting barley, reaping and binding by hand with leisurely movements. The women wear gay, ankle-length petticoats of imported cotton, but the men have homespun trousers and jackets, again recalling the Aran Islands. Gilgit's entire population is Muslim – different sects predominating in different regions – but the turban is here replaced by a soft cloth cap, turned up around the edges, which gives the men an oddly European appearance.

Today's landscape was a series of dramatic contrasts. The valley floor around Gilgit Town showed the fragrant abundance of early summer – fields of trembling, silver-green wheat and richly golden barley, bushes of unfamiliar, lovely blossoms and, most beautiful of all, a rock-plant with tiny, golden-pink flowers, growing so lavishly in the crevices of the walls that it was like a sunset cloud draped over the grey stones. Then the valley narrowed to exclude the early sun until there was room only for the river between the opposing precipices and we were alone in a barren, rough, shadowy world, where nothing moved but the brown flood-waters.

Next the track soared upwards, overhanging the river-bed, and it became so rocky underfoot that I was often carrying, rather than pushing, Roz. At one stage I couldn't get her up an impossibly steep gradient with kit 'on board', so I unloaded, carried Roz up, slithered down to retrieve the kit and, as I dragged myself up for the second time, admitted defeat. By now Roz has gallantly carried me through quite a variety of improbable terrains, but clearly she can *not* carry me through the Karakoram Mountains – nor can I carry her through them . . .

After some miles of this daredevil upward spiralling the track wriggled around a jutting thousand-foot cliff and I saw, far below, on the other side of the river, a fertile semicircle of land, hidden and tranquil at the base of a snow-capped mountain. A few of the hamlet's farmhouses were visible between willow, plane, sinjit and mulberry trees, growing tall and strong among neat little patches of corn and shimmering young meadows. Sunlight was brilliant on the dark green waters and white foam of a nullah leaping down the mountainside to join the mud-stained river, and through the still, clear air I could hear the faint shouts of men directing the donkeys which were walking round and round on mud threshing-floors.

After this the track descended to river level, before again climbing steeply, and it was almost as difficult to manoeuvre Roz down such a gradient as it had been to haul her up. My wrists ached from the strain of holding the brakes while I stumbled against rocks and slipped on the deep sand: I wished then that I'd had the good sense to heed my 'military advisers'.

Beyond the next pass the mountains receded slightly on our left and for a few miles I was able to cycle across the boulder-strewn moor, though a surface littered with sharp flints kept my speed down. Then, at 10 a.m., trees ahead showed that we were approaching the first hamlet on this side of the river, where the reaction to my appearance was rather disconcerting. Only a few old people and children were about, and the children, after one horrified look, either screamed loudly and buried their faces in their elders' laps, or bounded over the low walls and vanished. The adults, though more restrained, looked no less alarmed, and obviously didn't wish to improve the acquaintance, so I realised that apart from the physical difficulties of cycling here an approach on wheels is psychologically unsound.

Soon after midday I met the problem of finding shade – something uncommonly scarce at noon on a bare mountainside. It wouldn't have been too difficult to find a patch for myself but here again poor Roz complicated things as it was unthinkable that she should be left exposed to such a ferocious sun. So for her sake I had to walk further than was prudent, until an overhanging rock offered protection to us both.

Having slept soundly for two hours I woke to find it even hotter than before, though fortunately the track was now partly in shadow. Today's highest pass lay immediately ahead and to prepare for it I had a swim – one of the coldest of my life – at a spot where high, projecting rocks gave protection from the current and where there was a nice little 'strand' of soft silver sand between the water and the track.

From the top of this pass I could see the orchards and fields of another village about eight miles up the valley. The descent here was more gradual than most and we free-wheeled slowly down – if 'free-wheeled' is the *mot juste* for zig-zagging between boulders! Then, when the track ran level with the river, there was no space left for zig-zagging so Roz and I again exchanged rôles. Near the village a man came riding towards us – the first person we'd met since leaving Gilgit.

Colonel Shah had given me a map which shows that this village is twenty-one miles from Gilgit Town and as I reckon that I cycled no more than one-third of the way it's obvious that the time has come to be disloyal to Roz and temporarily acquire a more adaptable mount.

The food situation here is very grim – an acute scarcity of flour and no tea, sugar or salt left after the winter. Most people are living on goats' milk, eggs and mulberries – not my favourite diet when served simultaneously but this evening I was too starved to fuss. I wolfed five eggs and about two pounds of white mulberries – but stuck at the milk. This is odd as I've so often taken it in my stride before: yet I suppose five eggs do make an insecure foundation for goats' milk, which so undeniably tastes exactly as a billy-goat smells! Of course, in a few weeks' time, when the maize harvest has been saved and ground, there will be no shortage of flour and by then too the camel-caravans will have crossed the Babusar Pass with this year's supply of tea, sugar, salt and cotton.

I find that the people here are much easier to get on with than the folk of Gilgit Town – who make me wonder if they have not already lost something through their comparatively close contacts with down-country. This village has one tiny shop, in which a tubercular-looking young man sits on the floor chatting with a few friends and surrounded by almost empty shelves: after eight long months of commercial isolation only a half-bale of cotton and a few boot-laces and pocket-combs remain of the winter's stock. Yet to my surprise cigarettes are available, at 6*d.* for twenty, and I'm told that these are flown up regularly, though few other goods are imported by plane – air-freight charges would put them beyond the reach of most Gilgitis. But again I'm experiencing the dignified generosity of the very poor: when I produced money for forty cigarettes the young man looked quite hurt and firmly refused to accept it.

My arrival here caused no less of a sensation than in that other hamlet down the valley. However, this community is better prepared to meet an invasion by bicycle, as some of the older men have served in the Indian Army under the British and two have even been to Italy, so the peculiarities of European women are vaguely comprehended.

The village has a school as well as a shop and within minutes of my arrival the young teacher came hurrying to the rescue. He speaks Urdu, which is of no assistance whatever, and a very few words of English, which is of the greatest assistance. Supplementing these few words with scores of complicated signs, I explained my position and was assured that a suitable horse will be awaiting me at dawn tomorrow and that Roz will be respectfully cherished until I rejoin her.

I'm often astounded by the complicated explanations, discussions and arrangements which can be conducted through signs, even without a single mutually comprehensible word. Admittedly the usefulness of signs varies according to the intelligence of the local population; I found the superbly quick-witted Afghans the easiest of all in this respect. A language barrier does inevitably impede the collection of concrete information and the exchange of ideas, but it really is surprisingly flimsy when one wishes to arrange practical details and in unsophisticated societies it ceases to count where personal relationships are concerned. What can be an embarrassment when visiting Europeans, to whom elaborate signs may seem undignified, actually helps to overcome shyness and awe in primitive homes. When you ask for fried eggs by making noises like a hen after laying, followed by noises like something sizzling in fat, the whole household is convulsed with laughter and not only are fried eggs served, but you are unanimously elected as one of the family.

A local detail which absolutely astounds me is that the women knit heavy unbleached woollen sweaters for their menfolk *on an Aran pattern.* It's unmistakable – and they certainly didn't get it from women's magazines!

During the summer, in river-level villages, everyone here sleeps out of doors – either on the flat roofs of their little houses, or in their compounds, if they have them, or simply in village streets or in orchards; my bed for tonight is a charpoy under an apricot tree in the teacher's compound.

11

From One Saddle to Another

GULAPUR TO SHER QUILA RAKAPOSHI

GAKUCH, 7 JUNE

When we started our trek today at 5.30 a.m. the sun was up, but not yet over the mountains, and the valley looked very beautiful in the cool light, with the air soft and fresh, like spring grass. I was so happy that I burst into what it pleases me to call 'song', but the result obviously unnerved my mount and I had to desist abruptly. Apart from this lack of appreciation, she's a splendid pony – a sturdy, agile eight-year-old of about fourteen hands, with a curious pale golden coat, not uncommon in this region. I've rechristened her 'Rob' for the duration of our trek because her real name is so tongue-eluding, not to say unspellable. At first I found her nonchalant treatment of precipices quite terrifying; then I realised that if she avoided the edge of today's track she'd very successfully concuss me against overhanging chunks of cliff and by midday I'd become quite reconciled to the way she tripped along the very verge of the track, frequently dislodging stones which took a long, long time to reach the river. And by evening I'd become so trustful that I positively enjoyed looking down to see nothing whatever between me and the torrent, 1,500 feet below. Following the example of local horsemen I walked up the steepest gradients and rode down, so I'd the worst of both worlds, since it's far more tiring to ride down than up such sharp inclines. On some of the level stretches I had to dismount again, where the track was too narrow to take a rider, or was strewn with massive boulders which it seemed wisest for us to negotiate separately.

Over the first two or three miles beyond Gakuch the valley floor was very fertile. Then the track began to go up and up, winding round and round mountain after mountain, and the many other fertile patches which appeared below were all on the opposite side of the river. I often stopped to look down on those little hamlets – one could never tire of their beauty. In this part of the valley the river seethes along, a mass of white foam, with thin waterfalls from glaciers twinkling down cliffs to meet it, and today fields of unripe barley and wheat were being played on by a strong west wind until they too looked like rivers flowing east. A lovely shrub, with feathery, pale green branches which shade off to pink about twelve inches from the end, grows abundantly amidst the stones and sand by the riverside; usually it's a few feet high but some of the bushes were almost trees.

We met one other traveller today – a frail and half-starved-looking young man who was carrying a colossal wooden crate on his back and could barely stagger along the rough track under its weight. I gave him my lunch of four hard-boiled eggs and he ate them so fast I was quite alarmed, fearing he'd die of indigestion and that I'd have done more harm than good. Now I basely and bitterly regret my generosity, as I myself am almost dying of starvation and this village can't even produce an egg. At the moment I'm waiting while clover is being cut in a nearby field to be stewed for my supper. It's the very same as clover at home and I suppose (and hope) it's nourishing; they eat it often in Afghanistan, too, and when it was served there with grilled mutton I mistook it for spinach. I'll know now what to do next summer with the clover on my lawn!

We covered thirty-four miles today, arriving here at 6.45 p.m., and I had one delicious swim where the track dived right down to river level. Watering Rob is the big problem (I carry fodder for her behind the saddle) but we were lucky enough today with springs en route.

The filth in these villages is beyond all, the poverty is the most extreme, I've met since leaving home and the skin-diseases are too dreadful to be described. Everyone stinks to high heaven – even in the open air it's overpowering and inside the little stone huts it's almost lethal. Now two grinning boys of about twelve have just appeared beside me, carrying a hideous-looking cloth full of mulberries. The method is to lay a cloth under a tree, climb into the lower branches and shake the fruit down. I'm too hungry to resist their juicy sweetness so, in spite of the cloth, will devour them. They are, of course, the chief source of sugar for the Gilgitis – and I badly need sugar this evening after those thirty-four miles.

NAME OF VILLAGE UNKNOWN, 8 JUNE

We arrived here at 7.45 p.m. – half an hour ago – and so far there's no sign of any food appearing. I've had nothing to eat since a tiny bowl of stewed clover at 5.30 a.m.; this would be passable with salt, but without it it merely tastes like a slimy mess and anyway is *not* sustaining. Rob did much better than I today – we came to several grassy patches where she grazed contentedly while I wished that I was a horse too! The situation is maddening because in Pindi I asked those who are supposed to be authorities on this area if I should bring stores and they said that if I was prepared to eat local foods this would not be necessary: which just shows how little central authorities know about outlying areas. Though I must admit that this village is *very* outlying – if the path and my permit hadn't petered out here we'd soon be in China!

I was also told that there are no snakes in Gilgit and consequently I have been happily sleeping on the ground all over the place – yet this afternoon I met two thin, black-and-yellow eighteen inchers within an hour; they hissed at us from beside the track and Rob got very jittery. I killed them both with heavy stones, having a vague feeling that it's one's duty as a citizen to do so; then afterwards I got scruples about taking life without provocation and regretted my savagery. But now the scribe of this village, who most improbably speaks English (As She Should Not Be Spoken), has soothed my conscience by telling me that these snakes are a menace to the kids grazing on the mountainsides. He added that the adult goats never get bitten, which seems unlikely – if goats had a built-in anti-snake device it would surely operate as efficiently for kids as for adults. Possibly the answer is that this poison is not strong enough seriously to worry the adults. Incidentally, the same kids are besieging me at the moment, having discovered that I'm good at scratching between their incipient horns – evidently horn-growing is their version of teething troubles. They're the most charming little creatures imaginable and come in all colours from jet-black to snow-white, through nigger-brown, russet and beige with many wildly mixed piebalds. When stroked or scratched they wag their little tails frantically. A few moments ago I discovered that one of them has just consumed the entire five pages of Daphne's last, and as yet unanswered, letter but I suppose he'll survive. If some food doesn't soon appear I'll be following his example and consuming Patsy's six pages! Yet it's odd how much easier it is to bear extreme hunger than extreme thirst, which almost drives one mad. By this stage my stomach must be lined with mud, I've drunk so much of the flooded river – but though it looks like mutton broth it tastes delicious. As I wrote the last sentence the tiniest kid was getting himself on to my lap where he is now curled up happily sucking my left thumb!

We covered about thirty-five miles today through the wildest landscape I've ever seen. This Gilgit region really does something quite extraordinary to one's mind. The completely unbroken solitude and the absence of anything recalling the rest of humanity produce a unique feeling of liberation as one moves slowly through these tremendous gorges. Today the outside world and my own life – past and future – as part of that world seemed so utterly unreal that for a time I ceased to be aware of it and existed only in the present, acutely conscious of my surroundings and of physical sensation, but removed, in a dreamlike way, from myself as a person. It was a strangely relaxing experience – though in retrospect slightly eerie.

About five miles from here I got quite a scare when we came round a sharp angle of the mountainside to see, right in front of us, what looked like an impassable torrent raging down across the 'road' between huge boulders. I was about to dismount and contemplate the crisis when I realised that Rob was all set to cope. She turned left, went downstream about fifteen yards and then plunged in. The water was some twenty-five yards wide and at one stage she was actually swimming. (I'm soaked to the waist now and have nothing to change into.) Then she came out on the other side and climbed up through boulders and loose stones that I would have considered dicey even for a goat. After that she halted for a moment of her own accord and looked round as though to say 'Who's a smart horse?' so I lavished the appropriate praises and pats on her and off she jogged again. The joke is that if I'd had time to *think* about it I wouldn't have dared cross, yet we'd no alternative as it's out of the question to remain in the open after dark here because of snow-leopards and bears. (Apparently the bears are much the more dangerous of the two.) I've had my share of these nullahs ever since leaving Gilgit Town but this was by far the deepest. They begin to flow about twelve midday, when the sun has been beating for hours on the glaciers, are in full spate by 6 p.m., down to a trickle by midnight and dried up by 4 a.m. After the next few weeks they'll be finally dried up for the season, when all but the permanent glaciers have melted. It was very hot today – I should think at least 80°.

There has just been a pause to eat maize gruel out of an iron dish and drink tea with salt in it. They get salt and tea here from China (unofficially) and when one comes to think of it, it's a matter of taste and custom whether one adds sugar or salt or neither to tea. Having by choice acquired the salt habit in Pindi and district I was undismayed by this evening's brew – but I do feel guilty at eating their gruel and I can't pay them as they simply won't accept money.

Despite their filth, the people in all these little villages are truly delightful and are contributing as much as Rob and the scenery to the success of this trek. They have a simple, but easily aroused, sense of humour and I've discovered that imitating animal noises is the surest way to send a whole village into convulsions of laughter. Another way is solemnly to put my solar topee on the oldest and most respected member of the community – at this point they almost roll on the ground with mirth. They wear very distinctive and highly coloured costumes in this village and the women have quite lovely bead and silver necklaces and bracelets. As they are all Ismaili Muslims the women go unveiled. There are few traces of Mongolian blood and the majority are very fair like northern rather than southern Europeans. Their biggest worry is the colour of my face and arms: they cannot understand why I don't pull down my shirt-sleeves and shade my face from the sun!

I had expected a painful reaction to follow my sudden transference from Roz to Rob but there's a most convenient custom throughout Pakistan which has helped my muscles enormously. Since crossing the Khyber Pass I've found myself being thoroughly massaged from head to foot almost every evening, either by one of the servants of the families with whom I've stayed or, in villages, by kindly women who appear out of nowhere, knead me efficiently and disappear. I haven't yet established whether this is common form for all travellers, or is reserved for those who are self-propelled, but whatever the basis of the custom it's making my life here much less sore than it would otherwise be.

This village is at an altitude of over 10,000 feet and after dark the temperature drops sharply, so tonight I'm sleeping indoors – i.e. sharing a stinking mound of blankets with six no less stinking children. But the use of that adjective is not to be interpreted as a mark of ingratitude – I appreciate these people's hospitality even more than I do that of my wealthy hosts down-country.

GUPIS, 9 JUNE

If anyone ever asks you to drive three donkeys and a foal for twenty-four miles through the Karakoram Mountains, be *very* firm and refuse to do so – it really *is* more than flesh and blood was ever meant to endure. The position, as explained to me this morning, was that the four were being exchanged for a pony mare and foal from Gupis, but the latter was too young to travel for another fortnight whereas the donkeys were urgently required in Gupis, and a donkey foal, although looking so much frailer, is presumed tougher – therefore, would I please take the donkeys with me and save a villager the journey to Gupis? Green as I am I foresaw some of the complications and said, 'Couldn't a villager come with me, riding half the way on Rob, and when the pony foal was able to make it, couldn't a Gupis villager bring them up?' But no – it was in the bargain that the donkey village was responsible for herding both lots. So off I went at 5.45 a.m., armed with a long switch which would, in theory, enable me to steer my charges without difficulty.

Well, maybe a local on horseback could do it, but those donkeys knew they were on to a soft thing. Everyone remained happy while there was, on one side, a sheer drop of hundreds of feet into the river and, on the other side, an equally sheer wall of rock – then the brutes had no alternative but to go in a straight line. The fun started when the mountains receded in places, or the track dropped to river level and there came level stretches between river and track. Then the quartet merrily gambolled off at about ten times the rate they'd go on the road, in divers directions, through deep, yielding sand and thorny bushes, and between boulders and over streams and behind trees and around cliffs. (It's all right for you to sit back and laugh, but if *you* were galloping under a blazing sun trying to reassemble *in one place* a herd of apparently demented donkeys, you mightn't think it so amusing.) Rob was again wonderful – this is obviously a frequently recurring crisis in her life. She went after them like a sheep-dog and on the track kept reinforcing my rather half-hearted use of the switch by pushing the last donkey's rump with her nose; twenty-four miles at the pace of ambling donkeys is decidedly wearing. I passed a lovely pool, but did not dare to swim because the caravan would have been halfway to Peking by the time I came out. After twelve miles I saw that the foal couldn't possibly be driven any further without positive cruelty: from his point of view the whole idea was cruel anyway. (He was the smallest foal I've ever seen, with a mother hardly bigger than an Irish donkey foal.) So then I did what they do in Afghanistan with tiny foals and calves – tied his forefeet and hind-feet and put him across Rob in front of the saddle. I had to climb on to a rock to get him in place – he seemed amazingly heavy despite his dwarfishness – and he took a very dim view of the performance, as did his mother. (Rob was the only one to accept the situation philosophically.) By the time this was accomplished the two donkeys not involved had vanished and as I didn't feel like going into the unknown with the foal *in situ* I pursued them on foot, leaving Rob tied to a bush, the foal tied to Rob and the mother psychologically tied to the foal. A twenty-minute chase followed over burning sand and loose rocks (my biggest fear was that one of the wretches would break a leg) and then we were off again. We arrived here at 7.45 p.m., having had several pauses to dismantle the foal for feeding.

This village is a veritable metropolis – its one shop sells cloth and matches and three men from Lahore are posted here on a six months' meteorological survey – they almost wept for joy to see someone else from down-country. The area also produces *potatoes* so I'd a luxury dinner with the boys this evening – spuds and stewed clover and ghee. It would have been even more luxurious without the ghee. They make butter here by putting milk in an ill-cured sheepskin and sitting for hours rocking it to and fro on their knees. The whole family takes a turn and eventually you have butter. Then the stuff is put in another, equally ill-cured, skin and buried in the snow for two years. When resurrected the thing is allegedly a delicacy. If you want to be frightfully polite you can describe it as 'mature' – and if you survive it you'll survive anything. Sugar may be obtained by air from Pindi at 6*s.* a pound if anyone wants it. Nobody does. The people reckon to get enough from mulberries – surely the sweetest of all fruits – which are dried for winter use. Some time ago an American 'expert' came to demonstrate a better method of drying fruit, but the locals found it too expensive and have reverted to their traditional way. Incidentally, that American has become a legend in the valleys – they still giggle at the memory of him refusing to drink the spring water from the mountains without first boiling and then chlorinating it, and the kernel of the joke is that he got such violent dysentery in the end that a helicopter had to come from Gilgit to remove him.

I've come down a lot in the world today – to 7,800 feet. The Met. boys told me that the temperature in Gupis this last week has been between 80° and 88°. They have a 'Post Office' here also and once a week a runner goes to and from Gilgit (literally running in bare feet), armed with a six-foot spear against bears, wolves and leopards.

GAKUCH, 10 JUNE

The food situation has improved here since I left a few days ago – apricots are ripe now and everyone can have their fill, gratis, including cattle. These seem a rather exotic fodder for animals but transport costs are too high for fruit to be sold down-country and the people here can't eat it all. The enormous trees – like giant oaks – are laden with their crop; and in another few days plums and peaches will be just as plentiful. I notice that, though in general the people are pathetically unhealthy, most have exceptionally good teeth – possibly so much fruit?

We took it easy today, covering only twenty-two miles, during which I had three glorious swims. The barley is ripening fast now and the little fields with their grey stone walls look like patches of pure gold as one gazes down from high up on the opposite mountain. The colouring on every side here is so vivid and clear and the contrasts are so wonderfully effective in their simplicity that I just soak it all up like a sponge and hope the memory will sustain me when I get back to the hell down-country – if I ever do! The Met. boys thought the Babusar Pass would be negotiable by now on foot, though they said it definitely won't open to jeep traffic this year till mid-July. Apart from being squashed by sliding glaciers (and that would be sheer bad luck and is far less likely than being squashed by a bus in Pindi) they said the nullahs will be the chief menace. There's a PWD Rest House eight miles from the top, so I'll be sure of a night's sleep before crossing. Of course it's possible I'll have to give up at some point and return to Gilgit. (Don't worry – I won't take any foolish risks. I've often wondered what a *wise* risk is and now I know – obviously the sort I take!) I have decided to hitch-hike with Roz from Pindi to Lahore (172 miles), as we will be returning on this road in October, when the weather is more reasonable for cycling; there's no future in sweating along it for three days during the hottest fortnight of the year.

SHER QUILA RAKAPOSHI, 11 JUNE

I forgot to tell you about the pseudo-soccer match I saw in Gupis. Having delivered our herd to their destination Rob was dragging herself (and me) along the road to the Met. office when suddenly I came on the most unexpected sight – a playing field complete with twenty-two youths and a soccer ball. I know very little about soccer, but enough to realise that this is how it is *not* played. No one ever moved above trotting speed, no one ever tried to tackle anyone else, the referee never used his whistle, the ball was never headed and the two goalies sat cross-legged between the posts most of the time, looking abstracted. The real excitement from a spectator's point of view was caused by the fact that one side of the field had a sheer drop of 200 feet, so that the main object of all the players was to keep the ball from going into the ravine rather than to kick it between the posts. Of course it frequently *did* go over the edge and then followed a ten-minute interval, while the 'linesmen' stationed down there retrieved it, and during this pause everyone lay about in attitudes of utter exhaustion, as though they'd been playing their hearts out. What fascinated me was the way they avoided the ball if someone occasionally (to his own evident astonishment) kicked it hard – both teams showed more speed and agility in getting away from this dangerous missile than they did in pursuing it. The final score, curiously enough, was 0–0.

That evening, too, I had my first bottle of Punial Water, the local wine which sells at 1½*d* per quart. It's nice, yet can't be described by likening it to any other wine, as its taste is unique; but it definitely is wine and quite potent on an empty stomach. Grapes are as plentiful here as other fruits but are not cultivated in vineyards. Instead, the vines have grown to full size and are like giant fossilised serpents, often coiling from a walnut to a mulberry to a plum tree and so overwhelming the 'host trees' that it's difficult to determine their species. The wine is amber and rather cloudy and tastes faintly of that ill-cured sheepskin which plays a part in the production of most food and drink here.

We left Gakuch at 5.15 a.m., laden with apricots to 'keep me going'. I don't think that if I live to be a hundred I'll ever forget those glorious early morning starts, seeing the first shaft of sunlight come over the sharp, snowy peaks to stream down the valley, and listening to the sweet, excited bird-song and to the rush of the brooks and the whinnying of local horses greeting Rob.

We're now down again to 6,100 feet and it was damned hot by 11.30

a.m. I stopped at a tiny hamlet for four hours and met a most interesting man who spoke fluent English and gave me a lot of information about the locality. He got a government scholarship as a youth and is now trying to improve local farming methods. Aged 36, he's one of the twenty-eight children of his father's four wives. But he says that because he could not afford to feed children as he has now learnt they should be fed he refuses to marry. I thought him a very impressive character, absolutely dedicated to the task of helping his people. We sat outside his family's stone hut, in the shade of walnut and mulberry trees, beside a 'white-foam-and-green-water' torrent hurtling down from the mountain, with weeping willow and golden barley on the other side of the nullah; the glaciers on the mountains across the narrow valley look very beautiful against the deep, deep blue sky. He and I were given roughly-made wooden chairs and about twenty-two other people sat around on the ground, fascinated and uncomprehending, as we talked in English while drinking bowl after bowl of buttermilk. Some of the girls were very lovely in a Germanic sort of way, but most were so dirty and undernourished that one could only pity them.

It's just occurred to me that the inoculation I'd have needed most in this locality is the one I *didn't* have – against TB. The coughing and spitting – often of blood – are appalling and about twenty per cent of the people in these villages are clearly dying on their feet. The only consolation – a poor one – is that a case of young parents dying and leaving half a dozen children isn't the tragedy it would be in most 'civilised' communities, as the children will be as well cared for as possible by other relatives. The only essential for children *not* in short supply here is affection, and the result is an extraordinarily happy atmosphere in every family I've stayed with, despite the starvation and squalor. Each child is doted on by everyone from its tiny brothers and sisters up to its creaking great-grandparents.

I made an effort to get this family sorted out, but on discovering that the man on my left had sired three of the infants present – all aged between four and ten months – I gave up the attempt. One of his wives, aged eighteen and mother of four, looked at least forty, and the eldest wife, who was forty, had just had her sixteenth (seven dead) and looked seventy – but was very gay and cheerful. In this region wives are quite frankly bought; until recently they were exchanged for livestock, now they fetch £5 to £50 depending on their looks. If a man wants an exceptionally beautiful girl for £50, he'll pay £10 down and the rest on the instalment system. Beauty means big eyes, small mouth, curly hair, long neck, straight nose, white skin, good teeth and plenty of curves. If the beauty proves barren she will probably be divorced if she is a first wife, but another man who has already sons by his wife or wives, will buy her for her beauty alone; among Ismailis there is far less emphasis on virginity than among Sunnis or Shias. But adultery by the wife remains the crime of crimes; it is legal for the betrayed husband to kill both his wife and her lover on the spot if he catches them together. However, if the lover flees and the husband kills them apart it is murder, and he goes to gaol in Gilgit Town for eight years. I asked if murder for other motives was common but apparently it's almost unknown, so probably the corpse I found was that of a lover who got away and was killed afterwards. Theft of any kind is equally rare (possibly because no one has anything worth stealing!) and my friend couldn't tell me what the penalty is as he's never heard of a case. Girl-babies are considered bad luck and everyone concerned weeps with disappointment at their birth – which seems very odd in a society where their sale will later on bring money into the family. Boy-babies are saluted with gunfire and twenty-four hours of rejoicing, singing and dancing. Nevertheless I notice that the girl-babies receive as much kissing and cuddling from both parents and from everyone else as the boys, so the weeping must soon stop.

Leaving my hamlet, after a lunch of apricots and maize bread, I jogged along in a leisurely way towards Gulapur, where I'd intended rejoining Roz this evening. Then, about four miles from the village, a horseman came galloping towards us in a cloud of dust, pulled up and with a broad beam and a low bow handed me a visiting-card. I looked at it in some astonishment, which you'll agree is a natural reaction. Then the horseman signed that I was to follow him and he led me – by this time feeling slightly surrealistic – off the Gulapur track and over a swaying suspension bridge to a very good imitation of the Garden of Eden on the other side of the river. Finally I found myself beside a mounting-block outside the Raja's residence and there was my host greeting me as though we'd known each other for a lifetime! (He speaks adequate, though not fluent, English.)

This is quite the most fantastic set-up I've ever met. A new bungalow, very rough and ready, has just been built to replace the old stone fortress where all the other Rajas lived. Here I am installed with an oil-lamp, which is regarded in these parts as the last word in modernity (the ordinary people use the roots of the juniper bush as lamps because they burn very slowly for a long time), and with a lavatory off my room, which sounds good till you discover it is a board laid across a stream which runs through the compound. I presume our drinking water comes from the same brook and can only hope that it's taken from upstream. The place looks almost completely unfurnished, apart from about half a ton of silver polo trophies. The Raja himself is an absolute darling who reminds me of something out of a fairy tale – I suppose because life in this tiny state of 15,000 inhabitants is all so simple and crystal clear that it belongs to childhood stories rather than to adult life. He had no difficulty whatever in persuading me to stay for a few days, so I sadly said, 'goodbye, and thank you for looking after me so well', to Rob, who was then taken home by one of the Raja's henchmen. The postal runner passed on the other side of the river as I was leaving Rob so I hailed him and delivered a letter to Daphne into his leather satchel: presumably it will arrive in Ireland some day.

The Raja, who is forty-eight, has only one wife living (and one dead) which is very unenterprising of him as both his father and grandfather ran to four simultaneously. His grandfather helped define the Durand Line and was made KCIE for that and his father was an OBE, for no apparent reason except that he ruled his people well and justly. The present Raja has ten sisters and brothers and can't remember half their names.

SHER QUILA RAKAPOSHI, 12 JUNE

Life is pure bliss here – the Raja has offered me a present of a little farm under the mountains and I'm almost tempted to accept! Dinner last night consisted of stewed goat-meat and maize bread and cherries, and this morning after a breakfast of eggs and bread we set off on foot for a tour of the 'village', which is not a village in our sense of the word but about a thousand acres of fertile land with the little stone huts of the peasant farmers dotted around it and a criss-cross of artificial streams keeping the place green. The atmosphere is indeed of paradise regained – such perfect tranquillity, innocent of politics, budgets and rivalry of any kind. The Raja is accepted as father of the whole community and treats everyone as 'family' and that's that. After every harvest he checks the amount of grain in the state and decides whether any should be sold in Gilgit bazaar or not and the people accept his decision without question – that's his function as Minister for Finance. As Minister for Social Welfare he receives all families who have suffered any kind of disaster into his compound and supports them indefinitely – at the moment a hundred and twenty-four people are being maintained. As Minister for Justice he settles the disputes which the council of twelve men in each village of the state bring to his notice. This morning, while eating his breakfast, he received a deputation who reported on a dispute about a rope bridge near by. It has always been kept up by two villages, one on either side of the river, but now one village says that its people almost never use it, and that the other village should do all the repairs – so the Raja pronounced that this was fair enough and the dispute was settled in five minutes.

This morning I kept thinking of Delius' 'Walk to the Paradise Gardens' as we went through fields of golden barley being harvested by women and girls in scarlet gowns and silver and blue caps, then climbed up by very narrow paths beside sparkling streams through woods of walnut, apricot, plum, pear and peach trees to where we could look across at the pine woods on the summit of the opposite mountain and see, through binoculars, the ibex grazing – that was a *big* moment! Then we went higher still to where one of the streams forms a pool on a level, wide 'step' on the mountainside. And there, in the soft, dry sand, I saw the pug-marks of a leopard who comes here nightly to drink – another *big* moment. It looked just like an enlarged version of my cat Roarin's prints on my writing paper on a wet day! The Raja said leopards are harmless unless a man is caught out on the mountain ill or injured, when they may kill and eat him. We returned by different paths to the Residence, through groves of weeping willow and fiery blossomed pomegranate trees, past more fields of barley and green wheat, with every peasant we met stopping to kiss the Raja's right hand and discuss their problems with their 'father'. The Raja told me that three years ago he decided it would be best for the people if he abdicated and handed over the state to the Pakistan Government, but everyone rose in revolt at this idea and begged him not to – so he didn't. I can't help contrasting Punial with Swat. Of course Swat is far better off materially, but personally I prefer Punial, which is really an extension of Afghanistan. (I've come round in a semicircle so that here I'm quite near the Afghan frontier.) And though the Wali and his family are model rulers, there's no comparison between the Swat ruler-ruled relationship and that of Punial. (Admittedly the comparison is not quite fair as the population of Swat is 594,000 and the same degree of intimacy just isn't possible.) But the Walis' household lives on a plane completely different from the people's, whereas here the only real difference between the Raja's and people's standard of living is that he has meat (goat's) once a day whereas they have it occasionally. The Raja is an amazing man, with a very highly-developed sense of responsibility and a very poorly-developed sense of his own importance; he's the first person I've met since leaving Europe who is quite happy to do his own fetching and carrying despite a host of servants. He's at the people's disposal always, whether they come during his siesta or at meal-times they are never expected to wait. Every December he has to go to Pindi on business and this he hates above anything as he can't get adjusted to the crowds and noise and traffic. He says he doesn't like city people 'because they are not honest'. I know exactly what he means – not that they are dishonest in their dealings, but in their attitudes to life generally. He doesn't know much about his own family origins but thinks his people came from near Kabul in the 1860s and took this place by force – Sher Quila means 'Lion's Fort' and the area is so called because it's very difficult to conquer. He certainly looks a typical Pathan and the family are Sunnis, though all the people are Ismailis. There are two tiny mosques in the village as, of course, the sects won't worship in the same mosque unless it's unavoidable (how Christian-like can Muslims get?) and this afternoon I visited both. The Ismaili one is lavishly decorated with gaudy pictures of the old and new Aga Khan and Prince Aly Khan. The present Aga Khan came here in 1961 and the mosque is full of coloured pictures of him in local dress. The Sunni mosque is a little wooden hut in the Raja's compound – what we'd call a family chapel.

Last night while we were having dinner wonderful music (very Afghan-like) began to play near by and when I asked why, I was told that it was the traditional way of announcing that an important polo-match would be played on the following day. Afterwards we went to look at the band. One old, bearded man was playing on a sort of primitive flute and two drummers were beating with their bare hands on the tight-skin ends of earthenware pitchers, which seemed similar to Afghan instruments. Polo is the national game here and the children begin to practise as tots by running around hitting stones with polo sticks; the result is astonishingly like our national game of hurling. Of course the sticks are home-made – branches of trees cut so cleverly at intersections that they look exactly like the real thing – but the balls used in matches are orthodox, made of bamboo root and imported from East Pakistan.

At 4.30 this afternoon the band began to play again. Then, at 5, I threw in the ball and, as Michael O'Hehir would say, the game was on! What a game to watch! Never anywhere have I seen such a thrilling spectacle. Of course it was totally unlike polo as we know it; there are *no* rules in this version and every sort of attack and defence is allowed. Blood was soon streaming from over half the twelve players' heads and hands and backs but they carried on regardless. The pace was tremendously fast and the horses streaked up and down the pitch foaming with sweat. Polo sticks were broken and replaced by the minute and the ball flew all over the place like a meteor – as often in the air as on the ground. The band played non-stop in time to the thudding hoofs and wild, whirling, clashing sticks and the faster the game the faster the music, till the three musicians were in almost as much of a lather as the horses.

One thing I noticed was the complete absence of fouls as distinct from accidents. Though this was a tremendously important championship game no tempers were lost and no one deliberately went for an opponent – the injuries were as often as not received from a member of the same team during what I can only describe as one of the scrums, when the ball got stuck beside a stone wall and all twelve horses 'packed down' with every man leaning from his saddle and poking towards it through the frantic jumble of horses' legs – anything less scientific it would be difficult to imagine. The only law concerned time; after thirty minutes there was a ten-minute interval (but no change of horses – they were simply walked about by little boys while their riders mopped up each other's blood) and then the teams changed sides and I threw in the ball again and off they went. At this stage it was Sher Quila: 1 – Gulapur: 5, and the crowds sitting all around on the stone walls were silent and depressed. Then Sher Quila got going and scored four goals in rapid succession, which feat caused frenzied cheering. However, Gulapur soon came back with two, leaving it 7–5 and eight minutes to go – by now I was hoarse from yelling for Sher Quila! For those minutes the pace was incredible – the horses flashed up and down the field wheeling at each end like ballet dancers and the air was full of the noise of cracked sticks, new ones being flung out for the riders to catch in mid-air as they galloped by. With half a minute to go Sher Quila equalised, and the villagers nearly feil off the walls in their delight. At full time it was decided to play an extra ten minutes, and Sher Quila scored again, to win. I was quite exhausted by excitement and suspense as I scrambled off the wall: it took a full bottle of Punial Water to revive me! The visiting team spend the night here after these games as both men and horses are too tired to go home and I'm now being entertained by the band still playing vigorously for their benefit, on the other side of the compound.

The Raja has what I can only describe as a few toys, in which he takes a boyish delight, and one of them is a Japanese transistor radio presented to him by our mutual friend Colonel Shah. On this he listens to the 8 p.m. Pindi news every evening and the weather reports from down-country are the single depressing feature of life here; today the temperature on the plains has been 115° in the shade.

SHER QUILA RAKAPOSHI, 13 JUNE

This morning, after a 5.30 a.m. breakfast on the verandah overlooking the river, my host disappeared for a moment and then came trotting back carrying a sheaf of letters. With a shy, sheepish smile he looked rather timidly down at me and said, 'I think you are a nice woman so you won't laugh at me because I cannot read or write. But sometimes I get letters in English, so now will you read them out for me very slowly please and I will ask you to write my answer for me because I see you can do much writing every day.' So we settled down to his correspondence for the next three hours – I've rarely been so pleased by any compliment!

But it's astonishing, when you come to think of it – he and most of the villagers speak their own local language (which I won't even attempt to spell but which is a distinct language, not a dialect, though it has no alphabet) as well as Urdu and Pushto, and he also speaks Pharsi and English, yet they're all illiterate. (Pushto is known here as so many caravans have always come over the Shandur Pass from Afghanistan.) The young village schoolmaster, whose pen I have just borrowed, acts as scribe, reading and writing letters in Urdu, but he knows only a few words of English. I'm afraid his qualifications as teacher are rather limited, at least in history and geography; he thought that Ireland was one of the United States of America and he swears that the Gilgit River is the Indus, whereas in fact it's a tributary, meeting the young Indus at Bunji, about sixty miles from here.

This morning I went for a long ride on a grey stallion, around the mountain which rises right behind this valley to the north. He wasn't as restful a steed as Rob and I had no confidence in my ability to control him, but fortunately we met no interesting mares en route.

I stopped on the way back to investigate a flour-mill which must be a perfect example of the very first mill ever invented by man. It was built of the usual stones over a rapid mountain torrent. A large tree-trunk had been hollowed out to form a sloping pipe through which the water was directed to increase its force, and flowing under the little hut it revolved what looked like an aeroplane propeller. Going into the hut through a four-foot high 'door' I found an amiable, ancient and very filthy old miller superintending the processes. A stone (such as I have seen lying around villages all the way through from east Turkey) about five foot in circumference (or perhaps diameter is what I mean?), with a six-inch hole in the middle, is attached to the revolving propeller in the stream below and slowly turns on another stationary stone, grinding the grains which fall, a few at a time, in a steady stream through the (yes!) sheep-skin hanging suspended from a beam across the five-foot-high ceiling. The flour dribbles out from beneath the stone into a dirty wooden trough and that's that! Each little mill is a private concern producing just enough for one family. Usually the grandfather or great-grandfather, who is past his speed for work in the fields or on the mountains, acts as miller.

Punial is a relatively prosperous area for this part of the world and the people are never actually without food, but in most of the other villages around they spend the winter in a drunken stupor as they have plenty of wine but only enough food for one square meal a week. In August they begin to fatten a bull-calf and in December it's killed and the meat is buried in snow and used very sparingly throughout the following months. This and their dried fruits keep them from actually dying of hunger. The winters here are as cold as you'd expect and the families exist crammed thirty or forty together in little stone huts, keeping each other warm to supplement the heat of tiny wood fires and drowning their misery in the abundant Punial Water, which apparently intoxicates them much more quickly than it does me.

I got back here at 11.30 a.m., which is lunchtime, and after lunch went off again on foot to find a cool corner for my siesta, as there are so many flies in this house that it's impossible to sleep here during the day. Also it's much cooler up the mountainside among greenery and running water with a delicious little breeze blowing down from the snows. I found a delightful spot beside a whitely-foaming torrent and went asleep for an hour under a willow tree.

Some noise wakened me and I opened my eyes to see a ragged, bearded old man kneeling beside me and stretching out his hand towards my throat with a ferocious expression on his face. The thought flashed through my mind – 'Well, you were bound to be murdered sometime . . . ' and then before I could move he drew back and beamed triumphantly and showed me, crushed between his fingers, the ant which he had kindly picked off my neck! Actually, I've discovered long ago that contrary to my preconceived ideas ants *don't* usually bite. I couldn't count the number of times I've lain on a spot of ground swarming with them and they've simply continued to swarm all over me without doing any damage. However, this reminded me of the snakes, which I'd quite forgotten, so I bounded up, made my salaams to the old boy and continued up a glorious path around the lower slopes of the mountain. On the way down I came on another old boy sitting beside a stream trying to get a thorn out of his foot by prodding it with another, bigger thorn from one of the aromatic shrubs which flourish here. When he saw me he beckoned me over and signed that his eyesight was *karrab* ('bad' in Pharsi and Pushto and evidently in Urdu also) and would I please operate on the foot. A lifetime of going barefooted meant that the soles of his feet were like leather and I had to get out my knife and spend a quarter of an hour dislodging the thing. It was a brute of a thorn half an inch long but after the extraction my friend happily thrust his bleeding foot into the stream and firmly declined to come back here with me and have it dressed and disinfected – but perhaps our disinfectants would give these people blood-poisoning! I thought the whole thing enchanting: could you imagine any European peasant stopping a tourist and requesting her to attend to his revolting foot? But, of course, here one is merely another human being, if an exceedingly odd one, and it's taken for granted that one will help if necessary just as when one needs help it is unfailingly given without anyone stopping to consider inconvenience or cost.

Yesterday evening I staged a cigarette crisis: I had my last at teatime and they're unobtainable here. The Raja is a non-smoker (and non-drinker) but he produced a box of choice cigars (*very* mild compared with the quite uninhaleable Pakistani cigarettes) which I've been on ever since – they make me feel like George Sand's ghost!

After dinner tonight the Raja again urged me to accept his offer of a little farm here and settle down for life 'where Heaven and earth meets'. He had already questioned me very closely about my family and financial affairs (as do all Asians, quite uninhibitedly) and he said this evening that I'd be far better off farming in Punial rather than living on fresh air in Ireland! I thanked him very much and explained that I couldn't be happy permanently exiled from Ireland, just as he couldn't if exiled from Punial – but he wasn't convinced. As his card so clearly shows, he thinks Punial the best place in the world and he also thinks farming the only occupation fit for any self-respecting person, all other ways of earning a living being regarded as debased, if not actually immoral.

Where Heaven and Earth Meets

Raja Jan-Alam

Raja Jan Alam
PUNIAL
MOUNTAIN STATE
GILGIT AGENCY
West Pakistan

I really must uproot from here in the early hours of tomorrow morning and get to Gilgit by the afternoon – but it *is* difficult! I went for another walk before dinner, at river level this time, right down the valley; it runs due east–west, so when I was returning the last, long shadows were before me, and the few frail scraps of cloud overhead were golden, the leaves were showing silver in the westerly breeze and the air was laden with the evening scent of shrubs and herbs. I ate some wild raspberries – tiny and tart and very refreshing. I've also discovered that *un*ripe apricots are one of the best of all thirst quenchers. Now early to bed.

12

Duel with the Sun

SHER QUILA RAKAPOSHI TO BABUSAR

GILGIT, 14 JUNE

I left my Raja, who was looking disproportionately devastated by the parting, soon after 5 a.m. His grey stallion took me to Gulapur, where the locals had got adjusted to having a cycle in their midst – the teacher told me that they had crowded around Roz daily during my absence. Half the little boys of the village were demanding to be given a ride and as there are a *lot* of little boys in every Asian village, this meant that it was 8.15 before I got away.

At the hamlet which lies halfway between Gulapur and here I was waylaid by a deputation of elders and a delightful old woman ushered me into a room absolutely devoid of furniture. There we sat on a straw mat and I was given buttermilk with salt – an honour of which I was most appreciative, salt being so precious here – and a big plate of *paratis* – very greasy, but I love them if the fat is not *too* rancid – and a pot of tea with sugar in it, which is another mark of esteem. This banquet was a joint effort by the whole community; flour, ghee, tea, sugar, salt, tea-pot and china cups all came from different homes. (Normally tea-pots are never used; the leaves and milk and water and sugar or salt are put in a flat pan and boiled up together.) I really appreciated their kindness, which was obviously meant to atone for the way they had unanimously shunned me (out of sheer astonishment and fear of the unknown) when we passed through before; I will never forget that reception committee. Neither will I ever forget the number of flies in that little mud house: the air was thick with them and voices had to be raised above their buzzing. The room was packed to capacity with villagers, all sitting around beaming at me, and the girls took it in turns to sit beside me waving green willow branches to keep the flies off my person and food – a procedure which made me feel vaguely like Cleopatra!

Then, halfway between that hamlet and Gilgit, an old woman spotted me toiling uphill, dragging Roz through deep sand, so she pursued me with an apron full of the biggest and juiciest figs I've ever eaten; all in all this has been one of my better-fed days, reaching a grand climax with a four-course dinner at the mess tonight.

My first request on arrival here was for some anti-lice preparation; the brutes have been devouring me since that night when I shared verminous blankets with the children, and they have successfully put up a stiff resistance to countless applications of soap and water.

I've noticed since entering Pakistan that comparatively few people say their prayers publicly here, though the majority are Sunnis, as in Turkey and Afghanistan. At dinner tonight it became apparent that both Sunnis and Shias hate Ismailis even more than they hate each other – and that's quite a lot. They say contemptuously that Ismailis are not *real* Muslims, and accuse them of never praying to Allah and only worshipping the Aga Khan. How true all this is I wouldn't know.

The temperature here today is 101°and 112° at Pindi.

JUGLOTE, 15 JUNE

I'm often astounded by the odd conceptions people have about what constitutes beautiful scenery. Last night two United Nations surveyors, who have recently gone from Gilgit to Chilas by jeep, told me that the landscape was dreadfully dull and that I shouldn't bother to cycle but should wait for the jeep which brings supplies to Chilas every Monday. Of course I didn't believe them, knowing that the Indus Gorge couldn't possibly be dull, but when I saw how uniquely magnificent the landscape actually is I decided that they must be completely blind.

Today's run was a complete contrast to my ride up and down the Gilgit Valley, but was no less beautiful and even more desolate. During the whole forty-three miles I didn't see *one* man, goat, bird, blade of grass or any sign of life, whereas in the other valley I passed a few people and animals every day and villages were much more frequent, even if often inaccessible from my track.

This jeep road was 'cycleable' (slowly) for about thirty miles and I walked the rest through ankle-deep sand, which gave me the feeling that some invisible person was trying to pull Roz back all the time. We started at 4.30 a.m. and as I had missed my siesta yesterday I felt quite dopey by 11.30, but kept going till shade was found under a big rock. Then saying 'To hell with snakes!' I curled up on the deep, soft sand and slept soundly from 12 to 3.30. I woke to find that a strong breeze had got up, which made the air very pleasant, and after a meal of eggs and bread and apricots we set off again. The water situation was grim all day. This valley is much wider than the other and there are no streams or nullahs till you get to Juglote, while the river is always out of reach. Occasionally it's out of sight too, as the 'road' goes over sand desert with only two lines of boulders to mark the route to be followed. At other times, where the track wriggles round precipices of sheer, bare rock, it's visible 1,000 feet below, in the deep gorge it has carved through the mountains, and to be able to see and hear water you can't possibly reach is the quintessence of torture. I had to make do on six pints when I could have used at least eighteen. On arriving at the Juglote nullah I drank twelve pints just like *that* and I've drunk another six since I came to the hamlet itself. But for all its hardships I wouldn't have missed today's journey. Nanga Parbat is directly overlooking Juglote and was visible all the afternoon, thrusting up grandly from the wild array of surrounding peaks; it's definitely the second most impressive mountain I've seen, after Ararat, with Demavand a good third on my list. Lying east of the road it was a glorious spectacle at sunset, with the last golden rays pouring over the peaks to the west and being caught by the snow-laden summits of the Nanga Parbat range, whilst the Indus Gorge was already full of purple dusk and the surrounding desert was a still expanse of greyness.

The people here are reputed to be rather wild and I had trouble persuading Colonel Shah not to provide me with an escort. Finally I said, 'Where are you going to get (*a*) another bicycle and (*b*) a soldier who would ride and push it over the Babusar Pass?' He saw my point, and that was that! In fact I find the locals very kind, though admittedly they are much rougher types than in the Gilgit Valley. But I sense no danger here though I'm sleeping on a charpoy by the roadside.

My eyes are going queer again from this last week of writing by the light of juniper roots. We'll make another dawn start tomorrow, so bed now.

GONER, 16 JUNE

This is a day to go down in my personal history as having given me the toughest cycling of a lifetime, not likely ever to be surpassed, though it may be equalled tomorrow. I was up at 4 a.m. and we left Juglote at 4.30, after a meagre breakfast of dry bread and tea. Only apricots were available for my picnic lunch. I covered no more than forty-five miles between that and 5.45 p.m. but each one felt like four anywhere else and there was no time for a siesta as we were ploughing through deep sand from 8 a.m. onwards and climbing practically vertical hills, all in fierce heat. The temperature was almost up to Pindi heights because of the bare rock mountains overlooking sand-deserts devoid of plant life. What a landscape! The sheer magnitude of everything is overwhelming – the height of the mountains, the depth of the Indus gorge, the fabulous chunks of rock scattered about the desert (some are literally as big as what we in Ireland call a mountain, yet here they are simply bits of rock broken jaggedly off a nearby peak), the perfect stillness and the brutal sun; despite being half-dead by 2 p.m. it was an experience worth the exhaustion.

I'm three-quarters dead now and just waiting for some form of food before falling asleep. On yesterday's basis the traffic was hectic today – one tribesman and one jeep. The tribesman looked terrifying – armed with a spear – but actually he was very amiable and seemed thrilled to bits when I took his photo. The jeep looked no less terrifying going up a stretch of track 800 feet above the Indus on a surface that was literally loose slabs of blasted rock. All the passengers had to get out and walk up, otherwise even a jeep couldn't make this gradient. Similarly, all loads had to be removed and carried up and re-loaded at the top; it's inconceivable how even an empty vehicle can ascend these stretches: certainly the jeep is a wonderful invention.

I'm yawning so much that if no grub appears soon I'll fall asleep where I sit – anyway I'm now too tired to feel hungry. I think the heat would have finished me today but for the fact that five nullahs appeared during the last twenty miles. Not that they made much difference to the temperature, as all were in deep clefts between mountains and there was no growth around them, but I got into them fully clothed and soaked myself for about fifteen minutes from head to boots. After another fifteen minutes I was bone dry again yet these immersions kept my temperature down somewhat. The water was just pleasantly cool, not icy as in the Gilgit Valley – otherwise I daren't have plunged in when so over-heated. But as these nullahs are also from melting glaciers, this shows how hot the region is. Anyway heat shouldn't be one of my worries tomorrow as surely even in June the Babusar Pass will be cool. Beyond a doubt *I* find such heat absolutely prostrating: maybe other constitutions can take it better.

I crossed one suspension bridge today and on it was a marble plaque to the memory of seven German climbers and nine Sherpa guides who were killed while attempting Nanga Parbat on 14 June 1937. The mountain itself rises on the other side of the river and there their bodies still lie. All the Germans were under thirty years old – but perhaps they were lucky; challenging Nanga Parbat is a better way to die than fighting for Nazism.

I lost my toothbrush last week when it fell into the river. Washing my teeth is the one thing I fuss about – not that they are getting much to do these days. *Still* no sign of grub! And in this hamlet (without the Prince) there aren't even mulberries or apricots or wine: I can't imagine what the people eat. But they're very nice folk and I'm quite sure are doing their best to dig up something for me – I only hope they've not gone to the snow-line to dig up ghee!

Later. I was wakened at 10 p.m. and served with one *chapatti* of maize flour and a one-egg omelette.

CHILAS, 17 JUNE

Well, I was wrong – yesterday's effort was a cake-walk compared with today's. In fact the only enjoyable part of today's performance is this – sitting down to write about it after recovering (more or less) from the consequences.

We left Goner at 5.30 a.m. and arrived here at 4.30 p.m., having only covered twenty-eight miles, yet I came into the shade of this nullah in a state of total collapse, so decidedly at the end of my tether that I don't believe I could have kept going *one* more mile. The Tahsildar here told me that when I arrived the temperature was 114° – he didn't really have to say it! I had to walk all the way as the first twenty miles were through very deep sand, up and down very steep hills, and after that I was too dizzy from the heat to balance on Roz, even where the track was level. By 7 a.m. the sun was so hot that I was saturated through with sweat and as we only came to one nullah for wetting, cooling and refilling the water bottle, dehydration became my fear. I found shade once, under a rock, and slept very soundly from 1.40 to 2.50 p.m., although lying on sharp flints. After that the real trouble began and by 3 p.m. I was seriously worried: I had stopped sweating, which is a danger signal, and my mouth was so dry that my tongue felt like an immovable bit of stiff leather. By 3.30 I was shivering with cold, though the heat was so intense that I did not dare touch any metal part of Roz. After that I just kept going but don't remember one bit of the road – only that the green trees of Chilas were visible in the distance. I had just enough sense left, on getting to the nullah, not to drink gallons, but to lie under a willow and take mouthfuls at a time until gradually I began to sweat again and get warm. Then I rolled into the water and lay there for a few minutes with it rushing deliciously over me, after which I was able to walk another half-mile to the Tahsildar's house, where I drank gallons of buttermilk and salt followed by cups and cups of hot tea; but I couldn't look at food this evening.

Chilas is only 3,000 feet above sea level and is hellishly hot even amidst all the running brooks and dense green trees and shrubs –

because it's completely encircled by naked rock-mountains which relentlessly throw back that intolerable sun. The Tahsildar (a minor local government official) says that I must stay here tomorrow for a day's rest before going over the Babusar and I couldn't agree more! Not that the pass will be difficult after the last three days; once I get eight miles up (and I'll start at 3.30 a.m.) it will be cool, and it's heat, not gradients, that finish me off.

The horror of today's trek really was extreme with heat visibly flowing towards me in malevolent waves off the mountainsides and the dreadful desert stench of burning sand – which still persists here – nauseating me; the terrifying dehydration of mouth and nostrils and eyes until my eyelids could barely move and a sort of staring blindness came on, with the ghastly sensation of scorching air filling my lungs, and the overpowering drug-like effect of the wild thyme and sage, that grow thickly over the last few miles, being 'distilled' by the sun; and above all the despair of coming round corners and over hilltops time and time again, hoping always to see water – and never seeing it. I have often thought that death by thirst must be grimmer than most deaths and now my surmise has been confirmed. The irony of it all was that all day the vast, swirling Indus flowed beside me, inaccessible. But what a magnificent valley it is! Though I could have done without this afternoon's instalment, I wouldn't have liked to miss this morning's panoramas; the rough track soared up and up and up the sheer black and beige mountainsides till even the tremendous roar of the Indus was inaudible and it looked a mere bit of brown ribbon, coiling for miles in both directions between its colossal, but now dwarfed, cliffs. From these the desert swept flatly to the foot of gigantic peaks, some of them almost level with the track. Occasionally, on the other side of the river, there was an unexpected oasis, around a nullah, inhabited by Indus gold searchers. These are a brown-skinned people unlike the other tribes of the area and they are much despised by the local farming-folk, who consider that searching for gold is a menial occupation! (From my distance those meagre oases, as they stood out on the level 'table' of sand, reminded me of the little wooden trees I had as a child with my toy farm. I saw several of the 'gold-men' by the river's edge, perilously scooping and sieving in quest of that Indus gold which is supposed to be one of the best in Asia. Incidentally, a peculiar kind of precious stone is found around Punial and Gilgit – like an opal but better. I don't know if they belonged to ancient peoples or not but all local women have at least one in their necklaces.) Sometimes the 'gold-men' cross the river by inflating two goatskins, laying planks across them and paddling over; naturally they land about ten miles downstream because of the ferociously swift current, but they rarely have an accident.

Apart from the gold-men the only living creature I saw all day was a man who looked like John the Baptist gone to the dogs; I came on him unexpectedly and got quite a fright. He was stark naked with jet black, thick hair down to his knees, a beard to his navel, skin burned ebony by the sun and a mad-looking glint in his eye. What he lives on I can't think. I was getting out my camera when he gave a sort of insane gurgle and came towards me with hands extended, whereupon I fled – if that is the right word for scrambling through nine inches of sand up a mountainside with a bicycle! When I got to the top of the slope I looked back and saw that the apparition had forgotten me and was now sitting hunched beneath a rock engaged in the contemplation of his toes. Probably he would have been quite harmless, but I didn't feel like waiting to find out.

I notice that all the men of this village (population approximately 2,000) carry rifles just like the Afghans. They are very friendly folk, now gathered in force round the first bicycle to penetrate to Chilas; it's very funny to watch the 'bright boys' working out how a bicycle operates and then explaining the theory to their companions.

CHILAS, 18 JUNE

This morning I was told of a boy's report that when I arrived at the Chilas nullah yesterday, he was there and observed that I had the 'sun-devil' – their very graphic term for heat-delirium. Apparently I was talking loudly to myself as I reached the water; the frustrating thing is that the boy doesn't know English and I'd love to know what I was talking about. It was considerate of him to report on my condition as this signifies real heat-stroke and you have to watch your diet for a few days afterwards or acute diarrhoea is the result. No fats, eggs or meat are allowed; lots of salted lemon-juice is advised if possible (not possible here) and any fruit, oddly enough, *is* allowed. It's amazing how our instincts work; I'd had breakfast at 5.30 a.m., before this warning was delivered, but though ravenously hungry I had said 'No!' very emphatically to the eggs and had asked for apricots to eat with bread and salted tea. My other meals today have consisted of bread and apricots and gallons of skimmed milk and salt. I spent most of the day writing, sitting on a lawn beside a baby nullah under a vast plane tree. I went indoors for my siesta at 2 p.m. and was wakened at 2.40 by a frantic gale carrying fine sand which penetrated everything. But it was a wonderful relief, because when the wind died down the sky had become completely over-clouded and the temperature had dropped to 92°. A period of intense heat in this area (as in Pindi) is always followed by the temporary ease of a dust-storm. The Tahsildar thinks I should stay a few more days here but I feel fine this evening, thank God, and tomorrow Chilas will probably be unbearable again. I'd much prefer to get up to the Babusar hut and stay a few days there before going over the top, which would also help to condition my lungs for the height of the pass.

BABUSAR HUT, 19 JUNE

I'm sitting now beside a crackling fire of pine-logs with a cold gale sweeping through the surrounding forest and big, fat, damp, grey clouds drifting among the peaks and occasional splatters of rain gusting against the windows. The net result of all these delights is that I'm feeling thirty years younger, back in the climate I was born to. This reminds me of a March evening at home and I wonder what point there is in leaving here before October! It's such a strange sensation to touch things like paper and furniture and not feel them warm to the fingers and I can hardly believe that there's no sweat dripping off me on to everything. The last movement of the Choral Symphony would be *very* appropriate as background music.

I left Chilas at 3.40 a.m. in a darkness just beginning to be not total and arrived here at 12.45 p.m., having walked twenty-one miles from 3,000 to 12,000 feet – not bad going on a completely empty tummy – unless you count water! By this stage I've got adjusted to going without any breakfast (even a cup of tea), when I make early starts, though at first I found such asceticism a considerable deprivation; evidently the human mechanism can adjust to almost anything but extremes of temperature. Needless to say, my ribs are almost coming through my skin now: two and a half weeks gallivanting around Gilgit on the skin of an onion is the best way to shed superfluous fat.

Today was superb – as good as, though utterly different from, the Indus Valley. The track followed a big nullah all the way up and of course there were none of the vast landscapes of the past few days; the mountains are so close on either side that the sun didn't reach me till 9.15 – when I was too high for it to hurt – although it rose at 4.50 a.m. Also there were none of the dangers; really the Gilgit–Chilas road *is* terrifying, with those sheer drops as the narrow track goes steadily higher.

This region is quite densely populated now by the Indus Valley folk who have been moving up during the past fortnight, bringing their flocks to the summer pasturage. They have tiny 'summer residences', built of stone or wood, perched all over the mountainsides, some of the little houses being on stilts. They grow maize extensively and the terracing on these slopes is awe-inspiring. Usually the strips are too narrow and the slopes too steep for bullocks to plough so all is done by hand, even the five-year-olds helping. The whole valley floor is quite heavily wooded beside the nullah, chiefly with mulberry and walnut trees. The majority of males, from the age of twelve up, go armed, and are much addicted to murdering each other *à la* frontier tribesman, but they're amiable to me.

Three times today I had to cycle Roz down the hill I had just pushed her up to show a pop-eyed crowd of men, women and children how a cycle works; it's so easy to give them so much pleasure – they were fascinated by the performance. The men and boys always tried to push her back up the relevant bit of hill at the end of my demonstration but to their astonishment there is considerably more than meets the eye to pushing a laden cycle up a steep hill and they usually ended lying on the road with Roz mixed up with their legs and the rest of the crowd in ecstasies of laughter. They couldn't understand why I wasn't riding her up (!) and it was impossible to explain that bicycles weren't really invented for transporting people through the Himalayas, but that I'd have my reward on the other side with 120 miles of free-wheeling on a good tarred road.

I would have needed a cine-camera for the whole thing. It was comical to see the pandemonium when I first turned a corner of the road into a populated stretch of valley. From every direction they came pell-mell – down the steep mountainside from their work in the forests, across the valley from tilling their plots, wading waist-deep through the nullah, scrambling up cliffsides, leaping off the flat roofs of their little huts, deserting flocks of goats and donkeys in mid-journey, and all ending up standing inside the stone walls that line the road, staring at me in wonder and half in fear, until I smiled and said, 'Salaam Alaikum,' which they took as an invitation to jump the walls and crowd around, tinkling the bell, twirling the pedals, feeling the tyres, fiddling with the brakes, opening the saddlebag and asking where I was going to and coming from. Some of them made the Persian mistake of thinking me a boy and the rest called me Begum Sahib – a variation on the 'Memsahib' used everywhere else. They were *incredibly* dirty, making the filthy people of other areas seem clean. In Chilas I was told they never wash and I observed today that at least three-quarters of them suffer from a ghastly eye-disease which comes from dirt and has the ghoulish effect of making many of its victims look *dead* in the eyes. The stink when fifteen or twenty of them crowded round made me feel quite ill, despite the fresh mountain air. Thank God this PWD hut is here, as with the best will in the world I couldn't bring myself to stay in one of their homes, if only because the risk of disease would be too great. I was surprised to notice the great number of pock-marked faces; one would think that here they'd escape smallpox but I suppose their own dirt breeds every known disease. An odd thing was that they kept asking me to feel their pulses and those of their children; I simply can't understand this, so I must enquire as to possible reasons. Incidentally, all pulses felt seemed very weak and fast to me, but perhaps this is the altitude and normal for them; my own is racing too. They were continually inviting me into their huts for milk and *paratis* but I had to decline with an inward shudder – though with regret too because (*a*) I was hungry and (*b*) they looked so sad and disappointed! On arriving here I found that the only food suitable for my present condition was a sort of undersised broad bean about as big as a large pea with three to the pod (eaten raw). The other foods available are *paratis*, saturated in the rancidest ghee, and eggs. Quite apart from my diet I wouldn't have touched the *paratis* after that little brush with rancid ghee in Gupis. People here haven't even got the fruit on which the peasants of other Gilgit areas depend so much.

I felt the thin air today, from about 9,000 feet, and had to stop every half-mile for a few minutes to calm my heart. (I also have a theory that being undernourished does not help.) From that altitude there was a big change in scene for the pine woods begin here with gigantic trees twice the height of any other pines I've seen. I also noticed lots of holly trees and evergreen oaks – which always remind me of Castile – and there was green grass everywhere instead of arid earth. All morning the sky remained a lovely clear blue with a few pure white clouds – in welcome contrast to the brazen, colourless glare over the desert – but at midday it began to fill with grey rain or snow clouds. I'd anticipated being exhausted on arrival and going to sleep immediately, but I'm so 'toughened up' by now that I wasn't a bit tired, apart from shortness of breath, so after a fistful of raw beans I went up the mountain to collect firewood and enjoy the delicious coolness and gusts of rainy wind. From here one can see right down the twenty-mile length of the valley, which remains unclouded, to the Indus Gorge and the infinity of white peaks beyond. I don't wonder at people risking their lives to climb mountains; even getting up to 12,000 feet and standing looking down at what one has conquered is wonderfully satisfying.

This is a very adequate hut, furnished by PWD, but the summer *chowkidar* (caretaker) must have used the bedding himself as it's full of bedbugs. I have hurled it outside and I'll sleep on the floor rolled in the curtains from doors and windows, which are of thick material and easily taken down. I don't trust the charpoy – probably it has bugs in the ropes!

BABUSAR HUT, 20 JUNE

In spite of my anti-bug precautions I slept wretchedly because of sandfly bites acquired in Chilas the night after the storm. These take twenty-four hours to get troublesome and then they're hell. My face, neck, hands and arms are covered with tiny purple lumps, both itchy and sore, and I woke constantly to find myself tearing at them with my nails. It's so long since I've slept under a roof that it was disconcerting not to see the stars above me. The night sky here is a most brilliant and beautiful sight and is one of the few consolations of the hot areas. If one opens one's eyes for a moment the starlight is almost dazzling, and the Milky Way, with 'coal-sacks' and nebulae, is quite different from the same spectacle seen through an Irish atmosphere. I spent quite a lot of my first night at Chilas admiring it as the wind off the desert was like a dragon's breath – *not* conducive to sleep – yet indoors with no fans was even worse.

There were few ordinary flies in Chilas, which made up for a lot; by now I've got an obsession about them. It's not an hygienic obsession about flies on food (if they stayed on the food and kept off me I'd be quite happy) but they drive me mad with their incessant buzzing and tickling hour after hour – I suppose it's their slick 'smart-Alecness' that really infuriates. One *knows* they can't be killed but after a certain period of persecution one begins to slap frantically at them, hurting oneself in the process and leaving them totally unaffected, which makes one feel even more of a fool than usual. (There are very few here also, Allah be praised!) Personally I much prefer lice, some of which can be captured at intervals and vindictively squashed to death – very gratifying!

This morning I decided to risk eggs for breakfast, as it's almost three days since the heat-stroke, so I bought four and boiled them. Three were *very* bad and somehow that deadened my appetite for the fourth, causing me to revert to beans instead.

Opinions here vary so much about the state of the pass that I decided to go up some of the way today by a short-cut and investigate for myself. At 7.30 it was a heavenly morning with warm sun, cool breeze and cloudless sky, like a good May day in Ireland. Progress was slow, with lots of pauses to rest my pounding heart, as the short-cut is naturally a much steeper gradient than the track, but I enjoyed meandering along looking at the very lovely wild flowers in the woods and listening to the birds. Inevitably I got lost and it was 2 p.m. before I came out on the jeep track, 13,000 feet up, amid stony, barren moors. By now the sky was overclouded, thunder was crashing amidst the peaks and it was snowing lightly. (I could hardly believe that seventy-two hours ago and only twenty miles away I had been getting heat-stroke!) I didn't dare go higher because of feeling a slight nausea – caused by either altitude or starvation or both – so I walked down the six miles of track to here. There are three small glaciers completely blocking the road but on this stretch they will be very easy to negotiate on foot. Probably there are more and wider ones farther up; it was a pity I couldn't inspect the last two miles to the top for fear of over-taxing my ill-treated carcase. (I feel quite sorry for my own body these days, in a curiously detached and impersonal way; I'd like to be able to give it the feed it's certainly earned.) The delicate question now is whether to stay here another few days and get more acclimatised before pushing Roz up (good for heart) or whether to go over tomorrow and get a square meal on the other side (good for stomach). I think stomach will win because I really would be debilitated after another forty-eight hours on raw beans. (This evening my watch is repeatedly slipping down my wrist.) I have just got another three eggs – all that were available – and about a pint of milk, but the peasants are starving too, pending the delayed arrival of the camel caravans over the pass. They would share their last egg with me and are most reluctant to take money, which makes it all the more awkward. Fortunately the gradient of the track, except on the countless hairpins, is only about one in eighteen for the first six miles anyway. I don't understand why, when walking briskly down such a slope, one is completely unaffected by altitude, whereas going very slowly up one feels half dead; surely walking is in itself an exertion?

The things they can do here with pine-trunks and stones are incredible. All the way from Chilas the many bridges over the nullah are constructed of these materials only; I went under one to see how it's done but I'm not mechanically-minded enough to describe the technique. Of course this means that they cost nothing but labour, which is just as well, since they are swept away regularly every year.

Timber is one of the chief sources of cash here; it's cut high on the mountains, rolled down to the track, carried by men to the Indus, thrown in and fished out hundreds of miles downstream years later, by the contractors who have bought the trees and whose name is carved on them. The locals have a curious method of felling; they burn the trunk near the ground until it's thin enough to cut through with their tiny home-made axes. Great skill is required not to (*a*) set the whole tree on fire or (*b*) set the whole dry forest on fire. When the trees have been felled it's fascinating to see small boys steering the giant trunks down steep slopes to the track.

13

Two Wheels over Nine Glaciers

BABUSAR TO ABBOTTABAD

BASAL, 21 JUNE

For a combination of beauty, danger, excitement and hardship (of the enjoyable variety) today wins at a canter.

As I was resolutely chewing my breakfast of beans and one *chapatti* (made from about two ounces of maize flour and given me in honour of the occasion) an incoherent but kindly old man came along and told me that a pony-caravan had left the hamlet about three hours ago in a desperate attempt to cross the pass on the Mahomet-Mountain principle; they hope to collect essential stores from the camel-caravan which has now been held up at Butikundi for ten days. At the time I didn't quite grasp why the old man was telling me this – but before long I got the message!

Roz and I started out at 7 a.m. (it was rather a holiday feeling not having to be up at 4 a.m. to beat the sun) and it took me nearly two and a half hours to walk slowly up the six miles I came down yesterday in less than one and a half hours. On this stretch I passed several groups of nomads, the smoke from their little camp-fires sending an incongruously cosy smell across the bleak landscape. Equally incongruous seemed the persistent call of a cuckoo. Apart from this, the only sounds to break the distinctive silence of high places were the whistles of nomads directing their flocks and the careless melody of sheep and goat bells.

I reached the first glacier in good shape, but the sun was now high and I noted with some alarm that this great bank of melting snow had moved a few yards since yesterday. However, the pony-trail was encouragingly clear and we were soon safely over; it was at this point that the penny dropped and I saw the import of the old man's information. I stopped here to eat some of the glacier, remembering my last meal of snow in the mountains between Yugoslavia and Bulgaria. Already I was almost painfully hungry and apart from quenching my thirst the feel of the solid snow in my mouth was absurdly welcome.

For another mile the track remained clear, though so torn by the thaw that it resembled a river-bed. At this height no trees grow and the rock-strewn pastures, which in a few weeks will be a rich green, were wearily yellow after the long winter. Ahead I could now see a gigantic glacier, more than two miles wide, extending to the Top. The track disappeared beneath this about a mile to the west of where it crossed the Top and hoof-prints in the thaw-soft earth showed me that the ponies had branched off to take a direct route up, cutting all the hairpin bends which obviously lay beneath the glacier.

At this point I stopped to consider what I should do. To follow the track approximately would be much less exhausting than to take the short-cut, but it might be much more dangerous for someone ignorant of the idiosyncrasies of glaciers. So I decided to drag Roz up the direct route, not suspecting that what looked like a twenty-minute climb would take almost two hours.

By now clouds were dark and close, and a sharp wind sent gusts of little snowflakes whirling around me at intervals. I revelled in this and went bare-headed, enjoying the keenness of the air. High peaks surrounded me, cutting off the valley below, and it was a rare joy to move alone among them with the chaotic symphony of re-echoing thunder as background music.

I was now higher than I had ever been before and when I stopped at six-minute intervals to regain breath my heart-beats sounded as loud as the thunder. This suffocating sensation frightened me until I realised that the illusory feeling of repeatedly coming to the point of death was simply the mountains' way of teasing novices. By the time I was halfway up the ponies' wisdom seemed open to doubt – their trail crossed many outcrops of rock and every time I lifted Roz over one of these barriers I collapsed with exhaustion. In places the snow was so soft that I sank into it up to the knees. Elsewhere it was so hard that even the ponies' hoofs had made little impression and I kept upright only by driving my specially nailed boots into it at each step – a process which still further exhausted me. After about an hour and a half of this struggle I was at that peculiar stage when one doesn't really believe that one's objective will ever be reached, and when one's only mental awareness concerns the joy (to some incomprehensible, if not downright unnatural) of driving one's body far beyond the limits of its natural endurance. Then, having dragged Roz up another savage gradient, and over yet another litter of boulders, we suddenly found ourselves on a level plateau, about a quarter of a mile square. Sitting where I had subsided beyond the rocks, and still clutching Roz, I slowly assimilated the unlikely fact that we were on Babusar Top.

I was understandably anxious to photograph Roz at this historic point where, because of her owner's mental unsoundness, she had become the first bicycle to cross the Babusar Pass; but though I took three shots I doubt if the light was strong enough for a cheap camera. Yet, between the intermittent snowfalls, I had a clear view to east and south, where the sun was bright on a sparkle of angular peaks and on the flawless, smooth curves of the glaciers that united them.

By now the thunder had ceased and when the wind dropped the overwhelming silence of the mountains reminded me of the hush felt in a great empty Gothic cathedral at dusk – a silence which is beautiful in itself. However, I could afford no more than half an hour on the Top, for I was still fifteen miles from the head of the Kagan Valley. In my enthusiasm to get *up*, the process of getting *down* again had not been very seriously considered; possibly I was suffering from lack of vitamins to the brain, because I'd assumed that once on the south side all hazards would be left behind. This delusion was fostered during the first stage of the descent.

From the plateau I could see, about 1,000 feet below me, a vividly green valley some eight miles long and two miles wide, with a foam-white nullah flashing down its centre, and a reasonably-surfaced earth track descending at a comfortable gradient along the flank of the mountain, where snow had lain too recently for any growth to have covered the brown scree. On reaching the valley floor the track crossed the nullah and was visible running level along the base of the opposite mountains before curving away out of sight halfway down the valley. As we began to free-wheel I reflected that this was a delightful road to follow, with all the characteristics which thrill a wanderer's heart.

Half an hour later I was rapidly revising my opinion. The track's first imperfection was revealed when we arrived at the nullah, to find that where a bridge should be stood two supports, stoutly upholding nothing. I looked up and down stream with wild surmise. The ponies had not returned, therefore the ponies had forded the nullah at some point. But at what point? Unfortunately the ground here was so firm, and the bank so stony, that my diligent search for prints yielded no clues. Then, as I stood looking pathetically around me, in the faint hope of seeing some nomads, a solitary black cow (for all the world like a good little Kerry) appeared some twenty yards upstream, walking purposefully across the meadow towards the torrent. There was no other sign of life in the valley, either human or animal, and in retrospect I tend to believe that she was my guardian angel, discreetly disguised. But when I first noticed her I did not pause to speculate on her nature or origin. She was obviously going to ford the nullah for some good reason of her own, and we were going with her. I pedalled rapidly and bumpily over the grass to the point for which she was heading. There I hastily unstrapped the saddlebag, tied it to my head with a length of rope mentally and appropriately labelled 'FOR EMERGENCIES', and was ready to enter the water.

The cow, when she joined us on the bank, showed no surprise at our presence, nor did she register any alarm or despondency as I put my right arm round her neck, gripped Roz's crossbar firmly with my left hand, and accompanied her into the turmoil of icy water. It had occurred to me that if I found myself out of my depth this could become an Awkward Situation, but actually the water was never more than four feet deep, though its tremendous force would have unbalanced me had I been alone. My friend, however, was clearly used to this rôle and we crossed without difficulty, unless the agony of being two-thirds submerged in newly melted snow counts as a difficulty. I felt that there was a certain lack of civility about our abrupt parting on the opposite bank, after such a meaningful though brief association, but our ways lay in different directions and I could do nothing to express my gratitude. So I can only record here my thanks for the fairytale appearance of this little black cow.

I was now almost paralysed by the cold – soaked clothes are one thing in the desert and another thing here. After replacing the saddlebag, I couldn't tie it on, my fingers were so numb, so I had to rope it instead, before cycling over the smooth turf to the road about half a mile away. From here the track climbed steeply (which I considered frightfully bad form; having gone up *all* the way *to* the Top it should now have had the decency to go down *all* the way *from* the Top) and this was the drill for the next seven miles, switch-backing up and down or round the flanks of mountains – all snow-peaked and overlooking wonderfully green pastures with more and more of those quite indescribable flowers. The pink and yellow and red and blue and purple and gold and white blooms often grew so thickly that the meadows looked like some giant's carpet, with vast circular patterns of colour woven into the green background. (Isn't it odd how the finest flowers grow where there are fewest people to see them?)

But I had other, less aesthetic distractions on this seven-mile stretch, during which I had to cross eleven glaciers, the majority forty to fifty yards wide. Eight were 'natural', i.e. situated where they had formed in gullies over streams, and the others were from high up the mountain-sides and had slid down recently to their present positions. These were the ones which scared me, as I morbidly reckoned that there was nothing to stop them sliding still farther while Roz and I were in midstream, as you might say.

As before I followed in the steps of my thrice-blessed ponies (Allah be good to them!) but edging oneself and one's cycle across steep masses of snow and ice, where one slip would be fatal, is a slow process, and it was 4.30 by the time I'd crossed those few miles. The last two miles curved round a most beautiful lake about half a mile wide with sheer green mountains rising from the opposite side, their gullies a-glitter with glaciers. The water was a clear but dark green and one of the loveliest sights of my life was the perfect reflection of the white snow in that still depth of greenness. On my side of the slope, between road and water, was a natural rockery formed of small chunks of grey stone between which grew masses of blue and white flowers. At various points not far from the water's edge were 'icebergs' – the tops of glaciers which had slid into the lake and not yet melted. The lake is shaped as shown below, and flows away in a nullah (the infant Kagan River, of which much more later); and as I cycled towards the nullah's source I heard an odd, roaring noise in the distance. Before I'd time to diagnose it a movement caught my eye and I just saw a glacier disappearing into the water where the arrow points in my sketch. Wavelets began to lap the shore near me only minutes after, but the splash of the impact was most dramatic; it must have been a comparatively small glacier as none of it was left above the surface.

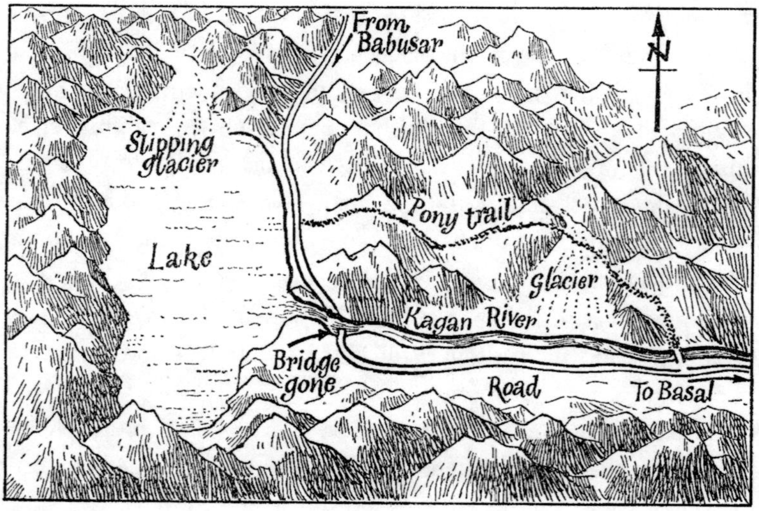

A few minutes later I came to the nullah and dismounted in disorder, confronted by the day's Chief Crisis. The bridge, which should have been where I marked it, was gone, and this time there was no question of fording as the water was some twenty feet below the road between sheer cliffs. (Here I began to feel that the day had contained enough thrills and that this was one too many.) I looked around in bewilderment, because of ponies there was no sign, yet it seemed inconceivable that they could have got through this impasse, as the road (see sketch) was overhung by a steep mountain strewn with great rough chunks of black rock. After a moment's gazing at this I suddenly, and reluctantly, registered the horrible fact that since the ponies were not visible they must have gone *over* this mountain, however far-fetched the deduction might seem. And then I still more reluctantly registered the even more horrible fact that I too must go over this mountain, and quickly too, for at 4.30 p.m. only three hours of daylight remain. (Also I knew that I would soon collapse from starvation.) So the next thing was to rediscover the ponies' trail.

To my surprise, this presented no difficulty (by now I expected everything to be difficult!) but to find it was one thing and to follow it was another. After the first few yards of carrying Roz up that gradient between those rocks my shins had been so badly banged about that I could have wept with pain, and Roz's back mudguard, severely injured while crossing the earlier nullah, was now completely torn off. Clearly this nonsense had to stop, for both our sakes, and the only alternative was to wear Roz round my neck. Thus arrayed, I proceeded upwards, still suffering from lack of oxygen, with my head sticking out of the angle between crossbar and chain and my vision obscured by the front wheel. Being in a weakened condition the ludicrous aspect of the situation struck me with special force and whenever I stopped to rest I wasted precious breath on giggling feebly at my own dottiness.

This trek lasted for about an hour and a half, of which at least half an hour was spent resting. The ponies' hoof prints were clear in the wet earth between the rocks, otherwise I would certainly have gone astray, not knowing the direction taken by the nullah. I was getting a bit desperate when I suddenly found myself crossing a level meadow free of rocks and ankle-deep in water from the thawing snows above. By now I felt so exhausted that I scarcely noticed the precipice at the edge of this meadow and almost went over on to the rocks 1,500 feet below. When I'd recovered from my escape I peered down to see seven little black figures (three ponies and four men) in the middle of a vast glacier beside the nullah. At first I couldn't understand how either men or beasts had got down there; then I realised that they must have used the glacier, which extends upwards for some 2,000 feet, bisecting the semicircular 'bite' out of the mountain, on the west side of which I was standing. But I still don't understand how even mountain ponies were induced to make that terrifying descent. And, observing the scene below, I noticed that three of the ponies had had it, and were resolutely refusing to cross the bridge of snow over the nullah. Personally, I shared their point of view.

However, our descent proved the simplest part of the whole journey. On reaching the glacier I shouted to attract the men's attention, and then pushed Roz over at the steepest point. She shot down at a rate that would have dislocated any lesser bicycle and was stopped by the bed-rolls which the men placed in her path. Next, I pushed myself over, at the least steep point, and half-rolled, half-tobogganed down – a painful progress, but one which at least required no effort. The pony-men had heard of my proposed expedition and when I arrived at their feet, in a bruised and breathless ball, I was greeted with joyful acclamation. Their leader, a very old and dignified man – who in Europe would not be allowed by his daughter to go out on a showery day – was almost in tears of relief, and ordered one of the men to carry Roz across the nullah.

We were now only a mile from Basal, and this snow bridge looked a fitting climax to the day. In two places the melting glacier had already caved in, and the pony-men had placed two planks of wood – specially carried for the purpose – across each five- or six-foot-wide crevasse. Standing on the verge, one looked down into the roaring water twelve feet below and, speaking for myself, I felt most unhappy to realise that at any moment – possibly the next moment – another wedge of glacier – possibly the wedge underfoot – would detach itself and collapse into the nullah. To add to the general feeling of insecurity the three ponies were thudding over the level snow between the crevasse and the bottom of the slope and I reflected that had they been trying they could have done no more to encourage its further disintegration.

However, the men's indifference to what I regarded as extreme peril calmed me down (I hadn't yet heard that six local men were recently drowned in a similar situation) and when Roz had been carried across the nullah I remained behind to give what help I could in persuading the ponies to venture over the planks. The unfortunate animals were lathering with fright and absolutely refusing to budge. Then I had a brainwave, which it took some time to put across in sign language, though it was simply a suggestion that if the rest of the party left the scene the three unnerved ponies might follow of their own accord. So I trotted across the boards firmly pretending that I was on O'Connell's Bridge and we all climbed the other side of the glacier to the road and made off briskly. Sure enough pathetic whinnies followed us and a moment later came the clatter of hoofs on boards and within five minutes the nervous ones had rejoined the party. This incident well illustrates the very low IQ of those men, who think that by cursing and kicking an already terrified horse they can influence him to do what he dreads. Of course they considered 'Begum Sahib' a genius for suggesting the obvious! In a way my device was cruel too – giving the poor creatures the impression that they were going to be abandoned on a glacier for ever – but at least it was short-term cruelty. The rest of this entry must wait till tomorrow as I'm too tired to finish it now.

BUTIKUNDI, 22 JUNE

To continue yesterday's entry: on leaving the narrow gorge with its snow-bridge we entered the head of the famous Kagan Valley – a very lovely sight in the light of the setting sun. Here the mountains all rise greenly to grey rock summits and on their gentle slopes graze buffalo, comically draped in heavy blankets, and huge herds of goats. Basal is what we'd call a 'townland', where the tribes-people camp during the summer when they bring up their herds, and the nearest hamlet is nineteen miles away. But there is a seasonal 'hotel' where the trans-Pass caravans stop. This consists of a tiny lean-to – not high enough for me to stand upright in – roughly built of boulders and roofed with pine-branches; there are only two walls so you can imagine the cold wind shrieking through at 14,000 feet! The proprietor, a young tribesman, sleeps outside in a goatskin tent and the fire is of dung, lit in a little hole in the ground. The fresh green leaves of a local weed carpet the floor and water comes from the young Kagan that rushes deafeningly by two yards away. I'll admit this accommodation doesn't sound luxurious, but after a day such as we'd all been through it seems positively Ritzy; it's only two miles from the top of the valley and I walked there with the pony-caravan.

On arrival we sat beside the tiny fire while tea was being made – me feeling so tired that I couldn't even attempt diary-writing. But after five tin mugs of Samson-strong tea (very sweet) I came back to life and wrote by oil-lamp for the two hours it took to cook our supper of lentils and bread. Dung is excellent fuel, just like good turf, but it's slow to cook enough for six ravenous people and the *chapattis* took what felt like weeks, each one being done separately on a flat piece of iron over the fire. (There are few bakeries in Pakistan and bread is usually made at home.) But I've been long enough in the East now to have forgotten how to feel impatient, so I enjoyed the cosy peace there in the heat while outside the blue sky faded to cold green and then was quickly black and filled with a glory of golden stars. Only the rush of the river and the deep breathing of the pony-men, who had all fallen asleep while waiting for food, broke the silence.

As we were eating, an extraordinary character came in – obviously a tribal chieftain of some sort as he was laden with gold ear-rings and bracelets and fabulous silver and stone necklaces and wore rings on every finger. He stood about six foot two in his bare feet and had the oldest face I've ever seen, yet was erect and vigorous. His long black hair and beard looked odd against the wrinkles and he had very sharp but kindly brown eyes and still excellent teeth. It goes without saying that he was filthy dirty and stank to high heaven – even more than the pony-men! He had evidently come to welcome them as the first over the pass this year and there was terrific salaaming and hand-shaking all round. On arrival he disregarded me completely but then he got used to the idea and became quite friendly. After he'd gone more strong tea completed the meal, which to me was the most wonderful I've ever eaten anywhere – despite the fact that I was sitting watching the bare-handed cook stoking the fire with dung in between kneading *chapattis.* Having taken turns puffing a post-prandial hookah the men went to sleep again and I continued writing till nearly midnight, when I curled up in my bedroll which was on hire for a shilling from the proprietor but seemed astonishingly free of inhabitants. I woke at 6.30 a.m. with an awful earache, as the cold had been intense all night and I couldn't sleep with my head covered because of the smell of the bedding. Also this evening I've a rotten sore throat and snuffles – inevitable after yesterday's wetting and freezing – but that's a small price to pay for the Babusar Pass.

We left Basal at 7.30 a.m. today, after tea and *paratis* fried in *fresh* ghee, and I took it easy, covering only the nineteen miles to this village. The Kagan Valley is so beautiful that one has to stop every hundred yards to sit and look. (Anyway, sitting and looking were about all I was good for today, as my back and shoulder muscles ache dreadfully from carrying Roz.) The Kagan River widens gradually and is a most beautiful shade of green as it races in the sunshine between great, grey boulders, bursting into violent cascades of white foam at intervals. For the first six or seven miles the road switched up and down green mountainsides and I had to cross three more glaciers (one tricky, two easy) and four rock falls brought down by the thaw. These presented difficulties as they were always at high points of the road overhanging ghastly drops. (One's 'head for heights' certainly improves in this area; six months ago I'd have shuddered even to think of cycling over loose rocks and slippery mud above such ravines.) I could see again the hoof-prints of the caravan, which had left Basal at 5 a.m., and the whole region was, by yesterday's standards, quite thickly populated with nomad herdspeople, though no dwellings were visible. I saw two magnificent eagles and the air was filled all day with lark-song. What a wonderful place this world is! Here was a valley of glorious beauty yet quite unique – different from the Ghorband or Gilgit or Indus Valleys – with its scintillating snow-peaks and regal fir trees, brilliant green meadows right up to the snowline and glistening glaciers in the gullies, waterfalls tumbling and sparkling everywhere and jewel-like wild flowers, rippling bird-songs and the faint, clean aroma of some unfamiliar herb.

We arrived here at 5 p.m. to find that some half-dozen wooden shacks make up the hamlet, plus a tea-house to cater for caravans. Coming round a bend I saw down below, in a deep hollow between the hills, the camel-caravan of fifty animals camped beside the tea-house and my pony-men busily loading up with their essentials. Then, as I came towards them, I noticed the fleecy coats and brightly-coloured turbans and marvellously-embroidered waistcoats of the cameleers – there was no doubt about *their* native land. I stopped the first one and said 'Afghanistan?' and he said 'Yes, Bulola,' and I shook hands vigorously and said 'Afghanistan very good and Bulola very good' (Bulola is the village next to Bamian), and he was as pleased by the meeting as I was, and we went off arms around shoulders, Afghan style, to have tea together. Then about fifteen other Afghans arrived and I told them where I'd been in Afghanistan and we performed the Afghan ritual of gravely admiring each other's guns and knives and they told me that I must time my return to Afghanistan to coincide with the King's birthday in October, when the national game of buzkashi is played at its best in Kabul. Again, as when coming into Afghanistan from Persia, I notice the remarkable superiority of these men in both mental and physical vigour, as compared to the peasants I've been with for the past weeks. It's possible to have quite a complicated conversation with the Afghans through signs and a few words of Pushto and English, they're so very quick on the uptake.

I'm now sitting outside one of their tents writing by firelight while supper is being cooked, having ridden with two of them to a hamlet up a tributary nullah to deliver cloth. The way was level grassland and never did I think horses could move so fast; it was a glorious sensation to gallop along the valley with the setting sun lighting up the snows ahead and my horse, having had nothing to do all day, going full stretch on the smooth turf. Fortunately I didn't want to stop him, as I don't believe I could have. I've been promised a trial ride on a camel in the morning.

NARAN, 23 JUNE

After an excellent supper of goat's meat grilled over a wood-fire, and lentils and bread, I slept soundly, rolled in snug sheepskins in a circle of Afghans around a fire which we kept up all night. I was wakened by the sun coming over the mountaintops on to our faces – such beauty to open one's eyes to! The soft, bright green of grass, the dark green of towering pines, the almost luminous green of the nearby river, the pale blue of the early sky and the pure white of glaciers between sharp, rocky peaks above smooth, sloping pastures. While the breakfast-water was boiling I was given my camel ride – very short and unsweet. (1) The camel knelt down. (2) I sat on the saddle. (3) The camel stood up. (4) The camel took one step. (5) I fell off. Fortunately this was exactly what the camel-owner had expected me to do and he caught me halfway to the ground. As these are the long-legged Arabian camels, seven to eight feet tall, this was a good thing. Actually the shorter, sturdier Bactrian variety are more common in Afghanistan itself. A camel saddle is a preposterous thing, like a wooden pouffe balanced on the hump; doubtless there are ways of *not* falling off, but my Pushto was unequal to following the owner's instructions.

After breakfast two men were going on another cloth-selling expedition to three tiny hamlets away up on the wooded slopes of a mountain and on invitation I accompanied them; we used mules for the very steep, rocky paths of the forest. Then I reluctantly left my friends at 12.15 p.m., having lunched off clover, bread and chicken; I tried to give them a present of cigarettes but of course they absolutely refused to accept it.

The weather pattern has been consistent during the past few days; it remains very sunny till about 12 p.m., then the sky quickly fills with clouds, the temperature drops and light showers freshen the air. It was delicious free-wheeling down-valley this afternoon with dense green trees all around and a grey sky overhead; except for the height of the mountains and the fury of the river, I might have been at home.

There was an amusing interlude today when I turned a corner of the track and saw a party of four unmistakably English people walking towards me. My astonishment was considerable, yet it was as nothing compared with theirs when they beheld a tattered and battered European female advancing with a bicycle from the northern wilds. Even English reserve could not withstand the shock, so they stopped to unravel the mystery and then told me that they came from Delhi and were camping on the banks of the Kagan. They thoughtfully suggested that I should stop off at their camp and ask the servants to feed me, and Mrs Haddow invited me to stay with them when I arrive in Delhi and gave me their address and telephone number on the spot. The farther one travels the more one becomes aware of the extraordinary wealth of generosity and kindness that exists in the world.

After ten miles I reached this village, to which a jeep penetrates twice weekly, and was sadly back in civilisation – if one may so describe twenty wooden huts plus a PWD rest-house with no mod cons whatever. I hadn't intended stopping here but the road was blocked by a landslide miles farther on, leaving no alternative. Naran is one of Pakistan's most famous fishing centres so enthusiasts brave what they consider the horrors of the rest-house for sport's sake, and this week a delightful Karachi family are staying here – husband, wife and five children. In conversation with them this evening I again noticed what is to me a most puzzling feature of Pakistani life. Here was a man educated, intelligent and widely-read far above the average, yet he was a travelling salesman; it's extraordinary that someone of such talent should be so wasted in a country where trained brains are at a premium.

KAGAN, 24 JUNE

The Karachi family and I started off for the 'Blue Lake' at 9 a.m. and got there at 11 a.m. after a glorious climb. (There is a jeepable road but that's miles longer.) This lake seems to be a volcanic crater, a mile wide and long, and it reflects all the snow-covered peaks that surround it on three sides. There was a cloudless blue sky above the green water when we arrived so the reflections were perfect. The surrounding glaciers are now melting but remain firm enough to be quite safe for walking so we went right round the shore; then a little breeze got up and a few clouds appeared and the beauty of the water colouring was beyond words. Just as we were leaving at 1 p.m. a party of young forestry students arrived with gallons of tea in flasks – very welcome – and I spent an hour talking with them and being photographed as one of the 'strange sights' they had encountered on their excursion. (If you could see me by this stage you'd appreciate the subtle humour of that description.)

I rejoined Roz at 4.30 after a late lunch of bread and hard-boiled eggs. It's a pity the 'reward' of free-wheeling down this valley is being marred by the temperature rising every mile. But each day different beauties surround me – I've never seen such tiny butterflies as today. They look like wild flowers taken to the wing, they're so fragile and delicately coloured.

I met another Afghan camel-caravan this evening and am staying with them tonight. It's wonderful how hospitable these people are; they saw me passing and signed to me to stop and have bread and tea with them. (They bring their own flour and make much nicer bread than the locals and drinking their green tea out of the familiar little Jap-made bowls was a pleasant change from the local brew, which is exactly as we have it in Ireland – strong and milky.) They're all delighted about the border with Pakistan being open again and are full of praise for His Imperial Majesty of Iran!

KAWAI, 25 JUNE

The Afghans and I swopped household hints last night: I told them that thyme added to their goat or chicken stew would taste delicious and they told me that the bark of the walnut tree, slightly moistened and used after every meal, was better than any toothbrush and paste. It seems extraordinary that they have never used wild thyme in cooking – they loved it in last night's stew, and I loved the walnut bark, which makes the gums tingle and leaves the teeth brilliantly white. I've been wondering for months how these people have such incredibly good teeth and this must be the explanation. No matter how filthy they may be otherwise, they are most meticulous about scouring their teeth immediately after eating.

We left Kagan at 6.30 a.m. and found the road so blocked by migrant traffic, moving up the valley to summer pastures, that it took us three hours to cover six miles. The road was all downhill, but cycling remained out of the question – one simply pushed and edged one's way through dense masses of buffaloes, cows, camels, horses, mules, donkeys, jennets, goats, sheep, kids, lambs, men, women and children. Of course, every day since crossing the Top I've been meeting these caravans, but today the migration was in full swing. Fortunately all the animals are blasé, widely-travelled creatures who take Roz in their stride. It was difficult for me, and dangerous for the riders, when a bicycle appeared suddenly in those parts where machines are almost unknown, causing horses and mules to shy and buck on the verges of precipices. (Today, *I* almost shied and went over a precipice when I saw my first machine – a jeep – since leaving Chilas a week ago!)

Recently, the government, who want to plant the high pastures with young trees, proposed to the Kochis that they should settle permanently on land in the Punjab, given to them by the State: but the tribes were so devastated by the idea that President Ayub ordered it to be dropped. For at least 3,000 years, and probably longer, these people's ancestors have been on this trek – up every June, down every October – and any other way of life would be as inhuman as caging a tiger. Actually they are quite well off by Pakistani standards, with their own meat, eggs, milk and butter, and clothing from their sheep and goats. To acquire supplies of flour, tea, sugar and salt they barter their superfluous animals. An incredible amount of silver jewellery is worn by the girls, from two years old and upwards, and by the women; some of it is very ancient and all of it is beautiful. On these long treks tiny babies are carried concealed in cloths on their mothers' backs, toddlers ride on their fathers' shoulders or on one of the animals and everything above the age of four walks sturdily, like a good Kochi. Often little girls carry top-heavy loads of pots, pans and miscellaneous household goods on their heads and sometimes little boys are in sole charge of a flock of thirty or forty animals. New-born or delicate foals or calves (except camel calves who can apparently cope with life right from scratch) are tied to some animal, other than their mother, or are carried on the men's shoulders. Puppies, hens and chickens go on the buffaloes' backs; when there's a halt one sees the fowls flying down and scratching and pecking while the humans make tea and the animals eat their fodder, and then when the signal is given to start again they fly back to their moving roosts. Each kind of animal wears a different-sounding bell and the result is quite symphonic.

It was much hotter today – uncomfortably so at midday, though it's pleasant again now. I'm stopping tonight at a *very* civilised rest-house, which just stops short of having a bathroom!

BACH, 26 JUNE

We're back to Hell today, yet we are still 4,000 feet up, so what will the true plains feel like . . . This afternoon I sadly said goodbye to the Kagan, which I had seen born from out of that high and beautiful lake; it is difficult to believe that this wide brown flow is the very same river we crossed by snow-bridge. It's quite an experience to follow a river for so long, right from the source, and to see it grow every day.

Twelve miles from Babbacot I joined the Muzzafarabad-Abbottabad road which I last cycled along exactly four weeks ago today. What a change! The countryside, then so green and lovely, is now burned brown and bone dry – you could almost hear it gasping for rain. I slept for two hours in the pine-forest but was afraid to smoke there in case the slightest spark would get amongst the tinder. I'm staying tonight at the American Presbyterian Mission Hospital here with a kindly missioner and his wife.

ABBOTTABAD, 27 JUNE

At last I'm really back to civilisation. It took me nearly two hours in the bathroom to get looking like an ordinary citizen instead of a tribeswoman, and my hostess very firmly took my shirt and pants and put them into the incinerator; they were long past being restored to cleanliness by any means known to mankind. I was dressed in Pakistani costume after the bath and then went off to the bazaar to get shorts tailored; I've suffered much in the effort not to offend Muslims but the heat is now so extreme that they'll just have to endure me in shorts. I got two yards of best khaki for 5*s*. and took them to a tailor at 6 p.m. At 9.30 p.m. the expertly-tailored garment was delivered to me here and the total cost was 10*s*. Of course I'd have looked like a vulgar picture postcard if I'd worn shorts a month ago, but having lost sixteen pounds in the last four weeks I'm relatively elegant just now.

At last the monsoon seems to be breaking here. I saw my first electric storm this evening and it was a sight of such beauty that I couldn't take my eyes off the sky for a moment. Then the rain came so forcefully that no one who hasn't witnessed such a spectacle could imagine it; yet they tell me that this is only a curtain-raiser, not the real thing! Roz has gone to hospital for a new mudguard and a brakes check; the latter were almost useless today after the fearful strain of the past weeks.

14

Running Repairs

ABBOTTABAD TO LAHORE

ABBOTTABAD, 28 JUNE

I'm staying here with the family who entertained me on my previous visit to this town. As you may remember, Farhat – one of my hostess's sisters – is a doctor, which has proved fortunate since I woke with dysentery at 2 a.m. and have spent half the day lying on my bed feeling pathetic and the other half on the hop. I'm not surprised – nor is anyone else – by this development. The recent combination of filthy food and flies and heat-stroke and over-exertion was bound to do some damage somewhere; I can only thank God that I didn't collapse until I got to this delightful family, each of whom is kindness personified and all of whom had the good sense to leave me alone today to cope with my misery in a private suite in their guest-wing.

My host is one of the wealthiest men in the area, and today I'm shamelessly revelling in the luxury of his new, palatial home on the outskirts of the town. Always, of course, there is the formidable ethical problem of such wealth as this co-existing with the poverty I've shared during these past weeks – a problem which lies at the back of one's mind and occasionally stirs uneasily. But ten years ago it would have stirred more often and more vigorously; by now it seems to me that prosperity as the West knows it today and poverty on an Eastern scale are equally harmful to the soul of Man.

This morning Farhat starkly prescribed 'starvation and sulphaguanidine tablets'. This prescription has been so successful that now my insides seem to be reintegrated and I look with disfavour on the starvation clause, having had too much of that medicine lately. But obviously Farhat knows best and I'm resigned to a plate of curds for dinner.

Today I've been reflecting on the benefits bestowed by the social anonymity of a traveller 'in the wilds'. To the peasants and tribesmen here one is merely a human being – outwardly strange but fundamentally one of them – and their spontaneous acceptance and hospitality is extended with an air of full and unselfconscious equality. In contrast, how deep is the gulf between groups of human beings in our society – go into a pub in Connemara or a café in rural Italy or even a posada in the remotest part of relatively unspoiled Spain and you find it impossible to establish the same easy *rapport*. You are at once noted as a non-peasant and are therefore someone to be envied, or admired, or despised, or kept aloof from, as individual temperaments dictate. Probably you will be treated most kindly by the peasants there, but at the deepest level you are automatically isolated because you have (they imagine) more money or more education or 'better' manners than they have. So I appreciate the chance to share the people's lives here for a time without regarding myself, or being regarded by them, as an intruder. Yet I also appreciate coming back to converse among friends who are on my own wavelength.

ABBOTTABAD, 29 JUNE

Today I wandered around the town in the sedate manner befitting my convalescent condition. In fact I felt as weak as a kitten and was good for nothing but sitting and talking, which I did at length with the Irish priests who run a big boys' college here, with the Irish nurse who has recently come out to the college as matron and who very kindly presented me with a pair of sunglasses to replace those lost crossing Babusar, and with a delightful Belfast Protestant missionary and her team of assistants, who fed me judiciously at lunchtime.

The sky was cloudless again today, after the monsoon's false start, but the air has been cooled and freshened by that storm and when I returned here at 6 p.m. we spent a very pleasant couple of hours sitting on the lawn drinking iced fruit-juices.

For this family the purdah system is in a state of flux. My hostess and her three sisters – all young women – observe it in Abbottabad, yet Farhat, who has spent some years in England, where she was accompanied by her youngest sister, obviously leads a European existence when practising her profession in Lahore. The second youngest sister is also married and lives in Mansehra, where I called to see her on my way to Bach the other day. Her husband is Assistant Commissioner there and she has a very congenial lot of in-laws with whom I spent a delightful afternoon, though I had no time to record my visit in the diary that night. The young couple joined us this evening for dinner and, observing them together, I was struck yet again by the high proportion of what are clearly happy marriages resulting from the Muslim tradition of arranged matches.

To me this has been the aspect of Eastern social life most difficult to understand – though one could argue that in a diluted form the custom was, until recently, prevalent in our own society. But since contemporary Western women expect freedom to choose their own husbands, it has taken me a long time to begin to understand the Muslim women's point of view. I have had prolonged discussions on this subject with a number of educated Muslims. The arguments which they put forward have not been entirely convincing, but the harmonious atmosphere that I have experienced in so many Muslim homes leads me to believe that their arranged marriages are just as likely to succeed as what they refer to, with faint undertones of curiosity and disapproval, as 'love marriages'.

The Muslim argument in favour of their system is simple. I've asked several women (wording my query as tactfully as possible) if they didn't feel deprived of a natural and inalienable right when someone else made for them what is the most important decision in most women's lives. To this they replied, 'No. It is our business to choose partners for our children, not for ourselves.' And each of them went on to explain, in her own way, that she considered youths and girls singularly ill-equipped to take the serious responsibility of selecting a life-partner. On the other hand parents know what's needed to make a marriage tick and continue ticking and they also know their own children – possibly better than the children know themselves at the ages of sixteen or twenty. Therefore, four parents in frank consultation are likely to arrange a more lastingly satisfactory match than two hot-blooded young things who can't see the trees for the sex. The arrangements concentrate on temperamental, social and financial suitability and leave the sexual aspect to sort itself out afterwards, with the cheerful assumption that all else being equal two healthy youngsters could hardly fail to enjoy each other physically. Indeed, the majority of women with whom I spoke on the subject assured me that the pattern of their marriages had been a steady growth of love and understanding on both sides. Personally, I can't help feeling that they miss the best of life's adventures by not falling haphazardly in love after the manner of us decadent infidels; but I do now understand the psychological mechanism of their system and can see its advantages.

I also discussed this question with a number of men here, who were emphatic that as youths they would have been terrified of the responsibility of choosing a wife; this unnatural (to us) attitude underlines the extent to which our mental and emotional processes are conditioned by our environment. Yet among a certain category of men – those who have now been educated beyond the average level of their particular social class – there is a new threat to domestic bliss. In the upper class boys and girls receive comparable educations, and intellectual affinity is therefore easily assured; but those less fortunate men, who may be the only literate members of their families, often find themselves married to women who bore them as companions because of their abruptly widened mental horizons. I've met quite a few of these victims of progress, who are usually employed as petty officials in small towns where there is an almost total lack of educated society. Inevitably they seize with tragic eagerness on the opportunity to talk to foreigners, and I sometimes wonder if, despite their inherent intelligence, they wouldn't have been happier left on an educational par with their kinsmen and neighbours. Mental loneliness is a painful thing and it seems cruel for the State to open a door invitingly and then shut it in a man's face by stationing him in a remote area. Someone, of course, has to fill those posts, but surely a man with a longer tradition of education and therefore more inward resources would fit them better than a poor devil who has simply had his appetite for learning whetted by a few student years on a scholarship.

A conspicuous feature of conversation with English-speaking Muslim men is the unabashed candour of their approach to sexual matters. This sounds as though I've been having a gay time talking pornography with a series of frustrated would-be lovers, and if one wanted to be frightfully Freudian it could be said that their penchant for talking sex with European women is a sublimation of their religion-fettered libidos. Yet none of these conversations was intended as a prelude to seduction and the odd thing is that what in a Western context might be regarded as embarrassing, if not slightly shocking subjects for discussion with a male acquaintance, are here rendered comfortably clinical by the matter-of-fact manner in which they are discussed. I find this extremely interesting. For all our Amorality or New Morality or whatever one likes to call it, we Westerners are still too dogged by Puritan obsessions to be able to call a spade a spade without inwardly pausing for everyone else inwardly to recover from the shock, which makes us look slightly immature in this respect compared with Muslims.

I'm reminded now of an incident at a dinner-party in Afghanistan where I was the only woman present; for diplomatic reasons the incident was omitted from the relevant Diary-entry and it has only now recurred to me. I was sitting in the place of honour, assimilating the pilau course and doing no harm to anyone, when the fellow-guest on my right suddenly turned to me and asked in too-good English, 'Did you ever see a man naked?' Perhaps there's a stock answer to that one but I didn't know it, and the best I could do, from amidst a mouthful of rice, was to say airily, 'Of course, Greek statues and all that.' Thereafter my neighbour could be observed silently turning over in his mind the unlimited interpretations of 'all that'. But his was an exceptional approach – though one I wouldn't have missed, however unnerving his query at the time. It certainly is a curious experience to be a woman travelling alone in Muslim countries. Most of one's time is spent in the company of men only, being treated with the respect due to a woman, but being talked to man-to-man, so that in the end one begins to feel somewhat hermaphroditic.

It's now 1.40 a.m. and for the past five minutes I've been sitting with the light off watching the weird beauty of another electric storm – a spectacle that must surely have inspired much folklore in these countries. I find it eerie enough myself and could almost believe that some demon-god is regulating the display, as vast sheets of quivering blue fill the eastern sky. Even now, with my reading lamp on again, that pallid illumination is perceptible in the room.

RAWALPINDI, 30 JUNE

This morning Farhat laid down the law on the subject of me and cycling and dysentery and heat-stroke. Her lecture ended with instructions to come here by bus and go on to Lahore by train. She herself is returning today, by air, to her hospital in Lahore and I've been invited to stop there. She will then give me another check-up and pronounce on my subsequent activities. Once upon a time I would have violently resented this situation but at the moment there's nothing I want to do less than cycle to Lahore. Thus are the mighty fallen!

The journey here seemed acutely prosaic when compared with Afghan bus expeditions. A healthy vehicle containing its legal quota of passengers left Abbottabad punctually and proceeded in an orderly fashion, arriving punctually in Pindi at 4 p.m. I was travelling along this route for the third time, and as I looked forward to the pleasure of staying with Major-General Ghawas' family, and of again meeting the Aurang Zebs, who are now down from Swat, I realised that I no longer feel like a visitor to Pakistan but like an adopted citizen. Everywhere I've made good friends, and this country, of all those so far travelled through, has become a true home from home.

Beside me in the bus sat a jubilant young man returning to his village to celebrate the birth of his first son. He told me that two perfect goat kids, of uniform colour and without blemish, would be sacrificed as part of the celebrations and their meat given to the poor of the village. (It's only one kid for a girl.) I asked him how many children he would like to have and he sighed and said not more than four but it was going to be very difficult as he and his wife were both under twenty and Allah didn't approve of contraceptives. At each stop he insisted on buying me an iced fizzy-drink – I never thought the day would dawn when I'd avidly gulp such a vile potation; temperatures of 109° in the shade have unexpected side-effects.

I received a tremendous 'welcome-back' from my friends here, and was delighted to find Colonel Shah, whom I'd already met at Peshawar, Bagdada and Swat, among those present. The evening passed in the usual way – sitting on the lawn within reach of mobile electric fans, sipping fruit-juices and talking. Social life here emphasises how nearly we Westerners have lost the art of conversation. Instead of switching on the 'telly' or dashing out to a show, how pleasant it is to sit and talk quietly about the books one has read or the people one has met or the places one has seen. And surely the individual exchange of ideas with our fellow-men is more worthwhile than mute dependence on what someone else's brain has devised for our entertainment.

The grafting of British military traditions on to the Pathan way of life has been more fortunate than most such experiments; possibly because both traditions have a certain affinity to begin with. Certainly the Pakistani army officers I've met are without exception the finest type one could be privileged to know; they seem to have evolved a code embracing the best of the two worlds which moulded them. It will be interesting to see whether this code is durable enough to be transmitted successfully to the next generation.

RAWALPINDI, 1 JULY

This morning Naseem telephoned and invited me to the President's House – where she and Aurang Zeb stay on their visits to Pindi – for dinner this evening. In honour of the occasion I then took myself off to the city's leading hairdresser and spent 5*s.* instead of the usual 1*s.* 6*d.* on a devastating hair-cut which has so transformed me that I get a shock every time I pass a mirror. Next my hostess and her three daughters passed what was for them a most enjoyable afternoon, equipping me with clothes appropriate to the Presidential Presence. Admittedly my wardrobe is unequal to that demand; at the time of writing it comprises Aurang Zeb's cast-off army slacks, my new shorts and two khaki shirts. Drastic measures were undoubtedly called for, but as Begum Ghawas and her daughters came up with garment after garment I began to wonder if they need be *quite* so drastic . . . Yet the end product was worth it all – you wouldn't have recognised me! In fact the President's household is the essence of simplicity as I knew from a previous visit, but the family's pleasure on seeing me in their national costume made the afternoon's sartorial marathon seem well worth while.

President Ayub doesn't live on the grand scale of the wealthiest Pakistanis; his domestic surroundings are more like those of the average army officer, with a comfortable but plainly furnished home where good, but not exotic, food is served. The man himself impressed me as being shrewd, honest, kind, and above all, utterly sincere. However, like many strong characters who are fighting a non-stop battle against widespread evils, he possesses a steely quality which doesn't make for easy approachability and since I'm unaccustomed to consorting with Heads of States I was myself rather more tongue-tied than usual this evening.

RAWALPINDI, 2 JULY

After breakfast Aurang Zeb called and took me to a most interesting debate of the National Assembly where I was promoted from the Distinguished Strangers' Gallery to solitary glory in the President's Box! Again I was impressed by the complete freedom of speech in the Assembly. Members may criticise as bluntly as they wish the régime in general and President Ayub in particular, and many members today were doing just that. I should think that a student of politics would be fascinated by the political scene here, which shows democracy at the crawling stage, before it has found its feet and begun to toddle.

Looking around the Assembly (which included four women members) I was struck by the complexities of trying to run a country like Pakistan as a united nation. The members ranged from near-communists through liberal Muslims to fanatically orthodox Mullahs; from white-skinned Pathans through brown-skinned Punjabis to almost black-skinned Bengalis; from wealthy hereditary princes like

Aurang Zeb through moderately well-off professional men to destitute representatives of the city slums; from men who spoke flawless Oxford English through men whose grammar and pronunciation were questionable to men who could only speak pidgin-English. And in the restaurant at the 11 a.m. interval the air was chaotic with Pushto, Urdu, Bengali, Punjabi and English, while the members (clad as variously as they spoke) sat arguing over their tea or coffee. Theoretically the unifying element here should be Islam but Pakistan's years of exposure to Western influence have brought her religion to a crisis of re-interpretation, so that it tends to disrupt at least as much as it unites, while individual citizens battle to adapt it to what they believe is best for the country, or to defend it from any change.

After so many hours in the blissful coolness of the new air-conditioned Assembly building it was quite nightmarish to step out into 108° in the shade at 1.30 p.m. Aurang Zeb took me back to the President's House where Naseem, he and I lunched together and where I had my two-hour siesta before being driven off in an air-conditioned state Chevrolet to meet an Indian journalist with whom I had an appointment. Poor Roz! I have to admit that air-conditioned Chevrolets are more suitable in present temperatures.

This Kashmir deadlock is a heart-breaking muddle and somehow all such muddles are made more muddled nowadays by the politicians' new weapon of mass-communication, which doesn't give international sores a chance to heal up but keeps re-infecting them. The Indian journalist to whom I talked this afternoon was a perfect example of just how terrifyingly irresponsible journalists can be when they want to give their public only what it wishes to read – or what its rulers wish it to read – and when objective truth is therefore utterly disregarded. Of course a certain section of the Pakistani press and radio uses exactly the same tactics of distortion and deception against India.

I had dinner with the Shahid Hamids, where the Aurang Zebs were fellow-guests. It was an enjoyable evening, but all the time I felt sad underneath, because tomorrow I leave Pindi and in a few days I leave Pakistan. At midnight the Aurang Zebs drove me home and I said *au revoir* (I hope) to the best friends I have made en route.

LAHORE, 3 JULY

What a name for a city! I'm staying in Farhat's rooms in the Lady Willingdon Hospital, which is beside the busy red-light district so I now know it only needs an 's' to make it true.

The Pakistani Railways must be a charitable organisation: they took Roz and me the 170 miles from Pindi in five hours for *3s. 6d.* The third-class carriage was quite comfortable, with fans and very nice fellow-travellers who, as usual, insisted on buying me so many Pepsis that I almost blew up. They also wanted to feed me the atrocious little tid-bits which are fried and sold on every platform; a fortnight ago in Gilgit I'd have given all I possessed for one of them but today my stomach somersaulted at the very sight of those greasy balls. So then they pressed me to have some of the fly-blown sweetmeats which are also hawked at each stop, and when I persisted in refusing they looked quite hurt, and one of them went off and bought me a roast chicken, to my great embarrassment. I tried to explain that I wasn't being upstage and 'memsahibish' about their sort of food, which I normally consume *ad lib.*, and that it was merely a question of my insides not being as democratic as my principles. But no one spoke English very well so the intricacies of the situation escaped them and they simply nodded and smiled and told me that the chicken was very good and sat happily watching me unhappily eating what they wouldn't dream of affording for themselves.

With every mile we travelled south the temperature rose, the flies multiplied, the dust thickened in the air and the flat landscape became more arid. We arrived here at 3 p.m., the most intolerable hour of the day, and my first impression was of a depressing dump of a city, all stinks and stenches and not to be compared with either Peshawar or Pindi. In fact Lahore is by far the most interesting of the three from architectural and historical points of view, but at the moment I'm a bit past being interested in the Higher Things of Life: I simply registered that it was even hotter than Pindi. The only thing that cheered me up, en route from the station to the hospital, was the phraseology of a young man who told me I'd find the hospital 'on the backside of the mosque'! When I did find it Farhat gave me a real Pathan welcome, but it was of necessity brief, since the staffs of these hospitals are grossly overworked. I then went to sleep until 8 p.m. – sleep being the only effective escape from this degree of heat.

LAHORE, 4 JULY

A deliciously fat mail, collected this morning, has put me in such good humour that Farhat thinks I must be getting used to the heat. On my way through the centre of the city I passed an RAC signpost saying, 'LONDON, 6,372 MILES'; it's nice to know the exact position! I'd resolved last night to be a good little tourist today and see some of the things one ought to see here, but after a ten-mile cycle to collect the mail I only wanted to lie on my charpoy under a fan, drinking *lassee* and reading and rereading my letters. It was too hot for me even to start replies; sweat ran profusely into my eyes when I sat up and dripped merrily on to the writing pad.

Then, at about 9 p.m., Farhat roused me from my not unpleasant lethargy by offering to take me to the operating theatre, where she was about to do a Caesarean. It was a most interesting spectacle and I was tremendously impressed by the cool efficiency of her team of assistants, all recently-emancipated young women in their early twenties. (Male gynaecologists are obviously not popular in the Muslim world.) Usually only spinal anaesthetics are given here as Pakistan can't afford anything else in her public hospitals; but the skill of people like Farhat more than makes up for the shortage of drugs and modern equipment. Watching the performance I even forgot the heat – though it was intensified by my mask and gown – and when at last a little black head appeared and the baby was hauled out I felt like cheering. He was a fine healthy son who roared like a lion after one look at this world – a reaction which in the present temperature I find quite understandable.

15

Out of the Saddle

LAHORE TO DELHI

BEAS, INDIA, 5 JULY

I suppose that when one has left Ireland to cycle to India the day on which one eventually cycles across that final frontier qualifies for Red Letters. Yet this evening I'm aware of no sense of triumph, elation, excitement or anything other than loneliness for Pakistan – though you may remember that on crossing the Khyber Pass I was too stricken by the parting with Afghanistan to feel any enthusiasm for Pakistan! Now it remains to be seen if a few months in India will have a similar effect; somehow I already doubt that.

Last night Farhat pronounced me fit to cycle again, providing I never cycle between 9 a.m. and 6 p.m., never cycle too far in one day, eat masses of salt and eschew too curried curries. So this morning we set off at 4.10 a.m. to reach Amritsar before the 'medical curfew'. Already it was bright and the sweepers were busy on the streets and lots of cyclists were buzzing around, although many lazy-bones still lay fast asleep on charpoys lining the pavements; it's odd to see half the population of a city sleeping in public. By 4.45 a.m. I was passing through the cantonment area where athletes were vigorously practising cricket, tennis and volleyball. Lahore is such a huge city that it took me an hour's fast cycling to get clear of it and we didn't reach the border until 6.15 a.m. Here there were virtually no formalities to be gone through, yet it was 7.30 before I'd finished drinking the inevitable tea and talking to three delightful Customs officers about my happy days in their country. Then I plucked up courage to go, and said my last *Salaam Alaikum* (God go with you); it will be too bad if I forget myself and use that greeting on this side! I'm trying hard not to be biased, but it's the objective truth that my reception at the Indian Customs post, though very polite, was markedly cold and formal. After the warmth and apparent joy with which strangers are welcomed at every Muslim Customs post I've passed, this one left me feeling slightly forlorn.

The Punjab is the most boring terrain I've ever cycled through. My only diversion today was the bird-life; a fascinating selection of beautiful unknowns were to be seen in every direction. On crossing the frontier, the two most obvious changes are the number of women in evidence and the comparative nudity of the men. Your average Muslim wouldn't dream of showing a knee, so it was quite startling to find myself suddenly surrounded by hundreds of loin-clothed bodies.

Some ten miles from the border I stopped for a cigarette and began to learn the ABC of travelling in India. I was sitting under a tree full of tailor-birds' nests, watching waterfowl fishing in a stagnant pond, when a Hindu peasant came walking along the road carrying two brass jars of milk balanced on his shoulders. I smiled and said '*Nemuste*', but instead of returning my greeting and passing on his way *à la* Muslim, he put down his gallons, came and sat beside me and tried to squeeze my arm while making what were obviously (even in Punjabi) improper suggestions. Knowing he couldn't understand English, I said what I felt – 'Go to hell'. So he went; not to hell, but off down the road. The motto seems to be that one curbs one's natural mateyness and refrains from greeting stray Hindus – which does not make life any more pleasant. Happily, this is the Sikh State, so I have them as buffers while I readjust; many Europeans and almost all Muslims distrust the Sikhs intensely on various counts and have warned me to beware of them but so far I find them very helpful, courteous and friendly.

Amritsar, twenty-three miles from the border, is the chief city of 'Sikhdom', but because of the heat I didn't stop to explore it; on my return in the cooler weather I hope to do my duty by the Golden Temple. About three miles beyond Amritsar I was settling down to have my siesta under a wayside tree when suddenly a dust-storm began. This sounds dire but it was in fact an enormous relief, because the gale-force wind was northerly and almost cool. Taking advantage of it I pedalled on through stinging whirls of dust that reduced visibility to about twenty yards, but even this seemed a cheap price to pay for the sudden drop in the temperature. Because of the wind we covered eighty-nine miles today, reaching this little village where I'm staying with the family of the local Sikh Superintendent of the Punjab Armed Police.

Sikh boy-children and adolescents are a trifle disconcerting; a religious rule against cutting hair means that their long locks, often tied in top-knots with coloured ribbons, give the impression that the country is populated almost exclusively by girls. The good looks of the race are quite astonishing, yet somehow not altogether pleasing. Unlike the proudly handsome Afghans, whose features are made additionally impressive by the spirit within, Sikh good looks are of a conventional, rather film-star type; they are reported to have the most regrettable effects on some Western women but I can't see the remains of my virtue being undermined here! Yet they are a fine race of people, tall and well-built, in complete contrast to their weedy, vegetarian Hindu neighbours. Also, of course, they are very astute businessmen and very unscrupulous money-lenders. One of their racial characteristics is a streak of mechanical genius; I'm told that most Indian bus and truck drivers in every state are Sikhs.

So far I haven't noticed any of the dire poverty one expects in India; but then the Punjab is the country's most prosperous state – partly because of its natural resources and partly because Sikhs are in general more on the ball than Hindus. An FAO official I met today told me that their work in the Punjab is much more productive than elsewhere in India because of greater and more intelligent co-operation from the locals.

However, if the poverty of India has not yet hit me the smells of India certainly have; one of these days I'll lose my grip on the situation and be forced off Roz to vomit by the wayside. Maybe that's one reason why I've lost my appetite so completely; even after today's cycle I couldn't look at food this evening though I haven't had a bite since 4 a.m. I just drink, drink, drink – *lassee* and salt and lemon and salt and tea and salt and mango-juice and sugar – glass after glass after glass.

SIRHIND, 6 JULY

We only covered fifty-eight miles today but even that nearly killed me. At 11 a.m. I took refuge in a dak bungalow for tea and a siesta and while the tea was being made I lay on the sitting-room floor under the fan and went to sleep. A few minutes later a piercing scream wakened me: the *chowkidar*'s wife had come in and, not being used to the spectacle of Europeans slumbering on floors, had decided that I was a corpse! Actually she wasn't very far wrong; this sun acts like a sleeping-drug on me and today I felt as if I'd had an overdose. You don't realise how exhausting it is while cycling on a level road but when you stop the yawning begins and you just want to lie down where you are and go into a coma.

Really, this Punjab is the most dire thing that ever happened. The landscape is flatter than Belgium, even more overpopulated and enlivened only by thousands of cattle, the majority at a most gruesome stage of emaciation. I feel as I did during the myxomatosis epidemic at home, when I carried a hammer around in my saddlebag and killed rabbits by the score every week; but it would hardly be politic to go along on Indian roads shooting cattle. I'm all for coming to terms with other people's religious angles yet it's exceedingly difficult to have patience with this cow worship; one has to see it in action to appreciate its full brutality and stupidity. But I suppose what we describe as the Hindus' cruelty should more properly be called 'insensitivity to physical suffering', and should not be regarded as an absolute yardstick by which to measure their national character. Hindu philosophy makes no discernible attempt to achieve that natural balance between the spiritual and the material which we consciously or unconsciously inherit as part of our traditional ethic, and to a people nurtured on such a philosophy the physical sufferings of both men and animals are of far less importance than they are to us. What interests me – although such a speculation may seem naïve to the learned – is whether the Hindu chicken or the apathetic egg comes first. In other words, did Hinduism encourage a resigned acceptance of material privations of every kind because some opiate had to be given to the relevant masses, or did these masses cease to strive for a reasonable degree of material well-being because Hinduism represented it as unworthy of Man's endeavour – or, in the case of the Untouchables, as a categorical impossibility? This brings us to the caste system, of which I've obviously had no experience yet, beyond a few brief discussions. These give me the impression that the sheer impracticability of upholding it in a modern city is destroying it throughout urban societies but that it still flourishes in rural communities, though possibly in a less virulent form than previously.

Then – to continue my jaundiced list of Punjabi abominations – there's the food . . . Curries are one thing but the local messes, that taste entirely of chillies, are quite another. And they even put the dratted stuff in your lemon-drink if you don't watch it – for alleged medicinal reasons. (Of course this also applies in the Pakistani Punjab, where unfortunate Pathan immigrants, like Farhat, simply can't touch the regional dishes and have to prepare their own food.) I find it quite impossible to swallow the average meal here – though today I was ravenous and tried hard – because of the acute burning pain in my mouth and throat, however much cold water I drink between swallows. Looking at it the other way round I pity the unfortunate Indian immigrants in Europe or America, who find our food not only tasteless but positively nauseating.

The little towns and villages along my route today were just smelly conglomerations of mongrel buildings – neither Eastern nor Western – inhabited by people who were on the whole unfriendly, unhelpful and of an unintelligence surpassing even that of the Persians. However, their unfriendliness has nothing to do with me being mistaken for a British traveller; already I've observed the almost total lack of anti-British feeling, which I surmise is not unconnected with their religious teaching. Several times already I've been assured that the average Indian harbours no resentment towards Britain for two reasons, which together strike a faintly comic note. The first reason is that Britain has done so much good for India and the second reason is that their religion inculcates the suppression of resentment. (I'll leave you to sort that one out for yourselves.) As an Irishwoman, I find myself having a curiously mixed reaction to this magnanimity. On the one hand I admire it and admit we could do with a bit more of it in Ireland, but on the other hand, being of good rebel stock and *not* a Hindu, I tend to despise it, having the strong conviction that no amount of good done to a country by a conqueror can quite compensate for the loss of national freedom and the dignity that goes with it. Yet in India's case it is a very moot point whether either freedom or dignity existed throughout the subcontinent in the centuries immediately preceding the British epoch. Incidentally, on almost every occasion yesterday and today when an Indian asked my nationality and I replied 'Irish', the response was, 'Ah! de Valera's country. He is a great man!' Whereupon I grinned all over my face and said, 'Yes indeed – a very great man.' It's nice to know that on at least one point I'm going to be in harmony with the majority of Indians! It's also nice to be in a country where the word Ireland conveys something; in most places en route it was impossible to convince the average citizen that Ireland was not my mispronunciation of either Iceland or Holland. And the occasional erudite individual who had heard of it usually remarked brightly, 'Ah, yes, part of Britain', which was infinitely worse than being a mispronunciation of Holland! I've had great fun at various points along the line speaking sentences in Irish for the delectation of the locals, and my passport has been scrutinised more often as a sample of Irish script than as an official document. Which reminds me of a philologically fascinating item I acquired a few hours ago: counting up to ten in Hindi is so like counting up to ten in Irish that even I mastered it in less than three minutes!

Ever since crossing the border our way has been lined by ruined mosques, burned and bombarded in many cases and providing a terrible monument to the berserk savagery which prevailed in this area at the time of Partition. Many of their walls are now derisively plastered with crudely sexy film advertisements that no Muslim country would allow inside its frontiers. Others of these once beautiful buildings have been converted into stables or cafés or, if small, into private dwellings; it reminds one of the fate of some Russian churches. All over this region I've been conscious again of the helpless anger evoked while cycling through the First World War battlefields of Northern France, where the aura of the futile wastage of human life has not yet been dissipated by time.

Having slept today from 12 p.m. to 5 p.m. I now feel inconveniently alert at 12 a.m.! Obviously the thing to do from now on is to cycle by night.

It was only when I crossed the frontier yesterday and saw the number of tractors in use here that I registered having seen none (apart from that Persian village) since leaving Bulgaria. Splendid progress is being made in re-afforestation throughout this area and thousands of young trees are thriving by the roadside. Incidentally, this grand trunk road from Peshawar to Calcutta via Delhi is the oldest highway in India, having been built by Akbar four hundred years ago. Its metalled surface is very well kept, considering the volume of heavy traffic, but the standard of driving is appalling and I cycle in constant expectation of a premature demise. The number of cycles, both in Pakistan and here, is astronomical: even the rickshaws are tricycles, with a little covered wagon for two behind. A thing that humbles me, speaking as a moderately proficient cyclist, is the skill with which Indians contrive to pedal a cycle through a densely-thronged street with an absolutely staggering load attached to both the rider and his machine. What in Ireland would be considered a fair load for a donkey is here a fair load for a cyclist, which makes one wonder if the Indians are as weedy as they look. But then a horrifying percentage of them do die in their forties of heart diseases. It still seems odd to see women cycling all over the place – and even odder to see husbands and wives walking along the streets together or sitting chatting in eating-houses. Of course these would be less common sights in the Hindu states as Hinduism adopted the purdah system when the Muslims were the ruling power; at first it was merely a status symbol in emulation of the ladies of the Royal Court, but I'm told it's now a feature of everyday life in many village communities.

If the monsoon doesn't break soon I'll go mad; however grim the rains are they can't be as bad as this – or so I like to believe. One must have some comforting thoughts.

NEW DELHI, 7 AND 8 JULY

What a topsy-turvy life this weather drives one to! We left Sirhind at 4.20 a.m. yesterday and as the sky was still overcast I kept going till 11 a.m., by which time we'd covered sixty miles, with frequent pauses for tea-drinking, as however overcast it is the similarity to hell remains marked. In one of my tea-houses a young and very moronic police constable took me for one of the two English girls who recently disappeared en route from Delhi to Lahore.

Perhaps it's the heat souring my sweet nature, but I like the Punjab less every day. The inhabitants' chief occupation seems to be squatting watchfully beside fresh cow-pats waiting for the sun to dry them to the point where they can be picked up and kneaded into shape for use as fuel when they're fully dried. I realise that this sight should move me to pity and compassion but somehow, in my present mood, it simply adds a final touch of squalor to the whole scene.

I slept at a dak bungalow from 11.30 a.m. to 5 p.m. and then set off again, having decided to take advantage of a full moon and travel through the night. Lots of crazy traffic kept my nerves permanently taut en route as half the population were also employing my tactics. I know now why the top of every Indian bus bristles with cycles: the owners go somewhere by bus during the day and cycle back during the night. However, this national habit of nocturnal travelling means that tea- and eating-houses remain open indefinitely, so I was able to refuel at will. I notice that Indian tea is of an extraordinarily poor quality, the best being exported, and as I'm a China tea addict anyway its only useful purpose here is to convey sugar to the system. But even for this it's not very successful as sugar is scarce in the Punjab – and strictly rationed in some other states because of an artificially created shortage attributed variously to political chicanery on someone's part and to the export of sugar to America in lieu of Cuban supplies. The result is that a nasty-tasting derivative of cane-sugar is used in many tea-houses.

An odd thing happened during one pause, when a truck driver offered me £28 in rupees for my watch! It's possible that he intended to swindle me with forged notes, but more likely that the offer was genuine, imported goods being at a premium here. Had this watch not been my father's, I'd have been tempted to do a deal, and may yet sell my camera (illegally) as all the photographs taken so far are worthless.

By the way, I forgot to mention that in Amritsar, two hours after I'd crossed the frontier, Roz's lamp was stolen. This was the first theft, apart from those cigarettes in Persia, since I left home. And yesterday five one-rupee stamps were swiped off the sitting-room table in a dak bungalow while I went to the lavatory.

Last night's run was by far my most enjoyable cycle since we left the Kagan Valley; the level plain, transformed by brilliant moonlight, looked quite beautiful. We'd covered the 104 miles to Delhi by 5.30 a.m., averaging a steady fifteen miles per hour on the flat road, and it was already quite bright when we entered the city. I felt that this was not the most appropriate hour to insert myself into the Haddow household – though knowing the Haddows as I do now I've no doubt they would have taken my inopportune arrival in their stride – so I curled up on the pavement outside Old Delhi Railway Station and slept there for an hour, with my head and shoulders on Roz's back wheel, among a multitude of slumbering Indians.

We must have gone astray somewhere on the outskirts, because we should have come directly into New Delhi, and when I woke I had quite a job to find my destination on Janpath, a mysterious boulevard which I'm secretly convinced runs in sixteen different directions, though the Haddows assure me that it goes in a straight line. Anyway, I kept finding myself on sections of it which were never the right section, and in the course of my disorganised peregrinations I saw enough of New Delhi to know I'm going to like it, despite its inevitable atmosphere of being a 'half-breed' city.

The Haddows, who have lived here for over thirty years and describe themselves as being among Delhi's Ancient Monuments, are the exact antithesis to the conventional picture one has of the British in India. Mr Haddow is a dentist, and having put down roots here they elected to remain on after Partition accepting their new status with a most laudable regard for India as a nation, yet not making any crackpot attempts to lose their own national identity. It's surprising how few of the old British ruling caste have had the grace to adapt thus to changing circumstances.

NEW DELHI, 9 AND 10 JULY

I seem to have recently developed the habit of one day entering people's homes as a guest and by the next day being metamorphosed into an invalid. Yesterday morning I woke feeling slightly peculiar but went to the new Diplomatic Enclave before lunch – partly on business and partly to see its proliferation of modern architectural curiosities. Allergic as I am to most modern architecture, I must admit that some of these buildings are a joy to behold. At the wish of the Indian Government, most Diplomatic Missions to Delhi have built or are building new Embassies in a special area allotted for the purpose and I couldn't help wondering if their general attractiveness was not partly due to the absence of older buildings near by. So often it's the conflict presented by the juxtaposition of old and new structures that numbs one's appreciation of contemporary design. But I wondered too if it was really necessary to expend such vast sums of money on such sumptuous Embassies in a country as poor as India is; on the part of socialist countries especially this seems an irrational acquiescence to the present violent contrast between wealth and poverty.

As I was cycling back to the Haddows' at midday I was suddenly attacked by the most violent belly-ache I've ever suffered and during the afternoon I began to run a temperature. However, thanks to Mrs Haddow's good care it was down again by midnight and the belly-ache had also subsided, so I slept quite well. But today my temperature has been fluctuating and I've stayed in bed so I have nothing to report – a day in bed in New Delhi is like a day in bed anywhere else.

Later. This evening I've been discussing my future plans with Mrs Haddow and we agree that cycling on the plains will have to be counted out between now and November. The spirit is willing *but* . . . ! So tomorrow, with Mrs Haddow's help, I shall look for some form of voluntary work here in India to keep me happy until Roz and I can get going again.

List of Kit

CLOTHES WORN AT THE START

1 woollen vest
1 pair of woollen ankle-length underpants
1 pair of gabardine slacks
1 pair of waterproof trousers
2 heavy sweaters
1 Viyella shirt
1 gabardine wind-cheater
1 woollen balaclava helmet
1 skiing cap
1 pair of leather fur-lined gauntlets

CHANGE OF CLOTHES

1 woollen vest
1 pair of woollen ankle-length underpants
1 Viyella shirt

TOILET ARTICLES

1 bar of soap
1 face-cloth
1 hand-towel
1 toothbrush
1 tube of toothpaste

MEDICAL SUPPLIES

3 tubes of insect repellent cream
100 Chlorinate tablets (for water purification)
1 ounce of potassium permanganate (against snake bite)
1 dozen Acromycin capsules

1 tin of Elastoplast
100 Aspirin
100 Paludrin tablets (against malaria)
6 tubes of sunburn cream

BOOKS

Nehru's *History of India*
William Blake's Poems (Penguin edition)

INCIDENTALS

1 .25 automatic pistol
4 rounds of ammunition
12 Biro pens
6 notebooks
4 maps
1 cycling cape
1 camping knife
1 Thermos flask
1 mug
Passport
1 money belt
£300 in traveller's cheques

ROZ'S SPARES

1 tyre
1 inner tube
1 lamp-battery
4 links for the chain
1 brake cable
3 puncture repair outfits
1 pump connection

Total expenditure from 14 January 1963 to 8 July 1963 = £64 7*s.* 10*d.*

Index

ALSO BY DERVLA MURPHY IN SPEAKING TIGER

Where the Indus is Young: A Winter in Baltistan

'Such is the author's love of travelling and of this untouched wilderness, that the lasting impression left by this book is one of sheer joy.'
—Colin Thubron, Sunday Telegraph

'It is her real reverence for natural beauty that gives her writing its special quality...Dervla Murphy is a writer one should be profoundly grateful for: her books are so much more than traveller's tales.'
—Daily Telegraph

One winter in the mid-1970s, Dervla Murphy, her six-year-old daughter Rachel and Hallam, a hardy mule, walked into Baltistan close to Pakistan-held Kashmir—the frozen heart of the Western Himalayas. For three months they travelled along the perilous Indus Gorge and into nearby valleys, making a mockery of fear, trekking through the forbidding Karakoram mountains and lodging with the Balts, who farm one of the remotest regions on earth. Despite the hardship, Dervla never forgot the point of travel, retaining enthusiasm for her magnificent surroundings and using her sense of humour to bring out the best in her hosts, who were often locked into the melancholic mood of mid-winter.

This hair-raising, quirky and vivid account of their adventure is a classic of travel writing.

ALSO BY DERVLA MURPHY IN SPEAKING TIGER

On a Shoestring to Coorg: An Experience of Southern India

'Dervla Murphy is the best kind of traveller: observant, high-spirited, open-minded, and impervious to discomfort...[Her] keen appreciation of natural beauty makes the tiny province of Coorg appear as an earthly paradise.'
—*Sunday Telegraph*

'One of Miss Murphy's most considerable gifts is the ability to choose, get into, live in—and take us back to—places where the world is as it was and probably ever shall be. She is a connoisseur of lost Arcadias.'
—*Times Literary Supplement*

'A travel writer of rare heart and freshness.'
—*The Observer*

One of the world's great travel writers, Dervla Murphy, and her young daughter, Rachel—with little money, no taste for luxury and few concrete plans—meander their way slowly south from Bombay to the southernmost point of India, Cape Comorin, in 1973. Interested in everything they see, but only truly enchanted by people, they stay in fishermen's huts and no-star hotels, travelling in packed-out buses, on foot and by boat. But instead of pressing ever onwards, they double back to the place they liked most, the hill province of Coorg, and settle down to live there for two months. In this book, Dervla Murphy creates an extraordinarily affectionate portrait of these cardamom-scented, spiritually and agriculturally self-sufficient highlands.

Dom Moraes (1938–2004), poet, novelist, and columnist, is seen as a foundational figure in Indian English Literature. In 1958, at the age of twenty, he won the prestigious Hawthornden Prize for his first volume of verse, *A Beginning*, going on to publish more than thirty books of prose and poetry. He was awarded the Sahitya Akademi Award for English in 1994. He has won awards for journalism and poetry in England, America, and India. He also wrote a large number of film scripts for BBC and iTV, covering various countries such as India, Israel, Cuba, and Africa.

Also by Dom Moraes

Green Is the Grass: Essays on Cricket (1951)

A Beginning: Poems (1957)

Poems (1960)

John Nobody: Poems (1965)

Mrs Gandhi: A Biography (1980)

Absences: Poems (1983)

Collected Poems: 1957–1987 (1987)

Serendip (1990)

Never at Home: An Autobiography (1992)

My Son's Father: An Autobiography (1968)

Out of God's Oven: Travels in a Fractured Land, co-authored with Sarayu Srivatsa (2002)

The Long Strider: How Thomas Coryate Walked from England to India in the Year 1613, co-authored with Sarayu Srivatsa (2003)

A Variety of Absences: The Collected Memoirs of Dom Moraes (2003)

Selected Poems, Ed. Ranjit Hoskote (2012)

Where Some Things are Remembered: Profiles and Conversations (2018)

Under Something of a Cloud: Selected Travel Writings (2019)

GONE AWAY
An Indian Journal

DOM MORAES

SPEAKING
TIGER

SPEAKING TIGER BOOKS
4381/4, Ansari Road, Daryaganj
New Delhi 110002

First published in the UK by William Heinemann Ltd. UK, 1960
This edition published in India by Speaking Tiger in paperback 2020

ISBN: 978-81-944729-5-7
eISBN: 978-81-944729-6-4

10 9 8 7 6 5 4 3 2 1

Typeset in Adobe Garamond Pro by Jojy Philip, New Delhi
Printed at Chaman Enterprises, New Delhi

Contents

Introduction

Adil Jussawalla, poet and archivist extraordinaire, told me about how he had first heard of Dom Moraes in the 1950s, when both were at school, Adil at Cathedral and John Connon and Dom at St Mary's, a Jesuit institution.

'I had a friend who had also been to St Mary's who told me about this prodigy whose essays were legendary,' Jussawalla said.

I thought about this when I saw a certificate Dom had won at St Mary's (Cambridge Section) on 1 December 1951. It was for the 'The English Essay Prize'. Only, the certificate was for a scholarship; the word 'scholarship' had been scored out and 'The English Essay Prize' inserted above it. That was what the Cambridge Section of St Mary's was like at the time; that was what the city was like; that was what the country was like. It was a time of making do. And so both young men of promise left and went to England to study. They had very different experiences there with very different results.

In 1959, Dom Moraes would come back to the city of his birth to write about it and about India. He was by now a certified prodigy; he had won the Hawthornden Prize in 1958, established by Alice Warrender for a work of the imagination, to be awarded to a writer under the age of forty-one. Dom wasn't yet twenty when he won it. Other winners were Vita Sackville-West and David Garnett. The very next year Alan Sillitoe would win it for *The Loneliness of the Long-Distance Runner*; later V.S. Naipaul,

Ali Smith and Jennie Uglow would all win it. In a book of poems called *John Nobody*, published in 1965, Dom would write, 'My agent tells me that I have a name/An audience waits for what I say.'

The confidence of that line is already clear in *Gone Away*. His prose is clean and clear; his lines are shapely and elegant. His writing could be a how-to manual for the young writer (and here Speaking Tiger is owed a huge debt of gratitude for bringing us *When Some Things are Remembered* and *Under Something of a Cloud*, selections of Dom's travel writings and reportage, recently, besides reissuing his autobiographies, *My Son's Father* and *Never at Home*). But the young writer might also see that the elegance, the clarity is hard-won; and these qualities make a beautiful carapace for his discomfort. It was this divine discomfort that shaped Dom's writing. I might go as far as to say that it was what produced most of it. His poems are precise and beautifully shaped. For a man who had no time for music, they were metrically correct, just as his prose sentences played to an inner beat. Both are saved from the bloodlessness of only-beauty by the underlying inferno of emotion that is only hinted at.

It is impossible to consider what these emotions might be, so well are they camouflaged in the presentation of reality we see in *Gone Away*. (For a Rashomon moment, you might want to read Ved Mehta's *Walking the Indian Streets*, which deals with much the same moment and many of the same events but tells another story altogether.) There is in this telling as much of Dom as there is of India—he says with fetching self-irony: 'I found myself very interesting.' We would call this self-implication today, the belief that you cannot tell the story without also presenting the prism through which it is told. Dom's father was Frank Moraes, one of the greatest Indian editors ever. This must have eased Dom's path and made some contacts easier. He had only to pick up the phone for Mulk Raj Anand to suggest that he come over right away. And when he went to Delhi and got to meet Khushwant Singh, he could get drunk and conflate Beowulf and William

Blake without a care in the world because everyone would only be gently amused. (Of Singh, he says, 'He is a rich-natured Sikh, with a curious fierceness and quickness of manner, shading down to a tender understanding.' I don't know how anyone could have put it better.)

Likewise, Narayana Menon was available to give him the latest army gossip and to play the veena for his young guest, begetting an interesting description, a strange description, of a kind I have not read before or since:

> The veena is shaped like half a pumpkin on a stick. The strings are of silver, and strung crosswise across the pumpkin-face. Narayana twiddled a few keys, tautening the strings, then bent over the instrument and began to play it. The long, very flexible fingers of his left hand struck the strings slowly, and a long-drawn-out succession of notes, like the calls of a mechanical bird, filled the room. Each faded out and was imperceptibly replaced by another, or overlapped and sang at different ends of the same golden bough.

Sometimes, you get the feeling you're climbing a set of stairs. First Mulk, then Nissim Ezekiel, then Khushwant Singh, then Narayana Menon....and drumroll! Pandit Jawaharlal Nehru!

More than anything, you feel in all this the sense of a watchful alien, not unsympathetic to local life forms but not quite understanding them either. Physical unease is easy to describe: the heat, the humidity, the air-conditioning 'spreading a coolness as unhealthy as the heat', the squishy feeling under his feet at the country liquor bar; however the unease of the mind, or the spirit, is often best when it is only suggested. In each portrait in *Gone Away*, in each interview, there is a sense of mismatch. In the best traditions of journalism, Dom Moraes is not expecting something but he seems unsure whether what he does encounter is what he should be encountering. He is in free fall through India, and the only thing that will steady him is to put everything into deadpan prose. And so there is no judgement made here, and the reader can make her own decisions as she goes along.

She may choose to reject Dom-as-Virgil on the grounds that he has been colonized only too well. She may choose to look at this book as being a precursor of *India: A Wounded Civilization* in which another brilliant prose stylist, V.S. Naipaul, turned his gaze upon the enigma of this country. But she cannot claim that the author has been anything but honest in his revelations of himself.

Now that we know who this Dom is, we can tell why he is so ill-at-ease in the country of his birth. We know it is not just a matter of privilege. He has had his fair share of knocks; a peripatetic childhood in the shadow of a famous father, a mother whose mental illness left scars of all kinds, early success which can be a cross to carry, the constant feeling of disconnectedness. We know it is not just a matter of belonging to a nation or to a nationality; no creative person can conjure up an unquestioning sense of belonging, except at great cost. (And it is the art that suffers first and most.) If you consider that this was the 1950s, a time that most people refer to as the honeymoon period of the Indian Republic, you can see how it can only have gone downhill from there.

There is something strange about reading this book now. I began by thinking of it as a period piece, for that country seems sometimes to be very far away. However, when Dom is on his way to Nathu La in Sikkim, his conversations with his driver seem to be the stuff of today's world. The Sikh gentleman who is the first voice we hear—other than Dom's own—is still to be found in airport bars and will still be saying much the same things. And the Tibetan Dom is interviewing says, in the voice of the interpreter, that 'he has lost his home. His home is in the country where the Dalai Lama stays, but he is not at home here. If he goes back to Tibet now, the Chinia will shoot him. His brother went back and him the Chinia took and shot.'

Through the veil of Dom's impeccable British accent, through the veil of his translator's inadequate English, we can still hear and relate to the plangent voices of these men, with their freight of love and despair.

Somewhere up in the mountains, somewhere in an airport, they are still saying the same things. That's what makes a book timeless.

JERRY PINTO
Mumbai 2020

A Preface

I was born in Bombay. It is the chief city of western India, and it squats on a forked island encircled by the Arabian Sea. It is a very blue sea, except where the sewers of the city disgorge into it; and above it the smoke of the factories hangs, so that passengers on P & O liners become aware of arriving at Bombay long before they actually arrive there.

My family came from a part of India that had been colonized by the Portuguese, which explains the family name, and also the family religion, which was Roman Catholicism. One of my father's sisters, indeed, became a nun and ended up by being beatified. My parents, however, were not religious. My father was a journalist; my mother was a doctor; both professions tend, I should think, to discourage one from being spiritual. Though my father worked for a British newspaper, he was a nationalist, and many of the people who came to the house when I was a child were nationalists just out of jail, or hiding from the police, or Communists who were officially underground. They taught me to play chess and lent me books. Because by the time I was ten I had read all the Russian novelists, my pet name was Domski.

I was an only child. I was never conscious of being lonely: I found myself very interesting, a vice that has persisted and because even as a child my father was wise enough to allow me complete freedom, I spent hours sitting in a corner of the sitting room listening to the talk of the revolutionaries, the Communists and anarchists, the young writers and the painters. They were thin and poorly dressed, often unshaven, and their dry insistent voices ate up the nights, on the verandah with the stars overhead in the silky black sky, and the splayed paintbrushes of the palm trees daubing the horizon with deeper shadows. All this while I had a secret. I could write. I wrote stories, essays, and poems, but mostly poems. When I was about ten I began to show them to my father's friends. They were all very kind. The novelist Mulk Raj Anand helped me to correct my stories; the painter Manishi Dey did a series of charming little watercolours to accompany my poems. I felt convinced that I was meant to be a writer.

Then when I was ten the first of my journeys began. After that I was to go away from Bombay and come back again and again. My father had been offered an editorship in Ceylon. We spent two years in Colombo, during which I wrote poems, bred dogs, budgerigars, and Siamese Fighters, dabbled in painting, and was lonely and miserable, then we returned to Bombay; my father became the Editor of the *Times of India,* but almost at once we were off again. My mother was ill and so my father was forced to take me with him on his travels. All this while, when he was being father and mother in one, he gave me the same perfect freedom. His only strong moral principle was the only possible moral principle one can have today—that people must be free to choose for themselves; and he held this principle too strongly to modify it in the case of a child. So whenever he went somewhere he would ask me if I wanted to come; and if, as I always did, I said yes, whatever the hazards or the expense or the dangers at the other end, he would take me. In this way, before I was fifteen, I had been with him through Australia and New Zealand, to Indonesia during the first days of Sukarno's administration, to Malaya during the heyday of terrorism, to Indochina when the Viet Minh threw hand grenades in the street outside our hotel in Hanoi, to Bangkok and the densely forested, bandit-haunted Mekong Valley, to Burma and Pakistan, and the borders of Red

China. All this while I watched, and wrote poetry. My dogs and budgerigars died, I gave away my tropical fish, I dispensed with everything but suitcases and the typewriter my father had given me. This typewriter became for me the symbol of my vocation. When I put my fingers on the keys I felt a vibration of pure power. Nobody else seemed to feel this in the finished product until one day in 1954, the poet Stephen Spender visited India. It was the first time I had ever met a real poet. Through the large opaque, sea-coloured eyes of Spender I seemed to see how it might be possible to write poetry. I showed him my poems. He liked them, and said he would publish some in *Encounter*, which he did. Also he asked what I wanted in do. Did I want to stay in India?

No, I said. I had never really thought of it before, but thinking of it now I said no. My family was an entirely English-speaking one. My father and grandfather had been at Oxford. The background of my life had been English. In the streets of India I felt uneasy, knowing neither the language, nor, because of not having come into contact with many Indians who were not from an English background, the people. I suppose I had always known I would leave India, but when Spender asked me if I wanted to, the answer came clear at last.

I left India in 1955. The combined efforts of Spender and my father had gained me admittance to Jesus College, Oxford, but I had a year to kill before going up. I spent this year in Europe: I wandered about in France and Italy, spending a month in Sardinia: then I went on to Greece, spending four months there, including a month in Crete looking for the minotaur. I finished up in Yugoslavia, snowed up in a Belgrade winter. I was staying with a beautiful widow, who used to take me to strange, faintly sleazy basement nightclubs where the opponents of Tito drank rakia, snarling and wiping the frost from their thick dark moustaches. All this while my eyes kept communicating power to my hand, and wherever I was I wrote, on iron tables of cafés, in trains and ships, or sitting on a rock in the sunlight watching the lizards licking their breakfast from the air. Then I returned to England and went up to Oxford.

About this time I met David Archer. He ran a bookshop in Soho. In 1933 he had published Dylan Thomas's first poems, in 1934 George Barker's, in 1935 David Gascoyne's, and in 1942 W.S. Graham's. Now, in 1956, he published my first book of poems. It was called *A Beginning.*

Meanwhile the Hungarian Revolution had broken out and I abandoned Oxford and shot off to the frontier, where I spent a couple of weeks. I returned by way of Germany to find myself in terrible trouble with the university, but also to find my poems a critical success. Finally, in 1958, they were awarded the Hawthornden Prize for the year's best imaginative work. This convinced my college that it would be a mistake to expel me. So they kept me, and in 1959 I became a Bachelor of Arts of Oxford University. If I pay my college dues regularly for three years I shall in due course become a Master of Arts, which would be nice for everybody.

Nobody had ever expected me to finish my three years at Oxford. I was always in trouble. When I felt like going to London, or even abroad, I always went; I brought up trainloads of drunken poets who turned the college into shambles overnight; I didn't turn up for tutorials. My college, however, had endless patience. This was especially due to my principal. He shielded me from the wrath of the disciplinary' authorities. Occasionally, in the quadrangle, he winked at me. We understood each other.

After Oxford was done, I felt a little strange. Mostly because I had fallen in love properly at last, and that confused me, who had always stood alone. My second book of poems was in the press, but I felt I should do something else. I felt I should go somewhere for a little by myself, to think about what loving somebody involved, and become more confident, if I could. I decided to go to India.

This book is the result. It was written with a particular person in mind, who was not with me. It is not really a travel book, nor is it political. It is a journal of what I did and felt during August–November last year, when I happened to be in India. So it may be too personal; but I hope, and I think, that that may be a good thing, because perhaps it makes the work more true.

I owe a debt of gratitude to my father for everything, to Marilyn Silverstone for reading and criticizing the manuscript, to Mr T.R. Gopalakrishnan of the *Indian Express* for typing it, and to James MacGibbon for infinite patience in waiting for it.

London, January 1960 Dom Moraes

Song

I sowed my wild oats
Before I was twenty.
Drunkards and turncoats
I knew in plenty.
Most friends betrayed me.
Each new affair
Further delayed me.
I did not care.

I put no end to
The life that led me
The friends to lend to,
The bards who bled me.
Every bad penny
Finds its own robber.
My beds were many
And my cheques rubber.

Then with the weather worse
To the cold river
I came reciting verse
With a hangover.
You shook a clammy hand.
How could I tell you

Then that wild oats died and
Brighter grain grew?

Now once more wintertime
We sit together.
In your bright forelock
Time gives me good weather.
All true love I know is
Patience and care.
Such grain as I grow is
Hued like your hair.

Going Away

Angst possessed me the afternoon I left for India, with the remembrance of fourteen swans on the Thames, and your bewildering kiss of goodbye. A small grey cobweb of rain covered the London airport. I sat in the bar till three, drinking double brandies, one of the impersonal community of the about-to-depart, masked in magazines. Outside the aeroplanes squatted among meadows of tarmac, looking derelict till their windows were blocked out with small disclike faces and one by one they lumbered into the air. It seemed a long time before ours did, but only a short time before it settled its wings through ridged greyish clouds, and came down on Düsseldorf.

On this interim soil the impersonality of my companions broke down; identities began to appear, like distressing flowers. At the bar a tall Sikh stood drinking whisky after whisky. He offered me a drink. 'It will not be long,' he said, 'before we arrive where we shall not be able to drink at all.' I was not sure whether he meant death or India, but accepted a brandy. He thought I should drink whisky, and muttered rather threateningly, 'Soon you will be glad of anything you can get.' The other passengers were mostly Indian families, the fathers plaintive in brown suits beside their gross wives, and children bleating amidst the debris of their teas. 'Too many children, bhai,'* said the Sikh. 'That

* Brother.

damn country is full of children. What is the use of them? They will grow up and do nothing. Otherwise they will grow up and become damn crooks like their fathers. As for me,' he added, 'my home is in Delhi, where the women are pretty, but I would not marry for anything.' We had several more drinks, and returned in jovial agreement to the aircraft.

On the way to Zurich I sat thinking sad thoughts about love and separation, but was continually interrupted by the Sikh, who now sat by me, discursing like Schopenhauer of the woe that is in marriage, and ordering round after round of drinks. By the time we arrived at Zurich I was in a state of deep alcoholic melancholy. I ordered the Sikh a large whisky in the airport bar with a Byronic toss of my head, and when we got back into the plane fell heavily and completely asleep.

At three next morning I was shaken awake. The Sikh leant over to me, pursing his lips redly through the coarse greyish hairs of his whiskers. 'Cairo.' I looked down, and saw many lights, and scrubby palm trees. We landed with a small succession of bumps. A few minutes later we were in another airport bar. All the children, awakened, were crying; the heavy-lipped mothers in their attempts at solace filled the room with noise. Sad with a hangover and the usual guilt, I suddenly felt extremely irritable. A mother came up to me, lamenting. 'Oh for Christ's sake!' I said. It was as if I spoke only to myself: she did not understand English. I had another drink with the Sikh, standing in the faint chirping night by a dry fountain. 'India is full of crooks,' he said. 'Why are you going back? Nepotism,' he said, and, liking the word, repeated it. 'There is no nepotism in Manchester,' he said, 'I have lived there for three years. A fine place. The cotton business is very good there, no bribery, everything honest,' and I like him felt suddenly nostalgic for the northern cities asleep now under rain three thousand miles away, save perhaps for policemen in wet oilskins alone in the oilskin-textured streets.

It was so gloomy, really, the unfamiliar colour of the night, and the unfamiliar birds ruffling awake as day broke, and stray dogs running across the airfield, and suddenly a haggard man before us with his hand outstretched as though in blessing. 'Beggars,' said the Sikh with contempt. 'Let us go.' I fumbled in my pocket, but he caught my arm. 'No,' he said. 'Give to one and you will get a hundred.' I remembered the phrase: it was the first advice ever given to me as a child.

We took off through the sunrise. The day resolved itself over desert and sea. We had now been joined by a teetotal Arab with a gun. The Sikh gloomed in his beard: I was sulkily quiet. The armies of fathers, mothers, and offspring, however, grew birdlike and sang for joy. They were coming home from a Europe that had not touched them. It had touched me, it had touched the Sikh: we were both apprehensive of the country to which we were coming across the sea, and 'I do not know,' said the Sikh, 'if I will like India. Let us have a drink.'

So we went on drinking till we reached Bombay. We knew when we arrived. The plane struggled down through clouds. Rain sprayed like buckshot over the windows. Winding themselves in their seat belts the passengers began to assume a new impersonality of the about-to-arrive. By the time we touched down they were all strangers again: and when I descended the ramp, though the Sikh was by my side, I was again alone.

We straggled over the puddled tarmac towards the Customs shed. At the edges of the airfield were ragged bushes, barbed wire, and refuse, and, beyond, purple hills helmeted in cloud. It was very hot. I took my jacket off and hung it neatly over my arm. The balconies were filled with brown faces, white clothes, fluttered handkerchiefs: an incessant watery mumble of talk rose from them. Suddenly I recognized my father on the steps of the Customs building.

'Goodbye,' I said to the Sikh. 'I hope all goes well.'

'Same to you, chum,' he said, and then, lifting his long hands in the Indian greeting: 'Ji namaste—go with God.'

~

The airport is ten miles from the city. It takes a long time to get from one to the other. I had forgotten: because the roads, narrow and tree-spiked, are full of people, all wearing white, drifting between the puddles, doe-eyed, sometimes holding hands. Kiosks selling fruit and food abut upon the road. The people did not hurry when the car pressed them from behind. They turned aside in a kind of languid chaos, and as very slowly we passed, stared through the windows, stroking their fingers gently over the sides of the car, red tongues protruding pleasurably between their lips. My father's driver was a bearded young Mohammedan, of a race that likes speed; he shouted hopelessly, blew the horn; his toe trembled above the accelerator, but it was half an hour before we reached the wide boulevards of the residential areas by the sea, and he could bring it down. Progress quickened, and we reached the great block of flats where I was to be installed: looking on the sea, with lawns, terraces, a swimming pool. When we went up the front door of the flat was already open: beyond stood a line of servants in white, each with two fingers to his forehead, 'Salaam, sahib,' they all sang softly at me, too respectful to smile. 'Salaam,' I said, smiling. 'The bearer will look after you,' said my father.

The bearer showed me to my room. 'I run your bath now, sahib,' he said. Gently he clapped his hands, and another servant appeared and ran it. The milieu was luxury, save that the water was dark brown. I did bathe in it, however, and when I emerged found the bearer outside with a drink, my case unpacked, and fresh linen on the bed. 'Dinner ready, sahib.' 'Thanks,' I said, 'I never eat dinner.' 'Young master must eat,' he breathed serenely. So I ate, while a fan hummed and clicked unceasingly overhead. Having to be Young Master gave me a strange sense of loneliness. 'It must be teatime for you in England now,' I thought, 'perhaps with chocolate biscuits. As for me, darling, I must see somebody.' So, after preventing the bearer from dialling for me, I telephoned Mulk Raj Anand.

I used to know him a long time ago, when I was a child. Since then he had become international, and I had seen him twice in London. He was the first Indian writer in English to live in England: he had been a London literary figure in the 1930s, and a friend of Forster and the Woolfs. His novels about the Indian poor had sold well in England then, and sell very well in the Communist countries now. Also, he had become the Editor of a well-known art magazine, and a member of the Indian Academy of Letters.

I had begun to feel neurotically a stranger, so it was a relief to find Mulk welcoming. In his warm husky voice, pleasantly breathless, 'Come and see me,' he said. 'Very soon. Come today if you like. Come tomorrow. You know my flat? Your father's driver knows it.' A pause. 'It is very nice to have you back.' And that comforted me in my state of Young Masterdom. So while still comforted, I retreated into my bedroom.

They had done it up for me. My old pictures had been rehung: there were magazines and a little pile of new novels by my bed (also a number of religious tracts, left by my mother), a flask, cigarettes, nuts, sweets, roses on the bookcase. I sat down on the bed and took my pills, feeling rather overwhelmed. I wondered how the Sikh was finding it all. Then I fished your photograph out of my case and stood you among the roses. I looked at you a long time and decided we both seemed a bit lost. So I put you under my pillow instead, and switched the light off. And was kept awake all night by the rain and the far-off commotion of the sea.

It was still raining in the morning. I was awakened by the cries of strange birds. When I drew the curtains and looked out into a sultry grey light, a hundred little parakeets, studding the dripping branches of the trees outside, sharply flirted their green wings and dived out of sight. I went back to bed to postpone the world. At eleven I remembered Mulk. The bearer helpfully sent for a taxi.

The driver looked curiously at me as I climbed in. I showed him Mulk's address on a slip of paper. 'Do you know the place?'

'Yes, sure,' he said.

The rain had stopped, but the sky was dreary and the streets filled with the same white-clad drifting crowds, apathetic and walking nowhere. We drove away through them, very fast, circled a Parsee fire-temple and several groves of palm trees, and returned to where we had started. The driver turned and smiled at me, pleased.

'This isn't right,' I said.

'Yes, sure,' he replied.

'Ask somebody.'

He asked somebody. Then, in a spurt of enthusiasm, he asked several others. They all gave us different directions. We set off again at great speed. He stopped several times to ask more people. Eventually, after a very long time, we drew up at a large house on the seafront.

'Is this it?'

'Yes, sure.'

I went up the front steps. The door was open, but I couldn't find the bell. So I coughed several times. Then I stamped my feet. Then I coughed and stamped my feet alternately for a couple of minutes. Nobody came. I turned away in despair and found a servant squatting behind me, watching me with interest. He had obviously been a spectator for some time.

'Does Dr Anand live here?'

He did not understand. I shouted the name several times. At last he put his hand gently on my wrist, nodding reassurance, and led me round to the side door. Then he pointed to the stairs and raised two fingers.

'Thank you,' I said.

Two flights up, I found a door and rang. A woman in a sari answered.

'Is Dr Anand in?'

'You have come to the wrong flat,' she said. 'Dr Anand lives on the other side of the house, on the ground floor.'

'I'm awfully sorry. I was told it was here.'

'You should never listen to people's directions in India,' she said briskly. 'They are always wrong.'

Hers turned out right. I found Mulk lying on a sofa in a room full of books, paintings, and a litter of manuscripts. By his side sat a very beautiful woman in slacks, his wife, the dancer Shirin Vajifdar.

'Hullo,' Mulk said. 'It is a long time since you last came home.'

He lay back on the red-covered sofa, small and composed, and his wife sat quietly near him. In the corner of the room a servant knelt, his hands climbing like brown spiders over a heap of books. Outside the garden was drenched with the last rain, shot through with vivid flashes of birdsong, and the crickets worked their small machinery in the grass. I began to feel curiously weightless, with the slow float of a headache. This precluded me from saying anything. With Mulk, however, it did not matter.

'You must write about the commercial film industry here. It's really fantastic. Hardly any of the stars can act, but they get £7,000 for each picture. They shoot six or seven simultaneously, you see. Besides, they only get about £1,000 officially, the rest is black money, paid under the counter, so they can't be taxed on it. The corruption is fantastic. You must write about it.'

'Yes.'

There was a pause, and for a few minutes we exchanged compliments, with gaps of silence: like a ritual dance, advance and retreat. It struck me suddenly that my whole morning had had this ritual quality: as if social intercourse was based on a system of flattery by misdirection: a conception of courtesy between individuals whereby neither could ever possibly be wrong.

'I would like to meet some young writers in Bombay,' I said. 'Could that be arranged?'

'There are none so distinguished as you,' Mulk said. 'In fact,' he added frankly, 'I don't know if there are any at all.'

'None at all?'

'The poets go into films, you see. Writing the lyrics for musicals. Nobody will publish their books, the magazines don't pay for poetry and the radio is not much better. They mostly marry young, they have families and it's all very difficult. Whereas the film people pay enough for the young poets to move out of their hovels in Kalbadevi into five-room flats on Marine Drive. In fact, they pay enough to make them stop writing poetry.

'I haven't read very much,' he added, 'but I can't believe anything important is being done in the Indian languages, except Bengali. Bengal has a living tradition, you see. But the rest of India is dominated by the bourgeois mind. It's a frame of mind that has come in since Independence. The petty moneylenders are the new rich, they despise the arts, the middle class don't bother, the poor are too tired to care. The artist gets no encouragement, anywhere. If you want to write about Indian literature outside Bengal, it would be better to look at the writer sociologically.

'Even among such writers as there are the jealousy is extraordinary. I know the six best Urdu poets. Not one of them will speak to another. The only time they ever meet is when they come here to dinner.'

'Isn't there anywhere else for writers to meet?'

'No,' said Mulk simply.

His wife had vanished, but there was a rustle of silk at the door and when I turned four incredibly beautiful Indian girls, high-breasted, long-necked Leda's daughters, floated their saris past us and were gone.

'My wife's dancing class,' Mulk explained. A shrill plaintive twanging started inside the house, and the tentative tap-tap of drums. 'It's a practice,' Mulk said. 'One of the few consolations,' he added, 'is that we have an evening of music and dance once a week. Otherwise it would be impossible. As it is I spend four days a week in Khandala, doing my writing. The real aristocracy in Bombay now are the film stars and the British advertising executives, and they are both mostly illiterate. It's frightening.'

He was suddenly very serious, moving his hands slowly in the air, as if threading a needle, and frowning with concentration.

'People attack me for being a Marxist. I'll tell you a story. There is a village near Khandala where the caste families evicted forty untouchable families who were trying to build a road. The case was put to the central government two years ago. Nothing has happened.

'When you're dealing with people like that, there is nothing you can do. One could fight the British, but one can't fight them, because they are petty bourgeois, they are nothing, and one can't fight the wind. I have bought two villages, and the untouchables have moved into them. But I can do nothing to get the petty bureaucracy out. If I lived in England I shouldn't worry, because there the bureaucracy seems to work. Here it doesn't, and I protest, and they call me a Marxist.'

We smiled at each other, and he jumped up, suddenly vivacious.

'Never mind. We'll give a party for you, and get some writers to come to it. We shall have some music and a little dancing. Would you like that?'

I said yes, very much, thank you, and could he tell me where to find a taxi, because I must go. Yes, he said, and gave me the directions carefully.

I went out and walked down the seafront. It was coming on to rain again and the cripples scattered along the pavement were huddling down, scaly tortoises, pulling ragged sheets over their heads like shrouds. I turned first left as directed, then first right, and found myself in a blind alley.

I stood and looked into it, in a somewhat ambiguous frame of mind. Mulk had obviously given me the wrong directions.

The Worst Place in the World

The city of Bombay is built on an island. Thus the sea exerts a considerable influence on the life of Bombay, more than I had suspected as a child, when, from the windows of my father's flat, I watched the triangular hills of the fishing boats like a row of teeth on the sea horizon. The cocktail parties to which I now went were always in houses by the sea: along the great boulevard of Marine Drive, or on Cumballa Hill or Malabar Hill. The sea is aristocratic in Bombay, lying under the lighted windows of rich houses, purring to itself and listening to the subdued thunder of cocktail shakers from within. If the sea were not there, one felt, there would be no parties.

The poor live inland, where they can neither see nor hear the sea. Factories spout like whales in the areas where they live, but these whales are marooned on concrete. In the tall narrow tenements around them the poor sleep ten to a room, or sleep on the pavements with their rags drawn up over their faces. They have never heard the cocktail shakers thunder in the corridors, unless they hire themselves out as butlers: and even then, a really poor man has too many lice to be a good butler. This is the folk wisdom of the rich.

These cocktail parties are extremely strange affairs. This is largely because Bombay is a prohibition state. Nobody can drink without a permit, and Indians have to declare themselves confirmed alcoholics before they can get one. You are not legally supposed to drink more than is allowed on your own permit. At some cocktail parties therefore, the host strews empty bottles of drink round the room, one at the feet of each guest. The idea is that if the police raid the party, each guest picks up a bottle and states that he has fetched along his own liquor, off his own permit. The need for such precautions leads to a certain tenseness in the atmosphere, which leads either to a general apprehensive silence or to furious quarrels where husband and wife reproach each other for their infidelities and threaten immediate divorce. Many such parties, of either kind, end in tears.

This, however, applies mainly to cocktail parties given by Indians. There are other sorts. For instance, there are the British cocktail parties. These are populated by executives who tell you yes, they are Oxford men themselves. While in England they live in Dorking or Esher and have elderly mothers. Their wives congregate seedily in a corner talking of their servants. Their skins have gone wrong in the heat and come out in dark splotches. They have all pencilled bright daring scarlet mouths on the ruins, and these mouths talk incessantly in marsh-bird voices. Such parties drag on a long time and end in Dorking gossip. Also there are the American parties, where you drink bourbon on the rocks. The women are cool and smart, and interested in local handicrafts. The men smile indulgently at them, often tell their guests that their wives are the most wonderful women in the world, and discuss office work. This sort of party is sculptured to a beginning, a middle, and an ending. The ending is usually pleasant in the sense that one gets too drunk to notice what is going on.

Apart from cocktail parties, Bombay has no social life, simply because unless you are a diplomat you cannot get enough drink, or you cannot afford enough, to be able to ask people to drop in of an evening. A bottle of whisky, for instance, costs £4 at the legal rate, and £5 in the black market. Moreover, there are no good restaurants, and since in any case you cannot drink with your meals, the atmosphere in such restaurants as there are is one of hopeless gloom. They are, as I imagine, restaurants must be like in an occupied city.

A few days of this made me very grumpy indeed. I spent the mornings in efforts to write, frustrated because it required no effort at all to sweat; the afternoons visiting people; and in the evening death and the cocktail party began again. The people I visited were Mulk, sometimes, who kept urging me to interview film stars; Nissim Ezekiel, a poet who deserves to be better known in England; Arun Kolatkar and Dilip Chitre, two young Maharashtrian novelists who look exactly like Rimbaud and Verlaine. All these, however, also seemed tired and frustrated in their attempts at writing. In each of them one felt a swaddled voice pinioned under the weight of the grits of the city.

Marilyn Silverstone gave me an idea, after these first few days. She is a *Time-Life* photographer, and had had a somewhat tempestuous career during her brief visit to India. Arriving at the time of the Dalai Lama's flight from Tibet, she had gone up to Tezpur, in the NEFA* area, to photograph his arrival. There had been many other journalists there, but Marilyn had gone a little beyond them all, in that, when the Dalai Lama boarded a special train at Siliguri, south of Tezpur, she had hopped aboard with the idea of getting some exclusive photographs. She had promptly been arrested by security police and interrogated for several hours under suspicion of being a Communist spy. Now, safe in Bombay, she became a little heated whenever she thought of this, but tried not to think of it too often. I trusted Marilyn's ideas, for their enterprise, and one evening she said, after I had been delivering myself of a tirade on Bombay: 'Why don't you go to some of these speakeasies, then? See how the other half lives.'

'Now just be careful,' admonished my father.

'It's all right,' Marilyn said sedately. 'They all have police protection.'

* The North-East Frontier Agency region of India.

It was discussed for some time, but I had made up my mind, and next day got hold of Marilyn's contact, a stocky, cheerful Indian journalist called Arthur. He arranged to pick me up that evening, and arrived in the original jalopy, carrying a large cloth bag full of empty bottles.

'I like to replenish my stock when I visit these bootleggers, see?'

With him was another journalist, known only by his initials: B.Z. He sat in the back, cheerfully describing his previous experiences in speakeasies, which seemed to be considerable.

'It's all balls about the police,' Arthur said. 'What police will come, man? They are all paid by these fellows, see? True, no, B.Z.?'

'Ah, yes, yes, true,' B.Z. said. 'You will see that, Mr Moraes. Where shall we go first, Arthur bhai?'

'Let us start with somewhere inside the city. He must see everything, no?'

Bombay at night, away from the sea, is curiously exciting. The darkness is bluish and smells of cooking food, excrement, flesh, musk, and oil, all mixed up. Every street is fronted with lighted shops and white-clad men wander hand in hand across the road, twittering and whistling. Cars have to nose slowly through this indolent float of people, their horns snoring in the humid air.

On the edge of the city, where it begins to give in to suburbs, Arthur stopped the car in a crowded thoroughfare. We climbed out into the noise of the street. People bumped gently into one and drifted away again. B.Z. rushed over to one of the shops and returned with three paans. These are a mixture of areca nut, spice, and betel wrapped together in a green leaf.

'Here, chew these. They help to digest the liquor.'

We went up a sidestreet into a decrepit tenement. It was entirely unlighted, and we had to clamber up four flights of stairs. On every landing homeless vagrants were stretched out, asleep. When we reached the top floor there was one light on, in a small room. We entered this. It was partitioned off to make a compartment in the back, from which rose the most extraordinary odour of fermentation and decay.

'That is where they do the brewing,' Arthur said.

The outer room was furnished with two chairs and a large bed, on which lay two small children, asleep. B.Z., chewing his paan, waved me to one of the chairs and shouted for the bootlegger. He emerged, a small corpulent man in underwear, from the brewery. He wore a Catholic scapular round his neck.

'Is he a Christian?'

'Sure,' said B.Z.; 'all these bootleggers are Christians.'

I noticed further proof on the walls. There were three pictures, one of Christ, balancing a raw heart in his hand, one of the Virgin Mary, and one of both together. There was also an embroidered motto. 'Sustain outburden, Lord Jesus,' this said. While I was looking at these and nibbling my paan, which had a sweetish, not entirely unpleasant taste, the bootlegger came out of the brewery again with three thick unwashed glasses and a milk bottle containing a colourless liquid. He slopped a large quantity of this into each glass, and added some soda.

I tasted mine without pleasure. It was rather warm, first of all, as if the bootlegger had been dipping his fingers in it. The flavour was curious, rather undefinable, but not agreeable. A mixture of coconut, rubber, and oil. I drank it very quickly.

'You like?' said the bootlegger, flattered. 'That very good stuff, master. No getting better than that. Two days old.'

'What is it made of?'

'You don't worry, master,' said the bootlegger. 'I no using only very good stuff. Molasses, rotten fruit, coconut, everything I putting. You drinking more?'

I refused, but smoked a cigarette while Arthur and B.Z. finished their drinks. Two government clerks came rather guiltily in just before we left.

'Now,' said Arthur, 'we go to a more high-class place.' The drink seemed to have made him jolly and rather schoolboyish.

'I will fill my bottles there.' We got back into the car and drove on into the suburbs. When we stopped again it was just off the main road, next to a plantation of palm trees.

We went off the road through these palm trees. There was a smell which suggested awful things, and the ground was soft and clinging underfoot, lending confirmation to these thoughts. Somewhere among the palm trees we came to a thatched shack. We went inside. It was again a small room, candle lit, papered with religious mottoes, containing several chairs, a large bed, where again a couple of children slept peacefully, and at one end of the room a crude counter behind which stood a pugnacious-looking woman in a red sari and spectacles. There were several unshaven young men in the room, all wearing white Punjabi pyjamas.

'Urdu poets,' B.Z. whispered. 'When they get drunk you will really hear something.'

A plump young woman in a cotton frock came round with more thick glasses. The liquid she poured out of a hair-oil bottle was brown this time.

'This is what makes this place high-class,' Arthur explained. 'These fellows put colouring in their liquor to make it look like whisky.'

It tasted exactly the same as the liquor at the first place. While we were drinking it, I watched the young poets. They were all sitting, chin in hand, in attitudes of dejection, occasionally drinking with a slight flourish. Suddenly, however, one sprang up, upsetting his chair, and began to shout at the top of his voice. I noticed that the shouting was more or less musical, and seemed to divide itself into lines, and the shouter flung out his hand in a great gesture, worked his eyebrows, and looked out of the corner of his eye to see how his friends liked it.

'Ghalib,'* B.Z. explained. 'He is quoting Ghalib, something about wine.'

---

* The great Urdu poet.

When the first young man had finished another leapt up and also began shouting and waving both his arms. One of the children on the bed woke up and began to cry. The plump girl in the frock rushed over, caught it up, and began industriously breastfeeding it. The poet went on shouting. At the end the others smacked their thighs with loud appreciative cries. A young man in underwear appeared at the outer door, looking surprised.

'That is the husband,' Arthur said. 'He has been watching for the police. It's a cooperative family, see. The girl who serves is his wife, his mother takes the payment, and those are his children on the bed. Have a drink,' he said to the young man, who accepted.

'I must go back soon,' he said.

'No, why, man?' Arthur said. 'The police won't hurt you.'

'Sir, no, but if any come for their payments, I must pay them before they come in here and frighten away the customers.'

'How much do you pay?' I asked.

'Arre, they are like flies. Five-five rupees I pay to the inspectors to keep away. But then every constable in the district comes, and brings his friends also. One-one rupee I must pay to each of them. I must be paying one-one rupee to two hundred constables and their friends every month, and five-five rupees to the inspectors. Altogether three hundred rupees a month I am spending on them.'

'And how much do you take in?' I asked.

'It varies, sir. Six to seven hundred rupees a month. This prohibition is a blessing, sir. Before this I was working as a sepoy for seventy-five rupees a month. Now, even with these sister-raping policemen, I am earning enough to keep my wife and mother and when my children grow up I will be able to send them to school.'

'Well,' I said, 'that's pretty good.'

When he had finished his drink, wiped his hands on his undershirt, and departed into the darkness, we decided to leave. 'At the next place,' Arthur explained, 'we will see a still.' B.Z., who was beginning to get drunk, was in that mood of bitterness that seems to go with drunkenness in Bombay. 'This bloody city,' he said, lurching. 'No fun in this bloody city.' We passed several loitering policemen, to whom he repeated this loudly in Hindi. None of them took any notice. 'The bootlegger pays protection for his clients as well,' Arthur explained. We drove on, deeper into the suburbs. Finally, after parking on the main road, we walked through a muddy lane, lined with palm trees, to another shack.

'A tin roof,' Arthur pointed out. 'This fellow has got so prosperous that he can afford to put in a tin roof instead of thatch. It used to be the best place in Bombay—all the journalists used to come here—till the proprietor took to drinking his own stuff.'

We stopped at the door of the shack. There was a peculiar noise from inside, like someone beating a carpet, mingled with squeals of pain, and then a little fat man curled up like a foetus came rolling through the doorway pursued by a large woman with a bamboo staff in her hand. She landed a final thwack and looked at us, arms akimbo.

'Gustav is drunk again,' she announced.

Gustav jumped up, dusted himself off, and said grandly to his wife, 'Woman, bring liquor for these sahibs.'

'Bring it yourself,' said the wife, and disappeared.

'Women do not know their place these days,' Gustav explained to us. 'However,' he added, 'I will be indulgent this time. I, Gustav, will bring the liquor. Please go inside, do not run away, Gustav flies!' And flapping his arms with many an unconvincing cackle he stumbled off into the dark.

We went in. There were benches and low tables set out in a long room lit by a single oil lamp. By its flickering light two men in their underwear were playing cards in a corner, a bottle between them. We sat and waited. Presently Gustav returned, reeling from side to side, and carrying a bucket. His wife, wordless with disapproval, came out of the kitchen behind the main room with three glasses. She dipped each into the bucket and brought it out half-full of a dubious fluid. 'One for me too,' Gustav carolled, with a shrill giggle. Still wordlessly, his wife stopped, dipped out a glassful, and emptied it over Gustav's head. Then she produced the bamboo and chased him out of the room.

'He will go back to the still,' Arthur said. 'Come and see.'

We went out, leaving B.Z. behind. Gustav could be seen in the distance scuttling across the fields. We followed, stumbling and slipping continually in the darkness. A strong and totally undesirable smell reached the nostrils. 'That is the wash,' Arthur said. We traced it—this was easy enough—to a lean-to in the field. A fire flickered inside. Gustav was squatting by this fire, over which hung a copper bowl. Over the copper bowl an earthenware vessel was suspended, and a smaller earthenware vessel hung above. Dense clouds of steam poured up, making us all blink and choke.

'The copper bowl holds the wash,' Arthur said. 'Rotten fruits, molasses, and all that. The smaller earthenware bowl holds cold water. The steam from the wash condenses on the top bowl and falls into the vessel below. That is what you've been drinking.'

'Have one with me,' said Gustav, owlishly, crouched over the fire.

But we went away.

'The smell!' I said. 'One can smell it a hundred yards away. The police...'

'It's all included in the protection money,' Arthur said cheerfully.

When we got back B.Z. was sitting in silent misery listening to Gustav's wife. The two card players continued with their game, and never looked up. The woman turned appealingly to us.

'You may think I am harsh with Gustav, sahib, but what else can I do? Our customers do not come because he is always drunk and sometimes he forgets to make a new boiling for them. I have to try and keep him in order. Otherwise, sahib, we would both starve.'

'This bloody city,' B.Z. said, shaking his head. 'There is no fun in this bloody city.'

I refused to take Mulk's advice and meet film stars, but when various colleges asked me to lecture I said I would, because I wanted to meet students. The first of my lectures was at what was described as a small college, that had been running for five years. The principal of this college, a worried man with grey hair, met me when I arrived and took me into his study for tea. We passed through several long corridors flanked by huge dismal classrooms packed with noisy students. Paper darts kept flying through the air. An ineffectual professor was saying something from each platform.

'Too many in this college,' said the principal sadly.

'I thought it was a small college.'

'Oh yes. Small it is. But that is comparatively, you see. We have two thousand five hundred students at present.'

'Goodness me, however do you manage?'

'We have two shifts a day, you see, morning and afternoon. Some also come for night classes. No, I tell you, Mr Moraes, there are too many.'

I felt apprehensive about my lecture, more so when I found that four hundred students had turned up, about a hundred of whom were girls. The girls sat in a block, separate from the men. There seemed to be the most extraordinary variety of ages among my audience: they ranged from twelve years old to about thirty.

'Don't you have any age limit?' I asked the principal.

'No, the only qualification is that they must have passed the matriculation before they can come here. Our youngest pupil is eleven.'

He grew sadder still. I began my lecture with a sense of shouting hoarsely across a vast abyss. The students' faces reflected total incomprehension. When I tried to be funny they looked grave. I ended the lecture quickly, and was startled at the volume of applause that came back.

'They are grateful to you,' said the principal, 'for getting them off their morning classes. So,' he added, 'are their professors. Otherwise usually in the morning the students are in a jolly mood; they throw ink-pellets.'

The older and better colleges seemed to produce more disciplined, but also more fatuous students. These colleges, founded mainly by missionaries or rich Parsees in the nineteenth century, are patronized by the richer people: the small new ones cater for the middle class. The poor do not go to college at all. The rich young of the missionary colleges were more Westernized than those in the college I had first addressed: they wore American bush shirts and often had American accents. Also, whereas the other students had said nothing, these were always asking questions. They were not really good questions. 'Have you read James Joyce?' they would ask, and proceed no further.

At one of these colleges I was talking to some students after my lecture when a young African came rather shyly towards me. I had noticed him during the lecture, as he had been the only person in the audience sitting alone. I smiled at him, and he came up a little more quickly. The Indian students talking to me immediately turned their backs, and I found myself alone with the African, who said a little breathlessly, 'I'm sorry to trouble you, but I have a few questions to ask you about life in England.' So I asked him to tea the next day. He said, 'Can I bring a few friends?' and I said 'Do' (in a privileged way) and then he left. The other students immediately gathered round, assuming attitudes of rebuke.

'You shouldn't demean yourself by talking to that hubshee.'*

I was surprised. 'What do you mean?'

'We *never* speak to him,' said a pretty girl. 'You've let us down by doing it.'

'They are not like us,' said a boy. 'They are not civilized.'

'Don't be absurd,' I said.

They were all very hurt. 'It's true. They are all savages in Africa. Some of them are still cannibals. Whereas we have a long history of civilization.'

'And they *look* so horrid,' said the pretty girl, pouting.

---

* The Hindi equivalent of 'nigger'.

'It is not colour prejudice,' one of the boys said. 'It is simply that we are a civilized nation and we do not want our country filled with black savages. They will corrupt our women.'

'Have you ever heard of Sir Oswald Mosley?' I asked.

'No. An Englishman? That is not the point. We are not objecting to Englishmen, but we do not like hubshees.'

The next day I had tea with the African boy, Charles, and three of his friends. They were all from Uganda, and had been studying in India for periods of between four and six years. Two were doing law, and two, including Charles, medicine.

They were all very interested in England, in university life there, and particularly in the colour problem. I said that it sometimes happened that a hooligan minority stirred up incidents, but that the government had always taken strong measures to prevent these, and that the majority of British people had no real prejudice against colour.

'How is it here?' I said finally.

The four looked ruefully at each other, and finally Charles said, 'Not easy.'

'I guessed that,' I said. 'Why?'

Laughter. 'Why do you think? It's not active, nobody ever attacks us physically, but nobody ever speaks to us either.'

'Don't you have Indian friends?'

They looked at one another again, checking over their experiences in subdued voices. Of the four only one had an Indian friend.

'The other students, don't they ever ask you home?'

'When they do that, they only do it once. And usually the reason for their asking us is that none of their family has ever seen an African.'

'Girls are more sympathetic than boys,' Charles said (there was a chorus of sniggers and 'You're telling us, old chap'). 'No, shut up, old chap. They sometimes agree to come out with us or they ask us home, but then it becomes too difficult for them and they give it up. Because if we go out in the street with them everybody stares, sometimes schoolchildren call out "hubshee," and waiters are rude in restaurants, and their families object, and it gets impossible.'

'I think it may be due to the caste system, or what's left of it,' one of the law students said. 'Caste after all began as a colour division. The proof is that even in the south, where the people are as dark as we are, there is prejudice.'

Charles said, 'It is not just in Bombay, but all over India. All our boys have the same story.'

'But,' said one of his friends, 'Bombay is the worst place in the world.' They all laughed quite good-humouredly.

'I don't think it is anything to do with caste, old chap, though,' Charles said. 'I think it's just simple racial discrimination.'

I saw the boys several times after this. I noticed that whenever we were in the street, people tended to stop and stare. One or two always shouted 'hubshee' and laughed, not behind their hands. The boys never took any notice, but walked with their heads up. I thought they were very brave.

'Your interviews are all fixed up,' said my father, 'with Nehru and the Dalai Lama. You'll have to go to Delhi. I have to as well, so we can go together.'

Later it transpired that Marilyn was to photograph various things in Delhi, so we all arranged to travel together.

The bearer packed my bag and dressed me, early one morning. Then he packed for my father and dressed him. Then he formed the servants up in a line at the front door to salute us as we left. It was just like when I arrived.

The sun had not yet come up, and it was a cool morning, but I was not entirely sorry to leave Bombay.

Hurricane in Delhi

One of the first things I saw in Delhi after we arrived, on the road straggling through dust-covered fields for ten miles from the airport to the city, was a camel caravan creaking toward Agra and the Taj Mahal, the camels floating along like elongated dragonflies with turbaned riders aloft. The weather too was Saharan, and the people along the road disposed like Arab tribesmen to siesta or gentle tobacco-chewing, on rope beds outside their huts. They seemed far less mobile than the people of Bombay: it made a change.

New Delhi is a scattered city. Coming from the airport there was a clump of houses here, a clump of houses there, part of a new building project, part of another, the great sandstone facade of a Mughal fort, before finally, in an avenue lined with heat-crimped trees, we reached our hotel.

My room was full of the soft thunder of air conditioners, spreading a coolness as clinging and unhealthy as the heat: to step out into the corridor was like entering a warm bath with all one's clothes on: they were sodden in seconds. Bearers floated on bare feet through the corridors with bowls of ice, answering innumerable bells. I drank some beer, took my shoes off, and lay down on the bed, wiggling my toes.

So I fell asleep for a while. When I went across to my father's room, it was already full of the beginnings of the train of visitors who appear, as if answering the Pied Piper's flute, wherever he goes. An employee of Krishna Menon's was unloading all the latest dirt from the defence ministry: American, English, and Indian journalists were scattered with glasses of whisky all over the room, comparing notes: the telephone kept ringing. I decided to strike out on my own a bit. I knew that Ved Mehta was in Delhi, so I looked up his parents' number and called him.

Ved was at Oxford with me, and came down when I did. He had been at Harvard before that, and he was now on his way back to take up a fellowship there, stopping off to see his parents en route. He has been completely blind since the age of three. I remembered, vividly, the last time I had seen him before he left England: we met in a pub in Chelsea; he was leaving for India the next day, and I, not expecting at that time to be in India myself, convinced him, and at the same time myself, that we would never meet again. The more we drank the sadder we got, it had been one of those evenings; in the end Ved had staggered away into the rain leaving me to console myself at the bar.

I got him on the line, after some trouble explaining my identity to the servant, and an astonished voice said: 'Is that really you, Dommie?' This is the name that I was always called by the more whimsical of my Oxford friends: it was originally given me by a little boy. 'Yes,' I said.

'What are you doing here?'

'I'll tell you,' I said, 'if you come and have a drink with me.'

So we arranged to meet that evening, and I hung up and sat down and tried to decide which group of visitors I should listen to.

Eventually, I joined the group around my father: this was where the official from the defence ministry was holding forth. He was a tall man in military uniform, braid and everything: he had a reticent habit of speech, enigmatic grunts and phrases being followed by long silences before they joined on unexpectedly with other phrases to make a sentence. Each sentence, therefore, took a long time.

In this onomatopoeic, meditative style, like a don constructing some elaborate theory on phonology, he spoke of the disaffection among the armed forces caused by the policy of the defence minister. Krishna Menon had recently made several army promotions over the heads of senior officers. General Thimayya, the commander-in-chief, disapproved of these, the phonologist said. Worse than that, he said, shaking his head at us, the army disapproved. The officers were splitting into parties for and against the newly promoted men: that is, by implication, for and against the defence minister and commander-in-chief respectively.

'Trouble,' said the phonologist. 'There will be trouble soon. You mark my words.'

'What does Krishna Menon gain,' I asked, 'by making all these unpopular promotions?'

'Hm. These fellows…who have been promoted…are mostly leftists. What he wants…in my view…is to have an army manned by leftist officers…behind him…against the time that Nehru dies.' He added: 'He has chosen the worst possible time. We have these damned Chinese…muscling in on the frontier. If he splits the army now…there will be trouble. We can't apply non-violent resistance now… If the peasants lie down in front of Chinese tanks…as they did in front of British tanks…the difference will be that the Chinese tanks…do not stop.'

'I think I'll have a drink,' I said. 'Shall you too?'

I opened my eyes next morning with pain and care, one at a time. I was in a totally strange bedroom. I looked at my watch. It had stopped. But it was broad daylight, and I had a moment when I thought I had amnesia, until certain unmistakable symptoms in my head put me right.

The door opened and Ved came in, looking terrifyingly spruce.

'Ved,' I said, dazedly. 'Where am I?'

'You're in the spare bedroom of my house, dear boy. Don't you remember? No, I don't suppose you do.'

'I haven't done anything awful, have I?'

'It depends on,' Ved replied judicially, 'what you call awful.'

He added, 'You were pretty sloshed when I arrived, Dommie, and you kept talking about the defence ministry. After that you gave a lecture on Anglo-Saxon poetry. I never knew you knew so much about it. Everybody there was fascinated, and there were hundreds of people there. Then I thought a little dinner would be good for you, so we went out. Then came the dog.'

'What dog?'

'We found a stray dog on the street. You wanted to take it into the restaurant for dinner, but they wouldn't let you. But you still seemed to think it was there. In fact you put all your dinner under the table for it. The man at the next table went rushing to the telephone to call up his friends. He wanted to tell them that they ought not to miss it, it was the only time this was likely to happen in Delhi. I told him that if you stuck around here for a few days, Dommie, the novelty would be sure to wear off.'

I buried my head in my hands.

'Never mind. Have a cold shower and some breakfast. Then we have some business. There were a lot of writers who came to meet you, but you didn't give them much opportunity. Unless they've changed their minds, I think we should call on them this morning.'

I had a cold shower and, feeling a little better, came out into the dining room. It was a house of broad, sunny verandahs, and the dining room was just off the largest of these. Outside the day was preparing itself to be hot, in a blue tent over the trees. Inside were Ved's father and mother and his sister-in-law.

I had prepared a little apology, but it was swept away. Ved's mother said, 'Poor boy, are you feeling better? Sit down.' I sat down, feeling I didn't deserve it. The sister-in-law, charming and cool in a pale yellow sari, said, 'Have an egg.'

'Thank you, no,' I said, 'I never eat in the mornings.'

'Yes, I noticed last night,' Ved's father said, 'that you seemed to be on a liquid diet.'

But he was chuckling, and I felt a little better. I had met him in London the previous year, and we talked for a while about that. I drank some coffee, and then Ved, in his most organizing mood, said, 'Come on, dear boy. We'd better start.'

I got up obediently. In the taxi I said, 'Your parents are charming. I do hope I haven't shocked them.'

'Oh no,' Ved said. 'There was only one thing they thought a little strange. When we arrived here last night I introduced you to my mother, and you clasped her hand and said, "I'm delighted to meet you. I've heard so much about you, sir."'

The first of the neglected writers we went to see was Khushwant Singh. He is a novelist, whose books have been well reviewed in England: he lived in Paris for some time, working for UNESCO, and I met him there with his charming wife, five years ago. I remember lunching with them in a restaurant with a huge sign outside saying: 'We speak a kind of English.' He is a rich-natured Sikh, with a curious fierceness and quickness of manner, shading down to a tender understanding.

When the bearer let us in, Khushwant was sitting cross-legged in a chair in the drawing room, writing. He had obviously only just got up, for his beard was still in bandages and he had not put his turban on.

'Who is it?' He peered over his spectacles.' Oh Ved and Dom. Has the Anglo-Saxon expert come to apologize?'

'Humbly,' I said; but Khushwant was laughing.

'Sit down. Have some coffee. It's Cona coffee, and quite good. And excuse me while I put my turban on.'

He returned turbaned and unbandaged. His beard was a little greyer than it had been in Paris, but otherwise he seemed much the same.

'I thought the line you quoted from *Beowulf* which you said described your state of mind in India was a misquotation, perhaps. "The Son of Morn in weary night's decline" you kept saying. *Beowulf* must have changed since I read it.'

'Don't,' I pleaded. 'What are you doing these days?'

'Well, I'm writing a history of the Sikhs. The Ford Foundation commissioned me to do it. Interesting work, you know. And I've just finished a novel. That'll sell in the States, I think: plenty of sex, triangles you know, and all that.'

The coffee was brought and Khushwant poured it. It was very good. 'But there's a new epic waiting to be written about India today, a satire. I don't know if you've been here long. Why, there's a whole novel to be written about the career of X. He's a high official of one of our most important states. He started as a hardware merchant and worked his way down into politics. He has a nose complaint, you know. When he addresses public meetings he quite often stops and gives himself a nasal douche at the edge of the platform. Also he has two sons who go around beating up all his critics and laying false charges against them. There was an ICS man he didn't like, a district judge, whom he had arrested in the fellow's own court. It would make a wonderful novel, really.'

'Are you going to write it?'

'Maybe, some day. Any high official's life would do, not just this one: they are all corrupt, they are all nepotists, and they all have peculiar habits. There's another one who is supposed to put down vice. He goes on an inspection tour of the brothels every week, and generally spends the night in one or the other. But at the moment I want to write about the villages of the Punjab. They are where I was born and bred. They're marvellous, you should go there, Dom, to the villages, anywhere really, though the ones I know best are in the Punjab: they are the last outposts of civilization in this country. The peasants are great rough Sikh labourers and artisans, and they talk in a picturesque, highly coloured kind of speech, and swear very variously and frighteningly well. They are rather like peasants were supposed to be in the Ireland of Synge and Lady Gregory.'

'Those peasants didn't swear.'

'True. But, you know, I would prefer to be in India now, as a novelist, than anywhere else. I would prefer as a man to be somewhere else, but as a novelist, no.'

'I saw Mulk Raj Anand in Bombay,' I said. 'He was saying how difficult it is for a writer to live here, because he has no other writers to talk to, and the atmosphere is depressing, and all that.'

'I don't see why it should be. I don't see many writers, but then I don't very much want to. I think life in cities in India is hell, certainly, because the whole country is administered by a bunch of corrupt puritans who operate in the cities. But I get away into the villages quite often, and there are always a few people one knows and likes anywhere one goes. And there's so much material. From that point of view this sort of country is far preferable to England, say. The London novelists write city novels, sex and sorrow and a lot of psychology for padding: novels about a certain way of life. In a country like India one has the material of life itself.'

We talked about Chelsea, where Khushwant used to live in London, and about Paris. He talked without a trace of nostalgia, but with that almost crude realism that is one of the most striking things about his novels. It seemed to me, as we went away, that his was the only possible attitude that a writer in England could take up in India, and live. Though, I thought, to take up this attitude one would need to have the things Khushwant had: a private income, comfortable circumstances, deep roots in the villages, and an interest in many other things beside literature. Without these, one would be forced to share in the general death.

Narayana Menon lives in a cool second-floor flat with a huge drawing room, furnished with broad couches and comfortable chairs, the walls palisaded with paintings by modem Indian painters. He waved his long hand towards one and said in his light and gentle voice: 'Do you like that? Husain's latest. He painted it only the other day. I think it's good, don't you? Come and sit down. No, no, don't apologize. There's nothing to apologize for. Will you have some gin or some beer?'

He is a slight, grey-haired man, with horn-rimmed spectacles on a thin mobile face. He has written a book of criticism on Yeats; during the war he was with the BBC in London, and he now runs the Indian radio network from Delhi.

'You've just been to see Khushwant? How was he? Was he very angry about the news?'

'What news?'

'Hasn't anybody seen the papers? The Chinese came into Indian territory today.' He picked a newspaper up and read from it. 'They crossed the border in the Subansiri division in NEFA, opened fire on our checkpost at Longju and overran it. Three of our boys have been killed.'

'What do you think Nehru will do?'

'Nothing. Protest. Take it as an aberration. In a couple of weeks they'll probably cross into Sikkim or Bhutan, one of those places. More aberrations. Then perhaps they'll cross into some other frontier territory. Ladakh. Then perhaps Nehru will think it has got beyond aberrations and send to the UN for a psychologist.'

'It's a bad time for this to happen, isn't it, with all this dissatisfaction in the army?'

'Well, yes. Though I doubt if the dissatisfaction will get beyond grumbling.'

The servant brought in gin-and-limes and a pretty little girl came in behind him.

'My daughter, Mala,' Narayana said, and his face grew gentler than ever as he watched his daughter say 'How do you do?' and go and sit down with the unique unobtrusive mannerliness that some Indian children have.

'She likes to hear me practise.' Narayana was also a famous veena player. We said, 'Why don't you? We'd love to hear it.'

'Would you really?' Narayana smiled. 'Mala, fetch the veena.'

The little girl's face lit up, and she dashed out and came back carefully carrying the wooden instrument in her arms.

The veena is shaped like half a pumpkin on a stick. The strings are of silver, and strung crosswise across the pumpkin-face. Narayana twiddled a few keys, tautening the strings, then bent over the instrument and began to play it. The long, very flexible fingers of his left hand struck the strings slowly, and a long-drawn-out succession of notes, like the calls of a mechanical bird, filled the room. Each faded out and was imperceptibly replaced by another, or overlapped and sang at different ends of the same golden bough. Mala leant forward in her chair with her eyes fixed adoringly on her father. The servant came and stood voluptuously at the door, his knuckles to his teeth, his eyes half-closed, moving a little with the music. When Narayana finished he looked up at us and laughed. 'Did you like that?'

We nodded, and he said, 'I did some experiments over the BBC during the war: playing European composers on the veena. They were quite successful, though of course there were some composers one couldn't do it with. But I've always wanted to try it the other way round: Indian music on European instruments. That would be more difficult, of course.' He stroked the stained wood of the veena affectionately.

'These things take about six months to make. Hand made, of course. There are only a few craftsmen left in south India who know how to make them. This one is thirty years old. I have another which is nearer a hundred.'

We talked for a little. Then Ved asked if Narayana had read the book by Nirad Chaudhuri, *A Passage to England,* which had been getting excellent reviews in the English press when we left.

'Yes. At least, I found I couldn't finish it. But it's well written. Chaudhuri, you know, has been praising the English way of life for years; but he had never been out of India till this visit of his which produced the book, and then he only stayed five weeks. So it's rather a lopsided book, I think, almost a pathetic book. And certainly most of the reviewers here haven't been very nice to it. One of them said Chaudhuri was like a dog trained to wag its tail when its master said "England." But of course the reviews were pretty lopsided too.'

'Do you know him?' I asked. 'I'd like to meet him. What's he like?'

'He used to work in All India Radio for a bit, and I knew him then. He's an eccentric, you know. He has the most extraordinary fund of information: he knows the date of the founding of Prague, and what porridge John Keats had, and things like that.'

'How does one contact him? Is he hard to see?'

'No, I'm sure he'd be delighted. I should think he feels a little lonely in India. I don't know where he lives myself, but ring up Khushwant and ask him, he would know.'

We said goodbye to him and to Mala and went down to our taxi. Narayana waved to us from the window.

'Ask your father what he thinks of the Chinese attack.'

When I got back to the hotel I found Marilyn in her room chuckling over the matrimonial advertisements in one of the newspapers. This is the modern form of arranged marriages: instead of having an astrologer as a go-between, as they did before, orthodox Indians now use the advertisement columns.

'What's so funny?'

Marilyn read out one of the advertisements between chuckles. 'Wanted one vegetarian virgin, skilled in H.H. affairs, for twenty-year-old cleanshaven bachelor. Caste no bar.'

'What on earth are H.H. affairs?'

'House Hold,' said Marilyn, and giggled furiously.

I went on to my father's room. It was filled with journalists and government officials, as usual: Connery of *Time-Life,* Atkinson of the *Daily Mail,* and in one corner, like Buddha in white ducks, Vincent Sheean. The telephone was ringing, as usual: as usual my father was doing several different things very efficiently, all at once.

While I was getting myself a drink I gathered that Nehru had just made a statement in Parliament over Longju. He had disclosed that for over a year China had been in possession of large tracts of Indian territory in Ladakh; that the Chinese had in fact built a road between Gartok in Western Tibet and Yarkand in Turkestan, that ran through the Aksai Chin of Ladakh and cut off hundreds of square miles of Indian territory; that they had established a military base at Spanggur in Ladakh, and a month before arrested a reconnaissance party sent there by the Indian government. Only three weeks ago, they had attacked the Indian post of Khinzemane, in the NEFA area, and pushed Indian troops back. Altogether they now controlled over a thousand square miles of Indian territory, and had recently announced their intention of making Nepal, Sikkim, and Bhutan, the independent border states, into part of the great motherland of China.

Nehru's speech had come as a bombshell. Everybody had known that there had been Chinese incursions into Indian territory before Longju, but nobody had realized their extent. My father was snorting like a warhorse that hears the trumpets.

'Why hasn't he said all this before? He's kept it a secret for a year. Why hasn't he taken any action?'

'Nehru is not a young man,' one of the Indian journalists said. 'And he has never faced this kind of situation before. He must be trusting in the goodwill of the Chinese not to come any farther.'

An American said, 'It's strange that he should trust the Chinese so much that he hasn't even told his own people and his own Parliament about all this for a year.'

They were all in that peculiar state of exaltation that marks good journalists when history is happening round their ears. For journalists operate in history, as poets operate in time. Both have an acute awareness of the past and of the present, and perhaps of the future: but whereas for the poet these are three separate cells, which with the lucky word he may make one, the speed of history sends the journalist skating forward through all three. Today the only one who did not seem to be skating upon history was Vincent Sheean; he sat calmly in a corner, occasionally joining, trumpet-tongued, in one of the many little arguments in the room, but part of none. I went and sat by him.

'Why don't you go up to the border states?' he said. 'You're young and footloose and you can afford to do it. Go and see what they're like, because in a year's time the Chinese may have got them.'

I said I would think about it.

India's troubles did not seem to come singly. When I awoke next morning, the bearer handed me the newspaper with an expectant look. Banner headlines announced the resignation of the three Indian Chiefs of Staff: Thimayya of the army, Katari of the navy, and Mukerjee of the air force.

I galloped round to my father's room to find him in pyjamas, a cup of coffee in one hand, and the telephone receiver in the other. When he had finished, 'Is this true?' I asked him.

'I don't know. If it is, it will probably be the first time in history that all three Chiefs of Staff have resigned simultaneously in any country. There'll be hell to pay for Krishna Menon. I hear he's furious this morning. He keeps chasing people out of his office.'

It was a pretty picture, but I did not dwell on it. 'What about Thimayya?'

'He isn't saying anything: except that the report came as a great shock. There must be some truth in it: but I think something's gone wrong somewhere.'

Then Marilyn arrived, then Sheean arrived, then Ved arrived, and then came the journalist armies, and the suite began to take on the aspect of an audience hall.

We all waited for the news from Parliament. The prime minister was absent. Krishna Menon was there, fobbing off furious volleys of questions from the opposition. Rumours were running all round the capital, and all the while Nehru kept silence and Thimayya kept to his tent. At four o'clock the news came through that Air Commodore Mukerjee, in London, had denied the rumours of the resignation. Admiral Katari was unavailable to anybody. Things were building up, however, for Krishna Menon.

Next morning the newspapers unanimously denounced him. Some demanded his resignation. The prime minister was to speak at midday. Marilyn shot off to Parliament with her cameras. My father went off with a host of excited French journalists. But Ved and I stayed in the hotel, drinking beer and eating pretzels. 'This is what I shall be doing in America,' Ved said. 'All this resignation business seems silly though. I don't know why people fuss so much about politics.'

Marilyn returned at one, dusty and exhausted, the cloth bags full of cameras swinging from her shoulders.

'Well, everybody said Nehru liked Krishna Menon, and this is the proof.'

'What happened?'

'He said that he had spoken to General Thimayya, and there was no question of his resigning. He said he had gone into Thimayya's grievances and found them extremely trivial.'

'Poor Thimayya,' Ved said. 'Did you get any shots?'

'Yes, I got two very good ones. One of Krishna Menon going into Parliament, looking like a thundercloud. And another of his coming out: and then he looked like a cat that had just eaten a sparrow.'

All the gossip in New Delhi is political. This is because it is not a residential capital, like London; it is a political capital, like Canberra. Most of the richer people are employed in one branch of government service or another, and around them the journalists buzz and whisper. Thus in times of comparative quietness the drawing rooms are filled with rumours of the impending fall of this minister or that minister; of who has Nehru's ear at the moment; of why the American ambassador went to dinner with the minister of food. In times like the one we were passing through, every rumour develops three heads and squirms through the teacups and the cocktail glasses, dipping a different head in each.

So there were many stories about what came to be known as the Thimayya affair, all entirely different. The one that seemed most reliable came from the phonologist in the defence ministry.

According to this story, the split between Krishna Menon and his Chiefs of Staff had grown wider and wider. In particular that between the defence minister and the army chief had assumed the proportions of an abyss. This was mainly over the promotions made by Krishna Menon, but another cause was alleged to be that Thimayya had asked that the Indian troops on the NEFA border should be supplied with automatic weapons, as they were inadequately armed in case of Chinese attacks. This request Krishna Menon is said to have refused: then came Longju, when inadequately equipped and outnumbered Indians were put to flight by the Chinese. Meanwhile Nehru is supposed to have summoned Thimayya on some other matter, and during the course of the discussion asked him whether the disturbing reports of dissension in the army were true, and what had caused such dissension. Thimayya answered frankly, and Nehru told him to go and see Krishna Menon.

When Thimayya arrived at the defence ministry, however, according to the story, he found Krishna Menon in a passionate rage. Thimayya was accused of deliberate treachery and of going over his minister's head. Krishna Menon is further alleged to have said that Thimayya should be behind bars.

At this Thimayya offered his resignation, and Krishna Menon told him he could do what he pleased. Thimayya is then said to have written a letter of resignation to Nehru. This reached the prime minister the next day. He summoned Thimayya, and asked him, in the interests of the country, not to resign. Thimayya accordingly withdrew his resignation and went home.

But that evening someone said something to somebody, and the next day the story broke. Thimayya's alleged reaction of shock is, in this context, understandable: by the time the report of his resignation appeared, he had already withdrawn it. But the whole thing had been dragged out into public, and in a public forum, if not in public opinion, Thimayya had suffered something of a setback. Yet Krishna Menon's victory, if one can call it that, was a Pyrrhic one. In the meantime, however, the gossip still went on, mingled now with a growing movement in the press urging that India should take up the Dalai Lama's case at the UN, and with news flashes stating that Chinese troops were moving along the Chumbi Valley on the Sikkim–Tibet border, that there was Chinese infiltration in Ladakh and Bhutan, and that Chinese troops edging along the NEFA border had replied when questioned that they were an entomological expedition in pursuit of rare butterflies.

All this was going on simultaneously when I went to see Nehru.

The Still Centre

In any shop or business office you enter in India, there are always two guardian angels brooding from gilded frames over the cashier. One is Gandhi, always, in these photographs, venerable, and the other Nehru, frozen into perpetual youth. Beautiful, young, he fills the gilt frame, one hand outflung to an invisible crowd beyond. One can feel this crowd vibrating outside the photograph, not quite getting what Nehru is saying but believing it anyway, because it is Nehru. When the outflung hand is lowered there will be yet another repetition of the thundered cry that has followed Nehru from podium to podium in India these thirty years: '*Jawaharlal ki jai*.'*

Today, after thirty years, the glass of the photograph has cracked. Long after I met Nehru in Delhi, I watched him address a crowd on the sea-beach at Bombay. Three hundred thousand people came through the rain to see him, not in real confidence but in vague hope that the ancient panacea would stream in under their umbrellas from the platform. Yet the moment Nehru began to speak, there was a disappointed murmur; the crowd seemed to realize that they had heard this before. The gathering began to fray apart and dissolve back into the rain out of which they had come: they were obviously all too aware that there would be no panaceas any more.

---

* Long live Jawaharlal.

There are several causes to account for this loss of grip. The most important is the failure of Nehru's foreign policy. Most Indians agree that India's line should be one of non-alignment: but not non-alignment as Nehru sees it. When the West does something wrong, he attacks: when it is the Communists, he always hesitates. Thus he condemned the Suez war and the Algerian butchery in the strongest terms; but he shilly-shallied about Hungary and he glossed over Tibet. He gave the Dalai Lama refuge, but he stipulated that the Dalai Lama should not use India as a political platform. The young and beautiful Nehru of the shop photographs, had he been exiled from his own country at the age of twenty-four, would have been very annoyed indeed if the country that gave him asylum had not also afforded him a political platform.

His economic policy has also brought protest, even from the small farmers who were the wall at his back in the old days. Nehru envisages a system of kolkhozes like those in China and Russia. His economic policy is tending more and more towards regimentation.

Ved and I had been lecturing to several colleges in Delhi. The students here were more sophisticated than those I had met in Bombay, and they talked a little more. I noticed that most of them were either Communists or left-wing Socialists, and I wondered why. One of them explained to me:

'We have all hero-worshipped Jawaharlal for years. We could even forgive him the mistakes he has made in the past, if he only showed signs of changing. But he has surrounded himself with misguided people, and they have fixed him in his course. He is too old to change. Therefore we have swung left, because there is nobody on the right of Nehru, and Nehru himself we do not want.'

Much later, students in Calcutta attacked the prime minister in much the same terms. The students have always been for Nehru, and their shift to the left is a sign that should disquiet the Congress Party. The illiterate electorate, which is in fact the majority, will probably still vote for it, because it is Nehru's party, and voting for Nehru has become a habit, and besides there is no other comparable figure. But the students criticize him; the newspapers attack him almost daily, his own ministers complain (behind his back) that he is dictatorial and will not take the advice of anybody except Krishna Menon, perhaps the most unpopular politician in India: the intelligentsia, such as it is, has forsaken Nehru, and it is sad, because he is still, and in spite of everything, the only man who could hold India to a stable democracy.

It was another hot day. Parliament was going into session at twelve, to try and tidy up the debris of the week's hurricane. My appointment with Nehru was for eleven-thirty. I arrived at quarter past eleven at his secretary's office in Parliament House.

This was a large room, flanked with filing-cabinets. Nehru's secretary sat in one corner behind a desk on which a telephone made constant small jangles. He nodded to me. 'Please take your seat.' One of the three armchairs in the room was already occupied by a stocky and worried-looking man in the national costume of jodhpurs and long white jacket. 'One of our ambassadors,' the secretary told me. From his looks he must have been a very peccant one indeed.

I took my seat, trying not to look at the ambassador, who was breakfasting off his fingernails, and lit a cigarette. Outside the room was a garden filled with tulips; between the garden and the room ran a broad corridor, culminating in tall mahogany doors with brass handles; a red-turbaned sepoy was on guard outside Nehru's office. The prime minister had not yet arrived.

Suddenly there was a stir at the door. Nehru stood in the corridor, a slight, stooped figure in immaculate white jodhpurs and high-necked jacket, a white Gandhi cap on his head. He wore in his buttonhole the red rose that has become a kind of badge of office, and in his hand carried a short sandalwood stick. Everybody in the room jumped up like clockwork. The ambassador, who seemed to have swallowed a fingernail, choked.

Nehru saw me, and lifted his stick to me with a smile. Then he looked coldly at the ambassador. It was eleven-twenty-three. 'I can spare you seven minutes precisely.' He walked through the tall doors that the sepoy had flung open, followed by a train of peons with files. The ambassador, a little sheepishly, brought up the rear.

The secretary winked at me. I smiled, nervously, back.

At eleven-thirty sharp the mahogany doors swung open and ejected the ambassador. A bell rang imperiously at the secretary's desk. He turned to me and nodded. The PM will see you. Go in, please.'

'This is terrifying,' I thought, but went into the corridor and towards the door. The sepoy clicked his heels, snapped into a salute, and opened it. I went straight through and became inextricably entangled in a curtain which I had not noticed on the other side. The door shut firmly behind me.

I struggled free of the curtain and confronted Nehru. He had risen from his desk, and was staring at me with a mixture of wonder and concern. He had taken his cap off. I looked at the high-domed, bald head, the beautiful face with its long, ambitious upper lip and hooded eyes, and said rather foolishly, 'How do you do?'

Nehru said gravely, 'Hullo.' He gave me a rather limp handshake and sat down again. His desk, an enormous teak desk, was set at right angles to the door. I sat down near him, on his left, facing the fatal curtain.

There was a long silence. Nehru had turned sideways in his chair, his fingers playing with a silver paper knife. He looked much older without his cap: one saw the deep lines in his face, and his eyes were more hooded even than one had thought, and entirely abstracted. I didn't know where to begin, so didn't say anything.

Finally, glancing at me for a moment, and then looking back past me to the tulips in the garden, he said, 'I've read your book.'

His voice was so soft as to be almost inaudible, but he spoke very slowly, with long pauses as if he were thinking each word out. There was another long pause, and I was just going to say something when he began again. I noticed later that this long pause occurred between nearly all his sentences.

'What are your plans now? Have you finished with Oxford?'

I said yes, and that I had another book of poems ready for the press, and was thinking of writing a book about what I did in India. He nodded.

'There have been a lot of books written about India.' He turned to me fully for the first time, with a small, fleeting smile. 'I've written some myself.'

'Yes, sir,' I said, and then, 'do you write much nowadays?'

'Not for the last fifteen years. There was no time. Going abroad…state affairs…that sort of thing. I did publish a bunch of old letters a little while ago… If I have time I can always go and dig some more up… I've got files full of the wretched things.'

I recalled an essay of his that I had once read about the Spanish Civil War. It was written in a peculiar succession of images that recalled a masculine Virginia Woolf. I asked him if he remembered it.

'I don't know.… I wrote so much in those days.…'

'If you hadn't been what you are, sir, do you think you would have been a writer?'

He seemed to wake up fully for the first time. He smiled with a swift and extraordinary interest that changed his whole face so that suddenly he looked young.

'That's an intriguing question.… I don't know what I would have been. What I wrote I wrote because it seemed politically necessary, or necessary to me to clear up a political confusion in my mind. I wasn't a poet, a creative writer, I was a political writer. I don't know…perhaps I would have been a scientist. Or a writer…? Yes, perhaps I would have been a writer.'

He turned back and again looked out of the window. In repose his face seemed old, petulant, and disinterested. But when he glanced at me again it lit up with that remarkable smile.

'What do you do in the afternoons? Don't you find it hot?'

I was rather taken aback, but before I could answer he said, 'Do you take your own advice, and choose the wise alternative to death, a nap in the afternoon?'

I recognized two lines from an old poem of mine. I was flattered but again at a loss for anything to say. Nehru said suddenly, bending away from me once more and looking out of the window: 'If you are going to write about India, you must decide which India you are going to write about.'

He looked at me. 'Well?'

'I don't know. I thought I might go up to the Tibetan border states.' For a moment he looked seriously displeased. The eyes hooded themselves like a hawk's eyes; the silver paper knife was tapped on the desk several times in quick succession.

'The Tibetan border states? Why?'

'I would like to have a look at them, sir.'

'Have a look at what?' Then again he back-pedalled, turned and looked out of the window at the stiff marching lines of tulips. He obviously did not want an answer, so I remained silent.

Presently he turned back to me. 'For natural beauty, mountains, that sort of thing, I would say...go to Kashmir and Kerala. I have...a local interest in Kashmir...being a Kashmiri. But it's very beautiful...the mountains...the snow...' I noticed he seldom made any gestures at all, except to fidget with the paper knife.

A peon came in with a file. He put it down on the desk, salaamed deeply, and withdrew. Nehru turned and began to read the file, initialling and signing each page. As he did so, however, the soft, slow voice continued to talk.

'Kerala...is the opposite of Kashmir. Scenically, and all that. But it is a most beautiful part.... There is no point in going anywhere in India and staying in a hotel, except in the cities. You must go to the villages. India is a poor man's country...a villager's country.'

He finished initialling the file and dabbed impatiently at the bell. The peon came in and took the file away. While this was happening Nehru again gazed out of the window, tapping the paper knife on the arm of his chair. He turned to me, but seemed for a moment to have lost the thread of his argument. Then he continued. 'You must go to the villages and live with the villagers. You must accept them for what they are. They are good people. It is difficult for people like you...people from Oxford and Cambridge, coming back to this country...to make that adjustment...because you are too sophisticated, that sort of thing...you have a preconceived notion of what you expect in the way of conversation and comfort.'

'You seem to have made the adjustment all right, sir,' I said.

He smiled again. 'Have I? I don't know.... Yes. I had to...at first it was part of my work, as a young man, and then I loved doing it. I suppose urban students in India would have the same trouble if they went back to the villages...it's unfair to attack people who have studied in England.'

I thought of an incident that had taken place during one of the lectures Ved and I had given. We had arrived at a college to find ourselves addressing the staff. No students were present at all. After the lecture I asked the principal, rather bewilderedly, where the students were. Couldn't we meet some? 'Oh no,' said the principal in a shocked voice. 'They are too badly educated to meet you.'

I told Nehru this story, thinking it terrifying but rather funny, and was rather distressed when he didn't laugh. Instead he turned angrily to his desk. 'Ridiculous,' he said, 'quite ridiculous.' He seized a pencil. 'What was the name of this college?'

I told him, and he scribbled quickly on a piece of paper.

'Quite ridiculous,' he said again, then smiled and added, 'haven't you seen any better colleges than that?'

I said I didn't like what I had seen of Indian colleges: too many students, too few teachers, too little contact between the two, and so on. 'I agree. But the country must have an educated majority.'

'Yes, sir, but at this rate the country's going to have a half-educated majority, which I should think is pretty dangerous.'

'We are still a young country.... All that will come in time.'

I felt a little disappointed in this reply, but looked at the clock, which said twelve.

'I'm sorry if I've kept you, sir.'

He followed my glance. Then he said, 'Parliament can wait for a few minutes.' After this he said nothing for a while, but sat gazing past me at the tulips.

Here, at the still centre of the hurricane that had just swept Delhi, everything seemed orderly but vague. The shadowy room was undecorated except for a few photographs, unfurnished but for the great teak desk and a sofa in the corner. Nehru sat with chin in hand for a few minutes. Then he put the paper knife down on the desk, picked up his cap and stick, fidgeted with a file and said, 'I haven't been able to read much modern poetry in the last fifteen years. Sometimes I wish... I had more time.' He rang the bell and a peon came in and picked up some files. The Cambridge voice shifted suddenly into a beautiful classical Hindi, giving orders. Then he turned to me. 'Sorry, but I must go.' He put his cap on. His face looked younger when he had it on. He put the stick under his arm and waved me through the door ahead of him.

'I'm sorry if I've taken up too much of your time, sir.'

'No, no, my dear chap. Glad to see you.' He patted me on the shoulder, gave me another limp handshake, and then walked off, slight, stooped, and beautiful, followed by a train of peons with files. The still centre moved off towards Parliament, and the regathering hurricane.

Out of a Journal

This morning Delhi is swept by the loose, wild rain that always follows days of heat and thunder. Frogs appear in ditches that have been dry for days; the awnings of the hotel bubble and drip; the trees turn green. 'God in his mercy has sent this'—Vincent Sheean, looking mock-solemnly at the sky—'It will cool Panditji's brow.' The lassitude of the last few days lifts from me. I occupy myself making and shaking Bloody Maries and Old Fashioneds in thermos flasks, Marilyn acting as taster, solemnly waggling her eyebrows in approbation. Wet journalists came into my father's room, but the rain seems to have broken a thread in the air. The talk is no longer of Nehru and Krishna Menon but of the weather.

I want to see Nirad Chaudhuri. Chaudhuri has no telephone. So I ring and ask Khushwant for the address. He seems a bit vague; somewhere near the Kashmiri Gate, he says, but if we go there and ask for Nirad Chaudhuri anyone will direct us: he is a known and beloved figure in the vicinity. Ring Ved, who picks me up in a taxi after lunch.

A long drive to the Kashmiri Gate: meanwhile the sun gropes through the clouds and the afternoon fills slowly with heat. When we reach the Kashmiri Gate, we stop the taxi and ask a passerby where Nirad Chaudhuri lives. He does not know. Conclude that he is not a local inhabitant and push on. An area of exceedingly tortuous streets all mixed up like grandmother's knitting. Heat-haze after the rain, making the road look as if it were covered with oil, and clouds of flies everywhere. Send the taxi driver to inquire at various shops, but draw a blank. Get out ourselves. Swarms of children immediately surround us. 'King of the world, give me money. My mother is dead, my father is dead.' We hold out some coins, they are snatched from our hands and all the children begin to fight over them, tearing one another with their nails. Their small bodies are like relief-maps, so far do the bones stick out.

Ask a photographer (Sikh) where Nirad Chaudhuri lives. He pushes his turban forward and scratches his head like a Mummerset man. First time I have ever seen a Sikh do this, and I watch in fascination. Finally takes his hand away from his head, fingernails coated in oil and scurf, and says do we mean a tall youth called Chaudhuri who goes to school? No, we say, but perhaps his father. His father, the Sikh says, is a lentil-seller by the Gate. No, we say again. The Sikh goes back to scratching his head. Then he asks is it an old man called Nirala? No, we say, a middle-aged man called Nirad Chaudhuri, a writer. Ved adds that he is a Bengali. The Sikh snaps his fingers triumphantly. 'Oh, that fellow! The Bengali Babu!' He gives us directions. As we drive off he runs after us shouting that if we ever want our photographs taken his is infinitely the best shop in Delhi.

Reach Chaudhuri's house, tall and wooden in a crooked street off the Kashmiri Gate. Climb three flights of groaning stairs. It is now very hot and my shirt is damp and heavy with sweat. Ved has a suit on and is worse off, but refuses to remove his jacket because he is wearing braces. By the time we reach the top floor we are both in a vile temper. We emerge into a broad verandah where a naked figure is asleep on a sheet. Ved bends and shakes it impatiently. 'Hai mai, brother, get up and call your master.' Figure springs up, wraps the sheet round itself to form a waist-cloth, and says with dignity, 'I am Mr Chaudhuri.'

Ved and I are dumbstruck. Chaudhuri, however, seems to take it all in his stride. 'Mr Mehta and Mr Moraes? I have seen your pictures in the papers. Please come in.' The main room is spacious but a little bare, the corners filled with heaped up books. Chaudhuri disappears for a moment, reappearing in a shirt and trousers. He is a small frail man with a sharp bespectacled face and a tiny moustache. We ask him about his new book.

'Oh I am *very* pleased about that. *Very* pleased. It has got some fine reviews in England. The English will understand such a book, you see. But here it has got bad reviews, of course. Here they do not understand.'

He gestures frequently, bobbing his head as he makes his points.

'You will not believe it, the Indians do not want to know me. No! It is the foreign diplomats who are my friends. I have been to ten parties in the last fortnight—*all* given by foreign diplomats! Now will you believe that? Is that not extraordinary? I get on better with foreigners, you see. I understand foreigners. Now one of my friends is in the French embassy. His is the last party I have been to. How tastefully his house is decorated! How gracious is the way in which he lives! Every man can be judged by his habits and surroundings at home.'

Ved and I remain silent. Chaudhuri continues: 'I am now writing a book about India. That also will be appreciated in England and attacked here. But I feel that if I write three or four books, perhaps I may achieve some reputation in England. Is that so? If you write three or four books do you achieve a reputation in England?'

I say cautiously that it depends on the books. Chaudhuri is very eager to know more. 'I want to settle in England, you know. I was only there for five weeks, in 1955, but I felt as if my whole life had been a preparation for those five weeks, and after that I feel myself at a loss till I can return.'

He says: 'How beautiful is Hyde Park! And there is so much tradition there in England! The eating places are like palaces—Lyons', the ABC. I feel at a loss for words. It seems to me a totally new view of London. If we had met in London I would have thought this a mad kind of poetry; here, with the Kashmiri Bazaar teeming below, the whole thing seems grotesque. I relapse into silence, while Chaudhuri talks to Ved about literature. He thinks *A Passage to India* Forster's worst novel because, he says, it was improbable: during British days a person like Aziz would never have been able to ask Miss Quested and Mrs Moore to tea or to picnics. He very gleefully adds that he had pointed this out to Forster. Forster, he says, had taken his point.

When we leave he says earnestly: 'I am glad to have met you, but take my advice, and return at once to England. If you stay here you will perish. They will not understand you here.'

Amongst the American journalists who drop in for a drink in the evenings is one with a statuesque and improbable dignity: when very drunk his upper lip trembles a little, as though he wanted to cry. He is to leave this morning and comes in to see my father but remains to breakfast with me off Scotch and water. By eleven he is imploring me to recite early Yeats and the Shakespeare sonnets to him and his upper lip trembles uninterruptedly, and fat little tears are squeezed out on to his cheeks.

'Repeat that. Repeat it. "That time of year thou mayst in me behold".'

'"When yellow leaves, or none, or few, do hang upon those boughs which shake against the cold"—'

'"Bare ruined choirs, where late the sweet birds *sang*." Isn't that beautiful, beautiful poetry? Come and listen, everybody. Repeat it.'

'You should pack, shouldn't you?'

'You must come and help me pack. And recite some beautiful poems. Will you do that? Will you recite some beautiful poems?'

So Ved and I go back with him to his hotel. When we get up to his room he points to three suitcases.

'That's it. My three beautiful suitcases. My clothes are in the cupboard.'

'We'd better ring for the bearer,' Ved says. We ring, and a slender young man appears.

'Pack this sahib's bags.'

'Bearer!' says the journalist, 'what's your name?'

'Jacob, sir.'

'You're a bloody Christian, Jacob. I bet your father was an untouchable, Jacob.'

'What's he saying?' the bearer asks in Hindi.

'No matter,' Ved says. 'Hurry up with those bags.'

The journalist says, 'Jacob, you have beautiful moustaches, my boy.'

The bearer says, alarmed, 'If the sahib feels like that I can get him the most beautiful girl in India tonight, for a hundred rupees. But I am a family man.'

'Never mind about that,' Ved says. 'Pack quickly.'

Presently the bearer says, 'I have packed two suitcases, sahib.'

'You're a Christian crook, Jacob,' says the journalist. 'Pack the third, you Christian crook.'

'Sahib,' says the bearer, reasonably, 'what with? There is nothing left to pack.'

'That's true,' says the journalist. 'You take the third suitcase, Jacob. Take it and remember me.'

'What is the use of a suitcase to me, sahib?' says the bearer. 'I have nothing to put in it.'

'Okay,' says the journalist. 'Unpack the other two bags.' When the bearer had done that, 'Pack all that stuff in the third bag,' says the journalist, 'and take it away, Jacob. Always be a good Christian.'

'You've got absolutely nothing left,' I protest.

'Jacob's got everything. Jacob likes it, don't you, Jake?'

'Yes, sir,' says the bearer, hastily withdrawing with his bulging suitcase.

'Just a minute,' calls the journalist. 'When will you wear my evening clothes, Jacob?'

'Sir,' says the bearer, 'at weddings and funerals.'

He disappears. It is too late to reason further. Ved and I each carry one empty suitcase downstairs, put them, and with more difficulty the journalist, in the airline bus, and wave goodbye.

Perhaps we should have tried harder to prevent him from parting with his clothes but so passionately misguided a gesture, I thought, had a native charm about it. Also I like the idea of a man who when the Customs asked him if he had anything to declare could answer with perfect and literal truth, 'Nothing.'

Drinks at Narayana's. His wife Rekha, whom I have come to know in the last few days, is there, as beautiful as a fresco from Ajanta. Mala, who has a cold necessitating mustard baths, sits like a cut flower, up to her calves in water, looking wistfully at the veena. Her father's long fingers dwell lightly on it, then move away. He tells me about Husain the painter, who is staying with him and Rekha. Husain came to Bombay as a young man. He was penniless and had to sleep in the streets: to earn a little money he painted people's names on suitcases and umbrellas. Then, one day, he started painting posters for Indian films. He became the most famous poster-painter in the business, earning an enormous salary. He kept it up for a year, then once more abandoned everything and returned to the pavements and the suitcases that needed names painted on. Meanwhile he painted his own pictures, and one day a Bombay art critic saw them and arranged an exhibition. Everything was sold. After that Husain had exhibitions in Paris, Rome, London, Berlin: after Jamini Roy he is perhaps the best-known Indian artist in the West. Now, staying with Narayana, he paints all night: all his new canvases are lined up on one side of the dining-room, as in an exhibition. The dining room smells of unseed oil and paint. Narayana and I stoop, peering into the pictures: some are still wet, they are all thickly painted in whorls, with opaque night-coloured blues and patches of red. Narayana adjusts his spectacles with a delicate forefinger. 'Don't say anything about them when Husain comes. He's very shy.'

In the meantime Han Suyin, the novelist, arrives, a tall and beautiful woman in a Chinese dress with a split skirt; she coils herself into a chair, speaking to nobody save Mala, but watching everybody with an enigmatic curly smile. She has just published a new novel with a Nepalese setting. I ask her what Nepal is like, for I plan to go there. 'Beautiful,' she says, 'but you must go and see, mustn't you? I can't tell you,' and she turns back to Mala.

When Husain comes he turns out to be enormously tall, lean but powerful with grey hair and a thick grey beard. He clasps a tankard of beer in long veined fingers and sits insecurely on a stool beside me. Like Han Suyin, he says nothing, but laughs silently at anything funny that is said. Presently he turns to me and says gently, not looking at me but at a point beyond my left ear, 'I am trying to write poems in English.'

I ask, what about? He replies, 'They are about the same things as my paintings.'

I ask if he will show me some. He withdraws a ragged piece of paper from his pocket and gives it to me. The poem is in rather unskilful free verse, but describes in an extremely precise and graphic manner the flight of a heron, and its manner of landing, dragging its legs for a moment as if it were injured, balancing on its wings.

Just at this moment three other painters burst in, one Krishen Khanna, in a honey-coloured woollen shirt that I immediately covet. He is the most promising of the younger painters. He seems, now, in a gay mood and immediately begins laughing and teasing Husain, who gives me the gentle, hooded smile of one who shares a secret, and replaces the poem in his pocket. For a little while all the room is given up to the newcomers. Krishen Khanna fishes Mala out of her mustard bath and hugs her exuberantly. They talk about prices and sales. When Krishen Khanna comes and sits by me I discover that he is a banker. This surprises me, and seems to surprise him too: as he tells me his eyebrows arch, his mouth goes round and wondering, as if he were Mala listening to one of Ved's Freudian fairy tales.

As the evening wears on Narayana and Han Suyin begin to argue about the Chinese incursions on the border. Narayana keeps saying that the Dalai Lama seems to him a symbol of freedom. Han Suyin disagrees: her eyes flash, she points her finger emphatically as she speaks, as if poking holes in Narayana's argument. The young painters cheer them on. Even Husain takes the opportunity to speak and begins to say something about painting, of which I can catch no more than a few words, for he talks very softly and with his head turned away. Mala, her sneezes reduced to faint protesting sniffs, is bundled off to bed by Rekha. We go on talking till late. I feel happier here than I have yet felt in India: these people are all my friends.

Breakfast with Malcolm MacDonald, the British high commissioner. He was commissioner-general in Southeast Asia before that. I remembered meeting him with my father in Singapore when I was twelve years old. Perhaps adults all seem gigantic to a child: I remember MacDonald being as tall as Stephen Spender, but discovering today that he is actually a small, slightly built man feel nonplussed and as if the basis of conversation has been taken away. But MacDonald is quick to make me easy, he talks about Borneo, Java, the Mekong Valley. As a child I saw some of these places and an interesting game begins, trying to relate ten-year-old memories to MacDonald's descriptions. Things come back: I remember for instance that the Javanese word for Mister is Bung, which used to amuse me greatly at the age of eleven.

A very English breakfast, with scrambled eggs, kidneys, and bacon. I horrify the butler by insisting instead on two raw eggs with tabasco sauce. MacDonald watches me mixing it with interest. 'Can you really eat that?'

'Oh yes, they're frightfully nourishing.'

'I would not eat those,' MacDonald says, 'unless somebody I

was in love with told me to.' He talks about the short stories he has been writing: 'I've been trying to write short stories since I was up at university. I've suppressed all the poetry I wrote then, but I keep the short stories and rework them over and over till I've got nearer to what I want to say.'

He has vivid blue eyes like stains in a bronzed face. Very *simpatico* and full of a nervous energy which one senses will be unleashed the moment breakfast's last kidney has disappeared. I am right: after breakfast, washed down with beer, he gives me a Dutch cigar and takes me on a flying walk round the gardens, pointing to various birds and giving me detailed information about their nesting habits. 'You must know about chaffinches?'

'No,' I say.

'Shame on you. A poet who doesn't know about birds.' He crimps the end of his cigar between his lips and leads me back to the houses, apparently disappointed by my lack of bird-lore.

'What do you think of all this Tibet business going on now?' I venture back in the enormous drawing room filled with Morlands and Sisleys.

He is silent, but presently says, 'The Dalai Lama is in rather a bad position, poor boy. I feel sorry for him. I can't think that anybody would prefer Delhi to Lhasa. Or Mussoorie to Lhasa for that matter.'

'He's coming to Delhi,' I say. 'I'm going to see him.'

'Oh, really? To persuade Nehru to take this business up at the UN no doubt. I wish he had a better chance.'

As I leave, still struggling with my cigar, he seems to think again of the Dalai Lama, and shakes his head. 'Poor boy. I'm sure he'd be happiest at Oxford.'

MacDonald was right: the Indian government has refused to take Tibet's case before the United Nations. They have done this for two reasons: firstly, that neither Tibet nor China is a member of the United Nations; secondly, that Tibet is an internal problem of the Chinese State, in which they do not wish to meddle.

Sophistry, I think: after all India has continually brought up the questions of apartheid in South Africa and French administration in Algeria before the Security Council, and has no more right to meddle in the internal affairs of France and South Africa than in those of China. Also, as Vincent Sheean reminds everybody with an ominous look in his eye, Germany was not a member of the League of Nations when they discussed Hitler's aggression against Poland.

The government is nervous. Chinese troops continue to move about on the border, not frog-stepping, not with caterpillar-footed tanks to tread on dreams of peace, but persuasively, Asiatically, butterfly-hunters with sten-guns. The press carry articles every day—my father is writing one now, scribbling in blue pencil as he does always on large neat sheets of paper—and there have been demonstrations in sympathy with the Tibetans: but a hundred blue pencils and a hundred thousand demonstrators will not remove the nervousness of an entrenched government. Modern politics run so strangely that perhaps that nervousness would only be brushed aside by a newly created nervousness, if an election were at hand.

But then India has nobody else to elect. The last man who seemed likely to be a successor to Nehru was Jayaprakash Narayan. Today Ved and I arrive, a little breathless and late, at a gathering on a terrace, which Jayaprakash Narayan is to address.

He is perhaps the only Indian politician (since Ambedkar, the untouchable leader, died) to have been educated in America. He spent seven years there, and then worked a short while in the Congress under Gandhi before he founded the Indian Socialist Party in 1932. He was then a Marxist Socialist, but drew close to Gandhi in his last years, and after Gandhi's death left the Socialist Party and joined the land-reform movement led by Vinoba Bhave. He has spent the last few years trudging through rivers and across deserts in remote parts of the country getting land for the peasants, more or less in retirement from active politics, but has recently returned to the political scene with a programme of Gandhian Socialism, which is really right-wing Socialism with a Tolstoyan basis.

Jayaprakash Narayan stands at the top of the terrace, looking at about forty people sitting on the ground. He is a man of medium height with a wheat-coloured face, beautiful and deeply lined at the forehead, these lines giving him a curious look of perpetual bewilderment. He wears homespun jodhpurs and an Indian kameez, a shirt that hangs free. He plaits his fingers together, not so much nervously as abstractedly, and considers the crowd.

My father arrives, and takes us up to meet him. With him is Minoo Masani, once a leader of the Socialists under Narayan, who has now transferred allegiance to a new right-wing party, the Swatantra. We have met before, and shake hands. Masani then introduces us.

Jayaprakash Narayan gives us a kindly smile and says something in a voice so soft that I have to strain my ears to catch what he is saying. He pats me on the shoulder and says, 'If you have any questions, please ask them. I won't promise satisfactory answers but I'll do my best.'

As we go back to find places on the terrace my father says, 'J.P. is probably the only politician in India who is an entirely good man.'

'Is he likely to become prime minister?'

'Why not?' Ved asks.

'You'll see in a minute,' says my father.

The first question has been asked. It is about the border situation. Jayaprakash bends his head and considers this in silence. It is quite a long silence. People begin to stir restively. Finally, raising his head, Jayaprakash begins to speak about the government policy. He disagrees with it, he says, but he can see why the government should act as they do. He gives several reasons for this. All governments have to act discreetly, he says. He explains why. It is not boring, partly because a great deal of it is completely inaudible, but partly, too, because he radiates an air of entire honesty, a groping, clumsy honesty that does not mind how much of a fool it makes of itself so long as what is to be said is said. Finally he returns to the point at issue and says that he feels that the borders should be defined more stringently. His answer has taken twenty-five minutes.

The questions go on. So do the answers. At the end the audience dries up and sits in respectful silence. Jayaprakash sighs and asks for a cup of tea. Immediately the audience dissolves: part of it rushes up to Jayaprakash to get his blessing. He is obviously thought of as a saint rather than a politician. I think certainly he is nearer to a saint than he is to a politician. When the crowd has thinned, my father, Ved, and I go up to him.

I ask him about Bhave. He smiles at the name, as though the sound of it made him happy. 'He is somewhere in the Punjab now, I think. The last I heard, he was in a village two hundred miles from Delhi. He seldom comes as close to cities as that. But now he may be five hundred miles from Delhi. He travels quickly, because he travels light.'

He adds, 'On the home front, I think a government that works on Vinobaji's premises is the only feasible one for this country. Of course, Vinobaji himself would not take office in it.'

'Would you take office?'

'I do not seek office.' And again the beautiful and human smile.

I ask about the Dalai Lama. Jayaprakash smiles once more.

'He is our most precious possession at the moment. It is strange that the home of the Dalai Lama should be in our country, though there was one* who made his home here before. But that one was no more than a political refugee. This one is also a symbol of liberty.'

I have heard these words before, from Narayana Menon. Also other words from others. Today the Dalai Lama has come to Delhi, he is staying in Hyderabad House, surrounded by security

* The thirteenth Dalai Lama, who fled to Darjeeling in 1910 to escape Manchu rule.

officers, and the drawing rooms chitter and quiver with the latest news about him. A man who saw him coming to Tezpur after his flight from Tibet asserts that there is a halo round his head. Vincent Sheean snorts and says belligerently, 'He's a child.' Marilyn thinks he looks a nice boy. I don't know which is true.

I am to see the Dalai Lama tomorrow.

Kundun

It was raining again. In the gardens of Hyderabad House the lilac-bushes dripped softly; water trickled through the channels of the rockeries and overflowed the normally arid bowls of the fountains. The great house which contained the Dalai Lama stood patiently in the middle distance, being rained on.

I saw all this from outside, through the great gates guarded by Sikh soldiers. Several tents had been pitched on the grass verge of the road to accommodate them and the security officers. A tangle of barbed wire lay, for no apparent purpose, in the grass: the Sikhs came carefully round it as the car drew up at the gate, and asked for my pass.

'I haven't got one.'

'Ha!' one of them said triumphantly. 'Then you cannot enter.'

'I have an appointment.'

'You must see the security officer,' the Sikh said.

So I climbed gingerly out into the rain and was led to a tent where a sad man sat with a telephone at his elbow. He picked this telephone up after I had put my case to him, and gloomily asked it for the private secretary. In a little while the telephone spoke volubly to him. At the end he nodded and put the receiver distastefully back on the hook.

'You are expected. The private secretary will meet you in the entrance. You may not take your car.'

I went back with the soldier who had brought me. He unlocked the gate and let me into the grounds. Then he trotted behind me, extending a small black umbrella that mushroomed from his fist over my head. A second soldier followed carrying the first one's rifle. In this manner, somewhat like a military funeral, we passed down the puddled driveway into the great porch.

A lama in brown robes stood in the porch. He was tall and elderly, and kept his hands in his sleeves. A rosary hung out of one sleeve. He said without pleasure, in English, 'I am the private secretary. Come inside.' We went into the entrance hall. Hyderabad House is now a state guest house, but it was formerly the Delhi palace of the Nizam, and the entrance hall is clearly the entrance hall of a palace: a huge domed roof, marble flooring, and grubby statues everywhere. Several groups of lamas, some in brown robes, some in black, stood talking softly under the dome that filtered a submarine light into the hall beneath. Their rosaries clicked softly. The private secretary deposited me on a sofa and went swimming away from me with prodigious strides, his robes floating about him. A young lama approached and sat, a little shyly, at my side.

He asked, in excellent English, if I had come to see His Holiness. Yes, I said. Was I a journalist? I denied this. He suddenly laughed and shook a finger at me: 'Ah, I see it, you are a poet. I see it by your hair.' To change the subject I asked him where he had learnt his English. He had been to school in India, he said.

'Then this isn't your first visit?'

'No, indeed, but I hope it will be the last.'

'Why?' He shrugged and wouldn't answer.

I asked him if he had come out with the Dalai Lama. He said yes. 'That was a terrible trip,' he said, 'a terrible trip. I do not like to remember.'

At this point the private secretary came hurrying back with a harassed-looking Indian official and a slender young Sikkimese in a bush shirt. The lama beside me vanished, and the official sat down in his place and said emphatically: 'You understand that the condition on which this audience has been granted is that you should ask no political questions?' I nodded. 'Please keep to that condition. Now, there are certain other things. Do not touch His Holiness. That is sacrilege. When the audience is terminated, do not turn your back on His Holiness. Leave the room backwards. Also, kindly do not ask His Holiness rude questions.'

'How do you mean, rude questions?'

'Do not ask His Holiness if he believes that he is a god.'

'It had never occurred to me to do so,' I said truthfully.

'Very well.' He beckoned to the Sikkimese. 'This gentleman is your interpreter. Please remember that he will not translate political questions. His Holiness will now receive you.'

The interpreter led me out of the entrance hall through a carpeted corridor that emerged on a square courtyard. This courtyard had taken on the air of a lamasery already: groups of lamas stood about talking, as in the entrance hall, and two or three sat on rugs turning prayer-wheels. The drone of their prayers came to me through the rain-cooled air. The interpreter paused at a doorway on one side of the courtyard, whispering to me, 'Prepare yourself.' Then he turned into the room, and I followed.

It was a big drawing room, full of sofas and occasional tables, and looking over the garden. In the middle of acres of carpet the Dalai Lama stood smiling. From his photographs I had always got the impression of somebody with an elongated body and enormous head: I was surprised to find him actually a sturdy, broad-shouldered, tall young man. He had clear skin and rosy cheeks, and wore black-rimmed pince-nez, slightly inappropriate-looking on the young face. His brown robe was open at the neck to reveal a tan shirt. He came forward and gave me an extremely firm handshake. The interpreter fluttered and kept trying to entice us to various sofas. Finally the Dalai Lama chose one by the window, pointed firmly to it, and turned to me, smiling. He gestured and said in English, 'Please sit.'

It was an enormous sofa. I sank into it with trepidation. The Dalai Lama sat beside me and the interpreter drew up a chair facing us. The Dalai Lama crossed his legs composedly, revealing under the robe brown brogues and a pair of red socks with yellow stripes. He spoke first. His voice was deep and clear, and he spoke rather fast, giving an impression of tremendous eagerness. He spoke in Tibetan, but looked at me all the while with brown intelligent eyes.

'His Holiness would much like to read some of your poetries,' said me interpreter. 'Is it possible for you to send him some poetries?'

'Yes, certainly. Has His Holiness read a great deal of literature then, apart from Tibetan literature?'

This was translated, and the Dalai Lama shook his head emphatically, the corners of his mouth turned down in a charming and rueful smile. I felt this was an answer, and was surprised when the interpreter began, rather hurriedly, to translate:

'His Holiness is familiar with all the literatures of the world.'

I asked, ignoring this fatuity, 'Is there any secular literature in Tibet? The recent revolt, for instance, did that produce any literature?'

The interpreter translated this. He addressed the Dalai Lama as 'Kundun', his usual Tibetan title, which means 'Presence'. As he ended each sentence he sketched a little obeisance with hand and head. Kundun thought carefully, and then answered.

'His Holiness says that he does not know of any literature, but there may be some. The difficulty about finding out would be that such literature manuscripts will be in Tibet and not India.'

'If they could be found I would like to try and translate them, if His Holiness feels that their publication in the West would help the Tibetan cause.'

The Dalai Lama nodded when this was translated, and smiled with his vivid smile. He leant forward, tapped me on the knee, and said something. 'His Holiness thanks you for your interest in the Tibetan people. He hopes to be able to send some of the young men of his people to your university, to Oxford, and to other Western universities. He will see if he is able to afford, and if possible he will send.'

'Does His Holiness not feel that young men brought up in an exclusively Eastern society in Tibet may have difficulty in the West?'

The Dalai Lama surprisingly began to answer this before it was translated. He shook his head emphatically at the start, then went on, talking quickly with many gestures of one long, capable hand, and occasionally reaching over to tap me on the knee. He smiled all the while, but usually a little wryly, the corners of his mouth turned down; it was only when he was genuinely amused or interested that the corners of the mouth lifted, the cheeks got pinker, and the eyes gleamed. Now he was explaining something unpleasant, and the smile was downturned.

'His Holiness says that the Chinese have already altered the structure of Tibetan society and introduced Western things. They have done this by force and brutality but they have altered Tibet in a way that has made it impossible for Tibetans to return entirely to their old system. Tibet will have to turn more and more to the West.'

I recalled the Dalai Lama's flight from Lhasa. 'When His Holiness left the Potala, we were told there was a great dust storm that prevented the Chinese from seeing him. Some people have suggested that this dust storm was sent by Providence. Does His Holiness agree?'

His Holiness shrugged his shoulders, and said something.

'Kundun says that there are many dust storms in Tibet at that season.'

I laughed at this. The Dalai Lama laughed too and again tapped me gently on the knee. 'How did His Holiness feel during the flight?'

This was answered briefly: 'Nervous.'

'Can His Holiness remember his childhood before he was chosen as the Dalai Lama?'

The Dalai Lama nodded.

'Does he have any clear memories of it? Did he feel any different to other children?'

The Dalai Lama looked thoughtful at this. The long hands moved as though sketching a childhood in the air. But he shook his head.

'His Holiness has no particular memory of that part of his life. He cannot tell if he felt any different from other children, because he had no standards of comparison. But his mother always said that he was the noisiest child she had ever seen.'

The Dalai Lama watched me closely throughout the translation. When the interpreter reached the last sentence, an expectant gleam came into his eyes, and when I laughed he joined delightedly in the laughter. He leant forward and said something to the interpreter.

'Kundun asks if you have any more questions.'

'Not if he doesn't want any more.'

The Dalai Lama looked pleased when this was translated. He smiled, rubbed his hands together boyishly, and spoke again to the interpreter.

'His Holiness says it is good that you have no more questions because now you can both talk properly. He says he is sorry he does not speak English, he is learning, but as yet he cannot speak it well. He asks you what you studied at Oxford.'

I said literature. The Dalai Lama nodded. The next question was about the methods of instruction. I explained the tutorial system. Again he nodded.

'Kundun thinks this is a good method. He asks you to describe the life in Oxford.'

So I found myself explaining scouts, landladies, the importance of the pub, the bicycle, and the river. The Dalai Lama listened to all this closely, occasionally stopping me to put in various questions. What was a punt? What academic dress did people wear? Why were colleges locked at midnight? Finally he made a quick switch of topic.

'Kundun wishes to know to how many countries you have been?'

And, after I had given him a list, 'How many languages can you speak?' As this was translated the Dalai Lama leant across to me and interjected inquiringly: 'Spanish?'

I shook my head. 'French, Italian, a little German, a little Greek.'

The Dalai Lama, seeming disappointed, asked again, 'Spanish-no?'

'Tell His Holiness I can't speak Spanish. Why is he so interested in Spanish?'

'He has seen a book of pictures about Spain. It seems to him a very beautiful country. He wishes that he could visit Oxford and travel to European countries, especially to Spain.'

'Does he plan to travel a lot?'

The Dalai Lama for the first time looked sad. His hands lay inert in his lap as he spoke. 'Kundun says that he cannot be interested in travel except in so far as it will help his country. He may visit some of the Buddhist countries, and if the Tibetan case is brought before the UN he may go to America, but he will always make India his base, and always return to it, because it is near his country.'

The Dalai Lama now spoke again, slowly and sadly. His face was grim, shadowed, quiet. He spoke for a long time. When he had finished the interpreter looked nervous.

'I cannot translate that.'

The Dalai Lama leant across again, putting his hand on my knee, and spoke urgently and even a little imperiously to the interpreter, who shook his head respectfully. He was sorry, he could not translate. I was divided between irritation and nervousness: nervousness because I was sure that in allowing the Dalai Lama to tap me on the knee, I was committing some awful unconscious sacrilege. I kept edging unobtrusively away, but he had obligingly humped himself along in my wake, so that by now we had traversed the entire length of the sofa and I was more or less pinioned against the farther arm. I hoped no lamas would look in. There was not much of my thought left free for me to feel irritated with, but I managed.

'Can't you just give me the gist of what His Holiness is saying?'

And then suddenly, coldly, precisely, the Dalai Lama lifted his voice. He spoke only a few words, but the interpreter looked up into his face and hurriedly began to translate.

'Kundun says that there are many people not far from here who speak of peace, truth, and goodwill. They are constantly lecturing others about this. They make promises in the name of peace and goodwill, yet when the time comes to keep those promises, they are always broken. This is as great a danger as aggressive militarism, in a different way.'

He hesitated.

'Kundun says there are two great forces in the world today. One is the force of the people with power, with armies to enforce their power, and with a land to recruit their armies from. The other is the force of the poor and dispossessed. The two are in perpetual conflict, and it is certain who will lose.'

The Dalai Lama added something to this. The interpreter again hesitated, but catching the Dalai Lama's eye stumbled on into a very curious remark.

'His Holiness says that this is the reason why there are so many suicides in the world today.'

There was a silence. The Dalai Lama's grave, stooped face did not change. I said rather lamely, 'That is quite true.'

The Dalai Lama spoke again. The interpreter said, 'Unless this is changed, the world will perish, Kundun says. Therefore every poet, every religious man, every political leader, should fight against this division till he dies. The teachings of the Lord Buddha also tell us this.'

'How does he think poets should do this?'

The Dalai Lama launched into a long, obviously detailed answer. He emphasized each point with a tap on my knee. His forehead wrinkled a little with concentration.

When he had finished, I asked, 'What did Kundun say?'

The interpreter, looking baffled, replied, 'He says poets must insert references to Tibet in their poems.'

The Dalai Lama shook his head helplessly at me, and suddenly laughed. We both laughed together once more, which was nice. I realized that I had been there for more than an hour, and that I should go. We all stood up and the Dalai Lama dropped his arm round my shoulders in a friendly gesture. He came quite close. I saw that the Dalai Lama has freckles on his nose.

He shook my hand with the same firm clasp as before, and stepped aside. I remembered what I had been told about not turning my back. I accordingly began to sidle out backward, crab-fashion. The Dalai Lama watched me for a moment. Then he suddenly took a few steps forward, dropped his hands to my shoulders, and turned me round so that I faced the door. He gave me a friendly push to speed me on my way. I heard his laugh behind me, for the last time.

Outside the door the grim black-robed elder lamas were standing, rosaries in their gnarled fingers. I looked back. Kundun was standing alone in the middle of the room as he had done when I came in. I waved at him across all those acres of carpet. He waved back, and briefly, the beautiful smile came again to his face.

Then I went away.

Ved had decided to come to Nepal with me. My father arranged that we should stay with a Nepalese general of his acquaintance. He armed me with introductions to the general and to Mr Gupta, his correspondent there, and the day after I had seen the Dalai Lama Ved and I left for Patna, en route to Kathmandu.

Living Like a Rana

From Patna we flew for an hour across the yellow flood-smudged plains of Bihar. Ved slept phlegmatically at my side, and I took surreptitious pulls at my hip-flask, avoiding the cold eye of the air hostess. Then the Heron began to flounder among clouds, and knobbly forested hills appeared below. The hills matured and became mountains: the Heron mountain-hopped, sailing between two scarred peaks, rising to miss a third, dropping between two more, and Ved awoke amidst the bounces. 'What in hell is happening now, Dommie?'

'Mountains,' I said. 'We must be nearly there.'

We were, for the Heron skipped neatly over a final peak, and slanted down to the Kathmandu Valley.

We landed on a narrow brown airstrip, with slate-coloured buffaloes scattering along the runway as the Heron came down. When we climbed out the sun hit us: a gross sun looking from the exact centre of the sky, frizzling the grass.

'For a seasoned traveller,' Ved said, 'your information is a bit unreliable. I thought you said it would be freezing in Nepal.'

'I thought it might be,' I said humbly, and we walked to the Customs building.

We were clearing our luggage when Mr Gupta came up. He was small and plump, in a brown suit, and he said, 'Mr Mehta and Mr Moraes?'

'Yes.'

'Your plane is very late. The general sahib came yesterday, he came today, but you did not come. Now he has gone to Parliament, but he has left you his car.'

We cleared our luggage, and Mr Gupta showed us to the general's car.

'I will see you later,' Mr Gupta said. 'You will be very comfortable in the palace.'

As we drove away, Ved said, 'What did he mean, the palace? We're not staying with the king, are we?'

'Well,' I said, 'this general probably lives in a palace.'

'This,' said Ved, 'is going to be quite something, Dommie.'

The Kathmandu Valley is very flat, but it is ringed round by mountains. It was these mountains, enormous and thickly forested, their shadows slanting into the lowlands, that were the first things one noticed, and we never got away from them. Wherever you go in Nepal the mountains come with you, in shadow or in substance: the eastern Himalayas; and away to the north, the Everest.

The valley is cultivated, mostly: the peasants grow rice, maize, and beans, buffaloes pull the carved wooden ploughs in the narrow acres, and everywhere the bearded speargrass waves in the wind, and red hibiscus coils suddenly out of the trees. We passed through three or four villages on the way into Kathmandu: Nepalese women, full-breasted and brown, dressed in tunics and skirts, pounded maize before every door, and the doors were as beautiful as they: very old, wooden, carved intricately, rather meaninglessly, but intricately; now and then they leant open and children fell squalling into each dirty street.

It took us about half an hour to reach the palace.

We reached it by turning off the main road and scrambling a hundred yards up a dirt track. People sat on each side of the track, mostly women, with cloths spread before them on the ground, covered with red peppers and speargrass drying in the sun. As we passed, they rose, making deep obeisance, unsmilingly respectful. I told Ved.

'They must be very polite people in Nepal,' Ved said.

'It's probably only that we are in the general's car.'

We drove through wrought-iron gates, shushed over a gravel drive winding through ornamental gardens, and arrived at the palace. It was a huge, ugly building, four storeys high, uncompromising in the green September, the Himalayas behind it.

The driver turned to us. 'The palace of the Rana,' he said.

Two servants met us in the high entrance hall of the palace. They took our bags, and led us through a courtyard to a flight of stairs. Then we climbed four floors, through winding corridors and anterooms, to a long gallery with rooms leading off it. All the corridors were hung with framed illustrations from *Picture Post, Titbits*, and so on, alternating with the heads of assassinated tigers, glaring soulfully through glass eyes, and photographs of dead Ranas, tiger-whiskered, soulful-eyed, clutching their jewelled swords. The servants showed us into a sitting room off the gallery. The gallery was obviously part of the general's own quarters; the sitting room was festooned in the same way as the corridors had been, and furnished with huge overstuffed chairs, elephant's-foot ashtrays, and beautifully carved Nepalese tables. Presents from Clacton stood on the tables. The tigers leered inexhaustibly from the walls. We sank into a sofa and the servants disappeared. We heard voices in the distance.

'I expect someone will come for us,' I said.

'Coo, Dommie!' Ved said, 'this really is a palace.'

At this point I became aware of an enormous Himalayan bear crouched next to the sofa. It glowered at me. I gasped.

'Now what is it?'

'There is a bear next to us. It must,' I added, groping for common sense, 'be stuffed.'

'Honestly, Dommie, I know you have a fantasy life, but what do you think? Have you ever known anybody who kept a live bear in their drawing room?'

'I only wondered,' I was beginning lamely, when the bear rose, snarled at us, and shambled loosely out through the farther door.

I was saved from the necessity of comment by the appearance of a plump, handsome lady in a sari. She floated toward us, smiling and making the namaskar. We introduced ourselves and she sat by us, smiling still. She was the general's wife, and she spoke only Hindi. In fact she was Indian, from the Kangra Valley, for the Ranas from time immemorial have married in India in order to keep the Rana blood uncontaminated.

I had picked up a little Hindi, by now, and was not as embarrassed as I might have been. Ved filled in my gaps.

'You look very much like your father,' said the Rani; she had a very soft, calming, dreaming voice, and I even forgot the bear for a few minutes. Then I felt I should mention it.

'There was a bear here a few minutes ago,' I said, feeling idiotic.

'Ah yes,' said the Rani dreamily. 'Which bear?'

'You have several?'

'Oh yes. That is one thing you must be careful about: don't go out at night; they don't see very well in the dark, and they might not know you were guests.'

And then, smiling, 'Would you like some tea? And then a bath? I know what boys are.'

It was very soothing. 'I will send my son in to see you,' she said. 'He is your age.'

The son came in a few minutes later. He was thin, pale, and bespectacled; he wore jodhpurs and a long coat, and on his head a bucket-shaped cloth hat.

'You are poets,' he said.

'Mr Moraes is,' said Ved. 'So he frequently tells me.'

'That is good, I too am a poet.' He paused and beamed.

We remained silent, so he went on, 'The best in Nepal, except for Devkota of course.' After another short silence, he continued, 'That is because I am the only poet of high birth: I am the only poet who is a Rana.'

'What are your poems about?' Ved asked.

'They are about the struggles of the poor. I am very liberal-minded, you see.'

The Rani brought in the tea. We drank it in silence.

Finally the poet said: 'You are here for long?'

'Oh, fairly long,' I replied.

'Excellent! I shall read my poems to you frequently in the evenings. It will help to pass your time.'

We finished our tea. 'Poor boys,' the Rani said, 'you must be tired. Your servant will take you to your room. Pannalal!' she called. A lean sulky Nepalese appeared and the Rani handed us over to him.

Our room was one floor up, at the top. It was a sort of hall, furnished with two vast mosquito-curtained beds. The walls were entirely covered with photographs of dead whiskery Ranas. Pannalal stood by the door, hands folded.

'The dining room is next door,' he said. 'You will take your breakfast there.'

'All right,' I said.

He remained where he was.

'It's all right,' I said. 'We don't need you.'

'I am your servant,' he said. 'I will stay here. You may need me suddenly.'

Suddenly there were footsteps on the stairs. The poet appeared.

'Is everything all right?' he said. 'If this dog here does not serve you properly, beat him. My father will see you for dinner at seven-thirty.'

He nodded, and went away. A minute later he came back.

'I have written four new poems today. I am very prolific. I have nothing to do all day, and I find poetry a good pastime. Shall I come before dinner and read them to you?'

'That would be a great pleasure,' Ved said limply.

The poet departed. Pannalal remained.

I fished the whisky out of my suitcase. 'I think we need a drink.'

'Yes,' Ved said.

We drank in silence, under Pannalal's eye. Then Ved said, 'It's an odd prospect.'

'Yes,' I said.

They were the last feudal overlords that the world has seen, these Ranas. Originally Indian princelings, they crossed the high passes into Nepal hundreds of years ago, and established themselves as the ruling class. The king still sat in Kathmandu, but the Ranas pulled the strings, and he danced for them. All over Kathmandu they built their fantastic palaces, where they lived, bearded pard men in jewelled robes, surrounded by the women they had abducted from their families, with the power of life and death over any Nepalese who was not a Rana. When one of them passed, any ordinary citizen who failed to do obeisance till he was out of sight was thrown into gaol. As late as 1942 the chief Rana used to ride an elephant through the streets of Kathmandu every month. The women of the town were required to stand outside their houses, and whichever took the Rana's fancy were immediately seized by his soldiers and taken to his harem. If husbands or fathers bothered the Rana thereafter they were gaoled. One village, Halembu, in the mountains, renowned for its beautiful women, was raided and the entire female population taken off to the harems.

One reason for this abounding appetite was probably that the Ranas were bored: they had nothing to do but copulate. One result of it was that over the years three distinct grades of Rana emerged: first-class Ranas, born of a legal wife, second-class Ranas, the sons of established mistresses, and third-class Ranas, the unfortunate result of slips that passed in the night. Every Rana, however, whatever class he belongs to, is born with the rank of a general. He is also born with a name: Shumshere Jung Bahadur Rana.

Nepal is an independent state. It has been invaded, but not often. For one thing, it was always difficult to get to the Kathmandu Valley, which is sealed in by mountains: Tibet to the north, Sikkim to the east, Bengal to the south, and Kumaon westward. The Gurkhas were the most successful of the invaders: they conquered and occupied the country in 1768, but in due course eddied away into the stream of Nepalese life and became one of the races of the country. Later, the Nepalese signed treaties with the British, and helped them during the Indian Mutiny and the First World War, supplying them with men, and, rather inexplicably, cardamoms.

Contact with the West had a strange effect on the Ranas. The British officers who visited Kathmandu brought whisky and soda in their mule-trains, and apparently offered it to the Ranas, who drank it, but seem to have felt a little irked at having been outdone. Accordingly they sent emissaries over the mountains to India; and next time the British came, they were offered a drink that put their plebeian beverage to shame. It was whisky and champagne. Excessive consumption of this elixir may explain why most of the Ranas in the nineteenth century died before forty.

The Ranas did everything in a big way. One of the sons of the house where we stayed told me of the time when his father wanted to send him to Eton. To finance the trip they had to approach the head of the family, the grandfather, a Rana of the Ranas. On being told of the project, he flew into a rage.

'No grandson of mine will be permitted to defile himself by crossing the black waters to England,' he said furiously. 'But I will be reasonable. If you like, you may hire all the masters from Eton and bring them here.'

Later, the grandfather fell ill. A British surgeon was fetched from India. When he arrived, he discovered that the old man's palace was on top of an unroaded hill; he could not imagine how he was to get his equipment up. He went to bed that night, still in a quandary, in a tent at the foot of the hill. He awoke next morning to find a road leading from the door of his tent up to the gate of the palace. It had been built in six hours by relays of slave-gangs working through the night.

So the Ranas lived on in their mad palaces, drinking their invented drink, begetting hundreds of children, taxing the men of Nepal and kidnapping the women, until 1951. In that year the Nepalese rose. The Ranas tried to seize the king, who fled to Delhi. They were overthrown. Most of them left the country and settled in Bangalore, a kind of Indian Cheltenham. There they still moulder, seedy old generals planning revolution over glasses of orange juice. The Nepalese Congress took over government and drafted a constitution. Elections were held in 1958, and the Congress, under the youthful B.P. Koirala, came in again with a crushing majority. It is a Socialist party, and such Ranas as remain in Kathmandu are now taxed for the first time in recorded history.

They were also required, in 1951, to cut down on their concubines (some houses had as many as seven hundred) and ordered to reduce this number by two-thirds. As a natural result, on the day when the order was executed, the streets of Kathmandu were filled by hundreds of loudly lamenting women with nowhere to go. Koirala solved the problem very resourcefully by marrying them off to the Assam Riflemen who had come in from India to help him keep the peace.

The peace has been kept so far. Though Nepal is a sovereign state, it relies heavily on India for aid, in road-building, for instance, and the training of troops. The Nepalese extremists have accused Nehru of colonialist designs on their country, but I think his interest is purely avuncular. Moreover India is interested in strengthening Nepal, for Nepal lies between India and Tibet, and in Tibet are the Chinese.

We were drinking rather gloomily when a plump young man in spectacles, with a round smooth smiling face, bounced in. Pannalal promptly fell to the floor, kissing his feet. The young man looked embarrassed.

'Get up, get up,' he said, and to us, 'I'm the general's second son, his engineer son. I came to see how you were getting on.'

'Oh, fine,' we said, and he laughed.

'You mean you're bored? Me too. Can I have a drink?'

'Do,' I said, and poured one.

'I thought,' said the engineer son, rapidly draining his glass, 'that you might like to have a peep round the palace.'

'We would indeed,' I said.

'It's very large,' said Ved doubtfully.

'Five hundred rooms. Don't worry, we won't go round them all. They're mostly full of pictures of my ancestors. We could have a look at the courtyard and the grounds.'

'Good,' I said, 'but have another drink.'

We had finished the bottle by the time we rose, and the engineer son was more expansive than ever. He led us down to the ground floor. It was a long way.

'Who lives in these five hundred rooms?'

'Well, my father has five of us, you know. Five sons. We each have quarters for ourselves and our families. Then lots of the rooms are guest rooms, drawing rooms, that kind of thing. And of course the maidservants have one wing.'

'Maidservants?' inquired Ved. The engineer son laughed and inserted an elbow into Ved's ribs. 'We had more of them before 1951, of course. About two hundred and fifty. Now I think the actual number is about a hundred and fifty. Useful girls, they do everything, ha, ha!' The elbow drove into my ribs this time.

We went out through a carved wooden porch into the main courtyard. The palace was rectangular and the courtyard a rectangle within a rectangle. It was very busy: men and women in loose tunics and felt shoes moved ceaselessly through it—the servants: the women almost all young and pretty. And on three sides of the courtyard there were shops. There were a blacksmith and a goldsmith, a cobbler, a tailor, a barber, a dispensary, and, in one corner, an anonymous doorway to which the engineer son pointed.

'That's the most important of all. The bank.'

He nudged Ved again, laughing.

'Who uses these shops?'

He looked at me, surprised. 'Why, we do. The family. We pay all these people, and they serve us.'

'What's the idea?' Ved said.

'When these palaces were built the Ranas had the idea of setting up autonomous communities in each one. All these people live in our house, and we take care of them. We feed and clothe them, and they serve us. It is like a little city. We even have a school in the grounds, for their children.'

'And are all the Rana's palaces like this?'

'They were,' said the engineer son. 'This is one of the last ones left. Things are changing. It was all very well, but the kind of life we led couldn't have gone on much longer: after all, not so long ago, I would have had the power of life and death over most of these people. It's a good thing,' he added surprisingly, 'that that's all over.'

We moved back through the house into the gardens outside. It was getting dark, and mist came bubbling gently in from the mountains. The engineer son shrugged.

'We'll have to see the grounds some other time. But I'll point a few things out. The stables and the dairies are over there. And the vegetable gardens. The fruit gardens are on the other side of the house. We keep the livestock beyond the stables: they have their paddocks there. Sometime I must show you our pigs; they are the best in Nepal.'

He said, 'We'll have to give it all up in a few years. The taxation is going up under Koirala.'

'Don't you regret it?' Ved said.

'No. I was a boy when the whole thing changed. I've grown up with it. It's the older people who find it difficult. You'll meet some this evening. Meanwhile, why not come up to my sitting room and have a drink?'

'A pleasure,' we said.

We dined with the general. He was a youngish fifty, and looked very much like his engineer son, except that he wore delicate gold-rimmed pince-nez. He made us a small effusive speech of welcome, but then said nothing: it was obvious that he didn't quite know what to do with us. In the uncomfortable hour after dinner he kept plunging across to one or the other of us, fetching a drink, a cigarette, or an ashtray: he would give it to one, stare searchingly into one's face, his lips rounding as if in surprise, and then plunge back across the room. The poet son sat sulkily quiet, annoyed because we hadn't been there to listen to his poems; the engineer son maintained a discreet silence; there was a third son, who had been at Sandhurst, who talked about shooting, and he was the only one who did talk. The Rani fussed over Ved and me, murmuring like a dove: now and then she asked us if we had any brothers or sisters. That was all, except for a very old Rana, a field marshal who sat hunched in a chair all through the evening. He was small, with a round starch-coloured face, the lips puckered in with age; he kept his tiny slippered feet together; his hands, dry leaves, lay together in his lap; He ate and drank with an almost inconspicuous flutter of hand to mouth, a sudden ingestion of the lips: after dinner he smoked, delicately, a cigar. He did not speak at all, except once. Ved was trying to draw the general out on some question of Nepalese politics, the general being a Member of Parliament, and Ved was not succeeding. Finally with a courteous little Oxford swivel of attention, he turned to the field marshal.

'What do *you* think, sir?'

The field marshal said in a high crackling voice: 'I wish the days were back when we chased the peasants through the streets with *whips!*' Then his face became once more starched and impassive, only he kept sucking in his lips after his remark, as though it had made him thirsty.

It was not a very successful dinner.

When we said goodnight, the general drew himself up, looked

over our heads, and said rapidly, 'I hope I have not forgotten anything that would make you comfortable.'

'Oh no, sir,' we said.

The engineer son winked at us and said softly, 'One for the road.'

'What a good idea,' Ved said, and we followed the drink-giver.

When, at about midnight, we stumbled back to our room, we found Pannalal asleep across the doorway. We stepped over him. 'Do you want the light, Dommie?'

'No,' I said.

We undressed in the dark. Ved was quicker than I was. He moved over to his bed while I was still fastening my pyjama trousers. I heard him struggling through the mosquito-curtain, and then came a yell of horror.

My first thought was of stray bears. I rushed to the light-switch and turned it on. Ved was scrambling out of his bed, which now contained a very pretty Nepalese girl. She didn't have any clothes on. When I turned to my bed, there was one there too. She laughed and made an unmistakable gesture.

Pannalal had now woken up. He stood doomfully in the door, wiping the sleep out of his eyes.

'What are these girls doing here?' I said.

'The general sahib sent them to entertain you. If they are not pretty enough I will fetch two others.'

'No, no,' I said, and cravenly retired into the dining room, leaving Ved to cope with the situation.

When I returned the girls had gone. Pannalal, looking very indignant, was going back to sleep.

'How did you get rid of them?' I asked admiringly.

'I said we both had a contagious disease.'

'Genius,' I said.

'Just a knack, just a knack, nothing at all,' Ved said, crawling back through the mosquito-curtain. 'Poof, they use very strong scent.'

He added, 'Apart from our other responsibilities, Dommikins, there are *two* of us in this damned room, after all.'

'Not to mention Pannalal.'

'Not to mention Pannalal. I don't think they believed me, you know. They'll probably think we are queer, and send us two menservants tomorrow.'

Several Priests

The general came up next morning as we were finishing breakfast brooded over by Pannalal. He polished one hand nervously with the other and said: 'How are you?'

Ved said, 'Very well, thank you, sir,' while I wondered how someone who had had so much power could be so shy.

'Everything is to your satisfaction?' inquired the general, like a hotel manager, and again Ved, who had just been complaining bitterly about the lavatory, said yes, splendid.

'I hope,' said the General, 'that the wolfhounds did not disturb you in the night. They are Tibetan wolfhounds, very fierce, which we keep in the grounds, and generally they howl at night.'

'No,' I said, 'everything was fine.'

Then the general gave a conspiratorial smile. 'I hear,' he said, 'that you are ill.'

'Ill?' I said, and then remembered Ved's alibi and nodded vigorously.

The general actually giggled. 'Fine!' he said. 'I am always telling my sons that nobody becomes a man till they have had a dose.'

Ved, who did not quite get what he meant, said, 'Of what?' and I produced a knowing smile.

'Don't worry about it,' advised the general. 'You will find your powers have increased when it is over.'

And he toddled off, rubbing his hands together with real satisfaction. 'What was all that about?' inquired Ved.

'Your contagious disease,' I said. 'They think we have the clap.'

'Good God!' said Ved puritanically.

'It was a fairly natural conclusion for them to draw,' I pointed out. 'Besides, our prestige has obviously gone up.'

'Except with Pannalal,' Ved said gloomily. 'Did you hear what the general said? They have bears in the drawing room and wolves in the garden.'

'Wolfhounds,' I corrected.

'And concubines in the beds. And, Dommie, the lavatory is awful. And I have the colic, Dommie. The colic!'

'Every cloud,' I said, 'has its silver lining.'

We went, in a jeep-taxi, to the airlines office. It is in the main street, the Jyuddha. This is a narrow frontier-town area meandered through by fleets of pedestrians and bicyclists, leading at one end into the green acreage of the Parade Ground, said to be the largest in the world, and at the other into the teeming market of the old town. We were confirming our reservations for Calcutta when a young Indian came up to Ved.

'Excuse me if I am forward: but are you Mr Ved Mehta?'

'Yes,' said Ved while I thought cynically how depressing it was to see him so exhilarated to be recognized in Kathmandu.

'I thought I recognized you from your pictures. And can this possibly be Mr Dom Moraes?'

I was overjoyed. 'Delighted to see you,' I said cordially.

'I am a professor of literature, one of the Indian professors loaned to the Nepal government. I heard that you were coming. A coincidence that I should run into you!'

'Come and have a drink,' I said automatically.

'I will do that when I come to England. You must come and drink with me.'

'Far from here?' asked Ved, who hates walking.

'Not so far. Two furlongs.'

'We'd love to,' I said.

We walked through the Jyuddha into the market. Here everything grew more congested. Wooden and brick houses, two storey tall, huddled into the roadway. We passed a temple of carved stone, outside which an enormous wooden chariot, thirty feet high, stood.

'That is the juggernaut,' said the professor. 'The chariot of the god. When the festival comes and the chariot is drawn through Kathmandu, they have to take down the telephone wires to give it free passage.'

We came to a narrow, cluttered street, which smelt of a lack of drains. 'This is the middle-class residential area,' the professor said, 'where I live.'

Children defecated in the middle of the road, dogs snuffed languorously at patches of old excrement, cows moaned in their dewlaps and ambled past. At intervals a rubbish heap spilled across the street and one had to climb over. Scattered over and around each rubbish heap, like lumps of grey wool flecked with blood, were the corpses of many rats.

'There was recently a cholera epidemic in Kathmandu,' the professor said.

The women and children looked rosy and healthy. They screamed at each other up and down the street, the mothers pounding their maize and drying their peppers by the fly-steaming rubbish heaps and in the carved wooden doorways. At length we reached the extreme end of the street. The professor led us through a gateway into a compound, a patch of grass with a few ragged daisies. Somebody had been using the entrance to the house as a lavatory. We negotiated the mess and climbed two flights of extremely narrow and circuitous wooden stairs to the two rooms where he lived with his wife, two children, younger brother, and sister-in-law.

In the main room there were a sofa, a table, and three chairs. Somebody had hung a reproduction of the 'Mona Lisa' on one wall, upside down. A few textbooks lay on the table, and some

Green Penguins in a corner. We sat down on the sofa. I felt a little uneasy, for the professor seemed suddenly depressed; he sank heavily into a chair, sighing, rubbing his face with his hands, and I was afraid he would think we despised him for the way in which he had to live. He had a sad and gentle face, with a little moustache, which he twisted uneasily between his fingers. His wife came out, her sari over her head, and squatted on the floor, not looking at us. The two children appeared with streaming noses, and the brother and his wife came silently to the two vacant chairs.

'Not like England, eh?' said the professor with a sad little laugh.

'It's charming,' I said. It must be difficult to find places in Kathmandu.'

'Ah, when a man marries, he can say goodbye to comfort,' the professor said.

He went into the other room and returned with a bottle of Rémy Martin. As he returned a rat scurried across the room, and he kicked angrily at it. His brother got up silently and fetched three glasses.

For a minute everybody was like a ghost. The room had power over us, silencing us all. Then Ved said, 'What very good brandy.'

The professor began to unlock his floodgates. 'You have no idea,' he said bitterly, '—how can you have any idea?—how badly paid we teachers are in India. Even I—I come here from the Indian government and I get paid just enough to keep myself and this, my family. You can have no idea,' he kept repeating, shaking his head.

Then suddenly he looked up and laughed charmingly. 'I am being foolish,' he said. 'Drink up your brandy and have another. Now, is there anything I can do to help you while you are in Nepal?'

'It would be nice to meet some students,' Ved said.

'That is a good idea. The Nepalese students, believe it or not, are far better than Indian students. They have more sense of discipline, and they are intellectually livelier. They ask questions.

My God, you have no idea what a relief it is to have students who ask questions! Also the girls in Nepal are much freer than Indian girls: you will notice that there is no inequality of the sexes in Nepal: the women talk freely, and they are interested in the outside world, and a far higher percentage of girls come to university here than in India.'

'There is a university, then?'

'Not as yet. They are building one near Kirtipur. As yet there are only colleges, and few of those. There are not enough teachers, you see. But already they have started giving the brighter boys scholarships to go abroad, to America and England, and so they are preparing the way. Those boys will come back to teach.'

'You find the students enthusiastic then?' Ved said.

'Oh yes. That can be proved by the fact that most of them have outside jobs, as clerks and stenographers in some of the embassies, and they come to college at odd hours, some even in the night. They are good students,' said the professor.

'It is all a result of these Ranas,' he added. 'While they were in power, they usually denied education to the masses because they were afraid that it might be dangerous. Now that it is possible to be educated, everybody wants it. The Ranas have always thrown boomerangs. All their little despotisms come back and knock them unconscious. It's impossible that they could ever return to power in Nepal.'

'We're staying with some,' I said.

'Ah, so? Which ones?'

We told him, and Ved launched into his grievance about lavatories.

'But, my good friend, you must not expect lavatories in a Rana's palace. They do not use lavatories.'

'They must use them sometimes,' Ved said surprised.

'No, no. You see, the custom is, when the Rana wants to' — he hesitated and ended daintily'—pass a motion, he will clap his hands, and one of the concubines comes running with a silver pot. Into this the Rana—ah—passes his motion. In the old days they used to do it while receiving guests. It was very'—he searched again for a word and came up with a rather surprising one—'irritating for the guests.'

'It must have been,' I said. 'What happened to the pot?'

'The concubine took it away and it was strewn on the fields as fertilizer. The excrement of a Rana was thought to be the best fertilizer. The peasants vied with one another to get it.'

He laughed and added dryly. 'It was the one useful thing the Ranas gave Nepal.'

Gupta panted up the stairs a few minutes later. He greeted the professor, kissed the children, avoiding nose-drips, and said, 'I have been following you from the pillar to the post. Would you like to look round the valley?'

'How many towns are there in the valley?'

'The valley is only thirty square miles. There are three towns, Kathmandu, Patan, and Bhatgaon. But Nepal is 53,000 square miles, you know, and if you want to see it properly you must go up in the mountains.'

'Let's look at the valley first,' Ved said, 'then the mountains."

'To go to the mountains you need horses. You can visit Thoka, Pokhra, Halembu, villages like that, for two days. But we can visit all the three towns in the valley in one day. By jeep.'

'I think,' the Professor said, 'they should also visit Kirtipur and Bhuttha.'

'Ah, Bhuttha you must see,' Gupta said.

'That is the Buddhist stupa, isn't it?'

'Yes,' said Gupta, 'I have a jeep below. Let us go.'

The state religion of Nepal is Hinduism, but there is also a Buddhist section of the community. In this, however, the two religions have interfused to such a degree that a totally new kind of Buddhism has emerged. It has little to do with pure Buddhism, and not very much, though more, to do with the Lamaism of

Tibet, which again is something distinct from Buddhism proper. The connection between Lamaism and Nepalese Buddhism lies in the fact that the majority of Nepalese lamas, like the majority of Tibetan lamas, belong to the Mahayana sect, in which the clergy are allowed to marry and have personal possessions, as opposed to the Hinayana sect, a rather more Trappist body. Bhuttha is the stronghold of Buddhism in the Kathmandu Valley. There is a great stupa, or Buddhist relic-shrine, in the village, and also a kind of monastery where lamas live, and a colony of Tibetan refugees. The whole community is ruled over by a Mahayana lama whose ancestors came from China through Tibet five hundred years ago and founded the stupa. He is called the China* Lama.

There are conflicting stories about the China Lama. The previous night we had been told that he had three wives and several dozen concubines in his house, that he brewed liquor in the basement, and that he extorted contributions towards the upkeep of the stupa. Gupta, today, said this was not exactly true.

'As to the number of his wives,' he said, 'I do not know. He certainly has many children. As to the concubines, there are many beautiful young girls on the premises, and naturally, people suspect that he has orgies, but I do not think that is so. He is really a very clever fellow, one of the cleverest in Nepal.'

We left Kathmandu by a dirt track climbing across a ridge or backbone of small hills. The sun was burning in the meridian, and the monkeys and buffaloes in the green rice fields by the road were swaying in a dazzle and stupor of heat. We went through a couple of villages, deserted save for the inevitable red peppers spread to dry on dirty clothes. The third village we came to, some five miles outside Kathmandu, we entered through a carved wooden gateway. A circle of mud-brick houses, thatched and patched and dusty, this village, and at the centre the stupa

* Pronounced Chee-na.

protruded from stone paving, the shape of a woman's breast, nippled with a staring golden mask of Buddha.

The jeep stopped at the end house and we followed Gupta up some more circuitous wooden stairs. One flight up, we passed through a curtained doorway, and the China Lama, sitting cross-legged on a chair fanning off the flies, canted a round, unevenly shaven melon-head sideways and looked at us through eyes small and dark as melon seeds.

He wore a crimson robe which left one plump, blue-speckled shoulder bare, and he stretched an arm out to shake hands. We sat down on a sofa. The room was furnished like mother's parlour in Tooting, except for strings of rosaries and scarf-offerings hanging on the wall. Through the single window the sun glittered from the blank golden face of the stupa's Buddha-cap.

'So,' he said in English, 'you authors from England are?'

'We have been there,' Ved said.

'Oh!' said the lama, rounding out his mouth and huffing slightly with his cheeks. 'You like?'

'Yes,' I said.

'You no surprise I can talking English? Many people very surprise, they come from whole world me to see, and always I can talking their same language. China Lama is most educated fellow. Twenty-four languages I can speaking.'

He told us what they were.

Gupta said, 'Lama sahib, Mr Moraes has come from seeing the Dalai Lama.'

'Ha! Good you are seeing that boy? He good boy, he Dalai, Rimpoche,* see? I his man.'

'In Kathmandu?'

'In all Nepal. All Nepal is knowing China Lama. Dalai Lama say he want any most little thing in Nepal, then China Lama is getting, see? You Buddhist boys are? Why for no? I Buddhist,

* Beloved: a title given to highly placed lamas.

I very good man. Dalai Lama Buddhist, he same to same God, see?'

I lit a cigarette. The China Lama shook his sharkskin-coloured head at me.

'I no smoking, no drinking, and I sixty-nine, going on seventy. Everybody say China Lama same to same forty-year-old man. See, I Buddhist, I doing what Buddhism say, Buddhism say, no must drink, no must smoke, no must make jig-jig with the ladies. I not doing like that, see? So I looking same to same forty.'

This aboriginal conversation was beginning to pall on all of us. Ved switched to Hindi, which was one of the China Lama's twenty-four languages.

'But that is Hinayana. I thought you were Mahayana.'

The China Lama brushed this aside. He burst into linguistic pyrotechnics and all his twenty-four languages turned the room into a tower of Babel. Most of the languages were incomprehensible Nepalese dialects, but there were snatches of Bengali, I thought I caught a few French phrases, and once he said *Jawohl.* When he had ended, a little breathless, he sat bolt upright and smiled at us.

'See how well China Lama can speaking? Now I show for you our postures of meditation.'

He turned his eyes to heaven and struck a succession of poses, naming each one as he did so. When he had finished, he recited a Buddhist prayer, wagging his finger at us, gravely.

'You want any more? I will do for you.'

'Thank you very much,' I said, 'we mustn't trouble you any further.'

'No trouble. Now I will telling you something how I live.'

He wagged his finger a little more and said, 'At three I waking up. Then half an hour I walking, to take some air. Then I eating some egg, then two hours I meditating.'

He showed us how he meditated. 'Then I praying. With one hand I turning prayer-wheel, so, with one hand I reading prayers. Two hours I praying.'

I tried to work out what time this would make it, but gave up.

'Then I drinking some tea, our Tibeti tea, I seeing my disciples, I eating some vegetable, for rest of day. Sometimes I going Kathmandu. Never I drinking, never smoking, never I eating except some egg and some vegetable, never I making jig-jig with the ladies, three hours I sleeping. You like?'

'Fine,' I said, and Ved said, 'Now we must really go.'

As we were leaving, a thin young man crept in on all fours. He crawled to the China Lama's small, plump feet and kissed them. The lama with one foot waved him aside into the corner.

'My disciple,' he explained unnecessarily. 'He fool.'

As we were leaving, I glanced back and saw through the window of one wing of the China Lama's house a number of exceedingly pretty Tibetan girls. They smiled at us and made 'Come-up-and-see-me' gestures: but we passed on.

I felt depressed, and Ved's lower lip protruded a little sulkily. Gupta alone remained cheerful.

'You have seen one of the great men of Nepal,' he said.

'It would be interesting to meet some Tibetans,' said Ved, ignoring the last remark. 'Do you think that is possible?'

Gupta stopped between two straw mats and asked the woman who sat sentry over the peppers drying on them. She nodded to a house close to the China Lama's.

'She says there is a great lama there who was abbot of a monastery in Tibet. Shall we see?'

'Yes,' said Ved with a determined look, and though I felt the whole expedition had a doomed quality about it, I trailed along.

We climbed more narrow stairs to the small room which the lama occupied. It looked out on to the stupa, it was furnished only with a chest-of-drawers, an iron bedstead, and a mattress on the floor. On this the lama sat. He was a tall, wiry man with a Sioux face, seamed deeply along the cheeks and forehead. His pigtail was wound round his head, forming a sort of bun at the back. He had wispy Tibetan moustaches, and two gentle slits for eyes. On the floor by the mattress lolled a young Nepalese, and standing on the far side of the room a Tibetan woman, obviously the lama's wife.

He was sipping butter-tea, when we arrived, out of an earthenware bowl. He looked up as we entered; his eyes rested on us, mild and inquiring. Gupta explained our visit to the young Nepalese, who translated into Tibetan. The lama smiled and thrust his tongue out at us in greeting. Then with a gentle float of his hand he invited us to sit on the bedstead.

The room was cool; a little breeze sifted through it. The walls had a few pictures of Tibet, cut out of newspapers, glued to them. On the floor by the bed was a small charcoal stove topped by a gently fuming iron tea-kettle. The lama asked if we would like some tea.

We said yes, and his wife fetched it to us, with worn careful hands, in the earthenware bowls, and with it a biscuit-tin full of small sugar-cakes. The language made conversation difficult: it had to come from the lama to the young Nepalese, from him to Gupta, and from Gupta to us. But all the while the lama smiled and turned toward us, touching us gently and alternately with his eyes.

'He is the Alakirti Lama from the Ando Monastery in Tibet. He came in 1956 even before the flight of the Dalai Lama.'

'Why did he come then?'

The lama gave a rueful little smile, turning his long hands outward to explain. His voice was deep and soft, but quick; he talked in little eddies; he clearly wanted us to understand his precise meaning, and because that was impossible the smile came often, rueful yet friendly and searching.

'He says his mind is very restless; he has no peace here; he regrets that he came. He came because the Chinese were taking the lamas of his monastery for forced labour, and confiscating the goods of the monastery; it was impossible to meditate or pray. But he wishes now that he had stayed: he says it is better for a man to die in his own country than to pray to the Buddha in someone else's.'

Gupta told the Nepalese that I had seen the Dalai Lama in Delhi. It was translated, and the lama made a swift little smiling gesture of benediction.

'Rimpoche says that it gladdens his heart to know that people from across the black waters are friendly to the Dalai Lama, for the Dalai Lama is the whole of Tibet, and without him there could be no Tibetan people. He asks if you are interested in Buddhism.'

'Very much so. He is Mahayana, isn't he? Ask him the difference between Mahayana and Hinayana.'

The lama looked thoughtful; then he explained, again with that queer simplicity that groped towards a perfect statement, tapping his pen case on his knee as he made a point.

'Rimpoche says the Hinayana do not mix with the world. They know no women, who are half the world to any man; they pray and fast in solitude. The Mahayana go forth into the world, they know women, and speak to other men. Thus by Hinayana a man attains Nirvana through himself; in Mahayana he attains it partly through others. Yet both are equal, for both are part of the Twofold Way.'

I had a sudden memory of a book about levitating lamas which I had once read. I asked about levitation.

'Some lamas say they can levitate, but Rimpoche has not seen this. He says for himself, man has enough grief on the ground, why should he wish to take it into the air?'

Ved asked how old he was. The lama looked puzzled for a second. Then he gave a gentle smile of apology and, lifting his heavy wooden rosary from the mattress beside him, told his years on the beads.

'Forty-seven.'

'How long has he been the abbot of Ando Monastery?'

'Too long,' said the lama with his smile.

'What is Ando like?'

The lama answered slowly, clicking his beads in his fingers. He bowed his head, and did not lift it till the translation had reached us.

'He says, once it was a small green field on the southern side of heaven.'

Gupta paused to laugh appreciatively at this, then went on:

'They had their yaks, and their land, they worked on the land, they prayed and honoured the Buddha, till the Chinese came. He says that the last time he saw Ando the Chinese were leading the young monks, bound, to Lhasa, and the western courtyard was in flames.'

The lama rose and went to the chest-of-drawers. He returned with a photograph. 'That is Ando.'

The picture was small and blurred, and brought no image to one's mind. When I handed it back the lama looked at it for a minute as if he did not really see it. Then he presented it to me.

'He wishes you to have it so that you may remember him when you are across the black waters.'

And round Ved's neck with the gesture of benediction, the lama hung a Tibetan scarf.

We rose to go. 'Tell him that we hope that soon, when the Dalai Lama is back in Lhasa and the Chinese have been driven from Tibet, he may return to Ando and live as he did before.'

The lama said something gently, laid a hand on my shoulder and looked at me for a long time. Then he did the same to Ved.

'He says that will not happen in his lifetime, but he thanks you for your good wishes. It has gladdened his eyes to see you. Nobody has come to him before from across the black waters. He will keep your faces in his heart. Go with God.'

The two great temples of Kathmandu are Pashupatinath and Swayambhunath. On the way back into town we stopped at

Pashupatinath. It is a place of pilgrimage for Hindus from all over Nepal and India.

The gateway was of carved wood, gaudily painted: gods with dry-rot on their foreheads surveyed us as we advanced towards the steps on bare and tentative feet. A riot of children appeared crying for alms. 'Give to one and you get a hundred.' There really were hundreds; those who were able-bodied mobbed us; the weaker children fell back, wailing softly, and returned to scrimmaging in the sacred rubbish heaps with dogs and langur monkeys.

Inside, down a flight of stone steps, the main temple stood in a sunken courtyard, surrounded by smaller buildings. There were sadhus everywhere, entirely naked, squatting under trees, with dusty beards and small, drugged eyes. One leant on a parapet, his face a mass of overgrown beard and hair; his flesh was ridged and yellow, like tree-bark. 'He is a very holy fellow,' Gupta said. 'He has been standing like that for the last twelve years.'

A noise of drumming and chanting rose from the temple. A smell of dead flowers and incense filled the air. It was all frenzy: an immobile frenzy drove the sadhus. Before the doorway of the temple stood a brazen bull, fifty feet long. The facade was of stone, carved with little wicked gods. We climbed the steps and stood before the sanctuary.

In the sanctuary, a small square cell, the air was thick with incense. Flowers lay at the feet of the god. I could only see the feet from where I stood: cubelike, unthinking stone toes, fallen arches. Three priests moved among all this; old wood-coloured men, warped in the middle, tortoise-necks writhing, naked under saffron robes that left the jellied flesh of the right shoulder bare, their faces smeared with red and yellow paint, incessantly wailing, mumbling, feeding the censer so that smoke poured blindingly up. One came to the window, mumbling toothlessly and extending a finger of his right hand. I felt a wet dab on my forehead, and then his left hand came up and lassooed my neck with a garland of dead flowers. For a minute I had a trapped feeling; then he let go. I did not wait for Ved and Gupta but hurried back to the jeep, surrounded by weeping, naked children; I gave them all the change I had, but more and more came, and more, and I was besieged in the jeep, rubbing again and again at the place of my forehead where the tika of wet sandalwood paste had been dabbed, and distributing English pennies in desperation, when the others arrived.

When we got back to Kathmandu we went straight to the bar of the only European hotel, off the Jyuddha, and ordered large brandies. The place was still under construction and the bar was full of carpenters hammering and sawing. There was only one other customer. Ved and I took the first drink in silence, while Gupta went on about plans for the next day. I rubbed the place on my forehead and did not say anything much.

'Anyway,' said Ved, 'it was an interesting day.'

'Yes,' I said. 'I wonder what the China Lama is doing now.'

The other customer at the bar gave a little jump of surprise. I glanced at him. He had taken off the crimson robe and had on an American bush shirt and palm-beach trousers, but it was still the China Lama. He was drinking a double whisky.

It was worth everything. I leant back in my chair and burst into helpless giggles.

The China Lama pretended not to hear.

A Village with No Walls

A flute playing in the garden dragged us out of bed next morning. Pannalal was clattering in the bathroom with buckets of hot water for our baths. It was very blue crisp weather outside, so I tried to whistle 'Greensleeves' till Ved, whose colic was unabated, implored me not to.

I went down instead, after my bath, and stood benevolently in the sunshine till Gupta arrived in a jeep.

'What do you wish to do today?' he asked.

I looked up to where the Himalayas stood, green shadows against the sky. 'Go to the mountains,' I said.

'Why not? While it is good weather you should go. Otherwise in rain it will be difficult. But you will have to spend the night there.'

So I went and told Ved, who continued to mourn over his stomach. We packed a toothbrush and a razor, and we left the palace at nine.

There were no clouds in the sky. The driver sang happily, and Gupta beamed at us. 'We will get horses at the foot of the mountains. We will visit Thoka, perhaps. Typical mountain village of Nepal. On the way we will see Patan and Bhatgaon.'

Patan is a little way up the valley from Kathmandu. It lies amid paddy fields, not a town really, a patch of town, starting suddenly and tailing away into huts to the east. There was a market on, when we arrived: wooden stalls had been put up, cluttered with fruit and vegetables: people bargained shrilly, but nothing ever seemed to be bought. We pulled into the centre of Patan, around a small temple-filled courtyard, which included a squat and celebrated Hindu shrine carved out of a single rock. The gateway to the courtyard was lined with the shoes of devotees. I had decided that I did not like temples, and the shoes were off-putting; it was almost as if they might get bored and come flip-flopping out while their owners were still prostrate before the god. One of the priests emerged, coughing and blowing his nose with his fingers. The smears of ochre on his face were roughed with sweat.

Gupta, who is a Hindu, advanced and made the namaskar. The priest replied. He was like a Catholic priest in some backward Italian town, planted like a fat persimmon in the sun, strong in parochialism, with bored eyes. His first words were even more reminiscent.

'The people do not make offerings at the temple as they used to. They are swollen up with selfishness and wickedness. I will teach them, I will teach the godless ones: no more blessings shall I give till there are offerings at the shrine again.'

He said this not so much in conversation as in proclamation, and the bystanders stirred uneasily and flickered an eye at each other. I cut in: 'How long have you been at this temple?'

'Twenty years. These rapers of their sisters have felt my wrath before now. If they are not respectful to the servant of the gods, he will blast their crops on the day of the harvest!'

'What is the history of this temple?' Ved queried. The priest looked at him with a severely practical glint in his eyes.

'Give me money and I will tell you.'

'Go to hell,' said Ved in English, and turned away.

But the priest raised one arm in the air, flapping and croaking.

'I know what it is that you say! Evil one! Have you no respect for the servant of the gods?'

The bystanders began to mutter ominously, obviously seeing an opportunity to reinstate themselves in the priest's favour without spending more than a little energy.

'We have annoyed him,' Gupta said. 'I think we should go.'

So we left Patan under something of a cloud.

Bhatgaon was much the same, only wilder, more straggling, with the same mud houses, and we hesitated in the main square, and finally Gupta said, 'Shall we continue?' and we said 'Yes, rather,' and so went on.

The mountains were closer, they rose towards us, always larger, and the track climbed through foothills, and eventually we had to get out and push, there was so much mud. Then we lumbered like a military tank to a village in the shadow of the Himalayas, and there stopped. Gupta climbed out.

'We will get horses here.'

The villagers gathered round us. They talked all together, quickly, and their hands slewed up and down. Gupta ignored them.

'They are not the owners of the horses. Keep close to me and do not enter into negotiations with elsewise persons.'

So Ved and I got out, and stood silent in a storm of voices, till Gupta, who had nipped up the street, returned.

'The horses are ready. Let us go.'

There was a short pause, while we instructed the jeep to come back the next day. Then, trailed by our adherents, we moved farther up the street to the headman's house, before which three sidling ponies stood, saddled, but rolling crimson nostrils, and gently and angrily flattening their ears.

In the midst of their pirouettes, we seized them, I feeling piratical, and came aboard. The saddles were wooden and horned, and hurt as soon as one sat on them. A trail of villagers clung to us, shouting, as we wheeled the ponies around and trotted out of the village.

It was midday.

For the only time in my life, I felt slightly anxious about Ved. As I bounced on the wooden saddle, I decided I must keep an eye on him. I was much aggrieved when he came cantering back down the bridle-path.

'Are you okay, Dommie? Do you want a hand?'

'No,' I said sourly, and followed the other two thereafter.

The road was steep, rock-strewn, and occasionally flooded. Progress was slow. Every now and then the ponies had to tiptoe along the edge of a precipice. At first it was all right: the precipice was low to the ground, and a fall would have meant a cut elbow, perhaps, and reminded one happily of one's childhood. Later it grew higher; a fall would have meant a broken neck. My pony insisted on the edge, and I kicked it despairingly. Occasionally, squinting down, I would see clods disintegrate from its hoof, and its previous foothold rain down crumbwise into the valley beneath.

All round the mountains got bigger, hairier, more menacing, and the valley dwindled to small Chinese roofs and rivers like saliva-threads from the sudden lips of the hills. I held the reins, pressed my knees tight into the pony's sparse ribs, and hoped. Finally we emerged from the edge into an area of trotted-up slopes, the trees steaming mist on either side. I had to lean forward on the pony to keep in sight of the others, and also, with the mist steaming in through my shirt, it became exceedingly cold.

'Are you all right?' Gupta shouted back through the mist, and I replied haughtily, 'Excellent.'

Then more climbing. The pony stuttered his feet every so often, and yawed his head back, and squiggled his behind, and riding became agony. The mist had fortunately blotted out any prospects of a fall, and my entire consciousness was concentrated on avoiding the next bump. Eventually we climbed to a village, where people came out and stared amazedly.

'Is this Thoka?'

'A few miles yet,' Gupta shouted back. 'Do you wish to dismount?'

'Yes,' I said, and slipped off into a dung-smeared street.

A girl came to my side, like Florence Nightingale, and said, 'Do you want a drink?'

'Yes,' I said again, and she brought me some Nepalese beer in a copper bowl.

I drank it and felt slightly better.

'Come on, Dommie,' said Ved enthusiastically, still from the saddle. 'We must go.'

We did, then, scrambling up a steep track dissolving now in the faint mountain rain, always higher; the wooden saddle unbearable each time the pony trotted: but luckily that wasn't often.

Finally, in the mist, the ponies clinging with slithery hooves to the edge, lights glimmered in the stew ahead, and Gupta called 'Thoka' back to Ved, and Ved called it back to me. So I stuck my heels into the pony's side again, and managed to arrive, at a species of canter, in a village of nervous mud huts sticking to the mountain. People came out to stare. We dismounted and looked around.

There were about twenty huts in the village, mud and thatch; a single narrow street; goats; a pig. The headman came out and showed us to his hut. We had been riding for five hours. Women brought us tea and a kind of popcorn. The doorway of the hut was filled with the rolling pony-eyes of villagers, darting away when we returned their look.

The hut itself was a low two-roomed building, with blackened beams across the ceiling, from which brass and copper utensils and ladles dangled. The only furnishing was a rope bed, on which we sat, and in the corner a broken-legged chair. The headman squatted on the floor in front of us. He was a wiry middle-aged man with quick eyes and bristly cheeks, over which he kept rubbing his hand.

'Where have you come from?' he asked, and when we told him nodded, impressed. 'You come from the capital. I welcome you. My name is Thapa.'

We exchanged namaskars and he said, 'How long will you honour us with your presence?'

'May we stay for the night?' Gupta asked, and Thapa spread his hands wide.

'It will be a privilege for us. We will give you a feast.'

And he clapped his hands and summoned his wife, and said to us, 'Do you drink spirits?'

'Some of us more than others,' said Ved, and the headman turned to his wife and said, 'Bring the drink of three waters.'

The wife returned in a few minutes with four copper bowls and a copper jug. She filled the bowls with a transparent liquid that had a curious smell of dry grass. Then she brought a copper dish with bits of pickled lime in it, and went away.

'Drink,' Thapa said; so I lifted the bowl and drank deeply.

It was as if the top of my head had been blown off. I closed my eyes and blew my nose. After some critical moments I felt a little better. I even laughed a little at Ved, who had just taken his first swallow.

'You don't like it?' asked Thapa, disappointed.

'It's remarkable,' I said. 'What is it?'

'We brew a liquor of one, two, and three waters. The difference is in the length of time it ferments. This is of three waters, the best and the oldest.'

'It's very good,' I said, and drank the rest. It got better, like most things, the more you drank. Also if you kept a bit of pickled lime in your mouth when you drank, as Thapa did, it went quite smoothly. One bowl of it, however, was enough. I staggered slightly when I rose.

The mist had lifted, and outside a damp world waited. The air was cold and good. We walked through the village. People came out of their huts to watch. Some of the young men joined us. They were small and sturdy, their cheekbones higher and their skins fairer than those of the people in Kathmandu, and were very friendly.

'It is time for the singing,' one of them said. 'Come and listen.'

'A concert?' I asked.

'No, no,' said the young man, laughing. 'You will see.'

A pale distinctive twilight; we walked to the edge of the village, where it abutted on the forest path. Scarlet hibiscus made wreaths among the trees. Thapa pointed.

'It is the guras,' he said, 'the flower of the mountains.'

The path came down from the mountain, lined on either side by enormous shadowy oaks. It ran parallel with the village for fifty yards then curled down the mountain again. The young men—there were about a dozen by now—lined up by the curve, some sitting on boulders, some standing. Gupta explained to me.

'The girls from the next village have gone up the mountain to cut firewood. Soon they will pass by, and the young men will sing.'

And while we waited in a twilight full of expectant whispers, other voices came from farther up the path, the bird-clear voices of girls, and seven or eight came into sight, each carrying a sort of wicker pannier full of firewood, walking with a swinging mountain gait towards us. The flowers of the hibiscus were twined in their black hair.

One of the young men stepped forward into the path, spreading his arms like wings to block their passage; a little self-consciously, swaggering a little, thrusting his chest out, he began to sing. It was a high wavering tune, with dying falls, as if a flute should have a voice and sing words. As he sang, he made cajoling gestures with his hand, looking uneasily every now and then at the other young men, to see if he was doing well. But the others looked embarrassed, and turned their heads away for the most part: a few laughed in the twilight, slapping their thighs. The girls had gathered into a little knot vividly miming first surprise, then anger, then indifference; but all of them cocked their dark eyes at the young men, and occasionally they giggled. At last, when the first singer had done, another took his place, and later another. The young voices piloted the high tune into the twilight gathering now to night, till it was lost; and at last the young men stood forlornly in the silence, looking at the girls.

Then one of the girls stepped forward. She gestured the young men out of her way, she stamped her foot, she mimed anger. Then she sang. Her voice was a soaring treble that broke on the high notes, but as she sang some of the other girls joined in, till it sounded like a little choir. The young men laughed again, freshly, and slapped their thighs: then the girls laughed too and moved forward, and the young men gave way. And the girls went on down the long path, still singing; and even when they had turned the bend and were out of sight the clear pure singing came back through the cold air. The singers stood staring after them long after they had disappeared, with their faces pleased and longing at the same time, like puppies after their feed. Mist came again, and we walked back into the village.

The young men cheered up on the way, laughing loudly and slapping each other's backs. I walked with Ved.

'What do you think of that?'

'It was very strange, Dommie. They were like little Nepalese angels.'

I walked ahead and caught up with the first singer.

'That song you were singing, it's very beautiful. What is it?'

'You like it?' he said, pleased and flushed, and the others laughed, slapping his back harder. 'It is an old tune of our people.'

'What are the words?'

'Oh, those we make up as we sing.'

'You improvise them?' I asked, genuinely surprised.

'Oh, yes. Each of us sings what he wants to say.'

'Can you remember what you said?' I asked.

'I can try.'

So I asked him back to the headman's hut. The other young men came too. We were all given copper bowls full of the liquor of three waters, and slices of pickled lime. Ved and Gupta talked to Thapa and the young men in one corner, all rapidly getting very drunk, and the first singer and I sat in another. Charcoal braziers were brought in by the women, for outside night had fallen in a final mist.

I got an old envelope and jotted down a translation of what had been sung to the girls:

'Since your childhood you have picked the red flowers from the
hibiscus tree.
Sixteen summers I have watched those flowers fall,
*But as yet I have not climbed to the summit of Dhaulagiri,**
As yet I have not understood the hearts of the people of Nepal.
Queen of the mountains, hibiscus-fountain, goddess of Dhaulagiri,
Come quickly, be gentle: the old men say time flies:
Come quickly to the forest, where your father will not see us.
Show me the hibiscus flower between your thighs.'

'What did the girls answer?' I asked the young man.

'I do not recall: they improvise their words too.'

'But did they say yes or no?'

'They said, "Not today,"' replied the young man, and laughed immoderately. 'That is what they always say.'

'But do you do this every day? Is it a custom?'

'No, not a custom,' said the young man. 'We do it because we like to do it. Who does not like to sing?'

Later, when we were all very drunk, the women brought in spiced buffalo meat and flat wheat pancakes, boiled eggs, and curds. Thapa tasted the food first, then the rest of us served ourselves. We each had a dish of beaten copper to eat off, and one of the women produced a teaspoon, but nobody used it. After supper bowls of warm water were fetched, for us to wash our hands in. Then we sat on the floor and smoked.

---

* A Himalayan peak.

'How long have you been headman?' I asked Thapa.

'Fifteen years now, ever since my father died. I am fifty years old.'

'You were a headman under the Ranas, then?'

'Yes,' Thapa said.

'Did you have much trouble under them? Taxation, things like that?'

'We were too far up in the mountains for them to bother us,' Thapa said. 'Sometimes, yes, sometimes they came, they took a pretty girl now and then. But even then, unless she was married, nobody objected. It was good for the girl; the Ranas fed and clothed her better than we could do in the village: what more could she desire?'

'Happiness?'

'My friend, you are sentimental. Happiness is to be fed well and clothed well. Even Devkota says that in his poetry.'

'Who is Devkota?'

'He is our great poet,' Thapa said with pride. 'He is the poet of the people of Nepal.'

'He is dying,' Gupta put in. 'He has cancer of the intestines and he is dying in Kathmandu.'

'Dying? Hai mai! What misfortune have the gods brought to Nepal?' There were tears in Thapa's eyes. 'It is hard that a poet should have to die.' He clutched his drinking-bowl, lifted it, and said, 'Let us drink to Devkota.'

So we all joined in the toast. Afterwards I said, 'Do you get books of poetry here?'

'Not books, my friend. I cannot read. But the poems of Devkota are repeated among us Nepalese. If my brother were here, he would recite some, but he has gone to Bhatgaon. Devkota was a sensible man, you see, for a poet. We can understand what he means, and it is always good sense.'

After a while Ved asked, 'What is life like in this village?'

'It is our life. It is as it has always been. The families who live in this village have known one another for two hundred years.'

'You live off the land?'

'Yes,' Thapa said. 'We grow the things we eat.'

'What happens if there is a bad season?'

'If one family's crops fail, the other families help it. After all, if the entire harvest fails, we would all starve together; so if one field does not bear, we all eat together. There are no walls in our village.'

It was past midnight. Thapa said, 'I have prepared a hut for you. Do you wish for women? My youngest daughter is a virgin.'

We said no. Thapa laughed.

'Too tired? That's right, it's no good when you're tired. But if there is anything else you desire, tell us and we will bring it.'

The hut had three rope beds in it, each with a straw quilt. It was cold; we were all tired and full of alcohol; we slept. I awoke sharply in the small hours to hear a deep creaky roaring outside. It died away into a muttered snarl, and then began again.

Ved was awake too. 'What's that?'

'Tiger, I think,' I said.

We listened, but there was no further sound. So we fell asleep again. Thapa's wife awoke us, bringing buckwheat cakes and raw onions for our breakfast. We washed at the well. Most of the villagers were standing round, including some of the young men from yesterday.

'Was that a tiger in the night? We heard something—'

'Yes, a tiger,' one of the young men said. 'He came quite close. The fires he did not like, therefore he roared. But he went away.'

'Do you have many round here?' I asked.

'No; it is too high for tigers. A few come, not many.'

He added, 'It is clear weather.'

'Yes.'

'If you climb a little higher,' the young man said, 'you will see Dhaulagiri and Everest. I'll come with you.'

We left Gupta in the village talking to Thapa, and climbed the slope. We took the path down which the girls had come the previous day. The guras bled through green leaves everywhere. As we climbed, the forest grew thicker, and the path little more than a furrow through the undergrowth. Brilliantly coloured birds flew away at our approach. There was no sign of human habitation anywhere, except here and there a felled tree. Presently we turned off the path, struggled through the forest for a hundred yards, and came abruptly into the open. We stood on the rocky lip of a precipice, moustached all over with smooth green turf. Purple and yellow poppies grew in the grass.

Our guide advanced to the edge of the precipice, and waved his hand outward.

'That way is Tibet, and there are the mother-mountains.'

I looked out from the precipice. In the brilliant sword-bright air one was able to see for miles, like an eagle. Ranges of small mountains, rocky or forested, stretched away before me; and at the very farthest point to which the eye could reach, beyond the hacked and rivered flesh of the smaller ranges, projected a line of snow mountains, like a row of teeth. 'Everest,' the young man said, 'Everest is one of those. Also Jalpaiguri and Dhaulagiri.' He paused, smiling back at us, lowering his pointing arm. 'Is that not beautiful?'

'Have you ever been that far?'

'Only with my eyes,' said the young man, smiling. 'Come, we must go back.' On the way down he plucked some guras flowers. 'If you have girls whom you love in Kathmandu, give it to them, that they may put it in their hair.'

'It's a very kind thought,' Ved said, 'but they are a long way farther than that.'

'Never mind. Keep it for them. The guras is red for many days.'

When we left the village Thapa and some of the young men walked with us a little way. None of us said very much, but smoked and spoke of the weather. The neck of my pony was hung with red flowers. Finally, where the track tilted steeply back toward the valley, Thapa stopped.

'We will go now,' he said, and smiled. 'Come back soon.' 'Come back soon,' the young men said, and we rode on towards Kathmandu, and I was sorry, because I did not think I would ever be able to come back.

Dying Poet

> 'Do not be too unmindful of the dead.
> Keep Kashi* burning.'
>
> —L.P. Devkota

Next morning we were visited by Dr Suman, the Indian cultural attaché. He is one of the leading Hindi poets: a large man with a heavy laughing face and thick black wings of hair stroked back from a centre parting. He burst into our quarters unannounced, followed indignantly by Pannalal, and flung his arms round me, crying, 'At last two poets meet!'

I agreed, after he had introduced himself, which he did not do for some while. I was feeling grumpy and a little saddle-sore.

'How long you are here for?' Suman asked.

Ved had to be in Calcutta the next day, in order to fly back to Harvard. 'Only another day.'

'A pity, a pity. But this evening,' he said, 'lots of poets can meet. I will ask all the Nepalese writers to come to my place, and we can hear their poems. You like drinking, eh?'

'Yes,' I said.

'Good! Which poet does not like? But now,' he added, 'I must take you to the ambassador; he wishes to meet you.'

We dressed, rather painfully, and went down to Suman's car.

---

* Benares: city of burning ghats.

It was a large Buick and he drove rapturously, frequently taking both hands off the wheel just to show us that he could.

'You should really have met Devkota. He is the greatest of the Nepalese writers. But his poor soul is flying away on the dark wings of cancer.'

He thumped me on the knee and shouted, 'Good phrase, eh?' The ambassador lives above the town, in a house with broad verandahs, surrounded by rose-gardens. He gave us tea on one of the verandahs; a host of dachshunds came and arranged themselves round our feet; it was like tea at Julian's house in Gloucestershire, even to the extent that the ambassador did a little painting and sculpting. Suman took me round the house and showed me the end products framed tastefully on every wall, or standing on occasional tables. There was one rather striking head of Han Suyin, enigmatic curly smile and all.

When we came back to the verandah, the ambassador was talking to Ved about Dickens. Eventually he turned to me with a charming and tactful smile, and said, 'I understand Dr Suman is arranging a meeting for you this evening with the Nepalese writers. It is a pity you could not meet Devkota.'

'We've heard a great deal about him,' Ved said. 'Is it possible to get his work in English?'

'He has himself translated some few things,' Suman said.

'A really great man,' the ambassador confided gently. 'It is a real tragedy that he is dying. The Nepalese queen mother offered to pay for his treatment in Russia a month ago, but by then it was already too late; now the doctors have given him two days.'

'Where is he now?'

'In hospital,' said the ambassador. 'But the whole history of his treatment in the last week is very peculiar. You know that the Bagmati, which flows through the valley, is a holy river? Well, the custom is, when a man is dying, his relatives carry him to the banks of the Bagmati and leave him there. The Pashupatinath temple faces the river on one side, and most people in Kathmandu are taken there. Last week his relatives carried Devkota there and left him for two days, but he did not die. So they had to take him back to hospital. Now they definitely think he is on the point of death, and apparently they're planning to take him back again.'

'He is a great man,' Suman said suddenly. 'He is a great poet. It is difficult with such a limited language as Nepalese to be a great poet, but Devkota has done it. Not only that, but by his work he has altered the entire course of the language.'

'And he is a very intelligent fellow,' said the ambassador with pitying eyes. 'And when he speaks, it is a kind of poetry: he thinks in poetry. I went to see him in hospital and he was not at all self-pitying, indeed he was sardonic. He said that while he was waiting to die by the river, with his relatives already singing his death-hymn, he determined that he would not die that day and be hurried off to the burning-ghat, simply because they all seemed to be anxious that that should happen.'

Ved and I sat silent. I said, 'I would like to pay him my respects.'

'He must be dead by now,' the ambassador murmured sadly, and looked deep into his rose-garden.

Later the professor called on us at the palace, bringing half a dozen students with him, three boys and three girls. They sat like mice while he held forth for a short while, nervously, on education. Then he waved at the students.

'Talk to these gentlemen,' he commanded.

The students looked at each other; then one of the girls said; 'Is England nice?'

I said yes, very. There was another silence, then another girl turned to Ved: 'Is America nice?'

'They know all about you,' said the professor with a contented chuckle.

'How are the cosmetics in England?' asked the first girl. 'Do they use lipstick there?'

One of the boys interrupted:

'What are the politics in England?'

'The government is Conservative. That is to say, a right-wing party. The opposition is Labour and Liberal. They are '—I hesitated for a description—' much the same as the Conservatives, really.'

'No Communists?'

'Not very many.'

'Then I shall not go there,' one of the boys said firmly. 'I am a Communist.'

The other boys nodded. The girls mocked them.

'Oh, you think of nothing but Communism.'

'And you think of nothing but cosmetics.'

'What are your politics?' a boy asked. We both said we were liberals.

'That means nothing,' said our questioner (I privately agreed). 'You must be Communists.'

'How would you apply your political views to Nepal?' asked Ved.

'We must have Communism.'

'Yes, but in what way?'

'We must,' said the boy firmly.

'Do many students belong to the party here?'

'Very many male students, yes. The girls are frivolous and do not care for issues of the day.'

'What would you say are the major issues of the day?'

'Communism.'

This went on for some time, then the professor nodded at them. 'You must go.' When the door had closed behind them, he turned to us. 'Those are my most intelligent pupils.'

'They all take English, do they?'

'Yes; but as you see, they are more interested in politics than anything else. They once supported Koirala's Socialist programme, but there has been a lot of CP activity in Nepal, and K.I. Singh has turned into the hero of the young people. Practically all the intelligent students are Communists.'

He added, 'They know nothing about it. But partly because they think Koirala is selling out to India, and partly because China is so close, they want Communism.'

When he left he said wistfully, 'I wish you had explained a little about the democratic system of government to them.'

'It would have been difficult,' Ved said.

'I suppose so,' said the professor.

In the evening the poet son appeared and said rather frostily, 'I am to take you to Dr Suman's party.'

'Ah,' said Ved, 'are you coming? How nice!'

His poor little olive branch withered at the poet's eye. 'It is after all a meeting of Nepalese writers,' the poet said. 'They cannot hold it without me.'

'And shall you read a few of your things?

'No. I only read to select audiences.'

We drove in silence to Suman's house.

Suman lived in a villa on the outskirts of the town. He came out to the trellised porch to greet us, and slapped us all on the back.

'I was unable to find any pretty ladies for you to talk to; they are all men,' he said, and led Ved by one hand and me by another into a large sitting room, with tapestries on the walls, where several grave Nepalese were sitting.

One, gaunt and pale, with a beret of starched linen, was introduced as Balkrishna Sama, leader of the old movement. Another, thickset and slant-eyed, was introduced as Vijaya Malla, leader of the new movement. They sat at opposite ends of the room, regarding each other without favour. The remnant were disciples of one or the other.

'Aren't there any of Devkota's disciples?' I asked Suman in an undertone.

'Oh, these are all Devkota's disciples,' said Suman airily. 'Nepalese poetry has only been going on for about fifty years, you know. Sama is the Chaucer of Nepal and Malla the Eliot, but

Devkota is the whole anthology from Chaucer to Eliot, so far as Nepali literature is concerned.'

And he pounded on the table.

'Drink, drink!' he shouted to his servant. 'O *Saki*,* let us look upon the wine!'

Gin and beer were produced, and platters of Nepalese delicacies: baked lentils, boiled potatoes covered with curry powder, tamarind kernels. 'Eat, drink, and be merry,' said Suman, 'for tomorrow we die. Let us read our poems,' he added. 'Sama sahib, you begin.'

After Sama had modestly declined, gradually begun to unbend, and finally put on his spectacles to look up his manuscripts, and we had all sat back to listen, the poet son said sepulchrally from the sofa into which he had sunk, 'This is an evening dull with poetry.'

Sama looked annoyed, Malla laughed, Suman wrinkled his whole face up in a wonderfully expressive grimace of disgust. But then the reading progressed. Each of the dozen or so poets read two poems each, and then translated, and one, Ghimiri, sang his poems. The Nepalese language, though it has its roots in Hindi, seems a more difficult language to handle: it has shorter words, and, I believe, fewer rhymes. The poems read out did not fall with any particular pressure upon the ear, and from the translations, their content was not particularly remarkable either. The older generation seemed mostly faux-Shelleys, fainting when they touched the night-dark tresses of their beloved. The younger ones indulged in surrealist juxtapositions: Malla, as he read, kept looking at Sama with a little crooked smile, to see if he was shocked. In both cases it seemed that the poets had taken their influences from English via Hindi writers. But the subject matter of both old and new movements was curiously similar: unrequited love, landscape-admiration, and little requests for salvation, though the younger poets occasionally threw in some social comment as

* Cup-bearer.

well. Thus all of them seemed to have a definite public in mind: a public which demanded a certain subject matter, and a certain already defined approach to those subjects. Every now and then, in the midst of the poem, a poet would raise a finger for closer attention and slowly syllable out some image of which he was really proud. All the others would smack their knees at this, with deep belly-grunts of 'Wah, wah,' or 'Shabash.'* Once Suman jumped up and rushed over to one of them and flung his arms round the poet, sobbing deeply and saying, 'Brother! Sensitive soul!' and it took some time to get the reading going again.

When Suman himself read, which he did last of all, his glass of whisky uplifted like a chalice towards which his luminous eyes rolled frequently, his poems were on unrequited love as well. Here again the Shelley influence was perceptible, but this time at one remove, whereas in the Nepalese poets it had been at two and clumsier. I tried to think precisely what it was that I did not like in this sort of poetry, and decided that, in the less advanced of the Indian languages (this excepts only Bengali, which is far ahead of the others) there has always been a restricted and highly conventionalized imagery. When a poet writes in the impersonal way in which most Indian poetry is written, refers, that is, less to himself than to a recognized background, he uses these stylized images as his basis, like a builder with bricks ready to hand. This is the way in which poets like Ghalib write, and it is successful. When the writer cobbles the old images together and adopts, in the poem, the stance of some chosen Western poet, the images lose their quality of ornament, and the stance its quality of power, because the two are fighting against each other.

But Suman loved his own poetry despite the faults he saw in it, which is one mark of a poet, and when he had finished, the tears were streaming down his cheeks. He seized my hand, asking in a choked voice, 'Good? Good?' There was obviously no room

* Well done.

for criticism here, it was not like someone throwing the latest manuscript over to one in the pub, so I said, 'Wonderful.' He beamed and cried, blowing his nose, 'Now the piece of resistance: you must also read.'

I recited two poems, a little nervously. I recite rather slowly, and they clearly thought that an ovation was required at each pause, and with Suman as cheerleader shouted, 'Wah, wah,' and banged their glasses on the tables between every line. This was very cheering. I laboured to the end and then had a long drink. Sama said, 'Devkota would have been glad to see you.'

'We fly away tomorrow,' I said.

'What time?' Suman said.

'Twelve-thirty,' Ved said, and Suman nodded.

'Is Devkota still alive?' he said.

'I saw him today, in the hospital,' Sama said. 'He is nearly dead, he can hardly speak. Tomorrow they move him to Pashupatinath to die.'

'I will arrange,' said Suman. 'I will arrange. Devkota will be happy. Any poet would wish for another poet to stand and wave at his train, when he says goodbye.'

I woke very early and went to the window as the sun struck free from the Himalayas: a welter of burning clouds: and then suddenly the same sun, like a new-minted coin floating over mountain and valley and river, a blue sky, and the Chinese roofs of the town showing up in the bright cold light.

It was our last morning in Nepal.

Peculiar, to leave a place. 'When I return,' I thought, 'if I return, I shall be older, stiffer, less drunk, more settled: I shall stay in a hotel and have breakfast in bed. For by the time I return there will be a Hilton Hotel, and there will be a motor-road to Thoka, and we shall drive there to take photographs of Everest. And the same for Ved.'

But meanwhile Pannalal was sneezing his way out of sleep, and

Ved was climbing through the mosquito-curtains and looking for his dressing gown. 'Hallo, Vedkins,' I said.

'Hallo, Dommie. Where the hell did I put my dressing gown?'

'Foot of your bed. I say, do you realize we're leaving today?'

'Yes. We shall have to send some telegrams.'

'Let's not,' I said. 'Far nicer to arrive in Calcutta with nothing fixed.'

'You old romantic,' Ved said, laughing.

'That's one of the things about leaving a place, one always has to send these damned telegrams. If we don't, we'll be able to breathe our way out of Kathmandu, not just leave, destination Calcutta.'

'Okay,' said Ved tractably. 'But I must send one to my father.'

'Come to think of it,' I said, 'I must, too.'

Pannalal fetched the hot water. We shaved and washed, and in the middle of it Gupta arrived.

'Suman says you want to pay your respects to Devkota. I will take you.'

'Is he in hospital still?'

'They have carried him to Pashupatinath today. He may die at any moment.'

'Oh, I say,' I protested, a little absurdly, 'one doesn't want to disturb him at this time.'

'No, that is all right. He will be glad to see anybody, especially two writers. He is alone, you see.'

We dressed, and went down to the jeep-taxi. 'Drive,' said Gupta to the taxi-man, 'to the ghats of the dead.'

It was a long drive, through the valley lying green and brilliant all round, before we bumped down a slope into a dusty village. The usual children surrounded us, asking for alms. Gupta waved them away like a cloud of gnats.

'The jeep can go no farther. The temple premises are down there, and the Bagmati beyond.'

We walked down from the village to where a wooden gateway let us through to an unpaved courtyard. Women were drying red peppers in the sun, and the overflow of children and dogs from the village harried our ankles. Little heaps of dung, from different sources, lay about.

'This is the temple.'

At the other end of the courtyard was another wooden gateway, and through this we saw the river, the Bagmati, a brown languid grease scumbling over stones between two wide banks. There was an extraordinary smell hanging over it, an unmoving, pervasive smell: a smell partly of burning, partly of excrement, and partly of death.

We walked down a flagstoned pathway, the river at our right. On our left a line of one-storeyed buildings, with stone floors and pillars, and wooden roofs, ran down to the long stairway leading into the temple. Two wooden rafts floated on the scummy surface of the Bagmati. Gupta pointed to these.

'There must be two people near to death. They will be cremated on those.'

A few steps farther there was a concrete projection into the river. 'That is where the king is cremated, and the Ranas.'

And then, pointing to one of the buildings on our left: 'The house of the dying. There we will find Devkota.'

This building consisted of a stone-pillared verandah, on which wooden trestles were laid, about ten feet apart. On most of these trestles lay undistinguishable figures, swaddled in sheets, most of them attended by one or two bored relatives, some unattended. The relatives hummed, in appropriately sepulchral voices, the final hymns, but there was an undersong, a deep tortuous humming, and as we came nearer we saw what hummed it: the verandah was black with flies; great clusters buzzed along the floor, and around the heads of the dying. A priest lolled on the steps, fanning himself to keep the flies off. He glanced up as we came.

'Where is Devkota?'

'The poet? I think he is dead.' He rose, yawning, and glanced leisurely along the line of trestles. 'No, not yet. There he is.'

He pointed, and we edged past the foot of deathbed after deathbed, till Gupta stopped, bowing deeply, and making the namaskar.

On the trestle before us a man lay on his left side with a dirty white sheet drawn up over him, so that only the top of his head showed. A woman with her sari over her face, in token of mourning, squatted by his side, fanning the flies away. Gupta said softly, 'Devkota sahib. Devkota sahib,' and the woman drew the sheet away from Devkota's face.

We moved to the side of his bed, and the woman signalled that we should sit down. One hand never ceased moving the fan over Devkota, so that the flies could not settle. We squatted on the floor.

The face that we saw was a mask, with thick dark hair drooping dryly above. Beneath the hair was a fine forehead, with large eyes that opened a little to look at us. Below the eyes the face had fallen in: the cheeks like craters, the lips sunken and wrinkled like a very old man's. But from under the dirty sheet two long hands projected from stalklike, sand-coloured arms, crept slowly together, and made the namaskar.

Then again the beautiful eyes closed, and he lay still on his side, his hands fallen. He breathed in deep painful sighs, and between each breath gave a faint moan. We sat in silence. Phlegmatically, the woman moved her fan.

After a long pause, Gupta introduced us. The eyes fluttered open. They were brown eyes, inanimate as lakes, so far had they gone into death. But when something struck them they reflected it: in flashes and for seconds. They were naked eyes.

One thin hand groped painfully over the mattress towards us.

I grasped the hand in both mine and squeezed it. It was very cold and dry. There was a long pause. Then the mouth unpuckered from its creases of pain. Very slowly, groping and whistling, it said: 'Cosmic conflagration….'

The woman, with the same complete resignation as had marked all her other movements, produced a chipped green thermos flask from the head of the bed. She opened it and took a lump of ice out. This she fitted between the poet's lips.

He sucked it for a while, still looking at us. Then he whispered again, 'I am in a cosmic conflagration...'

None of us said anything. The mask twitched in a summoning of strength.

'I am burning. This is like hellfire. Nothing...man has not invented a torture that can equal cancer.'

We were still silent. He whispered at me, 'I have read your work.... I know your friend's name also.... It is a miracle to find you here as I am dying.'

'We wanted very much to see you, sir,' I said.

'Cancer...it burns me, I am dying. If I was alive I would show you my poems. Have you seen my poems? Tell Sama,' he whispered to Gupta, 'to give him my poems.'

Then to me: 'Some of my poems I tried.... I tried to translate. Translation is a very difficult work...but I did my best....'

His eyes closed, he had gone away from us, and again came that faint regular moaning. The woman put another bit of ice into his mouth. After a while he looked at us again.

'I have so few words left to say.... I want each one to mean something...but now there is nothing I can say. They gave me blood transfusions: they said they would keep me alive a few days longer. But I grew tired of drinking human blood. So I have come here to die...

'My poems were too materialistic...they were too much of the world...but I will not renounce them. I am here in the temple of Pashupati, I am dying. But somewhere there is one inch of me left...one atom of me left, that will not allow me to let go. I pray that I may let go...if the god Pashupati were to come, I would beg him to crack my skull....'

He looked at us again, striving to say something with his eyes, but could not, and wearily they fluttered shut, and wearily opened again.

'You see before you the carcass…of a man who once weighed 175 pounds. Now it weighs fifty-two…it is a carcass…there is one inch of Devkota left…one atom…that too will die. What is the use of lingering here, in this misery? Pray for me…pray that soon I may die….

'They called me a Communist, because I went to Russia…. I was only a poet…pray for me…pray for Devkota, that he may die….

'Even if I go into hellfire, it would be better than this…pray that I may go quickly…for me… I am the most unfortunate of the writers of Nepal….'

And suddenly the mask tried to cry. The sunken lips twitched, but could not sob: they were too far divorced from human function: only tears slipped down from his eyes, to make lakes in the deep crater of his cheek. I clasped his hand in my hands, and at last he looked at me again. 'Recite some of your poems…let me taste a little peace.'

I came closer to him, so that he could hear properly, and began to recite.

I had just begun, when from one of the other beds came a wail of women, high and monotonous; the priest came rushing from the steps, officiously; somebody had died.

Devkota paid no attention; he fixed his eyes on mine and whispered, 'Recite.'

I went on. When I had finished, Devkota sighed. Behind me the relatives were carrying the dead man out to the burning-ghat. Devkota whispered one of the lines.

'"Earlier in Time I prayed to be forgiven…"'

And then, strengthening, 'Recite another.'

And when I had finished: 'You are a much more natural poet than I was…. I was always more mechanical…too professional… there was so little time.' And for the only time he tried to smile. 'You will forgive me for that?'

I squeezed his hand again, and he whispered, 'Recite some more.'

'I'll recite somebody else's,' I said, and thought of Edna St Vincent Millay's 'For Any Dying Poet':

> *Time cannot pluck the bird's wing from the bird.*
> *Bird and wing together*
> *Go down, one feather.*
> *No thing that ever flew,*
> *Not the lark, not you,*
> *Can die as others do.*

Devkota said, 'Yes, that is beautiful.... The image in the first three lines is bad...but I understand...it is true, perhaps....'

Gupta touched my arm and said, 'Your plane. You have only just time.'

He said to Devkota, 'They must go. Today they are flying to Calcutta.'

Devkota whispered, 'Will you not stay...two writers...will you not stay till I die?'

And I said, helplessly, 'I suppose we must go.'

Again the mask trembled, trying to weep. Then the lips quivered together. 'Give me your blessing on my road,' Devkota said. 'You both have mine on yours.... Go then.'

Ved and I both bent and kissed his forehead. It was like his hand, already cold. With a great effort he lifted his hand in the sign of benediction.

'Pray for me.'

So we walked away from that place. We stumbled through the dusty courtyard back to the jeep. My eyes did not seem to focus on anything properly. From the Basumati a plume of evil-smelling smoke rose, gently tickling the nostril, from the pyre of the man who had died.

Spider City

We packed quickly, thanked the general, who wished us better health, tipped Pannalal, who did not thank us, and drove to the airport to find the plane was late. So we fed off our fingernails till it came, and then rose over the Himalayas, rose away from the Chinese roofs and the dying poet and Thapa and the palace, and three hours later came bumpily down at Calcutta.

Rain poured from the sky: it was like landing under a waterfall. The great airport was full of people going somewhere. We stood in a floodlit lobby, feeling small and unimportant, while the rain hammered on the roof and the bus stood snoring placidly outside. When at last we left, all the roads were flooded.

The bus ferried us into the city, through flickering miles of tenements, past rows of lighted shops crowded with Bengalis prodding their umbrellas at the lightning, and decanted us at the terminal. We stood there, small and unimportant again, and discussed policy.

Eventually we got a taxi and drove round to several hotels. They were all booked up, and it was still raining. We wound up at a large hotel in Chowringhee, the main street. Crowds insected through Chowringhee, traffic lights flared green and red, pachydermatously the buses and cars shuffled through, umbrellas gleamed, rain fell, and Ved said bitterly, 'Here we are.'

We went into the hotel, up a stairway carpeted in red, with

flunkeys saluting us everywhere. This was clearly going to be expensive.

It turned out to be the most expensive hotel in Calcutta. We took the cheapest sort of rooms, not air conditioned, that is, and went up to them. Ved collapsed on his bed and groaned: 'What about money?'

'We are running short,' I said.

'Short! We shall have to write articles for the newspapers. Rush jobs. It's going to be just like London, in a month when one's broke.'

'Oh, for Christ's sake!' I said. 'Forget it and let's have a drink.' 'What do you feel like?'

'Champagne,' I said.

So Ved rang for a bottle of champagne.

When it came we suddenly broke out into laughter.

'It's no use, Dominie,' Ved said. 'We do have expensive tastes.'

After we had drunk the champagne we felt better. Ved said, 'What shall we do now?'

'There is a very good poet somewhere here,' I said, 'called Buddhadeva Bose. Let's get hold of him.'

We looked round. 'Where's the telephone?'

There was none. Ved rang for the bearer.

He came, a plump and satisfied man, rubbing his hands together, with a noise like the scraping together of two biscuits.

'Where's the telephone?'

'There is no telephone, sir.'

'Why not?'

'What is the use of a telephone, sir? Who uses telephones?'

It is the only time I have ever seen Ved really angry. He stamped both his feet. I had only seen this done once before and I stared in fascination. Then he smacked his hand with his fist.

'What do you mean, who uses telephones? What sort of talk is that? Go away. Go away quickly.'

The bearer looked suddenly discomposed. He squinted nervously at Ved for a minute, then hastened out. Then came shoutings in the corridor outside, and finally the bearer reappeared. He carried a tray. On it was a telephone. The flex trailed gracefully behind.

'My God!' I said, and began to laugh.

The bearer was hurt. 'I did my best, sir. Do you not like this telephone? It is a nice telephone.'

'Yes, yes. Very nice. Thank you.' I tipped him and he resumed his former poise. I looked up Buddhadeva Bose in the directory.

The pattern of the evening was already forming. Buddhadeva Bose was out.

'Now what?' Ved said.

'Let's go and have a look at the town.'

'I'm told,' Ved said meditatively, 'that it's full of vice.'

'Good!' I said.

Because I suddenly felt very tired, ill, foolish: Devkota was with me, he would not let me go; and I was so lonely for you, to tell you, to help myself by telling you, that it paralysed me: Devkota's face floated above an image of swans and the Thames and a sunny day. Perhaps it was only the champagne. As a child I used to go away by myself, when I felt like that; since growing up, I take myself into crowds instead.

The bearer was still hovering round. 'Where's the nearest bar?'

He named it.

'Is it lively?'

'I do not know, sir. I do not drink. But there was a murder there last month.'

'Then,' Ved said, 'it must be lively.'

'Only uneducated fellows go there, sir,' said the bearer warningly. 'My friend has never been educated,' Ved said.

We got a taxi and went to the bar. The city seemed vast: it was still raining, and neon winked sardonically through the rain. It was strange after Nepal.

The driver turned back to us. He was a Sikh.

'You looking for——?'

'No, we don't want food, we want a drink.'

'Not food, sahib,——. You not know——?'

Ved was quicker than I was.

'No, no. Just a simple drink.'

'Why you going that bar if you no want——? Very cheap there, very quick, they having beds upstairs. Otherwise you coming with me, I getting you fine girl, whole night spending, she know everything.' He lapsed into Punjabi.

'What's he saying?'

'I think it's better for you not to know, Dommie. It might corrupt you.'

We reached the bar, in a street of neon. As we got out of the taxi a thin man in pyjamas came up.

'You want——?'

'No,' I said. I was orientated by now.

'Very fine girls. Anything you want. English, French, German, Anglo-Indian, Indian, anything. I know one Spanish also.'

'No,' Ved said, and we pushed him out of the way.

'—— not wanting, —— not getting,' said the taxi driver from behind us.

'You philosopher, you,' I said.

We had to climb a floodlit flight of stairs to get to the bar. It was all one packed room, with a square of dance floor, and it was full of sailors. They were mostly English, but one heard Norwegian and French when the music stopped. This was not often. There were tables, all taken up, and a counter from which a huge forlorn cuckolded phonograph projected its horn, and the dance music brayed, and the couples dancing seemed to be anticipating the beds upstairs. In one corner of the room sat a row of decrepit Chinese and Anglo-Indian taxi-girls.

We found two seats at a table: an English sailor and two Chinese taxi-girls were in the other three.

'What colour is your brassiere?' the sailor kept saying.

The girls held the front of their dresses open, and the sailor peered in, looking a little bewildered.

'Pink,' he said finally, with an air of triumph, 'and *black.*'

'Do you like black brassieres?' he asked me.

I said, 'Very much.'

'Why not let's all go to bed together? The five of us? I know a way for five.'

'Some other time,' Ved said.

'Well, have a drink with me anyway,' said the sailor.

So we all had a drink. The taxi-girls said nothing, and the sailor tended to wander a bit. Presently another sailor came up. He had a broken bottle in his hand.

'Do you want to fight?' he asked.

'Get the hell out of here!' the first sailor said. 'Can't you see that these are my friends?'

'Well, that's all right, but what about a fight? Just a little one.'

'No. These are fine chaps. They like black brassieres.'

'Oh,' said the sailor with the bottle, impressed. He wandered off.

'Low class of clientele they get here,' said our sailor.

We ordered another round. One of the girls said, 'Do you want to dance?'

'I can't dance,' said Ved, lying, and I, being truthful.

The sailor put his head on the table and went to sleep. Presently he opened his mouth and was sick. 'I think we should go,' I told Ved. 'Come upstairs with us,' said the taxi-girls. 'Next time,' I said.

As we went out, two Anglo-Indian teddy boys came up. They had sideboards and leather jackets. One of them had a flick-knife in his hand.

'Do you want to give us your money, chum?'

'No,' I said.

'Oh well,' said the teddy boys, disappointed, 'if you don't, you don't.' They went away.

Outside, a man came up to us. 'You want first-class?'

'No.'

'Very fine. Very clean girls, English, French, German, Nepalese, African....'

'Oh, off,' said Ved despairingly.

More bars, more sailors, more whores, more pimps, and finally Ved said, 'It would be interesting to talk to some tarts.'

'What about, for Chrissake?'

'Oh, their life, their work, that sort of thing.'

'What are you going to ask them about their work?'

'Don't be coarse, Dommie. Prostitutes are interesting people. I once read a book....'

'If you want to talk to a whore, I must say it seems pretty simple here.'

We went outside. A lean Cassius-faced man came up to us.

'You want ——? I got fine selection, English, French, German, Chinese, Indian, very clean girls, all virgins.'

'How much?' Ved said.

'You want quick one or whole night?'

'Half an hour,' Ved said.

'Ten rupees for the girl and two for me.'

'Oh, all right,' I said.

We all got into a taxi. The pimp sat in front. The taxi driver, again a Sikh, turned to us.

'You not trusting this man, sahib. I knowing him well, he uneducated fellow[7], taking you uneducated girls. I knowing some fine girls, English, French, German....'

'Don't listen him,' said the pimp. 'He bad fellow, I not uneducated man, I going to college, failing BA.'

I could only remember an appropriate aphorism of the painter Francis Bacon: 'Put not thy trust in ponces.'

We drove into a narrow street, the houses leaning over us, narrow jigsaw-puzzle houses: no neon here, a dark world.

Presently the pimp waggled his hand and the taxi pulled up. We sat in the dark, the pimp had disappeared, and the taxi driver began a jeremiad:

'It is a pity that educated people like you falling in clutch of such fellows. Terrible disease you will get.'

'Where's he gone?'

'He gone getting girlies.'

Then the pimp came back.

'Lovely ladies coming,' he said, 'you wait, I not uneducated fellow, I bringing you real Jean Harlow girls.'

And two girls came sidling along the pavement, in short tinsel frocks, and stopped by the taxi. One of them thrust her head in the window. Her cheeks were ash-coloured with the wrong shade of powder.

'Don't you fancy us?'

'No,' I said, frankly.

We drove on. 'Uske umer bahuth uper the,' the driver said. 'They were aged girls, nearly thirty. You see how this fellow is cheating you.'

We circled into another street of dark houses. 'Nepalese girls here,' said the pimp. 'Young girls.'

He slipped something into the driver's hand.

'Sahib,' said the driver, 'I can tell you, this good house, nice girls here. This fellow fine fellow, not showing you wrong.'

The pimp returned. Behind him, walking on quick furtive mouse-toes, came two very pretty Nepalese girls. They were made up very heavily, and they stopped by the taxi.

'Do you want them in the taxi or do you want to come up?' asked the pimp.

'In the taxi,' Ved said.

So they climbed in. They smelt of some very strong Indian scent. The one next to me put her arm round me.

'No, no,' said Ved at the other end of the seat, 'you don't understand. We only want to *talk* to you.'

'We want to *talk* to you,' I told my girl, but she clearly did not follow.

'No, not that,' Ved said desperately. 'Talk. *Bathchit.* Understand? *Je veux parler.* What is talk in Nepalese, Dommie?'

'You pleased, eh?' the pimp said from the front seat. 'They very passionful.'

'Yes,' I said. 'Go back to where they came from.'

'You want go upstairs?'

'No. I want them to go upstairs.'

'You not like?'

'We tired, we sick, we going home,' I said. 'We pay.'

'You want us to undress?' my girl asked a little angrily.

'Why don't you ask them a few questions about their work?' I said bitterly to Ved.

We got back to the hotel reeking of Nepalese scent, and I said, 'I think we probably need another drink.'

We drank some brandy. Then I went to bed. I was awoken an hour later by Ved.

'For Chrissake,' I said, 'it's two o'clock!'

'I know. But we weren't very brave. Let's go out and talk to some prostitutes.'

'It's two o'clock.'

'I know. I know. But you wouldn't want all the taxi drivers to think us cowards, would you? We aren't cowards, are we?'

'Yes. Go to sleep.'

'We shall always be thought of as cowards, Dominie. We must talk to some prostitutes.'

I was just drunk enough to think this a reasonable argument. 'Oh,' I said, 'all right, all right.' And I dressed.

We went out and got a taxi. 'You want——?'

'Yes, yes, yes, yes,' I said.

'What kind of girl?'

'Any kind girl,' I said.

'No, Dommie. They must be indigenous.'

'Indian girl having,' said the driver, 'Anglo-Indian girl having. Indijuns girl not having.'

'Any kind of girl.'

So more narrow streets, and another house. The driver went up. He returned with two girls in saris.

'Lovely girls. Same to same film star.'

We got out. The girls disappeared into the house. 'Stay here for twenty minutes,' I said to the driver, 'otherwise I will eat your life.'

We climbed a flight of narrow stairs. They smelt like a urinal in Paris. The girls were waiting at the top.

They were both about sixteen, with mascaraed eyes, cheeks smudged with rouge, and the lips crimson with betel. They led us into a long room with benches in it, and we sat down.

The girls sat next to us. I suggested that Ved should begin to talk.

But before he could do so, a flock of girls came through the opposite door and sat on the benches as well. They were mostly Bengali girls, but there were a couple of Chinese, and a negress. All of them were in their twenties: they wore tinsel saris, or short cocktail frocks: all had carnivorous mouths of betel-lipstick. They sat down and giggled.

'You must choose,' said the first girls.

'We only want to talk,' said Ved piteously.

'The best kind of talk is done in the bedroom, light of my eyes,' cried the African girl passionately, and tried to unzip my trousers.

I leapt up in the posture of a Botticelli virgin and said, 'We must go.'

But three men stood at the door. They were small hairy men, with absurd pouting betel-reddened lips, and absently they were paring their nails with large knives. They looked at me and smiled, still absently, but pared their nails with great flourishes thereafter.

The girls fluttered away, leaving an aura of chypre. We were alone in the long room with the scent and the nail-parers. We walked towards them, with the sensation of coming down a long narrowing gangway. When we reached them I said, 'Get out of the way.'

The first man smiled pleasantly and turned the knife in his hands so that it pointed at my stomach. He said nothing.

I grasped Ved by the arm and plunged towards the doorway. We thumped softly, once, against the men; they disintegrated suddenly and we stumbled down the odorous stairs to the taxi.

Wind inflated my shirt, which had a neat knife-cut through one side. 'Back to the hotel.' The taxi driver greeted us with a fraternal smile.

'You having good——?'

'Wonderful,' I said.

'Yes, this good house.'

'We didn't have time to talk,' said Ved, disappointed.

The spider city winked its neon eyes.

It was four in the morning when we returned to the hotel. I slept till four that evening. Then I woke, shaved, drank a raw egg, and telephoned Buddhadeva Bose. I had never met him, but knew him by name as one of the leading Bengali poets. He is one of the four stars that flamed in the wake of Tagore. The others are Amiya Chakravarty, now in America, Bishnu Dey, and Sudhindranath Datta. All these poets have translated their own work into English, and some of it has appeared in the West.

Bose was in this time: he asked us to dine with him. I asked him to drink with us before that: eventually he said he would meet us at the hotel. We were drinking in the bar downstairs when he arrived: a very small man, with a keen and extremely beautiful face, a wide sensitive mouth, and thinking eyes. With him was his son-in-law, Jyoti, and a tall American, the poet Galway Kinnell.

Kinnell was on a Fulbright scholarship; he was on his way to Teheran, to teach there. He said little at first meeting, and Bose, too, was mostly silent: he left his son-in-law to do the talking. But once we had settled in the garden with our drinks, he began to talk, and at once I felt that peculiar and extreme gentleness which most poets carry with them like a cloak. 'You will be long in Calcutta?'

'I don't know,' I said. 'Ved has to leave tomorrow, but I want to go up to NEFA if I can.'

'Stay a long while,' Bose urged with a quick smile. 'It's rare that other poets visit Calcutta, and there is so much here to write about.'

'Are there many young writers?'

'All the young Bengalis are writers, but there aren't many good ones. A few. I'll arrange for you to meet them, if you would like that.'

'Where do they publish?'

'Well, I run a poetry magazine. *Kobita.* It has been going for twenty-five years. I was a boy when I started it, but we have grown up together. Shall we go now? The women will be waiting for us.'

'There's some Indian whisky,' Jyoti said. 'My brother-in-law said that he would get some ice and soda. He made me swear that Mr Kinnell and you were both poets. He never does anything for people who aren't.' So we got a taxi and went out into the warm rain-smelling night.

'They are bloodsuckers at your hotel,' Bose said. 'You ought to come and stay with me. I live in the Indian part of Calcutta: we are going there now. You ought to see that: it is better than this in every way.' We drove quite a long way, fetching up in a wide teeming street where radios wailed from the eating-shops, and cows mooned along the pavement. Bose lived in a flat above the street. We climbed to it and went inside. Bose's young son came out to greet us, his hands folded in welcome. His two daughters and wife emerged quietly from the kitchen, were introduced, and returned.

The room we sat in was cool and quiet. We could hear the trees sifting the wind outside. There were books everywhere, paintings, a desk: the sofa and chairs were covered with rough hand-woven cloths, beautiful and cheap. Everything in the room had a look of use about it; even the paintings were paintings that had obviously been used by quiet eyes.

Jyoti brought in some Solan whisky, cracked ice, and glasses; we drank. The soft bird-murmurs of the women stirring in the kitchen came to us occasionally, and a faint smell of cooking. Bose began to talk about Tagore.

'Nobody has ever realized, in the West, the extent of Tagore's influence on Bengali literature. He is more than our only great poet. He was our first great novelist: he wrote about eighty novels. He was our first great playwright. He wrote criticism that shaped the thinking of all the younger writers. He painted pictures to illustrate his poems, and he composed the music for his songs. He was a colossus: I think even in world literature there has never been anyone quite like him.'

'Did you know him?' Galway Kinnell asked.

'I knew him when I was a young man. It was the greatest honour possible to a young poet to be taken to see Tagore. We used to cut our hair, put on fresh clothes, chew cloves to make our breath sweet, and then not have the courage to say anything. That didn't matter. He talked all the time. He was very conscious himself that he was doing one an honour; he liked to patronize young men a little. He looked magnificent too, with that white beard and the high forehead. It was terrifying. Of course, his voice was rather squeaky, that was the only thing that made one feel he was human at all.

'He was a great man. He invented new metres, he refurnished the language and he was Bengali literature while he lived. There was Tagore: then there was nothing. For a young poet, it was difficult to grow in his shadow...'

The women came in, bringing dinner: Bengali food, soya beans and wheat-cakes and the famous hilsa fish, prickly as the coelacanth. Afterwards there was fruit, which the women quickly and neatly skinned for us. Then Bose brought out a dusty bottle of Benedictine. We sat drinking it slowly while Bose read out some of Tagore's poems. He read in an intent whispering voice, with a long pause between each line. The poems had a pure, lighted sound: strange to me, who have read Tagore only in English, and not liked it. Bose said at the end: 'You see what a great craftsman he was? He could say anything, but he always said it beautifully, musically. And it is true what Yeats said, "We must labour to be beautiful."'

He closed the book; we rose to go. Bose remained in his chair, smiling at us. 'You must come again, soon. Telephone me, Dom. We will come here and read some poems and create some peace.'

Ved was leaving next morning. I saw him to the terminal. He would be in London in three days, and standing outside the airlines bus, I told him to give my love to various people. I felt awkward, involved in the mechanism of a goodbye.

'It was quite a good time,' Ved said finally. 'Goodbye, Dommie. See you in New York some time.'

'Goodbye,' I said. 'Be good.'

I stood waving rather pointlessly on the pavement for a long time after the bus had pulled away.

Sargasso Time

'A tract of ocean covered with floating weeds.'

After Ved had gone, I started spending most of my day writing. It was so hot that I did this in a cold bath, the typewriter balanced on the soap-rack, the shutters pressed back like eyelids over the windows to keep the glare out, so that the room was in semi-darkness. It was very peaceful like that, but got a little lonely. I was glad when Jyoti called me up one afternoon and asked if I wanted to meet Jamini Roy.

Jamini Roy is perhaps the best known of Indian painters: the maestro figure. He has held this position since the 1930s. I remember, as a child, having a painting of his in my nursery, 'The Last Supper': small, flat bright-coloured saints with fish-shaped eyes, rigid in identical poses on each side of a small, flat bright-coloured Jesus. When Jyoti arrived with Galway Kinnell to pick me up, I recalled this.

'He's painted hundreds of Last Suppers,' Jyoti said with a smile.

'Really?'

'Yes; he has a few apprentices, you see: when he wants to get some paintings ready quickly, he draws the outlines and the apprentices paint them in. Then he adds a few finishing touches and signs it, and there you are, another Jamini Roy. The Last Supper is one of his favourite subjects for rush jobs.'

Jyoti was slender and bespectacled, with curly hair and a curious air of being simultaneously thoughtful and excited over everything. He made a strong contrast with Galway, big and powerful with a square jaw, features that seemed hewed from some pale grainy wood, and unchanging blue eyes. For a moment I looked at them both as though they were a painting, listened as though they were disembodied voices: Jyoti giving the world away in a word, Galway, in a soft Princeton drawl, giving away nothing.

We drove through the glaring afternoon. Jamini Roy lives in a white house away from the centre of Calcutta: a disciple in white robes opened the door for us; he showed us inside, to a long white-walled room. One felt drenched in coolness, though there was no fan. Perhaps this was due to the spaciousness of the room: it was totally unfurnished, save for benches along the wall, on which new-looking paintings were propped. The two adjoining rooms were similar. We walked from room to room looking at the paintings. They were all painted in the same manner of a highly stylized primitive: often there were seven or eight in a row, identical except for the colours: Last Suppers, Annunciations, and the three kings going to find Jesus, three bearded triangular-eyed figures poling a skiff over a curly two-dimensional ochre sea. It was a purely decorative kind of art. There was no real reason why any of the pictures should exist; yet they existed, and propped up like that against the white walls, they seemed to come out of a legend, and to form a world.

When we had looked at all the paintings we paused and looked at each other. We were alone: the disciple who had let us in had gone away. The rooms smelt faintly of paint and cedar wood. 'Jamini Roy will come soon,' Jyoti said. 'He generally has a nap in the afternoons.' We stared at the paintings; they smiled at us.

After a while there was a soft murmur of voices and the disciple appeared at the doorway, looked in to see if we were there, then stepped aside. Jamini Roy came in, an old man, in spotless white robes, folding his hands in welcome and smiling. He had white hair and a high forehead: a face in which, as in the faces of many old writers and painters, the lines were those of a sage or of a saint. Jyoti hastily stooped down to touch his feet in reverence.

Jamini Roy lifted him with one hand, and signalled to the disciple with the other. The disciple went out and returned with some wooden stools, and we sat down in a little semicircle. Jyoti explained who we were, and added that Ved would have accompanied us save that he had to leave.

Jamini Roy listened, then turning to me said that he had heard of Ved, and was he blind? Yes, I said. The painter gave his curiously sweet, illuminated smile, and began to speak. He had a soft husky voice, and spoke in a mixture of English and sign language.

'Painters are same as blind people. They also must see with nose and ears and fingers. But not quite same: they have their eyes. But sometimes they too must shut their eyes to see clearly. I would have liked to see your friend.'

'You paint a great deal?' Galway asked.

'It is my life. I paint always. When I am not painting with my hand I am painting inside my head. All those colours and shapes are always there: I am the one who must stretch my hand out and break them from the air, like fruit from a tree.'

The disciple came with cups of cool water. As we sipped it Jyoti and Jamini Roy spoke together in Bengali. Every now and then the painter gave his sweet smile, so that I thought at first Jyoti was being witty; then I realized that he was not, that Jamini Roy smiled whenever he felt happy.

'Are you a Christian?' I asked. 'Your subjects quite often seem to be taken from the Bible.'

'The Christian books are full of colours to paint with, if you look in them. I look in them. But no, I am not a Christian: I am a painter.'

And he began to ask me about England, about my plans for the future, and my methods of writing poetry. He seemed genuinely interested in them all. Meanwhile, the disciple was explaining some of the paintings to Galway, who was nodding rather vaguely. Jamini Roy smiled again.

'Do you like any of these paintings? Would you like one?'

Galway and I protested, but Jamini Roy shook his head.

'Choose one, if you like any of them.'

So at last Galway chose a blue cow feeding a calf, in a border of lotuses, and I chose one of the three kings in the boat. The disciple fetched them from where they stood, and then handed Jamini Roy a brush. He signed each one and smiled.

'I am glad you like my paintings.'

'Sir,' Galway said, clearly emboldened by his smile, 'I'm told your disciples complete some of your pictures.'

'Yes,' the painter said. 'They do as the disciples of the Renaissance painters did. That is not important. It is not the single painting that matters: to paint is my life, and one episode on the way is nothing in relation to the whole.'

He looked keenly at Galway. 'Is that not true? Do not poets feel the same?'

And, turning back to me, 'You must paint as you breathe.'

After a while we got up to leave the shady white-painted room, with the paintings standing quietly around the walk. The painter stood quietly in the midst of them, with folded hands, saying goodbye with a smile.

Later that day Galway dropped in at the hotel for a drink. The heat of the day had gone and the fan no longer washed one in warm air, but in cool. But it had been hot enough before to make us both tired, and even cluttering the drinks with crushed ice did not quite take the dust out of our throats.

I told him about the visit to the brothel, and he laughed.

'I thought it was much more glamorous than that in India,' he said. 'I thought it was all Oriental and silky.'

'Not this place,' I said. 'But in Benares it's certainly more Oriental.' I told him about the nautch-girls.

He looked interested. 'That sounds more like it. I'd like to see that.'

'I don't know if they have that sort of thing here,' I said. 'I could ask Jyoti.'

Jyoti, on the telephone, sounded surprised. 'You want to visit a brothel? My dear fellow I really wouldn't advise it. It's very dangerous.'

'Not professionally,' I said. 'But you know these nautch-girls, don't you? Galway wants to see that.'

Jyoti laughed and said, 'There's a special Calcutta type. Go to Bow Bazaar, you will find them there. But be careful what you do. And if Galway is going, on no account settle for the first price they offer. If they see an American they will try and fleece you.'

Galway and I sat on for a while, drinking. I didn't really want to go and watch dancing-girls, but two days of more or less immobility in the hotel demanded breaking. Finally I said, 'Well, we'd better go.'

Our taxi driver was again a Sikh. I told him to go to Bow Bazaar. He squinted appraisingly at us.

'No,' I said, 'we want to see a dance.'

He grunted in his beard.

We arrived in a crowded and noisy street, and pushed through to a narrow tenement. Noises of radio music came from here. People were asleep on every landing, swaddled like corpses in sheets. Preceded by the taxi driver, who kicked the sleepers to one side whenever they got in his way, we climbed three winding flights of stairs spattered with betel-spittings, and finally knocked at a little door. A man opened it and stared at us. He was a south Indian, wearing the sacred thread and a cotton sarong. The taxi driver jerked his head at us and said, 'They want to see your woman dance.'

'That's all?' asked the man. When I nodded, he glanced at us and said, 'A hundred rupees for half an hour.'

'No,' I said. 'Do you think we're Americans?'

'Your friend is.'

'Are you mad?' I said. 'He is a Hindu from Kashmir.'

He stared for a long while at Galway, and finally nodded. 'All right. Fifteen rupees for half an hour.'

We went in. It was one small room, with a glass-fronted cupboard in one corner, filled with Hindu religious pictures, pink plastic dolls, and cheap English crockery. On the wall above the cupboard was a tinted photograph of a slim dark young woman, heavily made up. The original, dressed in a white sari, was squatting on a cloth-covered mattress on the floor. She was not as young as she had been when the photograph was taken, and her make-up was even heavier: her dark face was ash-coloured with too much powder, purple at the cheeks with too much rouge. Her eyes were more tired than the eyes of the photograph. Also when she got up one could see through the thin stuff of the blouse the dark eyes of her breasts and the curled mouth of her navel, like a second, slightly obscene face wobbling beneath the one on top.

'You want Indian dance or English dance?' the man asked.

'Indian dance,' Galway said.

The woman gestured us to sit on the mattress, while she stood in the middle of the floor, in front of the cupboard, tightening the waist-knot of her sari and shaking her head as if to clear it. The man took a gramophone from beside the cupboard, put a record on, and wound it up. The wail of an Indian film song broke into the room. The woman, however, was tying on heavy anklet-bells, with slow, methodical, tired movements. When she had finished she began to dance. She stamped and shuffled her feet slowly, making the anklet-bells chink, swayed her arms, and rolled her eyes at us with bored seductiveness. When the record stopped she paused, wiping her face with the corner of her sari. The man put a different record on, and she danced with precisely the same movements. In fact they never varied, whatever the music, except that towards the end she ceased to dance at all, trying tiredly to give the illusion that she was doing so by occasionally moving one foot, or fluttering one hand in the air. After half an hour the man stopped the gramophone in the middle of a record and came over to us. We paid him and he said: 'Do you not wish to sleep with her?'

'No,' I said. 'My friend wanted to see a dance, that's all.'

'But, sir, you will enjoy it, she is very good.' His face worked pleadingly. 'I can recommend her, she is my wife.' And as we turned away he said, 'How shall we keep our children? I will give you a reduced price, sir.'

The woman stood with her head bent and her face to the wall. We thanked her for dancing, ignoring the man pleading at our elbows. She came slowly round to face us.

'It is true. How else shall we keep our children? Now that I am getting old, nobody comes to my bed.'

Shamefacedly we pressed a little more money into her hands and fled downstairs. When we got back into the taxi the driver said: 'Good, eh?'

Galway said awkwardly, as though thinking out his reasons as he spoke: 'I didn't like that at all.'

After that evening Galway and I often drank together. We drank usually in the hotel, but sometimes went exploring round the bars where Ved and I had been the first evening. Here, amongst the usual assembly of prostitutes, pimps, and sailors, shouting above the band, or whispering under, we talked about poets we both knew, or about London, or New York. One recalled the oddest things: I remembered a toy shop in a Knightsbridge arcade where I used to go when very unhappy, during my first days in London, in order to buy small delicate glass toys which I later smashed, one by one, in the fireplace of my flat, with a malediction against anything beautiful. Also an evening on the hillside above Agamemnon's tomb in Mycenae, when I pressed my ear to the grass and thought that I heard the old king humming to himself in the beehive cavern beneath. There was a moon above the hill, and I had a bottle of ouzo.

Calcutta seemed conducive to this: in the sweats of daytime and the nostalgia of the night, one fed on memories, drying them up quickly by sucking at them too hard. Also, of course, I was worried, because I didn't know where I was going to go next. All my life since I was fifteen I have travelled light, always thrown things away because I wasn't sure where I would be next day, and cherished a romantic ideal of myself as a wanderer. This ideal became a little ridiculous when one was stuck in a large expensive hotel with the minimum of necessities in one's suitcase, and a typewriter that had jammed through being dropped into a cold bath. The people with whom I had been going to stay in Assam were not available: I bit my nails and wondered.

From all this I was saved by a good angel in a brown suit. He came bouncing into my room early one morning, while I was swearing at the typewriter.

'Hah! You are having trouble with your typewriter? Let me see.' He seized the typewriter and shook it. Then he did something to the reels. Then he said, 'It is done. Nothing like a little mechanical ingenuity, hah?'

'Is it all right, do you think?'

'Certainly, certainly. But we have not been introduced, hah?' He shook my hand. 'I am Ajit K. Das, of the United Press of America. Here is my card. I am also a professor of economics in Calcutta University, and finally, I work for your father's newspaper. It was he who asked me to look you up.'

'I think Marilyn Silverstone mentioned you,' I said.

'Hah, Marilyn! I was with her in Tezpur when the Dalai Lama came. Fine, fine! Now let us sit down. Movement is essential sometimes, stillness is essential sometimes. Tell me your plans.'

I launched into a long mournful tale. He listened, unaffectedly tucking his feet under himself and tapping his knee with his fingers. His gold-rimmed spectacles caught the light. I watched him as I talked. I have a little game I play with people, which in my nastier moments I am proud of: I take notes of their mannerisms, chuckling to myself. I was just starting the first invisible chuckle when I noticed Das chuckling too. His eyes rested on me, intelligent, sardonic, and seeing. I stopped taking notes hastily.

'All is solved,' Das said. 'Ajit K. Das has solved your problem. Come with me to Sikkim.'

'Sikkim?'

'What is education coming to? You have not heard of Sikkim?'

'Yes, of course,' I said stiffly, 'but it's inaccessible, isn't it?'

'Inaccessible? Hah! You leave that to Ajit K. Das. He knows. See, the Chinese are on the Sikkim border. The rumour is that Indian troops are moving in. It is a wild place, with beautiful scenery. We can go up to the Tibetan border. Even if you go to Assam now, it will be raining like hell, and you will not be allowed to go into NEFA for security reasons. In Sikkim you have everything that you have in Assam, and better weather. Also more poetic. Will you come?'

'Yes,' I said.

'Hah! Good. You are a real good boy. Leave everything to me, I will arrange. Only meet me tomorrow morning at seven o'clock at the air terminal. I will fix it up.'

'Tomorrow?' I said weakly.

'Tomorrow. How long you want to stick in this damn place?'

'Oh, all right,' I said.

'Very good. We go to Sikkim tomorrow. Cable your relatives and dependents saying that you are in the care of Ajit K. Das. That will stop them worrying.'

He bounced out again. I fingered my typewriter. It worked. I got a little of my breath back. I decided I liked Ajit K. Das very much indeed.

Later, Galway called. 'Bose wants us to meet some students. And he's fixed up for some writers to call at his flat this evening for us to meet.'

'I'm going to Sikkim tomorrow.'

'Sikkim? A bit wild, isn't it?'

'Yes,' I said. 'When do you leave Calcutta?'

'This evening, after Bose's party.'

'What about these students?'

'Oh, Bose has it all fixed. We have to go to the university.'

So we took a taxi to the university, which is a little way from Chowringhee. A young man was waiting for us at the gate. He took us through a large entrance porch cluttered with grubby marble busts of previous principals to a small room where four other young men were waiting, sitting at a table, thin, intelligent-eyed, and a little spotty.

'These are some of the officials of the Students' Union.'

I remembered a few of the things I had heard about Calcutta students. The Bengalis, and especially the Bengali students, have always been the most vocal, the most intelligent, and the most anarchistic section of Indian society. Their resistance to the British in India was long and vociferous: one result was the caricaturing by Anglo-Indians of the Bengali Babu as always full of ideas he did not understand. The resistance came to its peak when thousands of students took part in anti-British riots. The spirit of revolt engendered then has not yet died down. A month before I reached Calcutta there had been further riots there: bombs had been thrown, and several people killed, including a policeman whose head was cut off. The authorities, alleging that the riots were instigated and organized by the students, had arrested many, and at more than one point had opened fire on crowds of student demonstrators. Who actually did instigate and organize the riots had not yet been proved.

Nevertheless the students of Calcutta are not orderly as students. They tend to go on strike, and not always reasonably. Bose, who is a professor of comparative literature at Jadhavpur University, had complained about their behaviour.

'There is a Spanish Jesuit teaching at the university,' he said. 'One day when the students were on strike, they surrounded him. They called him a dirty Catholic, and they pulled his beard.'

He added, 'The students who broke the strike were assaulted and abused. My own daughter was attacked. They are not disciplined at all.'

So when Galway and I sat down with these students, the leaders of the students of Calcutta, we were neither of us predisposed to like them.

'Can you tell us,' I asked, 'about the part that the students here played in the recent riots?'

'We will have to go into causes,' one of the young men said, 'before we can go into effects.'

He began to detail the grievances of the students against the food minister of West Bengal.

'We are after all interested in the country we are going to inherit. Food distribution is Bengal's main problem. In the old days Jawaharlal would have protested for us. But he has become too old and too entrenched in his position to protest for anybody. Therefore we marched to protest peacefully to the ministry. As we reached it, the police lathi*-charged. Five hundred students were arrested. Forty were killed in the firing that followed. Forty are still missing. More than a hundred are in hospital. At this very moment we are busy drafting petitions for the release of those arrested, and organizing funds for their defence. They have been held without trial for beyond the statutory term.'

'That's all very well,' I said. 'What about the ambulances that were burnt by the students? What about the bomb throwing? And the acid-bulbs? And the policeman whose head was cut off? And the assaults on students who broke the strike?'

'Any demonstration of this kind naturally draws hooligan elements. Our demonstration in the beginning was peaceful.

* Baton.

If the police had not charged us and fired on us the hooligan element would have had no excuse to do what they did.'

'But if this sort of demonstration naturally draws hooligan elements, why hold it? You must know the probable consequences. Why not do it some other way?'

'What other way?' one of the young men said bitterly. 'All the heroes of revolution in India have turned into pillars of the Establishment. Nobody would listen. It is the country we shall inherit, but if we draft a petition, the petition of the inheritors is put into a file by a government clerk and forgotten. If we are to gain anything, we must risk being associated with hooligan elements. If the government had not fired on us, why should they treat us like this now—gaoled, shot, held without trial, lying in hospital after police beatings, unable to speak for ourselves because we are already condemned? Is that part of the process of democracy?'

They kept repeating, bitterly, that there were no leaders in India any more. One of them quoted a line from Buddhadeva Bose to prove it. As intelligent students ought to be, they were familiar with the poets of their time and place, and the first quotation touched off a stream of others from Datta, Chakravarty, Dey, and Samar Sen.

Just before we left I asked what their political beliefs were. They were all Communists.

There was another quiet evening at Bose's flat, where six grave young poets had congregated to read their poems. They treated Bose with a reverence that differed widely from the attitude of young poets in England towards older poets. At the same time it must have been rather irritating for Bose: they treated him like something venerable and fragile: solicitously they plied him with his own whisky. The actual reading was much of a muchness, save that one poet read out a section of the *Iliad* which he had translated into Bengali. Aurally this was a successful translation.

The poet was a small man, with a thin voice, but when he read the poem took hold of him and the room filled like a shell with the murmur and thunder of the sea.

Bose read some of his own poems in the same incantatory whisper in which he had previously read Tagore to us. He seemed self-absorbed this evening, moulding a long hand over his forehead and staring out of the window. But when we left he stood up, taking my hand in both his. 'Come back to Calcutta,' he said, with a charming smile. We had arranged to do some translation together from the Bengali. 'You can't translate Bengali in Chelsea. You will *have* to come back to Calcutta.' With a mischievous giggle: 'Also there is no way back into India from Sikkim except through Calcutta.'

'Why are you going to Sikkim?' said one of the grave young poets. 'It is a savage place, and there are no hotels there. You will have to sleep on the pavements.'

They stood in a little triangle and stared pityingly at me. I averted my eyes and said goodnight to Bose again, then to all the rest. The grave forum opened and shut like a fan, letting us pass.

A Mountain People

> 'We dwell in freedom by necessity,
> A mountain people living among mountains.'
> —W.H. Auden

I write this in Gangtok. A thin small rain is falling in streets drifted over with mist. Almost my journey has come full circle, since the day I flew away from London, lonely for you. If I stopped thinking, this could be London, except instead of buses, tasselled mules jingle past under the window, prodded into speed by Tibetan muleteers in felt boots and slouch hats, like Western cowboys.

Inauspicious days...they began when we left Calcutta yesterday. I woke at four and drifted through the motions of bathing and dressing before fully waking up: then to the terminal, far too early, and unjustifiably irritable at Das for being late. He arrived exactly on time, bearing in his arms and about his person two movie cameras, a typewriter, a briefcase, and an airbag. His man followed, carrying a trunk and some rolled-up bedding.

I looked at all this, then at my own small case and typewriter. Perhaps I seemed surprised. Das obviously felt he should explain.

'I always provide,' he said, 'for the basic necessities. Among other things I have brought some rugs in case we feel cold on the Tibetan border, a raincoat in case of rain, and a small brass pot for washing.'

I was a little ashamed.

There was the usual long wait. Presently our flight was announced over the loudspeakers. We bundled out, staggering a bit under the weight of Das's basic necessities, to the aircraft. At this point we were intercepted by an embarrassed airline official.

'Sorry, sir. Announcement was not for you, sir.'

'Who was it for, for God's sake?' I said irritably.

'For the crew, sir.'

'The crew?'

'Yes sir. We have lost our crew, sir. We do not know where they have gone.'

We did not argue. We carried our cargo back to the lobby. An hour later a delighted official rushed up.

'We have found the crew, sir. We have put them in the plane.'

So the delinquent crew flew us off, and two hours later landed us at Bagdogra under a glaring sky. The airport sat in the middle of flat plains: green, spotted with buffaloes and a few men: but off to the north a rim of mountains stood, helmeted in cloud. Das indicated them. 'Sikkim is there,' he said laconically, 'and Tibet.' I was as amazed as a child.

It was very hot. We took a rickety bus to Siliguri, where Marilyn had been arrested. Before we left the airport Das pointed out a room on the first floor.

'That,' he said impressively, 'is the room where she was questioned.'

'Dear Marilyn,' I thought, and felt rather like a pilgrim.

We passed the green fields, the buffaloes squelching up from mud-wallows, the groves of bamboo, the pools full of children, and on every side the cool white speargrass wagging a thousand beards in the windless heat. Presently we crossed a wide, rough brown river; a few peasants stood waist-deep in the water, manipulating fishing-lines with idle flutters of the wrist.

'The Teesta,' Das said. 'We follow this river a long way, it comes with us into Sikkim.'

Siliguri was tiny and ramshackle. We got off at the railway station and loaded our things into the bus for Gangtok. This bus takes the mail from Gangtok to Siliguri and back every day, a journey of twelve hours altogether; the remarkable thing about it is that the same driver operates it always. He was bronzed and wiry, a Sikkimese, chain-smoking and a little sulky. He wore a vest and blue Chinese trousers, but when he got into the bus he took his trousers off and hung them neatly on a nail. I asked him why. He replied that the only reason he could see for wearing trousers was that they had convenient pockets in which money could be kept. While actually driving, he said, he had no need of money, therefore no need of trousers. This seemed logical.

The bus itself was a peculiar one. It was long and low-slung, and physically divided into three parts. The front seat, by the driver, where Das and I sat, was first-class; then came a section cut off on either side by yellow-painted iron bars, like prison bars, second-class; and finally a section shared by mail-bags and third-class passengers. The doors were fastened by a kind of peg on the inside. The luggage went on the roof. 'How long does it take to Gangtok?' I asked Das.

'Six hours.'

'And how far is it?'

'Seventy miles.'

'Seventy miles! Are the roads that bad?'

'It is not only the roads.'

'What then?'

'You will see,' Das said darkly.

We began our journey. After we had reached the outskirts of Siliguri the bus stopped, the driver got out, and we waited. The driver's assistant sat among the mail-bags, singing, I chain-smoked, and Das read the papers. Half an hour passed. 'Where is the driver?' I asked. Das asked the assistant. 'The driver has gone for his lunch.'

The driver returned some time later and the journey went on. The mountains rose taller toward us, dappled with cloud-shadow, hairy giants, clouds like wet linen clinging to their shoulders. An hour's driving found us high up, the bus like a mad beetle skidding along a road that wound tightly round the flanks of the mountains. The driver drooped a cigarette from the corner of his mouth and one hand constantly played with the horn. The horn was rather unique: it was apparently operated through the steering-bar, in which there were a number of little punctures, like the holes in a flute, and the driver ran his fingers over these, producing a kind of horrible melody. On one side the road dropped six thousand feet into a narrow valley, where the Teesta, stronger and clearer than in the plains, roared in foam over huge upended boulders and narrow sandbanks. On the other the mountainside rose vertically, bleeding a thick green vegetation out of its clay, great trees crowding for room, exploding ferns, and jammed among them enormous insecure rocks. Every twenty yards a midget waterfall spilled down the mountainside through a pebbled and mossy crevice, slipping at last over the road to drip towards the valley. Also, there were constant little wooden bridges slung over chasms where branches of the Teesta whispered to their stones. Most of the road signs said, *Danger, Bridge Unsafe for Heavy Traffic:* but the driver's foot was firm on the accelerator, and the bridges shook and creaked beneath us as if the bus itself was a great weight of rushing water. Sometimes also the road signs said. *Beware of Falling Boulders,* and indeed the great boulders balanced so precariously overhead seemed likely to fall out of sheer boredom, and bring the uprooted trees and porous clay down in a slow spin upon us. It was two hours of this, the Teesta always ploughing plain-ward away from us on one hand, and the untrembling mountains rising above us on the other, before we made our next stop, at a village sprawled across the mountainside, where a concrete suspension bridge went over the Teesta. Here the road split: one branch went on through the Himalayas to civilized Darjeeling, with its promenade and missionary schools, the other crossed the Teesta into Sikkim.

The village only had one goat-infested street. The half farther up the mountain was where people stayed, two-storeyed tin-roofed shacks with little slotted windows; the lower half was mostly composed of stalls selling fruit and condiments. This was still the Indian side of the border, but the people were all high-cheekboned and slant-eyed; the women selling fruit in the stalls were often young and very beautiful, with rosy cheeks and a shy downturned look of the face.

Two wandering Tibetans came slowly over the bridge, in their felt boots and cowboy hats, their robes kilted to the waist, and pouches tied to their hips in which each carried his private Buddha. All along the bridge down which they came, Tibetan prayer-flags flapped lazily in the wind to warn off the spirits of the dead. The Tibetans came slowly into the village and slouched down the street, bought fruit and sat down on the grass to eat it, coughing and hawking up the pink pulp like consumptives. When they kilted their robes higher one saw the beautiful embroidered linen belts of Tibet, and when they took off their hats, pigtails spilled over their shoulders and turned them in a minute from cowboys to Red Indians.

I was beginning to feel a little nervous; it was clearly wild country into which we were coming, and the mountains on the far side of the Teesta huddled impassably together, forbidding in their community. So I repeated C.'s remark to Das: was it true that one had to sleep on the pavements in Gangtok? I asked. C. had said so.

'That is an interesting remark,' said Das, 'because it only shows that C. imagines that there are pavements in Gangtok to sleep on.' This did not ease my fears.

We left the littered village after an hour or so, the Tibetans sleeping on the grass, the women crying their wares, children weeping, and at the far end of the street a goat trying to make love to a girl.

Then again the mountains, the slow climbing, the descents,

the bends, and always on one side the following and wandering Teesta, and on the other the hairy mountains.

Occasionally we passed people on the road breaking stones, squatting women, beautiful and wild-looking, men with slant sharp features, dying waterfalls and the growing, sprawling vegetation everywhere, forcing itself sometimes through the cracks of the road. Sometimes the road ceased to be road for a mile or so and became a bridle-path, so narrow that the off-wheel was always trembling on the edge of a terrible decision. It was all very muddy too.

We stopped in a town high up in the mountains. It was market-day, and traders had come in from Kalimpong, spreading their wares in the street, cotton and a little grain and food, and, largest of all, there was a sort of sidewalk department store: combs, sand-shoes, cheap fountain pens, plastic teacups and glasses, charm bracelets, shirts, caps, and, strangely, pink silk knickers. 'Is there much of a market for those?' I asked the trader.

He said yes.

'I shouldn't have thought so.'

'Well, they wear them as fancy hats, you see.'

We spent quite a long while here, because it was time for the driver's tea. When we took off again I went to sleep. When I awoke we were passing a Tibetan mule-train: the mules tasselled and decorated, laced lightly together, with the lead mule free, a mirror on his breast, a bell round his neck, the muleteers loping behind. Then again the Teesta, and a bridge: Rongpo, the Sikkimese frontier.

At the far end were the Customs, a modern police station (the only modern building in Sikkim) and a faded blue-and-gold border sign. We drove on, and now we were always climbing.

As we climbed, I saw cultivation in the narrow valleys for the first time since leaving Siliguri. The fat green earth was cut into wedges, parcelled, forced to bear: the wedges turned to terraces, climbing the foothills. In the mountains themselves an astonishing thing was the number of butterflies, thousands of unhealthily vivid scraps of paper struggling in the wind, and birds dressed in red velvet and blue velvet preening like courtiers among the leaves. Also, the branches of every tree were wired together by cobwebs, enormous cobwebs, billowing in wind, festooned with corpses, and one gross spider sensuously fingering the threads. Even the rocks had cobwebs on them, the butterflies hesitated above them, and the birds looked down and squawked. 'Beautiful, eh?' Das said.

The bus drew up at a village called Sinthan, the driver needed more tea. This was again market-day, vegetables and fruit spread over the pavement on horse-blankets steaming with flies: red-spiked lychees, guavas with their chalky flesh, ginger and peppers. Among the traders the Sikkimese women moved, the young pretty ones with their virgin's gait, like clockwork mice, the old ones like trees floating. A few Tibetans paced about, robes flapping laxly, and everyone looked happy and anxious. When we left, the ones I had talked to stood and waved from the unpavemented street.

More climbing; spiders and butterflies; and at last as we came round the bend of a mountain Das pointed ahead. High up on the next mountainside a few houses were strung out, tin-roofed or thatched. Gangtok. As we climbed nearer we passed caravans loaded with wads of yellowish, smelly wool. 'Yak-wool,' Das said. 'They have come through Tibet, through the Chumbi Valley and the Nathu La Pass to Gangtok.' It was dusk, and the caravan bells chinked rhythmically behind us for a long time before they died away.

As we entered Gangtok, the Last Post sounded from the Indian police station.

Talking and Men

'Rain, rain, and the clouds have gathered,
The eight ply of the heavens are darkness,
The flat land is turned into river.
Wine, wine, here is wine!
I drink by my eastern window,
I think of talking and man….'
—T'ao Yuanming (Tr. Ezra Pound)

In the first of day the mist that drifted over Gangtok all night would thin away into cold and brilliant sunlight, and across the far valleys Kanchenjunga come suddenly clear, like a white nail driven into the sky. It presided over the wakings of Gangtok. In the one straight street which forms the town proper the Indian traders peeled the canvas out of their windows ready for the Sikkimese women who minced in to buy vegetables. The Tibetans uncoiled their long bodies from the alleys where they slept, and the proprietor of the puppet-theatre at the top of the street came coughing and blinking out from under the stage and did a few yoga postures to start the day. There was also a mad beggar whose sex was indeterminate under grey rags, who shuffled and blubbered from shop to shop, holding his brass bowl out in the hope of a little breakfast. He could not speak, only weep, and the shopkeepers did not understand that language and would throw buckets of water over him. This happened every morning. Once I gave him eight annas; but he gave it to a little child.

I awoke more or less with the rest of Gangtok. The hotel we were in was the better of the two in the town; but it was more dosshouse than hotel. There were only three rooms, and six people slept in each. Das's bedding turned out to be of the essence, for the hotel provided none; only low pallets set head to head. The other occupants of the room were mostly Tibetans. They slept with all their clothes on and put their knives under the pillow. This alarmed me somewhat. I took my problem to Das, who was rapidly turning into a sort of father-figure.

'A lot of these fellows may be Chinese spies,' Das said. 'They are all certainly thieves. Keep your money in your sock.'

It was very strange to me. The room smelt of yak-butter from many Tibetan pigtails. The ceiling was entirely covered with cobwebs, swarmed through by black spiders which descended on silk threads at night and bit one. Once I took a glass of brandy to bed with me: when I awoke I found the surface of the liquid covered with a small woollen blanket of dead insects. There were also a great many rats who ran over one after dark. In the end I developed a technique. I bought a lot of matchboxes and kept them by me, and when the scurry of a rat came in the dark hurled matchboxes at the noise till it went away. In the morning the floor would be littered with these matchboxes, which I could never bear to pick up. In the morning, too, the single bathroom was full of people strenuously hawking up the accumulated phlegm of the night. The floor was always covered, as a result, with a slippery liver-coloured jelly, and I could never quite face going in.

Instead I would go out and blink at Kanchenjunga and the narrow street, where the mail-bus coughed slightly, waiting to start for Siliguri. Chiranjilal, the man who ran the shop under the hotel, would come out and offer me a cigarette. Our breath clouded in the bright air. 'What news from Tibet?' '

'Arre, sahib, the Chinia are moving troops to the border, a friend came last night from Yatung.' And he would shake his head at Kanchenjunga. 'What will happen to us if the Chinia come?' But then a pretty Tibetan girl would come in to have iodine dabbed on a cut finger and Chiranjilal would brighten. Massaging her hand, while she giggled and covered her mouth coyly, stroking her forearm a little, he would peer back at me, suddenly small and wicked: 'Arre, there are compensations in life after all.'

Our first visitor in Gangtok came on the evening of our arrival. The hotel had a kind of restaurant, a room with four tables and a curtained-off section for illegal coupling. It looked over the street, where after dark the puppet theatre got going. Drifts of people moved towards it, looked and went away. It was always the same show, the same puppets mincing and cackling on the same wooden trestle-stage against the same backcloth peeling a little more each day. Tonje came up from watching it. 'I watch it every night,' he said. 'It is restful to see the same thing every night.'

He was Tibetan by birth, but a naturalized Indian, and he was the only resident correspondent in Sikkim. He was stocky and walked with the swagger that all Indian hill people seem to have: arms swung back like wings, chest out and hips paddling. He wore always an open-necked shirt, a pale blue jacket, and corduroys, and on his head, with that slight touch of absurdity which I think a grateful thing in a person, a cloth cap exactly like that cloth cap with which the poet George Barker used to intimidate barmen in Chelsea. Also he laughed magnificently and very often, all white and gold.

Das had put his dhoti on to be comfortable and sat cross-legged in a chair by the window, gold-rimmed spectacles flashing, laughing his high laugh and drinking much tea. I had ordered a bottle of Sikkimese brandy, which was sweetish and rather awful, so I was drinking very fast, trying to become hazy enough to forget where I was going to sleep. Tonje, who did not drink, nibbled a

Sikkimese cake. He did not smoke either. 'No vices I have,' he said, laughing explosively.

'Hey Tonje,' Das said in that hectoring tone which was too obviously assumed to be less than lovable, 'what about these Chinese?'

'What about them, Ajit sahib?'

'You have filed any stories?'

'I say, Ajit sahib, I will tell you,' Tonje said. 'This place is full of their spies.'

'That I know,' Das said.

'These Tibetan muleteers. Many of them are spies. Many, many. I have discovered,' said Tonje, growing excited, 'they are paid three dollars a word for every message they send back to the Chinese.'

'That is very clever,' said Das. 'Did you get these statistics straight from Chou En-lai? Or do you discuss salary rates with the muleteers?'

'Ha, you only laugh at me,' Tonje said, laughing. 'But,' he said, 'they come to the frontier every day now. Chinese pickets come. Also by night the frontier guards see their searchlights in the Chumbi Valley. And flashlights near the frontier. Thirty thousand Chinese are in the Chumbi Valley, that is what the traders say.' They talked on, while the valley mist dripped through the windows and a religious procession passed in the street, the chanting drowning out the squawks of the puppets below. The mountain people were happy, but where the two journalists talked, a kind of sobriety, a kind of international apprehension, was created. As Tonje spoke of the Chinese manoeuvres on the border, a small ghost came into the room and squinted at us. Preludes, preludes: to what? For what? As the mist thickened in the valleys and the singers went home, and the brandy began to work, I decided I could go to bed. I left them still talking, over frigid cups of tea.

Next morning Das said briskly, 'We must get moving. Movement, movement, that is the thing, to keep moving, hah?'

'Yes,' I said meekly. Das bounced out to find a taxi. There are three taxis in Sikkim. Das returned with one of them, a Land Rover with a blasé Sikkimese driver and a boy, his assistant. 'Now,' he said, 'we go to the police commissioner. He is my good friend.' We went bumping out of the main street and climbed for a while. Above the main town the houses of the Indian officials in Sikkim are strung out across the mountain. The police commissioner lived in one of these. We drove down a dirt track to reach his house. It was guarded by Nepalese policemen, and a huge blowsy Tibetan stood on the verandah, spitting lazily into the rose-trellises. 'An Indian spy,' Das said. 'Good that we also have spies, hah?'

The police commissioner came out to greet us, a large Sikh, handsome as all Sikhs are handsome, and a little drowsy, a little far away. He took us into his drawing room, a large airy room with swords hanging on the wall and athletic trophies on the shelves. Das introduced me, and the commissioner smiled at me sleepily, twirling his moustaches in his fingers with a gentle contented motion. He was very nice.

'You don't mind,' he said, 'if I see one of my men?'

The Tibetan came in, shuffling and holding his slouch-hat in his hands. He smelt, inevitably, of yak-butter.

'When did you come back?' the commissioner said.

'This morning, sahib.'

The commissioner had a map in front of him. He drew it towards him and fidgeted gently with a pencil. As they talked he marked the map with tiny delicate lines. They talked in Tibetan which neither Das nor I could follow, but every now and then Hindi words came in and we understood snatches.

'*Chinia ko dekha, kya?* You saw the Chinese?'

'Sir, yes, sir. Thirty men. One officer.'

'*Kya karthe the?* What were they doing?'

'I didn't follow them, sir. They were going towards Khamba Dzong.'

'Why didn't you follow them?'

'Sir, I was afraid.'

The commissioner gave his gentle tired sigh. Then he said, 'Go to the bazaar. See if you can find anyone who has come in today from Khamba Dzong. If you find him, send him to me.'

'Sir, yes, sir.'

'Come for your money this evening.'

When the Tibetan had gone the commissioner sighed again: 'You cannot trust any of them. They are all liars.'

Das showed him some photographs taken on his last trip to Sikkim. He was gently pleased with them, stroking his beard, and giving a peculiar courtesy-laugh which consisted of murmuring softly 'Ha ha.' Then he clapped his hands, and a servant brought tea, cake, toast, Punjabi rice pastries, bits of omelette, cheese, and so on. Plate followed plate. My stomach, in a strange disorder already, received this somewhat coldly, so I did not catch much of the subsequent conversation.

'These Chinese on the border, commissioner sahib. What about them?'

'There are no Chinese on the border.'

'But we are told....'

'Sala, that is all bazaar-gup. I tell you, sometimes they come there, five or ten, but all they do is fraternize with the border guards.'

'Fraternize in what way?'

'They talk.'

'About what?'

'Arre, they ask our boys how many they are, where they are placed, what they are armed with, and like that. It is only fraternization.'

'And these lights in the Chumbi Valley?'

'I will tell you, that is simply these muleteers; when they lose some mules they take flashlights and look for them in the night.'

'But the searchlights?'

'Arre, these muleteers may be carrying portable searchlights also.'

'What about Indian army troops moving in as reinforcements?'

'There are none.'

'But we hear....'

'There are *no* Indian troops in Sikkim.'

'Oh, well,' I thought, controlling my rebel digestion, 'hadn't we better go?' The same thought had clearly occurred to Das.

'Well, commissioner sahib, we must not waste your valuable time. We shall take our leave of you. One thing, can you give us a pass to Nathu La?'

'Ha, yes, that can be done.'

'Thank you.'

'One thing, if you have your camera.... There is a football match at the school ground this evening.... Gangtok versus Kalimpong. Why don't you take some few photographs?'

'With pleasure, commissioner sahib.'

'I will give you the pass when we meet at the match.'

'Thank you, commissioner sahib.'

We left him, standing tall and indifferent among his policemen in the mist of the Himalayas.

Sikkim is the second of the three mountain kingdoms of the north. Nepal lies to the west; its border with Sikkim is where the yeti does whatever peculiar things it is supposed to do. Bhutan lies to the east, an impassable roadless mass of Himalayan forest. Northward of all three is Tibet.

Sikkim joins Tibet on its northern and eastern borders. There are two passes into Tibet: the Jelep La and the more strategically important Nathu La, to which a jeepable road has been constructed from Gangtok. Until a very little while ago it was far easier to get into Bhutan and Sikkim from Tibet than it was from India. In fact, until the end of the eighteenth century Sikkim was a dependency of Tibet, and its ruler was designated governor of Sikkim. The ruling house is descended from one of the gyalpos or princelings of Eastern Tibet, and the State religion is Lamaism.

Even now the palace, stalked through by Red Hat Lamas clattering their beads, with its carved wooden gates painted red, its devil masks mounted above the doors, and its long plaintive strings of prayer-flags, is what one imagines Lhasa to be like. There is a constant movement, now as always, of Tibetans to and from Sikkim. Through Nathu La, the mule caravans come tasselled and belled to Gangtok, and even into India as far as the trade station of Kalimpong. Then they come back, and the Tibetans buy pink plastic raincoats in Kalimpong, and drape them round their shoulders against the small ceaseless rain of the passes. Lots of them settle in Gangtok and Sinthan; they are called Bhotias. There was a shop opposite the hotel that sold yak-wool and yak-pemmican and Chinese army issue mugs and plates imported from Tibet, run by a Bhotia mother and daughter. They were very nice, and gave me Tibetan butter-tea and tsampa whenever I visited them. Their people had been in Sikkim for a hundred years; they had gone back to Tibet on a visit every year, until the Chinese came.

The Sikkimese are a fierce and independent people, and Sikkim only became a British protectorate in 1890. It passed over to India in 1947, and the Indian government took over the responsibilities that the British had held. That is, they were in charge of the external affairs of Sikkim, and of defence. Such defence as there has been in the past has been entrusted to armed constabulary, and, so to speak, our friend the police commissioner was almost the minister of defence. India, however, has kept discreet tabs on the internal affairs of Sikkim as well, so that although Sikkim has its own government, the public works department, which has built such roads as there are, is staffed and run by Indians, the post office is run by Indians, and there is an Indian political officer who serves as a kind of grey eminence.

The dewan, or chief minister of Sikkim, is also an Indian; he is usually from the Indian Administrative Service, and acts, among other things, as a liaison officer between the Sikkimese ruler and the Indian government. His office is on a hill above a park where a few miserable deer fetched in from the forest nibble at such herbage as grows between the wire-netting of their cages; when the wind turns a strong smell of deer droppings pervades his room.

Later that morning we saw the dewan. He was leaving next day on an eleven-day tour of the northern borders. He was large and pleasant and seemed delighted at the prospect of pony rides and walks up and down mountains and waking at the foot of Kanchenjunga every morning. But he denied that he was going to inspect the border defences. He did not fear Chinese incursions, he said.

'I do not believe that all this border trouble is more than a diversionary tactic. It is an old Communist trick, you know. Three months ago the world was very excited about Tibet. Now next month the case is coming up at the UN. Meanwhile what do the Chinese do? They take Longju, which is in any case disputed ground, they have a few skirmishes, they refuse to accept the McMahon Line, and the whole world gets excited about the Indian borders. Tibet is forgotten. It is very convenient to the Chinese that the world should forget Tibet at this stage.'

'But what about the new Chinese troops being moved to the border? Why should they bother to do that, if it is just diversionary?'

'You know,' said the dewan, 'as to that, the Chinese may be afraid that the Tibetan refugees in India will cause trouble on the borders.'

'But,' I said, 'there are supposed to be thirty thousand Chinese troops between here and Lhasa, and there are only ten thousand Tibetan refugees in India.'

'It may also be,' said the dewan, 'that they want to seal the border so that no more Tibetans can get out. You see, the more Tibetans leave, the worse the reputation of the Chinese government becomes. They have an interest in keeping the Tibetans inside Tibet.'

'What about the Indian troops in Sikkim? If you don't fear Chinese incursions, why move troops in?'

'We are not moving troops in,' said the dewan firmly. 'Have some tea.'

We left with the mist thickening and met Tonje outside the dewan's office. He flung his arms wide in a gesture of love and surprise. 'Ha, my dear friends! It is a pioneer you are seeing before you. I am going with the dewan to Lachen and Lachung. Pathless, leech-infested territory twenty thousand feet above sea level,' he said with relish, quoting from his next dispatch. 'My dear friends, no food is there, even! I will take,' he planned, furrowing his brow, 'some cold rice and bread, and many tins of beans.'

'And a lorry to carry it all in,' Das said coldly. 'Have some sense. If you travel with the dewan you live like the dewan: off the land. Off the fat of the land too, I think.'

'No, no,' said Tonje. 'This is savage country, my dear friend. Tigers,' he said, snarling, 'bears,' lurching slightly, 'and Abominable Snowmen,' and paused, foxed for a suitable gesture. 'Also there is great danger of being shot by the Chinese. I will take my pistol.'

'Do not endanger the lives of your companions in this foolhardy manner,' said Das.

But we left Tonje gesticulating on the steps of the dewan's office, his cloth cap awry, flushed with the perils through which he had not passed.

Das bounced for the remainder of the morning. He had plans for the rest of the day. We would go a little way up the Tibet road and interview some muleteers. 'Movement, hah? That is the chief thing.' Plans to leave Gangtok, however, necessitate passes. Passes are unobtainable of a Saturday. In small dispirited bounces Das lowered his sights to the football match at four.

The school ground (there is only one school) is cut out of the mountainside, near the Indian residential area, quite far from the bazaar. We arrived to find Gangtok society seated uncomfortably in a small pavilion, and the proletariat scattered about the mountainside in a mushroom-forest of umbrellas. It was drizzling and misty, and also very cold. The commissioner stood on the edge of the playing-field furling his beard in the wind.

'Ha, Das sahib. Have you brought your camera?'

Das waggled the apparatus at him, dolefully.

'Sit down,' said the commissioner, and added optimistically, 'it is going to be a fine match.'

We sat down and looked at the field. Multicoloured players were practising with slightly inappropriate violence. A favourite joke seemed to be to kick the ball very hard into the crowd, which brought roars of joy from the mountainside. The commissioner appointed one of his policemen the judge of the best player on the losing side. Then the match began.

It had only lasted a minute when the ball was kicked out of the ground. Since it was a six-thousand-foot drop into the valley, a new ball had to be procured. This took some while. It was eventually fetched. But the game had scarcely restarted when there was a roar of thunder, a thick grey rain swept down the mountains, and total invisibility supervened. This state of affairs continued for an hour and a half. During this time Das went to sleep, I used my hip-flask lavishly, and Gangtok society peered into the haze, occasionally exclaiming, 'Oh, that is very nicely played, sir!' The only thing resembling contact we had with the match proper, however, was when the ball was kicked into the valley, which happened frequently, and a wet referee appeared demanding another. Finally it was announced that Kalimpong had won. The rain cleared. The mountainside, now denuded of spectators, had turned to a waterfall, the playing-field to a lake. Illuminated by an unconfident ray of sunlight, the commissioner presented the trophies to the winners, while Das clicked his camera vigorously in the distance. Finally one small cup was left. The commissioner turned to the judge.

'Well?'

'Sir?'

'Who is the best player on the losing side?'

'How can I say, sir? I could not even see them playing.'

The commissioner roared very gently into his beard, like a peaceable lion. He was not, however, nonplussed. 'I will present this fine cup,' he said, 'to the entire losing side. They were all the best players.'

There was general applause. The commissioner beamed at us. 'You have taken pictures?' he said. 'Good. Have breakfast with me tomorrow, and I will give you the pass for Nathu La.'

So we tiptoed away across the flooded field to find our Land Rover.

When we got back to the hotel we found Tonje in the restaurant, eating and listening ecstatically to a programme of Indian film music wailed over the radio.

'Do you know what I am eating, Das sahib?' he crowed when he saw us. 'Flesh of swine I am eating! A heathen fellow I am!'

'I am not a Mohammedan,' Das said.

'But I am coming to say farewell to you both, my dear friends, for all our lives,' he said sadly, and then burst into high-pitched giggles. Das scowled and went up to change into his dhoti. He had had a rough time at the football.

Dusk was coming, and apart from the radio everything was quiet and misty. Gangtok breathed softly after the rain. Suddenly a mob of people galloped through the bazaar, doubled forward and with lips pursed as though each was chasing a thistledown. They turned at the top of the bazaar and came charging back in the same way. I looked at Tonje in surprise.

'Some poor bugger has just died,' he explained with a happy laugh. 'But what are all those people doing down there?'

'When a poor bugger dies,' said Tonje, 'the mourners,' he described a mourner with one hand, 'become very frightened of the ghosties.'

'The ghosties?'

'Evil spirits. Yes. The evil spirits come to take the soul. So these mourners make fat their cheeks, so, and they run in the street very fastly, and they go phoof! phoof! and thus the ghosties go away.'

The mourners ran up and down the length of the bazaar seven or eight times, and then ceased their activities. The puppet-theatre began its nightly performance. The mist smoked up from the valley, and I sent a boy for a bottle of Sikkimese gin.

'You should not drink so much,' Tonje said reprovingly. 'You will become an alcoholist.'

Das returned and we ordered dinner. The food was a mixture of Chinese and Bengali, all cooked in a pervasive kind of oil. I was surprised to find myself enjoying it till I remembered that my last meal had been the previous morning.

'Why you don't come to the north with the dewan sahib?' Tonje asked. 'Very interesting for journalists.'

'Too far,' Das said. 'Eleven days.'

'Come up to Dikchu with us,' Tonje said. 'Beautiful country. Mr Dom will write some poetries if he sees that.'

'How far to Dikchu can we go by jeep?'

'By jeep, seven miles. There is a landslide at the seventh mile. Then two hours' walk to Dikchu.'

Das considered, cross-legged, chin in hand.

'Acchcha. We will come.'

'Many Chinia there,' Tonje said gaily. 'We will frighten them away by going phoof! phoof!'

'That is enough of that,' said Das, dourly. 'I go now to sleep.'

Ups and Downs

Next morning we had to have breakfast with the commissioner, and Das insisted on my wearing a jacket and tie. We arrived to find a wiry shrewd-eyed Sikkimese in plain clothes also in the drawing room. He was introduced as one of the border guards. He had just been made an inspector, and we congratulated him. The commissioner smiled benevolently in the background, accepting his share of it all. He had just got up, and still had on the oil-soaked bandages which the Sikhs wear at night to keep their beards in place.

'We are having, you see, some trouble with the refugees,' he said. 'All the able-bodied Tibetans are offered jobs by the Sikkim government, working on the North Sikkim road. Recently there has been some discontent, they are fighting, really giving much trouble.' He sighed more gently than ever and turned to the inspector. 'I have ordered two constables to help you,' he said. 'If you need more take them. Go today to the road-workers' camp. If you find any trouble there, chalan* two or three of them. Nothing stops trouble quicker than a few chalans. And tell the others that those we have arrested will be sent back to Tibet. That will stop all the fuss.'

'Is that not a big decision to take,' Das said, 'to send them back?'

'Arre, the police are always justified,' smiled the commissioner.

---

* Arrest.

Das changed the subject. He turned to the inspector with his most professional, most dentist-about-to-extract-a-tooth-ish smile.

'So you come from the border?'

'Ji ha.'*

'Do the Chinese come to Nathu La?'

The inspector hesitated and looked at the commissioner who was busy unbandaging his beard. He found no help in those calm eyes. 'Ji ha,' he said.

'How many at a time?'

'Sir, most days five, never more than ten. They are only patrols.'

'How often?'

'Every day, sir, sometimes in the morning, sometimes in the evening.'

'Ha!' said Das. 'How are they armed?'

'Sir, with sten guns. But,' said the inspector, getting into his professional stride, 'they have old-type sten guns, with wooden butts like this.'

'And our boys have what?'

'Sir, rifles only.'

'This is a fine state of affairs, hah?' Das said excitedly to the commissioner. 'They have automatic weapons and we have only rifles. What will happen if they decide to attack one fine morning, hah?'

'We have applied,' said the commissioner placidly. 'We have applied for automatic weapons. But the government does not send.'

'Krishna Menon again,' Das said bitterly. 'Defence ministry. All our sten guns are rotting in the plains and here we have nothing.'

'Sir,' said the inspector with dignity, 'we are policemen, it is not our business to carry sten guns.'

'But you're doing army work,' I said, 'at least at the moment.'

---

* Yes, sir.

'That is true,' the inspector admitted. 'But,' he qualified, 'their sten guns have a range of one hundred and fifty or two hundred yards. Our rifles have a minimum range of three hundred but they go up to four hundred. Even to five hundred,' he said rather recklessly.

'Still,' said Das, 'a sten gun is a sten gun, and a rifle is a rifle.'

'True,' said the commissioner profoundly. He wagged his head.

'But,' said the inspector, 'our boys are good shots, and they know how to fight in the mountains. These Chinia do not even know how to hold their sten guns properly. Some are boys of fourteen and fifteen. They don't even have proper uniforms,' in a tone of contempt. 'Some are coolies straight out from China and they go in rags, like coolies. These Chinia can give sten guns to anybody, but they cannot make anybody a good soldier.'

He wrinkled his mouth with disgust, remembering.

'They are cowards as well. When a picket of five come to the border, three advance, an officer and two men; the other two stay behind covering our boys with their sten guns. And we go up to them unarmed, we are not afraid. They are women, sahib.'

'What do they talk about?'

The inspector suddenly revealed unsuspected histrionic ability. He imitated a soldier clutching a sten gun and said in a falsetto voice: 'What are you doing here?'

Then in his own deep voice, holding out empty hands: 'What are you doing here?'

'We are defending our border against aggression.'

'So are we.'

'How often do you come here? How many are you?'

'We come here every day.'

'Don't you have automatic weapons? Who is your general?'

'And like that, sahib,' said the inspector, with a gesture. 'Also, to prove that they are cowards, I will tell you that one reason they have not yet come into Sikkim is that they are afraid of wild animals.'

'What?'

'It is true, sahib. All the border guards know this. On their side, in the Chumbi Valley, they have few wild animals. On our side *we* have tigers and panthers and bears. They are very frightened of them. They always ask us have we seen any, are they very fierce, and like that. They are *very* frightened.'

'What do you say when they ask you?' I inquired.

'Sahib, we say that the tigers of Sikkim are the fiercest in the world, and that around the border they eat three men every night.'

He laughed charmingly.

'Each one of us border guards will eat three hundred in one night, when the Chinia come.'

After breakfast we rushed to the post office in the Land Rover: Das wanted to file some dispatches, and I wanted to send you a telegram. 'We must move quickly,' Das said. 'We must get to the seventh mile ahead of the dewan's party, so that I can take photographs. Come, come, come,' he said, whirling me into the post office. 'No gossip, Babuji,' he said to the postmaster. 'We are in a hurry.'

The driver and his assistant entered into the spirit of the thing with terrifying whole-heartedness. The North Sikkim road is a dirt track, clambering through gorges and ravines, and occasionally fording waterfalls, high over rock-strewn valleys. The driver chain-smoked his way along this dubious route at forty miles an hour, and in the back of the Land Rover the assistant, clutching Das's movie and still cameras to his bosom, giggled joyfully and shrieked him on. Das and I, sharing the front seat with the driver, attached ourselves to the struts and bounced for dear life. At last, where many little landslips had littered the track with fragments of rock, clay-heaps, and uprooted plants, and each new bounce took us tilting to the edge, the driver took his foot off the accelerator. The Land Rover shuffled through the debris, bumping still, but less hazardously. Occasionally it had to stop to make room for mule-files. It was during this part of the journey that Das suddenly grabbed my arm. 'Look!' he cried, like Saint Paul.

When I looked farther up the track, shrouded in mist where it climbed the mountain, I saw what I took to be another mule-caravan. But Das had already leapt out of the jeep, and, followed by the boy with the cameras, was sprinting to a rock at the edge of the road. Then as the lead mules came towards us out of the mist, I saw that their packs did not contain yak-wool, borax or herbs, but mountain-guns; and their drivers weren't Tibetans, but Sikh soldiers with rifles, their faces tired and fixed. More and more mules came down the mountain past the Land Rover, some carrying mountain-guns and ammunition, some camouflage-nets, others stores and clothing. And after and among them came the Sikhs, all carrying rifles and ammunition, cocking an eye at Das, who precarious on his rock was furiously working the movie camera. After the Sikhs came Gurkhas, their steel helmets swathed in netting, festooned with leaves and twigs, like many ungraceful Daphnes. There must have been five hundred troops and fifty mules. All through their slow passage Das stylized it on his rock, handing one camera down to the boy while he used the other, and occasionally bestowing delighted winks and salutes upon the passing troops. When they had finally passed, he leapt off the rock and came cantering back, reloading his cameras as he came. 'Quickly, driver,' he shouted. The boy tumbled in at the back as the Land Rover bumped away. Das dexterously reloading his cameras between bumps, yelled in my ear: 'We have beaten the world!'

'Why?'

'Indian troops in Sikkim! They may deny and deny, but we have seen them with our own eyes,' smacking his spectacles. 'We are the first civilians to have seen them!'

He yelled to the boy: 'Look behind, bahadur sahib, great general, and see if the dewan sahib's jeep is coming.'

We arrived at where a waterfall struck the road, bounced, and fell steeply into the rocky valley. As the Land Rover wheezed among boulders and water the boy shouted. We turned. Behind us the track followed the deep inward curve of the mountain, and at the far end of the curve a small train of jeeps was crawling jerkily towards us.

'Shabash, O beloved of the world!' said Das, and precipitated himself into the torrent.

I followed him. The waterfall on our right rushed smoothly down, like a white wall, exploding as it hit the track, and spray rained on us, while the swift water, freezingly cold, tugged at our knees. My position was a little worse than Das's, who, mounted on a rock above the torrent, was madly working the movie camera as the jeeps inched round into the curveway. Then he leapt off the rock and we both squelched back into the Land Rover.

'Chalo, chalo,' I said, catching Das's mood. 'Drive on!'

'Sahib, injin bundh hua,' said the driver gloomily. 'The engine is dead.'

'Then we must push,' Das said invincibly, and out we tumbled again.

Pushing a Land Rover through a waterfall is not easy. For one thing, we had to keep lifting boulders out of the way. For another, when we got into the middle the current was so strong that it flattened us against the car and shifted that a little farther towards the edge. All this while the dewan's procession was closing in on us from behind.

We managed somehow. As we dripped up on to reasonably dry land behind the Land Rover the engine coughed a little and began working. Das, the boy, and I fell into the back and we pulled away as the dewan reached the waterfall.

Das's camera was busy again. He knelt wetly and bucketingly in the back, shooting away as the dewan's jeep started fording the waterfall. It was much quicker about this than ours had been. Soon we found ourselves the leader of the cavalcade by about twenty yards.

'Scoop, scoop, scoop,' Das kept saying gleefully. I was so wet I didn't care.

Finally we reached a little village of thatched and tin-roofed huts spread down the mountain towards a valley now cross-hatched with cultivated fields. The villagers were lining the road with scarves and garlands, the prayer-flags fluttering in the thin mist overhead. Under the impression that we were the dewan, everybody began to salute and advance with the garlands. Das promptly rose and bowed. As we pulled up, however, the real dewan arrived. Tonje tumbled out of one of the jeeps behind him and came rushing through the mud, also with a movie camera.

Das hopped out too and they both levelled their lenses at the emergent dewan, like the nozzles of sten guns. The dewan wore his State clothes: a brown jacket buttoned at the neck, and jodhpurs, in his hand a sandalwood stick. He accepted the garlands and scarf-offerings and returned them with a gracious gesture. Then he walked with dignity to the edge of the road, accompanied by his entourage, and they all peed into the valley. Tonje and Das stopped their cameras hastily, and we joined ranks on the edge. Finally the dewan buttoned his trousers, and stood gazing seignorially at the village, as if in thought, gently tapping his leg with his stick. Then he climbed back into his jeep. We all scrambled for our respective jeeps, doing ourselves up as we went, and the cavalcade began afresh. The road was worse here. The landslip ahead had precipitated other minor landslips, and the track was flooded in many places and sputtered over by newly created waterfalls. When we reached the big landslip I felt inured, but even so was startled by what I saw. The entire mountain seemed to have caved in, leaving raw fissures in the slopes, and a kind of dwarf mountain had been created on the track: earth, rocks, and uprooted trees upside-down in the debris, while water flooded through.

The entire cavalcade drew up, and everybody got out and stood peering at the landslip. 'Is it safe to cross?' the dewan said.

'On foot, yes, sir,' said the private secretary, who wore leather shorts and a peaked cap. The porters with the dewan's baggage appeared labouring along in the Sikkimese manner, with their packs fastened by a strap round their foreheads. They began to negotiate the landslip, while the dewan poked it experimentally with his stick. Then we all climbed over. It was all right, save for one horrible moment, when, balanced on the slippery clay at the top, I looked down at the rocks of the valley three feet across from my right shoulder and several thousand feet beneath my right toe. Now we straggled through forest mud. Tonje, huffing and puffing under his camera, was my companion. Das galloped about the mountainside ahead, unbelievable in his energy, taking photographs. It took about two hours to get to Dikchu, a small high village, mist-wrapped and cold, and by that time even Tonje was speechless. Das still limped beside the dewan, taking notes. The villagers came out, did obeisance, and showed us to a collection of pallets outside the headman's hut. Here we sat down and were brought Sikkimese tea, which is mostly hot milk, and buckwheat cakes. It came on to rain. Presently Das rose. 'Good luck, dewan sahib,' he said. 'We go now back.'

Tonje saw us to the edge of the village with effusive goodbyes. 'Perhaps I may never see you again, my dear friends.'

'One can always hope,' Das said ambiguously. He was a little embittered by exertion. The villagers sent a boy with us as guide.

Das and I squelched back for two hours through ever-increasing rain. It was nearly dark by the time we reached the Land Rover, dumbly faithful at the far side of the landslip. The driver and his assistant were both asleep. We woke them and began our journey back in silence and very nearly in tears. I kept discovering leeches in my clothes. Das was too tired to worry about leeches.

We got back to the waterfall where we had stuck, and stuck again. We were knee-deep striving when a mule-caravan jingled up. The muleteers stood akimbo on dry land urging us to hurry. At length they were tired of waiting, and decided to try to take the mules across on the far edge. Four mules went over safely. The fifth stumbled in the stream and abruptly disappeared. There was a shriek like a woman's, and a heavy crash far below. The muleteers peered over the edge of the cliff, clicking their tongues. The mule had fallen about a hundred feet; and been brought up short by a boulder. It lay now straddling the boulder and heaving as if trying to bring something to birth. The mirror on its breast had splintered, and the tassels been torn away. It looked curiously nude without them, and blind, struggling against what it could not see. Thick mud-coloured blood dripped from its side.

Two of the muleteers took their knives out of their silver scabbards and began very cautiously to climb down to the mule. It was like a sacrifice, the animal on the mountain, mute and struggling to be comfortable, and the knife-carriers descending to it. But the Land Rover was now across, and we drove away.

We did not reach Gangtok till midnight. Das had fallen asleep and it was an effort to wake him. I was very tired, and aching and itching all over from bumps and leeches. I tried to think of you, but my mind was too tired to function. All night I could not sleep.

Tibetans from Tibet

'... existence is believing
We know for whom we mourn, and who is grieving.'
—W.H. Auden

Next morning Das said proudly, 'We may have overexerted, but still we have scooped the world, hah? We have films of the first Indian troops in Sikkim.'

'Good show,' I said idiotically.

'Now we shall go and see the PO,' Das said. 'He may be having some hot story.'

As we went down to the Land Rover Chiranjilal came out of his shop. 'Hey, Ajit sahib,' he said, 'the press attaché has been telephoning for you.'

'Now what does that raper of his mother want?' Das wondered agreeably. He went into Chiranjilal's shop to telephone. I talked to the driver and his boy.

The driver lolled back across the seat, a cigarette in his fingers, speaking in small blue puffs.

'You go to Nathu La soon?'

'Tomorrow or the day after.'

'I see no reason for it. It is a wild place. Yaks and savages live there, not civilized people like we have in Gangtok.'

The boy said: 'Also the Chinia are on the pass with guns.'

'Silence, boy,' said the driver. 'However,' he said, 'your friend the journalist may be interested in going tomorrow. Chhibar sahib is coming.'

'Who is Chhibar?'

The driver looked shocked. 'The Indian consul in Lhasa. He comes out tomorrow.'

'How do you know?'

'A friend of mine came from Yatung today. He passed Chhibar sahib's mule caravan. Chhibar sahib was in Yatung last night. He is spending today in Yatung and tomorrow morning he comes to Nathu La.'

At this point Das returned. His face was as sorrowful and angry as Saint Sebastian's.

'Imagine what those sons of bitches have done!' he moaned, climbing into the Land Rover. 'A government order to confiscate my films of the troops!'

'Surely they can't enforce it?'

'Arre, if I do not give in, they will never let me into Sikkim again. Those sons of bitches! Why are they frightened that the world should know? Two hundred feet of film,' he mourned, 'at sixteen rupees a hundred feet,' and another arrow seemed to whiffle home.

I tried to think of healing ointments. 'The driver says the Indian consul in Lhasa is coming out through Nathu La tomorrow.'

'Hah?' exclaimed Das. 'What is that?' He leant forward and began to cross-examine the driver. Finally he leant back with a small complacent smile. 'On this then,' he said, 'we shall beat the world.' He thought deeply, then looked up, beatific. 'Let us go now to the PO.'

The grey eminence, the political officer, Mr Pant, lives in a beautiful gardeny house on a hill-top. Pant is one of the best of the younger Indian diplomats. He was high commissioner in Nairobi during the Mau Mau troubles, is an expert on India's northern frontiers, and has visited Lhasa during the Communist regime. He is very tall and extremely handsome, with eyes that seem hooded and inward like the eyes of Nehru.

Now he received us in what, even without comparison with our own hotel, was a truly gracious-living sort of drawing room ('it makes you afraid to tread on the carpet, hah?' Das murmured) and offered us tea. Then he took a quick hard look at me and said with unflattering perception: 'Would you prefer some beer?'

'I would indeed,' I said enthusiastically. The beer was brought. It was very good, very cold Danish lager. I drank it and looked at the mist troubling the grass and smoked Mr Pant's Turkish cigarettes and felt happy. Occasionally, I scraped a little moustache of foam off my upper lip and listened to what Das was saying to the PO. He had launched into a long diatribe about his film. Mr Pant listened gravely.

'We can't let you release it, you know,' he said, shaking his head. 'I'm sorry, but we really can't.'

Das sputtered, and then with the true journalist's imperturbability began his questions.

Mr Pant was amiable and historically informative. 'Longju, after all,' he said, 'has always been disputed territory. The British mapped it as an unsettled part of India, that is, they collected no taxes there, they had no district officer, and so forth. On the other hand, the Tibetans have collected taxes there off and on over a long period. Since 1947 the Indian government has been collecting taxes there and making roads and that sort of thing, but it is disputed territory. The same with most of the other areas where the Chinese have moved in. We cannot say with authority that they have always been an integral part of India.'

Sometimes he became very acid. 'Don't you think,' Das said, 'that you should let me write that there are Indian troops in Sikkim? It might also warn the Chinese that we are prepared.'

'Do you think,' said Mr Pant, 'that they don't know? Do you think five hundred words in the *Indian Express* by Mr Das will send the Chinese running all the way from Nathu La to Peking?'

I intervened at this point. 'Do you think they will attack India?' I said rather crudely. 'After all, that's what it's all about!'

'This year, no,' said Mr Pant. 'If you were to ask me that next year, I don't know what I should say.'

He hooded his eyes at me and said in his beautiful deep voice: 'You are the poet.'

'I suppose so,' I said.

'Let me see what I can remember from the newspapers.' He closed his eyes. Then they opened again. 'You were at Oxford!' he said accusingly.

'Yes,' I said.

'So was I,' said Mr Pant delightedly. 'What college were you at?'

For the next half hour we wandered over Oxford, the grey stones wedged together with books, the bicycles, the Epstein in New College chapel, the dons like huge fruit-bats flitting through the dusk to the Hall. Das brought us out at the other end on to a dry table land of no nostalgia.

'Is it true, Apa sahib,' he said a little impatiently, 'that Major Chhibar reaches Nathu La tomorrow?'

Mr Pant looked irritable again. 'Who told you that?' He had Nehru's imperiousness as well as Nehru's eyes.

'Ah,' said Das in modest triumph. 'I have my sources.'

'Yes,' said Mr Pant, and I congratulated the taxi driver in my heart.

'At what time this will be?'

'He's supposed to get there at eleven,' Mr Pant said.

We wished one another cordial goodbyes. 'You talked so much,' Das said fretfully as the Land Rover took us away, 'I was not able to get a word in sideways even.'

Later in the morning we drove up the North Sikkim–Tibet road to inspect progress. The engineer in charge, a slim hairy man, came with us. We started on the same road along which we had come the previous day, but at the fifth mile branched off to the north.

The new road is cut high up on the mountainside. On one hand, the bald rock rose three hundred feet through the clouds, on the other, birds hung above immense gorges, cluttered with trees and veined with the silver blood of streams. Tibetan work parties sat phlegmatically chipping stones at intervals along the road. Little flocks of shanties pimpled the slopes. 'The labour camps,' said the engineer. 'We provide well for these refugees.'

The road as yet is a dirt track. About fifteen miles of it have been cut, but when it is finished it will be sixty miles long, leading to the North Sikkim–Tibet border. We went about ten miles. The first five were the easiest; then came the usual landslips, waterfalls, and, most terrifying, points where the road was only just wide enough to take the Land Rover, a thread on the shoulder of the mountain hung over the tree-packed valley. The driver smoked with one hand and drove with the other, occasionally I closed my eyes. The engineer pointed this out to Das and they both laughed happily.

We stopped at last by a work party clearing the debris of a landslip. They were Tibetan refugees, girls and men with brown mountain-lined faces, the exact colour and texture of sea-sand. They looked at us curiously. Das began to work the movie camera, and I wandered a little way up the road. There were butterflies everywhere, struggling from the foliage and the rocks and drifting off sideways to float over the valley. At one point, by a bed of straggling purple flowers, there were so many that they settled all over me, as in the legend of the prince. The undergrowth by the road smelt wet and herbal: to breathe this tart chill air was like biting into an unripe apple.

I came back to find Das had finished and was ready to go back. There was a tractor farther down the road and he wanted to film it in operation. 'Let us take some of these fellows with us,' he said, 'for local colour.'

So a dozen Tibetans piled into the back of the Land Rover, Das, the engineer and myself piled into the front, and we started back.

It was not a restful journey. The weight of the men in the back was unequally distributed. On the fly-walk above the gorge they canted the Land Rover over so that often it balanced on two wheels on the extreme edge. Vertigo had a queer physiological effect on me. The splayed paintbrush of each tree in the valley seemed to daub my eye with green: by the time we stopped the tractor my vision was completely green, like a mad camera: even the Tibetans had green faces. It took some time for this to wear off. I sat in the Land Rover composing myself while the engineer, perched high in the cockpit of the tractor, incited it to snort and heave in a baffled way. The Tibetans meanwhile stood sadly around. I wanted to talk to them.

'Tibeti janthe ho?' I asked the driver. 'Can you speak Tibetan?'

'Ese ese,' he said, which is Hindi for cosi-cosi.

I beckoned two Tibetans over. They were father and son, I think; they wore ragged blue trousers and vests instead of robes but they retained their slouch-hats. They smiled uncertainly at me and were silent.

'Tell them,' I said, 'I hear there is some trouble among the road-workers here. Ask them what it is.'

He asked them. They hesitated, then the younger one brought forth the flat smacking Tibetan consonants. He went on for a little while and stopped, waiting to be translated, his tongue thrust politely between his lips.

'He says they do not like it here. They do not get paid enough, they have not enough time with their families. He says this is not the work they want to do.'

The engineer had now produced a definite result. The tractor screamed and began to struggle down the road, Das trotting behind with his camera. I had to shout to make myself heard.

'What do they want to do?'

After a short exchange: 'He says in Tibet they are farmers.'

The older Tibetan now chipped in. He had to shout too, opening his mouth wide, revealing blackened teeth and a black lizard's tongue. His eyes were anxious, pleading like a bulldog's through wrinkled folds of skin.

'He says nobody understands their language here. He says he finds it hard at his age to become a foreigner.'

'Ask him if he wants to go back home.'

Presently the driver said: 'He says he has lost his home. His home is in the country where the Dalai Lama stays, but he is not at home here. If he goes back to Tibet now the Chinia will shoot him. His brother went back and him the Chinia took and shot.'

'But if he doesn't want to stay here and doesn't want to go back, what *does* he want to do?'

A short translation and the old Tibetan began his answer. He spoke with the same strange naturalness which had been the dignity of the Alakirti Lama in Kathmandu. The younger man shook his head in agreement. The tractor had stopped and Das was now taking still pictures.

'He says he wants to be back in Tibet before the Chinia came, when the Dalai Lama was in the Potala and the Tashi Lama at Shigatse, when he lived with his brother and their wife north of Lhasa. He wants those days to come back. He says why does India not drive the Chinia out of Lhasa? He says his people are fighting, and if India does not help they will all die.'

In the heavy silence that followed the cessation of the tractor's screams the old Tibetan and I looked helplessly into each other's eyes. I thought of Hungarian refugees on the Austrian frontier, cloth caps, cloth bags, muddy shoes, and always the same hard painful eyes. I thought of what the Dalai Lama had said in Delhi. 'The poor and dispossessed....' There was nothing I could do beyond what I did, the simple and meaningless compromise, a smile, a touch of the hand.

Only that morning I had never heard of Major Chhibar, but his name wove itself into a litany that was repeated all day, by Das, by Chiranjilal, by the shopkeepers in the bazaar. Chhibar had been three years in Lhasa. During the flight of the Dalai Lama his consulate, from which the first news had been sent to India, had been surrounded by Chinese soldiers. Now he was coming back to be the Indian first secretary in Gangtok. He had already been travelling fifteen days from Lhasa, through Gyantse, Yatung, and the Chumbi Valley, and the bazaar was full of reports from Indian traders coming back: that Chhibar had been detained by the Chinese in Gyantse and his diplomatic luggage searched, that the Indian traders in Yatung had appealed to him for protection.

Bazaars are good places for picking up news. Das wandered about while I sat with my friends, the Tibetan mother and daughter, in the back of their shop, drinking butter-tea, eating small pieces of dried yak-meat and flirting a little, to make myself feel younger, with the daughter, who was pink and pretty and giggled all the while, her knuckles to her lips. Das returned in the midst of all this, with a whole notebook filled with information and a cross look.

'That son of a bitch of a taxi driver wants three hundred rupees to take us to Nathu La. Have you ever heard such dung?' He sat down beside me and flumped his hands down on his knees, sitting four-square and rigid with indignation, as always when deeply moved.

'How far is it, though?'

'Thirty-five miles there and thirty-five back. Seventy in all. It is true that the roads are bad,' said Das, 'also we climb all the time, but three hundred rupees is a damn cheek.'

'Well, but who else is going to take us?'

'I have hired a jeep for a hundred and fifty,' Das said. 'It is outside now.'

So I went out and looked at the jeep. It was decrepit in the extreme.

'There aren't any waterproof door-covers,' I said as a preliminary objection. 'We'll get as wet as hell.'

'Those he can put,' Das said. 'Otherwise it is okay, hah?'

I pointed out a more fundamental lack. 'Where is the hood?'

'That is true,' Das said thoughtfully. 'Where is the hood?'

'Sahib,' said the driver, 'that is only a lid. I had to keep lifting it up and down when I wanted to look at the engine. It was too much trouble. Bahuth mushkil hua. Therefore, I removed the lid, and now there is no trouble.'

I know nothing about cars, but it seemed to me that if it rained, as it certainly would, the engine would get wet. I said so.

'No, sahib,' said the driver. 'Many times I have been to Nathu La. Never has there been any trouble. My boy has the heart of a lion, and is a fine mechanic. The best in Sikkim. Also I am the best driver in Sikkim. This is well known.'

'The offside tyre is flat,' I said.

'That he can blow up,' Das said. 'Arre, Dom, tell me, what other jeep would take us at this price? Every item missing means twenty rupees less.'

'Well,' I said, 'if he thinks he can do it....'

So it was settled. Das worked out the times on his fingers.

'Three hours to get to Nathu La. Chhibar is coming at eleven. So he would leave at eight. I have to file some dispatches in the morning. Say seven-thirty. Come at seven-fifteen,' he told the driver. 'Otherwise I will eat your life.'

In the hotel we ordered hard-boiled eggs, a loaf of bread, and a bottle of brandy for the morning, looked at the puppet-show for a little while through the window, and went to bed.

Tibetans from Peking

As usual I woke at five. I woke with a vague thought of hard-boiled eggs and liquor and a feeling that Julian and Del and Ved and I were going for a picnic along the Cherwell. Then I inhaled the foetid air of the bedroom and remembered. I went out on the terrace, shouted for a bucket of water, and splashed for a little. Day had come up over Kanchenjunga and there was a flavour of snow, woodsmoke, and herbs in the sunlight. I dressed and sat on the terrace, drinking brandy, watching the bazaar waking up, and reading *The Memoirs of Hadrian*. I knew when Das got up because his typewriter started raiding away and there were sleepy shouts of protest. At precisely seven-thirty he came out to me. He carried his cameras and typewriter, and, rather depressingly, his first-aid kit.

'Ready? Good. Let us go.'

The jeep had arrived. There was a slight delay while we put in eight gallons of petrol from the shop across the street. Then we drove uphill to the post office, and Das sent his telegrams.

The expedition seemed to have begun. But a hundred yards up from the post office, where the road became steep, the jeep suddenly ceased to work. It roiled gently backwards down the hill and stopped again exactly in front of the post office. The postmaster issued forth in some surprise.

'You want to file another message?'

'No,' said Das grimly, then to the driver, 'Son of a donkey, what has happened to your jeep?'

'Sahib,' said the driver, shamefacedly, 'now it will work.'

He started the engine and we climbed the hill again. At the top the jeep stalled conclusively. Once more we slid gently down to the post office. The postmaster had now been joined by his entire staff. They were laughing.

'Go back to the bazaar, O fatherless one!' Das said between his teeth.

But the engine had died completely. We coasted back under control of the law of gravity. Once in the bazaar, Das jumped out with murder in his eyes.

'Go to Chiranjilal's shop,' he said. 'I will settle with this bastard.'

Chiranjilal was all concern. 'It is five past eight,' he said. 'You will never get there in time for Chhibar.' He began telephoning various people to see if another jeep could be found. It was in vain. At eight-thirty Das returned in a fury.

'This driver has paid me back for the petrol,' he said, 'and I got our old Land Rover. But that driver wants five hundred rupees now.'

'I will talk to him,' Chiranjilal said.

So we all went out, Das, Chiranjilal, the two shop-assistants and myself, to where the driver straddled the front seat of the Land Rover, grinning hugely. A small crowd had gathered, including the Tibetan mother and daughter. Chiranjilal, Das, and the shop-assistants all shouted at the driver together.

The driver continued to grin, and occasionally to breathe smoke into the air, ogre-wise. Otherwise he gave no sign.

'These are very important sahibs,' Chiranjilal said. 'Chhibar sahib wishes particularly to see them. You will gain great honour from the dewan sahib if you take them.'

'My honour has already been taken away by these sahibs,' said the driver. 'I am being generous when I charge only two hundred rupees extra for it.'

'We will give you four hundred,' said Das, almost pleadingly.

'Five,' said the driver, adamant. I looked at my watch. Quarter to nine. Lost, I thought.

At this point the Tibetan mother, at the fringe of the crowd, lifted her beautiful aquiline head and called: 'Shame on you, Sanje, and shame on Sikkim. You should be privileged to do anything for these sahibs. And here you are bargaining for more money to give your unchaste wife for jewellery, and bringing your country nothing but disgrace.'

The driver looked at her, then looked back at us, and said sulkily: 'Two-fifty. Get in.'

I shot our preserver a grateful glance. She returned a broad wink. I laughed with relief. I could have kissed her.

We left Gangtok at about nine.

'Bahadur sahib,' Das said flatteringly, 'if you get us to Nathu La by eleven, we will call you Rajkumar, a prince.'

'Sanje is sufficient for me,' said the driver disagreeably. 'Do you think I have wings to fly to Nathu La?'

I offered him a cigarette, and said guilefully, 'If you get there by eleven, we will pay three hundred rupees.'

'Sahib,' said the driver, suddenly tractable, 'if you say half past eleven, I can do it.'

He sucked tentatively at my cigarette as we climbed out of Gangtok into the Himalayan track.

'It will be raining. There is fog ahead. I will try. Sahib,' he said, looking at the cigarette in his fingers, 'do you make these yourself?'

'They are made by a great sahib in Bilayat,'* I said, 'called Du Maurier.'

'Do you know this sahib?' asked the driver.

'Of course,' I said.

'If he comes to Sikkim,' said the driver, 'recommend me to him. He must be rich. I will take him to Nathu La for a thousand rupees.'

* England.

Then we passed into the mist.

Out of the mist, every so often, mules blundered like moths against the headlights. Behind them the tall shivering muleteers raised their arms in salute as we passed. As we climbed that spiral funnel towards the sky, the air thinned and rain began to whip tinily in with a knife-cold wind. I pulled the waterproof across the doorway, cutting off the view and saving myself from vertigo, for the track had narrowed to a strip of mud disintegrating in rain. We passed a huddle of shacks outside which cold policemen stood. 'Karponang,' Das said. 'Twenty-three miles still.' I looked at my watch again. It was ten to ten. 'Good going.'

Das said, 'Last time I passed through Karponang there were ten feet of snow. Mist everywhere also, you could not see even. I was coming back from taking medicine to the first Tibetan refugees, just after the flight of the Dalai Lama. My driver was driving with one hand and telling his beads with the other: he was a Buddhist. But I also thought we were going to die that day.' He hesitated and said: 'One should not bother about dying.'

Cigarettes gave one a strange ill feeling so I stopped smoking and squinted ahead through the mist-frosted windscreen. Only one of the wipers was working; it hissed and snicked to and fro; as a child I used to call them 'Vipers.' Presently we passed a gutted building.

'The old fifteen-mile checkpost,' Das said; 'It burnt down last year. Soon comes the new one.'

Ahead the mountainside widened and accommodated a kind of village with a worn wooden gate and a barbed-wire palisade across the road. A policeman came dripping out in a waterproof to inspect our pass. He took down the particulars, and nodded, unspeaking. We drove on. 'Nine miles to Chhangu.'

For the next half hour we leant slowly, noiselessly, through a cotton-thick mist. Rain fell. It was bitterly cold, and I draped my knees with one of Das's blankets. Then we moved out of the mist, to a cold burning of sunlight, and the unwinding road brought us down to a great lake. The mountains lay, wobbling gently, under the water; the water was powdery and blue, like an eye, like a pearl, and shivered all over by the risings offish.

'Chhangu Lake.'

We climbed again, till we had left the mountain hollow of the lake behind us. Mule caravans were now very frequent. The landscape was changing noticeably. All the way from Gangtok, the mountains had been humped and rough with trees. Now they seemed to have broken off in the air, jagged and pointed, and furred over with thick grey-green lichen, on which broken fragments of limestone lay. Among this lichen browsed enormous antediluvian animals, hung round with black hair, like woollen blankets walking, with horns splaying massively across their low brows. 'Yaks.' The driver pointed out a reddish flower coquetting in the wind. 'Poison-flowers, sahib. You only find them here. Touch, and you die.'

The sunlight burnt on, an icy fever, and wind tacked across the shelved valleys, altering the clouds. We reached another hamlet, another worn gate, more barbed wire. Yaks were browsing between the huts. One raised his great matted head with a deep sleepy bellow.

'Sherathan,' Das said. 'The last checkpost. Two miles to Nathu La. What's the time?'

'Ten past eleven.'

'Not bad. Good. Shabash, driver. Three hundred rupees for you. Chhibar also may be late,' he explained to me.

Now we were climbing all the way, above the blue sockets of two more lakes, anthology of the tears of all the rocks. The landscape had an undated quality, prelapsarian perhaps, and the yaks, shaggy and gentle because their eyes were hidden under hair, might have floundered to Adam's hand in Eden. Ahead, the road became well trained, covered with small slaty flagstones like fish scales. Then coming round a bend we saw it lift, under walls, to where a jeep was parked and three uniformed midgets stood. Das gave a deep sigh of achievement. I looked at my watch. Eleven-thirty. 'That is Nathu La.'

We pulled in at a small shelf cut into the mountain-top, a lichen-rusted hummock rising beyond. The shelf had for ornament a small stone boundary-post, inscribed 'Sikkim-Tibet Border'. Pools of water lay about, memorials of the morning's weather. A police officer and two constables greeted us with a request for our passes.

Then Das and I climbed the hummock, to look into Tibet. The sun had come out brilliantly and coldly, and the sky over Tibet was an icy blue. From where we stood the mountain slipped steeply down, dry and boulder-strewn, into the Chumbi Valley, a succession of folds in the ground, thickly forested, rippling to a narrow V. At the point of the V, across the valley, rose a range of forested hills. Beyond them the horizon was like a picture postcard, two scarred snowpeaks vivid in the frosty sky, and a glimpse of plains between and beyond. The police officer came silently up behind us, pointing out the higher of the snowpeaks.

'That is Chumbiladi.'

'Where does Tibet start?' I asked.

'My dear gentleman,' said Das, 'we are in Tibet. It starts from the boundary-post down there.'

'Where are the Chinese?' I inquired naively.

The policeman handed me his field-glasses. I followed his finger as it swept the Chumbi Valley. Where the valley turned into hills, at the point of the V, I made out a small concrete building among the trees.

'That is their checkpost, at Chumbithan. But who can tell where those rapers of their sisters are? They hide here and there in the jungle and watch us through field-glasses. But I can tell you, sahib, there must be a hundred or two between here and Chumbithan, and that is two miles.'

'Chinia aye the aj, kya?' Das asked. 'Have they come here today?'

'Ji nahin. No, sir. They will not come till Chhibar sahib has passed. This is their diplomacy'.

I turned and looked about. Huge cairns of stones littered the hummock, ominous and druidical. Above them hundreds of improvised prayer-flags, made of tattered garments, tautened in the whipping wind out of Tibet.

'What is all that?'

'When these Tibeti folk come back from Kalimpong or Gangtok they throw a stone at the border, to drive away the evil spirits from abroad. Also they put up those flags for good luck.'

Clouds swept over the sky, and suddenly mist rose everywhere, and Tibet was blotted out of sight as completely as if it had never been there. I could understand, suddenly, why the Tibetans believe that evil spirits live in these high passes. The cairns loomed gloomily; the prayer-flags hung limp, then whiffled in the wind. I found myself strangely exhilarated. 'It's the air,' I thought; then, as the wind sang over the pass, shivered, helpless with cold.

Das, drinking the wind like a tonic, rushed sharply about, posing the policemen, the drivers and myself in various places, against the cairns and flags, drooping over the boundary-post, and so on. He had given me his movie-camera to hold, and that hand had turned completely numb. I tried to talk to the police officer, but it was difficult to move my lips.

However, 'What do you think?' I said. 'Will the Chinese attack?'

'Sahib, that is what their officers tell everybody. The yak drivers and the muleteers say that the Chinese promise to be in Sikkim before next summer.'

'What will you do then?'

'Fight, sahib. What else? Only the sarkar* must give us material for us to fight with. Our radio transmitter here works only three hours a day. If the Chinia should come while it is not working,

---

* Government.

how can we let them know at Sherathan, so that our boys can be ready there?'

'Well, they can see Nathu La,' I said, 'through field-glasses.'

The police officer laughed.

'Sahib,' he said, 'the garrison at Sherathan has no field-glasses. They have asked for some, but the sarkar does not send. If there is fighting at Nathu La, our men at Sherathan will not see it till the Chinia are on their heads.'

The mist was thinning. He swept the Chumbi Valley with his field-glasses. Then he said, 'Someone is coming.'

I shouted to Das, who returned from his photography at a trot. He peered through the field-glasses, then passed them to me. Four or five men on mule-back were snailing up one side of the valley.

'It doesn't look like a diplomatic party,' I said.

'It may be some traders,' said the policeman. 'Let us wait.' I remembered the brandy. We squatted, all of us, under a cairn, which afforded some protection from the wind, and passed the bottle from hand to hand. Mist went over in little puffs. The brandy had a strange, fiery effect, fifteen thousand feet up: my ears sang and I felt sick.

As the mist lifted again for a minute, we saw the mule-riders plodding up from the foot of the hummock towards us. Das jumped up and shouted for his movie-camera. He began to work it as the first rider reached us. Three others drifted after him. They were definitely Indian traders: small heavily muffled men, with nervous rolling eyes, like apprehensive ponies. The first one dismounted, and Das was at him like a terrier.

'Welcome. Where are you from? Yatung, hah? Kya hal chal hai Yatung me?'

'Bahuth mushkil he Yatung me, sahib. Much trouble. Yesterday the Chinia killed an Indian trader there. Their people stabbed him and looted his shop. Therefore, this morning we left there, closing our shops. There are only three Indian shops open in Yatung today, where once there were fifteen.'

The police officer interrupted. 'Have you seen Chhibar sahib?'

'He was leaving Yatung an hour after we left, inspector sahib. We thought, if we came before, we would be safe; if we came after, the Chinia would eat our lives.'

'So,' said Das thoughtfully. 'He will still be one hour.' He glanced into the misted valley. 'Are there any Chinia down there?'

'Many, many Chinia,' one of the other traders said. 'They are in the forest, three furlongs down the valley.'

'Why don't we go down and look at them?' I suggested.

'That is what I also was thinking,' Das said.

Brandy and the thin air had brought on euphoria. I heard myself laughing and saying rather stagily, 'Two minds with but a single thought.'

'Arre, don't try these mad tricks,' said the inspector in alarm. 'If the Chinia see you they will shoot you first and then ask who you are.'

'Sahib,' said one of the traders. 'On my mother's life, it is a mad thing to do.'

'Driver,' shouted Das, 'bring my movie-camera.' He cast the kind of glance a professional spy might have cast into the valley. 'While the mist gives us cover, we shall start. Lend us your field-glasses, inspector sahib.'

'Sir,' said the policeman, 'on my mother's and grandmother's lives, I should forbid you. What will come to me if you are killed or taken prisoner? I will lose my job!'

'Come on, Dom,' Das said to me.

So I took a final drink from the bottle, borrowed the inspector's field-glasses, turned my coat-collar up against the wind, and followed Das into the valley.

The slope was strewn with rocks, which afforded precarious handholds. We had to let ourselves down backward, like mountaineers, and I felt acutely conscious of the wind flapping my jacket, the field-glasses dangling round my neck, and the unseen Chinese probably even now gloating over us through their field-glasses, like uniformed Fu Manchus.

I reached the bottom of the slope a minute after Das. He did not hesitate, but set off at a brisk walk down the valley. The ground was rough and tussocky, the mist had thickened and it was impossibly cold. My limbs were like stalactites: lifting one became a creaking, breathless effort. Conversation was out of the question. I simply followed Das, and we were suddenly among trees.

Here there was a clean acid stench of wet earth and herbs. A bird or two shrieked upwards through the leaves, but otherwise everything was grave-silent. Our feet scuffing through the undergrowth sounded like a forest fire.

We walked for about twenty minutes, twice passing clearings where ashes remained in ersatz fireplaces made of heaped stones. Then Das stopped. We were both breathless. We sat down and I lit a cigarette. We talked in whispers.

'There don't seem to be any Chinese hereabouts.'

'Certainly we are not seeing any. But we must have come the best part of a mile. If we push on, we will be near the checkpost. If I can get a film of some troops without their seeing me, we shall have scooped the world.'

I no longer felt any apprehension. It seemed to me reasonable that Das should want to scoop the world. Apart from the difficulty of breathing properly in this rarefied air, I felt quite willing to go on.

'Those fireplaces, do you think they were made by the Chinese?' I was beginning to feel towards the Chinese now as I might toward the inhabitants of Troizen or Zimbabwe.

'Perhaps by the Chinese, perhaps by some muleteers. Let us get on.'

We stumbled through the trees. In the forest the mist seemed to be filtered away by the leaves, but overhead the sky was still clogged with grey. This unrewarding sky was our only window to the rest of the world for another twenty minutes, till we stumbled out of the forest on to a bare ridge, littered with chalky rock fragments, between two hillocks. Here we sat down again. I looked round through the field-glasses. We were a good way into the valley: the two great snowpeaks looked closer and the barren hummock of Nathu La surprisingly far. I put down the glasses and lit another cigarette. Das drummed his fingers on his knee.

'If we pushed on a little farther, we would get close enough to Chumbithan to take a film of the checkpost. Do you think that is a foolhardy plan?'

The clouds rifted: suddenly and fugitively the sun glared from a waste of blue. Idly I picked up the glasses and looked round. The sun caught them, and reflected light flashed on one of the neighbouring hillocks.

A moment later, there was an answering flash on the ridge where we sat. Das looked up in surprise. The flash was repeated. I looked through the glasses in the direction from which it came.

On the neighbouring hillock, clustered together, was a group of Chinese.

There were about twenty, stocky and tough-looking. Two were in a drab grey-green military uniform with peaked caps. These two were looking at us through field-glasses. The rest stood behind, sten guns and ammunition belts hung over their shoulders. They pointed at us, and were apparently discussing us among themselves.

I told Das. He said very coolly, 'Let us get back into the trees in case they open fire. I will take a film.' We moved back to the fringe of the forest. Das fitted the tele-lens on his camera. He knelt down, swivelling it for focus. I was unnerved, but not unpleasantly. I tried to analyse what I was feeling. I hoped to God that they wouldn't think Das's camera was a sten gun and open fire. I could feel my own heart beating very fast, and I kept on swallowing. But after the initial shock had worn off, I was able to calculate a few things. First, they could not be less than half a mile away. If our information about their weapons had been right, we were out of range. Second, we were going to have to hurry back, for they would certainly send men after us. Das's camera had begun to hum by my side. I put the glasses back on the Chinese. Half a dozen men and one of the officers were already moving downhill. The remaining officer continued to study us through his glasses.

Das's camera ceased to hum. He stood up and turned to me.

'A scoop. You noticed those men coming down the hill, hah? They are coming to get us. Therefore, I think we will have to run.'

He nodded toward Nathu La.

'Run straight back. We must not stop for anything. Mind the field-glasses, they belong to the inspector. Come on.'

Of the next half hour I remember very little. I am not a good runner anyway and in the thin clear air of the plateau I was worse than usual. The initial stumbling gallop through the forest rendered me breathless; then my ears filled with a buzzing that shut out all other sound; finally I developed a burning stitch in my left side. That is the physical memory, and there is one visual image: when we came to a small pebbled brook in the forest, I collapsed beside it and lay on my stomach watching the weeds waver slowly in the flow of the current, two long-legged water-flies, and a minnow; the moss was cool against my cheek. When I looked up Nathu La seemed far and unreachable. I was willing to stay where I was. Das's voice, breathless but imperative, brought me to a kind of reality.

'Come on. We are nearly there. Quickly!'

So flight began again. I reached Nathu La in a daze, a small iron needle in my side. We scrambled back up the slope and sat down heavily amongst a solicitous group of policeman, traders, and drivers.

'We were beginning to worry,' said the inspector.

'We also,' said Das, and managed a smile.

The mist had come on again, and there was no sign of the Chinese.

We lay on foam-rubber-textured lichen, getting our breath, and in my case helping it along with the remains of the brandy. One of the traders came and squatted beside us.

Das, sighing, heaved himself indefatigably up and reached for his notebook. 'This Indian who was killed. Tell me about him.'

'It was done by the Tibetans,' the trader said. 'They came to his shop in the afternoon, and stabbed him five times. Then they looted the shop, took the money from the cash-box, and left.'

'Tibetans?' Das said with professional disappointment. 'I thought you said Chinese.'

'The Chinese say they themselves are Tibetans who have come from Peking. But these real Tibetans were hired by the Chinia, sahib,' said the trader. 'They did it in the daytime and the bazaar was full of Chinia policemen, but they did not interfere, though he shouted for help.'

'Ha!' said Das, and scribbled enthusiastically. 'How do they treat you, these Chinese?'

'Sahib, in the daytime we cannot move more than two hundred yards from our houses without a permit. After nine o'clock we cannot leave our houses also. It is gaol life. Also they have taken the custom from our shops, and anything they buy they buy on credit, and never pay.'

'Why don't you complain to the Indian trade agent at Yatung? He is there to help you?'

'Sahib, what can he do? They pay no attention. And if we leave Tibet, they confiscate all our goods. Now we, today, were only allowed to bring our clothes and ten rupees from Yatung. They only have contempt for us Indians. Every Saturday in Yatung they have a clown show with four clowns, and one is Nehru.'

'Good, good!' said Das, scribbling a little more. 'Who are the other three?'

'Eisenhower sahib, Churchill sahib, and Khrushchev sahib.'

'Why Khrushchev?'

'They are very angry that Russia has not supported them over the border dispute.'

'What do they say about the border?'

'Sahib, the officers say one day soon they will be coming. At the checkpost at Chumbithan they told us to say that in Sikkim.'

'It may not be as easy as they think,' said the police officer dourly.

'The Chinia are strong,' the trader said.

'How do they treat the Tibetans?' I asked.

'Sahib, all the rich men they have put to building a military road from Shigatse. Also in Yatung two weeks ago they took all the young girls away. They do this to keep the men from running away; also the girls are useful in North Tibet, because they are settling many Chinia civilians there, and they have no women.'

'What about the rebels, the Khambas? Is there still any fighting?'

'With them also, they took their families and put them in gaol, until the husbands surrendered. Them they shot or put to work on the Shigatse road.'

He sat by us, sighing, gathering a little dust in his hand and sifting it away with the slow movements of a tired man. I noticed how jumpy all the traders were. They had lines under their eyes, and all of them had nervous twitchy gestures of the hand.

We sat there, thinking, drinking, and then the inspector said: 'Chhibar sahib is coming.'

Through the field-glasses a file of mules appeared ambling up the valley towards Nathu La. It was a relief. We squatted on the hummock watching them all the way up the valley till they had reached us.

Chhibar came first. He was a large man, rosy and powerful, wearing a fur hat and leather jacket. As his mule crested the ridge, we all shouted, rather raggedly, 'Welcome!' He smiled and waved a hand. After him came his wife, a most beautiful woman in a ballooning quilted jacket that made her look like a little tent, and three Tibetan nurses, each with one of the Chhibar offspring in her arms. They were followed by a baggage-train, the muleteers prodding the mules with goads and shouting the Tibetan version of Gittup: '*To to to to to to to,*' on a rising scale. 'Very picturesque,' said Das, going happily to work with his movie-camera. When he had finished, the Chhibar family dismounted, and Das handed his camera to the driver and fished for his notebook.

'How was your trip, Major Chhibar?'

'Fine, fine,' said Chhibar, smiling gently.

'What are these reports of your being hindered by Chinese troops on your journey?'

'Untrue,' Chhibar sighed.

'The Chinese were helpful?'

'To me, yes,' emphasizing the *me.*

'And to other Indians? Say, the traders?'

'Less helpful.'

'Would it be true to say that the traders are in fear of their lives?'

'Perhaps.' So large, so gentle, so like a wall blocking off undiplomatic questions.

'How many troops would you say there were in Tibet?'

'I can't say. It is a difficult question.'

'In Lhasa, then?'

'It is a difficult question. Ten thousand—fifteen thousand.'

'And between Lhasa and Nathu La?'

'It is a difficult question. Perhaps the same number again.'

'So there are between twenty and thirty thousand Chinese in the area between Lhasa and Nathu La?'

'I would say so, yes.'

'Hah!' said Das, but at this point Mrs Chhibar came up to introduce the children, and I became occupied in teaching one of the little girls how to whistle, and missed the rest.

Then the Chhibars left in the waiting jeep, and Nathu La was desolate again.

I went up to the hummock to get a last look at Tibet. All I saw was mist.

Coming Back

There was nothing to stay for, and in Gangtok I realized how dead the journey had become. Das did too, I think; we left for Kalimpong next day: city of spies. We ate in a Chinese restaurant where the radio played music from Radio Peking, and the waiters loitered about, rather obviously listening to the conversation of the customers. A day in Kalimpong, then to Bagdogra again, and back to Calcutta. I kept flying, going from Calcutta back to Bombay. So I had to say goodbye to Das: though I had only known him two weeks, goodbye was sad and strange.

But then all goodbyes are, even the ones in Bombay, with the servants lined up at the door with garlands and tears, Marilyn getting a fit of hiccups and my father pressing my air ticket into my hand like a deathbed relic.

I planned to go to Manila and Tashkent before returning to London but that is another story.

Flying is as strange as saying goodbye: to be above the world, swimming in the blue bird-sea with the clouds under, the air hostess bringing round the drinks, the passengers suddenly peaceful and beautiful people. Above the chaos of world folded into world, for ever and ever, world where nothing ends because nothing has ever truly and beautifully begun.

But landing in London is my beginning, my perpetual peaceful return to your hand in sleep at last made actual. I will bring back yaks to you in my head, and lamas; rice fields drying in the sun, the living and dying of a world half-the-world away. I can bring you nothing else, because all the rest comes from you.

It is raining in London. November: cold: I remember that I have not got my overcoat. But I put the thought of you on to warm me, and diligently I advance towards the Customs.

TAMAM SHUD

ALSO BY DOM MORAES IN SPEAKING TIGER

Where Some Things are Remembered: Profiles and Conversations

Dom Moraes was not only one of India's greatest poets, he was also an extraordinary journalist and essayist. He could capture effortlessly the essence of the people he met, and in every single profile in this sparkling collection he shows how it is done.

The Dalai Lama laughs with him and Mother Teresa teaches him a lesson in empathy. Moraes could make himself at home with Laloo Prasad Yadav, the man who invented the self-fulfilling controversy, and exchange writerly notes with Sunil Gangopadhyaya. He was Indira Gandhi's biographer—painting her in defeat, post Emergency, and in triumph, when she returned to power. He tried to fathom the mind of a mysterious 'super cop'—K.P.S. Gill—and also of Naxalites, dacoits and ganglords.

This collection is literary journalism at its finest—from an observer who saw people and places with the eye of a poet and wrote about them with the precision of a surgeon.

Price: ₹499; Page extent: 208; ISBN: 978-93-88326-68-1

ALSO BY DOM MORAES IN SPEAKING TIGER

Under Something of A Cloud: Selected Travel Writing

Under Something of a Cloud spans a lifetime of Dom Moraes' work to select the very best of his travel writing. Featured in this volume is a vividly recollected childhood tour of Sri Lanka, Southeast Asia and Australia with his father, Frank Moraes, and his mother, Beryl, who was then rapidly sliding into madness; a darkly comic account of a trip to the Sikkim-Tibet border, amidst rumours that the Chinese would soon attack India; and a thrilling adventure among the Dani tribe in Indonesia who, at that time, were reputed to be cannibals.

Also included here are Moraes' sojourns among dacoits in the Chambal valley, one of whom, Lacchi, he helped spring from police custody; an evocative account of a 'madai', a fair where the Maria tribals of Madhya Pradesh gathered to barter goods and find life partners; and encounters with women victims in Ahmedabad, soon after the riots in 2002, which left him shattered.

With a keen sense for atmosphere, colour, understated wit and unfailing empathy for the underdog, Dom Moraes brings to life people and places like few other writers anywhere can. Not only will fans of the author love *Under Something of a Cloud*, it will also appeal to readers of world-class travel writing and connoisseurs of timeless prose.

Price: ₹599; Page extent: 236; ISBN: 978-93-88326-65-0

TRAVELS On My ELEPHANT

An Indian Journey

Mark Shand

SPEAKING TIGER

SPEAKING TIGER PUBLISHING PVT. LTD
4381/4 Ansari Road, Daryaganj,
New Delhi–110002, India

First published by Jonathan Cape 1991
Published in the UK by Eland Publishing Limited 2012
Published as a paperback in India by Speaking Tiger 2018

ISBN: 978-93-87693-08-1
eISBN: 978-93-87693-09-8

10 9 8 7 6 5 4 3 2 1

For sale in South Asia only

Text set by Nick Randall
Printed at Printworks, Delhi-92

For Clio and Tara, one small, one big, both loved

This reprint is dedicated to my wonderful daughter Ayesha

Contents

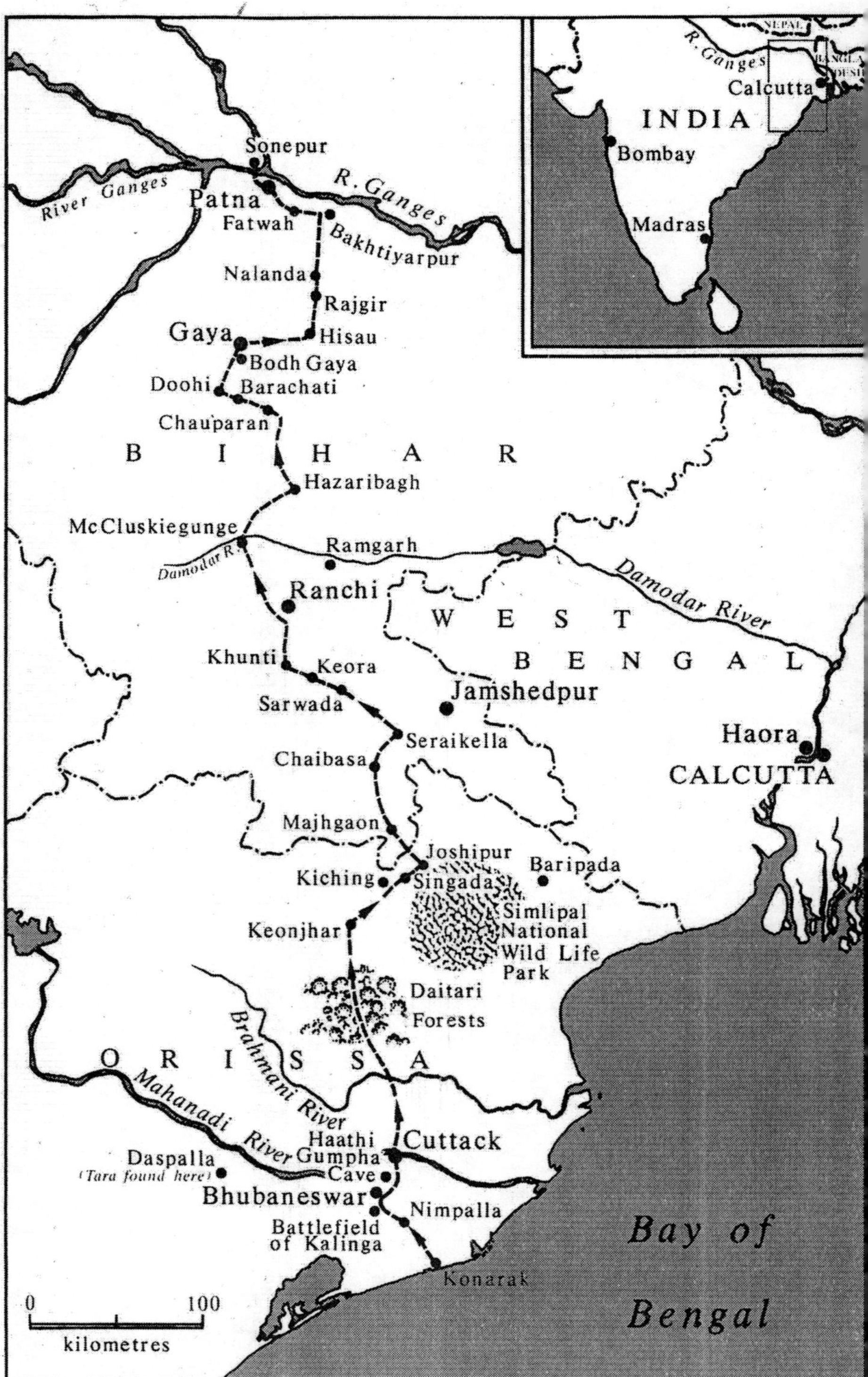

NEPAL
R. Ganges
BANGLADESH
Calcutta
INDIA
Bombay
Madras
Sonepur
River Ganges
R. Ganges
Patna
Fatwah
Bakhtiyarpur
Nalanda
Rajgir
Gaya
Hisau
Bodh Gaya
Doohi
Barachati
Chauparan
B I H A R
Hazaribagh
McCluskiegunge
Damodar R.
Ramgarh
Ranchi
Damodar River
W E S T
B E N G A L
Khunti
Keora
Sarwada
Jamshedpur
Seraikella
Chaibasa
Haora
CALCUTTA
Majhgaon
Joshipur
Baripada
Kiching
Singada
Simlipal
National
Wild Life
Park
Keonjhar
Daitari
Forests
O R I S S A
Brahmani River
Mahanadi River
Haathi
Gumpha
Cave
Cuttack
Daspalla
(Tara found here)
Bhubaneswar
Nimpalla
Battlefield
of Kalinga
Konarak
Bay of
Bengal
0
100
kilometres

Prologue

'AM I RIGHT in assuming that you want to buy an elephant?' the voice from New Delhi shouted down the telephone to me in London. Even through the hiss and static of the long-distance connection I could detect the apprehension in the voice.

'Yes,' I shouted back.

I was restless again. The last time I had been restless, I ended up being pursued by cannibals in Indonesia. This time, I had decided on a quiet jaunt across India on an elephant. This idea evolved from a drawing I had discovered while clearing out my grandmother's house after she had died. The drawing was of an infuriated male elephant about to charge a little Indian mahout or elephant driver. I took it with me and forgot about it – at least I thought I had.

A few days later I opened a book on India. Staring jovially at me from the page was a bewhiskered gentleman, wearing a dashing plumed hat, sitting nonchalantly astride an elephant. It was Tom Coryat, the eccentric Englishman who travelled to India overland in 1615, on foot, on twopence a day. When he reached the court of the great Moghul Emperor Jahangir, he wrote: 'I have rid upon an elephant since I came to this court, determining one day (by God's leave) to have my picture expressed in my next booke sitting upon an elephant.' I was now obsessed. With or without God's leave I was determined to have my picture expressed in my next book sitting upon an elephant.

I rushed to the library where I read a few classics on elephants. From the notebooks of Leonardo da Vinci, I received sound information:

> The great elephant has by nature qualities which rarely occur among men, namely probity, prudence and a sense of justice. They are mild in disposition and are conscious of dangers. If one of them should come upon a man alone who has lost his way, he puts him back peacefully in the path from which he

> has wandered. It is so peaceable that its nature does not allow it willingly to injure creatures less powerful than itself. If it should chance to meet a drove or flock of sheep, it puts them aside with its trunk so as to avoid trampling upon them with its feet; and it never injures others unless it is provoked. They have a great dread of the grunting of pigs and they delight in rivers. They hate rats. Flies are much attracted by their smell and as they settle on their backs they wrinkle up their skin deepening its tight folds and so kill them.

How could I go wrong? It seemed I had chosen a most practical and agreeable travelling companion.

Now I was telephoning a friend in New Delhi. 'Yes, I want to buy an elephant,' I shouted to him, as if this was the most usual of requests.

'You must be mad,' his voice echoed. 'Still, I suppose it's possible. India is full of elephants, but what are you going to do with it when you leave? I don't see your parents taking kindly to it residing in Sussex. Think of their beautiful garden. Why don't you rent an elephant?'

'Rent one?' I yelled. 'It's not a car.'

'All right, I'll see what I can do.' I could hear the resignation in his voice. 'Meanwhile I suggest you contact Pepita. I think she has an elephant.'

'Thank you so much. Goodbye.'

'Mark,' he shouted frantically. 'There's just one other thing. Where are you going to go on it?'

'Well, um ... er ...' I stuttered feebly. 'To be frank, I haven't really given it much thought yet.' In fact, I had not thought about it at all. I just imagined myself climbing aboard and setting off.

Pepita Seth is an unconventional English woman, married to one of India's finest actors. A scholar and talented photographer, she spent ten years in Kerala documenting the religious rituals of southern India. There she became obsessed with the elephant that so enriches Kerala's ceremonies and festivals. Now she lives in Delhi. I wrote asking if I could buy her elephant. Pepita replied promptly. Her writing paper 'ELEPHANT OWNERS' ASSOCIATION' announced what surely must be the most exclusive club in the world: No, I could not buy her elephant, she wrote indignantly. 'On the other hand I know where you can get one. The Sonepur Mela in Bihar, the world's largest animal fair. Elephants, cattle and horses have been sold there for centuries. I went three years ago and must have seen three hundred elephants. It happens sometime at the end of November, depending on the full moon.'

It was now the beginning of August and the Mela was not for another four months. I couldn't wait that long. I decided to leave for India immediately certain that I would find an elephant once I got there. After all, I now had a goal – a place to sell it. I just had to find one and ride to the fair.

I

Elephant Headquarters

INDIA SHOWS WHAT she wants to show, as if her secrets are guarded by a wall of infinite height. You try to climb the wall – you fall; you fetch a ladder – it is too short; but if you are patient a brick will loosen and then another. Once through, India embraces you, but that was something I had yet to learn.

When I arrived in Delhi it was my ladder that was too short. I wanted everything immediately. The monsoons had broken. Black, swollen clouds brought the usual rain, humidity and chaos. Roads were awash, taxis broke down, peacocks screamed. I perspired, worried and developed prickly heat – and I had only been there a few days.

Inevitably I consulted a fortune-teller. 'You are married, yes,' he stated wisely.

'No,' I replied.

'But you are having a companion, I think.'

'Yes.'

'You are most fortunate, sir. Soon you will be having another one. I am seeing many problems. But do not worry, sir,' he added brightly. 'They will only be getting worse.'

With characteristic generosity my friend had put his house at my disposal. It was to become 'elephant headquarters' and the mantle of co-ordinator had settled, however unwillingly, upon his shoulders. In the following week his elegant dining-room was converted into an operations area fit for a world war. Maps and papers littered the table, kit bags, medical supplies, mosquito nets, tents and food rations occupied corners. People dropped in and out. The telephone never stopped ringing and his staff worked overtime producing a continuous chain of refreshments. Game wardens, wildlife officials and forest officers, retired shikaris, politicians, journalists, government servants, ministers and just plain friends were contacted – all important people with tight schedules who went out of their way to help. Undeservedly, however, the bricks had already been loosened for me.

'Everybody's so kind,' I remarked to my friend incredulously.

'It is not you that they're worried about, it's the elephant.'

In this merry-go-round of madness I sloshed from office to office pestering people. I spent a morning discussing the reproduction cycles of the gharial, the Indian freshwater crocodile, and another looking at slides of seabirds. I was offered a camel and found myself buying a jade green parrot from a mobile bird seller, which promptly bit me. I listened carefully to mercurial advice on ancient routes and less carefully to lectures about pilgrimages and migrations affected by lunar and solar cycles. I heard about the great temples and festivals I would see, the jungles I would travel through and the tribals that I would encounter. 'And elephants?' I would eventually enquire hopefully.

'India is like an elephant,' I was told. 'She moves slowly.'

At last a vital brick fell out. Through my friend I met an important bureaucrat who had a deep knowledge of wildlife and, more important, was an expert on elephants.

'Orissa, the old kingdom of Kalinga,' he said, studying the map I had spread before him, 'is where you should go. For centuries the rulers paid their tributes in elephants. They were known as Gajpati, the Lords of Elephants. In fact,' he continued, 'you will almost certainly be retracing some ancient elephant route. You tell me that you are ending the journey at the Sonepur Mela in Bihar.'

'It was just an idea ...'

'Well, where did those elephant tributes go? To Pataliputra, the old capital of India, or Patna as it is known today. Sonepur is a few miles north of Patna, across the Ganga. Now,' he paused for a moment. 'In India every great pilgrimage or journey begins or ends at a temple or place of worship.' He smiled. 'In your case particularly an auspicious start would be of great importance. You might consider the great Sun temple at Konarak, the Black Pagoda. The main structure is supported by a carved frieze of two thousand elephants and the north side is guarded by two colossal war elephants which are so lifelike that, on moonlit nights, visitors often mistake them for the real thing.'

I now had a complete journey more or less mapped out, but still no vehicle. 'And an elephant, sir?' I enquired with diffidence.

'Your best bet is the zoo. I'll give you a letter of introduction to the director of the Nandankanan Biological Park. He's a helpful man and runs one of our better establishments. If anyone can find you an elephant, he will. Now, whatever you do, don't buy a Muckna.'

'Of course not,' I replied firmly, assuming more knowledge than I possessed. Obviously he did not believe me. He explained that a Muckna is a male elephant without tusks that suffers from a kind of inferiority complex and is usually exceedingly dangerous.

'Like a sort of eunuch,' I suggested brightly.

'Well, yes,' he replied, looking at me oddly. 'I suppose that's one way of looking at it. Of course, you will need a mahout and a charkaatiya.'

I must have looked perplexed.

'A charkaatiya,' he explained patiently, 'is a man who cuts fodder for the elephant. Its daily consumption can be as much as two hundred kilos. In certain areas, fodder will not be available, so you will have to buy it. It will be expensive. And,' he continued, 'it might be a good idea to get hold of a jeep. You can probably hire one in Orissa. You'll need back up.'

I swallowed hard. My entourage was growing. The idea of climbing on and setting off vanished. I would now command a small army.

His information was limitless. He advised me on the different types of howdahs, the price of elephants, their feeding habits, medical care, emergency tactics, mahouts and elephant commands (alarmingly there were eighty-four of them). Before I left, he gave me the letter and told me that when one is buying an elephant, there are five points to look for that one doesn't look for when buying a wife, and vice versa. Unfortunately, he could not remember what they were.

Back at the house I found my friend pacing the garden nervously.

'I'm off to Orissa,' I announced happily.

'I know,' he sighed. He was born in Orissa and had spent his childhood there.

'Well, don't look so miserable. You are about to get rid of me. Anyway you should be happy I am going to visit your home.'

'That's what I am worried about,' he retorted testily. 'You are bound to get into trouble, or else get lost. You must take somebody with you. What about the language? How on earth are you going to understand anything?'

I had become so obsessed with finding an elephant that I had not given this a thought. Two or three months of sign language could become confusing, in fact, unbearable. 'What should I do?' I asked anxiously.

'I think I know a man. He is a photographer. This kind of folly will appeal to him.'

'When can I meet him?'

'In about ten minutes,' he announced smugly. 'I have invited him for lunch.'

Ten minutes later a distinguished, well-built man, sporting a full moustache and wearing Rayban sunglasses, loped into the garden. He took off his glasses. 'You!' he barked fiercely. Puzzled I looked around me. The garden was empty. He then roared with laughter and held out his hand. 'I'm Aditya Patankar. We have met before – at Holi. But I do not think that you would remember me.'

I cringed at the mention of the Spring Festival of Holi, a wild, bacchanalian affair where people smear each other with coloured powders. Pulverised by traditional opium concoctions I had passed out in a fountain. He won't want to come, I thought.

'I don't know much about elephants,' Aditya said, to my surprise. 'As a child I was taken by my father to see the elephants in the stables at my cousin's palace in Gwalior. These elephants were used for ceremonial occasions and for the tiger shoots. About one hundred years ago the ruling Maharaja hoisted two of the great beasts on to the roof of the palace to ensure that the ceiling would withstand the stupendous weight of two Venetian chandeliers he wished to install. But tell me about your journey …'

Over lunch I weaved a beguiling tale of a well-planned expedition.

'I don't believe a word of it,' he said with a smile, 'but I will come. There is another reason. You see I'm a Maratha – my ancestors, of whom I'm intensely proud, formed a superb fighting force, and were reputed to have invented guerrilla warfare. Their barbaric reputation alone was enough to strike terror into the heart of India. Both Orissa and Bihar suffered from their swords. It will be interesting to retrace some of their exploits.'

I realised I was extremely fortunate. Already I liked this straightforward man with his loud voice and laughing eyes. We were an unlikely pair, I thought to myself – an Indian nobleman and an errant Englishman, thrown together by a whim, like some mad nineteenth-century expedition, except the quest was not for a lost city or a hidden treasure, but for an elephant.

Two days later we flew to Bhubaneshwar, the capital of Orissa.

2

An Original Elephant

THE LONG ARM of coincidence, in which travellers are often held, found the director of the zoo – the very man for whom I had been given a letter of introduction – travelling on the same flight. There were no elephants that he knew of for sale in Orissa, he told us sympathetically. In fact he himself was looking for elephants both for his own establishment and for a temple. He then suggested we try Madras. 'In the meantime visit my zoo. See the white tigers and the kangaroos that have just arrived from Australia.'

'Well that's that,' I said glumly after we returned to our seats. 'We might as well catch the next flight back to Delhi.' I turned to Aditya, trying to stay calm. 'What on earth are we going to do?' He was fast asleep.

Bhubaneshwar – the city of a thousand temples – was draped in thick black cloud, glistening from the wet kiss of the monsoons. A steamy heat hung in the air. Even the sparrows, those lively occupants of Indian airports, were silent, wilting on top of the announcement speakers.

At the hotel the receptionist asked politely, 'Sands, that is your good name?'

'No, it's Shand.'

'Welcome to the Prachi Hotel, Mr Sands. How long will you be staying?'

'Until I find an elephant.'

'First class,' he said encouragingly, with a slight inclination of his head.

We had barely reached the stairs when a room-boy approached us. 'You are looking for elephants, sir? I have one friend who has many. All sizes. Shall I call him?'

A few moments later there came a knock at my door, which I flung open to the surprise of an elderly man wearing a smart two-piece polyester safari suit. Behind him the room-boy struggled with a large suitcase.

'My name is Fakir Charan Tripathy,' the man said recovering his composure, 'I have elephants.'

'When can we see them?'

'Now, of course, sirs,' the man replied, opening the suitcase. Inside were rows of elephants made from ivory, ebony and sandalwood.

'Please be making a selection. Finest quality. Most reasonable.'

Aditya camouflaged his mouth by pulling on his moustache and explained that these would not meet our requirements. The man seemed confused. Then an expression of wonder crept across his face. 'Aah! You are wanting an o-r-i-g-i-n-a-l elephant.'

The room-boy said suddenly, 'I've seen many elephants.'

'Where?'

'Outside my house, sir. Often they are passing. My children love to see them.' He looked down at his hands in shame. 'I try to keep my family inside. We are very poor and I cannot afford to give away money or food. Only last week three ...'

'Saddhus!' Aditya exclaimed. 'They must be saddhus, and they can't have gone far. They will be stopping at every village and it shouldn't be difficult to follow their route.' He turned to me. 'You see, Mark, the elephant is revered in most parts of India. It represents the elephant-headed deity, Ganesh, our Hindu God of Protection. These elephants are usually ridden by con men masquerading as saddhus, or holy men – a powerful and very lucrative combination. They criss-cross the country, begging, living off the consciences of people much worse off than themselves. Now, you are to stay here. If they see that face of yours the price of an elephant will double. Mr Tripathy, will you come with me?'

'With pleasure. For a small fee. But there is just one other thing. Why is the gentleman wanting an elephant?'

Aditya whispered something into his ear. With a broad smile Mr Tripathy shook my hand before leaving the room.

'What did you tell him?' I demanded crossly.

'That you are an Englishman.'

'Well, so what?'

'Everybody knows that the English are mad.'

At three o'clock in the morning Aditya returned, tired but elated. They had located the elephants about sixty miles west of Bhubaneshwar in a small town called Daspalla. They were indeed begging elephants owned by saddhus.

'Did they want to sell?' I asked anxiously.

'We can take our pick. There are two females and one tusker. The tusker comes from Nepal and is a good elephant, or so they tell me. But what the hell do we know about elephants? We must get some expert advice …'

'What were they like?'

'Oh, devious buggers, they …'

'No, no, not the saddhus, the elephants.'

'Big. Like any elephant. I didn't really see them properly. Now let's get some sleep. You'll have plenty of time to look at them tomorrow.'

I found I couldn't sleep. All night everything I looked at became an elephant – the shadow of a swaying branch, the moon-filled clouds or even the television set. My obsession had indeed turned to madness.

It took most of the day to locate the zoo director who kindly agreed to lend the services of his chief mahout, Bhim. Our party had grown. There were now four of us. Myself, Aditya, Mr Tripathy, with his suitcase of elephants, and a young taxi driver called Indrajit, who had impressed Aditya with his driving skills the previous night. He was a handsome, courteous young man, who radiated energy and had dark fierce eyes – the kind of eyes that remain fierce even in jest. But I wasn't thinking about a chauffeur, I was eagerly waiting to set eyes on my first mahout.

In Delhi I had been lent a book on elephants entitled *The Elephant-Lore of the Hindus*, which had detailed the essential qualities required in an elephant driver:

> The supervisor of elephants should be intelligent, king-like, righteous, devoted to his Lord, pure, true to his undertakings, free from vice, controlling his senses, well behaved, vigorous, tried by practice, delighting in kind words, his science learnt from a good teacher, clever, firm, affording protection, renowned for curing disease, fearless, all-knowing.

The mahout was waiting at the gates of the zoo. Bhim was a man of indeterminate age, the colour of a walnut, bandy-legged and carried himself like a wounded soldier. As we got out of the car he executed a shaky salute, his arm and leg not quite in co-ordination. From the state of his bloodshot eyes, he was clearly suffering from a hangover. He climbed into the car and yawned, exposing the remains of three yellow teeth which wobbled when he spoke. 'Sleep now, sah. Very good. Haathi later.' He then passed out.

Aditya was not wrong about Indrajit. He drove with a cunning recklessness, the tropical landscape passing in a blur outside the window. We had only one accident when he swerved to avoid a bullock cart, clipping the back side-window against one of the animal's enormous horns. The glass exploded like a hand grenade with some of the fragments embedding themselves in Aditya's face. 'Lucky it wasn't my eyes,' he shrugged stoically, picking the glass out of his cheek.

It was late at night by the time we reached Daspalla. The town was deserted. There was no sign of the elephants. I felt as if I had been kicked in the stomach. 'Jesus!' I shouted, 'I just can't believe this. We've lost them. They could be anywhere ...'

'No sir,' Mr Tripathy announced calmly, pointing to large mounds like loaves of bread that decorated the road. 'Now we follow shit.'

We pushed on deeper into the night, our eyes glued to the black surface of the road, illuminated in the taxi's headlights, searching for the tell-tale signs. At intervals the trail would run dry and Mr Tripathy and Indrajit would make enquiries. Villagers, rudely awoken by the urgent shouting, would appear in their doorways, cocooned in blankets, looking bewildered and frightened. Reports regarding sightings of the elephants became equally bewildering – anywhere between two hours and six days. We reached a toll gate, where we received more accurate information. The elephants, we were told by the sleepy toll keeper, had definitely passed through. Did he perhaps know how long ago, we asked. No. Unfortunately his watch was not in working order. But he assured us it was not yesterday.

We were closer. The droppings were fresher and, as if on cue, Bhim woke up. 'Haathi close,' he said quietly, rubbing his bloodshot eyes, as he poked his nose out of the window. 'Can smell.'

We rounded the next bend. Three massive shapes loomed out of the night, their shadows dancing over the glow of a small roadside fire, around which lay bundles of vermilion and saffron rags.

'We'll pretend you're a tourist who has never seen an elephant,' Aditya whispered to me. 'Just stare in astonishment.'

As I got out of the car the rags suddenly billowed upwards and I found myself transfixed by three pairs of hot eyes that flashed like cash registers, curtained by matted tresses of long black oily hair. I forgot the necessity of our charade. As if drawn by a magnet, I was already moving towards the elephants.

Then I saw her. My mouth went dry. I felt giddy, breathless. In that moment the ancient wall crumbled and I walked through. With one hind leg crossed over the other, she was leaning nonchalantly against a tree, the charms of her perfectly rounded posterior in full view, like a prostitute on a street corner. I knew then that I had to have her. Suddenly, nothing else mattered and I realised with some surprise that I had fallen in love with a female Asian elephant.

As luck would have it, I had become enamoured with a perfect elephant, an elephant, even Bhim said, that made his heart flutter. She was young, between twenty-five and thirty years old and although in poor condition, due to mishandling and starvation, would in fourteen days in his care, turn into a lovely riding elephant. She had all the attributes – a healthy pink tongue unblemished by black spots, brown kindly eyes with no traces of white, the right amount of toenails, eighteen, five each on the front feet, four on the back, strong and sturdy joints and a perfect arc to her back. The other two elephants, he warned, were dangerous, and would quite likely kill somebody soon if they hadn't done so already. Take her, he advised me, it would be impossible to find better.

Anywhere between 10,000 rupees and 2 lakhs, I was told in Delhi when researching the price of elephants. A tusker is usually more expensive due to its ivory and prestige, yet a female is sometimes more desirable due to its temperament.

The odds were already stacked heavily in favour of the saddhus. To make matters worse a crowd had mysteriously assembled and was excitedly denouncing the saddhus as robbers and urging the 'rich firinghee' to buy all three elephants. My diary entry for the negotiations reads as follows: 'Their first price was 2 lakh. Our first price: 60,000 rupees. Their second price: 1 lakh 50,000 rupees. Our second price: 80,000 rupees. Their third price: 1 lakh. Our third price: 85,000 rupees. Their final price: 1 lakh. Problem. Stalemate. Holy men will not budge. Crowd now very excited. Go away and have urgent discussions over cup of tea. Tea delicious. Tripathy, Indrajit and Bhim advise stick to our price otherwise loss of face. Aditya says loss of elephant more likely. Return and offer 1 lakh. Holy men now refuse. Why? Holy men never go back on word and have hurt feelings. Aditya tells them will bring cash tomorrow. Holy men go back on word and forget about feelings but now want more. How much? 1,000 rupees. Why? In India, even numbers inauspicious, odd numbers auspicious. Bloody crooks. Agree. Crowd very disappointed.' (£1 sterling is approximately 26 rupees, give or take a little depending on fluctuations in the rate of exchange. 1 lakh equals 100,000 rupees, or £4,000.)

The mendicants, or beggars, told us that they would bring the elephant back to Daspalla. There they were more likely to find a suitable place to load her on to the truck that we would be bringing the next day. Before leaving I went to see her. I watched her flapping her huge ears, the ends of which were splotched with the palest of pink dots, as if somebody had flicked a paintbrush. I felt ashamed that I had bargained for her at all. I wanted to reach out and touch her, but found I couldn't, terrified that she might reject me. In the car on the way back I realised I didn't even know her name.

Mr Tripathy had forgotten about his suitcase full of elephants and now seemed as obsessed with acquiring an original elephant as we were. The next morning he and Indrajit went to organise a truck, while Aditya and I set off to find the zoo director to ask him whether we could keep the elephant there until we departed on our journey, and also if he would allow Bhim to act as mahout. We had reached the decision last night after three bottles of rum. Tripathy and Indrajit had vehemently opposed the idea, saying that he was too old, too weak and too drunk. Whether it was the alcohol or emotion I will never know, but the way that Bhim had accepted his position removed my doubts. 'Sah,' he said proudly, drawing himself up to his full five feet and executing another shaky salute, 'Raja-sahib, Daddy, Mummy, my family now. Bhim look after.'

The director was somewhat surprised and sceptical at the speed of our success. He readily agreed to let the elephant reside at the zoo, but wanted it outside the main park due to the quarantine regulations. The place he was suggesting was next to Bhim's house, which suited us perfectly. But, he warned us, although he had no doubts about Bhim's capabilities with elephants, he did have a drink problem. However, if we were prepared to take the risk, he would not stand in our way.

We found our transport was waiting for us at the hotel. The truck was a machine of magnificent chaos. It was difficult to ascertain on first inspection which was the front and which the back. It was the hippies' ultimate chariot, a relic of the Sixties and flower power, bedecked with garlands of flowers, effigies of gods, good luck charms and strings of fairy-lights that twinkled on and off prettily on application of the brakes. On the back was written, 'USE HORN PLEASE, OK' and underneath, 'TATA' which I thought was a message of farewell, but was in fact the make of the vehicle.

We set off to Daspalla stopping for a 'sharpener' in a bottle shop on the way. The proprietor, an ex-serviceman, excited by our visit, took out two bottles of beer and three glasses from a cupboard. The name of the beer was printed over a picture of Mohammed Ali standing over a fallen victim with his arms outstretched – KNOCK OUT, HIGH PUNCH, STRONG BEER, BREWED IN BANGALORE.

'On the houses, gentlemen,' he said, raising his glass. 'To England, India, elephants. God bless and the best of British luck.'

'That makes me proud to be an Indian,' Aditya said as we walked back to the truck. 'You have just witnessed something quite unique. In all my travels across this country, that is the first time I have been offered a free drink. It bodes well for our journey, my friend.'

'Luckily he didn't know you are a Maratha,' I remarked, 'otherwise his hospitality might have been of a different nature in view of the depredations committed by your ancestors in Orissa two hundred years ago.'

'Ah, the sword of the Marathas. Those were the days,' he said dreamily. 'You know, Mark, it was probably right here, on this very spot that my ancestors won yet another brilliant victory.'

'Actually it was at a place called Barmul Gorge which is somewhere near here. It was your last stand in Orissa. The English army, led by Marquis Wellesley, wiped you out.'

The mendicants were already sleeping by the time we found them in a deserted schoolhouse on the outskirts of Daspalla. I couldn't see the elephants but I could hear them feeding; sharp cracks of breaking branches punctured the still night air like pistol shots. Aditya squatted down beside one of the sleeping forms and I overheard a short, muffled conversation. The mendicant pulled his blanket further over his head, rolled over and went back to sleep. Odd behaviour I thought for a man who is about to receive nearly £4,000. Aditya stood up, his face registering a mixture of anger and disbelief.

'They won't sell. They've changed their minds.'

'You're joking.'

'I am not bloody well joking,' he hissed. 'You know what this bastard told me when I pointed out that he had gone back on his word and put us to a great deal of expense. He said it is our right to give people trouble. We do it all the time.'

Indrajit and Tripathy had now joined us. When Aditya explained the situation we had to restrain them forcibly from attacking the mendicants, who were now fully awake clutching an assortment of crude axes and spears, which I realised with horror they had probably used on the elephants.

'We are wasting our time,' Aditya said. 'There's only one solution. We will go to the police.'

The police station was empty apart from a bat circling a ceiling fan. From the back of the building we heard the sound of snoring. Indrajit disappeared. A few minutes later he returned followed by a disgruntled man with tousled hair, hastily tucking a khaki shirt into a crumpled lunghi. He waved us to a couple of chairs and slid behind a desk. He looked at me, as if he had just awakened from one nightmare and was now about to enter another.

Aditya explained the situation. The policeman blinked owlishly and painstakingly scratched out a report.

'In my opinion,' he announced finally, pushing back his chair and yawning, 'there is not seeming to be a crime committed.'

'There bloody well has been,' I shouted, losing the last vestige of self-control. 'They've got my elephant!' I threw down a visiting-card I had been given by a senior bureaucrat in the Orissa government.

To my astonishment, the policeman's eyes widened noticeably. In a matter of moments the entire garrison of the Daspalla Police Force were lined up in front of the desk and ordered to fetch the beggars. The posse returned with the man to whom Aditya had spoken. It would have given us some satisfaction if he had been driven at the point of a bayonet, or at least in handcuffs, but he seemed to be on excellent terms with his captors. He entered the station, helped himself to a cigarette from a packet lying on the desk, lit it from a match proffered by one of the policemen, and squatted down unconcernedly in a corner. A crowd had assembled outside the station. The majority were on our side, but a faction became demonstrative when a local quack told them I was buying the elephant in order to kill it. I would then, with the aid of a huge syringe, extract some magic potion which I would sell as an aphrodisiac. The police chief, sensing a riot, dispersed the crowd.

Up until now the mendicant had only revealed his name as Rajpath but when one of the police advanced upon him with a bamboo cane, he broke down in a well-rehearsed fit of histrionics, and whimpered that the elephant did not belong to him but to his boss who lived in a village near Benares in the state of Uttar Pradesh.

'Why in hell didn't he tell us that in the first place?' I asked Aditya incredulously.

For the next two hours a strange negotiation took place, during which the police acted as go-betweens. At one moment they would be deep in conversation with Aditya, Tripathy and Indrajit, the next with Rajpath through the bars of the station cell, behind which he now reclined. Meanwhile I waited outside and spent a pleasant night discussing the merits of the English and Indian cricket teams with one of the junior policemen.

In the early hours of the morning a solution was found. Mysteriously, Rajpath could now sell the elephant. Empowered by the owner, its destiny lay entirely in Rajpath's hands. He would be prepared to sign an affidavit to the effect as well as the sale deeds which we had brought from Bhubaneshwar. Both these documents would be witnessed officially by the police, and Rajpath would then set out immediately for Benares to deliver the money to the owner.

The deal was seemingly foolproof, except, I pointed out, for one salient point. In view of his previous attitude how could we trust Rajpath to deliver the money?

It was decided that Aditya would accompany him to Benares and conclude the negotiations with the owner personally. I had to fly to Delhi to sort out some visa extension problems. In the meantime, Mr Tripathy and Indrajit would keep watch over the elephant and we would meet back in Bhubaneshwar in a few days.

Arriving in Delhi, I found an article had already appeared in a national newspaper about my intended journey. The last paragraph read: 'more than anything else Mr Shand is looking forward to travelling at an elephant's pace in today's era of jet travel because it would enable him to absorb the surrounding elephant.' I assumed the last word to be a misprint; it should perhaps have read 'elements'.

My work finished I called on my friend and in his drawing-room ruminated over a name for my elephant. On a table there was a collection of miniature ivory elephants. He picked one up and handed it to me. It was exquisite. The body intricately carved in a pattern of tiny stars.

'In Hindi,' he explained, 'the word for star is "tara", more importantly Tara is one of our goddesses. What do you think of that for a name?'

'Tara, Tara, Tara,' I rolled it over my tongue. I liked it. It was a beautiful name for a beautiful elephant. A goddess and a star. She deserved nothing less.

A jubilant trio was waiting for me in the hotel room in Bhubaneshwar; Aditya handed me an impressive looking document studded with blue seals, a jumble of illegible signatures and a cluster of thumb prints. 'You are now the absolute owner of one female elephant named Toofan Champa.'

'Her name is Tara,' I interrupted.

'Then you are the absolute owner of one female elephant named Tara, aged about thirty years, height about seven and a half feet, with black forehead and black body, pigmentation spots on both ears, with eighteen toenails, six-inch tusks and healed wound marks on the centre of her back. By the way,' he added, 'Rajpath returned with me. An elephant, he tells me, takes time to get used to a new mahout. He'll work with Bhim.'

Over celebratory drinks he told me of his journey. At first he was worried that Rajpath might escape from the train, but the mendicant seemed so sad, and so subdued, that he spent the journey gazing mournfully out of the window until even Aditya began to feel sorry for him. When they arrived in Benares, Aditya employed the services of a lawyer, and they left by taxi to Lakeshar village, about two hours by road north-west of Benares.

The owner of the elephant, an elderly man, was obviously a figure of some standing. He lived in the largest house in the village and was not at all surprised to see them. Sitting by his side was one of the other mendicants who, it seemed, had gone on ahead to warn him. The rest of his family were also present. There were fifteen of them. At this moment, Aditya felt concerned. But everything went smoothly. The gentleman wanted to sell the elephant: there was no bargaining and the lawyer drew up the papers which were duly witnessed and signed. The money was then handed over, and each member of the family wanted to count it. This took time. Finally everyone was satisfied and the deal celebrated with cups of hot milk sweetened with sugar. As they were leaving the old man told Aditya that he would now buy another elephant. When he and his brother were young men and first married, their wives were unable to produce a male heir; a saddhu was consulted who advised them to keep 'Ganesh' near the house. They immediately bought an elephant, and some time later his brother produced a son.

'If he has to keep an elephant near his house at all times,' I remarked, 'what's it doing traipsing across Orissa?'

'He can't afford to keep it all year round,' Aditya explained. 'An elephant costs about 300 rupees a week to feed, which in India is a great deal of money. From November to March, our marriage season in India, he rents the elephant out. On such occasions, it is auspicious to have "Ganesh" present. During the rest of the year it will just sit eating money, so he makes a deal with mendicants like Rajpath. During the off season, he lends it to them and they make a lucrative living by begging. He also gets a cut of their takings.'

I was astounded. 'What a sensible arrangement.'

'It's actually quite a large business, particularly in the Benares area. Some of these landlords own up to thirty or forty elephants, or more. In many ways this is a good thing. Sadly, the use of elephants is dying out. Can you imagine India without elephants?'

Everyone in the hotel appeared to be involved in Tara's destiny. When I arrived, the receptionist told me my elephant had refused to get on the truck.

Aditya laughed. 'It was quite an event. These two' – he nodded towards Tripathy and Indrajit – 'were most upset. They wanted her to be waiting for you at the zoo. Indrajit even tried to ride her himself, as if she were some huge taxi. And poor Mr Tripathy nearly got flattened when she shot into reverse. The trouble was caused by the crowd. You can imagine the scenario – the shouting and jeering. She was a nervous wreck.'

'Where are they now?'

'On the road. Let's go and meet your new girlfriend.'

After driving about twenty miles we found them, taking shelter from the sun under the spread of a large banyan tree. It was, I realised, the first time I had seen her in the light of day. As often happens in life and love, she now presented a somewhat different picture. Even to my inexperienced eye, she appeared to be half starved. She lacked that roundness of girth that I had always associated with elephants. Her rib cage was clearly visible and her skin hung in folds like an ill-fitting suit. She looked at that moment exactly what she was – a beggar. It was only then, as I surveyed this immense bag of bones, that the enormity of the situation struck me. She was mine. I was the owner of an elephant, and the idea seemed so ludicrous that I began to laugh. Quickly I controlled myself for I thought – and this was even more absurd – that she might think I was laughing at her, and I had no desire to hurt her feelings.

I was also at a loss as to how to effect an introduction. She wasn't exactly an average pet, like a cat or a dog, or even a hamster, which one can pick up and cuddle or stroke and expect a contented purr or a wet lick or, in the case of the hamster, a sharp nip. However, she soon solved that problem. As I approached her nervously she stretched out her trunk and with the utmost delicacy began to explore the front of my shirt. She's making friends with me, I thought happily, enchanted by this apparent display of affection. It then stopped abruptly in the area of one of my trouser pockets into which she quickly inserted the tip of her trunk and deftly removed my lunch – an apple – and, with a squeak of delight, popped it into her mouth. It seemed the key to Tara's heart was going to be through her stomach. I dispatched Indrajit to buy her some food.

After two kilos of rice, which she consumed by poking her trunk into the sacks and sucking the contents out like a vacuum cleaner, four bundles of bananas and twenty-three coconuts, she seemed a little more replete and broke wind loudly as if to say thank you. As I watched her crunch up the last of the coconuts, her eyes, fringed by lashes long enough to suggest that they were false, closed contentedly.

3

Bandobast

IN HINDI THE word 'bandobast' means 'arrangement', and it was to bandobast that the next two weeks were devoted. On the 15th September the great festival of Ganesh was to be celebrated. We could not hope for a more appropriate and auspicious day on which to begin our journey.

Rajpath had spent five days with Bhim and Tara at the zoo handing over the reins of command. It was remarkable how quickly she adapted to her new master. Although the language of mahouts is universal – all originally derived from the ancient Sanskrit – local intonations are different. Rajpath's was strong and sharp. Bhim's was more sing-song and gentle. This encouraged me, for I had imagined an English accent causing terrible confusion. She was really a very clever elephant, though Rajpath told me before he left that she had one weakness: deep water. Always, he advised, shackle the front legs before her bathtime. Hardly a weakness, I thought. All elephants love water, even I knew that, and I forgot about it.

Her daily intake began with a morning snack consisting of thirty kilos of rice, wrapped in paddy, sprinkled with a few roots of turmeric (for digestion) and fed to her in bundles, like giant birds' nests, by Bhim. She then disappeared behind a mountain of fresh fodder, namely bamboo, the branches of Bud and Peepul trees of which she ate only the bark, and if she was lucky, some pieces of sugar cane. Having slowly worked her way through this she would reappear in the late afternoon when her larder would be restocked for the night. In addition she picked up tit-bits from the busloads of visitors to the zoo, and from my daily visits, when I would bring the icing on the cake – gur. Gur is unrefined molasses, and to elephants it is like foie-gras to a gastronome. They love it. The moment I arrived Tara would drop anything that she was eating, shoot out her trunk, flap her ears and stamp her feet like an impatient child. I became the candyman, and I admit the greater part of her affection at the beginning was due to this treat.

One difficulty remained. How were we to satisfy the appetite of such an enormous beast once the journey had begun? I had no idea where to find a chaarkatiya or food-gatherer.

'Not problem, Raja-sahib,' Bhim announced. 'My friend Gokul help us.' He introduced me to a shy young man with a mischievous face whom Aditya interrogated closely. Gokul's squeaky voice gained confidence with each statement, punctuated by laughter from Aditya. At last Aditya turned to me.

'Well?'

'He's our man. He's eminently qualified for the job. He has been a singer, an acrobat, a dancer, and most recently a tree feller. He now has a new ambition. He wants to be a mahout. Just like you.'

The legendary G. P. Sanderson, who was in charge of elephant catching operations in Mysore and Bengal in the late nineteenth century, reckoned a ton to be a good load for an elephant on continuous march. In his classic work, *Thirteen Years Among the Wild Beasts of India*, he also recommended that 'in hilly country seven hundredweights is as much as he should carry.' Now Sanderson was describing a male elephant and probably a large one at that. Tara was a female and in reality quite small, though admittedly at the moment she was doing her best to change her image. Her pack gear alone was substantial. It consisted of a soft quilted pad, about one inch thick, that extended from her withers to her rump and halfway down her sides. On top of this came the gudda or saddle, made of stout sacking stuffed tight with straw, six feet long, four and a half feet broad, eighteen inches deep, and weighing about one hundred and fifty pounds. It had a longitudinal opening which to some extent relieved the pressure on the spine, one of the most vulnerable parts of the elephant. 'Sore back,' Sanderson continues, 'often disables elephants for months, sometimes for years and may even result fatally.' On top of the gudda came the howdah, which can be an elaborate and ornate affair, but in our case simply resembled a heavy, four-legged rectangular table turned upside down with a cushion to sit on and rails at each end to prevent us falling off. The whole contraption was strapped on by means of one length of thick rope which went round her head and girth and up under her tail. To prevent chafing, it passed through a crupper, which was made not of leather but of metal, in the shape of a piece of bent pipe. 'Smoothness, not softness,' Sanderson insists, 'is the prime requisite in a crupper.'

Our personal gear, all the paraphernalia of a long expedition, tents, sleeping bags, cameras, cooking equipment, food, lamps, axes, kerosene, water, torches, and so on – hung from both sides of the howdah, so that the weight was distributed evenly and would rest on the upper part of her ribs, and not on her spine. This was all exclusive of her food, chains and shackles and, most importantly, the four of us. It became obvious, as I had been advised in Delhi, that we would need back up. With a vehicle to carry the bulk of our load, we could travel relatively unencumbered across the country, and then be supplied every few days at predetermined points of rendezvous. It sounded simple enough in theory, but whether it would work in practice remained to be seen.

Finding 'back up' was considerably easier than finding an elephant, and a jeep and trailer were kindly lent to us by friends for the duration of our journey. With the jeep came a driver, and without the driver we could not have the jeep, but there was, as Aditya and I agreed, something about Khusto that spelled trouble, though at that moment neither one of us could put our fingers on it. For a start, communication with him was a problem due to large well-chewed wads of 'paan' that were permanently wedged into his mouth, giving him the appearance of a squirrel with mumps. He was also more of a modist than a mechanic. The only spare part that he deemed necessary to take with him for this long and arduous journey was an extra rearview mirror, and he spent much of his time teasing his bouffant hair with the bright red comb he kept wedged in the back pocket of a tight pair of khaki trousers. Indrajit, on whose sagacity and faithfulness we had now come to rely heavily, also voiced his doubts about Khusto. To our great relief he insisted that he himself would come along as co-driver.

Although I knew he would decline, I asked Mr Tripathy to accompany us also. There were tears in his eyes. He clasped my hands, and I was as deeply affected as he was. 'I am too old for such things, sir. With my reward, I have decided to start a new business.'

I was intrigued. 'What kind of business?'

'I will become a miner,' he announced with marvellous inconsequence. 'I will find gold and diamonds. With my riches I will buy elephants.'

'But that was your last business.' I was now confused.

His wise old eyes filled with laughter. 'No, sir, o-r-i-g-i-n-a-l elephants. When you return to Orissa I will be selling them to you.'

4

Paint, Pujas and Pandits

WE HAD ASCERTAINED that the Sonepur Mela lasted two weeks, and that the peak day – Kartik Purnima (the day of the full moon) – fell on the 23rd November. Elephants could not be bought or sold before that auspicious date. To be on the safe side, we planned to arrive at the Mela around the 17th November, which would allow us sixty-four days to complete the journey. With the aid of some very out-of-date maps, we established a route. By my calculations (which were by no means accurate) the journey would be some seven hundred and fifty miles long, roughly the distance between John O'Groats and Land's End, or from New York to Chicago, or Sydney to Adelaide.

'Four miles an hour is a good pace for an elephant, but long-legged ones will swing along at five,' Sanderson wrote. Tara had the most beautiful long legs. Even if we were to be on the move for only four hours a day, starting early to avoid the heat, it seemed to me that we had plenty of time.

I could scarcely believe it. We were ready to begin our journey on the most auspicious day of the year. Some friends had arranged a special puja for our good fortune. Early on the morning of the 14th September, the day before we were due to depart, Aditya and I went to the zoo to watch Tara being made ready for the puja by some students from the art school in Bhubaneshwar.

Decoration of elephants is usually carried out by mahouts – specialists in the art, using chalk and coloured paste – who are familiar with the dangers, the vagaries and the fidgetiness of this large animal. They can work with assurance, secured by their knowledge. Understandably, the students were nervous. An elephant is a different proposition to the stillness of a canvas. They were also working in watercolours, and moved warily round her, applying dabs of colour with their paintbrushes. Tara now nervous as well, and perhaps annoyed by the tickling sensation of bristles on her skin, shook her head violently and flayed out with her trunk and tail, sending students, pots and paintbrushes flying.

Bhim and another mahout immediately took charge, forcing her to sit. They grabbed her trunk and her tail and held them tightly. Apart from her huge flapping ears Tara now remained steady enough for the students to work. With wonderful imagination, a trait seemingly inbred amongst artisans of Orissa, Tara was transformed into a bride. The insides of her ears were decorated with painted earrings of yellow diamonds and rubies, her forehead became a fringe of lacy pearls, her trunk a fretwork of flowers, lotuses, frangipani blossoms and blood red hibiscus, and around her legs appeared anklets of silver and gold. She emerged resplendent, a princess fit for the mightiest of kings.

When the truck arrived to transport Tara to Konarak, it was backed up against the side of a wide stone terrace about four feet high which fronted the zoo's museum, a long low building, from the roof of which bougainvillaea spilled. It was a venue, I thought, more picturesque than practical. The interior of the truck was littered enticingly with every kind of elephant delicacy – succulent stalks of sugar cane, thick sheaves of bamboo leaves and three or four large bundles of bananas. Bhim astride a closely hobbled, radiant Tara clanked up the steps on to the terrace. They approached the truck and then stopped. From where she stood she explored the back of the truck with her trunk. She crept all the way around it, testing and checking everything. She then leant forward, managing to reach the nearest of the delicacies which she popped into her mouth. Bhim urged her forward. She remained stationary. Two or three other zoo mahouts, armed with sticks, crept up behind her and began to beat the back of her legs, while another climbed into the truck and tried to interest her in the food. With a squeal of rage, she shot into reverse, scattering the mahouts and a group of enthusiastic onlookers in her path. She then halted and, regaining her composure, methodically consumed the contents of a flower bed which lined the other end of the terrace. Inevitably, a large crowd had congregated. They had not expected this added attraction on their day out at the zoo.

After three hours the experts (and there were a great many of them by then) decided that this was the wrong approach. I began to doubt their expertise and wondered if they had ever attempted such a manoeuvre before. The arrival of one of the other zoo elephants, a big docile female, who was in theory going to show Tara the way, proved it. She too refused to enter the truck. An impasse had been reached. There was only one solution. Tara, accompanied by Bhim and Gokul, would have to walk to Konarak, a distance of some thirty miles.

As I squeezed into the jeep, my backside wedged uncomfortably on a sack containing tins of corned beef and my head squashed at right angles against one of the metal roof struts, I agreed wholeheartedly with Louis Rousselet, who said of his travels in central India and in the presidencies of Bombay and Bengal that 'It is neither a slight responsibility nor a trifling matter to have to keep and maintain an elephant for a month or two.' I couldn't believe the amount of paraphernalia that had collected. Did an elephant journey really need all this equipment and all these people? But it seems I had got off lightly, for he goes on to tell us that 'a mahout usually takes his wife and children with him on the journey'.

It had been agreed that Tara and Bhim would meet us that evening at the government inspection bungalow, close to the great Temple of Konarak. By midnight there was no sign of them. A search party was sent out and returned without success. By 7.30 the following morning there was still no sign of Tara. The pandit who was to perform the puja deemed the early morning as the propitious moment for devotions. I had washed, had not taken food and was therefore clean.

For two hours I sat cross-legged in a sandy hollow outside the inspection bungalow which overlooked the Bay of Bengal. Facing me was a small, pink clay idol of Ganesh. Being a foreigner, I could not help feeling self-conscious and somewhat of a fool. Sand flies shot up my shorts and stung me on the backside. I was desperately worried about Tara. As the pandit muttered the last incantation in a cloud of incense, and I showered the little pink effigy with yet another handful of nuts, flowers and coins, news reached us that Tara had been located fifteen miles from Konarak. The Indians have a proverb, 'Listen to the elephant, rain is coming.' At that moment it started to rain.

In the driving rain, we piled into the jeep, pandit and all, to meet them. The old mahout was mortified that he had failed to reach Konarak punctually, but Tara had suddenly become lame in her front right leg and this had delayed them. The accommodating pandit performed a second puja, beside a little pond at the side of the road. This turned out to be a merry affair. As Tara's decoration had been washed off by the rain, Bhim anointed her forehead in a bright red powder, with the sign of the god Shiva, the Destroyer. The pandit blessed us all by dotting our foreheads with 'tikkas' and Tara was garlanded with marigolds and frangipani, which she happily consumed. At one point he blessed her by circling her head with sticks of incense. Thinking it was more food, she shot her trunk through the clouds of scented smoke. The poor pandit, already wary of this large, benevolent elephant, took a step back and fell into the pond.

It was now auspicious and appropriate for me to ride her, if only for a few yards. With Bhim tugging from on top of Tara and with the help of Aditya, Indrajit and Khusto, and a crowd of amazed local villagers pushing from below, I was hoisted on to her. In my panic I managed to climb aboard the wrong way round and found myself facing Bhim. I carefully turned round, and we set off to great cheers. It was the first time I had ever been on an elephant. I looked down the long drop, and as Tara gained momentum I knew I was going to fall off. Perhaps because I was sitting in the wrong position, her shoulder blades pumped up and down against my backside like pistons, and I felt myself going. Then I felt cold steel against my lower back and Bhim restored my dignity by hooking the curved point of the 'ankush' into my underpants.

In a way I had already started my journey. I felt elated, blessed and unbelievably smug. Leaning down, I kissed her on her large soft ear and whispered that I loved her. My confidence grew as we lumbered down that road. I turned and doffed my panama hat in what I thought was a most cavalier fashion, yelling at Aditya who was walking beside me, 'How do I look, my friend?'

'Ridiculous,' he said.

If the standard of our camp that night was any portent of the next two months, it looked like we would be in trouble. It was my fault, for the choice of the site in sandy ground amongst a forest of casuarina trees overlooking the sea was mine. I selected this scenic spot for two reasons. The first was that it was very close to Konarak, where the next morning we would officially start the great trek. The second was that I had developed a romantic idea of this journey. It was to be a journey of imagination, from the sea to the source, from the blue waters of the Bay of Bengal to the mighty Ganga at the ancient seat of the Emperor Ashoka's empire, Pataliputra. If only instead I had remembered my boy scout training. Tent pegs do not hold in sandy ground. I should have listened to Bhim, for chaining Tara to a slim, shallow-rooted casuarina tree was about as effective as tying her with a piece of string to a daisy.

It turned into a night of bedlam, not helped by copious amounts of rum which I had liberally distributed to celebrate our first camp. Khusto passed out. Bhim and Gokul could hardly stand. It was left to Aditya and me to try and control Tara. Three times she escaped, and in the process flattened an area the size of a football field. Dotted intermittently along the edge of the road were signs saying in big red letters: GOVERNMENT OF ORISSA FORESTRY DEPARTMENT. KEEP OUT. NEW PLANTATION. Eventually, under the threat of a ban on alcohol for one week, Bhim miraculously sobered up. With another of those shaky salutes, and after several attempts to climb aboard Tara, he announced that he was in full control and that he and Gokul would chain her to a sturdy tree about a mile down the road.

Aditya and I curled up inside a collapsed tent and fell asleep. One hour later we were woken by the sound of rattling chains and wild singing. Peering blearily out of the tent, I was amazed to see approaching us at top speed through the gloom, Bhim riding Tara, followed by a staggering Gokul. Mummy (Tara) had been a bad girl, Bhim informed us, and made a fool out of him. He had given her a good talking to and now Mummy knew who was the boss. Also Mummy had told him that she was lonely at the tree and wanted to spend the night near Daddy (Aditya) and Raja-sahib (me). So, with an incoherent mahout, a drunken chaarkatiya and a comatose driver, we spent our first night with Tara chained to the rear bumper of the jeep.

5

The Black Pagoda

AGAINST A FLURRY of protests I enforced a mandatory early-morning dip in the sea for everybody, to clear away the effects of last night's excesses. Only Tara was excluded after she had expressed great suspicion and then terror at the sound of beating waves and had run up the beach trumpeting, causing a group of amazed fishermen to drop their nets and dive for safety behind their boats.

As we entered Konarak the first rays of a glorious sunrise were illuminating the Black Pagoda, a temple of such solitary grandeur yet of such sensuality that my first impression was one of shock. I had been fortunate once, many years ago, to have visited an empty Taj Mahal on a bright moonlit night and had thought that nothing I would ever see could surpass it for its beauty. But the Taj Mahal is a mausoleum, a tomb, silent in its splendour while Konarak is alive, a constant motion of stone – celestial nymphs with swelling breasts and rounded hips, the rhythms of the lovers and the ecstasy on the faces of the erotic statues. Its energy is manifest in scenes of royal hunts and military expeditions, with infantry, cavalry and elephants marching in full regalia, speaking of the dream of an ambitious and mighty monarch.

Conceived as a celestial chariot of the Sun God, pulled by seven exquisitely carved horses and supported by twenty-four monolithic wheels, each of which represents the division of time, the temple was constructed by King Narasimha Deva the First of the Ganga dynasty of Orissa in the mid-thirteenth century AD. Twelve thousand men toiled ceaselessly for twelve years to complete this masterpiece, and it was named the Black Pagoda by the captains of coastal ships who used it as a landmark. Konarak is the peak of Orissan architecture about which it was said that the artisans 'built like Titans and finished like jewellers'. On the north side stand two lifelike elephants, their flesh rendered with wonderful realism. Between these stone elephants, dwarfed by their size, Tara made her ceremonial 'pranam' by lifting her trunk in salute. The head priest of Konarak came out to bless her.

In the shortening shadows of the Black Pagoda we set off triumphantly on our journey, applauded by a laughing crowd, many of them poking fun at the ridiculous figure striding out ahead, wearing a hat that had become a bonnet under its weight of garlands.

The countryside was lush, sensual and green (similar to Indonesia). Paddy fields dotted with clumps of bamboo and palm trees stretched for miles. Flashes of brilliant colour suddenly emerged as men in bright lunghis of emerald green, azure and saffron that had faded to salmon-pink stood up, gazed for a moment and then waved and shouted in greeting, their dark muscular bodies black against the green. Kites wheeled on thermals overhead and piebald and blue kingfishers hovered stationary above the fields. Then, wings pulled into their sides, they dived like arrows into the water and reappeared with frogs, fishes and small snakes in their beaks.

'What are those?' I said to Aditya, pointing to slim, glossy black birds with long, deeply forked tails that perched in lines on the telegraph wires, looking like a selection of chic little black hats displayed in a milliner's window.

'Drongos,' he said excitedly. Aditya was a keen amateur ornithologist and seemed relieved that my conversation was not going to revolve exclusively around Tara. 'They are clever birds,' he continued. 'They ride on the backs of grazing cattle and capture the insects that are disturbed by the animals' feet. With any luck, we'll see a racket-tailed drongo. They are much larger and have two long spatula tipped feathers like streamers in the tail. I have always longed to own one. They are superb mimics.'

Passersby stopped in amazement. Some just stared, open mouthed. Others turned their bicycles round to follow us and I overheard snatches of conversation with Bhim. 'Haathi-wallah, Konarak.' Then they smiled shyly clasping their hands together in greeting. But it was the children who went wild. At every village out they came, screaming and laughing and shouting. 'Haathi, haathi, haathi, haathi,' they cried and chased after us. One or two of the braver ones moved up in front of Tara and fed her bamboo and sugar cane.

At other villages we stopped and took tea, the best tea I had ever tasted, sweetened with sugar and cardamom. Tara was surrounded and paper bags of 'ludoos' (sweet yellow round cakes) were produced. She would delight the crowd by consuming the entire paper bag. Then she helped herself liberally to the piles of sweets and cakes laid out in trays in front of the shop. Sometimes her greed annoyed the owners and Bhim would smack her trunk smartly, reproving her, whereupon she would squeeze her small brown eyes shut like a naughty little girl. 'Mummy learn proper manners,' he told me seriously. 'She too greedy. She have bad habits. She Raja-sahib haathi now. She behave like one.'

Worryingly, Tara's foot did not seem to be getting better. She was walking with a pronounced limp, and it was Bhim who discovered the cause of this lameness – an infection caused by a wicked metal leg shackle with small spikes which pointed inwards that had been used on her by Rajpath. One of the spikes had caused a deep-rooted ulcer, but, Bhim told me, with hot-water compresses mixed with salt applied nightly she would soon be better. Until then, nobody was to ride her except him. The howdah, due to its weight, was abandoned. His knowledge of elephant ailments reassured me, but I fussed about like an expectant father.

It was a glorious day as I watched her plodding along in front of me, her tail swishing and her trunk shooting out from side to side, plucking at branches from overhead trees, flapping her great ears and munching with contentment. I felt wonderfully happy and patted her on her big, fat bottom.

'She really *is* lovely, isn't she, Aditya?'

'Yes, Mark.'

'No, I mean she is *the* most beautiful elephant in the world, isn't she?'

'Yes, Mark.' I could see I was going to drive him mad.

Considering it was our first day on the road, and that Tara was lame, we stopped and made camp by a wide river on the outskirts of a village called Nimpalla after covering a distance of only twelve miles. There are two basic requisites for a camp-site when travelling with an elephant: one is water, for bathing and drinking, and the other is a stout, thickly leaved tree to which one can safely chain the elephant, to provide shelter from the sun and perhaps obtain fodder. We were lucky to find both. Beside the river, a row of ancient Peepul trees stood like sturdy oaks. In a few minutes Gokul, with the agility of a monkey, and armed with an axe, had disappeared into the upper foliage and soon Tara's dinner came crashing to the ground.

For my benefit camps were, if possible, to be set up away from villages in the future. I had not yet become adjusted to the huge crowds I knew our entourage would attract. I realised I had no right to complain. I was travelling in their country, probably camping on their land. An elephant with a foreigner was understandably fair game, but I was still too much of a tourist to tolerate such human curiosity. As countless pairs of eyes scrutinised my every move while I struggled with Aditya to put up our ridiculously complicated tent, I was not in the most charitable frame of mind.

'Go away,' I roared, waving my hands like a demented marionette. A hundred pairs of eyes blinked once, my tormentors settled themselves more comfortably on their haunches and waited patiently for the show to go on.

'They won't go,' Aditya remarked quietly. 'Just ignore them.'

'Well can't you frighten them or something?'

'Perhaps,' he suggested, 'if you removed those white socks and covered up those ridiculous blue underpants they might think that you're a human being instead of a creature from outer space.'

'I'm going to take a bath with Tara,' I added grumpily, noticing Bhim leading her towards the river.

'That, my friend, will probably cause a riot.'

Watching an elephant take a bath is a delight in itself, but bathing with, or washing an elephant is something close to experiencing paradise. When I reached the river she was lying at full length with a contented expression on her face. Bhim and Gokul were busily scraping her with stones and the normally grey skin on her protruding backside was already turning black and shiny. Occasionally the tip of her trunk emerged like the periscope of a submarine, spraying them playfully with water before disappearing again and blowing a series of reverberating bubbles. I grabbed a suitable stone and, forgetting my self-consciousness, joined in the fun.

After half an hour my arms were aching, my fingers were bleeding, but I felt absurdly proud. Bhim, sensing my eagerness, gave me the honour of cleaning her trunk, her ears and around her eyes, something which usually only the mahout, who is most familiar to the elephant, will undertake, due to the extreme sensitivity of these areas. However, he made sure that the ankush was hooked around the top of one of her ears at all times.

'If Mummy feels that,' he explained, 'she give Raja-sahib no trouble.'

She didn't, except at one moment when she took a liking to my underpants (I'm glad somebody did) and dragged them half down. This caused hilarity among the crowd, now squatting on the side of the river bank. The whole process was then repeated on the elephant's other side. By means of a sharp command from Bhim, she lumbered to her knees and rolled over, creating a small tidal wave. Taking to my new job as a mahout's assistant too zealously, I found out the hard way that Tara did not like to be scrubbed on the soles of her feet. She was extremely ticklish, and being winded by the kick of an elephant was not an experience I would care to repeat. I still had a lot to learn, I realised, or rather she had a lot to teach me.

After feeding Tara we sprawled around a blazing fire, bloated from an evening meal of corned beef, lentils and rice, spiced with a few chillis. This was to be our staple diet, unless we could find the odd chicken or goat. None of us, it seems, were great chefs. Perhaps Indrajit might fill the position. Mugs were filled with carefully measured tots of rum and we drank each other's health, banging the tin mugs together and solemnly uttering the words, 'Jai Mata' (victory to the Goddess).

His inhibitions softened by the liquor, Bhim began to reminisce in a mumbling voice. 'Haathi, nicer than people. Only hurt if you trick. Never eat until haathi eat. If feed well always faithful. But not not steal haathi food. Haathi always know. Haathi wait. Then haathi attack. Many mahouts bad, steal haathi food. Bad mahout, dead mahout.'

I asked him why he had become involved with elephants. 'In blood,' he replied.

Many years ago his father was the chief mahout to the Maharaja of Mayurbhanj, so he had grown up with the elephants. But there was one incident that changed his life, and from that moment on he knew that his destiny was to work with the haathi. He was involved in a tiger shoot in the forest of Mayurbhanj organised by the Maharaja for some visiting dignitaries. His father and the other mahouts were riding the main elephants while he and another younger mahout, who were riding the supply elephants, became separated somehow from the main party. They ended up camping alone at night in the jungle. Bhim woke up to the sound of a tiger close by and then listened in terror as the tiger killed and dragged away the other mahout. His own elephant with instinctive protection had grabbed him by its trunk, pulled him between its legs and stood guard all night, trumpeting fiercely as the tiger stalked around. In the morning Bhim had ridden back to safety.

'Haathi, like Mummy. Guard child.'

Later as I lay in the tent I thought about what Bhim had told me. Even above Aditya's stentorian snoring I could hear Tara happily feeding – the crackling and crunching of branches followed by a contented munching. There was something reassuring about an elephant close by. It was like being guarded by a huge jovial nanny, and I fell asleep dreaming of tigers and temples.

A torrential rainstorm in the night was just a foretaste of the kind of weather that was going to dog us for the next two weeks. All the tents were blown down and the ground was ankle-deep in water. When I went to retrieve my air mattress from the mass of sodden canvas, it floated happily towards the river. In the half-light we struck camp quickly, cursing as we tripped over our tent pegs and guy ropes, serenaded by a deafening chorus of belching frogs which seemed to be laughing at our discomfort.

As another day's march began, Aditya and I walked gingerly. Blisters, or 'water bottles' as he more aptly described them, had begun to appear on our feet. Both of us were lame, and Bhim and Gokul had fever, shivering under umbrellas.

'Water bottle coming up under left big toe,' Aditya barked as he splashed along.

'Two water bottles under heel on right foot,' I replied wincing. 'God, they're painful! Do slow down, I can't bear it any longer.'

'Don't be so feeble. Crush them, forget the pain. Imagine what my ancestors had to endure.'

'Your ancestors,' I pointed out crossly, 'were generals and commanders. I bet they never walked anywhere; rode in great comfort on horses, I should imagine.' I turned to look at Bhim enviously, wondering whether I was ever going to ride Tara.

Our misery turned to laughter at the chaos Tara caused as we passed. Goatherds frantically tried to control their animals as they scattered bleating and panicking into the paddy fields. Bullock cart drivers on their way to the market, their ramshackle contraptions piled precariously with their wares, stood up and shouted, 'Hut, Hut,' mercilessly whipping their cattle like charioteers, urging them to pass us quickly. Sometimes they dismounted and covered the animals' eyes. It was to no avail. The bullocks, big enough in themselves, and sensing that something much bigger was threatening them, charged away uncontrollably foaming at the mouth, scattering their loads on the road. Three young men riding a small moped passed, whipping us in a fine spray. All three turned simultaneously, as if to double check that what they had seen was not a dream. The moped, out of control, snaked off the road and crashed into a muddy ditch. They were not put out in the slightest, laughing uproariously as we helped them out of their messy predicament.

Near the village of Hirapur we came across an exquisite and seemingly forgotten temple, surrounded by verdant paddy fields. We approached it by skirting a small lake in the centre of which stood a tiny, overgrown shrine, like a little gazebo in an English country garden. The temple was quite empty and of a curious design – a perfect stone circle about nine feet in height, standing open to the sky. Access was made by a narrow, low entrance way, which was no more than an interruption of the surrounding wall. Inside sixty-four perfect goddesses, carved in black chlorite, each about a foot high, sat in little niches facing an open pavilion in the centre. It held a beautifully seductive atmosphere and I imagined music, incense, flesh, colour, laughter, accompanying orgiastic love. The wall was built at just the right height so that people could not peep in. Later I found out that it was the Chausath Yogini Temple, one of only four in the whole of India, built in the ninth century AD. The goddesses or Yoginis were attendants on the goddess Durga, an image of whom at one time sat on the open pavilion in the centre. It was a place of worship exclusive to Orissa's kings.

On the main road we passed a tourist bus which screeched to a halt and reversed up alongside us. Excited cries of 'Slon, slon' poured out from the opening windows as I realised it was full of Russians. 'Slon' is Russian for elephant, and curiously the only word I know in that language. Tara, never one to miss an opportunity for food, worked the bus like a professional. Her long trunk dipped into every window emerging with oranges, bananas and apples, and finally a bottle of vodka which, before I could grab, she inserted into her mouth and sucked dry. Bhim reprimanded her fiercely by rapping the blunt end of the ankush on top of her bony head. This had about as much effect as hitting a hippopotamus with a lollipop, but I could see from the mournful expression on his face as he looked at the empty bottle, where his anger really lay. Luckily another was produced and we toasted each other uproariously.

'Do dra' (to the bottom literally, or bottoms up) came from the Russian contingent. 'Jai Mata,' from the Indians, a strange rumbling belch from Tara, and from the lone Englishman, 'Up yours.' With the aid of an elephant I had done my bit for 'glasnost' and 'perestroika'.

For a while the hot snap of the vodka warmed our bones and we swung along at a grand pace, forgetting about the rain. Bhim, looking like a cheerful, drowned water rat, sang a strange hooting melody that was muffled by the hood of the raincoat I had lent him. Tara now considered anything moving – whether a truck, a bus, a car or a cyclist – as meals on wheels and wandered, waving her trunk, into the path of these oncoming vehicles. Gokul hung on to Tara's tail giggling squeakily, performing an odd little jig. Aditya and I discussed blisters.

I struggled to keep up with him as he demonstrated what he called 'the loping gait' of a Maratha foot soldier.

Through the driving rain we could just make out the blurred outline of the Dhauli hills. On top of a prominent hillock, blinding white against a black sky, stood the Vishwa Shanti Stupa, the domed Peace Pagoda the Buddhists built in this century with Japanese collaboration, to commemorate the conversion to Buddhism of the great Indian Emperor Ashoka.

We took a short cut across some open fields to the River Daya, a river which was said 'to have run red with blood' during the horrifying slaughter of the battle of Kalinga, a massacre so enormous that Ashoka flung away his blood-stained sword and embraced the path of peace. It was on these very fields that the great battle had been fought. Under the black rainclouds, it was a bleak and eerie place. The wind moaned soulfully, pushing into us and making us shiver, less from cold than from something else, perhaps from the spirits of the one hundred thousand souls that had been slaughtered here. Tara sensed it too. She moved forward reluctantly, her trunk in the air, sensing, probing. Finally she came to a halt. Bhim tried to urge her and she let out a loud reverberating roar which I could only imagine was of terror. With her ears extended fully forward, she backed hurriedly away, then turned and fled.

'Mummy no like here,' Bhim yelled over his shoulder, struggling to gain control.

'Let's get out of here,' I muttered to Aditya.

'God knows how many elephants perished on this spot,' Aditya replied, shivering. 'This is an elephants' graveyard. After two and a half thousand years how is it possible Tara still senses that?'

Somehow I believed it possible, just as I believed the legend about the Emperor's conversion to Buddhism.

On these fields he had stood with a bloodied sword, gloating over the carnage around him. The skies opened and the Buddha appeared in a shaft of pure white light, holding in his arms a dead child. 'Give life back to this child,' the Buddha had pleaded. 'How can I perform such a miracle?' Ashoka had asked. 'You have taken so many lives,' the Buddha had replied. 'Cannot a man as noble and great as you give back just one life?'

We headed for the road that led to the Stupa where Khusto and the jeep were to meet us. There was no sign of Khusto. We waited an hour in the gathering dusk. Tara was fidgety and nervous, and her foot horribly swollen. We had to find shelter for the night and decided to head for the monastery, where the monks would certainly welcome us. We reached a wide, covered veranda with a large, shady tree conveniently near by.

'Perfect,' I said, jingling a brass bell attached to an iron grille. A faint smell of incense emitted from inside. There was silence. I rang again.

'Who is there?' called a nervous voice as a young Indian pressed his face up against the other side of the grille.

'Could I speak to the monks?' I asked politely.

'They are Japanese,' he replied.

'Well, that's very nice,' I said, 'but can I speak to them?'

'Gone away, in Calcutta.'

'Perhaps you could help us then. We need shelter for the night. We are all very cold, very wet and my elephant is sick.'

'You cannot stay here,' he stated firmly.

'Are you a Buddhist?' I asked.

'Yes.'

'Buddha Shuranam Gachami' (may the peace of the Buddha be with you), I greeted him.

'You cannot stay here,' he insisted.

'But we are weary travellers. We are not asking for much, just a roof over our heads and a tree to tether the elephant.'

'You are a foreigner.'

'Yes, but so what,' I shouted, starting to get angry. 'Buddhism is universal.'

'You cannot stay here. Please. It is a bad place. There are no lights and murders take place.'

Aditya shrugged. We limped off into the rain and several hours later found a deserted schoolhouse in the dark. After applying a hot poultice to Tara's leg, fashioned out of sanitary towels which had mysteriously appeared from Bhim's pocket, we collapsed in exhaustion, oblivious of our damp misery.

Early the next morning, as we were entering Bhubaneshwar, Khusto caught up with us. Through a paan-filled mouth, which did not conceal the smell of rum, he mumbled that he had had a puncture and got lost. Aditya and I decided that Indrajit could deal with Khusto. Tara's leg was our main concern and we pushed on to Nandankanan, which was on our route northwards, to consult the zoo vet. Bhim did not seem at all happy about our decision. Pouring scorn on the modern methods of medicine, he stated that it was he who always cured the sick elephants at the zoo. I was adamant; I could not bear to see her in such pain any longer.

6

In the Tracks of the King of Bliss

ON OUR WAY into Bhubaneshwar, we passed many young people beating drums, singing and carrying papier-mâché images – some gigantic, some tiny and, oddly, all pink in colour, for immersion in the river. It was Ganesh Chaturti, the last of the days dedicated to Ganesh, and their songs called upon the elephant-headed god to come back early next year. But the melancholic farewells were already alternating with excited hymns anticipating the god's return and it seemed to me that their continuity was like India itself, where the end of any event is always pre-empted by the birth of the next. The crowds turned, and it was as if they had found a new festival. To see an elephant on the day of Ganesh Chaturti was auspicious. A brass band, featuring trombone and trumpet players and a child dwarfed by a huge drum, joined us and we marched triumphantly into Bhubaneshwar like a circus parade.

At one time over seven thousand temples dominated the skyline of Bhubaneshwar, appropriate for a city that is called the 'Abode of the Gods'. It had started to rain as we approached the temple of Lord Lingaraj (the Lord of the Universe), the largest and most impressive of the temples in Bhubaneshwar, its vaulting spire soaring to a height of one hundred and sixty feet. The priests, seeing a foreigner, uncoiled themselves like pythons from wet stone entrances and slid menacingly towards me to extract money. But the sight of an elephant, or rather the sight of a 'firinghee' with an elephant, caused a clash of conscience; they didn't know whether to give to the elephant or to take from me. Being businessmen, they did neither.

At a busy roundabout a smiling policeman wearing a smart white solar topee hat and a cape saluted, blew furiously on his whistle and stopped the traffic to let us pass.

'Why be walking, sir?' shouted a rickshaw driver. 'I will be taking you anywhere for half price.'

'Patna? In Bihar?' I shouted back.

'Not being a problem, sir. Please be seated.'

'But it is at least seven hundred miles away.'

'Then I would surely die. Good morning,' and he pedalled away, his thin legs pumping furiously.

Indrajit and Khusto drove up in the jeep. We were now back to full strength. We instructed the two drivers to go ahead to Nandankanan to inform the vet of Tara's predicament. To rest her leg, we stopped at the Hati Gumpha cave (elephant cave) in the Udayagiri hills. Two stone elephants stand guard at the entrance. Inside, engraved on huge stone slabs, is the record of the reign of King Kharavela, the greatest monarch of Orissa, ruler of the mighty Kalinga Empire. Known as the 'King of Bliss, His Majesty the Mighty Conqueror, Sri Kharavela, the Possessor of Invincible Armies', it was he who pursued the Greek king, Demetrius, out of India. He came to the throne when he was fifteen years old and, in the twelfth year of his reign, led his vast army of elephants, cavalry and chariots towards north-west India, striking 'terror into the people of Magadha while making his horses and elephants drink from the Ganges'.

I liked the sound of this gentleman; perhaps it was just the name or perhaps it was that I, mounted on an elephant, was now firmly in the tracks of the King of Bliss. Like his royal elephant, Tara would drink from the waters of the Ganges.

As if to seal this bond, Tara's trunk suddenly snaked out and circled around the stone trunk of a guardian elephant. In elephant language this is the ultimate gesture of friendship.

At Nandankanan the vet made a perfunctory examination of Tara's leg and prescribed a week's course of strong antibiotics.

'How do I give an elephant pills?' I asked. 'In her food?'

'No, no, no,' he replied. 'This is a most serious infection. The course must be administered intramuscularly.'

'You mean injections?' I was terrified. 'I've got to give her injections! Oh, my God! I hate needles at the best of times. How on earth do I give an elephant a jab?'

'It is easy. Come,' he said. 'We will give her the first one now.'

I wished I had the confidence shown by J. H. Williams in his book *Elephant Bill*:

> One cut out all the fuss and just walked up boldly to the animal, gave it a good smack with the left hand and exclaimed, 'Hello, old chap.' With the right one thrust the needle through the hide and squirted in the vaccine. Then one gave it another smack and turned away, exclaiming, 'Come on,' to the next elephant. Elephants will bear a great deal of pain patiently and appear to understand that it is being inflicted for their own good, but they will only put up with it when the operator is full of confidence himself and feels he is making a good job of it, for an elephant can sense the absence of self confidence quicker than any other animal in the world.

'Can't you give her the first one?' I implored the vet, as I held a needle the size of a rocket-launcher in my shaking hand.

'No,' he replied firmly, 'you must learn immediately. Remember, plunge it in right up to the hilt. Once firmly in place, you can attach the plunger.'

'Which cheek?' I asked, nervously, standing behind Tara's enormous bottom. At that moment she turned her head and gave me a curious look.

'Either one. Whichever you feel most comfortable with,' he said airily.

After marking a spot in my mind I shut my eyes and plunged in the needle like a dart. With a squeal of rage she shot to her feet and trundled away with a broken hypodermic needle wobbling precariously out of her backside.

'That was very incorrect,' the vet remarked needlessly. 'It has to be a firm strong blow. Place the needle in straight. Now, we will try again.'

Tara was retrieved and made to sit. She gave me a look of pure venom. I repeated the process, this time with success, and even managed to pump the sticky fluid in efficiently.

'Repeat every evening for the next six days. You will soon find that she will become used to it. In fact, she will be grateful.'

Of this I was not convinced, especially when Bhim, who had been watching with distaste, came up and whispered in my ear. 'Raja-sahib,' he said slyly, 'Mummy in pain, Mummy know who give pain. Mummy cross with Raja-sahib. Better Daddy give injection. Raja-sahib hide. When injection over, give Mummy gur. Mummy then like Raja-sahib,' he smiled, winking at me.

As we were about to leave, after adding to our equipment a large box of hypodermic needles, syringes and glass phials, the vet pointed to two raised and hardened circles of skin on each side of her backside. 'You know what those are?' he said. 'Those are the marks made by the Lohatias, the men who in the olden days, when hunting wild elephants with lassoes, would hang on to the crupper ropes and spur their elephants on with a short club faced with iron spikes when extra acceleration was needed. This type of elephant capture was called Mela Shikar and the type of elephant used was known as a Koonki. They had to be very fast elephants.'

Looking at her now, as she stuffed her face with paddy, I wondered if she could catch a bus, let alone a wild elephant.

'Mela Shikar is now of course banned,' he continued, 'but it took place in north-east India, mainly in Assam. So you now have an idea where she might come from.'

Miraculously, Tara's leg already appeared to be improving. She could bend it more and we moved at a good pace over a wide, sandy, dry river basin in the shadow of an unfinished bridge. In the distance we could see the outline of Cuttack, the old capital of Orissa which, due to its unfortunate geographical position, wedged on a spit of land between two huge rivers, had been unable to expand. The capital was transferred to Bhubaneshwar in 1948. It was over one of these rivers that we now crossed.

Trucks and buses thundered perilously close. I had not adjusted to the fact that I was travelling with an elephant rather than a dog that might slip its lead, and I became foolishly anxious that Tara might disappear under the wheels of an oncoming vehicle. To my left, over a railway bridge, the Madras–Calcutta express train chugged imperiously. We were moving faster.

Cuttack was buzzing with an air of excitement, for the Russian circus was in town. Minibuses darted in and out of the traffic, their sides emblazoned with posters of svelte young ladies dressed in scanty sequinned outfits, balancing with arms outstretched on top of charging horses. Lions and tigers snarled from advertising hoardings and bicyclists with tannoys attached to the handlebars of their rusting machines excitedly described the entertainments of the Big Top. Pale-faced Russian artistes mingled with the crowd, and the circus strongman had managed to squeeze into a rickshaw's tiny seat. On his knee sat a dwarf. Tara and I greeted them all cheerfully but were met with a suspicious silence.

In the main square, fenced off, stood a marble statue of a splendid turbanned man with a beautifully refined face. Around his neck hung a garland of marigolds. He was the Maharaja of Paralakhemedi, a popular figure, responsible for making Orissa a state in its own right in 1936, separate from Bihar.

I was taken to meet the owner of *Samaj*, the oldest newspaper in Orissa. A venerable old man with exquisite manners presented Aditya and me with a wooden deity, and around our shoulders wrapped colourful appliqué-work blankets. He clasped my hand. 'Traditions are dying fast. What you are doing is an inspiration to the youth of Orissa.' Then he asked if I needed money. I was astonished by this genuine gesture of kindness.

On the outskirts of Cuttack we passed the ruins of the Barabati Fort. It was built in the thirteenth century and once consisted of nine courts, the first of which housed the elephants, the camels and the horses. All that remained was a crumbling stone entrance and a wide moat.

'This place has seen some action,' I remarked to Aditya. 'The Moghuls didn't behave too well, but it was your lot that really went to town.'

The invasions of Orissa had begun in AD 1205 with the purpose of securing the superior breed of elephants for which Orissa was famous. The most remarkable foray of all was made in 1360 by the Delhi Emperor Firoz Shah, who cut through the jungles of Orissa, crossed the Mahanadi river and occupied this fort, from which the King had fled. Here Firoz Shah spent some time hunting elephants, and when the terrified King sent envoys to negotiate for peace he replied, ironically, that he had only come to hunt and was amazed that the King had taken flight. The embarrassed Oriya King sent him twenty elephants and promised to do so annually as a tribute. Only then did the Emperor return to Delhi. Invaded and occupied by Mohammedans for five hundred years, the state of Orissa was plunged into further despair by the arrival of the Marathas.

'During the famine of 1770,' I reminded Aditya, 'when people were dying in their hundreds of thousands, you went completely berserk and, it is recorded, "raged like wild beasts across the country".'

'Tell me more,' Aditya said enthusiastically.

'It's not a nice story, but I must say you were efficient, in your extortionist greed.'

'Well there you are,' he replied. 'Nothing better than an efficient army.'

'Fortunately for Orissa your efficiency barely lasted a century. The British stormed the fort and the Maratha yoke was finally broken.'

'Bloody British,' he remarked with a laugh. 'Always poking their noses in where they're not wanted.'

Over the next few days we headed slowly northwards, gradually entering into rural Orissa, camping in government rest-houses and schools to avoid the discomfort of wet nights under canvas. The monsoons were still in full flow. Tara's foot had healed almost totally due to the injections that Aditya now performed expertly each evening. Bhim's sly plan didn't seem to be working as she paid rather more attention to Aditya than me. I was convinced that the vet was right; Tara was grateful to Aditya for healing her pain and they had become firm friends.

In preparation for my imminent training as a rookie mahout, Bhim had given Aditya a list of basic elephant commands which Aditya had written down for me phonetically. Mercifully there were only seventeen of them, not eighty-four as I had been told, and unless I learnt Hindi they just about covered everything. In the evenings, Aditya and I would wring out our wet, bloody socks and attempt to patch up the raw holes with Elastoplast, while I practised my commands.

Agit (Ah-git) – Forward/go

Peechay (Pee.Chay, like the name) – Back

Chai ghoom (like chime, like goon) – Right

Chi (like cheese) – Left

Chhee (like cheese again, but longer) – Dirty

Dhuth (like Dutch without the 'ch') – Stop, the most important command, which I never quite managed to master

Maar Thode (Ma, toad) – Break

A Dhur (A like Eh, Dur like Durbar) – Get this/get that

Oopar Dhur (Oo, pa, dur) – Reach up/grab

Mylay (My, lay) – Get up

Baitho (Buy, toe) – Down/get down on your knees

Theeray (Tea, ray) – Lie down/roll over on side

Theylay Chhup (Tea, lay, chap) – Drink

Bey (Bay) – Bitch

Lay lay (same) – Eat/take food/open your mouth. This one was pointless. Tara needed no encouragement

Utha (Oo, ta) – Lift

Bowl Bowl (same) – Speak/say thank you

This is easy, I thought to myself smugly, and was soon word perfect.

'I've learnt them,' I told Aditya. 'Test me.' I had hardly reached the 'Pee' of 'Peechay' before he exploded.

'For goodness sake, Mark. This is an elephant, not a dog. You sound exactly like that tweedy lady on British television who stomps around in green wellington boots saying "Sit. Walkies. Good doggy."'

'Barbara Woodhouse,' I interrupted crossly, 'was jolly successful.'

'Well, I can tell you my friend, this is a different ball game. Rather than speaking like some la-di-da debutante, put some life into it – "Dhuth,"' he roared.

Tara dug her front legs in and stopped dead. A mahout with lesser experience than Bhim would have fallen off. As it was, he lurched forward and buried his head in Tara's neck, almost swallowing the cigarette he had clamped between his teeth.

'Yes, I see what you mean,' I said humbly. 'I think I need a bit more practice.'

We stopped that night beside a lake surrounded by mist-veiled hills. For a change it was eerily silent; there were no people and only the soft 'clock clock' of wooden bells attached to the necks of the grazing cattle and the 'pit-a-pat' of something being thrown on top of our tents disturbed us. Tara, chained to a tree behind us, enthusiastically scooped up trunkfuls of earth and flung it over her shoulder, giving herself a mud bath. She soon resembled a giant molehill, but the coating of mud was an effective deterrent against the insects that were annoying her.

It was an evening of an old mahout's tales. Whether fact or fiction it did not seem to matter, and as the rum took effect Bhim, with his eyes closed, began to talk, not for our benefit particularly, or to anyone – just an old man's reminiscences because the time was right. He spoke contemptuously about the new methods of caring for elephants and of the people who claimed to understand them, but did not; of how it had been he who had been sent to capture a tusker rampaging in the jungles, causing havoc and destruction among the villages and to the people's crops, after all modern methods of capture had failed. The tusker had not been a wild elephant but a domesticated animal that had gone wild after being deserted by its mahout, probably a mendicant like Rajpath. Bhim had been sent for and had performed an old puja taught to him by his father, cutting the ear of another elephant, taking a little blood and offering it to a deity of Ganesh. Then he had been able to approach the tusker and within five days, soothing and comforting the distressed animal, had ridden him back to the zoo. He spoke of crossing the Simlipals, now a huge wildlife sanctuary, as a child, on top of a bus. The bus had passed under a rocky escarpment and he had felt hot breath and seen a flash of yellow hair as a tiger launched itself on to the bus and carried away the man sitting next to him. And he spoke of how the Maharaja of Mayurbhanj had presented the British Collector, who was returning to England, with a baby elephant; how the little calf had been hoisted by a 'big machine' on to the ship; how in return the Collector had presented the Maharaja with a thousand and one balloons of all different colours, shaped like animals, and of his amazement and delight seeing them float into the air around the ship as it slowly slid from its berth.

Later that night I was awoken by a soft tap on my shoulder and a rum-laced whisper in my ear.

'Come, quietly, Raja-sahib, you look Mummy sleeping.'

I crept outside and there, like a grey boulder, Tara lay quietly on her side, her trunk curled around her neck emitting a wonderfully soothing sound like bubbles escaping from a diver's mouthpiece.

'Mummy snoring,' he whispered. 'Mummy happy.'

7

Touch-me-not

OVERNIGHT, AS IF somebody had simply pushed a button, the monsoons left us, hurrying their black clouds further south. There was a distinct change in the air. It was crisp, alive; the early morning a few degrees colder and then warming as the sun rose. Autumn in India had arrived bringing with it long, hot, golden days of harvest, celebration and festivals.

As instructed by Bhim, we were to be on the look-out for the mimosa plant, otherwise known as 'touch-me-not'. If you caressed its small fern-like leaves they closed quickly, like a shutting book. The plant was an essential ingredient in the puja that was soon to be performed, where I would take on Bhim as my guru. Bhim called it the 'full control ceremony'. Once Tara had eaten the blessed offering of mimosa and gur, he explained, she would be as obedient as a lamb and I would become the complete master. I was sceptical about this – not that I doubted Bhim, but because I doubted my abilities in controlling Tara, who was becoming friskier as each day passed. All the same I eagerly scanned the countryside for this plant. I was going to need all the help I could get. I was also encouraged by watching Gokul. He had apparently undergone a similar ceremony before we had started at Nandankanan and now was riding Tara with all the ability of a seasoned mahout, urging her along with shrill, squeaky cries.

We were well into rural Orissa, where fresh droppings were abundant, signalling that we had entered elephant country. At the top of the giant bamboo groves ringing the paddy fields were tree houses, constructed like large storks' nests, access to which was gained by long rickety ladders. These were anti-elephant machans in which the villagers would sit at night and, by means of fireworks, crackers, shouting and flaming torches, attempt to deter rampaging beasts from demolishing their crops. In one village, where we stopped for tea, a young man, the local teacher, approached me.

'It is indeed,' he said, 'a wonderful thing that you are coming today. A gift from the gods.'

'Namaste,' I replied, delighted by this welcome but slightly bewildered.

'You, of course, will stop and help us?' he enquired eagerly.

'Well, yes,' now completely bewildered. 'If I can.'

'It is the tusker, sir. It has decimated our crops. It has already killed eleven of our people. You,' he said pointing to Tara, 'will catch it with your elephant.'

'Catch it with my elephant?' I answered amazed. Tara was happily rummaging around by the side of the tea-stall in search of food. The thought of the four of us with Tara engaged in some mad Mela Shikar chasing a highly dangerous elephant was absurd, and yet it was wonderful that he imagined it as being so simple. 'I'm sorry. You see we are just travelling through your beautiful country and we are not equipped to undertake such a task. Can't the government do anything about it?'

'The government,' he replied crestfallen, 'will do nothing. The tusker has only killed eleven people, sir. It must kill twenty-four before they are even considering taking actions.'

This was but one of many similar situations that I would encounter on my travels concerning the growing imbalance in India between the rural man and the natural life of the elephant living in harmony. Both are blameless and both are victims of greed; greed caused by the desire for timber, and the consequent massive deforestation. Elephants are creatures of habit. They have, for centuries, followed the same migratory routes in search of food. They arrive and find none: their larder has been cut down, and in desperation they turn to raiding crops on which the villagers' livelihood depends. The villagers are helpless and, even if they could afford to buy modern firearms, would usually be loath to use them. The elephant is a revered beast. Even when, which is seldom, a licence is granted to shoot an elephant that has been established as a rogue, more often than not the kill is not carried out. They revert to modern methods of trying to drug the animal, which in reality is an expensive and impractical situation. In a local newspaper I had read about a problem tusker that had killed and was causing havoc in another area of Orissa:

> Licences were issued to kill it. When the hunters took position closer to the pachyderm to shoot him, they found that tears flowed from his eyes and he

> was supplicant. They dropped their plans and the tusker returned to the forests. The experts are of the opinion that the best way to tackle the situation is to capture the pachyderm. For every untoward incident created by the animal, they contend, there has been enough provocation by the timber merchants and the others who depend on the forest produce. The Minister for Forests who was informed of the case, vehemently opposed all proposals to kill the elephant. He asserted that he would instruct the forest staff to have him tranquillised and deported to the zoo where necessary arrangements with Rs 1 lakh would be made to get him trained under an expert mahout from Assam.

Sadly, this situation is worsening. The Indian elephant is simply running out of living space. Recently a herd of thirty were creating havoc as close as twenty miles to Calcutta. It is fervently to be hoped that desperate measures like culling will not be introduced, and it is up to man to redress the balance. The tiger, which until recently was almost extinct, is beginning to make a dramatic recovery thanks to the resources and expertise made available to 'Project Tiger'. The elephant must now be given the same attention.

At Mandahat, we came to another mighty river, the Brahamani. Some people had told us authoritatively that it was six feet deep and could be crossed, while others shook their heads, knowledgeably stating that it had burst its banks. The latter were right: no one could ford it. We took a short cut along a road which would lead us to another bridge at Kabatobandah, where we hoped to meet up with the jeep. The road soon turned into a track, and then into nothing, as we found ourselves amongst fields choked with baysharam, a kind of bush with long wavy stems sprouting lilac bell-shaped flowers, also known as 'shameless' for its gregarious, prolific and deep-rooted growth. It is considered a virulent weed which causes the Indian farmer enormous difficulties. The baysharam gave way to bamboo groves that had been decimated by wild elephants. In turn the bamboo led into sal forests still being decimated by human beings, in which the sound of a falling axe was always audible.

Considering their size, it is remarkable how elephants can move so soundlessly. Tara's footsteps, at their loudest, resembled the shuffle of an old man wearing carpet slippers. Because of this quietness, we encountered everything with an element of surprise, whether animal, human, bird or insect. Aditya was particularly happy. When we saw the flash of a golden oriole, a beautiful yellow bird with a jet black streak through its eye dipping away with a raucous *Cheeugh*, or the long ribbon-like tail of a paradise flycatcher, he would jot down his sightings excitedly in a small book. At one point Tara disturbed a carpet of big yellow butterflies that exploded into the air. A single butterfly, more courageous than its companions, attached itself firmly to the end of her trunk and after several vain attempts to dislodge it, by swinging it from side to side, she finally blew it off with a large sneeze.

The sal forests began to thin out and we moved carefully along the ridges dividing well-tended paddy fields. In corners of these fields were small tribal shrines situated under the spread of large shady trees. Dedicated to the goddess Devi, they consisted of groups of exquisite terracotta figures of horses, camels, elephants and bears which were offered as gifts to the deity, to ensure a healthy harvest to the indigenous Mundas. In the distance we heard the sound of drums. Spurring Tara on, we reached a small collection of thatched huts with pink walls surrounding a muddy courtyard where a Munda party was in full swing. A chain of men and women, dark muscular people with full lips and handsome high-cheekboned faces, were pounding their feet drunkenly in ankle-deep mud, performing a kind of ritual hokey-cokey.

At the sight of Tara looming over their compound, they threw their arms into the air, moaning loudly. The drum tempo increased, they whirled in ever-decreasing circles and finally collapsed laughing in an exhausted heap. A young woman wearing a brilliant azure sari, moulded to the contours of her body, untangled herself from the group and undulated over to Tara. She knelt gracefully and touched Tara's feet in obeisance. Each of her companions followed suit, and then offered us leaf cups containing a milky fluid which they had filled from large terracotta gourds. This was 'handia', a local rice beer. At first it tasted slightly bitter and fizzy, but after numerous replenishments, one was filled with a sense of contentment.

The drums started again. We were dragged to our feet and whirled round the compound. Now as drunk as our hosts, we proudly showed our paces. Aditya performed a sort of martial strut. I attempted to show them break dancing, which resulted in my head becoming firmly stuck in the mud, my feet waving in the air. Gokul, the professional, delighted the audience by doing somersaults, handstands and back flips. Even Tara, after draining one of the gourds, flapped her ears and shook her head while Bhim squatted with the elders and concentrated on the more serious aspect of things – drinking. When we took our leave the women presented us each with a frangipani flower, garlanded Tara, and blessed us for a safe journey.

We reached a small river where a flash flood had washed away the bridge. A man sat forlornly on the bank drying out a bundle of soggy letters. He told us that while attempting to cross, he had been knocked over by the current and his bicycle was now caught in a bundle of branches in the middle of the whirling water. Bhim and Tara waded into the river. Directed by his sharp commands of 'Uhta, uhta,' Tara lowered her trunk and plucked the bicycle from the branches as if it was a feather, depositing it gently in front of the grateful postman.

Out of curiosity, I penned a letter to myself in London and gave it to him. When I returned home three months later it was waiting for me. The letter was slightly worse for wear, with an added message written on the back of the envelope. 'For Haathi-wallah from K. Rath, postman, thanking him sincerely.'

Guided by a full moon that washed the landscape in a pale light, we finally crossed the Brahamani over a long concrete bridge. It was late by the time we found the camp and by the look on Indrajit's face we knew there had been trouble between the two drivers.

'Khusto!' he spat fiercely. 'No good, he take rum. He always drunk. No helping either. I put tents, I cook, he does nothing. So I hit him. Either he go or I go.'

Aditya and I looked at each other in despair. We did not need a domestic squabble and we couldn't afford to lose Indrajit. He was invaluable. We checked the rum supply. Indrajit was right. Out of a new case of twelve bottles of rum one was missing. We found Khusto sitting in the jeep nursing a face that was even more swollen than usual. He mumbled something incomprehensible and turned his back to us insolently.

'Leave this to me, Mark,' Aditya said angrily.

For the next ten minutes there was an angry exchange of words punctuated by metallic slaps as Aditya banged his fist on the side of the jeep. It stopped abruptly. Khusto's voice had changed. He was now pleading. Eventually he shuffled into the firelight and muttered an apology to Indrajit and offered his hand. Indrajit took it hesitatingly and then with an angry smile touched him on the shoulder. The crisis it seemed was over for a time.

'What did you tell him?' I asked Aditya.

'Simple, my friend. He has stolen, so therefore he is a thief. I threatened to take him to the police station. That did it. I have told him that from now on Indrajit is the boss.'

'Do you think it will work?' I said.

'We'll see. Anyway, I don't think Khusto's bad, just foolish. He told me that all his problems stem from being born with too small a tongue.'

'What's that got to do with it?' I asked incredulously.

'I have no idea,' he laughed. 'Anyway we shall be without them for a few days. We are entering the forests of Daitari tomorrow and Bhim has announced that Tara is fit enough to carry the howdah.'

'What about my puja?' I insisted anxiously. 'Why can't we find this bloody mimosa plant?'

'Slowly, Mark, remember this is India.'

'Slowly indeed.' At this rate I was going to walk to Sonepur, I thought, as I finished my mug of coffee.

We were sitting round the fire which had been made in the crumbling porch of a deserted house near our camp. Bhim suddenly jumped to his feet and pointed into the dark confines of the house. 'Nag, nag!' he cried excitedly. Everybody immediately disappeared and I was left sitting bewildered.

'What the hell's going ...'

'Get out of there, Mark!' Aditya shouted.

'Will somebody tell me what's going on?'

'Nag, nag!'

'What in the hell is nag?'

'A snake, you idiot! Cobra!' Aditya yelled from the jeep, from which he, Bhim, Gokul and Indrajit reappeared armed with axes.

'Jeeesus! A snake! Oh my God!' I shot out of the porch and fled towards Tara who in the circumstances seemed to be the safest bet, noting on my way that Khusto had climbed on top of the jeep. The boys advanced quickly into the house and a tremendous mêlée started. Shouts and screams followed by the sound of metal ringing on stone. I returned as nonchalantly as possible.

'Well?'

'Nag escape,' Bhim stated crossly. 'Big, maybe seven feet.'

'Seven feet!' I cried. 'Well, where is it now?'

'Maybe tent,' he leered happily. A thorough inspection of our sleeping quarters was made, but none of us slept well that night.

Early next morning before setting off, Aditya and I took a detour to visit Bhuban, famous as Asia's most populated village. Our mission was more than one of tourism: we were to buy 'bombs', anti-elephant devices that Bhim said we might well need over the next few days. The houses of Bhuban are so close together that their thatched roofs join over the narrow alleys, cutting out the light, and only single-line pedestrian traffic is possible. None the less, in the maze of shops selling brass and metal objects for which Bhuban has a reputation, we located the bomb-seller.

The bombs were hard and round, about the size of golf balls, and were wrapped in brightly coloured paper. When thrown against something hard they exploded like army thunderflashes. These ethnic grenades scared the hell out of me, and it was hoped that they would have the same effect on a wild animal.

By the time we returned to camp Tara was fully loaded. Unhappy about this sudden extra weight, she kept whipping her trunk back trying to undo Bhim's knots. From the front she looked like an old bag lady. Pots, pans, kerosene stoves and old sacks filled with tinned food hung from one side. Over the other flank dangled tents, sleeping bags, pillows, axes and cameras. All this paraphernalia had been placed in two white nylon hammocks that I had brought from England, so that from the back she resembled some grotesque model, wearing gigantic shoulder pads. As a deterrent against the hot sun, the top of her head had been oiled and it gleamed like a patent leather shoe. When Gokul, eager to see her reaction, exploded a bomb beneath her feet, she displayed the same patience as a nanny with a small naughty child, simply turning her head and giving him a look as if to say, 'Silly child,' and continued trying to undo the knots. It was not surprising that she didn't react. Rajpath must have taken her through so many town festivals that she was now indifferent to ordeal by firecracker.

There are four ways to climb on to an elephant. The first, and the one that we were about to adopt, is the easiest for the passenger and the most uncomfortable for the elephant. With a command of 'Baitho!' the elephant kneels and one clambers up on to the howdah by way of stepping on to the top of the front part of either leg, grabbing on to the ear, and hauling oneself up. In the old days a ladder would be produced or one would mount from a special block. The second way is harder. Upon the command of 'Utha! utha!' the elephant lifts either of its front legs and, grabbing the ear, one steps on to the leg and is raised up like an elevator. The third is over the backside. The elephant lowers one of its back legs, and one simply catches on to her tail or the crupper rope. The fourth, the expert's way, and the way that I hoped one day to achieve, is by the trunk. It looks so casual, elegant and simple. The trunk is lowered to the ground; placing a foot about in the centre, one holds both ears and is hoisted up and over.

Having awkwardly, but successfully climbed aboard, I settled into the howdah and noticed Aditya about to mount with his boots on.

'Take off your boots,' I said.

'What?' he exclaimed crossly. 'Why?'

'I don't know why. But from now on, no boots when riding Tara.' For some inexplicable reason I felt her to be as sacred as the deck of a yacht and I was delighted when I saw Bhim nod his approval. Grumbling, Aditya untied his boots, threw them up to me and climbed aboard. Tara immediately rose to her feet and we were lifted gently upwards. Elephant-back at last, I thought happily. We really have started the journey.

8

An Angry Tusker

> I do not know why it is, but the instant I am on an elephant I do not feel afraid for myself or anybody else. When the tall grass shakes and the elephants begin to scream, I ask whether it is a tiger or a rhinoceros in exactly the same tone I should ask the servants whether it is a partridge or a pheasant.
>
> Fanny Eden, Indian Journals 1837–1838,
> *Tigers, Durbars and Kings*

FROM THE VERY moment that Tara took her first step forward, I was filled with a complete sense of security, cocooned, wrapped in cotton-wool. I knew that while this wonderful benign animal lumbered below me, nothing could go wrong. From twelve feet up the view was spectacular. The landscape took on a different perspective and one could see both far and near – the blazing yellow of a distant mustard field or the early morning goings on over a mud wall of a village. But it was the feeling of invincibility that struck me most. My imagination ran riot, and I became the 'King of Bliss' surrounded by a thousand elephants, revelling in the horror and fear of my foes.

The experts told me that it would be uncomfortable, tedious and even painful to travel in a howdah. How wrong they were. I found the soft swaying motion relaxing, almost too relaxing. On occasion, I fell asleep, and just caught myself before I slid off. To prevent this, I fashioned a sling from a length of rope and found I could lie back with my feet hanging over her backside. Then, after plugging in my Walkman, I could recline like a Maharaja, listening to the strains of Italian opera while a huge, never changing empty sky passed by overhead.

Occasionally, like a tiny silver arrow, an aeroplane would flash far above. I felt sorry for the passengers squeezed into their pressurized chamber, hurrying from one destination to the next, unable to see the beauty that I was so fortunate to be enjoying. Gradually I was slowing down, slowing down to the pace of a country in which if one moves fast, one misses everything – and like a patient tutor Tara was influencing me, showing me the way.

We were now climbing steadily and passing through Orissa's mining belt – a dull, wide, angry landscape, dotted with huge rocky escarpments gouged out and scarred by blasting and bulldozers. In the distance I could see the forested ranges of Daitari shimmering blue in the heat haze. It was hot. As elephants do not sweat, Tara cooled herself down by looping her trunk into her mouth, extracting a mixture of spit and water and blowing it in a fine spray over her flanks and under her belly. Elephants, like camels, can store water. They have a kind of shut-off valve system that they can open and close as they wish. As the sun became fiercer, she piled a bonnet of straw and leaves on top of her head. Her great ears, the smooth skin behind their wide spread knotted with thick veins, flapped rhythmically, acting as ventilation under which Bhim would occasionally stretch out his legs and manipulate her with his toes to urge her on. Each toe had a life of its own, pushing, probing and playing like the fingers of a concert pianist. Then he would sit back on the front of the howdah and work her head with the heels of his feet, pushing forward and down. No commands were necessary. It was all being done by touch. Bhim told me to watch his movements carefully and learn. A true master remains silent. Considering my appalling Hindi accent, this would certainly make life easier.

Another example of Bhim's expertise came when Gokul, who would be walking alongside us, would change into the driving seat. Tara's pace would then alter considerably and she would slow right down, however much Gokul shrieked commands at her. She knew instinctively that she was now in control and exploited the situation mercilessly.

We made camp under a lone Peepul tree on top of a small hillock by the side of the road. The heat had sapped our strength and we slept for most of the afternoon. In the evening I went to feed Tara her gur. She greeted me with an affectionate rumble, wrapped her trunk around me drawing me closer, searching my body for her treat. The vet at Nandankanan had also given me some deworming powder for her, a little of which I had hidden in a thick ball of gur.

'Lay, lay! Tara,' I commanded.

She opened her mouth wide, exposing tiny six-inch tusks on either side and I caught a glimpse of her gigantic molars. I placed the ball on her fat pink tongue which was as soft as a blancmange and watched the obvious pleasure appear on her face. It changed quickly to one of 'You can't fool me' as she delicately removed the ball, placed it on the ground, broke it open with her trunk, blew the powder out, remoulded it and popped it back into her mouth. She did, however, like some medicines. As I kissed her goodnight, she reached into the top pocket of my shirt and pulled out a new packet of Setlers which she swallowed whole with relish.

Over the next few days we crossed heavily wooded highlands which in some places were as high as three and a half thousand feet, to Keonjhar, the capital of this large hilly district. The rocky ground, called laterite or iron sandstone, was of a sombre dark reddish colour. When I picked up a stone I was surprised by its lightness and the large round holes, like those of a sponge. All ancient temples, forts and palaces in Orissa are built with this stone, and, mixed with gravel, so are most of the roads. Our progress was slow as Tara picked her way carefully avoiding the sharp stones to prevent injuring her sensitive feet.

As we reached the summits which, from below, appeared as sharp peaks, we crossed extensive tablelands filled with green paddy in which women, wearing a colourful blaze of saris and large cane cone-shaped hats, were reaping the harvest. As the sun reached its zenith they shaded themselves under the trees, singing and combing each other's hair in the heat. We heard them giggling as we passed and they waved shyly.

'It reminds me of summer in England,' Aditya remarked.

'I didn't know you'd been there,' I said.

'Yes, in 1970. I worked in Kent, picking hops, although I didn't sit around like these girls. I worked from 5.30 in the morning until 7 o'clock at night. He was a bastard, that foreman, a real driver of slaves.'

'That's probably exactly what he thought you were,' I joked, 'fresh off a boat that had sneaked in somewhere on the coast at night.'

'I most certainly was not,' he replied indignantly. 'I hitchhiked all the way from India. But let me tell you, I felt like one the way that I was treated. I don't have many good memories of England at that time.'

'Well,' I murmured philosophically, 'here we are now, riding across India together on an elephant. What could be more apt?'

At that moment Tara shot out her trunk and grabbed a pile of paddy that was laid out to dry on the roadside. Bhim picked up the ankush and jabbed the sharp spiked end into the top of her head. She squealed, violently shaking her head in pain. I watched with fascinated horror as a large drop of blood bubbled from her skin. With a roar of rage I tore the ankush from Bhim's hand, grabbed hold of one of the ropes and swung on to the ground.

'That's it!' I yelled. 'The journey's over. I will not have my elephant hurt. You can all find your own way back.'

I stamped off down the road. Ten minutes later Aditya caught up with me. I stared at the bloody tip of the ankush.

'Forget it, Aditya,' I said. 'You can't say anything ...'

'Now listen!' Aditya shouted. 'Who in hell do you think you are? Elephant Bill? What do you know about elephants? Bhim would not use the ankush unless it was absolutely necessary. Before you interrupt, let me tell you what he told me. Tara was stealing. And I have just had to pay that poor farmer compensation. It is not Tara's fault though. She was taught these tricks by Rajpath. Many mendicants literally hold people to ransom by getting their elephants to pick up the paddy, unless the farmers pay up. Bhim has to break Tara of the habit of stealing and the ankush is the only way to make her understand.'

I sat down and stared moodily at my bare feet.

'Come on, Mark. Elephants are big powerful creatures. If you start pampering them you are in trouble. They are intelligent, cunning and deceitful. Believe me, the old man knows what he's doing. If he fails to convert her now she will only get worse.'

'All right, I'm sorry,' I said, slightly mollified. 'I guess I have a lot to learn, but one thing is for sure, you won't find me doing that. Shameless bribery with gur rather than sharp jabs with the ankush is going to be my method.'

'We'll see,' he replied. 'Just wait until you start riding her.'

We walked back to Tara who did not seem at all affected by her punishment. She was pulling up roots, smacking them against her legs to remove the earth, then stuffing them into her mouth. We climbed back on board and Bhim pointed at her head. 'See, Raja-sahib. I fix.' A small poultice of herbs was attached to the wound. 'No hurt now. Bhim sorry, but Raja-sahib must learn. Mummy learning also.'

Apart from the numerous anti-elephant machans dotted everywhere, the paddy fields that we now passed were surrounded by anti-elephant ditches seven feet deep, five feet wide at the top, tapering to about two feet at the bottom. Wild elephants are powerless to cross them except during the monsoons when the ditches silt up. Around the planted fields there were fences of twisted creepers in which wild mint grew in abundance, filling the air with its sharp aroma.

Then we entered the silent darkness of the forest and all was still again. Tara suddenly stopped, her huge ears spreading outwards. She extended her trunk upwards and moved it from side to side scanning and smelling the air.

'Haathi,' Bhim whispered. 'Close.'

Aditya reached for his camera bag. In the process he knocked it against a metal strut. With a sharp downward gesture of his hand Bhim indicated him to keep still and with another instructed Gokul to climb aboard. There was no noise, only the sound of dripping water. Then a sharp 'Tuk, tuk, tuk' split the silence and a coppersmith bird rang its alarm bell.

From the corner of my eye I caught a slight movement. A soft sound, almost inaudible, was the only indication that the foliage was being gently brushed aside. Like ghosts, three female elephants appeared and stood motionless on the road in front of us. I could feel Tara trembling beneath me. The wild elephants let out a deep rumble and extended their trunks towards Tara. They seemed much larger than her, more muscular, their bodies sculpted like sheet armour on a tank. Then as quickly and quietly as they had appeared, they disappeared.

I let out my breath and was about to reach for a cigarette when Bhim gave another of his urgent hand signals. We heard a movement, as if the grass were being crushed by some huge, unidentified force and suddenly a large male elephant with tusks almost three foot long confronted us. The tusks were not white, as I had expected, but yellow, and the tips dark from where he had been digging in the earth. Tara was trembling violently and Bhim was having trouble holding her steady. We were so close I could see the flies clustered around the tusker's mean little eyes. Without warning he rapped his trunk on the ground, emitting a terrifying sound that somebody once described as like 'shaking a large sheet of thin metal' caused by air being driven out of the trunk as it strikes the ground.

'Quick,' Bhim hissed. 'He angry. Throw bombs.'

Gokul, who always carried a permanent supply like a kid with fireworks, hurled one on to the ground. Nothing happened. It failed to explode. The tusker took one step forward, throwing his trunk contemptuously into the air, emitting a terrible shrill trumpet, as if warning us to keep our distance. It was so loud, so enveloping that one's senses reeled. I shook my head to clear it.

'For Christ's sake,' I whispered in desperation. 'Throw another.'

Leaving nothing to chance, Bhim picked up a bomb, laid it on the flat of the howdah and hit it with the ankush. There was a blinding flash, a puff of blue smoke, and when it had cleared the road was empty. We could hear the elephants crashing away through the trees, as delayed shock set in. But in that moment of silence, before terror turns to laughter, the primal energy of the absent beast still vibrated in the void. It seemed almost impossible to go forward. The silence of the jungle was no longer tranquil. It had become predatory.

'What would have happened if we hadn't got the bombs?' I asked, shaken.

'Maybe trouble,' Bhim laughed. 'Forget tell you. Mummy on heat.' He pointed to the temporal glands, two small holes from which a black viscous fluid was oozing, on either side of her face.

I remembered my amazement when I had seen an elephant's erect penis at the zoo. It was at least four foot long and as thick as a man's leg.

9

Firinghee Mahout

WE CAMPED BESIDE bubbling brooks and bathed in clear fresh water. The fodder was abundant and Tara ate well. Gokul trapped fish by making an ingenious dam-like contraption from his underpants and a hammock. Once a large black water snake became ensnared in it. We were all fitter and stronger. Aditya and I were beginning to lose our city bellies. Bhim had changed. Gone was the alcoholic ravaged face. His eyes were clear and he walked erect like a proud foot soldier. He explained it was nothing to do with the exercise but due to the good booze he was drinking. In Nandankanan, he told us, each day he drank two bottles of local hooch spiced with fertiliser to give it a kick. The pain in his stomach was sometimes so bad he was unable to walk.

We stopped that night at our most spectacular camp so far, next to an exquisite little colonial bungalow overlooking a vast, calm lake, where water swept noisily over a large concrete dam. Aditya and I went to bathe at the bottom of the dam. We sat with our backs against the cool stone as the water thundered over us, crashing past boulders into the valley below. As we walked back, something colourful caught my eye at the edge of the lake. It was a little offering of flowery garlands from which burnt incense sticks were poking out. Thick green sal trees swept up almost vertically from the lake and the ground was a carpet of crimson fallen flowers, like discarded silk handkerchiefs.

The occupant of the bungalow came out to meet us; an elderly man with a shock of wavy, white hair, wearing a smart khaki uniform on which the brass buttons gleamed. He was the dam-keeper and he had lived in this remote and beautiful place for the last twenty years.

'Don't you get lonely?' I asked him.

'I have my dogs, sir,' which were pressing up against my legs. He winked at me conspiratorially and glanced behind at a curtained window. 'Occasionally I am having company.' For a second the curtain drew back and a pretty face peeped out before hastily disappearing. 'But it is my garden that is keeping me busy. Please follow, sir. It would honour me to show you.'

It was indeed charming. Bougainvillaea spilled from the bungalow roof and night jasmine twisted round its small columns. A carefully tended vegetable patch lay on one side. On the other, surrounded by a ring of flame-of-the-forest trees, was an immaculate green lawn like a manicured croquet green on which stood an ancient Atco lawn-mower.

'I am apologising for the state of the lawn, sir,' he said regretfully. 'I now have to do it by hand. I am not able to get spare parts for my machine. The blades were worn down many years ago. I could probably be getting a Japanese one from the mining company, but they are no good. They do not understand lawns like the British do. If it would not be too much trouble,' he continued, 'could you be sending me a spare set of blades?'

'Of course,' I replied, 'if I can. It will probably take a long time as I won't be returning to England for some months.'

He smiled. 'What to do? I have all the time in the world.'

The trees thinned out alarmingly as we began to descend. Great trunks lay like slain corpses along our route, on which men worked feverishly chopping and sawing as if they were dismembering their victims. I supposed it would not be long before the beautiful forests that we had travelled through suffered the same fate. Under bridges, in order to avoid detection, villagers panned for gold, sifting the silt brought down by the rushing streams through concave boards. Aditya tried to photograph them but they hid their faces. Apparently their activities were illegal and if discovered were punishable by heavy fines.

At the village of Harichandanpur we met with Indrajit, Khusto and the jeep. The vehicle was surrounded by people, who grew to a huge crowd by the time we joined them. Sensing a reception like this, Indrajit had wisely made the camp about three miles out of the village. We tried to shake off the crowd, but by the time we reached the camp, hidden by a small rocky escarpment and surrounded by mango trees, we found ourselves hemmed in by about five hundred people. Eventually even Aditya got fed up with them and hurled a well-aimed anti-elephant bomb. The result was most satisfactory and they fled, but not too far, only as far as the rocky escarpment where they sat, patiently like hyenas.

Indrajit managed to find a couple of chickens and provided us with a very passable dinner. I congratulated him profusely, hoping that this flattery would induce further culinary prowess; our food up until then had been somewhat bland. Just before falling asleep I remembered the mimosa plant.

'What about my puja? When is it happening?' I enquired urgently of Aditya, who was cocooned like a mummy beside me.

'Tomorrow,' he said sleepily. 'It's all arranged.'

'But why tomorrow? What about the mimosa? I can't do it without the mimosa. Tara won't listen to me,' I banged on anxiously.

'Tomorrow, because ...' He replied wearily, 'Bhim has decided it is an auspicious day. And as for the mimosa, well, do you really think it will make any difference?'

'Well, yes, I believe in those sort of things now. After all, India's full of them and you are always expounding the theories of the unknown and the supernatural, and the higher levels of cosmic consciousness.'

'Far out, man,' he replied and fell asleep.

We were woken in the middle of the night by a terrible commotion. Tins were being banged, people were shouting hysterically and the glow of fire lit up the interior of the tent. Aditya and I shot out to a scene from a Ku Klux Klan film as the villagers swept across the fields with lighted torches.

'What's going on?' we yelled.

'Bhalloo,' came Bhim's muffled and bored voice from the interior of his tent. 'Mummy not crying, so no trouble.'

Aditya laughed. 'It's a bear, Mark. It's been feeding on those ground-nut fields over there. The look-outs must have discovered it.'

The bear had succeeded in attracting the crowd away from us. Apart from one solitary silhouette, the escarpment above the camp was empty. I crawled back into the tent, contented.

'Rabbits and hares,' I said, poking my head out of the tent in the morning.

'What, where?' Aditya croaked, waking up quickly.

'No, no, it's only a silly English expression which you are supposed to say on the first day of every new month, and today is the first of October. But they must be the first words otherwise the charm doesn't work and is considered unlucky.'

'Just as well,' he yawned sleepily, falling back into his cocoon. 'Today is your puja. Today you ride Tara and you are going to need all the luck in the world.'

Against a lemon-tinged dawn sky we bathed Tara in a small, deep, circular rock pool that was choked with weeds and lilies. It was so perfect that it might have been made to order. Bhim and Gokul were worried about the possibility of snakes, so we threw buckets of water over her while she stood pulling at the weeds. When the crowds began to return, Tara was saddled quickly and we set off.

Indrajit and Khusto had already left on a secret shopping mission to Keonjhar. I guessed it might have something to do with my puja. I had seen Aditya slipping Indrajit a piece of paper. They were to meet us later on that day. I was consumed with curiosity and longed to interrogate Bhim about what part I was to play in this ceremony. I was still concerned about the absence of the mimosa plant. I wanted to know everything, but Bhim seemed very detached and pushed Tara along with clinical efficiency. Fields of ground-nuts – the poor man's almond – stretched out on each side of the road, broken by small hideouts – anti-bear machans. We had left the hunting grounds of the Haathi and were in the territory of the Bhalloo. Remembering the confusion he had caused last night, I saluted the bear again.

On a telegraph wire a handsome Oxford and Cambridge blue bird with a big head and a heavy black bill chuckled as we passed underneath.

'Roller or blue jay,' Aditya exclaimed excitedly, fumbling for his notebook. 'Your luck is in, it seems. The roller is considered very auspicious because of its colour. It represents the god Shiva, whose neck turned blue when he swallowed the poison of the world.'

'Far out, man,' I quipped nastily. I was still fuming about the lack of importance Aditya had attached to my mimosa plant.

Suddenly our progress was halted. Four policemen, astride bicycles, formed a road block. One of them was holding up his hands, as if stopping traffic.

'Good morning, Mr Sands,' he said.

'Good morning, officer,' I replied bewildered. 'Have you come to arrest me?'

'Good heavens no, sir, just to escort you.'

'Escort me. Why? Are we in danger?'

'No, no, Mr Sands. Just orders from headquarters.'

'What headquarters? Whose orders?'

'Bhubaneshwar, sir. I am not knowing who, but if you are comfortable we will begin.'

I never did unravel this mystery. It was a genuine escort and a very jolly one at that. Two policemen wobbled precariously in front while the two behind swerved to avoid the contents of Tara's breakfast which thudded down in front of them at irregular intervals. Buses and trucks and bullock carts were all pushed aside as the officer blew furiously on his whistle. One felt terribly important. The police station which they insisted I should inspect was spotless and neat, with gardens surrounding the pretty white bungalow built by the British in 1927. Inside it was cool, the cells were empty; there was no crime here they told me. Hanging next to a rack of well-oiled Lee Enfield .303 rifles and a bunch of handcuffs was a curious looking object like a grappling iron attached to a long rope.

'What is that for?' I enquired.

'For drunks, sir,' the officer replied. 'Many people are drinking now because of the harvest. Sometimes they drink too much and topple down wells. We fetch them out with that.'

At mid-day we passed a long granite ridge. Bhim pointed saying, simply, 'Puja.'

At a small stream the old man and I immersed ourselves in the muddy water to cleanse ourselves before the ceremony. Then we ascended to the ridge's bleak summit. It was an eerie, lonely place shrouded in metallic clouds. The wind tugged at our clothes and the clouds moved together becoming a monstrous black umbrella.

'It's going to rain,' Aditya said suddenly, breaking the silence. 'You know this is really extraordinary, it is considered ...'

'Yes, I know,' I interrupted flippantly, 'if it rains it is considered auspicious.'

'For once, Mark,' he said unsmiling, 'just try to be serious. For some inexplicable reason the gods are favouring you. Now pay attention, for Tara's sake, and I will tell you what to do.'

The jeep pulled up on the road far below and Indrajit and Khusto struggled up the hill, carrying an assortment of packages. Indrajit unpacked the boxes. On a big metal platter he placed bananas, two coconuts, bundles of incense and small arrangements of coloured flowers. I was told to undress and my waist was wrapped in a starched white dhoti, the traditional dress of the Indian when at worship. Around my neck was placed a saffron gumcha, a cloth about the size of a small sarong, and my forehead smeared with vermilion. Bhim was dressed identically. I faced him trying to keep a serious expression on my face. This was difficult as I could feel the cold tip of Tara's trunk exploring the back of my dhoti.

Picking up the offerings between my clasped hands I made my namaste to Bhim and placed it at his feet. I repeated this three times, each time bending to touch his feet. He placed his hands lightly on my head and recited a mantra. I completed my obeisance by a gift of money, 500 rupees, adding one rupee to make the total uneven and therefore auspicious. We both faced Tara. Her forehead shone crimson with the mark of Shiva. Bhim then uttered a mantra over Tara, circling her head with sticks of burning incense. We smashed the coconuts in turn and anointed her feet with the milk.

'Raja-sahib,' Bhim instructed, 'now make mantra to Tara. Then we ride.'

Caught unawares, I closed my eyes and recited in a loud pious voice a poem by Hilaire Belloc,

> When people call this beast to mind,
> They marvel more and more,
> At such a little tail behind
> So large a trunk before.

Luckily, the boys did not understand. They smiled approvingly at what they thought was an immensely powerful English mantra. On the other hand Aditya understood only too well and shook his head in despair.

Anxious that the next and most difficult stage of the ceremony went smoothly, I surreptitiously slipped Tara a large chunk of gur.

'Please, Tara,' I whispered in her ear, 'make this easy for me. Be nice. If you are', slipping another piece, 'there is plenty more where this came from. We'll have secret midnight feasts together. I won't tell Bhim. You know he doesn't like you eating too much as it upsets your stomach.'

She rumbled quietly and squeezed her eyes together as if winking at me in approval of our conspiracy. I might as well have been talking to the moon. When I placed my foot on her lifted front leg and grabbed her ear, she shook her head violently. I found myself being swung wildly – my dhoti unfurling – backwards and forwards like a rat being shaken by a terrier, and then with a spine-jarring thud, I landed on the ground.

'Traitor,' I muttered angrily, 'the deal's off,' and smacked her hard on her trunk. She looked only slightly remorseful but the next attempt was successful, only because I was aided by Gokul who pushed giggling from below, and by Bhim who pulled sternly from above until I was settled unceremoniously on her neck. Still, on reflection I didn't blame her. If I had been used to the nimble light tugs of Bhim, Gokul and Rajpath I would react similarly to the sudden dead weight of a hundred and eighty pounds hanging like a limpet from my ear. Determined, at least, to regain some measure of dignity, I dug my toes firmly behind the ears and said 'Agit.' Nothing happened. She remained stationary, turning her head to look at me with a puzzled expression.

'Come on, Barbara,' Aditya yelled. 'You can do better than that. It's not "Aaahgit," like "Amen," it's a short command and don't mumble. Yell.'

This time I yelled. To my surprise Tara lumbered forward and we set off down the hill.

'That's it,' he shouted encouragingly. 'Keep at her. She has got to learn that you are her master. Keep your back straight, have some pride. It is a great moment for you. You are the first "firinghee" mahout.'

As if my action had met with approval from the gods, it started to rain lightly, and then mysteriously stopped.

The eight miles to Keonjhar were sheer agony, chaotic and slow. I had now changed my riding position, sitting at the edge of the howdah to work her with my heels, digging them in continuously. Then, to guide her, I flicked my toes under her ears. After a mile I felt as if I had completed the Tour de France. My legs ached mercilessly and my toes were a bleeding mess. Oblivious, Tara wandered from side to side like a hungry locomotive, stopping at bamboo groves to feed at her leisure. However much I pleaded, kicked or cajoled, she did exactly what she wanted. It was like trying to steer a bulldozer for the first time. Bhim, perched behind me, did his best, rectifying my mistakes like a patient driving instructor.

'You just need practice,' Aditya remarked nonchalantly from where he lay sprawled on the howdah. 'You can't expect to be an expert overnight. Bhim has told me it will take at least a week before she will be used to you. During that time,' he said happily, 'you will be unable to wash, sit down or sleep. And do you realise,' he continued, even more happily, 'that as you are now Bhim's pupil you will have to do everything for him?'

'What do you mean?' I grunted, wiping the sweat from my face.

'Well, for instance, you must prepare his food, wash his clothes. All sorts of things.'

'Christ,' I said bitterly. 'I've come all this way to ride an elephant only to be turned into a bloody valet. The sooner I find that mimosa the better.'

The sight of this uncontrollable elephant on which sat a cursing, wild-eyed Englishman dressed like a saddhu, caused a variety of reactions in passersby. Women quickly ushered their terrified children to the safety of their houses. Some men shook their heads in total disbelief, while others doubled over in laughter. At one village, a group of men sitting drinking tea on a 'charpoy' laughed so much that it tipped over backwards, and six pairs of thin, brown legs waved like tentacles from underneath. Bhim spent a voluble afternoon alternately satisfying their curiosity, controlling Tara and pacifying me. Eventually he got fed up. In answer to the standard question of 'Where are you going?' he would snap 'England.'

At a small roadside house an old man with a long grey beard shuffled out from inside and stopped us. He sank to his knees, prostrating himself in front of Tara while she gently rubbed her trunk through his hair. A beautiful girl in a blood-red sari with a frangipani blossom behind her ear followed suit. After washing Tara's feet with water, she presented all of us with garlands of jacaranda flowers. There was a sudden sharp cry of pain behind us. A little boy, the girl's son, ran screaming to his mother, holding a small brown hand to his face. Blood seeped through his fingers. He had been standing too close to Tara's tail, watching in fascination as she whipped it back and forth to brush off the flies. The thick, long, hard hairs at the tip had struck him in the cheek, splitting it like a melon. Aditya quickly pulled out the first-aid kit and after cleaning the deep wound, patched it with Elastoplast.

'I am sorry,' I said to the girl and the old man. 'I'm afraid it will leave a nasty scar.'

'Sorry, why be sorry?' he said quietly. 'Your elephant has done my grandchild a great honour. He has been blessed by Ganesh. He will always be lucky.'

IO

Tara's Tantrum

BY THE TIME we reached the outskirts of Keonjhar it was dark and I was both hoarse from shouting commands and exhausted. Once an old British hill station, the town lay at some elevation and for the last ten miles I had forced Tara up steep inclines. After that the thought of spending the night under canvas was just too hideous to contemplate. I went to visit the Collector, a charming, easy-going man, who immediately arranged for us to sleep in the Circuit House, built by a former Maharaja of Keonjhar some eighty years ago, which was now usually reserved for visiting dignitaries and judges.

It was a splendid, solid example of English Colonial-cum-Indian palace architecture, spoilt only by a coat of vile mauve paint. We had the place to ourselves. After chaining Tara to a mango tree in the large, walled garden, we spread ourselves out in a suite of four rooms on the first floor leading on to a spacious veranda. It was surrounded by a pretty wrought-iron balcony, furnished with old-fashioned teak and wicker planters' chairs with extending leg-rests, marble-topped ebony tables and, best of all, a large refrigerator which we quickly stocked with beer. As we sat looking out over the twinkling lights of Keonjhar, a white-coated attendant filled our glasses and looked disdainfully at Indrajit's line of dripping clothes festooned around the balcony like mourning flags. Obviously he had been used to more respectable guests.

After the luxury of hot baths and a decent dinner, Aditya and I lay out in the long chairs in the darkness.

'We might spend a few days here,' he remarked, settling himself more comfortably and taking a long pull of beer. 'We're well on schedule and it would do us all good to take a rest,' he added, noticing me trying to sit sideways in the chair.

'No, I'm fine,' I winced. 'I think we should push on.'

'As you wish. But I was really thinking of Tara. Bhim has told me she is a little under the weather.'

'What?' I said, falling into his carefully laid trap. 'In that case, we must rest.'

Like Tara with her gur, Aditya had successfully discovered my Achilles' heel. Unable to walk, I crawled over to the side of the balcony. I could just make her out, dusting herself happily while leaning up against the tree, with one back leg crossed over the other.

'Goodnight, my love,' I shouted. She turned, lifting her trunk, emitting a half trumpet, half squeak, like a suppressed sneeze. I smiled happily. I was getting there.

In the morning Aditya and I set out in a rickshaw to visit the old palace of Keonjhar which we had been told was just a crumbling empty shell. The rickshaw driver's leg muscles bulged with the effort and his breath came in short, sharp bursts as we climbed steadily out of town. Then we picked up speed, freewheeling down hills lined with shops where men made metal pots, banging them into shape with small hammers. Out of the clouds appeared a fine crenellated wall overgrown with creepers, and furnished with tactically sighted look-out turrets embellished with arrow slits. Leaving the rickshaw we passed through an ancient gateway, its great wooden doors hanging askew from rotten hinges. We could make out the ruined palace overgrown with jungle and stained green with mildew, but still showing traces of former elegance. We wandered down a weed-covered pathway, choked with wild roses and shaded by towering palm trees.

At the main entrance, guarded by a pair of heavy bronze cannons moulded in the shape of tigers, we were met by a group of scruffy young urchins who announced that they were the keepers of the palace and would be pleased to show us around. They led us into the Durbar Hall which had been capped at one time by a fine frescoed rotunda and was now open to the sky. The floor was covered in bird shit. Graffiti was scrawled on the walls: 'The world is a servant to money' and 'Life is nothing but pain'. In the ballroom, they told us, a vast crystal chandelier used to hang from the ceiling, where a family of swallows now had their nest. As we felt our way along dark dripping corridors, bats erupted around us and screeched away, brushing our faces with their velvet wings. In the Deity room a black outline was all that was left of a solid gold statue, stolen twenty years ago, and in a corner, flaking with rust, was the Royal Nagara – a huge metal war drum. Noting my interest, one of the little boys explained with the air of a professional guide that there were once two war drums covered in human skin. In warning against invading armies, they would reverberate of their own accord.

'What happened to the other one?' I asked.

'Gone walking, sir. To lake.'

Under a large mango tree, which we were told was a thousand years old, stone slabs covered a dried up spring. Legend said that anybody entering the water disappeared. Keonjhar took its name from this. It means 'spring' in Oriya.

Our young guides ushered us into a large, pretty courtyard surrounded by small pavilions. In the centre stood a marble fountain designed as the open petals of a lotus flower. The floors of the pavilions had once been mosaic and were still studded with a few remaining pieces of lapis lazuli. An ornate, gilded, empty frame was propped up against a wall, a reminder of an opulence long gone. This was the entertainment chamber where once the Maharaja had received his visitors, plying them with opium-based sherbets and sweetmeats as they relaxed on silk bolsters, while dancing girls had whirled in front of them. To make his foreign guests feel at home, the ruler had commissioned carved scenes, which still ran along one wall – a two-masted ship in full sail; a lady in European costume with a small boy in knickerbockers hanging on to her full skirts; a train puffing over a bridge. One of the boys asked as we were leaving if we wished to meet Her Highness the Rajmata.

'The Rajmata!' Aditya exclaimed incredulously. 'She still lives here?'

We waited in a small, dripping courtyard surrounded by tubs of long cactus-like plants called 'mother-in-law's tongues' and from whose shape and sharpness they have taken their name. Where once we would have been forbidden to enter we now stood – in the old zenana.

The boys reappeared carrying in their arms an old lady dressed in a simple cotton sari and scuffed rubber sandals. After laying out a strip of torn Aubusson carpet, they placed her carefully in a rickety wicker chair. Behind her, in the gloom, her attendants fluttered about like ghostly moths, their faces veiled. The boys informed us that the Rajmata was unable to speak, but she could hear and see.

Aditya stepped forward and touched her feet in obeisance. For a moment the sad eyes cleared and she smiled gently, as if remembering better times; times when the palace had bustled with activity, times of glittering banquets, the rustle of silken saris, of colour, and, above all, of respect. Now she was reduced to this, a proud old woman left with nothing. A wave of great sadness swept over me.

The boys' devotion to the old lady was touching. No one looked after her now, they told us angrily as we were leaving. Her relations had abandoned her. She had been robbed at gunpoint three times. Everything had been taken. They had begged her not to keep her valuables under her bed, but like many old women she did not trust banks.

'You know these western states were once famous for human sacrifice,' Aditya told me on the way back in the rickshaw. 'Traditionally, the Rajas of this state had the right during their coronations to have a man brought in front of them, whereupon they would cut off his head, and give rent-free land to his family as compensation. After the British arrived and banned capital punishment, the Commissioner, on hearing of this custom, quickly travelled to Keonjhar to put a stop to it. As you can imagine, everybody was highly upset, but the Commissioner, a practical fellow, managed to appease the ruling Raja and solve the problem. The chosen man was duly brought forward. The Raja swung at him with his sword without actually making contact and the victim collapsed on the ground feigning death. He was then ordered to disappear from the kingdom and to be very careful never to be seen by the Raja. He was in fact declared dead and the family duly compensated.'

'Typical British ingenuity,' I crowed. 'At least we did achieve something.'

Early next morning, Aditya and I were woken by a frantic Indrajit and Gokul. 'Tara escape!' they exclaimed, 'in big tank [reservoir]. Won't come out.'

'Where's Bhim?' I growled, sleepily.

'Sleeping. Drink too much rum last night, so we take her for bath.'

'Wake him up now and meet us at the tank.'

When we arrived there was no sign of Tara. The surface of the water was calm. Alarmingly, the tank was enormous. (I remembered the case of an elephant that went for a two-hundred-mile swim, island-hopping across the Bay of Bengal. It took twelve years to complete its journey and the distance between some of the islands was at least a mile.) Suddenly from the far side of the tank, the tip of Tara's trunk broke the surface, blowing a spray of water like a fountain into the air. With a trumpet of pleasure she flung herself forward like a porpoise and disappeared again, delighting the large crowd which had by now gathered around the tank.

Bhim arrived carrying a spear, the ankush, a selection of fruit and a large sack of gur. 'Not Mummy's fault,' he said angrily. 'Gokul forget chain legs. Rajpath warn.'

Gokul squeaked with indignation stating that he was unaware of Tara's penchant and if Bhim had not drunk so much this never would have happened. Aditya calmed them down before a fight broke out, suggesting they should concentrate their energies on getting her out.

Standing in the shallows, Bhim started calling Tara, a banana in his outstretched hand. She immediately reacted, came surging across the tank to stop a few yards from the bank. In the meantime, as Gokul could not swim, Indrajit, armed with the spear, had managed to circle behind her. He waited, treading water frantically with the tip of the spear aimed at her backside. As she came a little closer and reached out her trunk, Bhim retreated, enticingly. She came closer still, almost into the shallows. With a quick lunge, she whipped the banana out of his hand, popped it into her mouth and reversed into the water. Turning to face Indrajit, who had been almost swamped by the wave, she blew a jet of water at him, performed a kind of elephant back-flip and surged away, trumpeting triumphantly. The audience applauded deliriously.

This ploy was repeated a number of times. All were unsuccessful. Finally Bhim turned to me. 'Raja-sahib call Mummy.'

Aditya had gone to call the police to see if they could disperse the crowd that were not helping matters. He returned with one policeman who upon seeing Tara cavorting in the water, tucked his bamboo cane under his arm and settled down to enjoy the fun.

I followed Bhim's instructions. 'Tara! Tara!' I yelled authoritatively, waving a lump of gur in my hand. 'A dhur! A dhur! Lay! Lay!' The people watching howled with laughter on hearing my accent. Some of them mimicked me accurately.

Again Tara came quickly across the lake. At the sight of the gur, she placed two large front feet on the muddy bank. I gave her a small piece and then as quickly as possible, grabbed hold of one of her ears to try swinging up on her back. She turned quickly. For a moment I was pulled through the water like a beginner trying to water ski, letting go as I swallowed a mouthful of dirty water. I started to swim back, gasping and choking. I felt something long and sinuous encircle me, and like a lifesaver rescuing a drowning man, Tara pushed me forward, depositing me in a wet bundle in the shallows. She trumpeted again and looked at me mischievously before returning to her watery playground. 'Mummy no come now,' Bhim stated. 'We leave her. Mummy come out when cold.'

That evening, almost twelve hours later, I was sitting on the veranda of the Circuit House when Gokul shouted excitedly, 'Tara coming!' Looking down, I saw her trotting happily into the garden. At last, I thought, thank God for that. Unfortunately our troubles were not over. Each time Bhim and Gokul tried to shackle her, she backed away, after ripping the chains from Bhim's hands and throwing them into the air.

We tried the old food trick. One of us fed her while the other tried to snap the two front chains together. It failed. After shutting the garden gate, we drove her into a small area surrounded by two walls. We advanced on her purposefully, shouting 'Baitho, baitho!' jabbing the spear into her back legs. She charged at one of the walls, almost demolishing it. Slightly stunned, Tara stood quietly for a moment. Seizing his chance Bhim quickly scrambled on to her and took control with the ankush. Gokul then chained her. She looked unusually remorseful, squeezing her eyes shut when I rapped the end of her trunk with a small stick.

Tara's tantrum was over, but I couldn't be angry for long. After all, it was Sunday and Gandhi's birthday. It was a holiday and she deserved some fun.

II

Death in the Jungle

WE HEADED NORTH-WEST into the state of Mayurbhanj, traversing a high plateau towards the great tiger sanctuary of the Simlipals. To our left, a few miles from the Bihar border where it looped down to its most southerly point, lay the ancient city of Kiching, in the tenth and eleventh centuries AD the capital of the Bhanja kings.

Having waited so long to ride Tara, I now dreaded it, the pain was so great. To ease the stiffness in my joints, I walked. We passed a procession of men carrying a small bundle wrapped in straw and strung from a long pole. A police chief idled slowly in a jeep behind. We stopped to talk with him. The bundle contained the body of a young tribal girl who had been found early that morning raped and mutilated by the roadside. Tara became increasingly fidgety as if the sight and the smell of this morbid situation was utterly distasteful to her.

Curious, I asked Bhim whether he had ever known an elephant to have eaten flesh. He shook his head vehemently, then narrowed his eyes as if searching for something that had happened a long time ago. Reluctantly, he recalled an incident. It had happened during a state occasion. A Maharaja was being carried in a silver howdah, on the back of a ceremonial elephant, ridden by its mahout. Suddenly the elephant snaked its trunk back, grabbing the mahout's leg and pulling him to the ground. As in the old days, when in certain states in India executions were carried out, the elephant stomped on the mahout's head, splitting it like a ripe melon. Gathering the gory contents in his trunk, it had blown out a bloody spray, spattering the Maharaja. Shocked and outraged, the Maharaja immediately ordered the elephant to be destroyed. The other mahouts, however, begged him to reconsider. This mahout, they told him, had for many years treated the elephant with the utmost cruelty. The Maharaja, passionately fond of this favourite elephant, believed their stories and spared it. The elephant never misbehaved again.

'There was one situation in which an elephant did actually eat a human being,' I told him. 'It happened in a zoo in Switzerland many years ago.' Bhim looked at me with disbelief. 'This elephant called Chang was punished for misbehaving and confined to his stable. Chang had a great admirer, a young girl who was so upset that she broke into the zoo overnight to feed and console him. She did not return home. In the morning the elephant keepers found traces of blood on the floor and, lying amongst the fodder, a human hand and a toe. On further investigation Chang's droppings revealed her undigested clothes, hat and handbag. The keeper persuaded the authorities to spare the elephant's life but some years later Chang grabbed his keeper and battered him to death against the bars. Chang was then destroyed.'

'Pah!' Bhim uttered contemptuously, spitting out a thin red stream of betel juice, and, leaning forward, covered Tara's great ears. 'No listen Raja-sahib, Mummy. He telling bad things.'

About eight miles from Joshipur, the point of entry into the Simlipals, I got on Tara and we joined a busy trunk road which straddles the continent from Calcutta to Bombay. The harder I was on her, the better she behaved and Bhim told me that I was beginning to make progress. My main problem, however, was avoiding the trucks that thundered by perilously close. I spent a tiring day digging my big toe under her right ear and shouting 'Chi, chi,' to turn her on to the verge. Once there, progress was even slower. It was lined with trees. At every one she helped herself to the overhanging branches, ripping them off and plucking the leaves, then stripping the bark before moving on to the next. Determined to put a stop to this greed, I banged the blunt end of the ankush repeatedly on her head. She simply shook her head and took no notice, occasionally showing her mild displeasure by blasting me in a fine spray of spittle.

She was none the less beginning to earn her keep. A number of the trucks that passed us would stop. The co-driver would stretch out a hand and place a coin in the tip of her trunk which she would then curl upwards and deposit the money on her head. Blessed by Ganesh for a safe journey the drivers would clasp their hands together, make their namastes and move on. Sometimes her trunk would shoot through the open window, almost demanding payment. When we reached Singada, our pockets jingled with coins. We now had established a way of financing our journey. Rajpath had taught her well.

A large weekly market was taking place at Singada. I threaded Tara through the mass of humanity and animals, causing a stampede. Bullocks and goats knocked over food stalls and Tara liberally helped herself to the spoils. Soon our jingling pockets were empty as we forked out compensation. Squatting in small groups, tribal women radiant in brilliant red and blue saris were selling 'handia', the local hooch, handing it out in coconut shells. Anklets jingling, others weaved through the crowds replenishing supplies, their smooth, strong, braceleted arms supporting large terracotta gourds on their heads. Everyone appeared to be drunk, throwing around their hard-earned money liberally, enticed by the miracles that were on offer.

Two travelling Rajput medicine doctors, wearing bright red turbans over strong thin aquiline faces, excitedly advertised the virtues of their wares which lay coated with flies in small trays in front of them. Most popular were the aphrodisiacs – dried intestines of snakes, toads' feet and a particularly strong brew of cobra tongues and boars' semen. At another stall a large crowd gathered round a man surrounded by baskets containing many different kinds of snakes. The crowd gasped as he rolled up his sleeves. Taking a snake's head, he forced its mouth open and plunged the fangs into his arm. Writhing in mock agony, he tied a bright red thread just above where the snake had struck, and then slowly straightened his arm. Miraculously he was cured. The threads, he extolled to the crowd, were blessed and stopped the effects of the poison instantly. He was a good salesman and business was brisk.

Short of Joshipur we stopped at a roadside tea-house. A dazzling array of trucks was parked outside. A small wiry man with slanting eyes, his face a deep ruddy colour, engaged me in conversation. He was Nepalese and a co-driver on one of the trucks.

'Take me with you to England,' he pleaded. 'I will be your bodyguard. I am excellent at fighting.' He pulled up his shirt exposing a livid lumpy scar that ran from his navel to his right nipple. 'I killed the man who gave me this,' he said proudly. 'These people,' he continued contemptuously, gesturing at some tough-looking characters who were sitting drinking tea, 'are weak. Nobody can match a Gurkha.'

'I don't need a bodyguard,' I replied. 'You see I have an elephant.'

'Ah, in that case you are in good company. It is not my lucky day.'

As we entered Joshipur, a motorcyclist wearing a uniform, goggles and a leather aviator's cap, slowed down, gave us a curious look and then drove on. He then stopped, turned round and passed us again. He repeated this manoeuvre several times, as if unsure of something. Finally he shouted, 'Are you Haathi from Konarak?'

'No!' Aditya yelled back. 'We are the Haathi from Calcutta. The Haathi from Konarak be arriving later.'

'More Haathis arriving?' he said puzzled.

'Yes,' Aditya said airily. 'Tomorrow one from Delhi and then another from Bombay.'

'Oh, goodness me, this is most confusing,' and the man raced off.

'Bloody officials,' Aditya laughed, 'that's fixed him.'

Joshipur is where one actually enters the park, but it is from Baripada, the capital of the state of Mayurbhanj, some forty miles away, that the permissions are granted. Through the window in the office I noticed a powerful radio.

'Would it be possible to send a message to Baripada?' I asked politely of a young bespectacled forest officer.

'It is not working,' he snapped nervously. 'Park closed. No one allowed in.'

'But your brochure', I argued, 'informs one that the park opens on the 1st October. It is now the 5th.' There was no answer. Two mystified Australians, who had come all the way from Delhi, were still waiting after four days to see the game park.

'We are wasting our time, Mark,' Aditya said. 'Indrajit should drive us to Baripada and we will find the man in charge. Maybe we can contact the Maharaja for whom you have a letter. He might be able to help. In the meantime, Bhim, Gokul and Khusto can stay with Tara.'

When we reached Baripada we discovered that the Maharaja was 'out of station' and the forest officer had disappeared, 'gone to the market', we were told. Through local information we found out the reason. There was a man-eating tiger abroad and it had just killed somebody in the south of the park. No one was allowed in. Desperate that we should cross this great game park, whose beauty had been extolled to me from the beginning of my journey through Orissa, I telephoned the authorities in Bhubaneshwar. I pleaded and pushed. The park was enormous, I argued. Over three thousand square kilometres. It was unlikely that I would bump into the tiger. Finally, we were granted full permission to go anywhere in the park, but only by jeep, not with the elephant. Reluctantly I agreed. It was better than nothing but I felt sad that I wouldn't be able to share this wilderness with Tara.

We waited three hours for the forest officer, a tall man with a limp handshake, who seemed anxious to be rid of us, issuing a letter immediately and nervously avoiding any reference to the man-eater. On the way back to Joshipur we stopped to stretch our legs at a roadside tribal shrine. Effigies of cows and horses and two black granite elephants stood garlanded by night jasmine. An old pandit came out of the shrine and blessed us. In the darkness Aditya and I looked at one another.

'Are you thinking what I'm thinking?' he said.

'Yes,' I replied.

We opened the letter and studied it under the jeep's headlights. It was addressed to the officer in charge at Joshipur.

> I talked with CWLW at ten p.m. today and he confirmed our earlier decision re the pet elephant will not be allowed inside Simlipal. They may keep the elephant at Joshipur. Accompany these persons in park jeep to Chahala and Barehipani but avoid Jenabil because of the man-eating problem. But do not tell them this. The roads are not OK. Tell that.

'But the people who collect honey from those sheer rock faces are deeper in the park. We'll miss seeing them,' I said. We had been told about them in Bhubaneshwar. Their methods of collecting honey were spectacular and unique to the Simlipals.

Indrajit came over and Aditya translated the contents of the letter. He was silent for a moment. 'Perhaps we lose park jeep in jungle,' he shrugged. 'If lost must go where we can.'

The next morning Indrajit, Aditya and myself left the camp. Earlier I had asked Bhim if he would like to come, but he wanted to stay with Tara. 'Mummy unhappy both Raja-sahib and Bhim go away three days,' he said. 'One day okay.'

The park jeep escorted us into the Simlipals. It was like entering another world; a world that had been untouched for centuries. The tracks were overgrown, lined by tall sal trees. The air was fresh after the monsoons. In sunny clearings peacocks stood motionless, fanning out their glorious feathers, and high above them mynah birds chattered noisily. At intervals we would catch the flash of gold and white and a spotted deer would turn to look at us before picking its feet daintily through the undergrowth. Everywhere was the evidence of elephants, old and fresh droppings littered the road. In the 1986 census four hundred and fifty elephants had been counted and as many as ninety tigers.

Through a bower of orchid-lined trees, we arrived at Chahala, an old shooting lodge of the Maharaja of Mayurbhanj, now converted into a tourist camp. It was gothic in design with vaulted ceilings and large open fireplaces. It had been painted a hideous violet and green. Surrounding it was a deep anti-elephant trench and beyond, strategically placed salt-licks for game. At five o'clock the next morning, as the mist still hung heavy in the air, we watched bison and barking deer approach the salt-licks, followed by a small herd of elephants, including two babies who held their mothers' tails with tiny trunks. From the distance came the deep cough of a tiger. The animals moved away quickly, the little elephants squealing in alarm.

From a raised log cabin at Barehipani, the source of the Buldha-balanga River, we gazed across a wide gorge and watched a thirteen-hundred-foot waterfall thunder beneath us. In Hindi 'barehi' means thread and 'pani' water. In the dry season, only a thread of water falls like a single silver arrow. The old forest ranger complained bitterly about the elephants. Every week, he told us, they destroyed his garden. Most years the log cabin had to be rebuilt because wild elephants rubbed their sides against the thick wooden poles. I thought sadly of Tara. How she would have loved this paradise where elephants roamed free, untouched and undisturbed.

As there was no news of the man-eater, our guides thought it safe to take us to Nawana, the village of the honey collectors. We descended from the hills crossing wide grassy meadows, alive with wild flowers. On the outskirts of the village, we parked the jeeps and entered a small mud-walled courtyard. It was empty except for a young man with one leg. The villagers, he told us, were far away on the other side of the park taking honey from the tree bees. It was only during the winter that they collected from the rock bees. I was bitterly disappointed.

'How is the honey collected?' Aditya asked him in Hindi.

'It is a dangerous business, sir. We lower ourselves on thick vines down the rock faces in which the bees make their nests in small caves. When we find a nest we light a torch and throw it in. The bees come swarming out and we collect the honey.'

'Don't you get stung?'

'Sometimes, sir. But we smear our bodies with herbs and always chant our mantras before work. On a good day we can collect twenty-five kilos of honey.'

'What happened to your leg?' Aditya asked, I thought rather impolitely.

He smiled ruefully and rubbed the stump. 'It is our wives, sir. They tie the vines on to trees at the top of the rock face. There they stand guard. Unfortunately,' he added, 'my wife liked another man. It was a long fall. I was lucky.'

I told the park rangers that I wanted to talk with the villagers when they returned from collecting honey. They agreed to let us stay at Nawana. They would return in a few hours to collect us.

'You want to go Jenabil? Now chance,' Indrajit said excitedly after they had left. 'Maybe seeing tiger?' Aditya and I looked at each other nervously.

'Well, why not?' I said to Aditya after some deliberation. 'We've missed the rock bees and we've come all this way. Let's go.'

The track was overgrown and from the absence of tyre marks nothing had passed this way for months. A tree blocked our way. Struggling to lift it we disturbed a herd of wild elephants feeding nearby, camouflaged by the solid green wall of the jungle. The ground shook as they crashed away, trumpeting wildly. At Jenabil the tourist lodge was empty. In the small village Indrajit found a man who knew where the tiger had killed. At first he was reluctant to take us, but with the promise of a healthy reward, he agreed. I told Indrajit to ask him whether we might catch a glimpse of the tiger. The man looked astounded and launched into an urgent tirade.

'This is not a joke, sir,' he replied angrily. 'This is a big, male tiger. It was a man-eater that killed my friend, and it will kill again.' Our bravado deserted us instantly. We fell silent. The man continued. 'We are poor people, sir. We go into the forest to collect lac [resin produced by coccid insects from which incense is made] from the trees. Each day, before entering the forest, our pandit tells us which side of the road to go to avoid bagh. That day there were ten of us. The pandit told us to go to the right but my friend, Sri Ram Naik, decided he would go the other way. A few days earlier he had spotted a good healthy tree. He was a brave man and had, on several occasions, fended off bagh with his axe. It is an everyday occurrence. We and bagh must try and live together. He was big man, like you,' he pointed at me. 'He took his young son with him. His remains are still there. The police were too frightened to go in to collect them. We must be very careful, bagh is still around.'

We reached a place where an axe cut marked a tree standing by the road. 'This is the place,' he said quietly. 'We go in here. Take sticks and make plenty of noise for bagh can be sitting two feet away and you will not see him.'

Aditya and I realised we were embarking on something both dangerous and stupid. We had no guns, only elephant bombs, which Indrajit cheerfully distributed to each of us. He seemed oblivious of the danger.

We stepped cautiously into the jungle, up to our waists in thick undergrowth. Large bamboo clumps, caressed by the wind, rustled urgently, warning us to take heed. We followed the guide in single file, Aditya and I firmly in the middle. Indrajit took up the rear. At intervals the guide would stop and check his route. Finding another cut in a tree, he moved on. We yelled. We shouted. We beat the bushes, feeling naked and defenceless. We reached a clearing. The bushes were flat, the surrounding trees raked with claw marks. Pointing at the dried muddy ground, the guide indicated large round indentations, the size of soup-plates – the tiger's pug marks.

On a small outcrop of rock, a faded blood smear; then a rubber sandal, and another – they were an odd pair. Close by a torn and bloody lunghi lay rotting in the ground. Finally a skull, gleaming yellow in the pale sun.

'It was here, sirs, that it happened,' he told us. 'My friend was looking up at this tree. Bagh struck silently from the back. From the other side of the road we could hear his screams. We rushed over, but he was already dead. The bagh had him by the throat. We tried to recover the body but bagh was too big and too angry. He came at us, and we ran.' Our guide shivered as he looked up at the tree. '"O my Father I am dead." Those were his last words. His son told us.' He shivered again. 'We must hurry out of this place, sirs. It is not safe.'

I turned the skull over disturbing a colony of ants, feeding on a flap of skin. There was nothing else. The man had been completely devoured. No bones; just the skull left as a warning. I wanted to take it but Aditya stopped me.

'Leave it,' he advised me. 'It has become part of his jungle.'

We collected the remains of his things. Now a small pathetic bundle, once worn by a strong, brave man. They deserved better than to rot in the jungle; we would take what was left to the Ganges for immersion in the holy river.

Our guide took us to the dead man's house. It was empty. His family had already left, paid a compensation of 2,000 rupees. A few broken cooking pots littered the floor. Stuck to a mud wall were coloured crayon drawings done by his children; of a field, of a cow and of a man looking up at a tree, behind him stood a yellow-striped cat with a big pink tongue and long whiskers.

If the welcome I received from Tara was an indication of her affection, I was a happy man. She positively vibrated with excitement, coiling and uncoiling her trunk like a giant watch-spring, straining against her chains and uttering sneezes of contentment. For a change she did not immediately open her mouth. She simply touched my face with the wet tip of her trunk and stood perfectly still, her eyes closed, resting against me gently. A feeling of pure pleasure swept over me and then one of equal panic as in just over a month I would have to say goodbye and would probably never see her again.

Bhim wanted us to visit his family in Baripada. As we left, Tara seemed almost resentful, hurling a branch petulantly into the air. Bhim's mother and father lived in an old tiled house which stood defiantly, like an ancient spider, in an encroaching cobweb of modern buildings on the outskirts of the town. In a neat room dimly lit by oil lamps and a small cooking fire, a tall, elderly man sat erect in a rocking chair. When we entered, he came quickly to his feet belying his age, and saluted smartly. Unlike Bhim, his face was curiously unlined, almost boyish, and, apart from one rheumy eye that glittered milkily in the gloom, he seemed in the best of health. When my eyes adjusted to the darkness, I noticed his wife squatting in the corner, fussing over some pots. After offering us tea, she returned to her place, but I could feel her accusing look boring into me. She mumbled something and Bhim laughed in embarrassment.

'She worried Raja-sahib take only boy England. Never come home.'

Aditya took both her hands in his, and reassured her that this was not true. She seemed to relax a little but still continued to eye me with suspicion.

The old man was anxious to talk of the old days, and in a soft proud voice told us he had been the chief mahout of the late Maharaja and during his tenure had often been to the Sonepur Mela. There he had purchased elephants for 6,000 rupees each and had taken three months to ride them back. At one time there had been twenty elephants in the royal stables. They were so well trained that during tiger shoots they had moved so quietly not even a leaf was disturbed on the trees.

He touched the rocking chair proudly. It had been presented to him by the Maharaja when he retired. As Aditya and I were leaving, he took me aside. 'Elephants are like human beings, Sahib,' he whispered. 'They like companionship. Don't leave her for too long. Every evening before you sleep, talk to her. Tell her stories.'

To check again if the Maharaja had returned we drove to Belgania Palace. Formerly built to accommodate royal guests during the Durbar administration, it was now his home, as the original larger palace in the city had been turned into a college. Situated on a small hill with commanding views over Baripada, it was a big picturesque colonnaded building, like a grand Florentine villa, the colour of burnt sienna, approached by a sweeping drive lined with flame-of-the-forest trees and jacaranda. An ageing chowkidar received us. We settled ourselves comfortably to start with, in easy chairs on a broad loggia, and then more nervously as a large, scarred Dobermann came and joined us. 'Brook you bloody dog. Get down,' a voice boomed as Brook began to take particular interest in one of my legs. A large, balding, unshaven man, dressed in a stained kurta and a dhoti, appeared. He looked tired. Black rings circled his eyes.

'Forgive me for keeping you waiting,' he said, 'but I was just finishing my puja.' With a smile he held out his hand and enquired our names. 'Patankar,' he said suspiciously. 'That's a Maratha name, isn't it?'

'That's right, sir,' Aditya replied proudly. 'I come from Gwalior.'

'Hmm,' he mused. 'Interesting. An Englishman and a Maratha. A friend and a foe. Two hundred years ago we suffered badly under the Maratha yoke. In fact, we joined forces with the Marquis Wellesley to stop you entering Bengal from the south. One of my ancestors, Rani Sumitra Devi, the adoptive mother of the *de facto* ruler of Mayurbhanj, was honoured by the British Government in recognition of her meritorious services. You must', he said pointedly to Aditya, with an amused twinkle in his eyes, 'have had a very nostalgic journey through Orissa. Anyway, we are all friends now. Let us have tea. I will call my wife.'

It was the kind of tea that one longs for on journeys such as this; cucumber sandwiches, cream cakes and endless Benson and Hedges cigarettes (my usual brand which I had not smoked for two months). They were supplied kindly by his wife, a member of the Nepalese royal family, a beautifully coiffeured lady, smelling wonderfully of Worth perfume, wearing a pale, powder-blue sari and dashing diamanté-studded glasses. To begin with she was a little shy but when our conversation turned to shopping she became very animated, eagerly praising the merits of Harrods and other famous stores.

'Where did you find your elephant?' the Maharaja asked.

'In a dreadful place called Daspalla,' I replied.

He laughed. 'Daspalla was famous for two things. The best elephants and the most stupid people.'

I told him of our journey through the Simlipals, which had once belonged to his family. On hearing of our exploits at Jenabil, his attitude was one of horror, telling us that our behaviour had been both foolish and irresponsible. However, he was grateful for the information and for what we had done.

'Sri Ram Naik always collected the resin from which I make my own incense. I knew him well. He was a splendid man.' As we were leaving, the Maharaja presented me with a plastic bag. I opened it. Inside were pieces of crystallised bark. 'This is resin,' he explained. 'Sri Ram Naik's last delivery.'

On the outskirts of Joshipur, we met up with two female elephants, the larger resembling an old and dusty tramp, dwarfing her little companion who hung on to her tail with her trunk. Both elephants were in poor condition – gaunt, almost skeletal. They stood listlessly, not bothering to brush away the flies that crawled over their eyes, from which dripped a white mucus. They greeted Tara placing their trunks into her mouth. Standing beside them she shone – a beautiful Maharani attended by two dowdy maidservants.

'Haathi no good,' Bhim said disdainfully. 'Both no see.'

We stopped to talk with their mahouts, mendicants who were working their way south through Orissa. By November, they would return to Benares, where the elephants' owner lived, a rich pandit who kept a stable of forty elephants. The elder man sported a curling, white moustache, his greedy eyes never leaving Tara. He offered to sell us the smaller elephant for 60,000 rupees. As if to show her off, he yanked down viciously on the ankush which hung from a rusty pin, piercing one of her ears. In resignation, she simply shook her head slowly. He then offered half this price for Tara. His contemptuous proposal was met with howls of derision from us, and we moved on laughing, ridiculing his impudence.

Then it hit me. My laughter died. A feeling of cold dread swept over me. I had been offered a price: however absurd, it was still a price and for the first time I became aware of Tara's destiny. In that brief moment, the entire context of what I was doing changed. It was no longer the romantic ride on an elephant across India that I had dreamed up so flippantly – a whim to satisfy my ambitions. It was reality, however camouflaged by the colour and the beauty – it was there, hard and completely unchangeable. Tara was my responsibility, her future life lay in my hands and every step she took brought me nearer to that moment. I tried to force it into the back of my mind. But it was now there, hanging like a relentless black shadow.

12

Double Dipper

IN A MATTER of a mile, the difference between Orissa and Bihar became visible. It was like suddenly parting the leaves on the edge of a rain forest and stepping into a scorched desert. Gone was the colour, the lushness, the laughter, the languid sensuality that manifested itself in Orissa, to be replaced by a harsh, suspicious and angry terrain. It showed in the quality of the tea, the sudden absence of fresh paan, the drabness of the lunghis, the condition of the villages and, above all, in the people. Our attitude changed accordingly. Bhim and Gokul became nervous and unsure of themselves.

Soon after we entered Bihar an incident occurred that exemplified this new feeling. An aggressive, stocky man with a bald head that gleamed like a billiard ball in the sun approached us driving a large loaded cart pulled by two bullocks. In an attempt to prevent the inevitable chaos, I steered Tara off the road and faced her away from the bullocks to allow them to pass as I had done in Orissa. He shouted at me angrily to get my elephant out of the way. I had already done this, but to avoid an unpleasant scene I moved a little further, at least two hundred yards off the road. He drove his bullocks forward, whipping them with a bamboo pole, and he had just come abreast of us when they panicked. Snorting with fear the bullocks raced along the road for a few yards, flew over a ten-foot drop to land in a muddy paddy field the other side, snapped their harness and made off quickly. Unimpressed as I was with his character I could not help but feel admiration for his driving skill. From a position with bullocks, cart and driver in mid-air, he landed the contraption like a seasoned jet pilot.

Unfortunately he did not reciprocate with admiration for Tara and me. He came stomping up the bank, gathering a few villagers on the way. 'This is my village and my road,' he spluttered furiously. 'Your elephant is a menace.'

'Excuse me, sir,' I interjected politely, 'this may be your village, but a road is built for the purposes of travel. Anybody can travel on it, including an elephant which, I would like to point out, is not a menace. If you recall, I moved off the road to let you pass.'

'Unless you give me compensation of five rupees I will impound your elephant,' he shouted. If he had been more civil and not insulted Tara, I would have paid gladly.

'How do you think you are going to impound my elephant?' I demanded angrily, flicking her behind the ear. She rolled her head and moved towards him. His eyes filled with alarm as this large beast loomed in front of him. He did not reply and we moved on.

Fortunately this feeling did not seem to be constant. At Majhgaon, a predominantly Muslim village, we were entertained royally by the elders, splendid old men in dhotis with long white beards. Delighted to see Tara, they crowded around her placing coins in her trunk, and even crushed paper money. Under the impression that the bank notes might contain something to eat, Tara investigated carefully, before dropping them despondently. Clearly, when she had been with Rajpath she had not received such riches.

One of the elders, the village tailor, took me into his shop over which a sign proudly proclaimed IMAM TAILORS, MAJHGAON. PERFECT FITTING LADIES AND GENTS. GOD MAKE A MAN, WE MAKE GENTLEMAN.

'If I may say so, sir,' he said, 'for an Englishman you are poorly dressed.' Measuring my waistline, he presented me with a pair of violet bell-bottom trousers and a matching shirt. 'Now,' he said, eyeing me critically, 'you look like a gentleman.'

Indrajit and Khusto managed to find a quiet campsite that night. To celebrate the halfway point of our journey we drank a great deal of rum. Unsteady and feeling inexplicably maudlin, I made my way over to where Tara was chained. I sat down in front of her and a feeling of great sadness swept over me. It was then that I knew I could not sell her. The two blind elephants and the sight of Tara when she had been with Rajpath, convinced me. I had to find her a good home. She would never be a beggar again. I drank more of the rum, wondering unrealistically if I could take her back to England. Not to some concrete zoo but to a wonderful estate where she could retire and live happily.

Many years ago the Duke of Devonshire had faced a similar situation. He had met a lady who enquired what she could bring back for him from her travels in India. He had replied jokingly, 'Ah, nothing less than an elephant.' To his astonishment, some months later, an elephant duly arrived. It was kept in a large enclosure in the grounds of his house in Chiswick, developing an undying passion for the gardener, who put the animal to work. The elephant brushed the paths with a broom held in its trunk, picked up grass cuttings and watered the plants with the aid of a can. Its dexterity and extraordinary intelligence did not end there. The Duke's guests were entertained after dinner as the elephant pulled the cork from the port bottle and handed it to the butler. Unfortunately, like many elephants, it developed a taste for alcohol and died of consumption in 1829.

Even as I realised I was fantasising I felt a presence behind me. Aditya settled himself beside me and we gazed in silence at Tara.

'You know, Aditya,' I said eventually, 'I ...'

'I know what you are thinking, Mark,' he interrupted. 'I feel the same. She has become part of me as well.'

'What are we going to do?' I asked desperately.

'I don't know. But Sonepur will be full of elephant experts, and I give you my word we will find a solution there.' Unable to shake off the feeling of unease, I went to bed.

Suddenly, late in the night, the fly of the tent was ripped open and Bhim tumbled drunkenly inside. 'No time left,' he shouted urgently. 'Journey soon over. Raja-sahib learn ride Mummy like good mahout. I watch today. No good.' He climbed on to Aditya's back, hooked his legs around his waist and proceeded to give a demonstration of toe movements. 'Daddy now Mummy,' he cried. 'Watch good, Raja-sahib, Bhim show you.' For the next half hour Aditya's legs were kneaded and crushed and his kneecaps grazed from the pressure of Bhim's horny toenails. Eventually Bhim exhausted himself and passed out.

'At least he's keen,' I remarked to Aditya as we carried him back to his tent.

'We were lucky to find him, Mark,' he replied. 'He cares.'

We climbed back into the tent. I was just falling asleep when a long, sinuous shape slid past the back of the tent, pressing against my head, which was wedged against the canvas. I sat bolt upright and shook Aditya. There was no need. He had felt it as well. I crawled quickly towards the front of the tent but Aditya grabbed me.

'Stay inside,' he said calmly, and yelled at Indrajit to investigate. A wild commotion followed. Then Indrajit poked his head in holding something long and bloody.

'Nag,' he said happily. 'I get it' – and he held up a five-foot cobra.

It was now getting cold in the mornings. We started later and later, waiting for the sun to rise, before facing the icy cold water when bathing Tara. We travelled slowly northwards passing people preparing to celebrate Dussehra, the festival which commemorates the victory of the warrior goddess, Durga, the consort of Shiva, over the buffalo-demon, Mahiasura. Drunkenly, they lay in the shade of large trees where hooch stalls had been set up. The powerful smell of 'handia' or 'raci', as it is known in Bihar, hung in the hot air. With nose and trunk filled respectively with this irresistible temptation, both Bhim and Tara were finding it hard not to stop.

One evening we became part of a travelling circus. As we set up camp we were joined by a band of roving snake-charmers, delightful, gregarious rogues sartorially resplendent in bright yellow turbans decorated with feathers. Around their necks on beaded strings hung little leather pouches containing remedial herbs to cure snake bites. They carried their reptiles in circular, flat wicker boxes; six cobras, a krait and two lazy pythons.

Their presence attracted an even larger crowd than usual who watched spellbound as the cobras undulated hissing from the boxes and danced to the rhythm of little wooden drums. Bhim, not to be outdone by this slick showmanship, delighted the crowd further by coaxing a variety of sounds out of Tara both from her front and rear end.

Once out of the intoxication of the tribal belt, we crossed a landscape bleached white from the smoke of a large cement factory. Nearing the town of Chaibasa, we could almost have been in England, on a sharp, sunny, frosty morning. Each leaf and blade of grass was covered in a fine white powder that sparkled in the sunlight. To avoid this white wasteland we took a small back road. Spanning it was a tall wooden bridge under which a fast river flowed.

I urged Tara forward. After putting one foot cautiously down, she backed away. No inducement could make her cross it. Without me so much as uttering a command, she simply took over and wandered further up the river bank. After testing the depth she splashed over. On the other side we met a man who told us that the bridge was unsafe. It was now only used by pedestrians and cyclists. Three weeks ago a taxi driver had driven his vehicle halfway across and the timbers had suddenly splintered. Luckily he had managed to reverse to safety.

Similar incidents of an elephant's extreme cautiousness have been recorded. One was during the Sepoy rebellion in 1857. A general, riding an elephant, had been leading his army towards a bridge which spanned a deep ravine. Similarly, persuasion proved useless – the elephant refused to cross. The general, trusting his elephant's sagacity, had the structure examined, finding that the enemy had cut away the main supports.

The outskirts of Chaibasa reminded me of an English country village. In British days the town had been the centre of administration for south-eastern Bengal. We crossed green fields dotted with clumps of giant mango and taller Peepul trees. In the distance the spire of a church trembled in the heat haze; fine sturdy trees, shading broad boulevards, gave relief from the hot sun and made a passing snack for Tara. It must have been a pleasant place to be stationed. But according to the Bengal District *Gazetteers*, a Mr Rickards wrote in 1854, 'There is everything in Chaibasa to make a person want to leave it ... it has not a single attraction.' And a Dr Bell in 1868 added, 'those officers who have mastered the Ho language and have become intimate with the people like this station, but with the executive services of Bengal generally it is regarded much in the light of a penal settlement.'

At a small bank we stopped to change travellers' cheques. The manager could not understand why I wanted to travel through his state. 'When God created Bihar, Mr Shand,' he told me, 'He was in a very bad mood.'

The exquisite church, whose spire we had seen shimmering in the distance, was of the Lutheran order and still retained its original stained-glass windows. Built a hundred and eighty years ago, it had an aura of dignity and simplicity, quite unlike its Roman Catholic rival nearby, a modern atrocity glittering like a seaside fun palace, complete with an ornate grotto-like shrine in which the Virgin Mary was lit by red and blue lights. Inside, converted tribals polished an already gleaming marble floor in which the giant gem-studded cross was reflected.

As we left Chaibasa for Seraikella, where we had been invited to stay by the Raja, we stopped to watch a game of cricket played by some college boys. A fine pull through mid-wicket sent the ball skimming towards us. It stopped just in front of Tara. She eyed this foreign object with interest and then cautiously rolled it around with the tip of her trunk. Satisfied the ball was inedible she stamped on it, embedding it into the hard ground. A group of players had by now run over. They stood in front of her silently, undecided about what they should do. One of them, braver than the rest, stepped forward.

'Excuse me, sir,' he asked politely. 'Um, could we be having our ball back. It is the only one we have.'

'Of course, I am sorry,' I said confidently, commanding Tara to move back and dig out the ball. Nothing happened. She stood firmly in place, flapping her ears. I repeated the command. Again she ignored me. I dismounted, rapped her on the trunk and dug the ball out myself. 'Here you are,' I said, embarrassed and furious at her behaviour, tossing it back to them.

'Maybe your elephant is liking playing cricket,' one of them suggested with a laugh.

'Oh yes, she is really very clever.' Taking the ball back, I tossed it at Tara. She did nothing. There was a soft thud as it hit her in the centre of her trunk. I repeated the manoeuvre to no avail. Eventually, I threw the ball back to the players. 'She's just out of practice.'

'You old bag,' I whispered to her. 'You let me down. You may be a slow learner, but that was pathetic. After all you are an Indian elephant. You should bloody well know how to play cricket.'

My accusations were a little unfair. Although an elephant is slow to learn, with practice it will repeat almost anything faultlessly, just like the amazing elephant cricket team that the famous animal trainer John Grindl of Bertram Mills's Circus succeeded in coaching. In his book *Elephants* Richard Carrington records that a pair of elephants would take up their stations at opposite ends of the arena, one with a cap and pads and holding a bat in his trunk, while the other bowled. On either side four or five others were ranged as fielders. At the word of command the bowler threw the ball down the pitch and the batsman took a ferocious swipe at it with his trunk. More often than not the bat connected and the elephant would plod down the arena for a run. Meanwhile, one of the fielding elephants would stop the ball and throw it at the stumps. It took Grindl several months of patient effort to perfect his act. He began by standing in front of the batting elephant, grasping both bat and trunk in his own hands. Another man would then bowl the ball and Grindl would guide the elephant's trunk to hit it. After many hundreds of attempts, the elephant grasped the idea and hit the ball on its own. A similar technique was employed with the bowler and fielders. Thereafter there was no holding them, and they would play the game with enormous enthusiasm.

In the blistering heat the road to Seraikella stretched before us unendingly. My stiffness had now almost vanished. Hard yellow calluses decorated the ends of my toes, but the sides of my legs were blue from bruising, where Tara's great ears hammered ceaselessly against them.

I was beginning to feel comfortable with her and perhaps she with me. My self-consciousness was vanishing and I barked at her fiercely when she tried to steal paddy or slow down unnecessarily. Considering she was supposed to be a

Koonki elephant, she moved remarkably slowly and I had continually to work on her to achieve an even pace. Gradually the habits of a beggar elephant were dying and I felt she was acquiring a new pride.

En route we picked up our first hitch-hiker, a young tribal who displayed great excitement on seeing a large dead snake in the middle of the road.

'What on earth was that all about?' I asked Aditya.

'Our friend has expressed a wish that the snake would come alive and bite him.'

'What ...!'

'He believes that it belongs to the lowest caste of snakes. It is, in fact, an untouchable. Therefore once our friend bears this mark, all other snakes will avoid him.'

We dropped off our logical companion on the outskirts of Seraikella. By the time we entered the town it was dark. Power-cuts added to the confusion as Tara picked her way with uncanny sureness, waving her trunk constantly as a blind man uses his stick. Elephants are short-sighted animals and rely on their remarkable proboscis to sense rather than see their way. At one moment we padded silently in a complete black-out, the next we found ourselves in the middle of a busy, brightly lit street. At the sudden sight of this huge animal, bicyclists fell off their machines and passersby shouted in alarm. A man on a brand new red Vespa suddenly swung out in front of us.

'Welcome to Seraikella. I am relation of the King of the princely state of Seraikella. Excuse me,' he added with an embarrassed laugh, 'that is not quite correct. I am relation of the ex-King of the ex-princely state of Seraikella. Please follow me.' Guided by this curious outrider, we made our way through a maze of twisting streets eventually arriving at a pair of large wooden gates, which were thrown open.

Waiting in the palace courtyard were the Raja, a plump, bespectacled man, and his younger brother, tall and elegant, who spoke perfect English. The Raja performed a small puja and anointed Tara's feet. Then he pointed to a huge, ancient frangipani tree, the roots of which were embedded in the wall, almost as if they had started life together. He told us we could chain Tara there. Bhim made a closer inspection of the tree and shook his head.

'Excuse me, sir,' I said to the Raja, 'my mahout does not think this tree is strong enough. I am afraid my elephant will destroy it.'

However much I appealed, the Raja insisted that it was the right place, telling me that the tree was five hundred years old, sturdy and particularly auspicious to the family, making it essential that Ganesh should rest there. As we followed the Raja and his brother, I heard the crack of the first branch being snapped off contemptuously.

Through a narrow porchway Aditya and I were led on to a spacious lawn where the Raja suggested we pitch our tents. He then disappeared to watch television and we settled down to talk with his brother.

I was interested to hear that Seraikella and Kharsawan, a neighbouring principality, were the only two states in all of British India that were never required to pay taxes to the British. In 1793 a friendship treaty had been signed between the ruling Raja and the East India Company in recognition of Seraikella's protection of the Company's salt industry, by preventing salt smugglers from entering the kingdom. Aditya was more pleased to hear that the treaty was also granted in connection with the help that the Raja's armies had supplied to the British against the ferocity of the Maratha invasion.

Then the Raja's brother spoke about the Chhow dance. Seraikella is famous for this dance, which is performed in honour of Lord Shiva. Now, the Chhow is almost completely organised and financed by the Raja's brother, himself a leading dancer, who has taken his troupe to London, Paris, Rome, Munich and New York. All the dancers are male. All wear masks. The choreography requires that the dancers should express the moods through the limbs alone, since if the mask is discarded, the face then becomes the major focus of attraction. The Raja's brother had arranged for us to see a performance – a dress-rehearsal only, he apologised – in the village of Govindpur.

We left the boys to put up the tents and drove with the Raja's brother to the village. In the mud courtyard of a farmer's simple home, the dancers were dressing for the performance. Lying incongruously among the terracotta milk urns and the cows, were big steel costume trunks covered in colourful stickers from grand hotels in Italy, England, Germany and other European countries. The dancers, all clad in costumes of exquisite finery, coloured their hands and the soles of their feet with vermilion, their faces now obscured by painted plaster masks. Surrounded by cattle stalls and lit by kerosene lamps, we were entertained to a superb display of the Chhow dance. Through the movement of the feet alone, as they leapt, turned and gyrated to the rhythms of the drums and other instruments, the dancers suggested not only the more traditional legends but also brought to life their own humble, daily occupations, such as fishing and hunting.

In the Peacock Dance, the young dancer managed to convey all the vanity of this colourful bird by moving only the upper part of his body to emphasise the extended fan of tail feathers. Another, dressed as a bee, seemed actually to hover, vibrating the sequinned wings attached to his back, as he darted around yet another dancer dressed as a flower. Sometimes, in this particular dance, the wings are made of stone, so one can imagine the stamina required.

What impressed me most was the avid concentration of the village audience, particularly amongst the small boys watching. I have found many times, when attending a dance in other remote areas, the audiences' concentration centred rather on the tourist, or the click of the camera. But here Aditya and I were totally ignored. The small boys' eyes were glued to the scene in front of them and, like young critics, they applauded a fine move or criticised a mistake.

On returning to our tents on the palace lawn, we discovered the boys in a state of considerable excitement. They were all vying for the attentions of the maidservant to the Raja's wife, a deliciously attractive young woman, who was heartlessly teasing them. All through the evening, I had received reports of how she had given Gokul and Khusto a 'dipper' and then Indrajit a 'double dipper'. Even Bhim, distracted for a change from booze and Tara, joined in, announcing firmly, to the derision of the others, that she obviously preferred older men as she had given him a 'triple dipper'. It all sounded somewhat pornographic until Aditya discovered that a 'dipper' was nothing more than a wink. The whole game was later put to an end by the Raja's wife, who banished the girl to her room.

Early the next morning I fetched Tara for her bath. Where once had stood a five-hundred-year-old frangipani tree and a wall, now lay a mass of splintered branches and crumbling stonework, occupied by an elephant with an innocent expression on her face. I unshackled her and headed for the river. Luckily, as it was the first time I had taken her alone to bathe, she was very quiet, almost lackadaisical, and behaved impeccably, but I was still very much on guard against her sudden pranks.

The River Kharkai was wonderfully clean and swirled its way across smooth, round boulders, having started its journey at the waterfall at Barehipani in the Simplipals. We waded into the cool, refreshing water. Tara sank slowly down on her knees, allowing me to dismount, and then rolled over happily on to her side. For an hour, I scrubbed her from the tip of her trunk to the end of her tail. Exhausted, I stretched out on her stomach and took the sun while she lay quietly, half submerged, beneath me. Around us a group of men went about their morning ablutions without concern, speaking softly to avoid disturbing us.

I rode her back to the palace, where I found a forlorn-looking Bhim standing nervously behind the Raja, who was surveying the damage. I apologised profusely.

Although I could see he was both astounded and quite upset, he assured me that it really did not matter. In another five hundred years, he told me, another tree would stand there. After all, he added, it would be something that he could tell his grandchildren.

He garlanded Tara with flowers from the fallen frangipani tree and we left. On our way out I noticed Indrajit looking anxiously at a high window in the turret of the palace. It opened slowly and a slim hand darted out dropping a single orange marigold. Indrajit picked it up and placed it carefully behind his ear. 'Double dipper,' he said happily. 'She like me the best.'

13

Full Control Ceremony

WE STARTED THE steep ascent of the South Bihar highlands, leading to the great ranges of the Chota Nagpur Plateau, which eventually wind downwards to the flatlands of the Indo-Gangetic plain and our final destination of Sonepur.

The gradient became progressively steeper, our path often blocked by boulders which had been swept down the hillsides during the monsoons. In places we were confronted by fallen trees, which Tara threw aside like twigs. In the early morning, the narrow tracks, lined with lantana bushes, became a tunnel of sparkling cobwebs filled with fat, black and yellow spiders which, being venomous, terrified me. Tara decided that a straight line was the best approach, and I spent hours wielding the ankush, brushing the spiders out of my face and then panicking as I felt something crawling down my bare back.

The sal forests were being systematically destroyed by the local villagers, for cash and for new fields. In deep valleys between the hills, the remaining topsoil and the trapped water yielded good rice crops and, on the peaks, where only a few trees remained, 'Jhoom', or slash and burn cultivation, was taking place.

We reached the summit of the South Bihar highlands and made camp, affording a fine view of the Chota Nagpur plateau, a watery blue massif in the distance. The tribals of this area, the Bhumias, are a wild and shy people, hunters who rightly claim that the forest belongs to them. Animists with long flowing hair, they wore head and arm bands made from snake vertebrae and knotted red loin-cloths. Most of them carried axes instead of bows and arrows, adopting an easier form of survival. They seemed out of place in this devastated landscape.

In the middle of the night Tara trumpeted loudly. I rushed over and found her straining at her chains, rapping her trunk on the ground and then signalling with it towards some bushes. I threw a bomb into the darkness. There was a scrabbling in the undergrowth and, in the beam of a torch, I saw the bushy back of a bear charging down the hill. I felt sorry for the creature, which must have been sauntering home, self-absorbed in the custom of bears, his belly full, to doze through the daylight hours in his lair. Confronted by this enormous and enraged elephant hissing and trumpeting loudly, he probably suffered terrible indigestion.

The next day, at a village called Biribanki we disturbed a colony of bats that blackened the sky and then returned to hang like clusters of black grapes from the trees. The villagers were disappointed to find that we were unable to shoot them as we were not carrying firearms. In this region bats are considered a great delicacy.

We reached a deep, impassable nullah or ravine. Indrajit coaxed the jeep carefully but when it could go no further he doubled back and arranged to meet us in a few days at Sarwada. We loaded Tara with provisions and set off, glad to be rid of the jeep and its mechanical problems. Now I could concentrate totally on Tara.

She was refusing point blank to listen to my commands and treating me with almost arrogant disdain. In a sulk I decided to walk for the rest of the day. We had entered the Bible belt and passed neat, white-washed churches in every village. Young girls with long hair gathered in pigtails and tied with pink ribbons, wearing blue skirts, white shirts, long socks and sandals, swept the courtyards with religious fervour. Two young boys fell into step beside me. Their names were Daniel and Imai, and they told me they were converts to the Anglican Church of North India. They were on their way, they said excitedly, to attend a five-day church seminar in the town of Muru.

'What religion are you belonging to?' Imai asked me politely.

'Well, I suppose Church of England, Protestant, but I don't take it very seriously. I go to church usually once a year at Christmas.'

'Once a year?' they gasped. 'But that is very bad.'

'I don't have the time, boys,' I continued poker-faced. 'You see, nine months of the year I live in England where I like to beat my wife, and when I go away I chain her up and come to visit my elephant. I never beat my elephant, though.' (Not much, I thought.) 'All men beat their wives in England. And drink. And do other things,' I said suggestively. 'Would you like to go to England?'

'Oh yes, sir,' Imai replied. 'Very much. I would like to see the beatings and drinkings and other things. In fact,' he continued wistfully, 'in our village we used to ...'

'Imai,' Daniel said sternly. 'That is enough. We will make a report of this at our meeting.' As we parted company, he turned and shook my hand. 'Sir,' he said sombrely, 'you may have a fit body, but you have a cracked mind.'

Completely out of context with the surrounding landscape, high upon a hill stood a magnificent red brick church with a high circular turreted spire. It was the Church of the Immaculate Heart of Mary, first constructed by Belgian missionaries in 1874. As the community grew and more money became available, the church was finished in splendid style in 1910.

The padre invited us in for tea, but banned Tara, who could easily have fitted underneath the large entrance. Instead she poked her trunk through the open window while I fed her a continuous stream of biscuits. It was light and airy in the nave, where the ceiling soared two hundred feet. The vestry walls were lined with clocks. There must have been fifteen or twenty of them, all showing different times – even a cuckoo clock which would chime wheezily and shoot out a rusty spring. As we were leaving, the padre pointed to the large collection of pouches attached to long wooden poles.

'Isn't it wonderful,' he announced in a condescending way. 'The people are so poor here that they are unable to give money. Instead they fill the pouches with rice.'

'Alleluia,' I said, and walked out.

We met up with the jeep near a village called Keora, where again people were celebrating the festival of Dussehra. Revellers lay unconscious at the side of the road, in ditches and the wisest in the comfort of small paddystacks. One man, more steady on his feet than most, hung on to Tara's tail, begging for a cigarette. Aditya gave him one which he promptly tucked behind his ear. He then stumbled forward in front of her and lay down and begged for another. Bhim shifted his feet fractionally behind Tara's ears and she reached down to grab the back of the man's trousers and dangled him in the air. By the perplexed look on his face, he seemed unsure of whether he actually was being held aloft by an elephant or simply having a drunken hallucination. He let out a scream of terror, whereupon she deposited him gently on the side of the road.

We pitched camp beside a wide, marshy lake filled with wild duck and surrounded by mango trees. Before eating, Bhim approached me holding something in his hand. It was the illusive mimosa plant.

Gently I took the plant from him, staring at it reverently. So this was what I had been anxiously searching for for hundreds of miles. I was a little disappointed.

I had expected something more exotic, instead of this lifeless green sprout that resembled a common weed. But, when I brushed its tiny fern-like leaves with my finger-tips, the plant became alive, the leaves closing rapidly – touch-me-not. Excitedly, I realised that in my hand I was holding power. The power that could tame an elephant. Bhim broke into my reverie: 'Raja-sahib. Now have mimosa. Now do "full control ceremony".'

The full control ceremony! This was my final puja. The puja that would turn me into a mahout! I ran down to the lake, bathed myself, combed my hair and put on my dhoti and gumcha proudly. When I returned to the camp Bhim presented me with a small ball of gur, wrapped in this precious plant.

'Well, I'm ready,' I said enthusiastically waiting for directions.

'This is your puja, Mark,' Aditya said. 'Between you and Tara. It's entirely up to you what you pray for, but after you have finished, feed her the offering.'

'OK,' I said. 'Just a moment.' I dashed into the tent and retrieved my copy of *The Elephant-Lore of the Hindus*. Turning to the chapters on 'Favourable marks' and 'Marks of characters' I knelt down in front of Tara and whispered, 'Oh, beloved Tara, who trumpets with a roar like clouds full of water. With sparrow-like honey colour eyes. Whose reddish trunk tip is as radiant as red lotuses. Whose back is long and curved like a bow. Whose temporal bosses are hairy, and large, like the swelling breasts of a lovely woman. With broad ears, jaw, navel and pudenda. With copper coloured lip and palate. You, that are beautiful, who has an odour like the white water lily, sandalwood, orange tree and lotus. Whose face beams and who has the cry of the koil [cuckoo]. You are blessed with the character of the god. O princess you are worthy of a king.'

'What did you recite this time?' Aditya asked. 'Humpty Dumpty?'

I ignored him and solemnly placed my offering of gur into Tara's mouth. She rolled it around inside for a moment narrowing her eyes at me, as if making a decision. Satisfied, she swallowed it, and reached out to touch my face with her trunk. Then she farted loudly. By the terms of the puja, the moment she swallowed that gur, she had accepted me as her master.

'Got you, you old bag,' I said triumphantly. 'Now you'll listen to me. Just you wait and see.'

I sat down for a while and watched her. I now felt I knew her inside out. Immediately she confronted me again with my own ignorance, proceeding to do something so clever, charming and human that it left me speechless with admiration.

She rummaged amongst her fodder and selected a suitable branch. Holding it in her trunk, she stripped the leaves away and began peeling the bark back. For a moment I thought she was simply going to feed. Instead after discarding the bark, she broke the branch into four separate lengths and laid them out in front of her. She selected one and sharpened it to a point against her chains. Satisfied with the shape, she began to clean methodically between her toenails like a manicurist, digging out the dirt, then wiping the tip of the stick in the grass. Her beautification complete, she blew spittle on her toenails and buffed them with the end of her trunk until they gleamed blackly. I later found out from Bhim that there are sweat glands between an elephant's toes. It is essential they are kept clean to prevent clogging.

Male elephants 'in musth' have been known to use the same process to clear the temporal glands, which can become blocked with discharge. On occasions, certain rogue elephants that have been shot have been found to have a broken piece of twig jammed tight, like a cork, into both glands. Some experts surmised that they had been driven mad by this and, unable to remove the blockage, had turned aggressive.

The next morning, my confidence unlimited, I decided to attempt the expert's way of mounting an elephant – by the trunk. With a certain panache, I grabbed both her ears, placed a foot solidly on her trunk and shouted authoritatively 'Utha! Utha!' I don't recall much about the next few seconds – just a slight sensation of air passing quickly under my lunghi. Then to my surprise I found myself sitting firmly on her neck.

'You see,' I said triumphantly to Aditya. 'That's due to the mimosa. I'm now the master.'

'Except that you are sitting on her back to front,' he replied acidly.

'That's just a small matter. I'll correct it in time. You see, I had my eyes shut. The most important thing,' I said smugly, 'is that I did it. You're going to try it next.'

Accompanied by Gokul, we plodded down to bathe in the lake. Wading into the shallows, Tara obligingly lifted her leg so that I could climb off.

'Chain her front legs, Gokul,' I said.

'Chains? No chains. Raja-sahib forget,' he squeaked. 'Wait, Gokul fetching.'

I stood beside her, holding on to one flapping ear. She looked out at the tempting flat surface of the lake and with almost an apologetic shake of her head, she whirled round and ran squealing into the water, surging across it like a stately liner, much to the annoyance of the ducks who took to the air in a flurry of beating wings.

'Come back you bloody nightmare,' I yelled. 'Come back at once. I feed you! I spoil you! I honour and praise you! and still you insist on making me look a fool. When I get you out of there things are going to change.'

Grabbing the ankush, I plunged into the water and swam out towards her. I circled behind her, jamming the ankush hard into her fat bottom. 'Move, you tub of lard,' I spluttered, treading water frantically. Whereupon she disappeared. Moments later I felt my backside being prodded. I whirled around and managed to clamber on her back, holding tightly by both ears. With a squeal of delight, as if I was now her new playmate, she dived, and I found myself being bounced along underwater as she tiptoed along the bottom of the lake. My ears began to pop. Remembering what Bhim had told me about an elephant holding its breath for the same length of time as a man, I somehow held on. Just as I thought my lungs would explode, we surged upwards, taking great gasps of air.

'You see, fatso. You cannot …' and before I could catch my breath, down she went again. This time I had to let go, spluttering to the surface. She popped up a few yards ahead and looked mischievously at me. 'All right, Tara, enough's enough. I'm going for help.'

I swam to the shore. She followed me closely. As I climbed out she looked sad that the game was over. Shaking with rage and cold I marched into the camp where Aditya and Indrajit were having breakfast.

'The all powerful mimosa,' Aditya crowed, and both of them collapsed in laughter.

'Where's Bhim?' I demanded. 'He's coming with me. And so are you.'

'He can't swim,' Aditya remarked, 'so what the …'

'I'm quite aware of that,' I replied icily. 'I'm going to use my lilo. He can lie on it with the spear and we can push.'

It would have been an odd sight anywhere, but on a remote lake in the middle of Bihar, it was a miracle. Drunken Dussehra celebrants shook themselves from roadside ditches and haystacks, rubbing their eyes in amazement, as if their hangovers could not possibly account for the sight. Passersby stopped and stared, and I heard the church bell tolling as if gathering people to see this unusual spectacle.

Bhim was decidedly sceptical about the lilo. He prodded it suspiciously, but I convinced him that it did float. Lying down gingerly, he held the spear firmly ahead of him, and we pushed out into the middle of the lake. Tara came whizzing over, fascinated by this new arrival. Poking the lilo, she flipped her trunk underneath it tipping Bhim into the water. The old mahout disappeared in a wash of bubbles. Aditya fished him out and, ignoring his protests, rolled him back on. With Bhim as the central attack, we closed on Tara, in a kind of 'V' formation, jabbing the spear continually into her legs and backside. At last we began to force her towards the shore.

'Boat sinking,' Bhim shouted anxiously. Indeed it was, and water began to lap over the sides.

'Hang on, Bhim,' I yelled. 'Just a few more yards.' Tara, perhaps realising that this was no longer a game, lumbered out of the water and raced at full speed towards the camp.

'Leave her to me,' I said firmly, following her. For the next two hours we played a kind of cat and mouse game. Unable to resist the large chunks of gur that I held enticingly in my hand, she would trot forward and slowly push out her trunk. I would remove the gur and with the other hand, in which I held a thick piece of rope, whack her as hard as I could. She would rush off squealing, bursting through the camp, scattering tents and pots and pans. In the end, her greed proved greater than her patience and, with a look that said 'the game's up', she stood meekly while I chained her front legs together. As I locked the final link, a bedraggled Bhim reached over my shoulder and punched her on the trunk.

'Now Bhim shoot Mummy!!' he raged. 'Like soldiers shoot great tusker, Ganges, dead, in water!'

We managed to calm him down, but it was only after he had finished the better part of a bottle of rum that he finally told the story.

The elephant, a big old tusker called Ganges, belonged to the Maharaja of Puri, the Gajpati – The Lord of Elephants. Ganges was a splendid, gentle animal, cherished by the family, being used only for the most important ceremonial occasions. The town of Puri is situated on the coast of Orissa, and early each morning the elephant's mahout, dressed in a red uniform, rode him to the beach where the fishermen would be unloading their night's catch. The mahout would make a selection for the palace kitchen and then Ganges would carry the fish back in his trunk. At the beginning, Ganges had clearly indicated his displeasure by refusing to perform this task. Being a herbivore, the stink and slime that cloyed his sensitive organ would have been most distasteful. However, being a disciplined elephant, and, no doubt goaded by vicious jabs from the ankush, he eventually carried out his duties punctiliously. One day, his dignity badly bruised, Ganges decided he had suffered enough. Throwing down his noxious burden, he charged at a tree, intending to smash his mahout in the overhanging branches. Somehow, the mahout survived the impact and hung in the tree until the elephant moved away. Ganges returned to his stable in the palace, where the Rajmata, the Maharaja's mother, as was her habit each morning was waiting to feed him. Alarmed by the absence of the mahout, she called for help. Obviously very disturbed, Ganges broke away before he could be chained, and rushed through the heavily populated streets of the town, where, amongst the crowds, he singled out and attacked passersby who were wearing red. Fortunately, only three people were killed and he finally came to rest in a nearby lake. By now, his mahout had returned, announcing that the elephant had gone mad. Acting on his recommendation, orders were issued to destroy the elephant immediately. As Ganges wallowed happily in the water enjoying his bath, a squad of soldiers lined the banks and emptied their magazines into him.

'Not tusker's fault,' Bhim said, his bloodshot eyes watering. 'Bad mahout,' and curled up next to Tara to finish his rum.

'How far is it to Ranchi?' I asked Aditya.

'About eighteen miles.'

'Right,' I said, climbing on to Tara. 'No stops. We're going straight through.'

Having perhaps sacrilegiously drawn a skull and crossbones with a white sunblock on her forehead, I dug my toes viciously behind her ears, rattled the ankush against the howdah and set off.

As elephants can sense fear in a human being, they can also sense anger. Perhaps it was this that vibrated through my body, transmitting itself to her, so that she finally realised I could no longer be exploited and began to respond accordingly. Gone were the days in which she would amble from side to side, travelling at her own convenience and pace. We fairly swung along. She misbehaved once, grabbing a handful of paddy from a passing cart. It was the last time she did it. Automatically, I stuck the point of the ankush sharply behind her ear. As she trumpeted in pain I winced, horrified by my actions. I felt instantly sick. Blood welled from where I had spiked her and I watched, mesmerised, as it spread over the side of her head.

'Good, Raja-sahib,' Bhim shouted from where he was walking behind. 'Now Mummy listen.'

Terrified that I had injured her seriously, I drew both my feet back into her neck, a trick that I had seen Bhim perform many times. Surprisingly she stopped dead in her tracks. Bhim inspected the wound.

'Not problem, not problem,' he consoled me. 'Not need medicine.'

But I was beyond consolation. After cleaning the wound with Dettol I stuck a large patchwork of Elastoplast over it, which she inspected suspiciously with her trunk before ripping it off, and throwing it on to the road. The blood had already dried, and I spent the rest of the day anxiously brushing away the flies.

We climbed steadily, up the southern fringe of the Chota Nagpur plateau. Cultivation surrounded us. There were no trees. This area had never recovered from the ruthless exploitation of the timber demands during the Second World War. We made camp under a large iron-girder bridge a short distance from Ranchi, the major city of this region.

The next day Aditya and I left by jeep to visit Ranchi, accompanied by a young crime reporter who had come out to meet us. He told us it was a relief to discuss elephants rather than murders. Bhim and Gokul in the meantime would make their way slowly around the vast town's outskirts towards Pisca, near where we had been invited to stay with the sister of a friend from Delhi.

In earlier times, the salubrious climate of Ranchi had induced many Europeans to settle, and going by the sumptuousness of the former Government House, they were determined to live well. About four hundred labourers and two hundred masons were employed in the construction of Government House. The woodwork was executed by Chinese carpenters. Portland cement was used as mortar. The floors and ballroom were lined in teak and the card-room in marble. The gardens, designed in an Italian style, were filled with imported plants. Once a town of great character, Ranchi was now almost completely industrialised, with the dubious honour of having the highest crime rate of any city in India.

We called on one of Ranchi's most venerable characters, a charming old Anglo-Indian lady called Marie Palit. A wildlife expert for thirty years, she had observed tigers from a tree-house she had built in the jungle. Now a sprightly eighty-five years of age, she told me she had started life in London, where she had studied to become a beautician and hairdresser in an establishment called 'Dolls', before marrying one of India's most eminent surgeons who had received the OBE. Her house was named 'Cobwebs'. When she had first moved to Ranchi some seventy years ago, the track leading to it was a tunnel of silken threads and she had been loath to disturb the occupants. Over tumblers of sherry she dreamily recalled a misty morning when the Duke of Gloucester, 'a charming man on a beautiful horse', had ridden over from nearby Government House to breakfast with her. A keen shikari in her day, she had shot everything except a hippopotamus and a man.

In the meantime, Bhim and Gokul were nearing Pisca. When we caught up with them, Tara was meandering from side to side, occasionally giving a small lurch as she tripped over one of her legs. Both Bhim and Gokul were asleep on top of the howdah – Gokul spread out on the back with a happy expression on his face – Bhim with his head on his chest, snoring loudly. As I got out of the jeep, Tara greeted me with a happy, lopsided grin and sneezed loudly. A blast of distinctly alcoholic breath hit me in the face. They were all drunk, having been to a roadside party. Bhim explained that the hot sun had made her thirsty, and it was impolite to let her drink alone.

Through some pretty, stone park gates, we could see a drive lined with jacaranda and wisteria bushes, at the end of which we could hear the sound of laughter and chinking of glasses. We had arrived at Tikratoli Farm. Our hostess was sadly in hospital, but her son was there to greet us.

On the lawns, surrounding a picturesque ornamental pond filled with rare species of water birds, a group of well-dressed men and women sat in easy chairs, chatting and draining the last of the pre-luncheon cocktails as if at some country weekend in England. We felt we were entering a dream as the scene was so alien to the vagabond life that we had led until now.

'Good afternoon,' I said as normally as possible, taking off my sweat-stained turban, as if I had arrived by car with my suitcases in the boot. I yanked hard on Tara's ear to stop her helping herself to the abundance of carefully planted shrubs.

'Welcome, Aditya and Mark,' he said expansively. 'Everything's arranged. Park your elephant over there,' he pointed to a suitable tree. 'Your boys' quarters are all prepared. Would you like to wash before lunch, or just get stuck into the drink?'

We spent an idyllic two days eating off china plates, using silver knives and forks, drinking out of pre-chilled beer mugs and bathing in big porcelain baths filled with piping hot water. Our travel-stained, filthy clothes were freshly laundered. We began to feel almost human again. Tara was utterly spoiled by the children of many friends who came to meet us, and the boys had an opportunity to have a rest and check out our paraphernalia. The jeep was stripped down and tuned. Tara's pack gear, which was coming apart at the seams after the endless days of travel, was repaired and patched up for the final part of our journey.

Our host arranged a press conference. Apart from one journalist who thought I was an 'exploiter' rather than an 'explorer' and another who was amazed I had not been at school with Rajiv Gandhi, it went off well. The State Bank of India presented me with a banner which read THE STATE BANK OF INDIA APPLAUDS THE SPIRIT OF ADVENTURE. I was delighted. My association with these institutions has never been amiable.

Lured by the comforts of Tikratoli Farm and the superb hospitality of our host, I was tempted to stay longer, but I could feel complacency setting in. It was time to move on. McCluskiegunge, Hazaribagh, the vastness of the Indo-Gangetic Plain, and the mighty Ganges lay ahead.

14
McCluskiegunge

> Our Homeland At Last. A Wandering Homeless Community Will Now Have A Real Home. The Land Of Our Dreams Is Now A Reality. Our Proud Possession Where We Can Get Together And Build Our Very Own Farms And Vineyards, Our Towns And Suburbs And Grow To Be One Of The Peoples Of India.

THESE WERE THE stirring words of E. T. McCluskie, an Anglo-Indian engineer from Calcutta, in the *Colonisation Observer* of 1933, after he had leased ten thousand acres from the Maharaja of Chotanagpur to build the first independent community where Anglo-Indians could make a life and grow into a nation through unity and co-operation. In its heyday, just before the war, three hundred Anglo-Indian families had settled in the colony, living in style in splendid villas surrounded by extensive farmlands. They brought with them every modern amenity; a departmental store, a club, a dispensary, a nursing-home. There were schools and churches. Hockey, football and cricket were played. Lavish balls were thrown, where the ladies rustled in the latest fashions from London and Paris, while gentlemen in black ties drank their chotapegs of whisky on the manicured lawns and discussed 'home', some of them never having been there. When the war came many able-bodied men, especially of the younger generation, joined the armed forces, never to return. Others fled in fear of reprisals from the Indians when the country was on the threshold of independence.

All that remains today are a few of the original families, possibly twenty-five, still living in their mansions, full of pride and spirit, cherishing memories of better times.

P. D. Stracey, himself an Anglo-Indian, wrote a somewhat harsh, but accurate, account in *Elephant Gold* of what the Anglo-Indian represented:

> I was a typical product of British Indian stock and western upbringing, an Anglo-Indian or Eurasian, as a person of mixed descent is known in India and further east. My community had evolved as a distinct entity among the many races of India and came to occupy a particular little niche in which traditions and respectability of a smug British pattern kept us aloof from the country in which we lived and earned our bread. We had once been of great service to the conquerors of India in building up the various strata of administration at a time when it was impossible to find enough people for the jobs which call for toughness and enterprise, but suddenly we had fallen on evil days. Still, we were the second line of British power, always at call to suppress unrest and disorder and to prop up authority during the period of India's struggle for independence. We were 'little Britishers' largely unconscious of the anomaly of our position, completely unaware of the indifference with which we were treated by the Europeans on one side and the Indians on the other, although, no doubt, in the eyes of the world, a tragic product of British rule in India.

Before 1946, the colony was for Anglo-Indians only and the land could only be sold to them. Subsequently, this restriction was removed, with the result that settlers sold their land, usually for a very low rate, to entrepreneurs who, over the years, have developed their own small businesses into thriving factories. When the wind blows from the north-west, the fumes of the largest open-cast coal mine in Asia blows its filthy, choking, smoke over McCluskiegunge. The mine is spreading greedily, and if nothing is done to preserve this unique settlement it might well become part of this monstrous pit.

McCluskiegunge, or the 'Gunge' as residents call it, spreads over nine square miles of heavily wooded, undulating hills, through which the Calcutta–Delhi railway line runs. In the old days, McCluskiegunge was filled with retired railway personnel and was a main stop on this line. Now the station is but a watering halt for the coal trains heading north.

Perhaps the term Anglo-Indian represented what I was when I rode into McCluskiegunge, an Englishman on an Indian elephant. For two days I found myself going through a series of mixed emotions: nostalgia, sadness and anger but, above all, admiration for the spontaneity and honesty of these people, who went out of their way to make me feel at home.

I passed white gateposts bearing the names 'Greenacres', 'Park Grange', 'The Nest', 'Honeymoon Cottage', 'Mini-haha' and 'The Gables', which led up carefully tended driveways in which labradors and terriers bounded down to greet me with their vigorous barking.

'Come here, Flossie, sit.'

'Jungo, you bloody dog, get down.'

'Sorry you weren't here a few days ago, you'd have met Podge, he got bitten by a cobra. Still, old Eva's bitch has just had a litter.'

'Come in, come in. You must be hot. I've just made some fresh lemonade, or perhaps you would like something stronger. Not a bad vintage this year. You can have guava, mulberry or elderberry wine. I suggest you try guava. It's got a bit of a punch.'

Stepping into the cool of verandas, luxuriant with bougainvillaea, I was shown proudly around the houses. Some were decorated with English chocolate-box covers pinned to the walls and prints of horses and foals, puppies and Beefeaters. Others were more elaborate. Heavy sideboards were littered with silver frames, holding faded photographs of friends and relatives back home. In the room of one house sat a Steinway grand piano, its woodwork eaten by white ants. Over well-trimmed hedges residents wearing panama hats and clutching secateurs and watering cans or baskets of cut roses, gladioli and large wild daisies, discussed their gardens and worried about the condition of their orchids.

I took tea with Mrs King, an elegant Eurasian lady, clad in crisp coloured chiffon scarves. Over cucumber and cheese sandwiches she told me that she had suffered a heart attack yesterday morning. That same afternoon she had destroyed a snake's nest containing thirty-eight baby cobras, but was determined to be up and about today to greet me. She sweetly presented Tara with a garland of marigolds. Nearby, I visited Mrs Matthews, a widowed Indian lady, whose husband had served as a doctor in the British army before spending most of the war as a prisoner of the Japanese. She now receives a pension from the British government in recognition of his services. Mrs Thipthorpe posed for a photograph in a red wool dress and pearls, proudly clutching her deceased husband's Service and Coronation medals, while Stanley Potter, the Gunge's oldest resident, whose house was called 'Dunroamin', lent me his valuable collection of the *Colonisation Observer*, dating back to 1933.

At 'Bonner Bhavan', whose grand wrought-iron gates were designed as peacocks, I talked with Dolly Bonner, a bitter but intelligent and controversial old lady who told me that she had never fitted in, warning me against visiting certain other residents who were not 'the right sort'. She really believed that between the time of British departure and Independence, the Anglo-Indian, who she considered to have a superior education and a greater understanding of administration than most Indians, was better prepared to take over the reins of government in the new India.

I lunched with Jit Roy, once a keen shikari, who brought his own food in a tiffin carrier – roast pork and potatoes. He carried his toothpicks in a small leather wallet. Immaculately dressed, he wore flannel trousers, silk shirt, a paisley foulard, and highly polished brown brogues, topped off by a brown felt trilby. A fan of the BBC World Service, he had requested a song on 'The Pleasure's Yours', in memory of an old friend and resident of the Gunge who had died recently, and had heard it was to be played for him that very night. Later I drank with Brian Callaghan, a former boxer who had trained in the same gym with Henry Cooper. He had returned to the Gunge to look after his sick mother.

The next day, at a pretty white bungalow nestling in the hills, we met one of the area's richest residents, eighty-eight-year-old Ida Mukerjee, an Anglo-Burmese lady who with a thirty-year-old boyfriend seemed determined to enjoy life to the full. Passionately traditional she had ostracised her son for marrying a local Adivasi (tribal) girl, forcing him to eke out a living selling fruit at the station. Four years ago, their young son had disappeared on a coal train heading north. Perhaps he had chosen this way of life at the station, in the hope that one day his son would return.

Kitty Teixaira, once regarded as the most eligible and beautiful girl in McCluskiegunge, had been dealt an equally tragic destiny. Her mother, a domineering possessive woman, had deprived her of any education, forbidden her to mix in society, keeping her a virtual prisoner. On her mother's death Kitty had inherited a large decaying property and no money. She had since married 'a bad sort' and, like Ida Mukerjee's son, struggled to make a living by selling fruit at the station. We met her there surrounded by three dirty snotty-nosed kids, a strikingly handsome young woman, with a haunting sing-song voice, dressed in a ragged sari.

'Keep away from Clem Mendonca,' we were warned. 'He's mad.' But we paid no heed, determined to meet the Gunge's most eccentric resident. It was dark when we arrived at the blacked out and silent house. We banged on a heavy iron grille, recoiling instantly as two snarling shapes sprang against it.

'Who's there?!' a voice growled from inside.

Nervously we introduced ourselves, as a powerful torch beam blinded us. Bolts were drawn back and a head poked out cautiously, scanning left to right. 'You haven't been to see those bastard Camerons?'

I shook my head. Earlier I had been told of a terrible feud that raged between the Cameron brothers and Clem Mendonca.

'Come in,' he said. 'But I'm keeping the lights out. I'll face them in the open, but I'll be damned if I'll sit like a duck in a shooting alley.'

We seated ourselves at a small table. The soft glow of a kerosene lamp illuminated an arsenal of crossbows, rifles and shotguns. Leaning against the wall was a thirty-foot aluminium boat. 'Captain' Clem Mendonca had served forty-five years in the Merchant Navy. Dapper and compact, he bristled like an angry otter. 'Glad you're not a Geordie. I'd have thrown you out. Worst crews I sailed with!'

Suddenly he jumped to his feet, crept over to the window and scrutinised the blackness outside, a pearl-handled Smith & Wesson .38 revolver appearing mysteriously in his hand. 'That's Cameron,' he yelled, and I just managed to stop him shooting Indrajit, who was smoking a cigarette. He noticed me eyeing the boat.

'I'm off soon,' he announced. 'Can't stand this place. Got to get back to the sea. No Camerons there – just you and the elements.'

The arrival of Bhim announcing that Mummy was lonely cut short our visit with Mary Morris. In five minutes, however, managing to look chic in a pink fluffy dressing-gown, this spirited elderly lady had captivated us with her wit and charm. Fortunately our paths would cross again.

A unique monument to a forgotten era, McCluskiegunge hopefully will survive. Already some influential people with the right values are starting to buy property for their retirement. This would have pleased E. T. McCluskie. He sounded a splendid man, and I found a tribute to him on his death in a 1935 *Colonisation Observer.*

> He might have built a palace grand, superb,
> Which rivalled many a Raja's rich demesne
> And revelled in a gay luxurious ease
> Like lordly Nabob. But he chose, instead,
> The better way: his fadeless name to write
> On heart and mind of a down-trodden race,
> With pen of fervent zeal dipped in gold ink

Of memory pure, eternal as the soul.
Let others grovel in mire of hoarded pelf –
'To serve' his maxim. And his deeds transformed
Lapra, waste village, into city fair –
McCluskiegunge! Fit for a worthy race
To dwell in, whose inheritors, while time doth last
Shall rise and call him blessed.

To avoid the long dull road route to Hazaribagh, we cut across the open coal mines of Ramgarh. If there was such a place as hell, this was it. Spread like some virulent rash across the landscape, the pits were linked by a roller-coaster of conveyor belts. Grinding excavators fed waiting trucks, like greedy prehistoric birds. In minutes, we were covered in a fine coal dust and were up to our ankles in black slime, choking and wheezing as the filth hit the back of our throats. It was Tara who suffered the most. Her trunk, which she continually dipped on to the track to find a safe route, became clogged with black sticky waste, which she blew out as if cleaning an old-fashioned fountain-pen.

We passed the towns of Daccra, Rai, and Bacchra, ugly places with ugly names. Crossing a glistening inky river, we washed our faces, a pointless effort, as if we had used a bar of trick soap. Brick factories, monstrous effigies to progress, belched smoke from their tall chimneys. Bhim told me that sometimes elephants were used to drag the steel cars up from the pits; his words were a chilling reminder for me of Tara's destiny. Most of the labourers were converted Santal tribals and I wondered whether they realised, when they took the good path from their quiet traditional life, that they would end up here.

After crossing the main Calcutta–Delhi railway line, we stumbled through a series of deep nullahs, and then, climbing again, reached a narrow forested plateau. As if a door had suddenly been slammed shut, hell was behind us. Along a narrow path lined with wild mint, jasmine and bridal bouquet, and alive with bird-song, we met happy groups of Santal tribals. The men stopped and offered us fruit, but the women and children, terrified of Tara, slipped quickly into the hedges. After we had passed, we saw them kneel, making their pujas in her footprints.

That night we camped close to a field of wild mustard, flanked by a clear bubbling river and a railway bridge arching gracefully over a deep ravine. It was a moonless night and in the limited radius of the firelight the area seemed to shrink to the size of a cellar, with a ceiling of stars, a wall of trees on one side and a crescent of tents, each lit by the dim glow of a kerosene lamp, on the other.

In the gloom, almost invisible, Tara stood quietly like a statue, occasionally disclosing her position by a rhythmic flapping of her ears.

Winding down off this razor's edge, in the morning we crossed the Damodar River, a roaring impassable torrent in the monsoons, but now like a mill pond. Egrets waited patiently for a passing minnow on little islands of exposed sand. The avarice of the Moghul emperors was excited by reports that diamonds were to be found in these rivers that criss-crossed the Chota Nagpur plateau. In fact, there is a legend that the Koh-i-noor diamond was discovered in the River Koel.

The track now petered out completely. Guided by two drunken tribals, Tara forced her way through thick Lantana bushes, disturbing partridge and 'jungli murghi', the Indian jungle fowl, a bird similar to a chicken but with a long tail, that explodes from its cover like a rocket. Finding the path again, we descended on to the Hazaribagh plateau, a patchwork of greens and pale golds where paddy and surguja were cultivated. In the distance to our left rose a misty mass of violet hills.

The villages were clean, large and well constructed. Courtyards filled with marigolds and sunflowers led into darkened rooms with thick mud walls. Instead of windows, there were a few strategically placed openings allowing the air to flow unhampered, making them deliciously cool. The roofs of the houses were tiled. Women were decorating the outside walls by a method of hand painting, dipping their fingers into a mixture of straw, ash and water and combing their fingers in long wavy strokes across the walls, creating swirling evocative patterns of trees and lotus flowers. When the painting dried the women would apply lime and red earth to add colour. With its tall cypress-like trees this terracotta landscape reminded me of the rolling hills of Tuscany.

Nearing Hazaribagh we encountered a small encampment of Birhor tribals. Traditionally nomadic hunters and jungle dwellers, their existence relies on the game that they can catch. They are a shy, little-known people who are now forced to change their ways due to deforestation, lack of hunting grounds – and by the lure of better housing donated by the government anxious to obtain the tribal vote. They are squat, dark and flat-nosed, similar to the aboriginals, wearing their hair long and straggly. Known as the 'leaf people', they construct their dwellings, resembling large hollow bonfires, from tightly packed leaves. If a Birhor builds a new hut, and it leaks once in two years, he is thrown out of the tribe. Masters of fieldcraft, they practise a simple and highly effective way of trapping game. For large animals, such as boar and hares, they use nets propped up on sticks, into which the game is driven, effectively entangling themselves as the sticks collapse. For birds, a small wire snare, like a noose, is used, which is carefully camouflaged by piles of leaves.

This encampment was unique, providing a contrast between those who succumbed to civilisation, living in new government-built houses, and those who still lived in the traditional leaf dwellings. The leaf house was tidy, the mud floor clean, while the government house was in chaos, pots and pans littering the floor and the wooden window-frames used as firewood.

We were accompanied into Hazaribagh by the Birhor medicine man, a splendid character carrying a sack full of oddities – lizard tongues and claws for cramps, silkworm cocoons for constipation and various roots for impotence. I saw him later selling his wares outside churches and government offices. He did thriving business, and the thought of some fat official suffering from constipation swallowing a silkworm, or dabbing his private parts with a root to improve his sexual prowess, made me very happy.

While taking Tara to bathe next morning, Gokul disturbed a nest of hornets and was badly stung. Jumping off Tara, he ran back to camp screaming. He was in severe shock, his body a mass of burning lumps. Meanwhile, Bhim went to retrieve Tara. Unaffected by the hornets that buzzed angrily around her, she was feeding happily nearby. An hour later he returned.

'Didn't you get stung?' I asked him incredulously.

'Once,' he replied smiling, pointing to a large lump on his head. 'But die, drunk. Eat Bhim blood.'

Later we drove over to see Mary Morris, whom we had met briefly in McCluskiegunge. She was staying at a large convent, formerly her family house and now a hostel for local Adivasi girls. By torchlight, owing to a powercut, we celebrated her seventy-fourth birthday over rum and fruit cake. She had been born in Ranchi and had left for London to train as a hairdresser and beauty specialist at the Mayfair Salon in Hanover Square. Having received her diploma, she had worked at grand hotels throughout Asia and became the Maharani of Jaipur's personal hairdresser. For a period in the Fifties, she worked at Steiner's in Grosvenor Street, where, she proudly informed me, her clients had included Yvonne Arnaud, Vivien Leigh, Jennifer Jones, Valerie Hobson and the Queen of Jordan. She had served as a nurse in Chittagong (now Bangladesh) during the war and escorted patients on ambulance trains from Calcutta to Lucknow. She had been awarded the 1939–45 medal, the Burma Star and the War medal.

She showed us postcards of herself as a vivacious young lady always on the arm of a handsome man, either in civvies or uniform. One portrayed her standing in front of the Taj Mahal surrounded by a large crowd of men. She laughed, her blue eyes twinkling.

'One woman with a hundred men – all to myself on a moonlight night at the Taj. Not bad, eh? Those, of course, were in what I called my salad days. Now I am just an old woman.'

'Not old, Mary,' Aditya said, 'just seventy-four and still capable of putting life into two weary travellers.'

'Flattery, my dear boy, will get you everywhere.'

That evening, Bhim decided Tara needed to get drunk. For once, it was not just an excuse so that he could join in, but because she needed a full night's sleep. She was very tired and the alcohol would act like an anaesthetic, ensuring her a long rest.

Mahouts often doctor their elephants, as we were to discover at the Sonepur Mela. Bhim prepared a mess of oats and gur in a bucket. He poured in two bottles of rum, moulded three or four sloppy balls of the mixture and shoved them into Tara's mouth. When drunk, elephants are like human beings – their reactions varying according to their characters. The naturally good-natured appear even more so, the aggressive become downright dangerous. Everybody, except myself, was dispersed. Bhim explained that although Tara would not cause any trouble, it was better she was with the two people she knew best and trusted.

At first nothing happened, then I noticed slight defects in her co-ordination. Tara always stood with one back leg crossed over the other and attempting this now, she found she could not feel her back legs at all, moving them from side to side with a perplexed expression on her face. Her huge head fell aslant and she began to whip her trunk up and down as if it were some kind of toy. Slowly her eyes closed. She became still. One of her front legs slid slowly forward, then the other. For a moment, in a most undignified fashion, she seemed to crouch like a giant cat. Finally, with a contented rumble, she rolled over and passed out.

'Mummy have hangover tomorrow,' Bhim murmured, opening another bottle of rum. 'Better Bhim as well. Then Mummy and Bhim ill together.'

15

The Land of the Buddha

A FEW YEARS ago, the inhabitants of Hazaribagh were terrorised by a man-eating leopard, which had killed with alarming frequency. Some people surmised that the killings were carried out by a pack of wolves which had acquired a taste for human flesh by consuming the bodies of deceased prisoners left to rot outside the prison. That prison, once Asia's largest, lay to our left as we made our way towards Hazaribagh National Park.

Tara was suffering from a hangover and would not be coaxed into moving faster than a shuffling amble. Bhim stopped regularly at small canals to enable her to slake her raging thirst. I felt sorry for her. Unlike humans, she could not sweat out the alcohol. To add to her misery, she carried a full load. We were taking a short cut over rough terrain to the Grand Trunk Road where the jeep would meet us in a day or so. Barring mishaps, we would arrive on the 7th November at Bodh Gaya, where I had arranged to meet my friend, the photographer Don McCullin, who was to accompany us for the last part of the journey.

We passed slowly through a herd of cattle. Around their necks hung wooden bells, emitting a sound like heavy raindrops hitting water. We stopped to talk to the cowherd, an Oraon tribal, who showed us a selection of these bells. Each was exquisite and of a different design, and each unique in its sound, enabling him to distinguish in which direction individual cows had wandered. Aditya offered to buy one. The cowherd refused saying that he would offend the soul of the tree from which he had fashioned the bell, having asked for the tree's blessing before cutting it down. The tree is always chosen and felled on a Saturday and the bell then made on Sunday. During its creation, no clothes can be worn.

In Assam and Burma, elephants also wear bells so that at night, when the elephants are set free, their mahouts can keep a check on their whereabouts.

However, blessed with that ingenious proboscis, they fill the bells with mud and wander undetected, stealing into cultivated areas to enjoy night-time feasts.

In the afternoon I tried to push Tara along at a faster pace. She kept crossing the road from side to side, as if selecting a special path. At first I thought it was due to her hangover but, after scolding her a few times, I realised this was not the case. At intervals, her trunk would swing up and deposit a pile of small rocks on to the top of her head. Then I spotted the reason for the obstinacy, which she was deftly showing me. The path was littered with small, sharp stones, and her slow, cautious movements were simply to avoid injuring the sensitive soles of her feet. This little show of sagacity gave me more pleasure, perhaps, than anything I had experienced with her so far. She had taught me so much.

We camped beside a dirty nullah, amongst a grove of date palms near a village called Kotapisi. Due to lack of firewood, I commanded Tara to uproot a thick palm stump which proved more obstinate than I had expected. She bent it backwards and forwards using one of her front feet, then loosened it more by using her full weight, pushing with her 'bushum'. Working steadily, she eventually ripped the stump out of the ground with a great tug of her trunk.

In the middle of the night Tara escaped. Following a trail of flattened grass, from dragging the uprooted date palm that she had been chained to, we found her in the middle of a lush paddy field. It was as if a combine harvester had been at work. Half the field was neatly cropped. We did not blame her. It was becoming difficult to satisfy her appetite, and unless we paid exorbitant prices, the owners of trees were reluctant to let Gokul cut fodder. We sat up all night, taking turns to watch her, leaving early to avoid an ugly scene. A final descent through dense jungle, from which we could hear the roar of traffic, led us to the Grand Trunk Road which links Calcutta and Delhi.

Delighted by the smooth surface of the tarmac, Tara swung along at a grand pace, unaffected by the diesel fumes from passing trucks that choked us and made our eyes water. It was a great shock. Suddenly the stillness of the forest, the clear bubbling rivers, the dazzling bird life and the colour and joviality of the tribals became a distant memory.

We stopped at a tea-house for breakfast. As the trucks pulled in and out, a few drivers threw coins at Tara's feet, which she picked up and placed on her head. We needed the money badly. It was Sunday and the banks were closed. The jeep had not as yet turned up. We were going to have to work the road. Bhim was indignant. Mummy was not a beggar now, he exclaimed angrily. She was a princess, and he refused to have anything to do with our venality, not that we had collected much by the end of the day.

'Generous bunch, the Biharis,' I remarked to Aditya as I glared at another passing truck, like a hitch-hiker glaring at a motorist who has failed to give him a lift.

'It's not so much that,' Aditya explained, 'it's because they don't want to stop. There are so many ambushes on this particular stretch that even the truck drivers are frightened. You wait until tonight. You'll find it difficult to sleep when the trucks join into one long convoy to cut down the risk.'

It was dark by the time we met up with the jeep. Suitable camp-sites were now impossible to locate. We ended up in somebody's back garden, just off the highway. Aditya was right – the constant rumble of passing trucks, the hiss of air brakes and the crunch of badly changed gears continued all night. To pass the time, we placed bets on Tara's height. Using the old method, we had to guess how many times a piece of string would wind around her foot (which was approximately twenty-four inches) to equal her height, taken at the highest point of her back. Khusto and Indrajit said twenty, Gokul, twelve. Aditya and myself, convinced we were correct, knowing Tara stood at seven and a half feet, from the sale document, stated five. Bhim, with a quiet chuckle, guessed two, a decision met with howls of derision. Extraordinarily he was correct. Twice around Tara's foot made her eight foot, just a few inches off her actual height. Going by Khusto and Indrajit's judgement, she should have been sixty feet tall.

The next day we continued along the Grand Trunk Road, the flowing artery of India that for many years has been the conveyor of life and legend.

'Prostitutes,' Aditya exclaimed excitedly, pointing to a colourful encampment of painted ladies sitting by the roadside, their eyes thick with kohl, smoking hookahs and chattering like mynah birds. 'Probably on their way to the Sonepur Mela.'

Seeing Tara, they cooed, whistled and called to us suggestively to join them for breakfast. They stroked my arms and legs, playfully pulling at my hair and smelling me. They wrinkled up their noses in distaste and started giggling.

'It's your fair skin, Mark,' Aditya explained, laughing. 'They find … how do I put it' – trying to be polite – 'you well, different. As a firinghee, they're saying you must be rich. So they're discussing prices. But because you are riding an elephant they are prepared to give you a discount.'

Bhim stood beside Tara, with a lascivious expression on his face, whispering to her quietly. Quite suddenly, her trunk shot out, grabbed the hem of the nearest sari and pulled sharply upwards. The girl gave a shriek of alarm and struggled to regain her modesty.

'Teach Mummy new trick,' he said happily, 'for Mela. Undress women.'

Aditya reprimanded him severely, but Tara was now enjoying her game. Like a dirty old man with wandering hands, she moved towards another victim and explored her bottom with the tip of her trunk. I stopped her immediately. Although I had heard stories of amorous elephants, this was going too far. Not only was she of the same sex, her actions were both unchivalrous and coarse, quite unlike the elephants that Edward Topsell described in *The Historie of Foure-Footed Beastes*. 'At the sight of a beautiful woman,' he wrote, 'they leave off all rage and grow meeke and gentle.' He then describes how an elephant in Egypt was once passionately in love with the same woman as the poet Aristophanes. The elephant annoyed the poet by putting apples into the girl's bosom and dallying with her breasts. Another elephant loved a Syrian girl 'with whose aspect he was suddenly taken and in admiration of her face, stroked the same with his trunke'. Apparently the girl reciprocated his affections and made him 'amorous devices with Beads and Coral and Silver and such things as are grateful to these brute beastes'. When the girl died the elephant was overcome with grief and expired romantically at her side.

At Doohi, a dirty crossroad town, we turned off the Grand Trunk Road heading northwards for Bodh Gaya, Gaya, Nalanda and Rajgir, the great centres of Buddhism. The countryside was monotonous; little irrigated fields criss-crossed by narrow footpaths and rough roads leading to endless shabby villages. Few trees lined the road, and most were protected by barbed wire. When Bhim took Tara to drink in scummy pools, he would bend down and whisper in her ear. 'Walk careful, Mummy. Water dark. Maybe hurt feet.'

At each village, young boys set off fireworks and exploded crackers, prematurely celebrating Diwali, the festival of lights, which takes place on the darkest night of the year, when Laxmi, the goddess of wealth and prosperity, is worshipped. As it is the beginning of the New Year, Diwali is particularly auspicious for traders and businessmen. People flock to the shops and markets to stock up with new merchandise. A man with a brand new bicycle, a machine totally foreign to him, hopped past us with his right foot on the left pedal. Another man, more expert, his bicycle loaded with planks of new wood, hammers and nails, was on his way to his brother's home west of Patna, where, he told us, a huge earthquake had caused terrible destruction and death a month ago.

'Was your brother's house destroyed?' I asked him.

'Oh no, sir,' he replied cheerfully. 'Just turning round. Now better view.'

As we entered the outskirts of Bodh Gaya we were joined by a tall, fleshy, loquacious German girl. She exuded good health and strode along behind Tara with her enormous rucksack as if it were a handbag. I became more and more irritated by tales of her travels through India; of how she hated the filthy food, of the lack of good accommodation and particularly of 'ze dirty Indian men' who were always trying to molest her. They must have been very brave, I thought, staring in awe at the size of her red, meaty hands.

'Haw, haw, haw, haw, haw,' she suddenly guffawed loudly, pointing at Tara's rolling bottom. 'Eet looks zo zilly. Ya, like ze wears ze pantaloons.'

I had had enough of this Valkeryian chatterbox. Nobody insulted Tara. I saw red.

'Listen Fraulein,' I hissed, 'it might interest you to know that according to the Sanskrit scriptures women were supposed to emulate the walk of the elephant, because it was so sensual, and,' I added, pointing to her large, wobbling posterior encased in a pair of tight shorts, 'you could learn something from that.'

She stopped dead and went crimson in the face. For a moment I thought one of those great meaty hands would come crashing down on my head.

'Vell,' she spluttered. 'I have never been zo insulted in my life. You ... you, focking Englishman,' and, with a swing of her pigtails, she stomped off.

I was still seething with anger as I rode into Bodh Gaya. The peace of the Buddha had not yet settled upon me, as I was confronted by a mass of Japanese tourists carrying white parasols, shuffling like anxious sheep in the wake of a shouting guide. A group of shaven-headed western Buddhists with sunburnt necks and arms, who wore their saffron robes self-consciously, were haggling with some enchanting Tibetan girls selling tourist knick-knacks from roadside stalls. As I came up quietly behind them, Tara reached out her trunk, tapping one of the devotees on his backside. He whirled around and uttered a strangled scream.

'Mon Dieu! Un éléphant ...!' and hurrying to get out of the way, caught the hem of his robe in one of his heavy, leather sandals. The robe unfurled quickly, exposing a tight pair of 'jockey' briefs, emblazoned with 'La Tour Eiffel'. 'Merde ...!'

I smiled reprovingly at him from my lofty perch. Clasping my hands together and bowing my turbaned head, I said 'Bonjour and Hari Krishna,' while Tara moved serenely onwards.

As we moved through Bodh Gaya towards the hotel where I had arranged to meet Don McCullin, I saw a familiar figure approaching. He was elbowing his way through a mass of pedestrians, his head down, swinging it from side to side, suspiciously clutching his stomach as if in pain. But I knew better. He was zealously guarding his moneybelt.

'Watchya, cock,' I said. His head jerked up like a turtle. A pair of eyes rounded in disbelief under big, bushy eyebrows.

'Gordon Bennett,' he growled, shading his face against the sun. 'Shand! Is that you? Who the hell do you think you are – Jesus Christ? I've seen some strange things in my life, but this takes the biscuit.'

'Don,' I said dismounting, 'this is Aditya Patankar.' They shook hands.

'Congratulations, Aditya,' Don said. 'If you have managed to survive with this lunatic, you must be as mad as he is.'

Bhim and Gokul saluted smartly. Tara, her manners impeccable, raised her trunk and trumpeted loudly in greeting.

'Hop on board,' I said. 'I'll send the boys back in the jeep to fetch your gear.'

'If you don't mind, mate,' Don said as he eyed Tara suspiciously, 'I'd rather walk for a while.'

To avoid the congestion in the town of Gaya, we followed the course of the River Phalgu, sacred to the Hindus, and believed to be an embodiment of Vishnu himself. Once it was said to have flowed with milk. We made camp on the far side, in a grove of mango trees, looking across to the old town of Gaya, a façade of ancient, greyish ghats splashed with colour as devotees came to bathe under the shadow of the great Vishnupad Temple. Far to our right, the sound of traffic crossing a narrow iron bridge rolled across the river flats like distant summer thunder.

Leaving Don to sleep, Aditya and I took the jeep into Gaya to stock up on rum. We bought lights and fireworks to celebrate our Diwali, and paid a visit to the police station where it had been arranged for my visa to be renewed. Beneath us on the river banks as we crossed the bridge, a multi-coloured carpet stretched as far as the eye could see. Bathers had laid out their clothes there to dry in the sun. Beyond, just visible as a black glistening speck, Tara was taking her bath in the shallows.

At any time Gaya is a busy, thriving metropolis: now, only a few days before Diwali, its streets were almost impassable. Like the great Maratha chief, Baji Rao, who in the mid-eighteenth century had sacked and plundered the city with an army of fifty thousand horses, Aditya drove with aggression and total disregard. Scattering pedestrians, ignoring police signals and blowing the horn imperiously, he hurled the jeep around the labyrinth of crooked alleys, shut in by high old masonry houses, many of them still loop-holed for defence against the marauding hordes. Streets were lined with shops, outside which merchants were wheeling and dealing; cotton weavers, grain dealers, grocers, carpenters, tailors, shoe-makers, blacksmiths, brass workers, silver and gold merchants, all shouting and gesticulating to the endless ribbon of passersby.

To be honest, I had been concerned about Don's arrival. Although I had travelled with him on many occasions, it is always difficult when a newcomer joins an expedition and fills one's head with news of home. I had become so immersed in this pilgrimage, so much part of India, that I wondered if I would resent an intrusion from another world. I need not have worried. By the time we reached camp Don, with his ability to fit in anywhere, had already become a cog in the machine, as if he had travelled with us from the beginning. Curious and fascinated by his slightly eccentric character, the boys took to him immediately and unable to handle the word 'McCullin' called him affectionately Meester Macleen. We dined well, courtesy of Meester Macleen and British Airways on tins of pâté, washed down with half bottles of Château-Latour.

I sat up with Tara until the early hours, waiting for that moment when she would rock slightly and then, in a slow, silent movement go down. Elephants are like horses; they get most of their sleep standing up and will lie down only when they are sure that all the world is at rest. Being immensely cautious animals they are at their most vulnerable when in a prone position. I sat in front of her, staring at her intently, wondering if in my presence she would make an exception. But she continued standing. It was not until Bhim appeared, like a ghost, and motioned me to move away that she finally sank down with a long exhalation of content. 'Mummy shy,' he explained in a whisper. 'If not see you, she sleep.'

Her repose did not last long; nor did anybody else's. I was about to enter the tent when something stung me on my foot, burning me with such ferocity that for a moment I thought I had stumbled into the glowing embers of the fire. 'I'm dying, I'm dying,' I shouted wildly. 'I've been stung.'

Aditya's head shot out. 'It's the big black scorpion. Bihar is famous for them,' he stated authoritatively. 'Don't panic, I'll get the anti-venom.'

'Oh, God,' I moaned, panicking, 'I'm done for.'

I hopped from one foot to the other while Indrajit played the beam of the torch on the ground.

'Ants!' he shouted. 'Quick, I burn.'

Returning with a tin of kerosene, he sprayed it around liberally, lit a match and the offenders were executed in a puff of blue flame. Shamefacedly, I crawled into the tent, the pain quickly subsiding.

'I have never been in such agony,' I told Aditya, who was putting away a large, long needle with an expression of some regret.

'They're only fire ants,' he laughed. 'They must be attracted by your sweet English skin.'

A sleepy growl came from Don's tent. 'You never change, Shand. Bloody hypochondriac.'

The next night we celebrated our own Diwali beside a trickle of a river, under a dramatic backcloth of the Rajgir Hills, circumvented by an old, fortified wall on top of which glistening white in the moonlight stood a modern Buddhist stupa.

The boys surrounded the camp with little clay pots, in each of which flickered a candle. Tara was garlanded and fed bags of ludoos. We gorged ourselves on a young goat which Bhim had prepared. Sweets were eaten, sparklers lit, and we toasted the New Year with quantities of rum, after which a highly dangerous display of fireworks took place, engineered by Indrajit. We took refuge behind the jeep as rockets snaked at low level through the camp and mortars exploded deafeningly overhead. Long after Aditya, Don and I had retired, the festivities went on. They finally ended in a furious but good-natured contest between Khusto and Bhim to see who possessed the biggest penis. We heard them staggering around drunkenly as measurements were taken with a piece of string. According to Indrajit, it was won, unfairly, by Khusto. Being the kind of person who became excited at the sight of two beetles copulating, he managed to maintain a fleeting erection. It was a merry evening and the boys enjoyed themselves. They deserved it; we had come a long way together and soon it would all be over.

16

The Mighty Ganga

RAJGIR, OR RAJAGRIHA as it was known in the sixth century, was the ancient capital of Magadha, the nucleus of the first great empire in India. The fortified wall, which we had seen the night before, was the boundary of the city, almost thirty miles in circumference. Here the Buddha himself had passed many years living in different localities. His favourite place was the Vulture's Peak, a high rocky outcrop on which he spent most of his time in contemplation. Sacred to Buddhists, Jains, Hindus and Muslims alike, Rajgir was crowded with pilgrims who had come here to worship and to bathe in its famous hot springs. It was also full of scavenging dogs and little horses pulling tourists around in gaudily decorated traps.

It is difficult to explain why elephants should display such uneasiness towards dogs and horses, considering that neither is capable of inflicting on them the slightest injury. Tara was no exception. On seeing a dog, she stopped dead, rapped her trunk on the ground and squealed in terror. According to *The Wild Elephant* by Sir J. Emmerson Tennant, Bt. – a man who was regarded by other more reliable elephant experts as prone to exaggeration:

> One instance has certainly been attested to me by an eye witness in which the trunk of an elephant was seized in the teeth by a Scotch Terrier, and such was the alarm of the huge creature that it came at once to its knees. The dog repeated the attack and on every renewal of it the elephant retreated in terror, holding its trunk above its head and kicking out at the terrier with its forefeet. It would have turned to flight but for the interference of its keeper.

Horses threw Tara into an even bigger panic. At the mere sight of their droppings, she shied violently. The moment she heard the metallic ring of their hoofs, she bolted. If Bhim had not controlled her quickly with the ankush we would have arrived at Sonepur in no time. Afterwards she stood shaking, bending her front legs in rapid succession, the effect of which was like sitting in the epicentre of an earthquake.

'Horse eat Mummy when baby,' Bhim announced with the utmost pragmatism. 'No like!'

The belief, however, that an elephant is frightened of a mouse must be an old wives' tale, for Tara had come into contact with both rats and mice on the road and had shown no alarm. The legendary J. H. Williams, probably the greatest authority on elephants, wrote in his book *Elephant Bill*: 'the idea makes an obvious appeal to the human love of paradox. But if it is true I can see no reason for it. It certainly cannot be because the elephant is afraid of the mouse getting into his trunk, since, with one snort, he could eject it like a cork from a popgun.'

For the next three days we marched north – and marched is the right word – like a small army across a desperate, barren and poor rural wasteland which eventually would lead us to the Ganges. It was fortunate that we were travelling with an elephant – admittedly a benign one, but at least her size gave our pathetic party some semblance of authority. I envied the great King of Bliss who had marched at the head of a huge army of a thousand war elephants. Still, considering the difference in military might, I felt he would have been proud of us forming a tight phalanx around Tara, armed with an odd axe, ankush and spear, and Aditya's large, metal tripod that we pretended was a machine gun.

Jeering crowds greeted us at most villages, taunting us with insults. I was riding Tara through one of these villages, followed by the inevitable mocking crowd, which I had found it best to ignore. A rock whistled through the air, hitting me on my back. Another followed, and then a fusillade broke out, striking Tara on her back legs and backside. I whirled her around and charged them in a shuffling clumsy way. To my satisfaction they fled into the safety of their village. In moments the culprits, a group of teenagers, returned. Egged on by their leader, a young man with a pock-marked face and wall eye, another rock came whizzing past, dangerously close to my head.

'Right, that's enough!' Aditya yelled. 'Let's deal with the bastards.'

Leaving Tara with Bhim, Don and I joined forces with Aditya, who was dishing out some heavy Maratha treatment to the ringleader. We grabbed another young man, but slippery as an eel, he wriggled free and escaped.

In India an incident of any kind invariably draws a crowd quickly. We were soon surrounded by a group of village elders carrying long sticks. Although we prepared ourselves for the oncoming fracas, we were surprised to discover that they had simply come to apologise. Following old traditions, they revered the elephant, but the younger generation, they told us, had no respect. Politely, they asked Aditya to release the culprit. They would deal with him in their own way.

By the time we caught up with the jeep at a village called Kachra (or appropriately 'rubbish' in Hindi) it was already getting dark. An angry Indrajit and Khusto were keeping another large crowd at bay while arguing violently with a man who they had accused of throwing a stone, splintering part of the jeep's windscreen. Deciding that this place was unhealthy, we moved on and camped on a raised rocky road, shadowed by a solitary Peepul tree, and were quickly hemmed in on either side by unfriendly villagers, muttering amongst themselves, eyeing our paraphernalia greedily.

'I don't like this situation,' Aditya said warily. 'We'll keep all the stuff in the jeep and just sit it out.'

He told Indrajit to bring out the tripod. With great showmanship, Indrajit assembled the 'machine gun' and squatting behind it, traversed the 'barrel' (one of the telescopic legs) across the crowd. They moved, fractionally. Our ploy did not seem to be working. Tara was not helping matters either. She should have been trumpeting fiercely and rattling her chains. Instead she stood quietly greeting each villager with an affectionate exploration of her trunk.

Suddenly, the crowd parted. Two tall men, bearing obvious authority, strode through.

'The local landlord, the zamindar,' Aditya whispered.

'Can I be being of assistance?' the elder of the two men boomed fiercely.

Aditya replied, 'It's these people. We have already had a few bad experiences and we are a little nervous.'

The man turned to the crowd. 'Chale jao! Chale jao!' he shouted imperiously, dispersing the people with a dismissive wave. 'My name Sri Ram Chandra Prasad,' he said, introducing himself, 'and this my son Ram Singhar. I am Thakur of Dehra. My village over there.' He pointed to a few twinkling lights in the distance. 'You are guests in my country. I bring food tonight.'

True to his word, late that evening a posse of villagers, led by the admirable Thakur, made their way across the fields with fresh bread, vegetables and water. Before leaving he extended an invitation to us to breakfast with him the next morning at his village. He would prepare green pigeon in yoghurt, a speciality of his house.

I caught a glimpse of Don's face. It was as white as a sheet. He had never been an adventurous eater.

We rode to Dehra, an oasis of white-washed houses surrounded by a grove of date trees. The Thakur proudly showed us his cattle, after which we climbed the stairs of his large house, where a fine breakfast had been laid out; fresh naan, sour yoghurt and tea scented with ginger. Fortunately for Don, there was no pigeon. I thanked our host for his help, adding that I was overwhelmed by his kindness. He explained to me that hospitality was a tradition in his family, learnt from a good Muslim who had lived for many years in the village until partition came in 1947. 'Always make guests welcome,' the Muslim had advised. 'Even if you can only spare a cup of water, it will not make you any poorer.'

Our route from there was trouble free. Word, it seemed, had gone out. We stopped at a police station to watch the Test Match on television. The police had been informed that 'three angry men, eight foot tall, were travelling with a mad elephant'.

On the 13th of November we arrived at a main road. To the west, some fifteen miles away, lay Patna. In front of us, the holiest river in India, the mighty Ganges, lay glistening dully as the sun played on its vast caramel-coloured surface. We had travelled from the sea to the source. We may not have 'struck terror into the hearts of the people of Magadha', like the King of Bliss, but with the same pride we watched Tara drinking thirstily from the Ganges, as the King of Bliss had once watched his army of elephants and horses being watered.

It had been organised that in Patna we would stay in a magnificent mansion overlooking the river, a private museum that included among the exhibits Akbar's sword and Napoleon's bed. Lured by the majesty of the Ganges, Don hired a little sailing dhow and arranged to meet us later at the mansion.

As we approached the outskirts of old Patna, the narrow streets lined with tea-stalls, paan shops and endless bicycle repair outfits became congested. While Bhim and Gokul stopped to buy paan, I rode Tara on ahead, Aditya lolling behind in the howdah. Hearing an approaching horse cart, her huge body began to vibrate violently. Before I could do anything about it, she took off like a racehorse.

Over a short distance an elephant can achieve a high speed, and the sensation I was experiencing was aptly described by C. F. Holder in his book *Ivory King*: 'I have felt on the one or two occasions which I have been on a bolting elephant as a man must feel if bestriding a runaway locomotive and holding the funnel with the crook of his walking stick to hold it in.' Except in this case I did not have 'the crook of the walking stick', the ankush having fallen off.

'Stop her!' Aditya bellowed from behind, as we flashed past terrified pedestrians, who were scattering as all our pots, pans and kerosene lamps flew like missiles in all directions. 'I'm going to fall …' I heard a sort of thud behind me. Catching a quick glance back as I clung to the sides of the howdah, I saw Aditya rising shakily to his feet from an entanglement of tents and hammocks.

'Tara, Tara,' I yelled. 'Stop! Oh, bugger! What's the bloody word? Dit! Dat!' Finally I remembered it and screamed out the command. 'Dhuth!' Too late, I saw a bus approaching us. To avoid a headlong collision Tara suddenly swerved, snapping the posts of an empty tea-stall. We came to an abrupt halt amongst a cascading river of cups and tea-urns. Facing us, his dark face a mottled purple, was the enraged owner.

'Er … I'm frightfully sorry, sir,' I gasped, wiping tea from my chest and arms, trying at the same time to stop Tara, who was now helping herself liberally to a selection of cakes that lay on the ground. 'You see my …'

'You! you!' the man stuttered furiously. 'Everything gone, ruined, I take you to court. I am getting big damages.'

At that moment, Aditya turned up limping slightly, followed by Bhim and Gokul carrying a load of our possessions which they had recovered from the roadside.

'Now, sir,' Aditya said. 'There's no need for that. I am sure we can come to some financial agreement.' After the man had cooled down, they assessed the damage, compensation was paid and dignity restored.

'Why in the hell doesn't she behave like this with me?' I exclaimed to Aditya in exasperation as we sat on the re-packed howdah behind Bhim, watching him thread Tara expertly through the traffic. Quite suddenly the most ludicrous image floated into my mind and I began to shake with laughter.

'What's so bloody funny?' Aditya demanded angrily. 'You bloody nearly killed me …!'

'Forgive me, I'm not laughing at you, but I've just had this vision of us appearing in court with Tara.'

In his book *Elephants* Richard Carrington records that during the last century in Cleveland, Ohio, a famous trick elephant had been the star turn in a circus show. There was some argument about the elephant's maximum speed and his trainer had bet that Pikanniny could achieve three miles an hour. The matter was then put to the test. Pikanniny completed the first mile in only eight minutes. At this moment, the local Society for the Prevention of Cruelty to Animals intervened, accusing the trainer of using his ankush too much and drawing blood. When the case came up in court, the trainer subpoenaed Pikanniny for his defence. The elephant arrived at the appointed time but the court had not been built to accommodate so large a witness and he was unable to squeeze up the narrow staircase. Obligingly the magistrate agreed to take the case in the entrance hall. There Pikanniny duly took the stand. When the prosecutor asked him if he had been hurt, the elephant shook his head from side to side, and when asked if he was generally well treated, he nodded and made squeaks of assent. Whether the course of justice was altered by Pikanniny's testimony is unlikely, especially as the trainer seemed to be connected with the performance. Still, as the elephant was found to be in good health and quite unharmed, the trainer was discharged. Pikanniny was congratulated by everybody and, like a star witness, received every kind of delicacy for his loyal support.

Late in the afternoon, we reached our destination, the entrance to Quila House, built on the foundations of the fort that Sher Shah had constructed in 1541. The high, imposing iron gates were closed and remained closed, even after we explained to the old, argumentative and highly suspicious chowkidar that we were expected. But Tara had spotted a luscious grove of bamboo on the far side. She lowered her head, pushing against the gates until they sprang open, sending the indignant chowkidar flying, and trotted triumphantly through. As we rode under an impressive portico, flanked by romantic Italian stone statues and a pair of blue and white Chinese water jars standing in niches, a small, well-groomed, prosperous-looking man, wearing a smart suit, in the top pocket of which was a row of gold Cartier pens, came running out to meet us.

'Welcome to Quila House,' he said excitedly. 'I've been expecting you. I'm Bal Manohar Jalan, but my friends call me Bala.'

'Thank you,' I replied. 'But I must apologise for our discourteous arrival. My elephant is usually extremely well mannered, but she does on occasions show a certain impatience.'

'I should be the one to apologise,' he said, dismissing with a wave of a plump gold-ringed hand the angry chowkidar who had chased us up the drive. 'We do have to be careful whom we admit. As you know, Quila House is a private museum. Please choose a suitable place for your elephant.'

I nervously surveyed an immaculate sweeping lawn. In the centre was a stone fountain, surrounded by neat rosebeds, in which an army of gardeners were busily working. Beyond, more men laboured in a well cultivated vegetable plot.

'She really is a very large and greedy animal,' I said, remembering Seraikella. 'It's quite extraordinary the … er, damage that she can do.'

'It does not matter,' he said expansively. 'Plants and flowers and trees will grow again, and it is not often we have an elephant as a guest.'

Eventually Bhim found a suitable tree, covered in a bower of bougainvillaea. 'Mummy here. But flowers soon go,' he whispered nervously, looking around, overcome by the grandeur of the setting.

The jeep arrived, having collected Don from the river. Our baggage was unloaded and we followed Bala across the lawn, down some steps and through a covered walkway of flowering jasmine. In front of us stood an exquisite marble pavilion, surrounded by balconies carved like lace, by its side a large tank choked with white water-lilies.

'I hope you will be comfortable here,' Bala announced anxiously, throwing open a pair of glass doors.

One could have been entering the home of an affluent Chinese gentleman in the nineteenth century. In the bedrooms, ornate opium beds, draped in mosquito nets, were strategically placed so that one could lie and gaze out at the Ganges. Polished rosewood and teak tables and chairs, elegant in their simplicity, filled the ante-rooms. Silk wallpaper printed with oriental court scenes lined the walls, and the doors were studded with blue and white Ming plaques.

'As you can see,' Bala laughed, noticing the expressions of astonishment on our faces, 'my grandfather was fond of Chinese works of art. But this is nothing. Later I will show you the main house and the collection. You will find that he really was a compulsive buyer. Come, let us have tea.'

On the main terrace overlooking the river, we reclined on charpoys covered in crisp, white linen as attendants served us tea from a silver service. We helped ourselves to cigarettes from heavy, green malachite boxes. Behind us, glowing pink and white in the setting sun, stood Quila House, a large, handsome two-storey mansion, built in the art deco style with a long, flat roof, its side elevation a series of tall bowed windows.

Sher Shah's fort was destroyed by a huge earthquake in 1934. Bala's grandfather, Dewan (Prime Minister) Bahadhur R. K. Jalan, built Quila House in this magnificent situation after acquiring the site from the Nawab of Gaya. It was by a quirk of chance that he had managed to purchase the land. He was travelling in the same compartment as the Nawab in a train going to Patna, when they struck up a conversation. It turned out that the Nawab was on his way to dispose of this property. At the station, the Nawab's carriage failed to show, so Bala's grandfather offered him a lift. When he delivered the Nawab to his destination he fell in love with the fort and made a deal to buy it there and then.

The next morning, after bathing Tara in the Ganges, we were shown round Quila House by Bala. I could not have imagined the scale and variety of the collection that spilled from one room to another in this wonderfully eccentric private museum. Bala told us that according to the last inventory over twenty thousand items had been listed. His grandfather had started his quest at the beginning of the century, buying in Kalimpong, Darjeeling and Calcutta, and moving on to the auction houses and art dealers in London and Paris during his visit to attend the Coronation of King George V.

Ancient Sanskrit scriptures lay in cabinets surrounded by the skins of cobras that had been killed in the house. Behind a pair of eighteenth-century Indian lacquer doors, which opened silently on oiled hinges, was displayed a complete George III Crown Derby dinner service, designed in its familiar bold pattern (as the King was short-sighted). We threaded our way through suites of Louis XV and Louis XVI furniture and towering display cabinets chock-a-block with nineteenth-century export Chinese porcelain. Smaller ones contained mutton fat and Imperial jade objects that glistened in the glow of the lights. Vast green celadon serving plates lay stacked up like common china in a soup kitchen. Propped up on an elegant Anglo-Indian table, was a set of Sèvres porcelain which had belonged to Marie Antoinette, hand-painted in an exquisite design of entwining roses and stamped with her cipher.

We sat on Napoleon's tiny four-poster mahogany bed, draped in heavy velvet curtains, and made cuts through the air with Akbar's curved sword, inlaid with gold and silver. Opening a strong safe, Bala pulled out the prize of the collection, a set of thirty-two solid silver Indian thalis, which belonged to Birbal, one of Akbar's nine 'jewels' or philosophers who advised him at his court. India's first Prime Minister, Nehru, was so overpowered with their magnificence that when he came to dine at Quila House he refused to eat off them. Somebody diplomatically whispered in Nehru's ear that other important statesmen and even royalty had done so, and the embarrassing moment passed.

Bala handed me the old visitors' books to leaf through. Viceregal guests, Wavell, Linlithgow, Dufferin and Ava; luminaries such as Mary Pickford and Aly Khan. The Maharajas of Dharbanga, Patiala, Jodhpur; Mrs Gandhi and the King of Nepal, whose brother is lucky enough to have the most romantic signature in the world – simply 'Himalaya' – all had passed through. In 1938 a British general had visited the house, his remarks typically brusque – 'Good show, bad taste.'

We were extremely fortunate to have arrived in Patna at this time, for the Chaat Festival of Bihar was about to take place. People gather from afar on the banks of the Ganges and, at the exact moment of the setting sun, immerse themselves in the holy waters, spreading their offerings on its smooth surface. The same ritual is repeated the following morning at sunrise. The belief is that the sun is harmful and its effects immediate, causing skin cancer, leprosy and other diseases. By making this puja, the sun's terrible wrath is appeased. For a state that has the worst reputation in India for violence and lawlessness, it is interesting to note that during the two days of the Chaat the crime rate drops so dramatically that the local newspapers have to work hard to fill their pages.

The terrace of Quila House, sitting high above the river, was the perfect vantage point from which to watch the ceremony. But Bala suggested that we should hire a boat for the evening and float slowly down the river past the ghats which line the banks of old Patna. As we drove to where we would board the boat, the streets were thronged with processions of people carrying offerings. The city was clean and the tarmac glistened from the water trucks that had preceded us. Above, a canopy of tinsel and fairy-lights formed a glittering tunnel. Brass bands of old men in red and khaki uniforms marched proudly, blowing curled highly polished silver horns. At moments, traffic would come to a grinding stop, enabling devotees to cross the road repeatedly prostrating themselves in their laborious pilgrimage to the river.

We boarded a large motor launch and slowly began to edge down river. A continuous stream of colour, like the flowing molten lava of an exploding volcano, ran thickly downwards as the masses descended the steps of the ghats carrying flowers, grain, little candlelit terracotta pots and garlands. On reaching the water's edge lit by the last rays of the setting sun, they made their puja, immersing themselves and spreading their offerings on the dancing waves. Their faces serene, there was no rush, no pushing or shoving, just a completeness, a sense of contentment and peace.

Looking up at the crumbling oriental façades of former palaces and opium factories and the massive wall and buttresses of the old fort, entangled with overhanging trees, the stains of history were indelibly painted on the worn surface of this city, one of the most ancient capitals in the world. It was founded in 600 BC when King Ajatasatru built a fort which later became the capital of Magadha. It was there that the might of the Mundas compelled Alexander and his legions to retreat back home. In 304 BC in the reign of the great Emperor Chandra Gupta Maurya after his defeat of the Nunda Empire, it came into its full glory. By then he commanded a vast empire stretching from Kabul in the north to Mysore in the south, from Saurashtra in the west to parts of Bengal in the east. The Greek ambassador Megathesnes described the scene:

> The public appearances of the Emperor Chandra Gupta were occasions of pageantry and grandeur. The Emperor was carried in a golden litter adorned with strings of pearls hanging on all sides. His linen robe was embroidered in gold and purple and before him marched attendants, carrying silver incense pans. The Emperor was followed by armed men and his immediate bodyguard was comprised of armed women. He rode in a chariot drawn by elephants. The King had a guard of twenty-four elephants and when he went forth to do justice, the first elephant was trained to make obeisance. In the King's pay, there was a standing army of six hundred thousand foot soldiers, thirty thousand cavalry and nine thousand elephants.

Later, the great Emperor Akbar lived in what is now Quila House, from where he conducted his battle against the Afghan rule of North Bihar. Akbar was acknowledged as the greatest elephant rider of all time. In the *Ain-I-Akbari*, the record of Akbar's reign, is written:

> His Majesty, the royal rider of the plain of auspiciousness, mounts every kind of elephant from the first to the last class, making them notwithstanding their almost supernatural strength, obedient to his command. His Majesty will put his foot on the tusks and mount them, even when they are in the rutting season (musth) and astonishes experienced people.

Early the next morning, feeling a little like the Emperor Akbar, I rode Tara down from Quila House through a continuous procession of delighted devotees. We passed a line of sodium lamps which glowed eerily through the mists rolling off the Ganges, like a gas-lit street in Victorian England. As the sun rose over the horizon, we stood looking down upon a crowd of three hundred thousand people, spread out like some endless richly brocaded carpet which undulated softly as the saris and dhotis of the bathing devotees danced on the surface of the water. Leaving Tara with Gokul, Indrajit and I waded far out into the river through a sea of floating flowers. Indrajit performed a small puja for Sri Ram Naik, the resin collector who had been killed by the tiger in the Simplipals. Wrapping rose petals into his blood-stained lunghi we attached his sandals and watched the little bundle float gently away, taken by the eddies, to mix with the other offerings of the festival.

The following dawn we returned to the river. In a few hours we would enter the Sonepur Mela. We worked hard on Tara until she shone like obsidian. Bhim anointed her forehead vivid crimson with the sign of Shiva. After oiling her head and toenails, we loaded her up and bade farewell to Khusto, who was driving home to Orissa. The jeep was now due back.

Indrajit was staying on for the Mela as our driver, since Bala had kindly lent us a small minibus to ferry provisions back and forth, and for use if there was any emergency. Don would accompany Indrajit in the minibus. Aditya and I climbed on to Tara, flanked by Bhim and Gokul in their smartest dark-green khaki outfits. I lifted my hand upwards and forwards, like some American cavalry officer at the head of his troop, shouting 'Challo' and we trundled through the gates of Quila House towards Sonepur and the great elephant mela.

17

The Haathi Bazaar

WE SHOULD HAVE been imbued with a sense of excitement and fulfilment, and moved accordingly through the quiet streets of Patna in anticipation of the end of our pilgrimage. Instead we moved almost reluctantly, knowing that each of Tara's steps was bringing us closer to the moment when we would finally have to part. No one spoke, each of us lost in our own thoughts, lulled by the quiet sound of Tara's soft shuffle. The view from my lofty perch had become so familiar, so natural, that I found it hard to imagine any other way of life. I gazed vacantly at the top of her broad head, at the little white patch of criss-cross healed scars, where the point of the ankush had been used, and I ran my toes through the sparse, springy hair of which I knew there were two hundred and ninety-seven separate strands. I felt the heavy thump of her large ears against my legs, a sensation that had once annoyed me, but which I now enjoyed. My hands caressed the sweat-stained wood of the howdah, and I wiggled my backside deeper into the old faded red cushion, wanting never to dismount.

We circled on to the approach road leading to the Mahatma Gandhi bridge, one of the longest in the world, a masterpiece of engineering, simple and elegant, spanning the vast reaches of the Ganges. A long tailback of modern conveyances – buses, trucks, tractors, taxis, cars and scooters – were waiting to pay the toll, revving their engines impatiently and belching out blue exhaust fumes. We passed them slowly, waved on cheerfully by the toll-keeper, for such an ancient mode of travel was untaxed.

At Hajipur we joined up with a group of elephants. Two or three of the large females – we discovered from their mahouts – were owned by a local landlord hoping to purchase a big tusker. Veterans of the mela, they were capable, quiet old men, with faces that had seen it all. They rode proudly with straight backs, becoming wildly enthusiastic about the firinghee mahout, asking me if I would do them the honour of leading the cavalcade into Sonepur. As we cut through back streets I heard them talking eagerly with Bhim. Breaking into elephant language unintelligible to the outsider, they were enjoying the chance to advise a newcomer, and, no doubt, cleverly trying to extract the parameter of Tara's price which would then spread like a bushfire across the elephant market.

Although Aditya and I had decided earlier that we would not sell Tara to anyone unless we were convinced they would provide her with a good home, secretly I did not want to sell her at all. To cut down this risk I would make her the most expensive elephant of the mela. I had the feeling, though, that Tara would attract a lot of attention. Apart from her obvious cachet – fame – she was a beautiful elephant.

Sonepur is similar in shape to an isosceles triangle. It is flanked by two great rivers; the Ganges from the south and the Gandak from the north-east which begins its journey in the snow-capped peaks of the Himalayas, thundering down to its confluence with the Ganges. The fair takes place on the right bank of the Gandak. On the auspicious day of Kartik Purnima, hundreds and thousands of people line the ghats to take a ceremonial dip in its holy waters.

The Sonepur Mela has a special significance for Hindus, owing to the temple of Hari Nath Mandir where uniquely the gods Vishnu and Shiva are worshipped together. Near to the temple a mythological battle between a crocodile and an elephant took place.

According to legend, there once lived two brothers, Jai and Vijay, devotees of the Lord Krishna who were asked one day by their king to perform a puja, and he was so pleased with their devotion that he showered them with gifts. The two brothers argued about the distribution. Jai thought they should be divided equally, but Vijay disagreed, saying that as he had performed a better puja, he should be entitled to more. Hurt by his brother's greed, Jai cursed him, saying he would become a crocodile in his next life. Vijay retaliated and said Jai would turn into an elephant. After some time they made up their differences and asked Lord Krishna to break the evil spell they had cast on one another. He was helpless to do so and in due course the brothers became a crocodile and an elephant. One day, on Kartik Purnima, the day of the full moon, the elephant was bathing in the river when the crocodile grabbed him by the leg. A fierce battle raged, continuing for thousands of years. The elephant, finally tiring, was about to drown and he cried out to Lord Krishna for help. The god appeared on his Garuda (eagle) and killed the crocodile with the Sudershan Chakra (wheel).

From that day on devotees have flocked to this place every year, paying their obeisance to Lord Krishna after bathing in the river.

Over the centuries the position of the fair changed. Sonepur, however, must have been the original site. According to old records, Raja Man Singh, one of Akbar's Mogul generals, camped there while advancing on Patna. The Haathi Bazaar is to this day still called the 'Garden of Raja Man Singh', and further records show that during Aurangzeb's reign, traders from far flung Tartar Desh and from Arabia used to come to the fair to sell horses.

Over the last forty years or so, Sonepur has been known as a cattle fair, but for thousands of years it was primarily a place for the sale of elephants, like three other smaller fairs in northern Bihar. For centuries these fairs were fed by elephant-catchers from the jungles of Assam, Bengal and Orissa, and must have been the main markets for the sale of war elephants to Pataliputra, the ancient capital of Chandra Gupta Maurya, whose vast army relied so heavily on these animals.

We approached the bridge spanning the Gandak. It was considered too narrow to accommodate the increasing volume of trains that stopped at Sonepur, an important junction on the north-eastern railway which, until 1950, boasted the longest platform in the world. Now a new parallel bridge takes the rail traffic across.

The cavalcade came to an abrupt halt. In front of us stretched a mile of mela traffic, waiting for the signal to proceed, as the oncoming vehicles inched across the narrow bridge. Bellowing cattle stamped impatiently against the wooden floors of their trucks. More were filled with horses neighing nervously, poking their heads out of the slatted sides. Some vehicles were unrecognisable under gigantic mounds of fodder, spilling over the back, the front and the sides. Business was brisk for the hawkers. They patrolled up and down the armies of bicyclists, selling fruit, ice-cream, newspapers and bags of sticky ludoos. We gained a few yards as the traffic was stopped on the far side and with a crunching of gears and hiss of air brakes, the procession would move forward. Tara was becoming impossible. One moment she would be swiping food from the hawkers, the next vibrating in panic at the horses, forcing me to use the ankush. Aditya swung down impatiently from Tara's back.

'We'll be here all day. I'll see what I can sort out.'

Half an hour later I caught sight of him signalling to me frantically to come forward. I bulldozed my way through, closely followed by the other elephants who were not going to miss this chance. At the entrance Aditya was standing with a smiling policeman who saluted smartly and waved us on to an empty bridge.

'How on earth did you manage that?' I asked Aditya incredulously, as we lumbered across.

'I told him you were related to the Queen of England and that royalty did not expect to be kept waiting.'

'Really?' I said, impressed by his ingenuity.

'No, of course I didn't,' he replied. 'I gave him a hundred rupees.'

To our right, a steam engine clanked across the new railway bridge. To our left, a vast shady grove of mango trees stretched out parallel with the river, under which I could see a few elephants standing. 'Haathi Bazaar!' shouted one of the old mahouts.

Urging Tara into a lumbering trot, with Bhim and Gokul running alongside, we reached the end of the bridge and, swinging left, thundered down into the 'Garden of Raja Man Singh'. We jumped off Tara, and to the amazement of incredulous onlookers the four of us danced a jig around her. Opening a bottle of rum, I poured half the contents down her throat. Each of us then took a swig and yelled 'Jai Mata Sonepur!' We had made it.

It was as well that we had arrived early. As newcomers, we needed to check the lie of the land and to learn the rules. The area between each mango tree, in front of which the elephants would be staked, belonged to a different landlord. We made our way slowly through the orchard, passing fodder stacked like giant teepees. Each landlord tried to interest us in his plot, offering discounts and special favours, knowing that Tara would almost certainly attract a large crowd. We settled on a site at the far end of the orchard which gave easy access to the Gandak some fifty yards behind and close to one of the main bathing ghats. Situated amongst the nearest row of trees to the river we would not be hemmed in. Elephants would stand in front and to the side of us, but not behind.

Our landlord, Lallan Singh, a delightful, wise old man, a veteran of fifty melas, took us under his wing, bustling and fussing over us like a kindly matron on our first day at school. I paid him 100 rupees, the traditional mela rent for the use of his land. (If the elephant was sold, the buyer reimbursed this amount.) Two large wooden stakes were driven deep into the ground and one of Tara's front and back legs were chained to each. An 'account' was opened with the fodder and firewood suppliers, who delivered in the morning and the evening of each day. To ensure some kind of privacy, Lallan Singh organised a large colourful 'kanat' (a rectangular canvas wall) to surround our camp. Between the two mango trees we draped Tara's caparison, the Union Jack, which hung grandly like a war standard. Tables and chairs were produced and by the time the tents were erected and a fire lit, we could have been guests in some Maharaja's grand shikar camp, lacking only uniformed attendants, popping corks from champagne bottles and a floor covered in richly embroidered carpets.

To ensure good luck and a good sale, our landlord performed the 'Aarti', a special puja. He circled our camp holding a terracotta bowl in which a holy flare burned. Then, standing in front of Tara, he raised the flame to her like a toast-master, chanting a few solemn prayers.

Lallan Singh then sat down with us and explained mela etiquette. 'When your elephant is sold, everything on the back legs belongs to the seller, the chain, ropes etc. It is customary to give the buyer the gudda [the saddle], the girth ropes, the bell, and any other decoration on the elephant, like silk cords and tassels. It is most important that your elephant is never unattended at any time, during the day or night. Accidents can and have happened frequently at the mela and a loose elephant can cause terrible carnage amongst "five lakhs" of people. Be very careful,' he warned us, 'to keep your money hidden, as the mela will be full of thieves. When your deal takes place, it must be done quietly, out of the sight of prying eyes and, if possible, in the presence of a few members of your entourage. A showing of people,' he explained, 'means power and wealth,' as we were to discover when approached by the local zamindars, who never went anywhere without a large armed bodyguard.

E. O. Shebbeare gives an ingenious description of how he dealt with this situation, in his book *Soondar Mooni*:

> I have assumed a companion because to go elephant-buying alone is a miserable business. Two heads are better than one when deciding what to buy and how much to pay; they are very much better than one when it comes to justifying your purchases and their prices before a critical audience when you get them home. There is another, more practical reason for hunting in couples; a proverb even more apt than 'two heads', is the one about 'safety in numbers'. As any policeman in the India of those days could have told you, a *mela* attracted more than just buyers and sellers, pilgrims and merry-makers; it was a magnet for every 'bad hat' in northern India. The reason was simple: since cheques were not accepted, a buyer before a sale or a seller after one was an object which no serious evil-doer could afford to overlook. My own security measures were simple. There was then, and may be still, a

practice in India of cutting currency notes in half. If a large sum was to be sent by post, one half of each note was sent first and not until these had been acknowledged were the second halves dispatched. Before going to a *mela* all the money that would be required was drawn from the treasury in notes of high denominations – hundreds, five hundreds, and a thousand rupees each. Each was cut in two and each half put into a separate pack clipped together in their right order. The packs were then slipped into the corresponding pockets of a pair of linen belts which my companion and I wore round our waists next to the skin. This ensured that the prospective robbers would at least be put to the trouble of committing a double murder.

By now a few more elephants had arrived. In front of us was a large tusker. To our right, attended by two mahouts, stood an old female with two terrible wounds in her flanks oozing a greenish pus. The owner, an overly helpful man from Orissa, explained that she had received these injuries while working in his cement factory. He was here to sell or exchange her for another. Looking at the suffering of this friendly, docile elephant I vowed again that I would never let Tara be maltreated.

Behind us, carpenters and builders were busily erecting marquees, fenced in by impregnable bamboo enclosures. These were for the different sects of religious saddhus who would soon be arriving. Our little set-up was somewhat dwarfed by the opulence of these encampments, particularly the kitchen facilities. Huge cauldrons and stacks of tin platters were being unloaded and carried inside, in readiness for the great feast on Kartik Purnima, which would feed thousands of devotees.

Further down the Haathi Bazaar rich zamindars had been allocated the prime sites, where entire canvas villages had been set up, in front of which stood their richly caparisoned elephants. Behind, surrounded by armed chauffeurs, their cars were parked, highly polished vehicles with blacked out windows; so the arrival of Don and Indrajit in the minibus added a certain cachet to our humble enclosure.

Already our presence had caused a stir and groups of people had started to gather outside. It was easy to discern between those who were merely curious and the professionals. The curious, straining on tiptoes, peered over the 'kanat' to catch a glimpse of the firinghee mahout. The professionals, tough, bow-legged men with sun-blackened faces and shrewd eyes, sauntered casually past Tara inspecting her with a well-assumed air of indifference. They would stop to have a few words with Bhim, hoping to glean a few titbits of information on pedigree and price. They would then report back to their bosses. These momentary inspections would take place continuously over the next few days. Unlike the hustling West, where fast decisions are the name of the game, a hasty deal is considered undignified in the East, and a strict etiquette is adhered to.

Aditya and I were worried about Bhim. He was not his usual pragmatic, cheerful self. His spirit had left him and he wandered around lackadaisically. Worst of all, he seemed to have lost all interest in Tara. Perhaps it was due to exhaustion or to thinking that once he had reached the mela his duties would be less arduous and he would have time to enjoy the fun. In fact, we eventually realised, he was simply overawed. Used to the relative quietness and routine of a zoo, he had suddenly been thrown into the lions' den, the 'Newmarket' of the elephant world, where true professionalism counted and one's knowledge was put to the ultimate test and carefully scrutinised. He was out of his depth and had lost his confidence.

Tara, too, was affected. Whereas she should have been in her element, as carts drawn by white bullocks continuously replenished her larder, she stood listlessly, a look of total resignation on her face. I began to think this was all too familiar to her. She had been here before, I realised, and my heart stopped.

At Gau-Dhuli (the hour of the cow dust), that quiet magic moment just after sunset, when the sky shimmered gold between the branches of the mango trees through the dust thrown up by the elephants, a group of men entered our encampment. Their faces showed a certain relief as they spotted me. The spokesman stepped forward and formally introduced himself.

'Mr Shand,' he said, 'we are the proprietors of the Shoba Nautanki [the folk theatre]. Thanking goodnews we have found you in time. Would you do us the honour of inaugurating our first show tomorrow? Already we have sent out this gentleman in a jeep to find you' – he pointed to a man who looked both exhausted and exasperated – 'and he has been travelling for five days. You will enjoy the show. There are many girls. Our theatre,' he continued proudly, 'has the reputation of the most beautiful women. But first we would like you to garland the statue of our local freedom fighter and then we will proceed to the theatre. Our last guest of honour was a famous dacoit. Now it is appropriate that the first English mahout should open the show. We will collect you tomorrow afternoon.'

That evening, when the muddy water was turning crimson from the rays of the setting sun, we bathed Tara in the Gandak, approached from a steep muddy bank, down which she slid on her bottom, like a child on a toboggan. She then proceeded to queue-barge into the elephant-filled shallows, much to the annoyance of the other mahouts, who were waiting their turn patiently. It was dark by the time Tara had finished her ablutions. Beneath us, elephants lay motionless, like giant prehistoric boulders. Then, as if infused suddenly by some unseen force, they erupted out of the water and lumbered towards the bank. Under the stars, we joined a silent cavalcade of returning elephants, this silence only broken by the soft shuffle of their feet, the swish of their tails and the flapping of their ears. An old mahout, riding the lead tusker, broke into song, swelling louder and louder as others joined in, then echoing quietly away into the blackness of the Gandak running swiftly beside us. I was by now so much part of this ancient brotherhood that my other world seemed like a dream as I felt the coolness of Tara's back beneath me.

Indrajit had built a blazing fire against the chill of the November night. We huddled round it, drinking with the owner of a big tusker. He was a landowner, but unlike most of the other zamindars, he himself rode and looked after his elephants. He was an honest straightforward man whom I felt we could trust, with a vast knowledge and love of elephants that bordered on passion. His family had always kept elephants. He remembered, as a child, coming to the mela with his father and counting over a thousand. The bridge is always closed on the day of Kartik Purnima and he remembered the latecomers trying to swim across the river. Due to the strong current, they had been washed away, mahouts and elephants drowning.

He admitted quite openly that his tusker was dangerous and only he could control it. However, unlike almost all the owners in the mela, he did not use drugs to quieten his elephant. There were now over a hundred elephants here, but he told us that Tara was the best he had seen so far. To an expert, she was obviously naturally fed and of a good temperament. He was not surprised that we were thinking of asking two lakhs for her.

'Bide your time,' he advised us, 'for her that is not an exorbitant price' – adding that if we needed any assistance he would be glad to give it.

In the middle of the night I was woken by the fierce shouts of 'Mahout!! mahout!!' – and running outside our encampment I found Tara, her stakes uprooted, about to escape. Bhim, who was supposed to be on watch, was fast asleep in a pile of sugar cane at the side of the kanat. I shook and reprimanded him. He apologised sheepishly and promised it would not happen again. But it was too late, the incident had been noticed. An unattended elephant, as we had been told, is an unforgivable crime in the strict mahout law of the mela and we had, as it were, lost face.

18

Mela Madness

AWOKEN EARLY BY the urgent shouts of mahouts and the chanting of saddhus, I walked to the side of the kanat and peered over. Though relatively empty last night, it was now as if an army had moved in quietly during the night and surrounded our encampment. The orchard was alive with elephants, swaying, feeding and dusting, while mahouts, wrapped in blankets, squatted beside fires, watching them carefully over rims of little terracotta bowls containing their morning tea. Arcades of hastily constructed stalls, like mini-bazaars, had mysteriously sprung up, selling paan, spices, food, cheap jewellery, clothing and medicines.

Behind us, like flowers in a desert, huddled little groups of families. When the sun rose, the women stretched languidly, turning bejewelled arms, ankles and tips of noses and ears bright gold as the first rays filtered through the smoke-filled air. Elephants ridden proudly by young well-muscled mahouts, their teeth a brilliant white against the black of their faces, raced each other down to the river. Like picadors, holding an ankush in both hands behind their elephants' ears, they showed off their skills and their mounts to the best effect. To the casual observer it would seem like a game but it was, in fact, in deadly earnest. Prospective buyers would be watching carefully.

Lallan Singh arrived with an electrician who ran a cable up one of the trees in our camp to connect a large high-wattage bulb. At night it would effectively illuminate Tara and, we hoped, keep the boys awake. I watched shamefacedly, but Lallan Singh consoled me. Three other elephants, he told me, had escaped during the night. It was only a precaution.

Our first buyer offered 70,000 rupees for Tara. This man, a magnificent actor, almost brought tears to my eyes. He told me of the wonderful elephant he had owned for thirty years, which he only rented out on very auspicious occasions. Just last week, tragedy struck when he was away on business. He had instructed his mahout to take the elephant to one of these very special occasions. The mahout, a lazy man, did not carry out his orders and when he returned he gave the mahout a sound beating. A week later the mahout disappeared, not before he had poisoned the elephant, which had just died. I declined his offer.

After Tara returned from her bath, I went shopping. From one of the many stalls specialising in elephant decorations, I bought her a beautiful brass neck bell attached to a bright crimson silken cord. Anklets made of bells and strips of silken material to hang from ears and tusks were also available, but I wanted to keep her looking simple, elegant, like a beautiful woman at a ball, wearing a plain dress, unadorned, except for one astonishing piece of jewellery. She did not need decoration.

I employed a specialist in elephant painting. After drawing a line that sharply demarcated the blackness of her oiled crown from the natural grey of her skin, he created with simple coloured chalks of purple, yellow, white and blue, a series of flowers and lotuses on her ears, face and trunk. In the centre, between her eyes, he traced a dazzling star. Taking down the Union Jack, we draped it over Tara's shoulders and when prospective buyers approached, Bhim and Gokul would dramatically draw it back.

As Don and Aditya had disappeared earlier to take photographs, I set off through the Haathi Bazaar, leaving Tara with the boys. My nostrils were instantly filled with the evocative smells of India – spices, incense, the heavy scent of the tribal women, mixed with the more pungent odour of urine and excrement, and I found myself thinking I never wanted to leave. Passing down the elephant lines, mahouts and owners alike called me over – not out of curiosity but because I was part of them, an elephant man, inexorably entwined with their way of life. I sat cross-legged by little fires and shared bowls of tea and littis, small balls of hot dough roasted over the ashes. I inspected their elephants, checking their backs for tell-tale sores and scars, and chuckled disapprovingly when, opening their mouths, I found patches of black on their pink tongues.

Easily now, I mounted the elephants by way of their trunks and tusks. I sat caressing their ears, and barked commands to make them sit. I watched a big male having part of its tusk sawn off, for a legal sale of ivory. The mahout first carefully measured the distance from eye to lip. After marking a spot which avoided cutting into the nerve, he sawed through it quickly. In India ivory fetches about 5,000 rupees a kilo. Magically, the tusk will grow back, just like a finger nail.

At one encampment stood a huge tusker, excessive in its ornamentation. Richly caparisoned in red brocade, bells hung round its neck and feet, yellow and red silken scarves dangled from its ears and tusks and its tail was braided with silver tinsel. The beast swayed from side to side continuously, its piggy little eyes transfixing everyone who passed, with a stare of pure venom. An old mahout warned me to keep my distance. This was a dangerous elephant, he told me. In the last ten days it had killed three people.

I counted a hundred and ninety elephants; last year there had been more than three hundred and next year probably there would be even fewer. It is inevitable that this way of life will, in time, die out.

Leaving the Haathi Bazaar I moved on to the other animal markets. For the first time, the sheer size of the great mela struck me. At the horse lines I watched a small snow-white arab, its pink eyes heavily kohled to highlight their dullness, its tail dyed the colours of the rainbow, being put through its paces. The rider urged him along at a furious pace, then suddenly pulled him dead on his hocks, whirling him about to perform a kind of 'pas' or, in military terms, 'marking time'. The horses were even more elaborately decorated than the elephants. Some sported headbands worked in gold thread, others had their legs encircled with brass bangles. One wore a necklace of silver and gold, containing verses from the Koran. They came from Rajasthan, the Punjab, Afghanistan and even Australia, watched over carefully by their dealers, old men with faces creased like parchment paper, shrewd all-knowing eyes wrinkled against the glare of the sun.

Beyond the horses, stretching for almost two miles, were paddocks crowded with cows, bullocks and buffaloes. Finally, I reached the bull pens, known locally as the 'jewel market'. Apart from the elephants, the bulls fetch the highest prices.

Making my way back to Tara I entered the shopping centres, a maze of streets lined with booths, overshadowed by the giant Ferris wheel of the fun fair and the Big Top of the circus arena. A crowd surrounded a pair of chained, moth-eaten bears. Goaded by their keeper, they shuffled miserably from paw to paw in time to a disco song. For five rupees you could dance with them.

A discordant screeching announced the bird market. Hyacinthine blue macaws from South America sat quietly on their perches, their feathers ruffled, swivelling their heads suddenly, blinking their baleful eyes. Nepalese mynahs chuckled and laughed, and a cage of little rice birds, so gaudy in colour that the owner admitted they had been dyed, hopped nervously from side to side. Outside, a shiny black mynah loaded and fired a miniature cannon, and for ten rupees would play cards.

The inevitable snake-charmers squatted at the sides of the streets, playing their flutes tunelessly to serpents swaying from wicker baskets. One snake-charmer, more enterprising than the rest, advertised 'a fight to the death' between a mongoose and a cobra. I hoped he had an unending supply of cobras, for inevitably the mongoose would win. Or perhaps he waited until he had attracted a large enough crowd to make it worthwhile.

Jugglers ferried their way through the crowds performing with extraordinary skill considering all the pushing and shoving. As I pushed and shoved I noticed an exceptionally tall man with piercing eyes bearing down on me. I tried to move, but it was as if I was hypnotised. Dipping a long large finger in a small jar of vermilion, he stabbed it against my forehead and demanded five rupees. I christened him 'dot man' and over the next few days, whatever preventative measures I took, he always managed to get me. Once, seeing him approach I slipped behind Aditya as the great finger shot out like a sword. I thought I had escaped. Aditya, obviously a seasoned mela veteran, simply ducked and I received it on the end of my nose.

'Your teeth pulled for only 20 rupees. Get a new set. A new look.' Dentists did a roaring trade from padded chairs operating foot drills. Naive patients writhed in agony as the dentists dug into mouths with what looked like pairs of pliers. In intervals between the shops bold placards hung advertising eating houses, their cuisine varied to suit the tastes of every caste and creed. The smell reminded me of the observation of the old planter who wrote in his *Reminiscences of Behar*: 'I cannot say the dishes look tempting while the smell of bad ghee makes you wish you had put a little extra eau-de-Cologne on your handkerchief before you left your tent.'

Passing brassière shops and signs advertising 'Genuine Siamese Twins' I entered the Bombay Bazaar. The smell of bad ghee disappeared in a wave of perfume. Here was everything for the lady. Women, young and old, queued up at scent booths, in which men sat cross-legged behind a thousand different bottles. After twirling cotton-wool on to long silver sticks, they dipped them in and dabbed them on the backs of waiting hands. Glass-bangle sellers displayed their incandescent wares on long tall poles. They fought a losing battle to prevent their eager clients from shattering fragile merchandise as the women pulled and pushed them up and down their arms.

In large mirrors, the ladies coquettishly painted on different hues of cosmetics and lipstick and applied kohl to their eyes, while others tried on gold nose and ear ornaments. Baskets filled with brilliant hues of sindoor (the powder used to make the 'tikka') sat in rows of tiny coloured mountains and gorgeous bolts of gauze, silk and cotton to be made into saris, fluttered like butterfly wings as they were gently unfurled.

As I moved on, persistent salesmen pressed me to buy their products; brasswork from Benares, inlaid boxes and trays and miniature Taj Mahals from Agra, enamel objects from Jaipur, beautifully embroidered shawls from Kashmir, and in one rather modern shop a Hell's Angel's leather biker's jacket and a pair of co-respondent brogues.

The ingenuity of the beggars knew no bounds. Beside a man sitting near the temple lay upright in the dust what appeared to be a human head – and it was just that. He had buried his colleague up to the neck and rubbed his face with paste to give it the colour of a corpse. Another simply walked around naked from the waist down, with a large padlock clamped through the end of his penis. Yet another had buried himself head downwards to the waist and was managing to breathe through the open ends of two bamboo tubes that just broke the surface of the ground. Unfortunately, he had neglected to hire an assistant. Passersby liberally helped themselves to his begging bowl.

On the other side of the temple, I came across the Naga Saddhus, who are fiercely ascetic and protect their privacy zealously. Trained in all forms of fighting they are treated with great respect. Their naked bodies daubed in ash, their faces painted white and vermilion, they resent any intrusion from outsiders, and woe betide anyone stupid enough to try and photograph them. I managed a short conversation with one of them. As a penance, he had not sat down for six years and supported his stiffened and deformed legs by leaning on a kind of wooden swing. He was most indignant when I told him that an elephant belonging to King Louis XIV did not lie down for the last ten years of its life and had worn two holes in the stone buttress with its tusks, on which it supported itself. I beat a hasty retreat.

There were the usual abominable sights of the poor unfortunate cripples. One was more terrifying and heartrending than anything I had ever seen. It was a young boy – or rather what was left of a young boy – just a small torso supporting a head, twisted and contorted by some hideous disease. He was pushed around in a little cart. On it perched a parrot, which took your money in its beak.

As I re-entered the Haathi Bazaar, I witnessed two extraordinary fights. Both had been caused by theft, and both were not without humour. The first was a clash of titans between two female elephants, staked next to one another. One of the females had stolen the other's sugar cane. She turned quickly on the thief and instead of using her head as a battering ram, she tried in the most ludicrous fashion to bite off the other one's tail. They whirled around trumpeting and squealing in a cloud of dust, looking like squabbling schoolgirls pulling each other's hair. Three or four mahouts, armed with spears, waded in quickly and put an end to this farce.

The second fight was decidedly one-sided until an unusual intervention stopped it. A thief had been caught and was being punished in typical local fashion. His hands had been tied behind his back and his feet bound together. Two hefty men wielding long bamboo sticks proceeded to give him a sound beating on his head and the soles of his feet until he was a crying, bleeding wreck. The women, I noticed, particularly enjoyed this spectacle and joined in enthusiastically kicking the unfortunate man's ribs with sturdy feet, their toes encircled by gold rings, like knuckle-dusters. He would have been killed but for the sudden arrival of a tall, pale, sweating Englishman, a camera slung around his neck, wearing a floppy sun hat. I looked more closely. It was a friend of mine, a travel editor for a glossy London magazine. He waded bravely into the mêlée holding his hands above his head shouting 'Bas, bas,' the only word he knew in Hindi. When this had no effect, he clasped his hands fervently together as in prayer, fell to his knees and cried 'por favore, por favore!!' Immediately the beating stopped and the crowd became silent. He called the police, who took the bleeding man away.

There was great excitement in the camp when I returned. Tara's price had gone shooting up, from 70 to 90,000 rupees. This offer had come from a man, Aditya told me, who had a dishonest face and apparently owned a hotel in Delhi. The man had said his elephants were well looked after and simply took tourists for rides once a day. Unfortunately, one of them had been hit by a bus.

19

Swept Away

OUR PROCESSION INTO Sonepur town to garland the statue of the freedom fighter was most impressive. The grandees of the Shoba Theatre supplied us with a bodyguard and I felt terribly important. Forming a phalanx around us, they spearheaded a path through the gaping onlookers. Our entourage, however, did not quite match that of the Prime Minister of Nepal who arrived in Sonepur in 1871 with a bodyguard of three hundred Gurkhas and a harem of pretty, lively Nepalese princesses.

My self-importance now blown out of all proportion, I expected a tumultuous welcome to greet me. Instead, there was an infuriated, sweating policeman, trying vainly to control the traffic, roaring uncontrollably around the monument, and a madman juggling ludoos. One of the grandees placed a garland of marigolds in my hand. Self-consciously I climbed over the fence protecting the statue, looped the garland over the marble head, and feeling I should somehow justify this honour that had been bestowed upon me, bowed deeply. As I climbed out, the madman dropped his ludoos, grabbing me fiercely in a sticky embrace.

Again cocooned by our bodyguard, we soon reached a large building like a warehouse, constructed from wood and corrugated iron. Its front façade was painted gaudily with ladies cavorting in various stages of undress. Tannoys noisily advertised the delights of the show to an eagerly waiting crowd, pushing and shoving to get nearer an entrance controlled by four large policemen wielding large lead-topped bamboo canes with clinical efficiency.

'Welcome to the Shoba Theatre, Mr Shand,' the spokesman shouted. 'As you can see it is very popular. Come. We will go through the back.'

Inside it resembled an aircraft hangar. At one end, shrouded by a gauzy curtain, was the stage, the backdrop a grove of palm trees set against a starry night. Below, in the pit, fenced off by large iron palings, sat the orchestra tuning their instruments in a cacophony of discordant notes. Behind the pit were the best seats, costing 25 rupees, and separated from them by a triple-stranded barrier of barbed wire, was standing room only, at five rupees per person. The theatre put on three shows daily and could hold a crowd of eighteen thousand people.

We sat sipping tea and eating cakes in the wings. Aditya and I were introduced to the artistes – highly painted, plumpish ladies in sequinned outfits, their male partners squeezed into tightly fitting jumpsuits, brocaded like matadors' costumes. The building vibrated suddenly, as the gates were opened and a surge of people fought their way in.

Behind the curtain, a row of chairs had been placed beyond a large red ribbon. A barrage of arc lights hit us as we sat down. I felt inordinately self-conscious and nervous. Sweat began to trickle down my back. The star of the show, Miss Shoba, whose appearance caused a roar of excitement from the crowd, blessed and garlanded us. Long speeches followed. The Master of Ceremonies, wearing a smart, navy blue blazer with shiny gold buttons and white bell-bottomed trousers, introduced me as the famous English mahout and gave a lengthy account of my adventures. The crowd became instantly restless, longing for the show to start.

The band struck up, the gauzy curtains lifted and a pair of scissors were thrust into my hands. I stood up, sawed through the ribbon and stammered a few appropriate words, which Aditya then translated. Miss Shoba reappeared and led me off the stage to a small smattering of applause. I wanted to leave immediately to see Tara but Aditya insisted it would be impolite. We must stay to watch at least one act.

I'm glad we did. A seductive girl dressed in a black, transparent sari worked the crowd into a frenzy. The origins of the dancing girl go back to the Gandharva women, renowned for their beauty and skill in dancing and singing. In the old days when the fair was a meeting place for Rajas, zamindars, big agriculturists and businessmen, the girls made a good harvest. Fees of 500 or 1,000 rupees were a common feature for a few dances. On some of the more noted dancing girls, lakhs of rupees used to be spent for more personal services.

The seductress of the Shoba Theatre undulated across the stage, singing a ballad of obviously erotic content. She was singing about her lover, with whom she was in bed, complaining he would not make love to her. Aditya translated: 'Why do you not come to me, my darling? My breasts are young and firm.' There was a groan from the crowd behind us. 'My thighs are as soft as satin, my crop green and young, ready to be irrigated.' This brought the house down. Turning around I saw the barbed wire bulging outwards as the crowd pressed against it, frantic to reach her, followed by the whacks of the police sticks as they rained down on unprotected heads.

It was a relief to be back in the relative peace of the Haathi Bazaar. Smoke rose in eddies through the rich foliage of the mango orchard from the fires round which mahouts were huddled, their animated faces illuminated in the ruddy glow, as they traded tales and secrets of their ancient craft. To reach our camp we had to thread our way carefully across a carpet of sleeping people. Inside, feet and arms protruded from under the kanat.

Relieving Gokul, I took the next watch over Tara. She still was not her old self. There was something else, an uneasiness about her, which immediately transmitted itself to me. I felt that sick feeling in the pit of my stomach that precedes impending disaster. She seemed to be trying to communicate with me. When I started to feed her sugar cane, she suddenly grabbed my arm and held it firmly in her mouth. She pulled me even closer and we rested against one another, like lovers in a long embrace. Eventually, she released me and lay down.

All down the orchard, in night air hazy from the smoking fires, elephants lay sleeping. Disturbed by something, one would silently rise up like a monstrous spirit and then settle down again as it realised that all was well. Surrounded by six hundred tons of these huge animals, soothed by their snoring, like a ward of asthmatic old men, I felt for the first time a sense of vulnerability. I had never really given it a thought before, but as I looked back on the journey, I realised how much I had taken for granted. At any stage Tara could have killed me. Or any of us for that matter, as simply as swatting a fly. Now I understood that she had always been in control. My destiny had been in her hands. With that realisation, once again, she had taught me respect.

The day before Kartik Purnima, we took Tara down to the Gandak for her bath. We passed the saddhu encampment. Its entrance was guarded by two wild creatures carrying tridents. Inside the saddhus were busily preparing food, churning great vats of stew in readiness for the feast the next day. Among their dark skins, I noticed an old pale woman with long grey hair, dressed in a sari, sitting quietly in the back of the marquee. At first I thought she was an albino, but looking closer I saw she was a white woman, a firinghee, and I waved to her gaily. There was no response. She sat like a stone, staring blankly. Later I found out she was deaf, dumb and blind. Fifty years ago she had been accepted by this sect, which had looked after her ever since.

As we stood patiently in line with the other elephants, waiting for a space in the river, a fight broke out between a large tusker and a female bathing side by side. Throwing off the mahouts washing him, the tusker lumbered to his feet and charged the female who was being ridden by her mahout out of the water. His tusks, even blunted (as they have to be by law), gouged a great rip in her side. She toppled over, squealing, blood bursting from the wound, in the process crushing her mahout. The tusker charged again, enlarging the wound, then turned as if to run up the bank. Tara and the other elephants scattered in alarm. Immediately, mahouts rushed into the river. Surrounding the tusker, they stuck their spears viciously into its legs, flanks and trunk, forcing it back into the water where they managed to chain both its back and front legs. It was then led away. The poor female, badly gored, struggled to her feet, blood streaming down her flanks. From underneath the mahout emerged, miraculously unhurt.

Disturbed by the excitement, we had neglected to chain Tara's front feet together. As she entered the water she flipped me off and swam out about twenty yards. There she started to perform her dolphin act, plunging in and out before turning on her back to float for a few seconds, like an old lady in a swimming bath. Indrajit and I struck out towards Tara but we were unable to reach her. The current was far too strong and we struggled back to the bank. We watched helplessly as she was being swept away. Unless we could somehow cut her off, she might easily drown.

Bhim and Gokul rushed back to the camp. Immediately Aditya arranged a posse of mahouts led by a large, unpleasant individual with a scar running down his face. He demanded, before he did anything, a fee of 600 rupees. Everyone thought this an exorbitant sum but I would gladly have paid anything to get Tara back. Two boats were arranged. Splitting into two groups, we pushed the boats out of the shallows and were at once swept down by the current. Excited crowds ran up and down the river bank, desperate not to miss the action. We caught up with Tara a mile down the river, where she was struggling, whirling round and round in a strong eddy. I dived in, followed by two mahouts. In a second we were pushed back and just managed to catch hold of our boat. Panicking, Tara lurched towards the bank and somehow extracted herself from the current.

She sat blowing in the shallows. From the other boat, a mahout jumped into the water. Crooning gently, he approached cautiously and patted her backside to soothe her. Then he crawled up her back and sat astride her. She surged off again trying to throw him off, shaking her head and rolling. Like a champion rodeo rider, he managed to cling on, steering her to the bank.

He was the same man who had painted Tara. When I thanked him, he told me with a smile that 'the little one' was only playing and he would come later to decorate her again, since most of his handiwork had been washed off in the river. I rode her back to camp, followed by a phalanx of mahouts carrying raised spears. Feeling again that unpleasant coldness in the pit of my stomach, I was convinced that this time she was not playing. It was as if she had sensed some bad omen and had made a desperate attempt to escape.

20

Elephant Trading

AT LAST IT was Kartik Purnima. From three o'clock in the morning a continuous wave of people surged past, and sometimes through, our encampment, on their way to the bathing ghats. The eastern horizon started to show a hint of red. As the visibility increased I saw it would have been difficult to insert a stick between the solid mass of people stretching down from our camp.

I was deeply impressed by the orderliness of the proceedings. Again there was no jostling, pushing or shoving. When a child fell from its mother's arms – a frequent occurrence – the crowd instantly withdrew like a wave, opening a small gap from which it was plucked to safety. As the sun rose battalions of different sects of saddhus marched to the river, carrying their holiest men on flower-decked palanquins, heralding their arrival with the blowing of trumpets. The first elephants started to trundle down, and the crowd again parted magically to let them pass. Convinced that Tara wanted to escape, I waited until the crowds had thinned out before taking her for the ritual bath. While we waited, we were entertained by a troupe of transvestites, whose performance was brazenly suggestive. One was totally outrageous. Wearing a long black wig, and a gold-threaded tribal dress which when he pirouetted revealed his long black hairy legs, he winked and blew continuous kisses through thickly rouged lips that barely camouflaged his heavy moustache. Recognising a good portrait, Don photographed him. The transvestite took this zealous interest to be of the romantic kind, and each time Don left the camp he had to take evasive action to avoid his advances.

Just after midday, preparations for the cremation of an old woman took place at the side of the river. Her body lay on a bamboo pallet, cocooned in a simple white sheet, scattered with marigolds and rose petals. Her neck was wrapped in a blood red silk gumcha, her face in death, serene. As the sharp rays of the sun lanced downwards, illuminating her composed features, she almost seemed to smile. The pallet was then lifted and placed on a funeral pyre. Before 'the dom' (the undertaker) lit it, a young boy, her grandson, came forward and placed a single red rose in her gnarled, clasped hands. The fire ignited in a burst of yellow flame and a thick black plume spiralled slowly upwards, for a moment blacking out the orb of the sun. Gathering her ashes, the family spread them on the smooth, fast surface of the Gandak, transporting her to rest in the holy Ganges.

We bathed Tara in the mid-afternoon. The multitudes of people had largely dispersed by then, but space was still cramped. Elephants and devotees bathed side by side, in complete harmony amongst a floating carpet of droppings and rose petals. I felt weary and oddly depressed, and could not find the energy to scrub her. As she lay in the water, I stood by her head idly stroking her trunk. Perhaps it was because I realised that this was one of the last times that I would be bathing her, or perhaps it was because I knew that I had failed in my role as her protector. As I rode her up the bank towards the camp, under a tunnel of gently flapping saris in yellows, reds, saffrons, vermilions and greens, where the women had draped them in the trees to dry, not even the riot of colour could lift my gloom.

Kartik Purnima was the day when elephant trading began in earnest. Groups of powerful zamindars wearing 'Jawahar jackets' (coarse handwoven silk waistcoats) and dhotis were waiting to see me. Each one was surrounded by a posse of armed guards carrying ancient shotguns. Like Mexican bandits, they wore bandoliers filled with cartridges.

One of them offered a lakh, which he said was the highest price ever paid for a female elephant. He had just sold his elephant for 75,000 rupees, he informed us, and she was undoubtedly the best elephant of the fair. He promised that his elephants were only kept for prestige. After all he was a rich man. Why should he need to rent her out? Another zamindar offered one lakh, 5,000 rupees, and whispered urgently in Aditya's ear. It was a bribe – of any woman I desired, to be delivered anywhere, any time, at my convenience. They all left disconsolately. One group stopped at the next camp, to talk with the owner of the injured elephant. He listened to them and then nodded reassuringly in my direction.

'What's he up to?' I asked Aditya.

'He's managed to sell his elephant, somehow, for 40,000 rupees. He's already pestered me about selling Tara. He's acting as middle man for that zamindar on a commission basis. We will have to be careful. I don't trust him. I've asked our friend who owns the tusker to keep an eye on things. If we have any trouble, he will come over immediately.'

Further down the orchard, I watched a deal being negotiated in the traditional way. The prospective buyer and seller sat side by side, with a blanket covering their hands. The joints of the fingers represent different amounts of money. The buyer presses the first two joints of the first finger of the right hand which, for instance, represents 5,000 rupees. The vendor in reply squeezes the same, but also pinches the first joint of the purchaser's next finger, raising the price to say 5,500, and so on. A bargain was struck almost immediately. The two men got to their feet smiling, and clasped their hands together. The beauty of this lies in its secrecy and simplicity. The vendor may sell well below what he had asked, but no one but the purchaser would know.

Later, Aditya drove Don into Patna as he was leaving for Delhi, and then for London the next day. Suddenly I was alone. The mela seemed to close in on me, and feeling adrift on this sea of alienness I crawled into the haven of my tent. I was sitting quietly when, a few moments later, Indrajit, looking anxious, poked his head around the flap. I noticed he was carrying a spear.

'Come quickly,' he said, 'people make trouble with Tara. Bring ankush.'

I hurried outside. Surrounding Tara, Bhim and Gokul was a large group of unruly ruffians led by the scar-faced man who had organised Tara's rescue. One ruffian was carrying a knife. I noticed him edging slowly around her hindquarters towards the rope that tethered her back legs. Scarface stared at me insolently and pointed to Tara, then back to himself, as if announcing he was taking her. I realised they must have been employed by one of the zamindars. They had bided their time until Aditya, whose presence gave us some kind of authority, had left the mela, leaving me virtually defenceless, unable to speak the language.

Heavily outnumbered, I looked towards the camp of our friend who owned the tusker and was alarmed to see he was not there. Bluff seemed the only alternative. I was about to try to charm Scarface when, suddenly, a vicious, uncontrolled anger exploded inside me. I didn't care any more. I had had enough. The pressure had become too great. I lunged at him with the ankush, knocking him backwards.

'Listen, you shithead!!' I hissed. 'Nobody takes my elephant. Not even over my dead body. If I catch you near her again I'll kill you.'

He had no idea what I was saying, but understood the intonation. I must have looked like one of the Naga saddhus – naked apart from a lunghi, my hair knotted and wild and my mouth drawn back in a rictus of hate. We stared at each other for a moment, eyeball to eyeball. With a forced laugh, trying to save face in front of his cronies, he turned and walked away. He stopped suddenly and shouted something at me.

'What did he say?' I asked Indrajit, shaking with emotion.

'Fat man warn you. He come back later.'

It was midnight before I heard the sound of the minibus. I pulled Aditya into the tent.

'You know what happened while you were away?' I said through clenched teeth. 'We got threatened by those bastards. They said they're coming back later. We'll have to go to the police.'

'We'll go first thing in the morning,' Aditya said. 'But now get some sleep.'

At first I couldn't. I sat at the entrance of our tent. Above the kanat Tara's trunk reached up and over, and she stared at me with sad eyes.

The police station was in the English Bazaar. Aditya had an introduction to the Superintendent of Police who, surprisingly, turned out to be a woman. To my knowledge, only three women in India hold this exalted position. As we approached the police lines, situated opposite the pig market, I was still in a deep rage. I imagined myself dealing with a masculine, humourless, domineering lady, characteristics with which I, as an Englishman, was only too familiar in the highest echelons of our government. We walked up a red gravel path bordered by a sweeping lawn that was surrounded by neat flower beds. It was like entering another world. Gone was the stink, the noise and the confusion of the mela, as we entered an opulent canvas oasis. Smart candy-striped marquees were pitched neatly, their sides draped in floating mosquito nets. Butterflies and birds played in the trees, and the air was filled with the sound of droning bees.

We were ushered into the coolness of the largest tent by a smart sergeant wearing highly polished brown boots. The floor was covered in clean white linen and I winced as I left a trail of dirty footprints. We sat down on a luxurious velour sofa. In minutes, we had been served hot coffee from a silver pot and I helped myself to a cigarette from the box on the polished teak table.

'Mem-sahib will be with you shortly,' the sergeant announced, saluting smartly.

As I gazed out into the garden I began to feel strangely at home. Up until Partition this whole area was known as the English Bazaar. I found myself torn between two worlds – the real India of the mela – and here, where my western upbringing reasserted itself. When the Superintendent of Police arrived I found myself automatically adopting the manners of a guest at an English country weekend, leaping to my feet politely. I couldn't have failed to do so anyway, for she was quite unlike any other police officer I had ever encountered.

'I am so sorry I have kept you waiting. I am Kumud Choudhury. Please sit down.' She held out her hand, shaking a thick mane of freshly washed hair. 'This bloody dust gets everywhere,' she complained, 'I have to wash my hair at least twice a day. How on earth are you surviving? If you need to take a bath, feel free to come here.'

Aditya explained the situation. She rang a bell. Immediately two officers appeared and saluted. With a quiet authority, she ordered them to take us back to the Haathi Bazaar and deal with the problem. She even offered us a policeman to guard our camp, adding that, if she had time, she would love to come and see Tara.

'I'm sorry about your floor,' I said as I got into her green Suzuki jeep, which flew a smart stiff pennant.

'Don't worry about that,' she replied, laughing. 'A fresh one is laid down every day. But are you sure you would not like a bath? Apart from your accent, I cannot tell whether you are Indian or a foreigner.'

'That's my problem,' I replied. Thanking her, we drove off.

21

God's Will

IN FORMER YEARS, the Sonepur Mela was the occasion for a large sporting and social gathering of Europeans. Where we were driving now, horse racing, polo, gymkhanas, cricket matches and lavish balls had taken place in the past.

We slowed down as we passed the encampments, so that the zamindars could clearly see that we were now under protection of the Superintendent of Police. As I breathed in the evocative smells of the elephant camps, the reality of the situation bore in on me once again and I found my emotions being torn one way and then the other. Inside our tent I asked Aditya, helplessly, 'What do we do now?'

'I'm afraid you're going to have to sell, Mark,' he said quietly, 'and you'll have to find a buyer here.'

'NO!' I shouted. 'I just can't sell her ...'

'You have no alternative. What are you going to do with her? Take her to England? The wheeling and dealing here is nearly over. Due to the poor quality of elephants, only a few have been sold. When I was driving back last night, elephants were already moving out of the mela. Please be reasonable. I know I am being brutal, but she is, after all, only an elephant.'

'She is more than that,' I yelled angrily. 'How can you say that after all we've been through together?'

'You have completed an extraordinary journey, Mark. You have become a mahout. The boys feel you are one of them, and consider you a brother. But your western side is now showing. You're too emotional. India is a hard place. Here, people have to survive. Life has to go on. If you can't face it, let me deal with it.'

I couldn't face it. Sitting in the tent in despair, I could hear the commotion outside as the zamindars bid furiously against one another. They had returned in force. I covered my ears. I did not want to know, and as the dread and panic churned my stomach, I almost vomited. I pulled down the flap of the tent, blotting out the colour of the crowds, and Tara herself. A wind had blown up, pushing dust into every nook and crevice of the tent. I sat despondently and found myself writing her name in the dust on my pillow.

Aditya poked his head into the tent. 'The best price we are going to get is one lakh, 15,000 rupees,' he said wearily. 'The prospective buyer has given me his word that he only wants Tara for prestige and good fortune. She will not even be used at weddings. He's given me his address and you will be free to visit her at any time.'

'Just hang on a little longer,' I implored, trying to buy non-existent time. He shrugged and left the tent. Praying for a reprieve, I thought I was dreaming the very English voice calling my name. I clambered out and stood bewildered in the middle of the encampment before two English women who were old friends of mine. We stared at each other in astonishment.

'Anne! Belinda!' I shouted. 'What on earth are you doing here?'

'I might ask you the same question, Mark,' Anne replied, looking in amazement at my appearance. 'We've come to buy an elephant – what else? Bob wants one.' (Bob is Anne's husband, Belinda their daughter.)

'Why does he want an elephant? What about the golf course?' I pictured Tara straying on to those immaculate greens and rampaging up and down the fairways. 'And what about your horses? They'll go berserk.'

'No, no, no,' she replied in exasperation. 'Not for the Tolleygunge Club. For Kipling – our jungle camp in the buffer zone of Kanha National Park in Madhya Pradesh. Bob wants an elephant to take the guests for rides.'

'Bob wants an elephant,' I repeated parrot-fashion.

'Are you all right, Mark?' Anne said, looking at me oddly. 'You haven't gone deaf or something? Yes, an elephant.'

'Well,' I heard myself saying, in a distant echo, 'I've got an elephant. You can have her. I'll give her to you. She's the best elephant here, or anywhere for that matter.'

'You've got an elephant!? I can't believe it. What on earth are you doing with an elephant?'

I told her briefly of our journey. 'Go and see for yourselves. She's a princess.' A crowd of zamindars was still gathered around Tara, inspecting her carefully. 'Tara,' I said. 'Bowl, bowl.'

As if she sensed my happiness, her little brown eyes lit up and she blew a long, shrill trumpet. I hugged her fiercely and she wrapped her trunk tightly around me.

Anne and Belinda took no more than five minutes to make up their minds.

'She's beautiful,' Anne kept repeating. 'She's so pretty, and she's got such lovely kind eyes. Are you sure, Mark? I mean, this is not exactly an ordinary present. Of course we will always regard her as yours.'

'Absolutely convinced,' I replied. 'She'll be so happy with you and thoroughly spoiled. You have no idea how extraordinary this is. I can't begin to tell you how relieved I am.'

The zamindars, altogether confused on hearing that Tara was no longer for sale, became highly aggressive, and Aditya had to call the police again.

'I think you should take her as soon as possible,' Aditya advised. 'I'll arrange another truck and we'll find you a new mahout. Unfortunately Bhim has to return to his job in Bhubaneshwar.'

An elephant mela is full of mahouts looking for jobs, but first we asked Gokul. He thought it over but declined. It was too big a move for him and he had to think of his family. The man who owned the tusker offered his assistance and introduced four candidates. By now I could spot a mahout immediately, by his carriage, straight-backed and proud and by his build; sinewy, slight and bow-legged. However, picking a good mahout is an instinct inbred, a knowledge only gained or handed down from a lifetime of experience. I turned to Bhim.

'Mahouts ride,' he said. 'Mummy choose.'

Each one, in turn, rode Tara, their styles and commands differing, yet all clearly experts.

'Well?' I said.

'Him,' Bhim replied, unhesitatingly, pointing to a middle-aged man with gentle eyes, a Muslim called Mujeem.

'Why him?' I was fascinated. We all were.

'When mahout finish ride, Mummy kiss. Others Mummy not kiss. Also Mussalman,' he added with a grin. 'Not drinking like Bhim.'

Everything was arranged. A truck would arrive early next morning and Indrajit volunteered to accompany Tara to Kipling. Aditya and I would go down there in a couple of days' time to meet up with Bob. I said goodbye to Anne and Belinda who had to return to Calcutta.

'How can we ever thank you enough,' Anne said. 'Bob will be so thrilled.'

'I should thank you. I now know that she will be in good hands – with friends. Look at her,' I said happily, 'it's as if she already knows.' Tara was stamping her feet impatiently, ordering Bhim with urgent signals of her trunk, to bring her some more sugar cane.

'Well! How about that!' I exclaimed to Aditya excitedly. 'What luck! Let's get really drunk!'

Exhausted from the pressures of high level negotiation, we sat around a small fire reflecting on the day.

'Right, Aditya. I'm going to teach you the famous drinking song from the time when we ran the Sonepur Mela.'

Aditya sighed wearily. 'Oh God. Not another childish English ...'

'No, you idiot,' I interrupted. 'This was written by Mr Hodgson, a very handsome man, who by the way, ran off with the wife of an Indian Army Officer. He also made Hodgson's Beer, known in the English Bazaar as "rare good stingo".' Raising my voice in military style I sang:

Who has not tasted of Hodgson's pale beer
With its flavour the finest hops ever gave?
It drives away sadness – it vanishes fear
And imparts a glad feeling of joy to the grave.

O to drink it at morning, when just from our bed
We rise unrefreshed, and to breakfast sit down,
The froth crested brimmer we raise to our head
And in swigging off Hodgson, our sorrows we drown.

Or to drink it at tiffin when thirsty and warm,
We say to the khidmutgar 'bring me some beer',
Soon, soon do we feel its most magical charm,
And quickly the eatables all disappear.

Or at ev'ning when, home from our ride we return,
And jaded and weary we sit down to dine,
We ask but for Hodgson and willingly spurn
The choicest – the dearest – the rarest of wine.

Then hail to thee, Hodgson! of brewers the head,
Thy loss we in India would sadly bewail;
May you live long and happy and when you are dead,
I will think of you daily whilst drinking your ale.

Raising his empty glass for a refill, Aditya roared in lusty Maratha fashion, 'Then hail to thee, Hodgson! of ...' when with a crack like a pistol-shot, the chair on which he was sitting collapsed. In the process of trying to break his fall, Aditya buried his arm in the red hot embers of the fire. He was wearing a long-sleeved nylon shirt which promptly burst into flames. For a moment, Indrajit and I were too stunned to do anything. Then we leapt forward to pull him free. As gently as possible, we patted out the still smouldering shirt. The air was filled with the smell of burning flesh, and something glistened white in the charred skin. It was bone.

'I seem to have burnt myself,' Aditya said, gazing at the hideous wound in fascination. Being obsessed with medical matters, I knew that if the wound was not covered immediately, infection would set in quickly, particularly here in the filth of the mela. Aditya could lose his arm.

Indrajit and I bundled him into the bus and drove like lunatics to Hajipur, where we found a hospital. In the emergency room an overworked doctor was dealing with the victims of a bad car accident. The floor was awash with blood. A man lay with a leg half amputated. Another man was sitting quietly, smiling strangely, his glistening eyeball hanging by a thread against his cheek-bone. Shards of sharp glass were embedded in his head, like arrows.

The doctor took a quick look at the burn and gave me some dressings. 'Put these on and go immediately to the main hospital in Patna. I am sorry. I cannot dress the wound myself, sir. As you can see I am most busy.'

With amateurish clumsiness I bound up Aditya's burn. Not once did he complain or show any sign of pain. He was extraordinarily brave. If it had been me, I would have been screaming, demanding a helicopter to fly me out. In Patna, the wound was cleaned and dressed properly and he was pumped full of morphine. They wanted to keep him in, but he insisted on leaving. At five o'clock in the morning, we reached the camp, where he collapsed.

The sunrise turned the Gandak into a smooth carpet of gold as Bhim and I took Tara down for her last bath. The journey was over. Today we would go our separate ways. As I scrubbed Tara, Bhim sat on her neck, rubbing her head, talking to her quietly. Tara's trunk lifted up to touch his wise old face. I realised he was saying goodbye so I waded back to the bank, to leave them together. As he rode her towards me, they were silhouetted against the huge rising sun. The sharp rays reflected off the droplets of water on Tara's skin, and she could have been wearing a cape of pearls.

I held out a lump of gur. Her manners now impeccable, she stretched out her trunk, plucked the gur delicately from my hand, rolled it into a more suitable shape and popped it into her mouth. She then rumbled softly to say 'thank you'.

'You see Raja-sahib, Mummy no longer beggar. Now royal princess.'

We struck camp, rolled up the tents and packed up our belongings. Bhim formally presented me with the ankush, an object I had once so hated. Now its smooth cold surface was as familiar as my own hands. In a few days, I thought sadly, I would have to hand it over to the new mahout.

The truck arrived. There was now only one last obstacle to overcome – getting Tara on to it. Bhim climbed on top of her for the last time. Whispering encouragement into her ear, he moved her slowly forwards. She put one foot inside, checked the wooden structure carefully with her trunk. Then, with a suspicious squeal, she backed out hurriedly, her head held low. A phalanx of mahouts carrying spears rushed at her from behind, jabbing her in her backside and legs. She whirled round trumpeting in rage, flaying the mahouts with her trunk. They fell back. She then rapped her trunk hard on the ground and stood defiantly, her sides heaving, blood dripping down her legs. I could hardly bear to watch her pain, even though I was determined she would get on this vehicle which would carry her to a happy new life.

'Wait! wait!' Bhim shouted suddenly to the mahouts. 'If Mummy see, not go. Maybe go backwards.'

With strong feet movements against her neck Bhim urged her backwards into the truck. Cautiously Tara planted one back leg inside, then the other. She was now half in and half out.

'Now,' Bhim shouted, 'come with spears.'

A solid wall of sharp points rushed towards her. Squealing in terror she reversed hurriedly into the truck and the big steel-lined doors were slammed behind her.

Encased in this foreign wooden prison, Tara went berserk stamping her feet, swaying from side to side. Her trunk curled around the top edges of the open box, as if trying to pull herself up. The truck lurched alarmingly and, in her fear, a continuous gush of urine and runny excrement poured through the floor-boards. The mahouts clambered up the sides of the truck. Using their ropes like lassoes they trussed her tightly. Bhim and I climbed up and peered inside. Tara's eyes rolled in terror and she squealed, reaching out desperately to us with her trunk.

There was one last rope to tie, the most dangerous, the one that would secure her back legs. From the top of the truck Bhim shouted down to Gokul who was standing on the ground looking miserable.

'You go my son. Mummy not hurt you. Then you proper mahout.' It was his final test for the young man – Bhim's last lesson. Gokul lithely clambered up the side of the truck and dropped in beside her. Rubbing her ears to soothe her, he moved quickly underneath her legs. Tara became still, obediently lifting one leg and then the other, to step into the open nooses. Bhim bent forward and kissed her once on her forehead. As he climbed down, tears were streaming down his face.

The taxi arrived to take Bhim and Gokul to the station. I embraced them both tightly and thanked them. I couldn't face a prolonged farewell. I had become so close to them. Now they would disappear from my life for ever. Bhim saluted smartly. As he got into the car, he wound down the window.

'Bhim happy now. Mummy go good place. But remember Raja-sahib, Mummy miss you. Haathi do forget. See her by six months. Not forget,' he called as the car drove away.

When the truck moved slowly through the Haathi Bazaar, all the mahouts scrambled to their feet, clasping their hands together and shouting – 'Go safely, little one. Our blessings are with you.'

As we reached the road leading to the bridge, a police escort was waiting – a last kind gesture from the Superintendent. The truck joined the queue of vehicles inching down the road. Tara lifted her trunk and let out one last shrill trumpet, but the sound was drowned by the roar of the traffic.

Epilogue

ADITYA AND I flew to Delhi. Three days later we left for Kipling Camp. I tried to dissuade Aditya from coming. His burn was giving him great pain, his usually sun-blackened face had turned pale and was covered in a permanent sheen of sweat. But he insisted on accompanying me, to see that Tara was happy.

Kipling Camp nestled in a grove of trees, rows of little white-washed bungalows, surrounded by luxuriant forest, where Tara could gather her fodder. Near by, a clean river flowed, spilling into deep rock pools. Tara could not have found a better home. It was wonderfully peaceful. Bob was there to greet us, a kind man, his gentleness camouflaged by a brusque manner. He was enthralled by Tara, and had already made plans to build her a proper stone stable, and quarters for Mujeem.

Indrajit and Aditya left the next day. I would see Aditya again in Delhi, but Indrajit was going back to Bhubaneshwar. We shook hands formally. Indrajit's fierce eyes softened for a moment and I realised how fond I had become of this loyal man, as he told me of how the journey had changed his life: of how much he had learned and benefited. I would never forget him.

I spent two idyllic days with Tara. Everybody left us alone, respectful of my feelings. She was still a little shaky, not quite her old self, affected by the long truck ride. Her neck was a mass of sores and abrasions where the ropes had cut into her. We explored her new territory together – going for long rides in the quiet forest – wallowing and playing in the rock pools. In the afternoons, she would stretch out in the lengthening shadows and I would lie on top of her and write my diary. In the evenings I would watch her feeding on a new delicacy prepared by Mujeem – large doughy chapatees, as big as serving dishes, which she would chew slowly, her eyes squeezed tight, in total bliss.

On the evening of my last night, my stomach started to churn with the dread of having to say goodbye. I needed something to numb my feelings. I needed to get drunk and leave with a hangover. Bob kindly gave me a bottle of whisky and after dinner I joined her.

Tara was already lying down. I settled comfortably between her legs, my head propped up on her stomach. However, she wasn't going to let me drink alone. As we shared the whisky, I told her of my home, the land that I lived in and why she would not be happy there. In reply, she occasionally rumbled. Before I passed out I vaguely remembered feeling something long and warm encircle my neck and draw me closer.

I awoke with a start in the early hours. The mist was heavy on the ground. Something was poking me urgently on my backside. I rolled over, my head throbbing. She was standing over me, looking disapproving, signalling towards a pile of sugar cane. I fed her for the last time.

As the car was taking me out of the camp later that morning, I asked the driver to stop. I walked slowly towards Tara, my mind detached, floating. Holding her tail, I clipped off three long springy hairs, the only memento I would take with me. It was then that Tara gave me my last lesson: elephants do weep. When I kissed her on her eye, one hot salty tear fell, staining my cheek. I walked quickly back to the car. We moved slowly away. I forced myself to look stonily ahead. But, as we rounded the corner, I turned and caught one last glimpse of her standing quietly, looking at me. Then she was gone, swallowed up in India's dust.

Afterword

'WITH ONE HIND leg crossed over the other she was leaning nonchalantly against a tree, the charms of her perfectly rounded posterior in full view, like a prostitute on a street corner. I knew then that I had to have her. Suddenly, nothing else mattered and I realised with some surprise that I had fallen in love with a female Asian elephant.'

Twenty-five years have passed since this meeting with an elephant whom I called Tara. It was a meeting that was to change my life – a life which, although filled with adventure and fun, had been going nowhere. Through Tara, I found a real purpose, more than that – a passion. For the last 10 years I've been heading up one of the most successful elephant conservation charities in the world, and if it hadn't been for my love affair with Tara, God knows where I'd be.

* * *

But how did it happen? How did a posh, privileged, fat, little boy with a fiendish temper end up one steamy, Indian monsoon night, deep in the jungles of Orissa, buying an elephant? It was a circuitous 35-year route, detouring through the respectable and the disreputable, the fast, the furious and the far reaches of adventurousness.

A love of animals developed early on. Spending my childhood holidays in the English countryside, often with an old gamekeeper, I developed my natural affinity with, and love of, nature and the indigenous wildlife. And at the same time, during lengthy shopping trips to Harrods, I would give my mother the slip and escape into the pet department, a deafening and exotic emporium that smelled of hay, birdseed and fur. I spent some of my happiest times there, wandering through the bewildering and magical labyrinth of cages that squawked, squealed, chirped, grunted, roared, growled and dazzled with myriad exotic species that conjured up for me the mysteries of far-flung lands. It was here that I bought 'Charlie', much to my mother's horror – a glossy mynah bird that woke me up every morning saying 'I love you' in a broad Irish accent. It was here, to my mother's even greater horror, that I took possession of 'Tiki', my cunning and swift Indian mongoose which nearly gave an elderly lady a heart attack in an Italian restaurant by climbing up her stockinged leg, on to her lap and on to the table, to help her open the clams of her *spaghetti alla vongole*. And it was here, perhaps, that a passion to discover the mysteries of those distant places was awakened in my child's mind.

Expelled from public school at the height of the swinging sixties for smoking dope, and excelling only in History of Art, I was sent by my father, who thought it 'might put some spine in the little bugger', to Australia. I spent a year down under, working on sheep and cattle stations, and as a guard on an Opal mine in Cooper Pedy, bang in the desolate and blistering heat of central Australia. I travelled round the country with two friends in an old car and even made some money by investing in the booming mining market. But, I could have made more. I still kick myself at the wasted opportunities, but considering my character, I can well understand my father's hesitation in sending more money. In those days, I was offered beach-front property, for a dollar a mile, in Northern Queensland. It is now the Gold Coast.

But it was India, where I stopped on the way to Australia, that awoke a passion and love that has and will remain with me for the rest of my life. I was supposed to stay a few days. I stayed a month. I don't know what it was, but I believe you can fall in love with a country with the same passion that you can fall in love with a person or, in my case, an elephant. I felt immediately at home. I had lived there in another life, at another time. It was that smell – the smell of incense, cow-dung, smoke, shit, sweat, burning fires, Chamoli and Champa blossoms, sandalwood, disinfectant, frying curry leaves, chilli, chai and moth balls. It is a fragrance so heady that I've always thought if a great parfumier could bottle it, the scent would be the most intoxicating in the world.

Returning to the West, after a number of false starts in business I founded Obsidian in London with a friend, Harry Fane, selling objets d'art and jewellery by the great jewellers of the Art Deco period, such as Cartier, Van Cleef and Arpels and Boucheron. It was perfect for me, combining travel and art. We were both good salesmen, and Harry took care of the finances, which were not my strong suit. Like posh swagmen in linen suits, with sacks of beautiful booty over our shoulders, we hit the rich and famous, the old and new wealth in the money-drenched capitals of the Americas: Caracas, New York, Dallas, Houston, Los Angeles, Palm Beach and Miami. In the mid '70s, New York became the party capital of the world with the advent of the infamous nightclub, Studio 54. It was hedonistic, decadent, glamorous and fuelled by the drug of the moment – cocaine. Although this period remains a complete haze I made many good friends.

Every year, to escape the partying, socialising and selling, Harry and I set off for the magical island of Bali for two months. There, a friend designed and built us a beautiful Robinson Crusoe house on a surfer's beach. We lived a bohemian life, chilled-out and very anti-social. We had a sign on the door to the property - *'If you are a friend of a friend fuck off'*. This didn't endear us to the growing expat community, but it was an effective deterrent against 'friends of friends' who thought it was perfectly normal to come and visit us or, even worse, stay.

I had a boat, a 20ft local *prahu*, a kind of outrigger used for transporting horses and cows between Bali, Lombok and Borneo. I named it the *Gin Pahit*, an Anglo-Malay term for 'gin and bitters'. We made many fantastic journeys through the pristine islands of the beautiful Indonesian archipelago. If anything, these trips to Bali and the Far East just increased my passion to seek adventure and travel. The moment we became successful and opened an office in Jermyn Street, and I found myself in a suit going to work every day, I quit. I felt bad about leaving Harry. But I think he understood, and he went on to make a major success of the business.

My experience on the *Gin Pahit* inspired me to think of sailing round the world. Financing the trip was not going to be easy. Sailing can be one of the most expensive occupations, likened to tearing up ten pound notes while standing under a shower. But perhaps I could follow in the footsteps, of rather the wake, of my intrepid ancestor Admiral of the Fleet Sir Henry Keppel, and write a bestselling book? My maternal grandmother, who was immensely proud of her sailing ancestors and had written a book about them herself, might act as a secret weapon in helping me persuade my parents to release the last funds I possessed in the world. As soon as I'd secured the minimum necessary, I set off for Thailand to stay with friends, find a boat and plan my journey.

An amazing tale, told to me in the early hours of the morning in a bar in Bangkok, gave me the bestselling angle I'd been looking for. I should have remembered never to believe a story told under the influence of too much drink. Apparently, during the Second World War, a very young Catalina flying-boat captain used to fly regular missions from Sydney to Bougainville on Papua New

Guinea, to supply the allies against the invading Japanese. His flight path took him over a beautiful island called Rennell, with a large volcanic cobalt blue lake at its centre. As he swept low over the lake, he saw hundreds of canoes, paddled by beautiful, topless girls with flowers in their long oiled hair. They would wave at him longingly and blow him kisses. He would wave back longingly and return the kisses. It all became too much for him. He landed the flying boat on the lake, sunk it and entered paradise. My friend paused for a moment, took a long gulp of beer, before uttering the words that would seal my fate. 'Apparently,' he said 'He is still there. He has many wives and many children. His name is Sexy Tyler.' How could I resist? I was going to sail to Rennell, find this elusive character living in paradise and write his story.

I bought a boat, found a more experienced sailing companion, Tim, and eventually we set off from Fiji. Although it was the hurricane season, I was determined to haul anchor. We'd lost too much time restoring the 28-foot, eight-ton, twin-keeled yacht and I was terrified that Sexy Tyler would die before I arrived. But we never made it to Rennell.

It was sunrise on a glorious Friday morning as we motored quietly out of the lagoon into the vast Pacific Ocean and headed due west to our first port of call, the New Hebrides, or as they are known now, Vanuatu.

In our rush to get going I had forgotten to buy a sextant, but Tim did not seem concerned. 'Don't worry,' he reassured me. 'I'll navigate by dead reckoning. Vanuatu is due west. We'll follow the sun. I know a bit about astrology. I'll set the course on auto pilot.' I gulped. 'Dead reckoning'. I didn't like the sound of this.

I was right to be concerned. We nearly died on that first passage. It usually takes a maximum of four days to reach the New Hebrides from Fiji. You really can't miss these islands. There are around twenty in the archipelago and the majority are very large. Somehow it took us fourteen days. We ran out of food and more importantly water. We were forced to drink distilled seawater. I had also run out of cigarettes. In desperation, I started cutting up rope and rolling it in newspaper to smoke. And it was here that my love-hate relationship with sharks intensified.

I've always admired them, but facing starvation I also came to hate them. I'd sit with my legs hanging over the stern, holding a long line stretching out about a hundred metres or so into the wake. Fish were abundant in those days and every few minutes I'd feel a tug and pull the line in as quickly as possible. As I reeled in, there would be another tug, a more violent one and the line went limp. The sharks had taken not only the fish, but the lure and the hook as well.

We eventually made land at Port Vila, the capital of Vanuatu on the island of Efate. I remember cheers of derision from the locals in the port bar as we limped in, and they toasted us with ice-cold Fosters. I could taste the drops of condensation on the tins as I looked at them. Never had a cold beer tasted so good. As we took our first long gulps an earthquake hit the island. Clutching our tins of beer, we ran out as the bar disintegrated around us. An ominous sign, perhaps?

We re-victualled, cleaned up the boat and headed north-west to the capital of the Soloman Islands, Honaira. We anchored about half a mile offshore, opposite the yacht club. We heard that a hurricane was approaching, put down storm anchors and waited nervously. Then news came that the hurricane would miss Honiara, but that we should expect strong winds. Tim decided it would be better to head for open sea, rather than be near land. I was not convinced, but respected my captain's experience. I went to start the engine. It would not start. It had totally seized up. If the hurricane was to hit us we were sitting ducks. It was April Fool's Day – April 1st 1982.

Hurricanes are fickle, and this one turned round and hit us at full force. Everything happened so fast. Wind speeds soared to 60 knots onshore. This is why Tim had tried to get out into the open sea. Yachts are designed, when hit sideways, to roll 360 degrees, to capsize and right themselves again. You lose your masts and most of your deck structure, but you can survive. If you're hit head on, the boat will pitchpole – flip backwards and break in half. The waves were now seven metres, crashing over the stern and sweeping onto the deck. The boat was like a bucking bronco – one moment sitting on her stern, the next burying her prow in the waves.

Tim and I were being hurled around in the main cabin, trying to grab anything to hold on to. Then the galley stove came off its hinges and hit Tim on the side of his head, opening a deep wound. I decided we had to get off, otherwise we were dead. I managed to tie Tim to one of the 20 litre plastic jerry cans used for storing water and I literally flung him overboard. I quickly followed. I don't remember anything else. The next thing I knew, strong hands were pulling me out of the massive pounding surf. We found ourselves huddled in the yacht club holding cups of hot tea. We were both cut to pieces, lacerated by the coral while being swept ashore.

I will never forget those wonderful people. They saved our lives. One of them was a doctor who stitched up Tim's head and did his best to patch us up. They told me to sleep. I couldn't. I burst into tears and cried all night as

I watched my beloved boat fighting for her life, illuminated by the headlights of the many vehicles lining the shore. Winds had now hit 80-85 knots (about a hundred miles an hour). Palm trees were uprooted and crashed against the yacht club. The waves were up to twelve meters. The boat had no chance. Early in the morning, I saw her rise up once more, topple backwards and snap in two like a matchstick. I was numb. My dream had ended. I had lost everything.

After several months sitting in total depression in Bali, I received a letter – one of my father's very special letters – which read: 'I think it's about time you stopped feeling sorry for yourself, contemplating your navel under the bodhi tree, and got back home'. Shortly afterwards a friend introduced me to one of my heroes, the legendary war photographer Don McCullin. I'd always been in awe of and fascinated by Don. He seemed such a complex man and came across as incredibly depressed and very grumpy. I love grumpy people. But I also felt an enormous compassion, lying under his gloomy exterior. Don had given up covering wars. He had a row with the editor of the *Sunday Times*, a newspaper he had risked his life for so many years. He now wanted, as he put it, 'To get rid of the rubbish in my mind and record the disappearing tribes of the world, before it's too late.' He asked me to accompany him to Indonesia, as I knew the area well.

We made many fantastic journeys, particularly to the Mentawai Islands, off the west coast of Sumatra where Don took stunning photographs of the Sakkudei people, who have now been wiped out. In 1986, joined by my friend Harry Fane, we set out on expedition to the remote Asmat area of South Irian Jaya – Indonesia's largest island. It was here in the 1960s that Michael Rockefeller was supposed to have been eaten by cannibals. We went to find out.

In 1987, I proudly published my first book, *Skulduggery*, an account of that journey. It got one review in a free property magazine. It read something like:

'This book should be called *Carry-on up the Jungle* – a farcical attempt at travel-writing.'

This was not encouraging. However, I was lucky enough to have the late great Abner Stein as my agent and the late great Tony Colwell as my editor at Jonathan Cape. With their support and perhaps because my publishers needed to recoup their losses, they gave me another chance to write.

* * *

I had long wanted to write a book about India, the country that fascinated me most. I felt my soul was in India. So in 1988, I set off and came face to rump with Tara.

During that journey, through Tara I got my first inkling of the dangers facing her wild Asian cousins. I remember that in rural Orissa I was approached by a local teacher who was convinced that Tara and I had been sent by the Gods to catch a rogue elephant which had decimated his village's crops and already killed eleven people. This was but one of many similar situations that I would encounter, exposing the growing imbalance in India between rural man and the natural life of the elephants. Both are blameless and both are victims of greed, greed caused by a desire for timber and space, and the consequent massive deforestation. Elephants are creatures of habit and have for centuries followed the same migratory routes in search of food. When they arrive and find that their larder has been cut down, in desperation they turn to raiding the crops on which the villagers' livelihoods depend.

Over one hundred years ago, the American naturalist Charles Frederick Holder had recognized the inevitable. He wrote, '*The Asiatic elephant is said to be holding its own. But the rapid advance of the British in the East cannot fail to have a fatal effect and extermination is only a matter of time. They are the last of a powerful race worthy of earnest efforts of preservation. The question of their extinction rests with the rising generation*'.

Unfortunately, the rising – or should I say exploding – generations (India's population alone is over 1.2 billion) have failed to address this urgent problem. It was only on returning home from my journey with Tara that the full impact of the experience began to take effect. Elephants, like India herself, move slowly and subtly to educate humans, and Tara had been a clever and instructive teacher.

What had started as a whim soon turned into a passion. I came to realise that Asian elephants had once roamed in their millions from Syria to China, but that now they were reduced to pathetic little herds in equally reduced forest fragments. Today it is doubtful if as many as forty thousand elephants survive in the whole of Asia. Africa's elephant population is over half a million.

Unlike the larger, mammoth-tusked African elephant, the Asian elephant does not suffer to the same extent from poaching because only certain males carry ivory. Ironically however, and I say this with no prejudice because I adore all elephants, the African elephant has benefited from a highly emotional public outrage at their bloody slaughter for ivory. Appeals to help fund this fight have been so lucrative, positive and widespread that the Asian elephant, like the proverbial poor relation, has remained in the background waiting patiently for some crumbs. It seemed to me that the world had forgotten there was another elephant.

So I became what is now socially fashionable in western capitals, a person with a cause. But – to borrow an Indian expression – 'what to do?' I had no qualifications or scientific knowledge and, as I was to find out, the closed and rather arrogant coven of Asian elephant experts and NGOs did not take a mad Englishman's journey on an elephant across India seriously. They thought it was a publicity stunt. If I was to be taken seriously, I needed credentials. I needed to get out to Asia and really understand the problem. My old mahout, Bhim, had told me 'Rajah-Sahib there is only one way to learn about Haathi – be with them.'

Fortunately my book, due to Tara, was beginning to make waves and I was soon approached by independent documentary film-makers to write and present films on the Asian elephant. The first was with the Hollywood actress Goldie Hawn. Others followed and I wrote another book on my experiences with elephants. But what was most important was that the Asian elephant was finally getting some exposure in the West, and I was getting real hands-on field experience.

In the early nineties, I was approached by Fauna and Flora International, founded in 1903 and the oldest and most prestigious conservation society in the world. I was made a vice-president alongside the legendary Sir David Attenborough and David Bellamy. Perhaps I was finally being taken seriously. Fauna and Flora International had started to support Asian elephant conservation, particularly in Sumatra, Indonesia. It was a real learning curve for me. I spent a lot of time in the field, studying conservation and seeing how a charity works. But for my purposes, Fauna and Flora was too diverse. I wanted to concentrate only on the survival of the Asian elephant. To my knowledge such a charity did not exist. So on 1st September 2002, under the patronage of the late Rajmata of Jaipur, Sir Evelyn De Rothschild and five friends with the same passion, Elephant Family was born.

* * *

We began as a welfare organisation, concentrating on improving the life of captive elephants in Jaipur and Sumatra. But soon we realised that every elephant in captivity reflects a failure of conservation efforts. It is like sticking on a plaster. There are many welfare organisations doing great work, but Elephant Family's mission is to save the *wild* Asian elephant from extinction, before it is too late. We had to look at the bigger picture.

And we had to move fast. Ninety percent of the Asian elephant population had been wiped out in the previous hundred years. Ninety-five percent of their forest homes had been destroyed to make way for plantations, farms, mines, roads, railways and villages. And the situation was getting worse each year. The boom in the economy and in the human population had been catastrophic for the region's wild places. The last remaining elephants were forced into tiny pockets of forest where they were competing with their human neighbours for food, water and space.

When they don't have enough space and food, elephants can cause chaos. When stressed, disorientated elephants clash with poor subsistence farmers and villagers, causing deaths on both sides. In India alone, a person kills an elephant and an elephant kills a person every single day of the year. By corralling them into ever smaller areas, we have changed the psyche of this peaceful herbivore into that of a dangerous, paranoid animal that will seek revenge. Elephants are the only species that are intelligent and big enough to take on humankind. And they won't go quietly.

Elephant Family is dedicated to ending this daily battle between people and elephants. We are saving vital stretches of forest while we can, and reuniting isolated groups of elephants by reconnecting pockets of forest with 'elephant corridors'. These corridors of protected land act as elephant highways, joining up forest fragments and allowing all wildlife – including tigers and orangutans – to roam freely, to find new sources of food and, crucially, to breed successfully. We are giving elephants the space they need. And we are helping poor rural communities protect their livelihoods so that their families can live safely in the last remaining elephant habitats.

There are over eighty-eight identified elephant corridors in India alone. Four years ago, in partnership with the Wildlife Trust of India, we set out to save the most important corridor of all, linking Tirunelli and Begur Forest Reserves in Kerala, South India. It is a lifeline for 6,500 elephants, the largest population of elephants in Asia.

Just six kilometres long by a kilometre wide, the corridor was home to fifty-four human families in five settlements. Four of these settlements have been relocated to brand new safe homes where they are now able to grow crops without the fear of raiding and dangerous elephants. We are just in the process of relocating the last settlement. Already, there have been sightings of other wildlife including tigers, leopards and spotted deer using the corridor. This is another reason why it is so important to save the Asian elephant. It is the apex species. Elephants are the guardians of the forests as they need the maximum amount of space. If you save them, you save all the other species that share their habitat.

* * *

To start a charity from scratch is not an easy task. It takes real graft and belief. One person who has stayed with me from the beginning of this roller-coaster ride, Ruth Powys, is now the Director of Elephant Family. She instilled into the young and inexperienced team a passion and commitment that has made Elephant Family the success it is today. And a little later, we were joined by a kharmic beauty called Carla Vincent, whose Zen-like calm spread to us all.

Funding is always a problem. I have spent most of the last ten years with a begging bowl. On reflection, I realised that my past life hadn't been such a disaster. I had made so many friends, many of whom have supported me with the utmost generosity. But you can't just rely on major donors again and again. Donor fatigue sets in. The charity sector is highly competitive. You have to think out of the box and find other ways to raise funds and awareness. And you have to make it fun!

Initially, we took the traditional route by holding a grand dinner and auction called the 'Elephant Durbar'. Its success was partly due to the fact that the event was held in a beautiful private garden in Richmond. In addition, in 2006 my sister Camilla married The Prince of Wales. Overnight, the demented young brother, the black sheep of the family, became a little more respectable, perhaps. Both have been long and loyal supporters of Elephant Family and kindly attended the event. In The Prince of Wales, I am lucky to have as a brother-in-law a truly brilliant ally, a legend who has contributed massively himself to conservation and the environment. But those traditional ways of raising funds are no longer sufficient.

Apart from her extraordinary work ethic and her refusal to fail, Ruth Powys possesses that rare ability to think out of the box. In 2005, we got involved with the fashion photographer, Bruce Weber, an avid elephant nut. He created a group of life-size metal elephant frames and dressed them in Haute Couture fashion for a shoot for *W Magazine*. The elephant frames were built by an eccentric and brilliant topiary artist from the States, Topiary Joe.

We never looked back. Elephant Family began to hit the headlines starting with 'Elephants in the Park' – a herd of ten beautiful life-size willow elephants covered by elephant blankets designed by top fashion designers. It was also the year that 'Date an Elephant' was launched. It's a charming and much more personal adaptation of 'Adopt an Elephant'. On Valentine's Day, elephant daters receive personalised photographs and love poems from special elephants with different characters, chosen from our welfare projects, written painstakingly and beautifully by one of our team.

In 2008, the Survival Tour rocked off – thirteen life-size topiary elephants created by Topiary Joe, Ruth's twin sister, Mary, and her husband, Derek, in a barn near their home in Clonakilty, Ireland. They travelled right across the UK and Ireland and were showcased in spectacular locations. Audiences from these two exhibitions had now reached thirteen million and significant funds had been raised from the sale of the elephants and the blankets. Most importantly Elephant Family was growing a reputation as the charity that did things differently.

In 2010, we staged the largest outdoor art exhibition to date, in London. Two hundred and sixty elephant sculptures were placed across London, all painted by top artists, fashion designers and architects. It caused a sensation. At the auctions, conducted by Sotheby's and online, we raised over £4 million from the sale of the elephants. The top price – £155,000 – was paid for a fantastic elephant creation by the Scottish artist Jack Vettriano.

In 2011, Ruth dreamed up 'Jungle City'. One of the objectives of this new exhibition was to unite the conservation movement in Asia. We partnered with six other charities working in Asia with different species. A hundred and thirty elephant, tiger, orangutan, crocodile and hornbill sculptures, again painted by fantastic artists, were hidden across Edinburgh and raised over a million pounds.

This year we changed shape. Elephant Family, in partnership with Action for Children put on the largest egg hunt ever, sponsored by the jeweller, Fabergé. For forty days and forty nights, two hundred and ten giant eggs designed and created by top artists were hidden across London. We broke two Guinness World Records - for the most expensive chocolate egg ever sold, and for the most entrants in an egg hunt competition. We raised over one million pounds for the different charities and artists such as Zaha Hadid, The Chapman Brothers, Marc Quinn, Sir Peter Blake, Bruce Oldfield, Sir Nicholas Grimshaw and Nicky Haslam headlined the event with others.

Elephant Family has grown. We now have thirteen projects in four countries: India, Thailand, Malaysia and Indonesia. Campaigning is a high priority. If you can't encourage conservation, or put pressure on the governments and major companies, you're hitting a brick wall. I am deeply proud to have played a role in this wonderful charity – probably more proud than of anything else I have done in my life. We are now the UK's biggest funder of the endangered Asian elephant. To date we have raised £9.7 million for their conservation. Not bad for a charity that celebrates its tenth anniversary this year.

* * *

It's fitting to end with Tara, who is the true founder of Elephant Family. Over the years, I've visited her regularly at her home in Kipling Camp, Madhya Pradesh, where she lives like a pampered princess. She wakes up, eats, sleeps, swims, has a massage, eats and then goes back to bed – day in, day out. I would swap her life for mine any time. If I ever feel the need for motivation, all it takes is a few days with her to relieve the stress and fill me with hope again.

People ask me all the time how old she is. I know it is impolite to ask a lady her age. However, I will disclose that we celebrated my sixtieth and her fiftieth birthday last year when she consumed a cake which took four strong men to carry. I hope she does not read this. She, like most vain women, has always lied about her age.

Though she is getting older, she is just as beautiful. The tops of her ears are curling over, and she has lost two sets of molars. But this has not affected her appetite. And she is in better shape than me, with my two replaced hips. She doesn't frolic so much now in her private swimming pool in the local river. She sits quietly, her eyes (fringed by lashes long enough to suggest that they are false) closed contentedly. Occasionally, she will flick her trunk out of the water, spraying us with cooling water as I rest my head against her back – two old friends, enjoying the evening of their lives together.

I remember when I had finished my journey, the old elephant hands of Assam told me that I could now retire. 'You have performed Haathi Dhun,' they said. 'You have given life back to an elephant. From now on your life will be gilded in gold.' How could I think of retiring? I did not save her. She saved me.

Mark Shand
London 2012

ELEPHANT FAMILY

Protecting Asian elephants and their habitat

To find out more about Elephant Family's work, or to donate to the charity, please visit www.elephantfamily.org

Bibliography

NOTE: I have referred to some of these books in the text and they have all provided helpful background information.

Harry Abbot, *Reminiscences of Sonepore*, Star Press, Calcutta, 1896.

Salim Ali, *The Book of Indian Birds*, Bombay Natural Society, Bombay, 1979.

George Franklin Atkinson, *Curry and Rice: The Ingredients of Social Life at 'Our Station' in India*, Day and Day, London.

R. D. Banerji, *History of Orissa*, vols 1 & 2, Calcutta, 1931.

A. L. Basham, *The Wonder that was India*, Sidgwick & Jackson, London, 1954.

Hilaire Belloc, *The Bad Child's Book of Beasts*, Duckworth, London, 1938.

J. Moray Brown, *Shikar Sketches with Notes on Indian Field Sports*, Hurst & Blackett, London, 1887.

Richard Carrington, *Elephants*, Chatto & Windus, London, 1958.

Jane Dunbar (ed.), *Tigers, Durbars and Kings: Fanny Eden's Indian Journals 1837–1838*, John Murray, London, 1988.

Gerald Durrell, *Rosie is my Relative*, William Collins, London, 1968.

Emily Eden, *Up the Country: Letters from India*, Curzon Press, London, 1978.

Franklin Edgerton (tr.), *The Elephant-Lore of the Hindus: The Elephant Sport (Matanga-Lila) of Nilakantha*, Yale University Press, 1931.

Abu 'L-Fazl, *Ain-I-Akbari*, translated by H. Blochmann, Calcutta-Asiatic Society of Bengal, Bengal, 1927.

Robert Fermor-Hesketh, *Architecture of the British Empire*, The Vendome Press, New York, 1986.

Bamber Gascoigne, *The Great Moghuls*, Jonathan Cape, London, 1971.

C. F. Holder, *Ivory King*, Samson, Low, Marston Searle & Rivington, London, 1886.

Samuel Israel and Bikram Grewal (eds), *Insight Guides: India*, Harrap, London, 1985.

Ramchandra Jain (ed.), *McCrindle's Ancient India as described by Megasthenes and Arrian*, Today & Tomorrow's, New Delhi, 1972.

Anne Morrow, *Highness: The Maharajahs of India*, Grafton Books, London, 1986.

Cynthia Moss, *Elephant Memoirs: Thirteen Years in the Life of an Elephant Family*, Elm Tree Books, London, 1988.

Naveen Patnaik, *A Second Paradise: Indian Courtly Life 1590–1947*, Sidgwick & Jackson, London, 1985.

An Old Planter, *Reminiscences of Behar by an old Planter*, Thacker, Spink, Calcutta, 1887.

Louis Rousselet, *India and Its Native Princes: Travels in Central India and in the Presidencies of Bombay and Bengal*, revised and edited by Lieutenant-Colonel Buckle, Scribner Armstrong, New York, 1876.

G. P. Sanderson, *Pack Gear for Elephants*, Calcutta, 1887.

G. P. Sanderson, *Thirteen Years Among the Wild Beasts of India*, W. H. Allen, London, 1890.

Ivan T. Sanderson, *The Dynasty of Abu*, Cassell, London, 1963.

E. O. Shebbeare, *Soondar Mooni*, Victor Gollancz, London, 1958.

P. D. Stracey, *Elephant Gold*, Weidenfeld & Nicolson, London, 1963.

Sir J. Emmerson Tennant, Bt., *The Wild Elephant*, Longmans Green, London, 1867.

Edward Topsell, *The History of Foure-Footed Beastes, describing the True and Lively Figure of Every Beast … Collected out of all the Volumes of C. Gesner and all other Writers of the Present Day*, W. Jaggard, London, 1607.

Leonardo da Vinci, *The Notebooks of Leonardo da Vinci*, arranged and translated by Edward MacCurdy, George Braziller, New York, 1954.

Francis Watson, *A Concise History of India*, Thames & Hudson, London, 1974.

J. H. Williams, *Big Charlie*, Rupert Hart-Davis, London, 1950.

J. H. Williams, *Elephant Bill*, Rupert Hart-Davis, London, 1959.

Colonel Henry Yule and A. C. Burnell, *Hobson-Jobson*, John Murray, London, 1903.

GAZETTEERS

Bengal District Gazetteer – Gaya, 1906.

Bengal District Gazetteers – Saran, 1908.

Bengal District Gazetteers – Singhbum, Sareikela and Kharsawan – Calcutta, 1910.

Bihar and Orissa District Gazetteers – Saran, 1930.

Bihar and Orissa District Gazetteers – Cuttack, 1933.

Bihar District Gazetteer – Singhbum/Patna – Bishar, 1958.

Bihar District Gazetteer – Saran, 1960.

Bihar District Gazetteer – Ranchi, 1970.

Bihar District Gazetteer – Patna, 1970.

Hazaribagh Old Records (1761–1878), 1957.

Orissa District Gazetteers – Puri District.

Acknowledgements

ABOVE ALL, I would like to thank Naveen Patnaik and Aditya Patankar, whose friendship, support and patience really made this all possible.

Foremost, for unending generosity with their time, knowledge and resources my sincerest gratitude is due to: Sri Bijoyananda Patnaik, Sri Martand Singh, Ajai Singh of Maksudpur, Maharaj Kumar Anang Udai Singh Deo and Maharaj Kumarani Vijay Lakshmi Devi of Patna, Maharaj Kumar Ranjit Singh of Wankaner, Sri Bal Manohar Jalan, Tavleen Singh and Pepita Seth.

I am deeply grateful to the following people, all of whom in many different ways contributed so much:

In India Rajmata Gayatri Devi of Jaipur, Maharaja Gaj Singh of Jodhpur, Maharani Vasundhara Raje of Dholpur, Maharaja Pradeep Chandra Bhanj Deo of Mayurbhanj, The Raja of Seraikella, Mahijit Singh Jhala, Rani Sunita Pitamber, Sri Bijoy Sorangi, Sri Brijendra Singh, Mrs June Lal, Sanjiv Lal, Rajkumar Braja Bhannu Singh Deo, Bheem and Reeta Dev Varma, Hershad Kumari of Jamnagar, Amita Beg, Sri H. S. Jassal, Bittu Saghal, Doctor Duke Chawla, the late Sri Babla Senapathy, Sri S. K. Patnaik, Sri Nand Kishore Singh, Sri Arun Pathak, Sri Ashok Singh, Sri Nilmandhab Mohanty, Sri N. K. Panda, Kumud Choudhury, Sri B. C. Verma, Peter Carter, Toby Sinclair, Gudu and Christina Patnaik, D. K. Lahiri Choudhury, Doctor Kumar Suresh Singh, Pramod Kasliwal, Kumar Ashok Singh Diggi, Deepak Rana, Sita Ram Singh, Bishwanath Singh, Ranjivoy Singh, S. P. Singh, U. P. Singh and the people of McCluskiegunge. For their generous hospitality and impeccable service I would like to acknowledge Mr P. R. S. Oberoi and the managers and staff of the Oberoi hotels in Delhi, Bombay and Calcutta.

In England Belinda Burton, Mariuska Chalmers, Mitchell Crites, Simon Elliot. H. E. The Deputy High Commissioner for India, Mr Salman Haidar, Sir Geoffrey

Howe, Sir Owain Jenkins, Harry Marshall, Don Munson, Marjorie Naisbitt, Doctor John Price, Joan Phillips and the staff of Sussex Secretarial Services, John Hatt, Abner Stein and Beverley Sturdy. From my publishers Jonathan Cape: Georgina Capel, Jenny Cottom, Rachael Kerr, Hilary Turner, Sarah Wherry, and in particular my editor Tony Colwell whose care and erudition is legendary.

I can never begin to thank Gita Mehta for giving me so selflessly her guidance, knowledge, encouragement and time; my mother and father for their total support and allowing me to use their home to write this book; Don McCullin for being as always an indefatigable travelling companion and friend and Bob, Anne and Belinda Wright for giving Tara such a wonderful home at Kipling Camp where I know she will enjoy a long and very happy life.

Finally, I would like to thank the many unnamed people who I encountered in Orissa and Bihar, whose welcome, spontaneity and sense of humour made this journey so memorable for me. I shall never forget them.

M. S.
London
October, 1990

Digesting India

PRAISE FOR *DIGESTING INDIA: A TRAVEL WRITER'S SUB-CONTINENTAL ADVENTURES WITH THE TUMMY*

'Part memoir, part travelogue with lashings of history, literary references and unbridled fun, this collection of eight essays takes the reader on a whirlwind ride through India and the food (and alcohol) it holds... *Digesting India* will leave you chortling and hungering for more.' —**Preeti Zachariah, *The Hindu***

'You really do not have to be a foodie to enjoy Zac O'Yeah's *Digesting India*...this Scandinavian-born author, settled in Bangalore, who has been exploring the sub-continent for over three decades now never ceases to surprise himself, and the reader with the everyday magic of India. This time, he discovers it through food.' —**Sukant Deepak, Indo-Asian News Service**

'*Digesting India* is in-depth and immersive, filled with anecdotes that many readers will be delighted to come across.' —**Anjana Basu, *Outlook India***

'A droll and deeply researched new book by Zac O'Yeah reveals to India the food, booze and culture of its backstreets' —**Samar Halarnkar, *Mint***

'O'Yeah brings a lot of knowledge and research to his writing, but wears all of it lightly—the tone is light, the puns keep flowing...All through the book I felt like immediately booking myself a ticket to the place he was writing about and at the end, wanted to undergo the same adventure—try the foods, learn about the place, see the landmarks and talk to the locals.' —**Sidharth Bhatia, *The Wire***

'O'Yeah's writing is humorous, insightful, and delightful, tempting the reader to binge on this country's delectable, sometimes unknown, offerings on each page...*Digesting India* is unputdownable.' —**Sharmistha Chaudhuri, *India Today***

'Zac O'Yeah's new book, *Digesting India*, harks back to the good old times when travel writing was about slow journeys, memorable encounters, subtle observations, tongue-in-cheek humour, deep dives into a destination, and more.' —**Avantika Bhuyan, *Mint Lounge***

DIGESTING INDIA

A Travel Writer's Subcontinental Adventures with the Tummy

(A MEMOIR À LA CARTE)

ZAC O'YEAH

SPEAKING TIGER

SPEAKING TIGER BOOKS LLP
125A, Ground Floor, Shahpur Jat, near Asiad Village,
New Delhi 110049

First published by Speaking Tiger Books 2023

ISBN: 978-93-5447-506-1
eISBN: 978-93-5447-507-8

10 9 8 7 6 5 4 3 2

Typeset in Dante MT by SÜRYA, New Delhi
Printed at Printworks, Delhi-92

For Mita & Rahul, and the great life!
I hope this book will tickle like a pickle!

'What, for instance, could hing mean
to your salt-and-pepper accustomed tongue,
of what do lichees taste to you?'

—*Food of Love*, Anjum Hasan

CONTENTS

Prologue

It's one meal I'll never forget. Ever. About to catch a bus to Nepal the next morning, I celebrated a successful tour of India. I was a rather inexperienced backpacker so I had reasons to be happy despite the fact that I munched on an only slightly dubious tandoori chicken in a somewhat seedy drinking den in Patna. I bet you can guess what happened next. Yes, exactly that.

Illustration: Paul Fernandes

At 3 a.m., I made a desperate dash for the commode where the resulting World War I-class bombardment of poison gas was so explosive that the toilet door flew off its hinges. As is well known, travellers' stories evolve as one grows older, but this is exactly how I remember it thirty years later as a mature, responsible tourist.

Wishing to put that ignoble moment behind me forever, get it off my shoulders so to speak, is one good reason why I wrote this book. In fact, I've never told anybody of my discomfiture, not even my wife, but in hindsight it is a hilarious episode to throw into a travelogue to raise the stakes.

Like I told you, I wasn't as experienced then. In retrospect, my theory is that the chicken, before turning zombie on me, had been entombed in putrefying marinade for too long. Perhaps a week, maybe even a month—maturing extra rapidly from young chick to elderly hen thanks to the lengthy power cuts that were common back then. It might have been waiting for me for a year, considering how well it had been marinated, until all hell broke loose...motion. But did I make the bus to Kathmandu? Yes, thanks to about 1 kg of Imodium that turned my intestines into a solid block of concrete.

A decade later, around the turn of the millennium, I had become a hardened professional travel writer, flying across the world on assignments. One sunny day I was being taken by a stubborn, officially-appointed guide to every single batik shop in Sri Lanka. He seemed hell-bent on getting me to buy enough hand-printed textiles to clothe the entire generation of 1967 in hippie fashion. Just then, I experienced tell-tale eggy burps reminiscent of that night in Patna; only this time it was evidently a gastric malfunction derived from dicey seafood at the previous day's five-star hotel. The only reason I continued to go along with my guide was a feeble hope that the next shop might provide me with a customer loo. Ultimately, I found relief in a grimy backyard bathroom. For days afterwards, my tummy continued to feel like a carton of champagne bottles about to self-detonate. As I was checking out on my last day, with the train to Colombo about to leave, the manager refused to let me go as he perused a ledger seemingly forever and kept asking, 'Why didn't you order food from the room service? We have king prawns.'

'Kindly book me a tuk-tuk [as rickshaws are called in Sri Lanka]. I need to be at the station in seven minutes!' I said.

'Sorry, phone is out of order.'

Too late to return to the suite to 'do a number two', I simply threw 1,500 LKR on the counter to cover tips for the room service meals that I never had and ran. I was lucky. As I was jogging towards the railway station, a tuk-tuk stopped beside me. 'Colombo train?' he asked.

'Yes, yes!'

'Train is 8.45,' he said and pointed at his watch. It showed 8.45.

Fortunately, goats were leisurely grazing on the tracks and the train was delayed as usual. I asked the stationmaster for the nearest restroom, because by now my tummy felt pretty much as if the aforesaid champagne bottles believed that New Year's Eve was minutes away.

'It'll come,' he replied.

'What will come?'

'Toilet is on train. It'll come in half an hour.'

Needless to say, a nearby coconut grove got its fair share of fertilising that morning and I wrangled a funny column out of it. A third time, an intestinal catastrophe was caused by one of those oh so delectable fried mussels known as kallumakkai, which are a specialty served in Thalassery, the fishing town in northern Kerala. Out of culinary curiosity, I had been snacking on them all day and one individual must have been in a sour mood at being deprived of its shell and thrown into sizzling oil, only to see its life pass by in agonising reminisces of happier days playing water polo with other mussels.

It clearly didn't like what it saw inside my bowels and knocked on all emergency exits at 2 a.m., sending me out of bed to projectile vomit into the wastepaper basket. Afterwards, considering that we had been on such intimate terms, I decided to name it Fred to pay homage to that exotic Franco-Cajun turtle soup served at the Galatoire's in New Orleans where, as per tradition, after setting down the tureen the waiter always leans forward to whisper, 'Its name was Fred.'

According to scholars there are world records in this specific field among tourists, with the highest known score so far being 37 t.t.b./h. ('trips to bathroom per hour'). In three decades on the road, I've occasionally felt like I'm about to breach that impossible limit, but it's never gotten that bad. By now, you're obviously wondering why I am going on about such farty aspects when you bought a supposedly arty book. This collection of travel memories isn't in actual fact about unsavoury experiences. The larger point is that I've had thousands of astonishing meals ranging from fried silkworms in Shanghai to the national dish of boiled super-hot chillies in Bhutan, from the weird rotten shark delicacy so treasured on Iceland to curried goat intestines in Zimbabwe, from the primeval pizzas of Naples to the raw meat sandwiches of Denmark, all of which gave me tons of ideas for stories.

And it follows that since 50 per cent of my writings are about local delicacies, I've naturally suffered as many forms of tourist diarrhoea as there are dishes in the average cookbook, ranging from 'Delhi-belly dancer-tummy', 'Calcutta-chromosomes' and

'Kathmandu killer-craps', to 'Beijing-burps', 'Istanbul-intestines', 'Moroccan motions' and 'Zimbabwean zumbas' as they form an integral if annoying part of travel.

On the one hand, if I played it safe, I might not have suffered inconveniences but would have had no stories to tell you. Some backpackers tramp on for years without snafus, spending their lives on the road eating yoghurt and nuts, starved of any destination's gastronomic heritage. Here, I'm reminded of a guide published in London in 1911—*A Handbook for Travellers in India, Burma and Ceylon,* which complains that: 'As a rule, the food supplied in hotels and railway refreshment rooms in India is not very good. Outside the really large places and cantonments, the meat, with exception of bullock hump, is often lean and tough, the fowls are skinny, and the eggs ridiculously small.' The helpful handbook warns prospective tourists: 'Bread is fairly good, but this cannot be said of the butter, and milk is not free from danger. Aerated water should be drunk in preference to plain water, even in private houses; and the water in hotels and refreshment rooms should be absolutely avoided. If the traveller leaves the beaten track, he should have a tiffin (luncheon) basket, containing knives, forks, and other simple fittings and supplies; and, as a matter of fact, whenever any long journey is undertaken, it is well to be always provided with such a basket of potted meats, soups or bovril, biscuits, jam, tea and sugar, some spirit, and soda-water, which is good and cheap in India, as this renders one immune against the accident of detention, or of failure to obtain an eatable meal at a railway refreshment room.'

The same attitude prevails even today, 112 years later, among foreign visitors to India. As for me, if it weren't for Fred and his bacteria-infested friends, I wouldn't have written this book, in which eating habits become an essential and deeply intertwined part of the larger narrative of places and culture. The above examples, distasteful as they may seem to dignified readers who would rather spend money on a decent poetry collection, illustrate three important aspects of successful voyages:

a) The need for preparation (never go on the road without Imodium);

b) Ditto for adjustment (learn to use coconut groves creatively);

c) And to be human (give even the most painful memories a name like 'Fred' or 'Donald' or something suitable).

For me, travel has always been about exploring—be it cuisines or cultures. After having munched on alligator sausages in Louisiana and barbecued kangaroos in Australia, I've been looking to expand my horizons with the aid of books like *They Eat That? A Cultural Encyclopaedia of Weird and Exotic Food from Around the World* and, not to forget, *Dinner with a Cannibal: The Complete History of Mankind's Oldest Taboo*.

A crucial aspect of travel, one that not everybody keeps in mind, is the importance of analysing oneself and one's reactions—both physical and mental—to what happens on the road, and in so doing learn new things. What have my tummy chronicles revealed to me?

a) The best-laid plans don't always work;

b) One ought always to make the most of the situation.

In other words, we could for instance rely on catching the ferry from Calcutta (as it was called once) like the chivalrous Phileas Fogg in *Around the World in Eighty Days*, but our train might run out of railway tracks somewhere in Central India. In Jules Verne's 1873 novel about those early days of tourism, this unforeseen change in the plan results in the memorable scene where Fogg rescues a virtuous maharani from a sati pyre and later weds her. A dire situation with a happy end! Not every trip needs to result in marriage, even if it has happened to me once, but the idea is to be prepared for the unexpected.

The art is therefore about learning to adjust when conditions change and, for example, courteously accommodate another passenger when the bus is overcrowded. Mistakenly assuming that the day before Friday the 13th ought to be safe for travel, I was once robbed of all my money, VISA card, valuables etc., by miscreants on a train in Assam, while I was engrossed in Rohinton Mistry's novel *Such a Long Journey*. When I reported the crime to the ticket-collector, he offered me rice and curry on the house. Seeing my plight, the other passengers fed me chai and ciggies that I gratefully chain-smoked to steady my nerves, until I got to Delhi where the hotelier recognised me from previous visits as an unfussy guest and offered me free accommodation until I got my situation in order. He also uncorked a bottle of Bagpiper and poured me a drink. I stopped tearing my hair out and after a few pegs, I knew I had a great feel-good story to sell to a travel magazine. At other times, when I've had no such luck, I've slept on railway platforms in Salt Lake City and rural Punjab, or flea-infested bus stations in Africa, or under a bush in some Copenhagen park.

Discomfort is the price that a frequent traveller pays in the hope of a bonus at the end. And, after all, minor disasters are merely *minor*—when compared to the many journeys of a lifetime. There's indeed something ridiculous about expecting everything to be 100 per cent glitch-free. Staying and eating five-star is not necessarily a safeguard against everything bad, so one may as well dive right into the adventure.

Situations where one negotiates the unexpected and manages to retain an optimistic approach, rather than boarding the next flight home to sulk, are the moments when one's resolve is tested in order to make it possible to reap rewards later—hopefully. At least in theory, these instances enable us to understand more about ourselves (and how to deal with life crises) and other people (humans are essentially kind and social). Incidentally, I learnt the art of patience in the Himalayas when I reached a bus stop on a winding mountain road and asked the uncles hanging about if the semi-deluxe limited-stop express was expected soon.

'Yes,' they agreed.

I waited with them but nothing happened.

'Is it coming today?' I asked an hour later.

'This week for sure,' said one of the men who knew a bit of English.

'This week! Why didn't you tell me it may not come today?'

'Or next,' he replied coolly.

I walked to the nearest village to find lodgings until a slow bus eventually came, but I also realised that these uncles by necessity spent much of their lives waiting for transport that might or might not show up—while I was free to move on. That was my first real trip anywhere in the world, but it was followed by much more learning through travel. The moral implication is that we should interact with strangers (who are actually the real people, we're the strangers who pass through) roughly in the same way that we interact with our own friends. Of course, to call ourselves genuine artists of tourism presupposes that we have backup plans—scans of important documents in the Cloud, sufficient insurance coverage, a global SIM and, don't forget, that mandatory Imodium to bring up the rear—because the solutions we think up on our feet are only as useful as they turn out to be.

Nonetheless, the moment you make it down alive from a steep peak after having lost sight of the trekking path in the mist, or talk your way out of a tricky situation in which desert militia are about to pepper your taxi with machinegun fire and you reach the coast of the Red Sea, it will seem that no matter what absurdities you've gone through, the trip was so worth it that you immediately want to do it again. At least I did. As with most art forms, the end thus justifies the means. You're feeling richer and spend hours at the backpacker café in Dharamsala or sit in a pub in Britain bragging about your exploits. Like Baron von Munchausen's legendary feats, your travails and triumphs grow with each retelling. If you sell your story to a publisher, you might even get your travel expenditure reimbursed.

The final step, then, of any trip is its dissemination or else it will lose its meaning. The click-and-go generation might be satisfied with WhatsApping selfies, but that is no long-term solution because as the saying goes: Elephants have memories, humans only Facebook. For older generations, holiday documentation was about embellishing one's trophy display case with Russian dolls, German schnapps glasses with the names of different cities printed on them, and porcelain plates where the mouth of the British Queen grins at the spot the *chateaubriand* should sit. I too have stocked up on fun objects to use in daily life—a Greyhound thermos mug on my desk reminds me of an American overnight bus journey, an empty pack of Maghreb brand cigarettes reminds me of smoky nights in Marrakech bars, a soft silk shawl from Antakya takes me back to the Mediterranean end of the Silk Road the same way the polychromatic T'ang porcelain camel with broken legs on my windowsill transports my mind to its other end at Xi'an.

As we know from thousands of years of human experience, the primary form of documentation is the written journal. Julius Caesar kept a belligerent one when he tried to conquer Britain and Germany in the first century BCE, jotting down notes regarding the weird habits of the Celtic and Teutonic races. The scholarly monk Xuanzang (also spelled as Hsien-tsang in mustier tomes) did so too when he toured India in the seventh century CE, noting how far it was to walk from one Buddhist monastery to the next, searching for the origins of faith. His *Journal of West Countries in Tang Dynasty* is perhaps the best 1st millennium guide to backpacking in India and remains in print as a valuable source of information for archaeologists. American humorist and author Mark Twain, ditto, on his trips round the world in the nineteenth century. Their writings are now invaluable records of locations and how these appeared back then, knowledge that otherwise may have been lost forever.

It's worth keeping such journals for their own sake—whether you publish them or not—because they may show their true value when one least expects it. In the case of what you are about to read, these are my finest pre-pandemic experiences from the road. So this might turn out to be a memoir of a lost world, but I'm hopeful that if things work out well—and the corona virus that had disrupted our lives since 2019, is replaced forever by Corona-beery cheery nights at pubs again—this book will serve as an inspiration to return to the joys of travel.

❖

Speaking of which, the pandemic that hit the planet in 2019 is still an on-going phenomenon as I write this in 2023, resulting in irritating travel restrictions. According to the latest updates, it may take years before things completely normalise. If they ever will, that is. This notion is, to say the least, a nightmare for those of us who enjoy travelling, sampling unaccustomed flavours and exploring cultures other than our own. For someone like me, who has viewed those viral food delivery apps as nothing but culinary malware—clickable edibles and mass-manufactured monotonous meal kits travelling to me rather than me venturing out to look for interesting items to ingest—this so-called new normal was indicative of a stomach-upsetting paradigm shift. It indeed looked like the beginning of a bad, unappetising time.

I'll never forget that moment in early 2020 when I realised to what extent times were about to change. I happened to be walking in Bengaluru's bazaars, when I heard the yells of, 'Corona! Corona!' Momentarily distracted (there had already been talk of a lockdown in the city to stop the virus and so I was wearing my anti-pollution mask to play it safe), I looked around and noticed teenagers dressed like villainous extras in some Kannada gangster flick, pointing in my direction. Then it clicked. *I* was the corona.

I hurriedly headed for the Chickpete Metro station to put distance between me and the rowdy pretenders. Two days later, papers reported on how a foreign tourist, who arrived in town from an ashram in Puttaparthi on 22 March 2020, the first day of curfew, found it impossible to get lodgings in the Majestic area, which, apart from hosting the railway station and main bus stand, is also the hub for budget accommodation.

The elderly foreigner was hounded across the roads by a wild crowd. Alert journalists and policemen rescued the hapless tourist before he was lynched and even fed him, as it seems the only word the starving, panicky man could utter by then was, 'Banana. Banana.'

The normally traveller-friendly area had—virtually in the blink of an eye—turned on visitors in a way one would never have imagined. Sure, one could maintain that these misguided local gents were only indulging in mischievous timepass—what else to do on a curfew day but turn vigilante? Yet it set me wondering how this situation will affect the relationships between inhabitants and tourists in what was hitherto arguably the most hospitable country in the world. As a personal testimony to this, I just have to think about the decades that I've lived in Bengaluru and how I've come to take it for granted that strangers everywhere—in the neighbourhood, on buses and trains, in markets—will greet me with a merry 'Had your coffee?' and be eager to strike up a conversation. Is it all over now?

I realised, when I read in the newspapers about another foreign tourist who had to wait fifty-five days at Delhi Airport before getting a flight home, that the travel restrictions hit too close to home for somebody who has spent half of his life travelling. In my own case, considering how much I had been travelling for my writing work in the previous decades, I was happy to be at home—on one of my occasional breaks between journeys—as a newspaper had offered me an all-expenses paid trip to Los Angeles that spring. For whatever reason I had been tardy about it but if I had boarded the plane, I'd have had to spend the next couple of months sleeping on a park bench in Hollywood. Or until I was jailed for vagrancy.

I was even starting to get wary of myself. Was I touching unsafe surfaces when I closed the gate outside my house? Even my usually helpful pharmacist had been bitten by the mental bug, although we were both masked and he was also wearing protective gloves, and neither of us was coughing and we were separated by the counter—a protective wall of clear plastic and 4 ft of air. When, after doing my other purchases, I asked for cough medicine, he took a step back, looked at me askance and said, 'We don't have any. Why do you need it?' He'd drawn his own conclusions and before he dialled some emergency helpline, I hastened to defuse the situation. 'Simply to have in case the worst happens. Pray god it doesn't.'

Something had definitely changed. Afterwards, I met a lady who worked as a maid for one of my neighbours (so we always greeted each other), but now she was lying on a quilt spread out on the pavement and looked like she was starving. Still, she smiled at me. 'Coffee *aitha*?' I asked, as we do in Kannada, before realising that she could probably afford neither food nor coffee. I gave her the 200 bucks left in my wallet before dashing home.

Our frustration over the pandemic may result in xenophobia, but who will we blame? The Chinese? But as Mahatma Gandhi argued with reference to colonial oppression, one cannot dismiss all Britons as bad merely because some of them upheld an unfair colonial system; likewise, just because the pandemic may have come from a particular food market in Wuhan, we should not stop eating chopsuey. It just doesn't make sense to allow social distancing to become a rabid distrust of everybody, especially since the only way life can go on is if one believes one's fellow humans to be responsible enough to follow the guidelines issued by authorities in a crisis.

Tourism—which earned India approximately $200 billion annually and employed forty million people pre-pandemically—definitely ushered in an interest in what was previously considered alien. When I was a kid in Sweden, there were few Indian restaurants but nowadays, there's a curry house on every second corner (helped by the fact that so many Swedes have holidayed in India and return home realising that the generic curry powder on the supermarket shelf doesn't compare favourably with fresh-ground masalas). Simultaneously in India, even smaller towns nowadays have eateries serving Conti staples. This is admittedly to simplify a complex matter, but the notion can be expanded to encompass, say, other Indian cultural exports such as yoga, Booker-winning novelists and Bollywood dance. Thanks to tourism, the culture of India has thoroughly penetrated the western world, whether we talk of the voluptuous creaminess of korma or mind-altering ideas like karma.

A futuristic non-tourism world, should we imagine it, might be like Disneyland (for kids) and Las Vegas (for adults), where we sightsee replicas of the Eiffel Tower, the Empire State Building, pyramids, Greek temples and so on. In Las Vegas, I ended up in a Roman-themed casino where guests could walk into an air-conditioned piazza of outdoor cafés situated under a perpetually sunset-rosy sky—just like being in Italy, but without the hassle of actually flying to Rome, not to mention the risk of ending up marooned for weeks at Leonardo da Vinci Airport because of all the possible global disasters one can think of.

Some hospitality properties were converted into workation (to break the tedium of WFH) or 'coronacation' hideaways where customers selected their preferred comfort from three to five stars and degree of 'self-isolation', contactless services via QR codes and Apps, vacation packages turned into 'vaccination packages' with immunity-booster cuisine. The general trend was an obvious preference for domestic destinations—rather than falling sick in a downlocked foreign country.

As a travel writer, I observed all of this with ever-deepening puzzlement. What were they doing to the world's hotels? Was my next hospitality industry reality check going to turn into a tedious hospitalisation? Or worse—as hotels increasingly attracted work-from-homers and turned themselves into office suites, I apprehended that the next time I was going to take a break from work, I'd find myself in a smaller replica of my own office instead of a relaxing room far from any desk. Scary thought.

Or perhaps this was the end of tourism as we know it because cyber-tourism took off in a big way at the same time.

App- or web-casting guides walked you through sightseeing itineraries for $30-40 and you didn't even have to put on hiking boots. Foodaholics learnt to fry *okonomiyaki* from Japanese chefs, how to boil Turkish coffee in an Istanbul café, or fast with meditating Buddhist monks, a Dharavi-dweller showed foreigners how to make perfect vada-pav online and Bengaluru foodies convened on video-conferencing apps to gorge on home-delivery biryanis. Dating went virtual with cafés in cyberspace serving signature Non-Fungible Token-tea—not to mention non-fragrant, non-caffeinated. And the nibbles may look Instagrammable, but in the metaverse they won't taste of anything. So, are we finding ourselves in a world where, if we cannot go to the Taj Mahal, that monument of love comes to us—in a virtual form to be viewed through sterilised 3D-glasses, downloaded as a software simulation which, if it has viruses, will only be bugs in the programme? The signs are already there considering how much online services benefit from the real world coming to a physical standstill.

Big questions. To look for small answers, for the first time ever I went to a palmist who answers vital questions—love-life, afterlife—at Rs 101 a pop. My query? *When will I again travel the world?* Possibly I was getting desperate, for I had strange nightmares about eating my camera. But I didn't tell that to the chiromantic practitioner, lest he think I'm weirder than his ordinary clientele.

After studying my palm, he instructed me to shake cowries while praying to any god of my choice, and then chuck the shells onto the table top. Unfortunately, he said rolling his head 180° this way and then 360° that way, envious sorcerers in my immediate social circle had engineered a black magic spell which is why I hadn't travelled. Unless I hired him to search my home for hidden hoodoo jujus, there was no prospect of journeys. At that moment, I snapped back to my senses because a year before I had lived in a different house, which was demolished months back, so any jinxed hex would have to be in some landfill. Yet, my problem remained—for a travel writer, I'd travelled unusually little since the end of 2019.

❖

Writing this book, I had my Hamlet moment as I walked past a spot that used to be crowded with snack hawkers. Now there were perhaps two, with few customers in sight. It seemed as sad as a Shakespearean tragedy. But the moment I dug in my pockets for loose change, I felt the stirrings of comorbidity. I carried on. Repining, I reverted, then changed my mind for the umpteenth time. Seeing a couple of fearless youths enjoying spicy snacks, masks down, I gave in to my inherent herd mentality, praying for herd immunity, and...*shabash!* Whatever it was, I forget exactly, probably a greasy roll stuffed with curried goat liver.

Years from now, the nexus between Wuhanese wet markets and gluttons' wet dreams may seem like a trifling conundrum, but had I foolishly put myself in mortal danger or was I merely giving in to a wholesome urge to enjoy life again? What's healthier: To go on existing indefinitely in a state of paranoia or to redevelop an appetite for existence? For isn't it true that the French word 'restaurant' originally meant a soup kitchen where one went to be physically restored to health?

But after the exquisitely brief pleasure of having fast-food again (it took me under seven minutes to gobble it down) after seven long months I worried for seven days that I might get COVID-19. I heard the clock of death tick like Edgar Allan Poe's tell-tale heart through the next nineteen nights, had nightmares about eating nineteen barbequed pangolins or two kilograms of bat fritters in a Wuhanese chophouse, yet as this goes to print, *I'm still standing* (two inches taller than Elton John).

It's worth remembering how, about 111 years ago today, Mahatma Gandhi debated 'whether the profession of a clerk or book-keeper is better or more respectable than that of a hawker. A hawker is an independent man. He has opportunity of studying human nature which a clerk slaving away for a few pounds per month can never have. A hawker is master of his own time. A clerk has practically no time he can call his own. A hawker, if he chooses, has opportunity for expansion of his intellect which a clerk cannot dream of.' Food hawkers aren't necessarily doom-bringers, because those that I personally observed were stricter about wearing masks than the common people I met. So I told my paranoid mind to focus on something worth worrying about instead.

Street-food may not be the healthiest option, but it can't automatically be equated with junk-food. Luxurious restaurants apart where patrons peer into kitchens behind glass walls, vendors with pushcarts are among the few chefs that customers can see in action. Wherever you go in India, if you are unexpectedly hungry, your easiest choice is street-food. Competitively priced, available at most hours, usually made fresh to order, it is what locals love to eat—so, a great way to befriend a new place. Furthermore, paying attention to the where and what also helps: Does the snack look like a petri dish?

In Kolkata? Grab a kathi roll near New Market. Mumbai? First thing to do after alighting from the train is to head towards the vada-pav stalls outside the station to get the yummiest pick-me-up of potato dumplings in a crusty bun. Delhi? Take the Metro to Chawri Bazaar and head up-street to Shyam Sweets, a kiosk dating back to the 1910s, for their legendary bedmi aloo.

And here, I'm not only thinking of India for in many other countries like Taiwan and Turkey, roadside cuisine has reached the highest possible epicurean echelons too.

In fact, the world over travellers encounter tantalisingly pocket-friendly short-eats: Meze in the Mediterranean, tapas in Hispanic lands, and in the country of XXXL T-shirts there's even a saying that, according to my American friend James, goes something like 'every candidate for US President is required to show their face and eat a Philly cheesesteak sandwich to prove that they are one of the common people. This is an election year qualification ritual.' So, after visiting the White House in DC, I obviously had to take the Amtrak train to Philadelphia and try out the most calorific 'Born in the USA' meal-on-the-go. Essentially, this is a hashed steer steak with plenty of onion smothered in gooey cheese, stuffed in a sub and preferably had at Pat's (where it was invented in the 1930s). Bill Clinton, Humphrey Bogart and Frank Sinatra all sampled it there, and it's the reason why cabbies are fatter in Philadelphia than elsewhere. The scariest junk I've ever eaten was at Whiz, a temple of terrifying tuck in San Francisco, whose 'corndog' is an indigestible cornmeal-battered hotdog on a stick, deep-fried until it becomes positively lethal. A suicidal treat that swiftly turned into a heartbreaking threat as my left arm tingled like a kathak dancer's ghungroos. Soon afterwards, I was diagnosed with high blood pressure. But eating it felt as deliciously sinful as having a Maggi-noodle Schezwan paneer dosa or chai-Maggi (tea cooked with instant noodles) in Bengaluru.

Even if it might be bad for my health, I sorely miss the *choudoufu* or 'stinky tofu' that's been fermented until it trumps the most matured of European cheeses in terms of olfactory orgasms, cooked in porky lard and served with a drizzle of garlic soy. If that's not your scene, then the *bao*—as the name implies a Cantonese cousin of the Goan pav (but in China we're talking steamed pork-patty-buns stuffed with slurps of crab roe broth)—should hit the gastric G-spot. The only things I found hard to digest in China were oil-fried scorpions, skewered chicken sphincters and animal genitals in general, but at least I tried.

So what if it's not the optimal fitness diet? One Bengaluruan foodie friend asserted that the grubbier the grub, the better it'll taste—because decontaminated squeaky-clean canteens can only serve tasteless nourishment. In the US, I asked a connoisseur why he loved corndogs and the expert retorted, 'We're not meant to live forever. We do our best to prolong our lives with medications, but Mother Nature dishes up temptations to curtail our lifespans. Every species understands this. Just look at lemmings, that don't have to eat corndogs to commit mass suicide.'

If one were to analyse this from a spiritual aspect, junk-food is divisible into junk (evil) and food (necessity): The necessary evil. After reaching that conclusion, I felt pretty much alright with my relapse to wayside cookery. Because there's nothing that beats the real deal, those spicy sauces blending with one's drool as one devours up hot snacks. Even if the world is full of museums dedicated to our collective memories of edibles, including a recently opened one in Tamil Nadu where Indian food traditions are traced back to 13,000 BCE, an Instant Noodle Museum in Japan and two Museums of Pasta in Italy, travelling in a hurry to where the next curry awaits is at the top of my post-pandemic agenda. Oh, and there's actually a Curry Museum, in…wait a minute…Yokohama?

Salivating, I search for its webpage to find that Yokohama's curry-themed exhibition was created to honour reinterpretations of Indian dishes—such as curried chocolate and curry cocktails—but has now shut down. Interestingly, curry arrived in the port town, with its large expat community of foreign traders, when Britons sailed eastwards from Calcutta in the late 1870s, packing Indian food in their tiffin-carriers. Once transferred into bento boxes, this became a Japanese staple. It seems the Japanese got hooked on curry's British avatars because their imperial aspirations led them to perceive it as sophisticated food fit for a global empire. *Kare*, as they call it, is milder and sweeter than its Indian prototypes, and remains the topmost comfort food in Japan. Coincidentally, the English word curry is an Indian loanword—its origin seems to be the Tamil 'kaari' which may be translated as 'black-peppery vegetarian broth'.

Another example of curry being adopted abroad was exhibited at the Currywurst Museum in Germany, celebrating Berlin's bizarrely beloved curry-ketchup-spiced pork-sausages that fuelled the labourers who rebuilt the city after each World War. Until the pandemic hit the food business, some seventy-three million currywursts were sold annually in Berlin alone, with another billion portions being eaten across the country! Come to think of it, even in Scandinavia where I grew up, no feast was complete without a jar of curry-pickled herring on the table and those scrumptious *smørrebrøds* of Copenhagen, topped with piles of *karisild* (curry-pickled herring), are as Danish as it gets. Appetisingly enough, the Indian tourism organisations cashed in on the country's foodie fame by modifying the monumental 'Incredible India' campaign which took place around two decades ago, into an 'Incredible Tiffin' drive in the 2010s.

I suppose you've guessed by now—since you probably picked this book up as you think a little like me—that I too prefer to have my curry on a plate before me rather than in a museum, relish the intimate feel of stepping into welcoming eateries (rather than having to masticate ambience-deprived delivery-food), and love looking at what's cooking if there's an open kitchen (instead of 'representative' web images). Furthermore, despite incongruous touchlessness being the new F&B menu card rule, India is the original finger food-country and will remain so, or to quote the magisterial culinary critic Pushpesh Pant from his epic *India Cookbook*, 'an Indian gourmet does not use knives, forks and spoons: the fingers, assisted by a variety of breads, are best to fully enjoy the temperature and texture of the food.'

When the British high commissioner visited Bengaluru and made the mistake of tweeting an image of himself eating a masala dosa—that quintessential and iconic southern quick tummy-filler referred to as 'the world's best pancake' in international food and travel magazines—with fork and knife, the Twitterati blasted him with comments like 'Ayyo, karma, how to teach you guys about civilisation only! Eat with hand saar, holistic sensory experience will be!' as reported by *Deccan Herald*. After thousands of Tweeters petitioned him to stop applying cutlery to South Indian food, His Excellency ate another dosa the next day—by hand—and admitted that 'it tastes better'.

Ayurvedic experts and yoga masters will any day enumerate the innumerable health benefits of using elegant mudras—essentially shaping one's fingers into whichever piece of tableware that best fits the food—to tuck into grub. The tactile feel of food against the fingertips is said to improve digestion and whilst the rest of the world relies on cutlery, we who eat with our right hand (and not the wrong one, mind you) can at least be sure that the fingers that fondle the roti are properly sanitised. As the ancients always said, hand over those forks and fork it in with your hand. What may be considered bad table manners in another country is the supreme sophistication in the Indian tradition as it was at ancient Rome's banquets.

It also requires elaborate cooking techniques to match—softer meats, suitably cut vegetables and breads that can be used to mop up gravies.

Anyway, to get on with the show as they say, here's my panegyric to Indian hospitality, to eating and travelling and to enjoying food on the road in a post-pandemic World 2.0 again…oh, and one last thing—the sharp-eyed reader might wonder how come I mostly write about old places, time-tested restaurants, antiquated watering holes and the glory of the past. There's an easy answer to that: It would be futile to even think of writing a book about restaurant culture in the present when the present becomes the past three weeks down the social-media timeline, but the slightly older past—the one we may cherish, the one that existed up to three years ago—doesn't necessarily have to change as long as we write and read about it.

—Zac O'Yeah

Bengaluru, 2023

I

A Town Called Beershop

(Regarding Bengaluru)

'Verily, thousands of visitors, from other parts of the State as well as the country and from abroad, pour into the city every day; aeroplanes, trains, buses and cars bring visitors of all classes and from all walks of life.'

—Old tourist brochure (that was new when I first came to town)

Author in Koshy's Cafe, Bengaluru.

Photo: Raghav Shreyas

Whenever I tread down the lane where Premier Bookshop once stood, my face turns into a sentimental emoticon. Sitting behind a cluttered counter, the proprietor T.S. Shanbhag—always dressed babu-style in his trademark semi-synthetic half-sleeves and polyester pants—was quick to recognise regulars and knew what we wanted, whipping out the latest arrivals of interest from the unruly stacks packed three rows deep, throwing in whatever discount he felt I needed to be persuaded. No haggling was expected.

It was always exciting to lose oneself among the books, as long as one remained slim enough to fit between the shelves that, in their own way, were a healthy incentive not to consume too much beer in pub city. Despite there being barely squeezing space inside the shop, it is a well-known fact that back in the 1980s, the proprietor caught celebrated history writer Ramachandra Guha getting pre-maritally kissed by his wife-to-be—as confessed in Guha's essay 'Turning Crimson at Premier's'. As we see in that revealing passage, it was possible for two people to fit in there, once upon a time, but as the collection grew it seemed increasingly doubtful that one could have romantic encounters in the narrower and narrower space. Only intellectual.

'Even in the old Bengaluru known for its hospitality, grace and charm, Shanbhag stood out for these qualities. He was personally acquainted with his customers and his books,' writes Suresh Menon in his memoir on booklove, *Why Don't You Write Something I Might Read?* Premier's well-stocked selection was intelligently put together, so more than a shopkeeper one could claim that Shanbhag was a curator of literature and, hence, in charge of intellectual developments in the city in those days—and, for me, crucial as an ally to build up my home library. But he shut shop in 2009 because CBD rentals were becoming impossibly high even for as tiny a shop as his. Besides, he was well past retirement age and he told me that he felt like calling it quits anyway after running it for nearly four decades. Fans of the bookshop held a function to felicitate him for his service to them. Sadly, he passed away from COVID-19 in 2021, I learnt, as tearful local newspapers paid tribute to the premier bookseller to Bengaluru's bibliophiles.

The loss of this legendary shop was a big blow to culture. At that time, when everybody ordered books online, it looked like the city centre was becoming illiterate. Thankfully, the Raj-era Higginbothams (74, M.G. Road), after having been boarded up for years, revived, smartly renovated back to its former glory. The chain was founded in south India in the 1800s, branding itself as 'official booksellers to His Royal Highness'. As one of the city's original bookshops it remains something of a hallowed relic.

Higginbotham's neighbour, the venerable Gangarams, founded in 1965 and once the biggest bookstore on M.G. Road, was not so fortunate. It shifted to a smaller space in 2013 and became less eclectic. Strand Book Stall, related to the Mumbai bookshop of the same name and specialising in lavish art books and remaindered imports, as well as Fountainhead that pioneered the trend of bookstore book launches with Arundhati Roy's *The God of Small Things* back in the late 1990s, and the smart Sankar's Book Stall, all went out of business and vanished without a trace. Even the beloved Variety Book House & Magazines Shop shut down both its showrooms. Their model had been to sell magazines from all over the world at discounts; this was the shop for cultural journals and comic books; whether one wanted years old copies of *The New Yorker* from New York or the most recent issue of *Rock Street Journal* from New Delhi, they always delivered. But increasingly, people accessed online magazines, which lead to a slump in sales.

Even the pavement booksellers were getting scarce. A lone book pirate occasionally pushes his cart along M.G. Road still, but the uncle who used to spread out an array of non-pirated books on a ledge hasn't been around in years.

To cut a long story short—browsing offline appeared to be doomed and the main reason why I fell in love with the city seemed lost. But then the other day, I decided to survey the scene and down Brigade Road, I slipped into the first alley on the left. At 71, Brigade Road Cross there is a secret treasure untouched by modern commerce: Select. Founded in 1945 by the passionate book collector K.B.K. Rao and run by his 92-year-old son K.K.S. Murthy today, its survival seems nothing short of a miracle.

Originally, it was run from a garage owned by a British bibliophile in nearby Museum Road, but as the stock grew with the inclusion of collections left behind by departing ex-colonialists, it moved into a bigger space. Luminaries who frequented this quirky repository include the Nobel laureate C.V. Raman, author Ruskin Bond, playwright Girish Karnad and the afore-mentioned Ramachandra Guha who eulogises the shop in his essay collection *The Last Liberal*, declaring it to be his 'favourite of all India's second-hand bookshops'. So, what is this celebrated shop like today?

Downstairs are a few impossibly crammed chambers while a locked storage hall upstairs holds the rare books with an estimated 70,000 titles—and also lithographs, maps and other collectibles—which apparently have included autographed copies of Rabindranath Tagore's Nobel Prize-winning *Gitanjali*. Bibliophiles can borrow the key from Sanjai Rao, grandson of the founder, and if a book isn't available, he'll try to track down a copy—this time he offers me two out-of-print books on Bengaluru that I've been hunting for. One is still plastic-wrapped and unused; the other is in fine condition despite being fifty years old—he tells me that he recently unearthed it from the bookshelf of a person in the older parts of town. I'm aware that one can buy it online for Rs 5,000 which is way above my budget, so I ask how much he wants for both.

Rao thinks for a moment and suggests, 'Let's say 1,650, shall we?'

I agree immediately, but I ask him why he doesn't demand more.

He says, 'It wouldn't be correct, because now the books have found the right owner.'

I celebrate my good luck with a pitcher of draught at Pecos, the retro rock & roll bar in another nearby alley that also serves up mean tacos and makes you feel that John Lennon might be alive and chanting mantras in the loo. There's reason for cheer as some newer bookshops are thriving so well that Church Street is again becoming a regular tourist destination for Gutenberg-worshippers.

One trendsetter is Krishna Gowda. Gowda's has been a remarkable journey for somebody who once peddled books on the M.G. Road pavement. Founded in 2002, his Bookworm gradually expanded to four branches in the area, out of which one was exclusively dealing in children's books. Once the pandemic lockdowns ended, in 2021, he consolidated his empire into one outlet in an old colonial era bungalow down the street, which gave him even more display space. The bungalow also has a garden where he will set up a book café. On my first post-pandemic visit, I suggested to him that this must be India's biggest bookshop. Humbly, he answered, 'Blossoms is bigger.' Having visited every significant bookshop in the country, I was about to correct him, but then again if Gowda prefers to be humble, then who am I to argue? Apart from a huge second-hand selection, he also sells the latest titles at an attractive 20 per cent markdown—which results in spectacular sales figures that

Ramachandra Guha with Rajmohan Gandhi at the launch of *Gandhi: The Man, His People, and the Empire.*

*Photo: Zac O'Yeah [**All images except where specified:** Zac O'Yeah]*

in turn make authors love the welcoming Gowda, who usually greets every writer he recognises with, 'We've sold a thousand copies of your books, please sign another fifteen today.' It is also a haunt of journos from the nearby editorial offices because whoever lingers long enough is served free coffee and as for me I left with Rs 4,000 worth of books, but paid only Rs 2,500 and that complimentary cuppa was thrown in, too.

The other major store that has, for decades, been specialising in an eclectic mix of new and used paperbacks is Blossom Book House, just a few steps away from Bookworm. I was introduced to it some twenty years back by renowned bibliophile Pradeep Sebastian when it had just been opened by Mayi Gowda (not related to Krishna Gowda) who gave up an engineering career to fill a minuscule cubicle at the back of a shopping complex with around 1,500 books. Business took off and it has since then, true to its name, blossomed into two gigantic stores diagonally across from each other, making Blossoms (as fans calls the shop) probably the biggest second-hand trader in India, selling on an average 1,500 books a day—a feat that has earned it listings in tourist guides from the *Lonely Planet* to *Frommers* as one of the city's must-dos. The main branch (84/6, Church Street) sprawls across three storeys—the ground floor showcasing the latest sold at discount, plus travelogues, cinema and philosophy; upstairs, one finds fiction (with a substantial Indian selection); and the top floor is exclusively for non-fiction (great collections of biographies, dictionaries, handbooks, self-help, you name it).

A special feature of Blossoms is a framed letter written by Rabindranath Tagore in 1931. The unique document was found, by chance, tucked inside a book. Their newer outlet (2, Church Street) is a veritable supermarket of literature with graphic novels aplenty, yards of non-fiction, tons of novels, plus free mineral water dispensers and loos, so one can technically go on browsing forever as there's basically no need to leave the shop. The combined retail space of both Blossoms is approximately

750 sq m, holding nearly half a million books, which is quite an expansion from the original 18 sq m hole-in-the-wall premises. This phenomenon has even inspired a fan-page that collects quirky conversations called 'Overheard at Blossoms':

Guy 1: Why are you going there, da? That's romance section.

Guy 2: Yeah, I know, dude. I want to see if they have one book.

Guy 1: Full romance books you're reading? Are you Romeo or Devdas?

Guy 2: No, dude, I saw one chick in my bus reading some Nora Roberts book. I thought I can say I also read it if I get the chance to talk to her.

Guy 1: Dude, you're my guru from now, da!

The spirit of Church Street is best illustrated by the fact that new independent stores, such as The Bookhive owned by the enthusiastic young Keshava R who loves to source difficult-to-get titles for his devoted customers, keep opening to give literature more and more space in this marvellous place. All the proprietors I chat with suggest in their various ways that they're not into it for huge profits, but a love for books as products and a deep engagement with the trade is at the heart of the matter. Also, the fact that there are so many of them, makes bookshop-hopping more fun than trying to find something readable online.

After loading up on literature the best thing to do is, at the end of Church Street, to cross Saint Mark's Road and spend the rest of one's afternoon at the bohemian Koshy's. Run by the always cheerful Prem Koshy, this 1950s multipurpose breakfast-to-dinner café-cum-bar is a culinary-literary landmark that wears its patina of timelessness lightly. It inspired literary sensation Vivek Shanbhag's globally bestselling Kannada novella

Ghachar Ghochar in which much of the action takes place in a fictionalised Koshy's. The novel's title apparently means 'tangled up beyond fixing'.

Koshy's other habituès include, apart from aspiring Hemingways and alleged CIA agents who eavesdrop on thinkers, intellectuals such as Ramachandra Guha who has been a regular for more than fifty years and in his essay, 'Café, Memories of Lime Juice and an Owl on a Moonlit Night', calls it 'an always-welcoming place in a chaotic and ever-changing city'. Hence, one might consider Koshy's an oasis for bibliomaniacs who live in the slow lane, as compared to all those cyber czars in the fast lane of gastropubs in Koramangala and microbreweries of Indiranagar. If one is to believe their motto: Top people have something more in common than an entry in Who's Who—they always think of Koshy's, when they think of dining out.

Some say this was where political dissidents convened during the Emergency in the 1970s (perhaps mistaking the Saint Mark's Road address as Marxist Road?). Curiously, the café is often filled with legal professionals (due to the high court being a stroll away) while at the same time, members of the LGBT community used to meet at a nearby table in those days when it was illegal to be nothing but a heterosexual. Before the Internet was invented, newspaper editors caught up with the news here—*Deccan Herald, New Indian Express, The Hindu* and *The Times of India* have their offices within walking distance. And it seems that even the late Queen Elizabeth of Britain came here to eat roasted chicken back in 1961. So all things considered, their motto does sound quite accurate.

Here, beer is cheap, coffee even cheaper—ah, how can one ever stop thinking about that powerful smell of the old-fashioned 'cream tray' with its concoction of tar-strong decoction with pewter pitchers of hot milk and cold cream that resurrects even the brain-dead, unlike the chicory-laden adulterations at most vends? Chicory is something that I expect in a salad but not in my cuppa. After a sip, life begins afresh; the loose wiring of the mind hooks up; random dots connect into words; untangling, they paint poetry...all thanks to coffee. No wonder then that an estimated two to three billion cups are consumed daily in the world, making coffee the second biggest business product after oil.

Koshy's is, as the crow flies, situated just 200 km from where the beans grow in the Western Ghat hills, guaranteeing its freshness. Statistics suggest that in the US people spend no more than the two minutes it takes to grab their decaf-to-go in a takeaway shop, in the UK folks sip theirs for twenty-five minutes on an average, but at Koshy's, nobody drinks up in less than two hours because they talk so much between sips. Whereas in many countries—say Italy, the typical café is like a bar where you get your caffeine shot at the counter because sitting down involves surcharges, here, we are talking of a living room where you can spend your life leisurely.

Other than that, the chaotic menu is a motley ledger of colonial-style Anglo-Indian standards such as spinach-au-gratin, non-south-Indianised North Indian dishes, Asian odds and ends, a special Kerala curry-and-rice section, plus off-menu options that only those in the know may order (like organic wild mushrooms or grilled pig's brain, and once I even scored a rare treat of tasty testicles).

Sorting through the day's booty and already regretting that I gave some tomes a miss, I know that next month, once I've read what I bought today, I'm going to do this same tour all over again—because even if Church Street has no church (well, actually, tucked away behind Koshy's one will find the town's oldest cathedral, Saint Mark's, inaugurated in 1816), it certainly is the place for book adoration.

❖

At the time I settled in town, I had published a few novels in my native Swedish language, but mostly made my living off travel writing. Due to my interest in other cultures, I searched for Bengaluru books, but after a good decade in town, I hadn't seen a single local thriller. Until fairly recently, indeed, crime fiction used to be dominated by British and American locations and concerns, but nowadays we read globally bestselling detective novels set in places like Botswana, Japan or—somewhat surprisingly—in Sweden, which is otherwise believed to be one of the least crime-ridden parts of the world. So why not Bengaluru?

My favourite bookshops did stock Asian crime stuff—I remember finding Japanese thrillers by Keigo Higashino at Bookworm, at Premier I bought *Bangkok 8* by John Burdett, translated Bengali detective story collections and *The Blaft Anthology of Tamil Pulp Fiction* are always available at Blossom Book House, as are sometimes second-hand copies of out-of-print 1970s pulp classics such as the 'Jaz Zadu' series by Shyam Dave about an IMFL-guzzling James Bond-character who 'attracts beauties and bullets with equal ease'. But nothing typically Bengaluruan, at least not in the first decade of the 2000s (later on, local writers have addressed this lacuna).

Anyhow, one day in 2008, I sat down in my favourite dive (it was located in the Majestic area of town if you must know but has, thanks to the ongoing gentrification, been demolished since) and wrote the first lines of what was to become the 'Majestic Trilogy', a project which was to occupy me for a decade until the third and final book was published in 2018. People sometimes ask me about my audacity, to even think that I as a foreigner can write novels set in Bengaluru, by and large without using foreign characters as an alter ego through whom to view events and cover up my ignorance. It was admittedly a gamble, yet the fact that I've received movie offers both from Kannada filmmakers and Bollywood suggests that many think it works. But the truth is that I was just having a beer in Majestic and after several beers too many, I strongly felt that every self-respecting city ought to have a library of detective novels dedicated to it.

In Sweden, for example, there are villages like Fjällbacka, home to approximately 1,000 souls, which have been the setting of serial-killer hunts in novel after novel. Realistic? How many semi-professional killers would it take to decimate 1,000 villagers? It defies logic, but you read the books (or stream the movie versions) because Fjällbacka is depicted as quaint and yet appears to have a darker side. That, in a nutshell, is the success story of crime fiction and why it is a global sales phenomenon, keeping publishing houses alive and kicking. And one thing led to another, the first idea spawned the next, and soon the matrix of my novel began to unfold.

A fictional detective is something of an urban explorer, so writing (or reading) such books can be a way of getting to know a place better. The detective character, be it logic-fixated amateur sleuth Sherlock Holmes of the late nineteenth century, the professional gumshoe gunslinger Philip Marlowe in the early twentieth or feminist icon Lisbeth Salander with her super-IQ in the twenty-first, has always been a bit of a misfit; obsessive and neurotic, constantly probing what goes on in cities after sunset, the stuff that most of us remain blissfully clueless about—whether made up or real, fiction or fact, who can tell? Does it matter?

Yes and no. I go to New York and buy an Ed McBain paperback or Paul Auster's 'New York Trilogy' to land in town; in Stockholm I pick up a Sjöwall-Wahlöö novel for local colour. Before going to Mumbai, *Sacred Games* by Vikram Chandra does the needful. It doesn't matter so much that McBain fictionalised the Big Apple as Isola, or that much of Chandra's city can't actually be found on maps. It's deep atmosphere us readers are after. A pioneering crime writer when it comes to using exotic locations, H.R.F. Keating became notorious for having largely written his 'Inspector Ghote' series without visiting Mumbai, where most of the books are set—just like Walter Scott based his war drama *The Surgeon's Daughter* in Bengaluru, 'this fine and populous city' where the 'rich pavilions of the principal persons flamed with silk and gold…' Several of Scott's relatives and friends had served in India, while Keating too had his methods, but I'll return to this matter in detail later. For now, we may note that in his how-to manual *Writing Crime Fiction*, he states that all the world's exotic hotspots are open to the plot and 'it is not altogether necessary, if your mind is constructed that way, actually to visit your chosen locale'. I beg to differ.

The attractiveness of 'crime fiction guided walks' grows organically in the footsteps of the booming thriller industry—whether it be Sherlock Holmes tours in London (to his mock-up home at 221B Baker Street, 'the world's most famous address') or Philip Marlowe bus rides in Los Angeles. (The late Raymond Chandler, incidentally, loved showing visitors the settings for his plots.) Trailing fictional heroes and villains is a global pastime. From this follows one important conclusion: Place, milieu and atmosphere are oh so important for a fictional sleuth. In the case of my own creation, the semi-heroic wannabe hero Hari Majestic, the hallowed ground is the aforementioned Majestic area.

Furthermore, I wanted to avoid creating a stereotypical literary detective—the overweight, middle-aged, divorced cop (if male) or the nosy spinster aunty (if female), or any of the other varieties of 'classic' investigator characters. Hence, the Hari Majestic of my novels was a week-old orphan when found under a seat in the third row at Majestic Talkies. That's how he got his surname. In his late twenties in the first book, he is a reformed tout who has turned into something of an unofficial trouble-shooter, a Mr Fix-It. People come to him with their problems—missing siblings, cheating spouses, suspected scams—and since he knows Bengaluru like I know my own nostrils, he's the perfect private investigator.

A reality check was required to understand what proper detectives were like. So one day after a few beers as I was literally cart-wheeling towards the Majestic bus stand, spotting a sign for a detective agency, I dropped in. Already on the staircase, I got the vibe that I wasn't going to find chain-smoking private eyes with brandy bottles in their shoulder holsters. Instead, a notice stated that job applicants must be well-groomed, freshly-shaved and with a proper haircut. I touched my own chin and realised that I should have visited a barber first.

It turned out that an Indian detective bureau is like any other open-plan workplace; this could be, say, an accountant's office or even a low-end call centre, if it wasn't for all the staff looking so ex-army. They also didn't care much for PR, I found, when I asked for a public relations person. After several unanswered questions, I was ushered into a glass cubicle where the head of the bureau sat behind a desk covered in spiritual promotion materials rather than beer ads.

Brimming with excitement, I asked my first question: 'What do real detectives work with?'

The boss replied, 'That I can't tell you, because it is secret.'

I tried again: 'If I wanted to hire you, what could you do for me?'

He stared out through the window and his all-detecting gaze was fixed on some enigma in the distance. 'Supposing you wanted to buy that house over there and needed to know who owns it, we could find that out.'

I glanced at that very same house, but no, there were no suspicious criminals lurking on its terrace—and if I really wanted a house, I might go to a real estate agent rather than a secret agent, but I found it wiser to say: 'So, is that what detectives do for a living?'

He shook his head vigorously. 'Not at all; I simply said that supposing you wanted to know.'

'And how much would it cost me to hire you to do that?'

He looked at me doubtfully and said, 'That I can't say, it's a secret.'

So instead I googled and found out everything I needed to know, watched plenty of Kannada action flicks of the so-called 'Machchu Longu'-type (named for the elongated machetes used in gang wars before handguns became popular) and became a fan of the wacky ones by Real-Star Upendra, the king of cool one-liners, and his closest rival at the time, Challenging-Star Darshan. I wondered what a literary equivalent of such films might read like. After all, Indian cinema follows a different logic from Western, so shouldn't that colour the literary plot and its protagonists as well? A typical Indian action movie includes elements of comedy and romance, song and dance, without being self-conscious about it; likewise a comedy will have romantic scenes and action sequences; and a romantic movie may be comical as well as action-packed. This has obvious roots in that ancient theory of dance, theatre and music, the

Natya-Shastra, which states that any artistic work must have a dominant mood, rasa, without neglecting the eight *bhavas* (emotions) such as for example *hasya* (comedy), *rati* (love), and naturally, also *vira* (heroism) juxtaposed with *bhayanaka* (terror).

By contrast, Hollywood (and Western storytelling in general) seem to follow the strictures of 'the dramatic unities'—propounded from Aristotle onwards and refined in the era of French Classicism: Credibility in theatre is created by avoiding mixed registers and hybrid art forms such as, for example, tragicomedy. This tendency remains very much alive today in the West. But India is too diverse for anything so simplistic. I therefore set out to write a romantic tragicomic thriller in Bengaluru.

The private eye became my key to unlock the city's geography and chronicle how crazily it changed. When I observe Bengaluru, when I meander through town, it's like I'm hiking through a magical manuscript forever in progress, a poem that will never be completed but will always remain in flux. Like no other place I had known, this city appears to follow a will of its own. In a street corner adorned by a colonial-era bar's lazy verandas, there would be a glass-and-steel shopping mall topped by a food court coming up before I emptied my beer. This kaleidoscopic urbanism intrigued me. Just when I thought I knew my whereabouts, the kaleidoscope shifted and everything tilted.

Writing books is, in fact, a little bit like trying to stay alive here: A chaotic activity; you must kill your darlings; tear into pieces what you've previously written and rewrite upon the ruins of your earlier ideas; stretch your limits to conquer new ground; attempt the impossible—just like the city itself does each day.

Some people complain about the uncontrollable growth,

how Bengaluru swells at an impossible pace, the lack of heritage awareness and how everything old-worldly is torn down. This may be contrasted against the pride of provincial newspapers as billions of venture-dollars flow into the city. The other day I saw this stressful headline as I was leisurely enjoying my pilsner: 'Bengaluru is now the world's fastest growing tech hub, Mumbai sixth.' London was #2 on that list, after pubtown, and it made me worry that ale might soon become more expensive in Bengaluru, charged in sterling pounds or perhaps bitcoins instead of Indian currency. Yes, I too do regret the loss of the past, as rapid change can be unsettling, but as an author I also find it incredibly stimulating.

When I was writing the first novel in the trilogy there was that heritage cinema hall called Majestic (which lent its name to both the area and my hero) but as I was writing about it, real estate developers tore it down. It was insane, but I didn't take tension—after all I had immortalised it in my novel, which is all I could do to preserve it. Around the same time, the Central Jail which was conveniently located at the edge of Majestic and where ladies used to line up at lunchtime to bring tiffin-boxes to their incarcerated husbands, a sight which featured in my novel, was reformed so to speak—into what is now the twenty-acre Freedom Park, a site for public meetings.

It felt as if I was writing local history at the same time as history was being erased around me. The eternal construction sites, the suburbs pushing city limits another kilometre out with every passing year—art produced in a place like this might, I reasoned, defy ordinary imagination, the way that Bengaluru itself does, to all appearances expanding fast enough to swallow the entire world. And here I was, right in the middle of it.

As a matter fact, if I hadn't broken journey at Bengaluru City Junction in the early 1990s, I don't think I would have been a novelist today. It takes a little luck, and much cheap beer, to help us find our true callings.

It is strange how cinematically I recall, in vivid Technicolor wide-angle, that morning when I got off the train, filling my lungs with the nippy but peculiarly brownish-beery and somewhat sambar-flavoured Deccan air, and crossed the footbridge above the roar of the Majestic bus stand where the humongous BMTC fleet of battering rams on wheels was revving in unison, preparing to take on the potholy streets. According to statistical calculations, there are more potholes per kilometre here than anywhere in the solar system.

The buses seemed to be breeding more buses like randy rabbits as I watched them (6,771 municipal at last count), but once I left them behind I was in Majestic—a peculiar interzone, which not only catered to a floating populace but was the traditional home to the film industry: India's fifth largest, the so-called Sandalwood that produces a hundred features per

Majestic, the area in Bengaluru with most cinemas per sq km—a classic movie poster.

year. Despite geographical shifts over time, even today Majestic remains home to production houses, shops that rent out filmy equipment and sell props like fake handguns and duplicate police uniforms, and trade in DVDs both genuine and pirated, not to forget cinema halls seating over a 1,000 each (in this age of increasingly smaller-screen movie-viewing), which makes it any cineaste's joy...and it was like coming home.

Little did I know at the time that this town was to be a vital part of my future. Long before I planned on becoming a writer, I'd been journeying for months through the harsher north of India—and had my encounters with the usual tourist traps in Delhi, Varanasi, Agra and Rajasthan—so by then, I was battle-hardened and my only concern was how to survive on less than a shoestring. The boarding and lodging house in Majestic that I checked into wasn't the best in India, but at the rate of Rs 85 a night I wasn't complaining. They even had running hot water in the mornings. There were no special tourist attractions nearby, therefore no need to carry out any sightseeing agendas. I spent my days in those bookshops around Church Street as well as in the nameless second-hand bookstalls that used to proliferate due south of Kempegowda Circle.

Browsing through piles of always dusty and often mouldy tomes was sure to leave one's throat parched. This phenomenon poses serious health hazards to any bibliophile. Mercifully, the distance between these intellectual havens and the nearest dimly-lit ramshackle pub was rarely over fifty steps, so as day turned into night my brain would be further stimulated by cheap 650 ml bottles of UB lager. With a faintly mildewed paperback in my hands and a bladder designed by the almighty bladder-designer to harbour a six-pack, I read for hours.

Having decided to break journey for a bit, I ended up spending a month or two in Majestic, which also had the maddest bazaars for basically everything a traveller might need—an enchanting place where temples stood next to cinemas with their larger-than-life cut-outs of cine gods; separate mythological universes cheek by jowl.

Later, I realised I liked it because Majestic is large-hearted enough to accommodate pretty much everybody and as if to prove it, I came across a thriving migrant food culture. The back alleys featured modest Malayali eateries serving the world's coconut-oiliest chicken fry, extra-spicy Andhra biryani joints and Bengali canteens cooking authentic mustard fish like the tiny Babu Moshai hidden in the maze of narrow lanes, and the area has even lent its name to a local variety of Chinese cuisine, 'Mejestic' style, famous for its chowmein-stuffed grilled sandwiches and Schezwan bhelpuri. Just being there was like doing a culinary tour of India and I'm reminded of R.K. Narayan's words in one of his rare travel stories: 'In any big road, apart from the Bangaloreans themselves, it is always possible to pick out men of other provinces—the South Canara man, the Bombay merchant, the cooly [*sic*] from Telugu and Tamil land, the long-shirted Bengalee [*sic*], the Parsee, and the Sikh driving a military lorry. It almost looks as if Bangalore were a junction of all the provinces in India.'

It was love at first sight, or smell. It's hard to explain how one can fall head over heels for a few tumbledown city blocks and a fistful of alleys like Majestic. But the sudden, unexpected homely vibe that's provided by easy-on-the-purse food, affordable accommodation, jolly people and an abundance of beer came as a pleasant surprise. Or perhaps due to some karmic coincidence, I was a South Indian in a previous lifetime who had found his way home. For years to come, I kept bouncing back like a malfunctioning email. Hardly a year went by when I didn't, for some reason or the other, find myself in

Bengaluru. If it wasn't a literary festival, then I was writing for a travel magazine, or just coming to see friends, and in the end, I wasn't particularly surprised when I got wedded to a Bengaluru-based girl in the year 2000.

Even then, living as a happily married man in a salubrious suburb and accustomed to the brain-rattling spice spectrum of Indian morning meals, I end up getting on a bus to good old Majestic once in a week or so, to revisit those haunts and wallow in my private urban nostalgia.

Only after settling down in the city did I learn that Majestic, which I was so backpacker-sentimental about, was something of a terra incognita for the average upper-middleclass city-dweller, where people simply didn't go unless they were after pirated films or other illicit fun. A bad place. Years later, as I was writing my detective novels and reading about the underworld, I learnt that rowdies planned gang wars over plates of vada-sambar-dip ('curried donuts') and tumblers of filter-coffee in the very Kamat Hotel that I habitually ate at.[1] Several Kannada gangster flicks had taken their inspiration from the area—including a 2002 blockbuster starring Challenging-Star Darshan in his debut lead role—titled *Majestic.*

But to be truthful, regarding crime, I've experienced very little first-hand. During my first sojourn in the early 1990s, I went to the Thomas Cook office on M.G. Road to exchange traveller's cheques (this was at a time before ATMs) and carried back Rs 10,000 stapled together into a brick. It was in my pocket when I, sauntering towards my lodgings in Majestic, was accosted by six to seven local gents who all had the build of large Old Monk rum bottles.

I instantly knew they represented the underworld dons who had instructed their staff to perform shakedowns on naïve backpackers, collect contributions towards their 'social work' and add 'tourist tax' to their development fund. After surrounding me, one said, 'Give us twenty bucks.' I was prepared to give up my whole stack of cash, but when I heard that request the only thing I could do was laugh. My merriment confused them and I took the opportunity to sneak off even as they shouted after me, 'Come back!'

My second run-in was more recent and grimmer. As I stepped out of a pub feeling humane, I noticed a fellow customer lying on the pavement, which has always been considered natural behaviour in Majestic. Only this time, I witnessed three urchins rifle through his pockets and snatch his wallet. Which again is only to be expected, but when they pulled off his pants, I felt an urge to object because, in other circumstances, it could have been me and what would my wife have said had I come home undressed from the waist down? As I gently pointed out the wrongfulness of their deed, the ringleader (who must have been about eight) pulled a switchblade and suggested that I mind my business if I wanted to retain my own garments. Times had clearly changed.

With plenty of cash dispensing machines, today's prospective robbers would typically have taken me to one of these, forced me to surrender my ATM card and key in my PIN so that they could help themselves to my bank balance (therefore I always leave debit cards at home when I go to paint the town red). Travellers are nowadays also advised against many of the deceptive bargain tourist experiences to be had such as cheap massage offers at shady 'spas' that can be fronts for activities that result in jail-sightseeing for purchasing erotic services.

Those days are clearly over when lodges were cute and resembled The Best Exotic Marigold Hotel—in the feel-good flick starring Dev Patel as an hotelier taking care of retired Britons like Judi Dench in a Kiplingesque environment. Not many know that even if it was filmed in Rajasthan that's so much more colourful with its camels and palaces, the novel that the movie is based on, *These Foolish Things*, was set in Bengaluru. Its sobriquet used to be, as everybody knows, 'Pensioner's Paradise' and the retirees in the book (should you read it) are being taught to communicate in Kannada, rather than Rajasthani. For lunch, there's no laal-maas but a 'coronation chicken' typical of the town's Anglo-Indian heritage and the hotel in question is a spacious colonial cotton-trader's bungalow from 1865, 'with flowered bedspreads and mismatched, cream-painted furniture' and there's 'an air of somnolence about the place: ticking clocks, creaking ceiling fans and, from the kitchen, the distant clatter of pans.'

'The longer you stay in India, the less you know,' thinks one of the protagonists, a feeling I sometimes share. The author Deborah Moggach appears to have actually visited town but many local references are misspelled: Puttaparthi is for some reason called Pattipurnam, Cunningham Road is fictionalised as Cunningham Street, the obviously Catholic Saint Patrick's Church is labelled as Anglican, turkeys are bought from Gandhi Market which is an unlikely name for a slaughterhouse, Bengaluruans speak Hindi to one another...and which lodge that fictional one was modelled on—purportedly near the crossing of Brigade Road and M.G. Road—I'm not quite sure of, as the Dunroamin Retirement Hotel obviously is a figment of the author's imagination, though it reminds me of the long gone Victoria Hotel. Some descriptions of Bengaluru are amusing such as when one of the retirees 'walked past the United Ice Cream Parlour and Khan's Video Rental, past the Hideaway Pub—The Hot Spot That's Really Cool—a throbbing den into which he had once unwisely ventured, to find its customers of kindergarten age. The road was being dug up in the torpid

Indian manner; one man squatted with a bucket while another man, clutching a spade, listlessly tipped in teaspoons of rubble.'[2]

Even if tourists can't check into this hotel, there's plenty of lodging houses in Majestic including one named after the biggest ever local movie star Rajkumar who kick-started the golden age of Kannada cinema. And that is why Majestic once had the greatest number of cinemas per square kilometre—an incredible twenty-two of them (though only a handful remain)—and remains the place to go if one prefers, rather than streaming at home, a single-screen hall and the company of other wild fans.

What more does a writer need in life? Ah, yes, there's the matter of beer.

❖

'Where did they go?' I gently lament as I stagger like a camel crossing a desert with the high-altitude Deccan sun augmented by global warming and shrinking green cover, hammering down on my balding pate.

The name Bengaluru is, according to folklore, slang for 'beer galore' that harks back to the colonial era. And it isn't far off the mark. If you were ET and landed anywhere in town, like I did, in the 1990s, there'd be a handy watering hole next to your UFO as attested to by statistical data (three per square kilometre was the norm). Therefore this city attracted lots of aliens who wished to get 'Bangalored' as it was called in those days. Slide in through the darkest door in sight, find a comfortable seat away from the sun, and within seconds an unfussy waiter brings a 650 ml lager while other clients mind their own bad habits.

With the outsourcing boom resulting in a hike in disposable

income, those jolly yesteryear pubs were torn down. Today, if I happen to be thirsty, I must locate the discreet elevator that takes me to a mall rooftop where, invariably, there's a hoity-toity cocktail lounge, where fruit-infused beer-on-tap is misspelt 'biere' and hard-selling waiters force me to sample overpriced, over-perfumed microbrews.

Being an aficionado of unfashionably seedy taverns where 'beeru' is served by the 'pintu', I'm unapologetically backward-gazing these days. For example, I spent so many years lounging in the cane chairs at Dewar's in Bamboo Bazaar that drunks mistook me for the portrait of Queen Elizabeth that hung behind the bar. The come-as-you-are, become-as-drunk-as-you-

Bengaluru's most nostalgic bar—Dewar's, Bamboo Bazar.

must Dewar's, born in 1933 and gone in 2010, was like a caring mother, a seafaring father, a homely bungalow where labourers in loincloths mingled with us khadi-clad intellectuals and everybody felt safe as the sturdy rosewood tables were too heavy to be used in bar battles. And the rattan chairs too light to cause harm with. The beer snacks were excellent, too. According to the grapevine, the extravagantly generous breadcrumb-coated fish fillets and other dishes like mutton balls and dry brain fry were introduced by an Irishman; after a few pegs to clear the historical haze, regulars recalled his name as Mr Dinky, but he went home to Dublin some years after independence, maybe in the 1960s.

Sarovara in Lavelle Road was another unpretentious beer hall. Across the street from the Bangalore Club where non-members were not welcome, it offered a passé ambience and great prawn fry to go with the chilled brew. Ultimately, the building was sold to some random luxury hotel and today one can only revisit it by watching the gangster epic *OM* (1995), the Kannada equivalent of *The Godfather*—its larger-than-life 'Machchu Longu'-type bar fight directed by Real-Star Upendra was shot at Sarovara and its gardens. Yes, in those days pubs in the Garden City used to have lavish gardens.

Others that vanished post-2000 include the already-mentioned Victoria Hotel that had cool verandas for an afternoon beer, overlooking its vast green grounds (nowadays occupied by Central Mall), and the nearby Carnival, half-garage, half-dive catering to the pub city's trademark drunk drivers—get a fix and get your two-wheeler fixed at the same time. Less known but equally stunning watering hole Kishore (picturesque gingerbread bungalow at 95, M.M. Road) recently reopened as the non-boozy but charmingly named Beerappa's Foodcourt while others are most likely awaiting demolition such as the art deco Highway (40, Broadway Road), which used to be a favoured drinkery among ruffians who conducted their wheeling-dealing in the Russell Market's so-called thieves' bazaar.

An era of gold-coloured inebriation is simply over, its legacy more or less lost. It all began with a Scotsman who founded the Castle Brewery in 1857, giving Bengaluru's beer an over 160-year-pedigree. Ale was an expensive cargo to ship from England, not to mention that 'old Blighty beer' sometimes went bad on the way so that whatever reached Indian shores had frequently turned fairly foul. One report calls imported beer 'thin and sourish' and therefore it made sense to start breweries across the country. At that time, the town's population had just crossed 130,000, half of them living in the Cantonment's infantry camp, (half in its neighbouring walled old city,) making it the biggest 'English' town in southern India, which was enough to warrant a beer industry. As the demand for potable drinks grew, another called Bangalore Brewing Company was built to cater to army needs in the 1880s on the spot where UB City shopping mall sits today. These, and another three, including the famous Nilgiri Brewery that had been set up some distance away in cooler climes at Ooty, merged into the United Breweries in 1915, known for its classic UB pilsner which remains a perennial favourite. Business thrived and huge barrels of beer were carted across south India.

Initially, brewing was a medical strategy to provide the troops and populace of the 'Civil & Military Station' with a health drink—a mildly alcoholic, bacteria-free beverage, which could be drunk like water and wouldn't be as harmful as the cheap hooch they got from illegal hawkers who peddled spurious concoctions outside their barracks. Despite the many virtues of coconuts, when distilled to arrack it ruined their gastric systems that were already under assault from exotic bacteria. Getting over-drunk was also a first step towards immoral recreational activities with the outcome that the troops 'filled the veneral wards' as one academic paper puts it. In the 1860s, the India Office issued cautionary orders 'to prevent the soldier from getting access, by surreptitious means, to the more fiery and deleterious spirit to be found in the Native bazaars'. Instead, they were given sufficient money to cover a daily beer ration and a fistful of hangover pills. Around the same time, corroborating this so to speak, *Allen's Indian Mail* (in an article on brewing) calculated that there were at least 200,000 beeroholics in the country—armymen, merchants, planters, Eurasians, Parsees, etc—in need of daily pints which worked out to 120,000 hogshead barrels (equalling a total of 25½ million litres). Remarks the editor: 'The question of supplying ourselves with beer becomes, then, one of great economic importance.'

If the above numbers are correct, it works out to 350 ml, or a very small pintu per punter—which is way less than, say, the daily Czech per capita consumption of 500 ml. The actual quantities required would probably have been much larger if ale was indeed the safest beverage in the tropics. The popularity of 'Bangalore beer' as a brand spread quickly all the way to Madras, Hyderabad and other English settlements where the climate was too hot for brewing—though even this beer did risk spoiling and was occasionally pronounced 'to be as bad as ever' so that for example, in the year 1900, brewers had to undertake 'to turn out high-class beer' instead of yucky gunk.

It is estimated by experts that their brews would have resembled British IPA (a strong beer) rather than lager, i.e. nothing like the modern-day dainty Kingfisher but rather what is labelled as Superstrong, with an alcohol content of 7-8 per cent similar to that of punchy Knockout which is beloved by hard-drinkers in downmarket joints even today.[3] Apart from 'English beer', they also brewed a 'Native beer' with the difference that it contained a very small quantity of malt while jaggery was used as its base, producing more acidic beer (according to colonial reports) that kicked like a mule so that one got tipsy cost-effectively.

Over time, the military personnel got many neighbours—like missionaries, who tried to save their souls after settling down around the Cantonment in areas still commonly known by colonial names such as Benson Town, Cleveland Town and Richmond Town—and for obvious reasons, few could live without the #1 tropical health drink, namely, beer. An 1875 government gazetteer refers to 'Public Rooms' (i.e. pubs) located south of the military barracks, between Saint Mark's Cathedral which was born as the garrison chapel and Trinity Church (where Winston Churchill used to go when he lived in town), basically in the area where Koshy's stands today. Although Koshy's itself is only seventy-plus, it remains the go-to place to understand what colonial taverns looked like—for example in the fine-dining hall a slightly elevated corner space may be what remains of a stage where a jazz orchestra played dance tunes and their kitchens still cook the colonial staple of Fish & Chips. Interestingly, the adjacent building, which now houses the Hard Rock Café, used to be Blighty's Tearooms, a posh hotspot for teetotallers.

In the 1890s, another gazetteer listed four exclusive beer taverns—huge halls for sinking tankards in and old maps locate these more specifically on Brigade Road, towards the corner of Residency Road, and where Resthouse Road reminds us of the presence of one large colonial hotel—identified on an 1885 survey map as Mayo Hotel—that would have been surrounded by these 'public rooms'. Newspaper ads from back then promote 'invigorating' Indian Pale Ale from the Nilgiri Brewery on sale from godowns at 5, Brigade Road, 'strongly recommended by the Medical profession'. The Opera House, formerly a cinema and now housing a mobile phone store, was then a British event venue and party hall. Fazlul Hasan in his seminal *Bangalore Through The Centuries* lists three of these turn-of-the-previous-century Brigade Road watering holes as Adelphi Shades, Elysium and New Inn, where colonial bohemians supped and guzzled, and paddies got plastered after attending service at the Saint Patrick's Church down the road—which is still standing even if those pub-crawling Irishmen are long gone. Also, I glean from memoirs by Bengaluruan elders that there was a Ye Olde Bull & Bush at the bottom end of Brigade Road when they were young (so I'd guess that would be in the mid-1900s) and many also refer to a popular hangout near the corner of M.G. Road that may have been named Bascoe's.

By the time I settled in town, Old Vic was the last genuinely antique bar in that area, but tragically the Victoria Hotel it was housed in was demolished and replaced by a mall. The bacchanalian Chin Lung now rules the beer scene attracting youthful alcoholics from the nearby colleges.

However, the aptly named Funnel dance hall on South Parade (repurposed as a newspaper office in the renamed M.G. Road) seems to have been *the* place to drink the night away. An article on partying in town, *The Boogie Woogie in Bangalore* (published in *The New Yorker* in 1943) praised the unbelievably good local beer while the correspondent described his attempts at hooking up with loose women at 'Funnell's' [*sic*] where 'the chances are good' to pick up a Danish or Czech chick, so after some rum for lunch at the dance hall the correspondent fast-forwards to 'two o'clock in the morning [when] you start learning the Boogie Woogie dance' before, jump-cutting to the next morning, waking 'up laughing and with no hangover'. Obviously, the beer was breathtaking.

While that delightful drink was brewed, as already

mentioned, in the compound now housing the UB City Mall, southwest of the Cantonment, a distillery came up to produce what in due time became known as IMFL, an acronym said to have been coined by booze manufacturers at the time of independence to differentiate industrially produced 'Indian-Made Foreign Liquor', essentially neutral sugarcane spirits coloured to appear like brandy, gin or even whiskey, from artisanal hooch. Judging by maps from the 1850s, the Central Mall was where the city's official 'Arrack Godown' stood with a convenient bar right across the street, where Mayo Hall now stands. One may hence conclude that things were really beginning to look better for city-dwellers.

These establishments were mostly geared towards the English and Anglo-Indians but people from the walled town, a mere kilometre and a half away, also benefitted from their existence as Janaki Nair notes in *The Promise of the Metropolis: Bangalore's Twentieth Century*, to 'many from the old city area, they spelt an unmatched social freedom' because apart from non-veg and alcohol, these were public spaces where women and men co-mingled without social taboos. 'Cantonment people were alcoholic in a mostly harmless and very euphemistic way,' adds Peter Colaco in his memoir *Bangalore: A Century of Tales from City & Cantonment*. According to Wikipedia, which always makes me think of a bar where every drunkard has something to say about everything, a scholar (writing as early as in 1853) observed that 'Drunkenness was also common in the Bangalore Petah, across all classes of people.'

Going to the 'Cant' to drink was something different from hooching on moonshine in a quaint, or creepy—depending on one's mental makeup—bazaar hut; it was a celebration, limitless fun, a liberal ethos suited for romantic occasions, something that to an extent still holds true except that one needs more cash to satisfy one's cravings for fun and sin as the price of a beer at Koshy's is somewhat costlier than the Rs 2 it was back in the mid-1900s.

I've been reliably informed that wining and dining in the 'Cant', even if conservatives deemed it a den of debauchery, was seen as a crash-course in cosmopolitanism before one's first foreign trip. Meals came with knives and forks and one was expected to order beer in English rather than, like I habitually say, *'Ondu pintu kodi.'*

These were the pub city's roots, then, growing parallel to the first half of the twentieth-century's temperance movements, almost as if synchronised. Mahatma Gandhi recommended in 1946: 'Every bar or, failing that, a place next door to it, should, so far as possible, be utilised as a refreshment and recreation room.' And post-independence, when parts of the country obeyed the Gandhian diktat—for as he pointed out already in 1938, 'our freedom will be the freedom of slaves if we continue to be victims of the drink and drug habit'—and went for prohibition, it was never an option in this city where the various brewers and distillers owned schools, hospitals, newspapers, cinemas, cricket teams and, ostensibly to mark the creation of Karnataka state in 1956, one of them patriotically launched what was to become the country's top beer: Kingfisher.

What we know as today's archetypal Indian pub was invented as late as in the mid-1980s after draught came around and two booze giants faced off. Ramda's was backed by the Khoday distillers and The Pub, by United Breweries. Draught beer cost Rs 5-7 a mug in 1987, by when another fifty pubs had joined the competition, serving an estimated 35,000 mugs a day. So when I finally set foot in the city just a few years later, there were innumerable dives that called themselves pubs, no matter if they poured from the keg or out of a bottle or just shandied together a concoction of brandy-flavoured soda that looked like beer. Already on the train heading south, in the early 1990s, a Mumbai businessman excitedly enquired what the difference between a pub and a bar was since he was going south for the first time in his life. It took me time to explain but, in the end, he was enlightened when I told him that jolly pubs focused on beer-cheer and camaraderie, sleazy bars on getting sloshed and anti-social. It was at that moment I understood how important Bengaluru was to civilisation.

According to a 2011 census there were 1,330 sit-down bars (out of which 300 were what one might call, strictly speaking, pubs proper) and 830 stand-up-drinking-dens in town, yet very few genuinely prehistoric—'first-generation pubs' in businesspeak—remain. The Pub, which by when I drunk there had turned into the city's earliest theme-pub, NASA, designed to feel like being inside a space shuttle, has been replaced by a Mumbai-*ishtyle* cocktail disco. Who even remembers Underground, once an M.G. Road institution made to look like a tube station and thus a precursor to Namma Metro, the city's rapid transit network? And did you ever go to Black Cadillac where the johns were named, respectively, Olivia Newton-John and Elton John? I miss them all. In my quest to live in the past, I never ever go to the microbreweries of Indiranagar and Koramangala—no matter how hep they are, even if there were (prior to the pandemic) over sixty to choose between, all cooking beers on site. I prefer the traditional entertainment district of Majestic any day.

The area is rather congested nowadays but nicely compact, so it's better to ditch one's rickshaw and enter on foot. I habitually get off outside Janatha Bazaar, once the flagship department store in town, now looming forlornly, vacant and fenced-in as if it too will be demolished notwithstanding being a most astonishing heritage building—it effortlessly blends royal Mysuru dignity with colonial architectural details such as Tudor arches. Apparently, the complex with its lavish teakwood and wrought iron staircases was known as the Asiatic Building back in the 1940s. In due time, it was taken over by the Public Works Department and turned into a shopping complex in the mid-1960s. At the time of writing, the demolition has been stayed as the conservation organisation INTACH is trying to rescue it.

Out of the aforementioned bars, a majority are concentrated in Majestic where the lion's share of the city's annual consumption of 455 million beers takes place and which seems to have put India (where hard liquor and hooch are way more popular generally speaking)—on the #23 spot globally when it comes to beering. In dicier dives corks are popped as early as 8 a.m. in order to fulfil the day's quota. Bills are usually settled in advance, perhaps the bartenders still recall Winston Churchill famously skipping a bar bill of Rs 13, approximately the cost of fifty-two pegs at the time, as he hastily decamped at the end of the nineteenth century—lugging only his 'campaigning kit I sped to the Bangalore railway station and bought a ticket for Nowshera.' Wherever that is and what he drank there isn't known, though at that time he despised whiskey, 'the main basic standing refreshment of the white officer in the East', but regarding brandy and soda 'there was much respectable warrant'. So presumably it was fifty-two brandies that he never paid for.[4]

More significantly, while living in a rented bungalow which stood near Trinity Metro station (on the north side of M.G. Road) he picked up his reading habit that eventually resulted in a Nobel Prize-winning writerly career, self-educating for up to five hours a day to make up for being 'an uneducated man' as he himself put it: 'So I resolved to read history, philosophy, economics, and things like that; and I wrote to my mother asking for such books as I had heard of on these topics. She responded with alacrity, and every month the mail brought me a substantial package of what I thought were standard works.' He was awarded the Nobel for Literature in 1953, the only Bangalore-inhabitant to ever receive that particular honour (although the IISc professor C.V. Raman won a Nobel in Physics in 1930), and it is believed that Churchill spent the prize money mostly on booze.

Most bars in Majestic are invariably of the 'stand and tank up' variety where patrons aren't encouraged to linger if they can no longer stand on their feet, but there are also several decent sit-down joints for a more meditative mug. Life here

Majestic Drinks—starring in a typical Kannada comedy flick.

is still very be-who-you-are and no bouncer will look twice at your bathroom slippers. Bars match this blatant lack of dress-code with a limited menu, sometimes the chef stands in the street frying the preferred bar nibble of heavily marinated cauliflower (a vegetable introduced by those colonials) in the 'manchurian' manner (a dish so essential to bar culture here that criminals have committed murders because of it), but most serve nothing more elaborate than 'congress'—the quintessential Bengaluruan roasted split peanuts spiced up with curry leaves, chopped onion, cut chillies, shredded carrot, tangy masalas and a squeeze of lime. This was apparently invented by the Iyengar community, which consists largely of teetotallers but operate many of the city's bakery counters and condiment vends. Ah, the name? Well, it was invented in 1969 when the Congress party split, which makes sense in the Bengaluru kind of way.

Talk of the Town (2nd Cross) may to the uninitiated look like an average fast-food counter, but open the discreet door behind the open-air grill section and you will find yourself in a rather gorgeous if shabby, dimly-lit bar that dates back to the 1970s and is decorated with replicas of the jovial Paul Fernandes's drawings of vintage Bengaluru. I habitually line my tummy with piquant chicken and too much beer, before exploring other backstreet drinking options.

I've heard from friends in the film industry that the bestselling whiskey in Majestic is Director's Special, usually to be followed by a spot of casting-couch-surfing. A well-known filmy bar is the cavernous Green Hotel in a quiet B.B. Naidu Road backyard. It was inaugurated by a superstar in 1990 and its board is still adorned by the motto: 'Film Industry's Favourite Place.' I doubt the celluloid stars drop by for afterwork pegs anymore because they've moved on to five-stars with plush lounges, yet the cobwebby heritage décor and cheap drinks make one feel like the good old days aren't over yet.

For one last port of call, I stop at the next corner where Port of Pavilion (1st Main Road) rules the nightlife. It was once a cultish Karnataka coastal eatery, which still cooks up a mean fish biryani, but has over the years grown into a versatile nightclub spread across several floors. I prefer the relaxed beer hall on the covered roof and after seven beers (I know, I know, that's too many), I am admiring the perfection of their chicken ghee roast and decide I must spend the rest of my life here. But there's one jarring note: I hear loud music thumping and there seems to be a party going on to which I hadn't been invited.

I ask the waiter. He does a nudge-nudge type of movement, and reveals that there's a 'ladies' bar' hidden behind an unmarked downstairs door. I suddenly lose interest in the chicken at the prospect of seeing real-life chicks. For a detective novelist, any experience like that is grist for the mill.

As soon as I enter the secret bar, we talk entirely different prices for drinks. Yet the sofas are crowded with men who are happy to pay through their noses to ogle the twenty or so girls in tight blue sweaters and jeans. Mind you, this is not a dance bar. Dance bars—local euphemism for 'striptease without removing garment'—were banned long ago. The ladies stand smiling, holding bill folders, pretending to be waitresses and the lads seem satisfied with that. Despite the far from raunchy entertainment, I read in the papers that it gets raided by the police regularly.

The phenomenon strikes me as surreal, but then there's lots of strange stuff going on in Majestic. The very next morning newspapers report that the police had, that night, descended upon two lodges around the corner, seizing cash and arresting fifty-nine gamblers who had booked rooms to play teenpatti over the weekend. It appears their luck ran out. But having fun in Majestic doesn't necessarily end with a jail sentence, especially if one doesn't break many laws. I've downloaded the Penal Code App to my smartphone and check before I do anything it might advise against.

❖

There are two eyes on my plate. They are not ogling ghoulishly or anything like that, because they're nicely covered in dark gravy and I bite into one...hmm, unusual. Experiences like this are only to be expected when one visits Shivajinagar, home to the slaughterhouse area of Bengaluru. My guide, Mansoor Ali who is devoted to exploring everything edible in town, is unwavering in his resolve to have me try all the 'sparepart items' available—otherwise known as offal.

Semantically speaking, offal encompasses every non-muscular, edible part of an animal's carcass, but various cultures have different preferences and taboos about what may be consumed and what can't. In many Germanic languages, such as my mother tongue Swedish, *avfall* means waste, discards or general refuse and basically the word can be deconstructed into 'fall off', i.e. the bits and pieces that fell off a carcass, by-products from when a butcher does his job of cleaning the meat. The word offal came to English through ancient Anglo-Saxon or Viking invasions, like a substantial portion of the English vocabulary that has its roots in Old Norse. And naturally, we Scandinavians love our old-fashioned black puddings—ancestors of Scottish haggis—that are in fact loaves baked of blood and meal, commemorating the times when Vikings ritually killed animals to drink their blood. I suspect the word may also be etymologically linked to ancient Roman cuisine, where the Latin word *offellae* denotes meaty morsels and titbits that, however, were considered much more gourmet than what we call offal. Actually, animal spareparts were known as *lumulus* in Latin.

Indian 'sparepart' dishes being exceptionally innovative, foodaholics are curious to try, to take an example, batti chutney which is not what you'd think—pickled bats—but rather balls of goat's liver and spleen mixed with plenty of chillies and garlic in Andhra Pradesh. Catholics around south India take pleasure in gravies with pig's blood such as Goan sorpotel or Mangalorean kaleesankiti; curried fish-heads are crowd-pleasers in Odiya eateries, while one of the most creative snacks from the inner Himalayas is a sausage made of barley stuffed in sheep's intestines and then steamed—it seems to be party food there and I found it the perfect complement to a tumbler of local apple wine.

All these examples suggest that I am on a mission of historic importance. Our spareparts tour starts at 11 a.m. with the 'sira' for breakfast, served both as dry-fry and in rich gravy in two separate bucket-sized dishes with hot Kerala parathas on the side. Apart from those hypnotising eyes, it contains other parts from the head of a goat (except brain which is made into a separate dish called 'brain' according to the menu card). So there's for example tongue that I find to be quite delicate with a spongy texture like an exquisite shitake mushroom. These dishes are available at New Hilal in a particular street known as Broadway Road—which in its entirety is something of a legendary hotspot among gluttons—lined with grills, falooda stalls and teashops serving suleimani. Everywhere meat hangs on skewers, covered in marinades ranging from deadly red to spooky white and scary green, Central Asian-origin delicacies such as sizzling kebabs on coal grills awakening distant memories of Turkic warriors roasting meat on swords over campfires, while keema samosas splutter in boiling oil.

Not every eatery dares put spareparts on the menu (so as not to scare tender-tummied customers). To get the best, one must know where to go and what to order, which is why a cicerone and expert on local food ethos like Mr Ali comes in handy. So when I heard about this curated 'Sparepart Walk', I jumped at the opportunity to explore the links between cooking and culture in an area where perhaps angels don't necessarily fear to tread, but mortals may feel queasy about.

After the exhilarating New Hilal, we pick our way down an overcrowded street to the huge multi-floor Taj for goat trotters' soup. Then we head to the nearby Saqlain Kebab Centre renowned for its robust chunks of fried liver (kaliji) and barbecued kidneys (gurda). Unlike its neighbours that offer AC or 'family rooms' for their better-quality clientele, this is as grubby as it gets—no tablecloths and instead of napkins we are given pages of *The Times of India*—but the food is truly superb, for example the canteen's nalli soup with its melt-in-the-mouth chunks of gooey marrow.

Over steaming brain masala and Iranian flat breads at Hamza Hotel (our next stop on Broadway Street), I get chatty with my walking companions. Somehow, I had expected to attend a macho jamboree featuring a bunch of hard-core carnivores out to challenge each other's non-vegetarianism. But instead I'm largely surrounded by dainty madams and strangely enough one pure vegetarian sahib who doesn't touch the food—it seems he is accompanying a non-veg friend for moral support like somebody who might buy multiplex tickets for a midnight screening of *Texas Chainsaw Massacre* in 3D without really being a horror cineaste. Another is a food-blogger who's obsessed with disinfecting the utensils. One lad claims that everything reminds him of his grandmother's cooking except that her offal came in semi-gravy as opposed to 'dry-fry' like here in Shivajinagar. For him this is a trip back to his childhood. Yet another turns out to be an Indian-origin nurse based in Minnesota; she has a healthy appetite, but does make the important argument that offal shouldn't be eaten too often. 'Today's lifestyles wouldn't support this kind of diet.'

'So, what would be best from a medical point of view—once a year?' I ask.

'Twice a month is fine,' she says with a big smile.

Before we part, I ask Mr Ali how come, since we've eaten almost every other weird cut, there's no scrotum on the menus? He blushes briefly and says that private parts are not eaten in India; it is a very Egyptian thing. But then the blogger says that she has heard that people in Mumbai actually eat testicles. *Takatak!* Then again people in Mumbai have always been wilder than us temperate folks in the south.

❖

The journey from Bengaluru takes two hours but I feel transported to a weird twilight zone of colonialism, into what old Bangalore perhaps was like in British times. Lavish bungalows—some inhabited and others barely standing—and pretty churches dating back to the 1800s dot the tranquil landscape of Kolar Gold Fields. The mines were given evocative names that contradicted their hellish nature—so there was a Coromandel mine, an Oriental mine and so on.

For a century, KGF was India's biggest goldmine. The area was designed to resemble a corner of rural England and with a population of nearly 40,000 around the turn of the 1900s, it was indeed a thriving idyll, as long as one stayed above ground. A colonial-era guidebook states that The Gold Field 'extends for several miles, presenting a very busy appearance with its numerous tall chimneys, mills, shaft-heads, buildings, and bungalows of all kinds' and even today it could be a major tourist attraction but, strangely, this ghost-town-in-the-making has stayed off the radar.

I first head for Bullen Shaft, the only one of the abandoned mines which, unaccountably, the owners forgot to shut. The others are all fenced in and guarded by watchmen who are least likely to let tourists sightsee. I must fight my way through thorny weeds and before I know it, I almost step into a bottomless pit. It's scary since the KGF is on the top-ten list of the world's deepest mines. Even if I survived a fall, would I find my way out of the extensive tunnels that form a 1,300-km-labyrinth some 3 km under the earth's crust?

'There is a slight heaviness in the chest and my ears are going dull, I can't very clearly follow what my friend is saying. "Are you feeling funny about the ear? It is due to the great pressure we are in...We are now at sea level...We are below sea level now, a thousand feet below sea level,"' wrote R.K. Narayan in a travel story published in 1944, describing a visit to the mines and how he experienced 'a strange feeling: oppressive and light at the same time, and difficult in the ears, nostrils, and chest, and the temperature is around 90° or 100°. Since I am not sure of being able to bear the temperature and pressure further down I have to content myself with seeing the mine at this level.'

Next, I stop at a ghost mansion perched atop a hummock from which the mining boss viewed the goldfields—its ceilings have collapsed and the halls are empty but were once furnished with mahogany tables, upon which butlers set down cooling cucumber sandwiches and the tea boy poured aromatic Darjeeling from a silver pot. Only the fancily polychromatic floor tiles remain in place. To save it from antisocials whose activities (piles of empties indicate alcoholic consumption and a makeshift stove, illicit non-vegging) it now facilitates, this could be turned into a world-class mining museum chronicling a millennium-long gold fever. Some even say it dates back to the Harappan era—or as Pranay Lal writes in *Indica: A Deep Natural History of the Indian Subcontinent*, 'archaeologists believe that the Kolar Gold Fields have been mined since ancient times, perhaps even from the time of the Indus Valley civilisation.' An old gazetteer of the area posits that the Harappans sourced their gold from Kolar, and certainly, India's gold industry was known to classical European scholars like Strabo and Pliny. The latter described how gold-hungry ants 'the size of Egyptian wolves' carried gold out of caves. Because of this, Wikipedia (that global asylum of lunatic facts and fictions) believes that Pliny travelled from Rome to visit these goldfields, but the fact of the matter is he merely noted down hearsay recorded by his fifth century BCE predecessor Herodotus, who never visited India either, and Megasthenes who may have been the first Greek ambassador to north India but his diplomatic affairs never encompassed the south.[5]

Even the bard of Britons, Shakespeare, seems to have heard of Indian goldmines long before Kolar became part of Britain's colonies, as he remarks in *King Henry the Fourth*, 'as wondrous affable and as bountiful as mines of India.'

In any case, the area was considered important enough by the Gangas and Cholas to fund the upkeep of its temples, so Kolar definitely mattered in ancient times.

Mining went on here for centuries using traditional methods like digging by hand (but no ants) to depths of 70-80 m and this is how the process was described by the first Englishmen to witness it around the year 1800: 'The miners extracted the stones (how we are not informed) and they were passed from hand to hand in baskets by the miners who were stationed at different points for the purpose of banking the stones. The women then took them to a large rock, and pounded them to dust. The latter was then taken to a well and washed by the same process as that used when washing the earth for gold, when about an equal quantity of gold was found to that procured from an equal quantity of the auriferous earth.'

Although colonial surveyors obviously knew about the presence of gold, it took a long time before the gold rush kicked off in the early 1880s. Industrial mining was considered unprofitable since the yellow metal was so deep underground, but eventually the fields became a hotspot for venture capitalists that saw an important resource to exploit, which in turn led to Kolar being one of the first towns to get electricity in 1902, long before the rest of India got powered up.

Life was leisurely for the colonial families then, as narrated by a British lady who spent her days cooking and eating: 'I may begin by telling you that we usually rise about half-past six, when the menkind go off to their offices, or underground, as the case may be. We have tiffin between twelve and one, and dinner at half-past seven. Breakfast is generally at about eight...We get mutton and beef from the local butcher, and also good bread from the bakery on the field. Our butter comes from Bangalore, and from there we obtain peas, potatoes, French beans, tomatoes, cauliflowers, vegetable marrow, and lettuces, and also fruit, such as apples, peaches, grapes, plantains, custard apples, melons, and sometimes pine-apples.' As unlikely as it may sound today when the city's population is counted in double-digit millions, Bangalore was celebrated for its orchards—the best European fruits and berries 'all ripen well' and 'are common there' another old colonial visitor stated, which could be how it earned its moniker, 'Garden City'.

These were, perhaps, the ingredients that went into what George Orwell described in his autobiographical novel about India, *Burmese Days* as 'not meals so much as orgies, debauches of curry and rice' and judging from old documents even the tiffin, that supposedly light snack, would consist of the previous day's done-over meats reconstructed into pies washed down with Mulligatawny soups, alongside curries with rice and roasted fowls, cheeses and freshly-baked breads topped by jellies, all chased with a few stiff drinks or at least a bottle of Madeira. Sunday tiffins would be even more overindulgent, often comprising twenty different items featuring up to four kinds of curry, mountains of ghee rice, roast beef with Yorkshire pudding, various egg preparations, steaks or chops or at least a fore-quarter of lamb, prawns and fish, vegetable stews, puddings and fruit salads and beer that had been cooled with ice shipped from as far as Alaska via Chennai in the days before refrigerators. The 1878-printed *Culinary Jottings for Madras, A Treatise in Thirty Chapters on Reformed Cookery for Anglo-Indian Exiles* by nom-de-plume Wyvern provides us latter-day gluttons with twenty-five menus to drool over. It turns out that tiffin, despite being widely used in many Indian languages to suggest a light meal, is not an Indian word at all but a colloquialism for monstrous over-eating coined by the Britons in 1807.

I quite unsuccessfully try to enter the 1890s' vintage KGF Club to fortify myself with a drink, but it opens only at 6 p.m. It is said to be the fourth oldest golf club in India. I spot, through a grimy window, a rotting piano in its decayed ballroom with wooden teak floorings dying to be waxed as I prick up my ears for any ghostly echoes of mildly indecent songs. But there are no ghosts in sight. Everything is allegedly gone, including the English-imported brass door knobs, the sterling silver cutlery with the club's emblem...yet, the distinctly Victorian building could be turned into a tourist attraction with a great dining hall, the way it is said to have been once upon a time—licking my lips outside the windows, I imagine menus consisting of 'bad word curry' (minced meatballs), 'Grandma's country captain chicken', 'dak bungalow chicken', 'devil pork' and 'railway mutton curry'.

Exclusive clubs like this dotted the Cantonments of India and can today provide us with a telling image of the erstwhile empire's soul. Make-believe places simulating 'home', i.e. England, they demarcated a boundary against the India outside of them (a bit like gated communities do today). Typically set in Anglican flower gardens, they had libraries full of mildewed books that fed more insects than intellects, game rooms for shooting billiards (one of the KGF clubrooms still holds a hundred-year-old snooker table), and dusty heads of dead animals rotting on walls above bars where gin and tonic was the choice cocktail as it was believed to prevent, even cure, malaria. There was some truth to this notion, as the tonic water gets it bitterness from quinine, a bark extract traditionally used to treat fevers and inhibit malarial parasites. On the other hand, to offset its bitterness bartenders used a liberal dash of gin and unfortunately this combination of alcohol with quinine severely harms the liver. In *Burmese Days*, Orwell wise-cracked about how colonials returned to Britain 'with a wrecked liver and a pineapple backside from sitting in cane chairs' as he, at the same time, elaborated on how in 'any town in India the European Club is the spiritual citadel, the real seat of the British power, the Nirvana for which native officials and millionaires pine in vain.' A joke at the time went that 'when two Englishmen meet they form a club, if there are three, they form a colony, and if four, an empire.' And so wherever the foreign traveller went in British India, the club was where he met everybody who was anybody worth knowing—of course limited to other Englishpersons, dolled up memsahibs (if he strayed into what was called 'the hen house' i.e. separate bar serving diluted drinks) or more often stiff-lipped gents who sipped their G&Ts with their sweaty legs propped up on the extended arms of wicker chairs variously called 'Bombay fornicators' or, as in the books of Kipling, 'long-chairs'.

I'm told there are still Anglo-Indian aunties, descendants of middle-level mining staff, who breakfast on vodka in their bungalows before heading to this club for G&T nightcaps. Suitably inspired by that, I proceed to assess the KGF beverage situation.

Old-timers recollect that there used to be a KGF brewery which produced a beverage with the simple but striking brand name 'Beer' and that was sold exclusively in a town called Beershop. Life was easier then when things were called by their true names and all of KGF had only one beer shop to supply that essential commodity. Somebody points out its site on B.M. Road but it is now occupied by a nursery school and a small chapel, side by side. My informant is unable to decide which of the two structures used to be the shop (this may be linked to over-consumption-caused memory loss). Basav Biradar, an expert on local history who has made a documentary film on the rise and fall of the mining industry here, clarifies: 'In early 20th century Mysuru princely state, liquor could be sold only through authorised shops. In KGF, there was only one shop called the beer shop, so Beershop became the local name for Andersonpet according to the gazetteers of the time.'

Additional scant facts I ferret out suggest that this shop owned by Anderson & Co was founded in the late 1800s. Andersonpet was then merely a rural bazaar serving the adjacent mines and their staff. Since its prominent feature was the sale of beer the nickname was apt. In 1904, the township was formally christened 'Anderson Market' and whilst that might be a more sober name, it lacks the magical appeal of Beershop.

The Beershop doubled as a tavern and later got licensed to supply liquor ('grog' in KGF's Anglo lingo) as well as the native staple arrack until it developed into a downmarket toddy shop that was most likely shut down when traditional palm wine was prohibited in Karnataka some decades ago. Men still called the town 'Beershop', ladies preferred to pronounce it as 'Bishop' and I imagine the conversations that must have taken place weekly, on Sundays which was the shandy day at the Andersonpet Market: 'Dearest, I'll pop over to Beershop to purchase pig mutton.' Madam: 'Oho, will you ask the bishop for blessings too?'

I find two booze counters around the corner from the defunct beer shop in the O. Daniel Road bazaar—named after the one-time local doctor O'Donnell who is unlikely to have been amused at the corruption of his name. New Lucky Liquors and Littar Flower Wines respectively carry on the Beershop heritage, despite being archetypical stand-up guzzle dives. The beer is no longer brewed locally—it's shipped from Bengaluru. Post-refreshments, one can get entertained across the street at 1920s' picture house Lakshmi Talkies, which miraculously survives in this era of streaming and downloading. When a new blockbuster is released, tickets go for ten times the normal rate and audiences get so excited that they must be mildly lathi-charged by constables before they can enter the theatre and enjoy the film.

One would think that a town called Beershop deserves a pub scene, but truth is its economy was hit hard when the mines shut, and like the legendary beershop, vintage vendors such as the English Warehouse—where everything from Coleman's Mustard and special sauces like Sutton's 'Empress of India', to tinned European vegetables and Atlantic herring and corned beef shipped from Cork, English jams and jellies, bottled Mediterranean olives and jars of Parmesan cheese from Parma were sold—closed in the early 1960s as there were only three Britons left in KGF by then, with the last European mining superintendent retiring in 1964. According to a report in *Deccan Herald*, the ex-mine workers have it hard since then and, as of March 2022, there were '30,000 families living in British-era sheds without roads, drains and other infrastructure.'

But as recently as twenty years ago, Anglo-Indians gathered for New Year's barn dances with ballroom orchestras playing tunes of the past. However, today, KGF serves up none of the Eurasian cuisine that nostalgic foodies wax lyrical about such as fishy kedgeree for breakfast ('mess of re-cooked kippers' curried along with hardboiled eggs in chicken broth, i.e. a non-veg permutation of khichdi), no dinner rolls with masala chops, no aubergine bakes or devilled chutney, none of what I read about in Bridget White's evocative *Kolar Gold Field: Down Memory Lane*. But this otherworldly place could revive—imagine if instead of flying to say, Scotland, one took the train to KGF to eat scones at bungalows-turned-heritage-B&Bs, followed by a round of golf (yes, there's still a golf course) and if craft pubs housed in former clubs offered potted ox tongue. Indeed, KGF could be a goldmine for the leisure industry.

Eventually, I stop at the New Imperial Bakery which used to deliver hot-from-the-oven loaves every day at 4 p.m. and is possibly the only remaining shop from old times. Back in the day, flour would be imported from America to avoid the local variety which was often adulterated with sand to weigh more. These days demand is down, so the jolly baker fires up his huge oven only occasionally to prepare items like the fabled Kolar muffin or seasonal hot-cross buns. The great grandson of the bakery's founder is understandably proud to show off the interiors where firewood is stacked neatly ahead of the next baking-day. A lazy cat lounges between glass jars on the hundred-year-old counter, but there are no more stick-jaw toffees or curry puffs, so I make do with a plastic bag full of orange and pineapple biscuits. For a bite of that bread, the only souvenir that a tourist can carry home of the golden age, I will have to revert to KGF another day—preferably a century ago, as soon as time travel becomes possible.

II

Looking for Malgudi

(The Imagined India)

'Green of several shades we saw, mountainsides lightly coated with verdure and fern, the dark foliage of trees rising hundreds of feet from the valley, light green, dark green, pale green, evergreen and every kind of green shade, were offered for our delectation...'

—*The Emerald Route*, R.K. Narayan

R.K. Narayan's home in Mysuru, now a museum.

Lyrical descriptions of food, hunger and eating in novels can go on echoing in one's head—or stomach—just like gushing depictions of nature. In my notebook, the most unforgettable lines are from R.K. Narayan's *The Guide*. 'He had a craving for bonda, which he used to eat in the railway station stall when a man came there to vend his edibles on a wooden tray to the travellers. It was composed of flour, potato, a slice of onion, a coriander leaf, and a green chilli—and oh! How it tasted—although he probably fried it in anything; he was the sort of vendor who wouldn't hesitate to fry a thing in kerosene, if it worked out cheaper. With all that, he made delicious stuff...'

Counted among the world's great writers, often mentioned in the same breath as Balzac, Chekhov, Dickens, Faulkner and Gogol, his many admirers comprised the likes of E.M. Forster, Graham Greene, Somerset Maugham, John Updike, Germaine Greer and even the exigent V.S. Naipaul—but, being Naipaul, with reservations. In *An Area of Darkness* Naipaul noted that the 'virtues of R.K. Narayan are Indian failings magically transmuted. I say this without disrespect: he is a writer whose work I admire and enjoy.' Essentially, Naipaul's grievance was that Narayan's fictional India hadn't prepared him for the factual India that severely culture-shocked him during his first visit to the country of his ancestors—suggesting that his own shock was made worse by Malgudi.

One of the less studied aspects of his writings, by the way, is how Narayan employed food to great effect in his stories. *The Vendor of Sweets* has edibles in its title; *The Man-Eater of Malgudi* suggests that humans can be part of the food chain; the protagonist in *Waiting for the Mahatma* suffers from a gnawing craving for freshly-cooked South Indian dishes, but is instead offered stale short eats: 'Kara sev, vadai and potato bonda…' In his short story, 'The Martyr's Corner', the focus is exclusively on junk-food—the protagonist being one of those hawkers who peddle goodies from the roadside every evening: Narayan's olfactory imagery excels in describing the dosai 'looking like layers of muslin', and chapattis with free-flowing chutney, duck's eggs 'resembling a heap of ivory balls' for those in need of protein, a sight so tempting that 'even a confirmed dyspeptic could not pass by without throwing a look at it'and to top it all there's puffy melt-in-the-mouth bondas too.

Ah, those lethal bondas! Salty and deep-fried, they mess with my BP, my medication must be upgraded, I burp from undigested chillies, the spicing drives my guts nuts. And it is in *The Guide* that Raju, the reluctant guru, is forced to undertake a fast by his devotees. He gets hungrier and hungrier by thinking of that bonda which used to be on sale at the station where he once worked as a tout, until it takes on hallucinatory powers. It heightens the dramatic tension unbearably as we approach the story's culmination.

It is an ironic tale. Initially, Raju benefits from the meals brought by villagers to the temple ruin he's squatting in (they think he's a holy man), but when drought strikes the land, there are no more free lunches coming his way. This forces him, eventually, to turn into a genuine saint—to conjure up rain through self-mortification. He goes along with it even if he knows that he has no supernatural powers. In the process, he's transformed from an egocentric crook to a self-sacrificing altruist, from being a tout (or, as he preferred to call himself, a *guide*) he turns into a guru by accident. But this story had a curious side effect on me. For years, I was unable to pass one of those deep-frying roadside chefs with their vats of boiling oil—probably spuriously recycled like Narayan suggested—without buying a piping hot globular bonda. These deadly globoids always came with lashings of mint chutney which may well have been churned out of greenish gutter water. I knew bonda wasn't healthy to binge on, but whenever I saw one I recalled Raju's starvation and had to eat it, as if to support his cause.

Interestingly, Narayan wrote *The Guide* not at home in Mysuru but in California—where his productivity was hampered by one singular disagreeable factor: The lack of vegetarian fare. Back in the 1950s, vegetarianism hadn't caught on there, nor were there any South Indian canteens unlike today when Bengaluruan IT experts rule Silicon Valley. In those days most menus in the Bay Area featured nothing but beefsteaks. Americans would question (as described in *My Dateless Diary*):

'Are you a vegetarian by conviction or religion?'

'I am a born-vegetarian. I cannot eat anything except rice, greens, and dairy produce.'

'Extraordinary! Wonder that you are alive.'

Eventually, in order to endure, the novelist bought a hotplate and lived on curd rice (his favourite dish, always had with lime pickle) until he finished the manuscript. His predicament is clearly mirrored in the hungry protagonist of the novel.[6]

The choice of bonda as a literary device is apt, considering that this Udupian dish has been a part of Karnataka's culinary legacy since at least the twelfth century. Food scholar K.T. Achaya terms it a variant of vada but historically speaking, bondas must have been stuffed with other vegetables because potatoes originated in Peru and are a distinctly colonial-era addition to the Indian pantry that only gained widespread acceptance as a household ingredient in the late nineteenth century.[7]

I was eventually cured of my addiction by climbing the colossal cliff at Sravanabelagola, known for its massive monolith of Jain saint Bahubali who starved himself to death about one millennium ago—on that very spot—after realising the vanity of hungering for power. The climb up and down the rock made me ravenous, and again, Narayan's lines replayed in my mind—the drooling Raju's fantasy of the ultimate gluttony, to 'eat bonda for fifteen days without a break', and the pain of his starvation heightened by the crowds of onlookers, 'picnic groups enjoying themselves all over the place'. Once I got down from the hill, to the bus stand where there was, as at almost all bus stops in India, a snack-frying man, my appetite for patently insalubrious edibles suddenly vanished. If those ascetics could starve themselves to death, I figured that I could at the very least abstain from bonda-hogging and lose inches from my podgy bonda-shaped BMI-world-record-breaking waistline.

Since then, I've not eaten a single bonda.

❖

Bengaluru has an endless Outer Ring Road. Cars like speed-addicted oversized cockroaches on growth hormones, horny and honking lorries, and buses resembling pregnant dinosaurs whiz past. The noise is deafening as I—the only fool on foot—

share the 'pedestrian space' with the occasional murderous scooter taking a shortcut through the wrong lane, dodging their exhaust and dust tails.

The city's roads are home to an astonishing ten million vehicles including seven million two-wheelers, about 1.5 million three-wheelers, over two million four-wheelers, with more being added at the rate of one vehicle per minute—altogether causing about 200 pedestrian deaths per year. Intriguingly, this is despite the fact that traffic moves slower and slower as it is estimated that the average speed of vehicles in the city was 35 km per hour in 2005, ten years later this had come down to nine per hour, today one shouldn't be surprised if travelling 5 km by car takes an hour. It is the secondmost congested city in the world, after London, and on an average a motorist is estimated to spend 200 hours annually in traffic jams. There's even an expression used by rickshaw drivers for certain times of day when roads get 'doubly-jammed' and if you buy a 'pre-owned' car in Bengaluru, you will notice that the gearbox hasn't been used from third gear upwards, while first and second are likely to be completely worn out. Anyway, I count myself lucky that there are a few inches of space for pedestrians as I'm reminded of the oft-shared joke—'In India we drive on the left of the road. In Bengaluru, we drive on what is left of the road.'

However, I'm not really studying the vehicular mess, but only strolling through Doddanekundi, once a probably charming ancient village by a pond of the same name, 20 km outside the town centre. The name of the locality is generally interpreted as 'jungle full of jackals', but now the flora and fauna have been swallowed up by the ever-expanding city and it's just one more suburb dotted with malls and drive-ins. Curiously enough, despite everything pointing to the opposite, Doddanekundi is nowadays best known for its bicycling culture, with cyclist clubs and the city's first cycling lanes laid out between its IT-parks, to 'tackle vehicular congestion by incentivising non-motorised travel and promote shorter non-motorised urban commutes' according to an article I read.

But that's like more on paper, I'm thinking as I recite to myself Darwin's immortal words—from *On the Origin of Species*—in which he seemingly explains why it is important that I make it alive through this traffic, or how the 'preservation of favourable individual differences and variations, and the destruction of those which are injurious, I have called Natural Selection, or *the Survival of the Fittest*.'

My quest is beginning to seem absurd before it's properly begun. I'm looking for Malgudi, that gentlest of places characterised by a completely different pace of life—quaint bungalows and cheerful bazaars populated by astrologers, printing presses, painters of signs and talkative men. If one googles this fiction created by Narayan ninety years ago, a quick search throws up several modern candidates in present-day India. One Malgudi is a gated community south of Chennai ('inspired by R.K. Narayan's ideological concept'), another is a pharmacy near Mysuru University, a third is a café called Malgudi Junction in Kolkata, and then there's a Malgudi restaurant on Bengaluru's outskirts.

The latter is said to offer delicacies of the four southern states, and a special 'Malgudi menu', which is why I'm searching for it. After a seemingly endless survival exercise on the Ring Road, it appears before me like a mirage—built to resemble a traditional home with wooden pillars, it has a swing on the porch, a tray of help-yourself bananas by the door, and walls covered with reproductions of drawings by Narayan's brother, the illustrator R.K. Laxman. Aunties in saris demolish huge thali meals, sinking their hands into veritable culinary landscapes

Malgudi Days Museum—closed on Tuesdays.

consisting of mountains of rice and oceans of sambar; soft-spoken software techies tank up on non-veg with beers...Non-veg? Beers?

What would Narayan have ordered, I ruminate as I peruse the menu card. The Malgudi section is a mishmash of southern appetisers such as chicken-65 (supposedly invented in 1965 in Chennai), chicken-95 (invented, well, thirty years later I presume) and Malgudi spl. chicken, but much as I've internalised his novels I can only recall two chickens ever being cooked and neither was considered edible...and once chicken pullao is even suspected to be a murder weapon, another time chicken is declared outright disgusting:

> 'I don't eat those things!' he cried.[8]

Therefore, I flip to the Tamil vegetarian selection. Narayan came from that side—born at a time when Bangalore was part of the colonial Madras Presidency—and towards the end, he returned to his birthplace Chennai where I was fortunate to be invited home by him in the late 1990s. He had stopped giving formal interviews and was unwilling to answer the same questions about Malgudi's symbolic meaning, so I didn't know what to say at first but soon any nervousness evaporated as it turned out he preferred to discuss Tamil food habits. The subject interested me too. Despite that, and considering that it is rumoured that he was twice fielded as India's candidate for the world's highest literary award, I just had to sneak in the question of whether he hoped to receive the Nobel Prize for Literature.

'No, I don't need a Nobel Prize. What would I do with it?' he said and quickly changed the topic. 'So exactly which Indian dishes have you eaten?'

I named all that had found favour with me and he appeared pleased that I enjoyed both dosa and idli, because dishes like these couldn't be had in Europe, he explained: 'The temperature wouldn't allow a proper fermentation.' A Tamilian would know. The constantly warm climate—Chennai's seasons are sometimes only slightly jestingly characterised as hot, hotter and hottest—was used for great effect in creating fermented goodies. (Later, I learnt from a chef in the UK that it usually takes a minimum thirty hours to ferment dosa batter in London even in summer). The less we talked about fiction, the more communicative he became and so we chatted about basically anything but writing. Now and then, the grand master of Indian literature inspected his potted plants with a critical eye but seemed to be entirely unsentimental when declaring that some of them did not seem to be particularly alive—for that is the course of nature.

'I think that all things, humans included, go through a phase of decay towards the end. So this is entirely natural, all this,' he said alluding to his own aged body and the fact that he had stopped giving interviews about his books, only then to ask as one writer might, with comradely pleasure, of another, 'Would you like to see my study?'

It was at this moment that I think he realised how much our meeting meant to me and the moment that I later felt the greatest gratitude for. He made his way slowly through the apartment he shared with his nephew, with the support of a crutch, over to a chamber where he kept a cot and a writing desk. He sat down to sign a copy of his autobiography for me and then rested his hand on a pile of papers.

'Are you writing something at the moment?' I asked.

'No, this is my correspondence. Every now and then, I have a typist write out letters for me, but mostly I let the mail lie here and go through a phase of decay. It's like a natural process. I imagine that if I wait long enough, these will disappear.' He then asked me to write to him sometime, he enjoyed receiving letters. But he added, 'If you don't get a reply, you'll know why.'

In case you wonder, I did post a letter, but I never heard back from Narayan. But our conversation about food stuck in my mind, so Tamil grub it is. Sandwiched between the non-veg offerings there's a short list of veg and I do the usual travel writer thing and order what I've never heard of before, hoping for an exciting discovery.

The munakai soup is a light sambarish preparation with drumsticks and I can imagine it being eaten in Malgudi. Their varthalkuzhambu—supposedly one of the most classic Tamil dishes—turns out to be over-spiced garlic pods pickled in salt, a bitter and sour assault on the bowels. Hmm, Narayan may have opted for the standard meals that seem to be a big draw.

As I empty my plantain leaf, I'm even more determined to find the real deal—the actual Malgudi. There are clues.

Internet sources useful for various degrees of disinformation situate Malgudi near Coimbatore (from where Narayan's wife hailed and where his daughter later settled after marriage).

In Tamil Nadu there are, in fact, several candidates such as Lalgudi, roughly 100 km from Rasipuram which is what the initial 'R' in R.K. Narayan's name stands for. And the town of Mangudi has an even more deceptively similar name. But what if it's in Karnataka instead? I've found evidence for such a notion in the Doordarshan series *Malgudi Days* by playing the video in slow-motion. Recall the episode about the mailman who doesn't deliver an inauspicious letter on a wedding day? The footage of the post office flashes the zip code 577 411 in passing. It happens to belong to a small Malnad town called Agumbe (with a population of 180 joint-families)...Malnad... Agu...Malgu...umbe? It's a 71.4 per cent match.

His cinematic adaptations give hints. When Narayan scripted his first and only feature for the silver screen, the now lost Tamil low-budget satire *Miss Malini*, it was shot in Chennai and portrayed life in that town. But when he rewrote his screenplay into the novel *Mr Sampath—The Printer of Malgudi*, the plot obviously moved from Chennai to his imagined Malgudi. This book was then adapted into the Hindi movie *Mr Sampat* and it was again a Gemini production filmed in their Chennai studios. Despite the Hindi-speaking characters, its sets look distinctly South Indian such as the Hanuman Vilas Hotel, an archetypal vegetarian café that can still be experienced, for example, in the older neighbourhoods of Bengaluru. By the time his novel *The Financial Expert* was 'adopted' [*sic*] into Kannada as *Banker Margayya* it seems that Malgudi had finally been located in geography, in the Malnad ('hill country'). Watching the movie, I spot the name Koppa on a signboard—a town some 30 km from the hill station Agumbe. Another clue that firmly settles matters came when Malgudi made its biggest-budget appearance in the award-winning Dev Anand-starrer *Guide*, for regardless of its box office success, Narayan preferred the humbler small screen televised version simply because the Bollywood version was shot in Rajasthan and Gujarat, which didn't fit Narayan's own image of Malgudi at all—'they had discarded my own values in milieu and human characteristics,' he lamented in his autobiography. But he felt that Shankar Nag's acclaimed *Malgudi Days*, with a stellar cast of senior Kannada actors, largely shot in Agumbe, really did justice to Malgudi.

A clear lead, if there ever was one. But before leaving the metropolis, it must be pointed out that Bengaluru isn't entirely irrelevant in the search for Malgudi, for it was here that Narayan came up with the name. It happened on Vijayadashmi Day in September 1930, an auspicious moment to set pen to paper according to his grandmother (who was very dear to Narayan and about whom he later wrote the biographical novel *A Grandmother's Tale*) and so that's when he began writing his first novel *Swami and Friends*.

Narayan had recently graduated but was unemployed. Staying with her in the big city, he waited for his future to somehow reveal itself, loafing about in the streets, planning, and then buying an exercise book in which to write his novel. 'As I sat in a room nibbling at my pen and wondering what to write, Malgudi with its little railway station swam into view, all ready-made, with a character called Swaminathan running down the platform'. The station had a banyan tree, a stationmaster, and two trains a day, one coming, one going.

In the completed book, the station scene features at the end, as the backdrop to the climax when his friend goes away on a train and leaves Swami devastated. 'All the jarring, rattling, clanking, spurting, and hissing of the moving train softened in the distance into something that was half a sob and half a sigh.'

As for myself, I'm booked on an overnight train that passes Malleswaram station without stopping. Next morning, reaching the temple town Udupi, the nearest railhead to Agumbe, I plan to hire a taxi and, with some luck, I'll find a cabbie named Gaffur, like the driver in Narayan's stories.

The coastal air is as sweltering as if breathing hot steam. Since dosa happened to be one of Narayan's favourite snacks, the first thing I do is to have a gigantic metre-long masala dosa at the Mitra Samaj canteen by the Krishna temple, where the pure-veg Udupi cuisine received its recognisable form 500 years ago as a monastic diet for the area's priestly class. Chefs-to-be train from their teens in any one of the temple kitchens that have perfected the art of high-quality sattvik food (no onion-garlic, no foreign veggies except chillies). To quote food writer Shoba Narayan, from her book *Food and Faith: A Pilgrim's Journey Through India*, dosa originated in this 'small, dusty town, no different from those dotting interior India. Its temple and cuisine, however, hold an outsize place in the local, regional, national and even international imagination.' In an article in the *Hindustan Times*, she brings up the possibility that it was invented so that the devout could 'hide forbidden onions inside the dosa folds'.

Unsurprisingly the holy town's name has become synonymous with the world's perhaps most wholesome and pocket-friendly vegetarian menu. Local, yet global—Udupi serveries were a secular version of refectories, bhojanashalas or temple feeding halls, and they rose to fame in Bombay around the time of World War I, as workers from Karnataka migrated there. With chefs hailing from Udupi, the dishes were familiar, comforting, and—accustomed to mass-feeding—their service was quick. Ten years later, there was an Udupi canteen in Madras (well, Chennai) perhaps much like the one I had seen in the aforementioned film and by the time of independence many towns had Udupi Bhavans, prototypes for the ones that nowadays can be found even in Silicon Valley, California, which is increasingly becoming another suburb of Bengaluru. A joke goes: What did Neil Armstrong see when he landed on the moon? A vegetarian Udupi hotel serving masala dosa!

There and then, life already feels very Malgudi. Once I get into a taxi, the driver's name turns out to be Krishna Prasad, which roughly translates as 'food consecrated to god' and which isn't bad at all considering that the Udupi Krishna temple is the main tourist attraction in these parts. He is exceptionally efficient, too, and drives up the narrow ghat road so fast it is like bungee-jumping uphill.

The 55-km journey to Agumbe, which sits at the top of a pass connecting the Deccan Plateau with the coastal belt below, is a tunnel of emerald greenery, areca nut plantations and rubber-tree nurseries. When he first visited Agumbe in 1939, Narayan described the view towards the ocean as 'a spectacle which is worth travelling a thousand miles to watch.' On the ascent up the serpentine road, we run into a cloud after the third hairpin bend and as we drive into Agumbe, following another dozen increasingly scary bends, the mist is so thick that it's like entering a fading photograph of a town...or hamlet, as this turns out to be.

Ah, finally I'm in Malgudi! Everything looks like the TV series but less crowded. There are barely any people. No cars. It's so quiet it is magical. Central Agumbe is essentially a T-junction, called 'circle', with a post office, a bus stand, some shops and canteens such as the roomless Hotel Kubera, as well as a bank and a school with a faded board outside—I decipher the name 'S.V.S. High School'—could this have been the Albert Mission College featured in the TV series?

A winding side lane, Car Street (where I still see no cars), takes me to a village square with the Srivenugopalakrishnaswamy temple that appears familiar and a primary school where kids like Swami and his friends crowd the classrooms, and a ruined pilgrims' hostel built in 1906—the year of Narayan's birth. People use the ruin to dry coconut husks.

Everybody I speak to, from the postman to the shopkeepers, remembers *Malgudi Days* which was filmed in 1985-86. When asked whereabouts the shooting happened, they all say: 'Everywhere.' Most villagers got walk-on parts, doing cameos in the series that transformed Agumbe into a bustling small town if only for the duration of the shoot. The film's crew and cast numbering more than a hundred were all lodged with the villagers. Apparently, an 18-ft equestrian statue of the British resident, Sir Frederick Lawley (cheekily executed in the form of a caricature by Bengaluru-based artist John Devraj), was put up at the T-junction that was turned into a proper 'Circle' for a time.

The key location, where the filmmakers spent months on end, is Doddamane ('the big house') in the main street.[9] This private home, erected in the year 1900, has a grand front veranda adorned with pillars and a central courtyard. The first episode that took place in the house was 'Maha Kanjoos', the memorable story of a miserly grandfather and his mischievous grandson.

Kasturiakka is the matron of the house and sits on a cot in the inner veranda, in the company of two other ladies. Before I quite know how it happened, I have a steaming tumbler of kashayam in my hand: A milky, lightly-spiced (with basil leaves, I think, and something else I can't quite put my finger on) health beverage trusted in these hills. Kasturiakka's hospitality is the stuff of legend. Visitors to the village can stay in an upstairs room and pay as they like, but she doesn't allow filmy folks anymore. She talks about how the shooting turned everything upside down. Listening to her, it is easy to believe that one has indeed stepped into a different world. The family is proud of how clean Agumbe is and claim it hasn't changed at all since the eldest among them were children in the 1930s. When I step out again, I get a funny feeling that the slow pace here really does adjust one's inner biorhythms to Malgudi time. The air is fresher, dreamier than elsewhere, remarkably so. Or maybe it's because of the fluffy wet clouds that wrap themselves around everything including my toes.

Whiling away Malgudian days at Dodda Mane, matrons with Kasturiakka in the centre.

But however close to an ideal village Agumbe might seem, with its kindly, unhurried, educated inhabitants, there are things missing. Where, for example, is the railway? Arasalu station, a 77-km drive north, on the rather obscure line from Shivamogga to Talguppa, was used for the TV shoot. Its abandoned colonial-era station building was recently developed into a charming Malgudi museum, housing props and memorabilia, well worth a detour if one happens to be passing nearby. And there's no clock tower in Agumbe. There's also no Lawley

Extension, suburban living belongs in Agumbe as little as traffic jams do.

The station at Arasalu has been renamed as Malgudi Station—confusing for passengers wishing to get off at Arasalu—but should you happen to buy a ticket to the Malgudi Express, one of the slowest trains in Karnataka, you will end up over 200 km due south, in Mysuru where Narayan spent much of his life.

Indeed, the Malgudi map drawn by Clarice Borio and reproduced on Narayan's request in one of his books, if tilted to the right, and then a bit to the left, bears a striking resemblance to a map of Mysuru. The river Sarayu for one is quite obviously based on Kaveri, south India's great sacred river. Green Hotel on Hunsur Road used to be part of the Premier Studios that was renamed the Malgudi Film Studio in his novels. The fictive Market Street with its Bombay Anand Bhavan, feels much like Sayyaji Rao Road with the real-life Bombay Tiffanys sweets and snacks shop (limited seating on two metal-topped benches) in the factual market building, which is surrounded by any number of places that remind me of, for example, Malgudi's Regal Haircutting Saloon and other sundry enterprises. The Palace Talkies resembles the genuine Prabha Theatre. While many other theatres have shut down, it survived the pandemic lockdowns in its futuristically upgraded avatar as Prabha UFO Digital Cinema. And the imagined clock tower must have been inspired by the nearby genuine clock tower, a few hundred steps north of the palace.[10] Sampath—the printer of Malgudi—is said to be based on a real-life printer, who printed Narayan's own *Indian Thought* publications (cheaper editions of his writings for the Indian market), and it is a curious but little-known fact that Narayan, at the Metropole Hotel near the railway station, observed a tout or tourist guide in action one day, which triggered his bestselling novel *The Guide*.[11]

In short, Narayan didn't bother to hide his tracks. And for sure, Lawley Extension could well be a portrait of Yadavgiri, a suburb behind the station where Narayan, in the winter of 1947-48, purchased a 55x36 metre plot worth about Rs 5,000 and over the next four or five years built his graceful two-storied home. If one didn't know, one would pass without a second glance as it is dwarfed by its posh neighbours. But a useful landmark is the Paradise Hotel, where Narayan and his brother Laxman dined in the 1980s and which stands across the street. Writing this, I sample bisibelehulianna, a Mysuruan VFM all-in-one-dish that is part veg biryani, part fiery sambar gravy and part mystical puree of hot-hot spices. And so I find that much here in Mysuru fits my mental image of the world of Narayan.

The house had shockingly enough been sold to a builder and was about to be demolished a decade ago, in 2011. Waking up to this cultural calamity, booklovers demanded that this irreplaceable legacy be rescued, so since 2016 it's been a museum where visitors may check out the author's library which includes a big fat biography of his mentor Graham Greene, his shirts, muffler and grey jacket. Before the pandemic struck in 2019, already 17,000 fans had taken the opportunity to pay their respects.

It's strangely moving to see the old-fashioned kitchen and imagine him making himself a cuppa—a fastidious caffeinist, he apparently had an impressive collection of eight percolators. I recall publisher David Davidar mentioning, in a preface to a collection of Narayan's stories, that 'after offering me some superb home-brewed filter coffee, he showed me around the house that he'd had constructed to his specifications, especially the many-windowed study on the top floor from which he could look out upon the town which had provided much of the raw material for his stories.' Although he generally ate meals and slept in the joint-family home in nearby Lakshmipuram, he used come here to write in his 'office'. The study that Davidar refers to, is a sunny bay-room with eight windows that offer panoramic 180° views of the entire city, plus playful birds and squirrels.

R.K. Narayan in his study (in Chennai).

Eventually, I find a conclusive clue in Narayan's essay 'Misguided "Guide"', where he talks extensively about the aforementioned Bollywood movie *The Guide*. The film team (that included the Nobel Prize-winning scriptwriter Pearl S. Buck) apparently came all the way to Mysuru to see the setting of the book—and Narayan writes, 'I showed them the river steps and a little shrine overshadowed by a banyan on the banks of Kaveri, which was the actual spot around which I wrote *The Guide*. As I had thought, nothing more needed to be done than put the actors there and start the camera.'

So there, he admitted it! He also took the moviemakers to the top of Gopalaswamybetta, the highest peak in the Bandipur National Park, up a steep jungly road where one might encounter tigers or elephants. 'At the summit I showed them the original of the "Peak House" in my novel, a bungalow built fifty years ago, with glassed-in verandas affording a view of wildlife at night, and a 2,000-foot drop to a valley beyond. A hundred yards off, a foot-track wound through the undergrowth, leading on to an ancient temple whose walls were crumbling and whose immense timber doors moved on rusty hinges with a groan. Once again I felt that here everything was ready-made for the film.' It is easy to imagine his disappointment when *The Guide* was shot in Rajasthan and Gujarat instead of his beloved Karnataka.[12]

It is a well-known fact that Narayan liked to saunter about in his hometown for inspiration and socialise with the various characters he met on the streets (talkative men, printers and vendors of sweets, and other oddballs), which he thought of as part of his 'office hours', or at least that's what he once told fellow writer Ved Mehta. In an obituary, Khushwant Singh described his own visit to Mysuru and how 'being with Narayan on his afternoon stroll was an experience. He did not go to a park but preferred walking up the bazaar.' There, Narayan stopped 'at shops to exchange namaskaras with the owners, introduce me and exchange gossip with them in Kannada or Tamil…' which gave Singh an insight into how Narayan got 'material for his novels and stories.'

Without Narayan to guide me, I spend a day walking in his footsteps, from his childhood's Bojanna Lane where formative experiences took place, to the family's house in Lakshmipuram, a fancier area with a clear Tamil vibe. And I recall how he typed his first stories on a second-hand typewriter. To get his friends to listen, he treated them to coffee, running up such a long bill that he had to sell the typewriter to clear his dues. But it must have been worth it, as he remarked, 'the cup of coffee blunted the listeners' critical faculties and made them declare my work a masterpiece.' Without a typewriter, he had a typist hammer out his handwritten manuscripts on demi-sized bond paper.

Following clues in *My Days*, I next walk to where his typist lived by the Jaganmohan Palace. Narayan made it a point to reach the house before the man could finish his breakfast, to follow him to his stall, Venus Typewriting Institute, through the narrow alley by the temple on the corner, now the ostentatiously named Srisribrahmatantraswatantraparakalaswami mutt, to Santhepete Bazaar behind the Hardinge Complex.

Leaving the typist to his work, usually Narayan walked up to the market, opposite which still stands a bookshop he frequented in the hopes that it'll stock his books one day—but when I ask for Mysuru-related literature, the proprietor only shows me expensive, lavish books on the maharajas. When I specify what I'm interested in, it turns out they have a single thin paperback by Narayan tucked away at the back. After I pay for it, I continue to a nearby stationery shop, R. Krishnaswami, which was another of his hangouts. The proprietor remembers him and says they kept a chair out in front, where Narayan sat down to watch people and take notes. I ask what pencil he used and am shown their enduring bestsellers.

The local Apsara brand is cheap at Rs 6 so Narayan bought those when he was short on money, so I buy a packet, but when he could afford it he'd upgrade to Staedtler pencils. 'A hundred years ago we were one of only three shops in India to stock these, the others were a shop in Bombay and another one in Madras' I'm told.

And as I get myself a luxurious Rs 625 set, I hope they'll bring me Narayan's blessings.

❖

Apart from being a hub of literary tourism, Mysuru is renowned as a foodie fairyland with its reputation resting primarily on the local variety of Karnataka's most world-famous dish, namely the 'Mysore masala dosa'. Like the Russians who have their blinis with vodka, the French who have their creamy crêpes, the Swedes who have...well, don't really have anything comparable as R.K. Narayan discreetly hinted during our conversation about dosas when I had travelled to Chennai to meet him.

It's interesting how, if one eats one's way from coast to coast, dosas mutate. They can be as thick as pancakes but with a smaller-than-Udupi diameter in Tamil Nadu; softer with spongier centre but crisper edges in Kerala (appams); on the east coast in Andhra Pradesh zesty dosa-like pancakes are known as pesarattu with the spices mixed into the batter, in contrast to which Tulu Nadu on the west coast has its gossamer-like non-spicy neerdosas ('water pancakes') and then there are the utterly buttery bennedosas of central Karnataka. Elsewhere on my trips, I've chomped on non-veg egg-coated dosas stuffed with minced mutton, or had stacks of them alongside Malabari chicken gravy; in Bengaluru's bazaars rice pullao-stuffed dosa is the stuff; while faddish experiments have spawned the Punjabified butter-roasted paneer dosa, but then again thanks to health-conscious restaurateurs, one also gets 'olive oil dosa'—just to mention some varieties on Indian tables.

Of all the notable Mysuru products that attract tourists, the dosa is perhaps the most emblematic yet most impossible to carry home as a souvenir. More easily packaged mementoes include the GI-tagged Mysuru silk (from a factory founded in 1912 by the maharaja himself), GI-tagged sandalwood oils and soaps (world-famous since 1916), likewise GI-tagged Mysuru incense, or sinfully sweet ghee-laden Mysore pak (also GI-tagged and best had at Guru Sweets whose owner invented this home-grown chickpea flour fudge in 1935), and last but not least, the GI-tagged Nanjangud-rasabalehannu which is a special variety of tiny bananas superior to all other plantains anywhere in the world, with matchless aroma—as I bite into one, it reminds me of sweet, ripe, juicy strawberries (India is the world's #1 producer of the sweetest bananas).[13]

There may be a deluge of burgers and pizzas on the contemporary Mysuruan fast-food scene, but the dosa remains the city's greatest bestseller and is, now and then, fielded as a 'national dish' whenever matters of gastronomic symbolism is debated. A global poll has put it at #4 on a list of 'Top 10 Dishes to Eat Before You Die' and for its Indian market, the conservative McDonalds junk-food empire, realising that they can't ever hope to beat local fast-food, found it necessary to introduce a McDosa masala burger.

Another great place for dosas in Mysore—this is where the maharaja goes when he craves a dosa.

Every good canteen in Mysuru prepares its dosa the same way (well, almost): Urad dhal and rice batter must be mixed in the exactly right proportions, then soaked and fermented overnight after which it is shallow-fried at the ideal temperature until its surface becomes perfectly golden brownish, crusty on the outside but fluffy within. An added signature smear of flaming-chilli-garlic-onion 'disco paste' for heightened tastiness is the hallmark of Mysuruan dosa. It is finally filled with the correct stuffing known as 'palya' that is basically curried potato mush. Narayan's own favourite came from a 'hotel' near his Lakshmipuram residence, a well-known eatery that was regularly frequented by late Kannada cinema legends Ambarish, Dr Rajkumar and Vishnuvardhan. When Dev Anand visited Narayan's 'office' in Yadavgiri, the Bollywood hero was plied with these fabled dosas 'and other South Indian delicacies' brought by Narayan's nephews. Known until recently as Ramya Drive-In, the eatery was recently shut down due to the pandemic.[14]

My first stop whenever I arrive at Mysuru by rail is unfailingly the neat Hotel Ashoka (Dhanvantri Road), a short walk from the station. A traditional eatery, it transports me to a gentler Mysuruan era and their dosa is top class, no doubt. Also, it isn't as crowded as the touristy hangouts. One noteworthy detail about the orthodox dosa is that it is folded into a half-circle, such as at Ashoka, and never rolled like crêpes or twisted into a cone (like elsewhere). The turmeric-yellow filling is a buttery melange of smashed spiced-up potatoes and fried onion lightly seasoned with mustard seeds and chillies.

Even if the potato stuffing isn't an old concept, some form of dosa has been in existence for 1,500 years according to the scholarly K.T. Achaya who found mentions of 'dōsai' in ancient Sangam literature—which means that the dish is as old as Mysuru itself.[15] It's generally assumed to have developed its modern shape in Udupi, as noted, but the enigma that scientists can't quite crack is whether it's a fried, flattened idli or if the idli is a compact, steamed dosa![16]

However that may be, the Mysuru dosa developed into

what we eat today when public eateries became a rage in Karnataka during the first half of the 1900s. As compared to the traditional set dosa—a stack of pancakes with veg gravy or palya on the side—stuffing a dosa with masala was seen as progressive as it speeded up serving and eating, and it could at a pinch be parcelled as a travel snack by wrapping it up in a banana leaf (though it does get soggy rapidly); hence an optimal snack.

Despite being the preferred bite to break a busy sightseeing schedule, for some strange reason one cannot eat dosa whenever one craves it. It's only served as 'tiffin'—and this is generally true across the south—in the mornings until about 11 a.m. and then again from 3 p.m. until when dinner service commences. However, some unorthodox holistic joints geared towards foreigners do cook dosa for lunch, as with multiple yogashalas and mystic research centres to pick from, Mysuru has become the hub of yogic holidays in the world. The local gurus teach a range of Hollywood heroines in search of that perfect physique and burnt-out pop stars; and following in their footsteps, a couple of thousand foreigners join the city's 150 or so yoga studios *every month*. In 2016, yoga was even recognised by UNESCO as an 'intangible cultural heritage' of global importance.

For these yoga tourists, dosas are stand-ins for crêpes when they feel culinary homesickness. They contain only about 350 calories but are nutritious, high in carbs and protein, rich in amino acids and probiotic qualities thanks to the fermentation process, and being fully gluten-free they're the perfect repast for today's increasingly gluten-intolerant health freaks.

So, to sample yogic dosa, and that too for lunch, I check out Dhatu Organics & Naturals (Adipampa Road), a combined ecological grocery store and café in the Gokulam area known for its upmarket meditation centres, kombucha juice bars and sourdough pizzerias. A couple of English girls sit at the next table, eating grilled veg platters and discussing their course in ashtanga it seems from the snippets of conversation I overhear. Although ashtanga is another Mysuru invention, in this case, the girls worship a Mysuru-based Spanish yogi! At another table, a health-conscious yet overweight techie works on his laptop. As I browse the menu, my attention is caught by a millet dosa served with sprouted green gram curry. Yummy!

It is a non-greasy, fibre-rich energy booster. At this moment, if it sounds like there's a deficiency in my personal health consciousness I have a small confession to make. I occasionally practice breathing techniques like pranayama along with friends, but as a person whose natural circumstances consist of unthinking non-veg hogging and brain-numbing beering, I doubt that any veggie utopia can reform me or steer my 'journey of self-discovery' in a more preferable direction. I tried staying at an Ayurvedic retreat once. Deprived of red meat and without even a single espresso in sight to accompany the ciggies I had smuggled with me, there was nothing to do other than observe myself—'witness' as the hypnotic guru with a twenty-five-year-long-CV of ashram-hopping put it—but which only served to freak me out. After doing his best to improve my sordid life via chakra-cleansing-cum-balancing, he asked me how it felt.

'Terribly hard,' I blurted out. 'Whenever I try to think about what you tell me, my mind thinks of something else.'

'That is because your mind is like a drunken monkey. It jumps whichever way it fancies.'

'Oh, that is good to know, it explains a lot,' I replied, thinking that's fine, I just have to learn to live with a tipsy simian jailed within my skull, and squeeze in the odd banana through my ears to keep it calm. During the morning yoga, my creaky bones felt irreparably damaged and the one time I performed suryanamaskar in the yogashala, I fully appreciated how poorly equipped my body is to manhandle anything more complex than a computer keyboard. So I've kind of decided to hope against hope that karmic laws have some paragraph that might let slack souls like me off the hook.

In a world where food is becoming increasingly complex, Mysuru is sheer bliss for the authentic down-to-the-roots preparations on offer and so eating dosa in excess gives me a strong sense of upholding cultural values, even if I feel stuffed like a dosa by late afternoon. Within marching distance east of the bus station stands the somewhat nondescript Mylari Hotel (Nazarbad Main Road), which interestingly enough has been certified by China as the 'best dosa hotel of Asia', if not in the entire universe. Their opening hours are tricky, so one must time the visit well—they fire up the dosa grill at 7.30 a.m. and again at 4 p.m., but shut whenever they run out of batter, which doesn't take long. The establishment seats maximum sixteen, so being early is being wise.

Their dosa is spongy, thick and almost as soft as idli—perhaps constituting that missing link between the two?—and its cloying nature is enhanced by how they cook on aromatic wood-fire rather than gas flame, and it comes not with thick palya or tangy sambar but a mild mix-veg masala typical of Karnataka cuisine, and chutney which I believe is made from fresh coconut lightly seasoned with just some chillies, black mustard seeds, curry leaves and maybe some other top secret ingredients. I order two more because the first was so velvety that I could go on eating until the shop runs out of batter!

Eventually, I force myself to stop, my conclusion being that the Mysuru dosa will feature on my list of five essential things that I would take to a desert island—the other four being beer, Bengaluru, books and my wife's phone number.

III

South by Southwest

(A Passage through Kerala)

'What on earth were you doing with yourself in India for five years?' said Isabel.

'Playing about,' he answered, with a smile of kindly mockery.

'What about the Rope Trick?' asked Gray. 'Did you see that?'

'No, I didn't.'

'What did you see?'

'A lot.'

—*The Razor's Edge*, Somerset Maugham

Toddy shop in Kumarakom.

You know you're in Kerala when you step off the train, walk right into the nearest shack and are served smoothly soothing and slightly sweetish appams accompanying a sublime fish curry—for *breakfast*. Now that's what I call a hospitable attitude! But actually, fish curry is considered a completely normal thing to eat the first thing you do as you open your eyes. And my eyes do open wide and water a bit...because, typically for Kerala, the fiery curry is packed with flavours ranging from chillies, coconut, coriander, cumin, curry leaves, garlic, ginger, mustard seeds, pepper, tamarind, turmeric and many others I can't tell apart, yet without being too spicy to enjoy for breakfast.

A breakfaster's self-combustion is prevented by those delicately plump and spongy palm-sap fermented rice flour batter pancakes called appams, that are sweeter than their dosa relatives, and which have curiously cushioned centres encircled by lacy edges. Appams, also anglicised as hoppers (which presumably is how the colonials pronounced the word), are sheer food artistry, 'perhaps the most beautiful of Indian breads' to quote food expert Pushpesh Pant. The appams are cooked in a special wok-shaped cast-iron appachatti—an implement that accounts for the appam's unique structural features. Widely consumed since time immemorial, they seem to have special links to Kerala's Christians, with varieties such as pesahappam or 'INRI-appam' prepared exclusively for the pesaha that commemorates the crucifixion (it is even embellished with a palm leaf cross). Hence these are said to have originated in that community, which blended ancestral Syrian influences with adopted Indian habits—an intercourse that gave birth to the omnipresent appam.

This shack has no name that I can make out, the owner speaks only Malayalam, but what a fishy welcome! Still peckish, I order fried fish with the delicate scent of coconut oil and go on munching until it's almost lunchtime: A perfect start on a day of sightseeing which immediately makes me forget the long train ride to Kozhikode.

It is a historically known fact that people travelled from afar to shop for spices here—the ancient Greeks and Romans, the medieval Arabs and Chinese, and later, the who's who of colonials whether Portuguese or English, French or Dutch, all came and sampled Kerala's flavourful pantry. Therefore, I dream of culinary fireworks as I follow evocative street signs: Sweet Meat Street is where the city's trademark dry fruit halwa has been on sale for over 600 years and where I also buy chunky pepper-and-jaggery coated banana chips. The Silk Street is the more or less official 'Food Street' lined with scores of enticing eateries—including The Chinese Factory, which isn't as old as one might wish but a modern pan-Asian fusion diner where Japanese *teriyaki* squids effortlessly rub their rubbery shoulders with pepper-grilled paneer and chicken fried rice. Halwa Bazaar needs no explanation because that's where the good stuff is made. Finally I arrive at the narrow, winding, cacophonic Big Bazaar where truckloads of spices are being unloaded into impossibly tiny shops. Everywhere a melange of piquant scents hangs heavy in the air. Not for nothing is Kozhikode known as 'City of Spices' and prowling through Big Bazaar it gets quite easy to imagine what things may have looked like 500 years ago when foreigners traded Portuguese silver, Italian velvet, English woollen fabrics and whatever else Europe produced, for spices.

Coincidentally, one of my favourite English writers, novelist Somerset Maugham, loitered on the city's beach in the 1930s—at a time when a tourist handbook describes the town thus: 'Facing the sea are the houses of the European residents and the custom house, and also the club. There is a great appearance of neatness and comfort in the houses even of the very poor in Calicut; and the whole place is rendered very picturesque by the fine trees and groves of cocoa-nut palms in which it is embowered.'

The 'beach' isn't particularly conducive to swimming but it's rather a quiet neighbourhood where I stay at the Beach Hotel, something of a landmark that was originally built as the British club back in 1890. Luckily it hasn't been significantly modernised since the town's name was Calicut and it oozes antiquity out of every creaky floorboard. I had requested the suite where Maugham plotted his novel *The Razor's Edge* sometime in 1938, but the staff didn't seem sure of who Maugham was. 'Your mom? What's her name?' In any case, the 75-sq-m room I move into is bigger than my compact flat in Bengaluru. Then again, Maugham was a bigger writer than I'll ever be. So I am not complaining, especially since the ex-club retains the most exciting bar in town.

The only kitchen to have survived long enough to have served Maugham, at least in theory, is the French Bakery in Kooriyal Lane. Set up in 1932, when there was only one Frenchman left in town (a watchman assigned to guard a colonial shed), it was nevertheless beloved by other colonials.

Unfortunately, it retains none of its 1930s' character—it looks like any other canteen that does bakes and snacks, with nothing strikingly Parisian about it. Whatever they serve, however, like fish fried in sweetish coconut oil, would approximate what Maugham sampled of Kerala cookery during his sojourn. And being a hardcore Francophile (Maugham had migrated from Britain to the south of France in 1928), he'd obviously have gyrated towards this bakery to pick up some 'hot cross buns' whenever he felt peckish.

Besides, he was a steadfast 'breakfast man'—who wisecracked somewhat ambiguously that 'to eat well in England you should have breakfast three times a day'—though I'm not sure if he would have considered fish curry to be a substitute for traditional English breakfast. Although this three-month sojourn was his first and only visit to India proper, he'd earlier travelled widely in Asia (including Burma which was then part of British India) and so must have gotten used to Asian food. Yet the only meal he describes taking pleasure in, according to *A Writer's Notebook*, is a freshly-shot peacock, which he feels bad about in a moral sense but on the other hand, its 'flesh was white, tender and succulent; it was a welcome change from the scraggy chickens which are brought to the table evening after evening in India.' As we see, he wasn't thrilled by Indian culinary skills. Touring across Burma in the previous decade, with a fulltime Telugu cook in his entourage, he wrote how he was served 'bony, tasteless fish; if not, [tinned] sardines or tunny; a dish of tough meat, and one of the three sweets that my Indian cook knew how to make.'[17]

I like to imagine that the spiritual-minded Maugham tried meditation cross-legged on the floor of the room at the club. And at the bakery, I buy a slice of cake with the word 'Coffee' piped onto it in cream as I consider how Maugham, for the rest of his life, fancied returning to write more about India. Up to now 'the shadow of Kipling lurking over the country' had inhibited him, he told another India-inspired novelist colleague, E.M. Forster, in a letter. But here, he met a different India from the one in Kipling's nineteenth-century stories and regretted not having come earlier.

Apart from entries in *A Writer's Notebook* (1949) and an essay about Hinduism, 'The Saint', in his last book (*Points of View*) that was triggered by his encounter with Ramana Maharishi, India formed the backbone of *The Razor's Edge*, perhaps his greatest masterpiece in which a long lost friend turns up after ten years and is full of mysterious stories from when he 'knocked about the East for a bit' including two years at an ashram in Kerala, 'a beautiful country of green hills and valleys and soft-flowing rivers. Up in the mountains there are tigers, leopards, elephants and bison, but the Ashrama was on a lagoon and all around it grew coconuts and areca palms.'

It is quite certain that he based the ashram described in *The Razor's Edge*, which he located at some distance by train and bullock-cart from Thiruvananthapuram, on a brief visit to Ramana Maharishi's abode in neighbouring Tamil Nadu.

On his travels, however, rather than roughing it out at ashrams he lived comfortably as a government guest, or was 'sumptuously entertained' by many maharajas, or stayed at posh clubs in cities like Bombay where, to his irritation, at the Yacht Club—where Indians weren't allowed—he was pestered by pompous colonials, 'doddering old fools' as he called them in a letter posted from there. Before coming to Kerala he had seen churches in Goa and after breaking journey in Kozhikode, he peeped into the Library in Thiruvananthapuram, where he was pleased to spot his own novels in the collection. He liked Kerala a lot: 'It is green, cool and quiet. You get a very curious impression of pastoral life, peaceful and primitive, and not too hard.'

Next he toured Tamil Nadu where he most likely celebrated his sixty-fourth birthday by the temple in Madurai (on 25 January): 'People talk all day long at the top of their voices, but in the temple they talk more loudly than ever. The row is terrific. People pray and recite litanies, they call to one another, vociferously discuss, quarrel or greet one another. There is nothing that suggests reverence and yet there is a vehement overwhelming sense of the divine that sends cold shivers down your spine.' Then he had his darshan of Ramana Maharishi when he famously fainted. The truth was that after 'a dull, hot drive along a dusty, bumpy road', he demolished a 'picnic luncheon' which, half-way through it, made him swoon. Once he came to, he was too sick to get up for the darshan in the ashram, so the Maharishi came to Maugham. 'He asked me whether I wished to say anything to him, or to ask him any question. I was feeling weak and ill, and said so; whereupon he smiled and said, "Silence also is conversation."' After fifteen minutes, the Maharishi smiled and walked away. Of all the spiritual masters Maugham met, and who gave long discourses, this encounter made the greatest impression.

'I heard later that my fainting had given rise to fantastic rumours. The news of it was carried not only to various parts of India, but even reached America,' he reported in *A Writer's Notebook*. 'When I was asked about it I was content to smile and shrug my shoulders. In point of fact that was neither the first nor the last time I have fainted. Doctors tell me it is due to an irritability of the solar plexus which presses my diaphragm against my heart and that one day the pressure will continue a little too long.'

Another meeting that didn't go according to plan was

on his visit to Mysuru, as a guest of the maharaja, where he wished to meet R.K. Narayan. He'd published three novels in England by then, but when the maharaja's secretary made enquiries no local intellectual knew of him as Narayan was not yet commercially successful in India. Hence Maugham was told, 'There is no novelist in Mysore. We may, however, find you one in Bangalore.' Ironically, Narayan's home stood less than two thousand metres from Hotel Metropole where Maugham stayed. He planned to return the following winter but, as we know, World War II blasted off in 1939.

During the next week, I lunch my way through the town's menus and in the afternoons, I pop into shed-like toddy shops where the drunks wait out the hot day. As per government rules, Kerala doesn't have many bars, but there's always a toddy 'shaap' or 'shappu' around the corner where fish is frying from morning to evening. One drunkard I have a heart-to-heart tête-à-tête with turns out to be a Malayalam writer who calls himself 'God's own poet' and he pulls out a sheaf of printouts to prove it. He makes me read the manuscript of his collected works in English translation as we sip our toddies. Is he perhaps Maugham's reincarnation?

Other highlights include the art deco-eatery Deevar (near the south end of Sweet Meat Street) where a hand-written menu on a board offers all kinds of tempting seafood. I order a kingfish steak and succulent prawns, pronounced 'frowns' by the waiter, cooked to perfection, aromatic, and the total bill comes to next to nothing. The chefs of Kerala realised long ago that what works best with seafood (or in fact, any food) is the oil of *Cocos nucifera*--the humble coconut. It has blessed Malayalam cuisine since the beginning of time by adding a mildly nutty fragrance that enhances the briny nature of marine creatures. It has many miraculous functions apart from the aromatic cooking oil that is extracted from it. Coconut also provides a nutritious, re-hydrating and refreshing juice; its sap can be fermented into wonderful toddy, a single tree producing up to 30l per day, or turned into vinegar, or distilled into arrack (believed to be the mother of vodka). Freshly-grated coconut makes the perfect base for chutneys, desiccated, it thickens gravies and moderates spice levels. It also yields palm sugar (jaggery); flour to make cookies from; coconut cream and milk that can become ice-creams, custards and sweets. It supplies coir to make rope; fronds to construct huts with; and its wood is perfect for carving kitchen utensils out of...which is why the coconut may be called 'God's own nut' if you know what I mean.

When I ask locals, they all recommend the Mappila biryani with date chutney—evidence of those past Arab links—at Bombay Hotel (Court Road), which has nothing to do with Mumbai. In 1949, when it was founded, 'Bombay' simply meant modern or 'fancy', but nowadays it is one of the more timeworn and plainer eateries in the upscale beach area. It has no ambience whatsoever, but is packed with lunch-goers throughout the day and is considered to be the second best option in town. Its snack counter is a snacker's heaven and for dessert, my eyes zoom in on the chemmeen cake which turns out to be not sweet at all but a medium-spicy seafood pie. It is amazingly amazing!

Ambling randomly, I happily stumble upon the town's classiest seafood restaurant, Kingsbay (Customs Street), down an alley towards the northern end of the beach. Housed in a grand building, it sports an eclectic menu. I order their house special, prawn-stuffed crab cheese bake, but the crabs haven't been fished out of the sea yet. So instead I ask what's freshest and the maître d'hôtel calls out to the kitchen. Someone yells back in Malayalam. It turns out that a consignment of mussels is being offloaded, so I order a plate—rich ghee roast is in vogue—and have it with another plate of luscious squids stuffed with spinach and cheese.

Eventually, all foodies will find themselves at Paragon (Kannur Road) in a bizarre location under the Red Cross Road railway over-bridge, and somewhat far from the beachfront. It opened in 1939 (sadly Maugham missed it by a year), and is known as the town's #1 restaurant, without a shred of doubt. This mini-empire with its hyperbolic slogan of 'best seafood in India' and three dining halls (seating 240 eaters) is always thronged by patrons hogging monstrous amounts of biryani. But there's much more on the menu which showcases everything that's fresh in the fishing harbour and I'm spoilt for choice. My order hits the table surprisingly fast considering the complexity: Tawa-fried prawns in a chilli-red masala, pan-fried mussels with caramelised onion, and kingfish in a creamy mango-coconut-milk curry which appears to be something of a specialty. It is a meal that I shall return to, again and again, in my sweetest dreams. And I'm proud to report there was no burping or indigestion that night.

But being a certified tourist, I must push on. About an hour's train journey north from Kozhikode's edible joys, lies a nine-square-kilometre-fragment of the French territories in India—Mahe. A so-called 'factory' or warehouse-cum-residence was built in 1722 in which exportable commodities were stockpiled—but this historic patch of Parisian outreach might today appear to someone passing through as nothing but a busy stretch of highway lined with countless cheap bars. But the moment I turn into a leafy by-lane I'm on a different planet. Vintage bungalows, check; church, check; spooky graveyard, yeah it's right there; and following a charming riverside walkway, I even chance upon a boathouse from where folks are taking catamarans for a spin.

Mahe recently got its first heritage hotel. The meticulously restored colonial-era Villa De 1945 brims with teakwood fittings and stained-glass windows. With only fourteen rooms it's terrifically exclusive and I spend leisurely evenings sipping tea on a huge balcony overlooking the town's quiet boulevard, peculiarly spelt as 'Bulu Ward Road' on street signs. In the dining hall, I sample chemmeen kizhi (shrimp steamed with

French colonial grandeur at Villa De 1945, Mahe.

coconut and circumspectly selected spices), roasted mussels (to die for unless one is already dead), and oh-so-light-fried veggies. For breakfast there's puttu, a tubular steam-cooked loaf of ground rice seasoned with coconut shavings—I've seen it translated on English-language menus as 'steamed rice cylinders' which rather makes it sound like an engine part—typical of the

Nairs, the warrior caste of Kerala, who used to cook rice this way in bamboo tubes known as puttukutti. It is normally served with curried legumes. Not exactly *Français* fare, but a deadly diet all the same.

It is believed that these colonisers' only significant contribution to Indian menus is *le omelette*, a fifteenth-century concept that translates into omelette. French fries may also be of Parisian origin, but they reached via the Brits, hence they are commonly referred to as finger chips in India.

There aren't any grand sights, no Eiffel Tower or Notre Dame, which means one spends one's days simply chilling. Even the government museum must be the smallest in the world—it's the very opposite of the world's largest museum, the Louvre—displaying a random table from colonial days, a couple of swords and a gramophone recording of 'La Marseillaise', but nothing that sheds light on how their Indian entanglement may have affected the Francophone culinary cosmos. Of local spices, I know as much that the occasional pinch of pepper may go into a *sauce béchamelle*, whilst *le curry poudre* is added cautiously to their aromatic palette that is more reserved than Latinate people's in general. They rely more on herbs to collude with the innate sapidity of raw materials or as the *bons mots* go, 'cabbage soup should taste of cabbage', which obviously no Indian diner would agree with.

Nevertheless, the *Larousse Gastronomique* encyclopaedia contains unthinkable 'Indian' dishes such as *cari de poulet* (chicken curry with ham!) and *choux de bruxelles à l'Indienne* which translates as 'Brussels sprouts moistened with curry sauce'! In this context, it is noteworthy that they are the only ones to ever have proposed a law to regulate curry: Apparently in the 1880s it was decided that curry powder must be mild and cannot contain more than 1.7 per cent pepper! Primarily, this weak blend is used when stale leftovers need a makeover. Today, a beloved spice mixture goes by the name of *vadouvan* adapted from Tamilan vadavams (sun-dried masala balls) they came across in south India, to make mildly Indian-flavoured soups, seafood preparations and, especially, duck stews.

Part of a bas-relief based on M. Mukundan's novel *On the Banks of the Mayyazhi.*

Although turkeys don't originate east of Turkey, but are American, they were christened *dinde* which stems from *coq d'Inde*, 'Indian cock', demonstrating how mixed-up the lingua franca is—if you pardon my French. Yet it shouldn't be forgotten that in other colonies, Creole connoisseurship gave birth to *rasson*, a rum-spiked savoury soup clearly derived from South Indian rasam which colonial adventurers carried with them to the Americas. In fact, many bars south of the Vindhya Hills serve a shot of rasam alongside drinks so the pairing isn't as crazy as it seems.[18]

Between meals, I watch the slow action at a laidback harbour where fisherfolks mend nets and check out a rustic temple complex notable for Mahatma Gandhi having visited it in 1934, telling the people that 'whether it is French India or

British India it is one and the same country. The same blood flows through my veins that goes through yours, the same soil, the same atmosphere, the same manners and customs and many things too numerous to mention are common to all of us. But for the difference in the uniform of your police and the French language I read here and there I would notice no difference whatsoever.'

At Tagore Park, an open-air bas-relief depicts the plot of a Malayalam novel on colonial tribulations—*On the Banks of the Mayyazhi* by local author M. Mukundan—set when streets still had names like Rue de I'Eglise and Rue de la Residence, and where the 'half-French would continue to play a role in the life of Mayyazhi, but they were never to achieve the same measure of greatness and nobility. Poverty and its attendant evils were to force them to lead mean lives. Beggars and prostitutes were to be born amongst them.' Speaking of fiction, my next stop is the riverside Le Café in the hopes of sampling something like a *café au lait* with a Proustian madeleine cake to bolster my mental faculties. But they have none of that, no turkeys *à la Cordon Bleu* either—no, they only serve Indian filter-coffee along with tapioca fritters. These are tasty though: kappa or cassava as it is also called, is a regional staple also eaten as chips or as mash—but seem like a completely fictive Continental café snack. It's another matter that in reality Marcel Proust didn't eat the madeleine either, though he propelled it to worldwide fame in his autobiographical novel, *Remembrance of Things Past*, but he rather gnawed on dry rusk that inspired him to write the immortal passage on how memories are triggered—'No sooner had the warm liquid mixed with the crumbs touched my palate than a shudder ran through me and I stopped, intent upon the extraordinary thing that was happening to me.' Personally, I get a bigger kick out of mashed tapioca drowning in something fishy.

The town's self-appointed patisserie on Railway Station Road is merely another typical bakery-cum-cakery, which offers no baguette (the elongated breads that Napoleon supposedly designed thus so that his soldiers could carry their lunch in their pant legs—not true), nor *brioche* (that Marie Antoinette suggested the starving plebeians should eat before getting herself guillotined—true). I'm ready to give up my frenzied search for Romantic flavours when I come across the cool diner Café Eiffel (near Tagore Park), which has quotes by Napoleon on the walls and where I munch on a halal chicken cheeseburger and, what else, French fries?

And thanks to having been part of France until 1954, Mahe follows different excise and licensing regulations, hence the bars offer tremendous value even if some resemble Dickensian nightmares: Drinks are sold at Maximum Retail Price though sometimes a nominal 10 per cent is added if one elects to sit in their dining halls, where snacks include fresh prawns fried golden—in what else but coconut oil?—or plump mussels pan-seared with onion, chilli, coconut chunks and curry leaves. Everything is uniformly mouth-watering.

Bar-hopping classics include Cee Cee's in an oldish bungalow with a huge kitchen and the day's almost-alive catch hiccupping in a well-lit fridge, but I personally prefer to frolic at the Foreign Liquor Palace which, despite its name, has no *château*-trained sommeliers on duty. But it's a friendly enough dive towering right by the Mahe Bridge with priceless views all the way to the azure-coloured Arabian Sea. The banter is good-humoured in a slurry mix of Malayalam and another language that might be English, only occasionally getting semi-aggressive. Within moments of the first sign of belligerence, a drunkard stomps over and says, 'Sorry.'

I say, 'Okay.'

He says, 'No problem?'

I repeat, 'No problem.'

Then he says, 'Nice to have met.'

That's French manners in Kerala for you. Chilling totally, I ask for another super-strong beer and watch the sun slowly set over the Mayyazhi River estuary (jokingly known as the English Channel). However, barflies should be aware that Mahe gets sleepy by 9.30 p.m., so last orders are served at 9.23 p.m., giving drunks approximately seven minutes to drink up that final beer before doors shut. On the other hand, they open early, so the party restarts with wet breakfasts at 9 a.m. Stepping out at 10 a.m., I run into mildly inebriated gents who beg for money to pursue sunrise binges. I suggest to them that coffee might be healthier at such an hour.

A couple of kilometres further up the coast, my feast continues as I get my first kick right after stepping off the bus plying on National Highway-17. I've been in Thalassery (once anglicised as Tellicherry), for approximately three minutes and am already having a salivating seafood experience.

The Shabna Tea Stall isn't the world's fanciest café, but they do 'stuffed mussel' or ari-kadukka which is the town's #1 snack. Best described as a shellfish married to a plump idli, the whole mussel is first filled with rice paste and steamed, then the resulting cake is pried out of the shell and fried with various spice powders.

What a miracle! I have two. Then three. All washed down with oversweet instant coffee. After checking into a room with a balcony at the Paris Presidency, which is part of the Paris Restaurant founded in 1942 bang in the centre of town, I find that it has over the years branched out into four establishments—all standing side by side in Logans Road. Skipping the fancy 'multycousine' section, I track down the original in a heritage building around the corner, at the back, which used to house one of Kerala's first newspaper printing presses a long time ago. There's no proper menu card but it is always crowded, open from morning to early evening, dishing out snacks and meals at a laidback pace.

Despite its name, there's again nothing French about the cuisine at Paris. I guess it's called so because it is 10 km north of Mahe, so the nominal theme is continued just like that only. For starters, I sample their trademark light and fragrant Thalassery fish biryani. It too testifies to the influence of Arabs, but more than merely a mutation of something alien, this biryani is an artwork in itself. Made using short-grained rice that grows in the region, it reminds one of ghee rice but it has actually been baked in a sealed container before getting wedded to the separately cooked aikora whitefish, that translates into 'Indo-Pacific king mackerel'.

I end up ordering lots of this particular fish—curried, fried or any other way it is available—and each time, the result is magnificent. But even if I seem to have discovered the world's tastiest fish, to tell you the truth, I've really come to eat fresh mussels. Having been born and brought up in Scandinavia where mussels are eaten as a snack, in soups, steamed or stewed, in pastas and on pizzas, yes, as practically everything but dessert—I had been for years dreaming of Thalassery, after being told by a couple of Malayalis I once met on a train, that the town is the major mussel fishing port of India. I've never heard anybody rave so much about the delicious kallumakkai (as they call mussels), as those two did, so I added a mental note to my must-go list.

It strikes me as I stroll in Thalassery that two millennia ago Europeans called shellfish *thalassa*—peculiarly enough it's a Greek word meaning, variously, 'ocean' in general, 'seafood' in particular, and it invokes the goddess of the oceans whose name coincidentally also was Thalassa. That gluttonous gourmand of antiquity, Apicius, devoted a full chapter called *Thalassa* to the enjoyment of shellfish in his pioneering *De re coquinaria*, Europe's first known gourmet cookbook commonly dated to the first century. In it, he described how to fry scallions lightly with crushed pepper (imported from Kerala, naturally) or oysters seasoned with pepper and cinnamon, or mussels cooked with ajowan, cumin, mint, pepper and something called malabathrum—the identity of which remained a mystery for the longest time. According to Pliny the Elder, Rome's leading expert on natural science, this was a 'most esteemed' herb with a scent 'superior to any other' and its name indicates that it was imported from Malabar. It is believed to be what we today call tejpat, i.e. cassia, a fairly common ingredient in Indian cooking, but which the Romans willingly paid through their noses for. Anyway, without attempting any too complicated guesswork, the town's name is surprisingly apt, so much that even a mummified Roman mariner might find himself quite at home in Thalassery's kitchens.

Out of the 7,500 tons of green mussels harvested annually in north Kerala, this town is one of the top producers of 'edible bivalve' as these are scientifically labelled. The harvesting is done manually with 'pickers' going out daily in rickety boats to the mussel beds during the season that lasts from September to June, diving as deep as ten metres to scrape shellfish off the rocks where they like to plant themselves. Hence the Malayalam name for mussels—'the fruit on the rock' or kallumakkai.

After lunch, I'm gallivanting on the beach in the hope of seeing my favourite shellfish in its fresh, pre-cooked state. On the way there, I did browse for pickles and condiments in a supermarket at Harbour City Mall, the only shopping complex in sight. They stock seafood pickles, but there are no preserved mussels available. Pepper is another thing to shop for—in Europe the classiest type of pepper is still branded 'Tellicherry Black' even if the godowns of Thalassery, that traditionally supplied this spice to the world, now appear abandoned. (The ancient pepper warehouse in Rome, too, is long gone. I found just a few bricks remaining of it at the Forum, but it was once the perhaps most important building in the city, where pepper was kept

The world's freshest mussels for sale in Thalassery.

under tight security and sold as if it was silver or gold.) Today, foreign buyers bypass Thalassery and do business directly with planters in the hill districts—or buy from countries that produce cheaper but less aromatic pepper, like Indonesia, Malaysia and Vietnam. At the mall, I also chanced upon the Mambally's Royal

Biscuit Factory outlet which practically invented the plum cake in its Indian avatar in 1883 to supply a British spice planter who missed English cakes. Only slightly paradoxically, it was made with French-imported brandy from the colonial competitors in Mahe (maybe as a soft rebellion against British colonialism?). They still bake the same cake though I'm not sure about the brandy's nationality, but it ranks as perhaps the best I've eaten—moist, rich and toothsome.

The fish market is situated right behind the mall where, in the alley leading down to it, geezers sell live mussels out of straw baskets. Seeing those heaps of black-shelled treasures, I'm ready to relocate to Thalassery instantly. A few steps later, I spot the colonial pier at which spice ships docked to pick up pepper and cardamom. Somewhere very near it, the English factory with its godowns and residence of the supervisor, opened in 1683 to facilitate exports. Travel was slower then, so dry items with long shelf lives, like spices, were the ideal trade goods. The boats coasted along the seashore, anchoring at night to catch fish for dinner—but it was no luxury cruise, because apart from abundant fresh seafood, passengers had to carry their own supplies, utensils and bedding. To sail from northern Kerala in say, the 1800s, to what was then Bombay took ten days—and to think that now Mumbai is just a nineteen-hour train ride away.

As per nineteenth-century accounts, there weren't many roads leading into the interior from the ports. Most people trekked through the jungle. Provided that there was some semblance of a track, those who could afford it journeyed by bullock carts—but the bullocks hade to be changed every five miles (i.e. hourly) which made it a slow mode of transport—or somewhat classier two-wheeled carriages known as 'nibs' that were 'waterproof, with Venetians and glass windows'. If the path was very narrow a *manshiel* would have to do, 'a kind of open-sided cot slung to a bamboo pole which projects far enough in front and rear to be placed with ease on the shoulders of the bearers. Four of these men are brought into play at once, while four others run along to relieve their fellows at intervals.' By this latter method one covered 80 km in a day and crossing from Kerala into Karnataka, where much of the cardamom and pepper grew in the hills and jungles, took at least two days—what is now a bus journey of mere hours. And it was brought home to me how arduous travel must have been the time I trekked across the mountainous border on jungle paths: although the forest rangers warned about tigers and wild elephants, pointing out fearfully big pugmarks and so-called 'elephant laddus' (cannon ball-sized poop balls deposited by pachyderms), the worst part for me was falling off the steep track into thorny bushes and cracking four toes. And at the end of the day, I pulled some thirty or forty saturated leeches out of my socks.

Uphill from the old pier stands the 1708 CE fort with an 1830s' lighthouse staring forlornly out to sea. Today, the Brits have been replaced by courting couples whispering sweet nothings, the chicks suitably impressed when dudes boast about future sports careers abroad. Coincidentally this was a base for Arthur Wellesley, the future Duke of Wellington who is frequently credited with having introduced cricket to Kerala—of which there's no conclusive evidence; historians I've spoken with suggest that there may already have been a cricket club or at least a sports ground in existence when Wellesley arrived. Also, he allegedly taught the game to local dhobis, but the first solid evidence of Indians playing cricket in Thalassery stems from some half a century later—therefore all one can say for sure is that the town has been the national sport's Mecca for less than two centuries. Despite having been a heavy-gambling booze-hound in his youth, Wellesley shaped up here and probably lived in what is still known as the Wellesley Bungalow, strategically situated between the fort and the town's cricket pitch. Fighting wars against Tipu Sultan gave him a reputation for being a great strategist—indeed, after returning to England in 1805, he crowned his career by defeating Napoleon at Waterloo. As a gastronomic footnote, he is said to have introduced cocktail cherries to India and his last act was to posthumously lend his name to the pie-like dish known as 'Beef Wellington' which he, weirdly, had nothing to do with (the earliest recipes appear circa 1900). Yet it is possible that he enjoyed a comparable dish here, maybe a kheema dosa, without calling it by any specific name.

Not quite ready to give up my quest for shellfish, I spend the next few days hunting for more mussels in Thalassery. I try the Rara Avis on Logans Road, a fashionable dining option recommended to me by a fisherman no less, but the sad truth is that they make creamy fish molee (with aikora) and soft but firm elegantly bowl-shaped appams fried until the surface gets perfectly crispy...but their kallumakkai dry-fry is done to death.

Then I find the Jubilee Hotel (opposite Old Bus Stand) that celebrates 'the traditional Malabari foods' and rejects the use of MSG or food colouring. The shallow-fried prawns are perfectly executed, but their mussel biryani is made with sadly departed shreds of overkilled shellfish. Not sure who to blame, except myself, when I experience an intestinal catastrophe in the middle of the night, I brush it aside as the price any glutton must pay on occasion.

Things improve at Hotel Adithya Non-Veg which is a steamy joint located by the fort entrance, actually featuring a colourful photograph of mussels on the wall. After I've explicitly explained that I'm not interested in anything cooked in a murderous manner, they rustle up parathas and the very best avial I've had, with lots of diced carrot, chopped drumsticks and beans, sliced plantain, yams and other veggies soaked in mild coconut milk, that perfectly complements a big wok of mussels in spicy gravy.

To properly identity what I've eaten, I ask the waiter, 'What do you call this lovely mussel dish?'

He beams at me and exclaims, 'We call it *Ma-Sa-La.*'

I imprint that on my mind. According to online sources, Mosons Pickle Factory some distance northeast of town, bottles a mussels and dates mixture under its Beevi's brand. My rickshaw drives me to the sleepy Palayad Industrial Estate, and we go in circles until I catch the strong smell of vinegar wafting through the palm trees. It turns out that Mosons doesn't officially receive visitors and there is no such thing as a guided tour, but I buy a bagful of jars with pickled mussels, squid and prawns at wholesale rates. Their stickers say 'Spicy' and I am happy to report that they're correctly labelled—even a tiny sampling sets my nose hairs fuming.

Nearby stands a nineteenth-century bungalow with shaded verandas and a roof of Mangaluru tiles. It is listed as one of the few attractions worth visiting in Thalassery, so I dutifully check it out, only to find that the bungalow is in use as a technical school. To enter the campus requires taking a written permission from the principal. In the compound, the students sit under shady trees and look at me as if I'm some weirdo tourist. Which I obviously am.

It's name is Gundert Bungalow and on its veranda wall hangs a painted caricature of a bearded foreigner, presumably Mr Gundert himself. Suddenly I recall how, in the centre of town on Gundert Road, there's a prominent statue of the selfsame personality.

This encounter with memories of Hermann Gundert—a German who played a significant role in Kerala's cultural development—sets off the strangest chain of associations in my spiced-up brain. It has to do with heavy metal and how that term came to be coupled with a particular form of Western music. And in a way, it all started in Kerala about 175 years ago, when the mother of one of Europe's greatest Nobel Prize winners was born in these parts.

En route to Calcutta in the 1830s, the missionary Gundert fell so much in love with south India that he decided to skip Calcutta and stay put. He ran a school on the porch of this bungalow and when not busy teaching, invited pundits to discuss Indian matters. In the process, he learnt Malayalam fluently enough to become a rather influential writer in the language, publishing a grammar and the first proper dictionary. He was also involved in local language newspapers. Furthermore, Gundert introduced the German model of gymnastics, which is why Thalassery is known today as the home of the best acrobats and circus artistes in India (logically, the bestselling writer John Irving's novel *A Son of the Circus* opens here). All this led to Gundert's appointment as inspector of schools, overseeing an area covering most of Kerala and much of present-day Karnataka as well.

Living in India, Gundert got hitched to a fellow continental European lady from nearby Mahe, and in 1842 they had a daughter named Marie. After the family moved back to Germany due to health reasons, their daughter in turn married a Herr Hesse and gave birth to Gundert's grandson who was also christened Hermann. Little Hermann had free access to grandpa Hermann's vast library, which contained many books on and from India. He was fifteen when grandpa passed away in 1893, which was also the year junior Hesse had his first rebellious drinks and smokes. He had by then gone through a somewhat sad period at the seminary he studied at—he was supposed to become a missionary like his elder namesake, but ended up a manic-depressive misfit who tried to commit suicide. After a stint in a mental asylum, he took a job as a bookshop clerk in the German town of Tübingen (in whose university, incidentally, Gundert's collection of manuscripts from Kerala is housed). He chucked it up at the age of twenty-seven when his first novel was published. What would become his biggest blockbuster appeared in 1927, the year he turned fifty: *Der Steppenwolf.* Some twenty years later, Hermann Hesse was awarded the Nobel Prize for Literature.

One of the main streets in Thalassery is named after German Nobel Prize laureate Hermann Hesse's grand-father.

A Californian hard rock group of the 1960s named itself Steppenwolf after Hesse's novel. The singer John Kay hailed from Germany but wasn't—as far as I know—related to Hesse, except perhaps in a metaphysical way. Hesse's magnum opus was, in those days, gaining the status of a hippie 'Bible' due to its hallucinatory passages that were good to read as one puffed on a spliff, gnawed on peyote and dropped acid, and so it struck the band as a perfect replacement for their much lamer original name, The Sparrows. In 1968, Steppenwolf released their third single on which Kay sang about riding a motorcycle and the 'heavy metal thunder' it made. The song was called 'Born to be Wild' and it went on to become the biggest ever riff-based rock superhit—partly because it featured on the soundtrack of the LSD-infused low-budget road movie *Easy Rider* starring Dennis Hopper, Peter Fonda and Jack Nicholson. And so, in one stroke were born the new musical sound known today as 'heavy metal' and the cinematic genre called 'road movie'.

As a teenager, I was heavily into Steppenwolf and their brand of psychedelic hard rock, so it was the music that led me to read *Der Steppenwolf* and its account of mental self-realisation. And now, many years later, I'm probing Hesse's intellectual roots in this small fishing port. The writer did, before World War I, undertake a journey towards Kerala to trace his own 'Indian' background. Unfortunately, he caught a stomach bug and suffered from heat stroke—the tropics were too much for him—so upon reaching Colombo he took the next available boat back home, without ever setting foot on Indian soil or snapping selfies (like I do) before his grandfather's bungalow. Furthermore, he had met impoverished Hindus and Muslims on the journey and was very upset at the subjugation of Indians under British rule. Yet he was taken by Indian philosophical ideas, which made him write the Buddhism-influenced novella *Siddhartha* some ten years later (and its 1970s film adaptation was shot in Rishikesh and Rajasthan—places the Buddha never visited—by Ingmar Bergman's ace cinematographer Sven Nykvist, with Shashi Kapoor starring as the Buddha).

Personally, I'm quite Buddhistic and never bothered with stomach bugs as long as they bugger off soon enough, so despite already spending one night spewing my guts out, as

I mentioned a few pages back, my seafoodish quest goes on. Hoping to have my karma fulfilled, I ask one waiter where to sample authentic fare. He says knowledgeably, 'You must eat in "kallu-shaaps". They serve the best. Avoid the "shaap" to the south of town, because they mix chemicals in their toddy. Only go to the one on the north side.'

'Kallu' is the Malayalam word for toddy and 'shaaps' were, as the esteemed reader recalls, already explored during my stay in Kozhikode, but this one is said to be the 'shaap of shaaps' in the whole of Kerala.

'Address to tell auto driver?'

'Pen drive!' he exclaims.

I'm sure he's pulling my leg, but later sipping on a musk melon juice in a fancy café, the owner's friend, a knowledgeable chap, sidles up and asks me if I am *that* food writer. I admit I might be 'that one'. He mentions some article I wrote about Kerala ages ago and introduces himself as Biju Aravind—tourism consultant who hopes to put Thalassery on the map. I ask him about a toddy shop called 'pen drive' and it turns out to be well known to him.

'Yes,' he corrects me, 'Pinarayi has the best toddy shop. I'll take you there for lunch.'

So, the next day we meet at the apparels showroom where he's a managing partner and drive 7 km north of town towards Pinarayi, to where the road follows the broad Anjarakkandi River through a hamlet called Kaliyil. A fish stall stands on the riverbank among scattered oyster shells and facing it is a sight for sore eyes—namely the Model Toddy Parlour, an unpretentious whitewashed establishment with a prominent 'non-smoking' sign outside. The interiors are squeaky-clean, airy and—at least in the daytime—very bright.

It's an extremely picturesque location for a bar. The kind

you'd want to spend your life in—like the other customers seem to be doing. Even if it is rather early on a Monday the shack is full of dining drunkards. There's no menu as such but to check what's cooking, we peek into the kitchen where a multitasking lady attends to pots of boiling fish curry, squid 'koonthal' masala and mashed kappa—the typical well-seasoned tapioca purée that goes nicely with fiery curries. We order plates of everything from the bare-chested mundu-clad attendant. The ubiquitous mundu is a national dress for gentlemen in Kerala, akin to the kilt of Scotsmen, and being made of light cotton it provides air-cooling for body parts that shall not be mentioned in a proper book like this.

In another chamber, a huge clay pot is filled to the brim with frothy kallu. I have been sampling toddy before, but this is certainly the best—if toddy was champagne, this would be its Dom Pérignon and I would, after a few bottles, be James Bond. I'm told that the luxurious beverage is harvested every morning at 4.30 a.m. by expert toddy-tappers. Apparently, the toddy industry gives employment to over 50,000 people and if all 'shaaps' were like this Model Toddy Parlour then it should be a good thing—for despite alcoholism being injurious to health (or so they say), the 100 per cent naturally fermented and soothing palm-wine seems to be an organic alternative to industrially distilled hard liquor. More like wholesome sweet-sour buttermilk than booze, it is merely mildly intoxicating, complementing the sizzling seafood perfectly as it moderates its spiciness—tawa-roasted prawns redolent with coconut oil and curry leaves, squid in explosively peppery gravy and tangy fish curry. The zing makes me finish the toddy quickly and so we order more bottles, until life feels unbelievably wonderful.

Before I leave town with my knapsack full of pickle jars, I hit two or three bakeries to parcel ari-kadukka and chemmeen unda—rice-stuffed mussels and prawn-stuffed rice balls—for the road. At the bus stand, as I'm ready to board the '7.1 digital LED smoke effect laser show bus' to my next destination, a drunkard comes up and stares incredulously, as if he can't believe my stupidity: 'Are you leaving?'

I don't know him from Jack O'Bedlam, but he acts as if we're buddies. Is he perhaps one of the 'happy to meet you' guys in one of the bars I've tried out? I say, 'I'm so sorry, but I am.' I'm wondering whether I ought to explain that it is part of my job as a travel writer to always move on. But he merely waves sadly as he tightens his mundu which is on half mast, and says: 'Please come back again soon.'

From here, I'm on my way to Kannur, about an hour's bus ride from Thalassery, and if one googles for grub there one will get many hits on a particular Internet-viral lunch-only canteen called Odhen's, with rapturous rants about the most unbelievably marvellous fish meals.

Furthermore, the prosperous town recently got its own airport and is expected to become the next great tourist hotspot of 'God's own country', although at first glance it looks more like one big shopping mall, like a suburb of Dubai. As it is too early for lunch, I have brunch at the renowned MRA Bakery (Station Road, next to Kannur junction), often suggested as the second-best option if one can't get a table at the fabled Odhen's. Unlike Odhen's, it's open from morning to evening and turns out to be a huge air-conditioned complex with a bakery and confectionary taking up the ground floor, and a vast dining hall upstairs. So, not exactly your standard neighbourhood cake shop.

Characteristically for morning meals in Kerala, there's mulakittath, a violently chilli-red but unexpectedly silky fish curry served with appams, those deadly-yummy pancakes that

I am already thoroughly addicted to. I must refrain from also ordering avial, that lovely coconut-milky veggie stew, as I plan to demolish a lavish lunch two hours later. But I do gorge on their nutty baklava—the best I've come across outside Turkey (the Topkapi Palace kitchen of Istanbul is the native place of baklava though many other parts of Turkey will also claim it as their own) and these are just perfectly flaky, buttery, cardamommy, creamy, cinnamony bite-sized pastries soaked in honey syrup and topped with shredded pistachios. I buy a boxful in case I get peckish.

To rebuild my appetite, I catch a rickshaw to Fort Saint Angelo (a.k.a. 'Kannur Kotta'), situated at the end of a road lined with old colonial churches and cemeteries, about 3 km from the centre. It guards the Mappila Bay with its fish market, which supplies the freshest catch to kitchens in town. The fort is a tranquil spot to roam around in, across manicured lawns, and I skip a museum that anyway seems permanently shut, but trace the cannon-studded red lateritic walls facing the Lakshadweep Sea. This was, namely, established as a Portuguese factory in circa 1500 CE and everything could have proceeded peacefully, if it wasn't for Vasco da Gama. Unhappy with the trading deal the raja offered, da Gama belligerently fortified the site with a palisade and stationed 200 soldiers here to terrorise the populace. Luckily, the Dutch captured the fort in 1663 and initiated cordial relationships with the royal family to whom they eventually sold it. But less than two decades later, power-hungry Britons stole the fort and made it their chief military base in Kerala. So, the eclectic architecture blends Portuguese with Dutch and British elements—including an eye-grabbing skull-and-cross-bone decorated tombstone set in the wall commemorating the Dutch commander's wife Susanna, who died here in the 1700s, aged only seventeen and a half years.

As soon as its staff deem it fit to let in tourists, I check out the comparatively dull Arakkalkettu Museum. It is situated within a cannon shot's distance from the fort in a royal durbar hall by the fishing harbour, but there's hardly anything worth seeing except blurry Xeroxes of faded documents, dusty daggers, vintage telephones and random furnishings. The walls are studded with stern signs yelling, 'Do not touch the antics.' How I wish I had experienced some antics!

Yet I can't avoid imagining an adventurous past when the medieval Moroccan globetrotter Ibn Battuta—pioneer among travel writers—in the 1340s sat in one of the chairs on display, perhaps used one of the antique telephones to phone home (like ET, you know) for some Moroccan takeaway, as he munched on spice-laden Malayali food and gossiped with the lord of the house who owned a fleet that sailed to Oman and Yemen; 'one of the most powerful sultans', noted Battuta of him. South of town, Battuta visited orchards crammed with coconut trees, pepper creepers, and as for bananas, 'never have I seen any place in which they are more numerous or cheaper.' He sampled many different varieties here.

The food-obsessed Battuta also gave an account of a feast served to him further up the coast in Honavar, in present-day Karnataka, where he found the men peaceful and women uncommonly handsome. The food was served to him on a plate 'which they call *ṭālam* [i.e. thali]. A beautiful slave, clad in silk, comes and causes to be placed before the prince saucepans containing the food. She has a large spoon of copper with which she takes a spoonful of rice and serves it on the plate; she pours ghee on it, and places some pickled pepper in bunches, green ginger, and pickled lemons and mangoes.' The mango, coincidentally, is said to be one of the main reasons why so many Muslims travelled to India from abroad, including—it is claimed—Babur who was so enamoured by Indian mangoes, that he thought it necessary to father the Mughal dynasty.

As Battuta tucked in, a curried fowl was brought out, followed by 'another species of fowl' and then even more, in an endless stream of delicacies. 'When the different kinds of fowl have been done with, there follow diverse sorts of fish and more rice with them. After the fish, they serve vegetables cooked in butter, and milk foods, also taken with rice.' Eventually, the royal repast is rounded off with buttermilk!

Feeling envy over the royal treats Battuta savoured, I feel it's time to head to Odhen's, named after renowned restaurateur Othenan whose sons nowadays run the canteen, which is counter-intuitively pronounced as 'Onden' locally. In fact, it's such a landmark that the road it is located at is known as Onden Road. Whatever one does, one is advised not to reach any later than 12.15 p.m. as the food will invariably run out quickly (they stay open only until 3.30 p.m.; Sundays closed). Latecomers end up queuing endlessly in the sweltering heat, though if one doesn't get a seat one may instead check out another nearby attraction: Room #309 at the Hotel Blue Nile. Just around the block, it's been preserved as a shrine in memory of footballer Diego Maradona's 2012 visit, with everything intact as he left it—including the prawn shells from his supper! But at twelve o'clock there are still empty tables and I quickly grab a stool. Gents and ladies sit waiting in expectant silence, facing the kitchen from where a thick fume of coconut oil bursts into the hall. The atmosphere is that of a temple moments before the theyyam dancer takes the stage.

As if on cue, the first waiter waltzes in, handing out banana leaves to one and all. In his footsteps tap-dances the rice man with a cauldron of 'boil rice', the typically plump reddish grain that is preferred in Kerala, dishing out a huge scoop on each leaf in a choreographed manner as the patrons carry on the ceremonial routine by patting the rice down into circular discs. This is followed by the meals man who, using his ladle as if it were a flamenco dancer's wooden castanet, apportions out the set lunch of sambar—a more veggie-rich Kerala variety of the southern standard curry—and dry vegetable pooriyal, plus ladles of mathi (sardine) curry, cucumber-curd pachhadi (a lightly cooked version of raita) and pickles. Finally comes the senior waiter, who performs a most seductive belly dance with his tray sumptuously weighed down by the seafoods of the day. I pick their incredibly attractive bread-crumbed aikora fillet (my darling kingfish), koonthal (squid fry), and chemmeen (prawns) shallow fried with crumbly peppery coating. As usual, the rich coconut oil lends the meal a uniquely sweetish note, reminiscent of hair oil perhaps, which may be an acquired taste but I do find it irresistible. The meal goes well together with a steel tumbler of hot kanji vellam, watery rice gruel drunk as stomach-calming soup on the side.[19] By the time I go to wash my hands, another fellow gastronome is already claiming my seat even before the banana leaf is cleared away.

IV

Tamil Tuck, Deccan Dining and Goan Grog

(Circumambulations in South India)

'He is a good companion who enjoys dining with ordinary people.'

—*Purananuru*, lyrical Tamil anthology compiled between first and third centuries CE

Andhra coast

In the morning, I get off the train at Tiruppur, a nondescript town on the Tamil side of the Ghat Mountains. It's at the heart of the cotton-growing Kongu Nadu region which encompasses much of north-western Tamil Nadu. Pankaj Mishra, the only other travel writer to have written about the town (as far as I know), dismissed it as being 'to underwear what Sivakasi was to firecrackers' in a couple of hours—and as few pages—in his celebrated 1990s' travelogue *Butter Chicken in Ludhiana*, before scuttling onto a bus for Kerala.

True, it's one of those places where no tourists go, there's virtually no information online, no guidebook recommends it, my trusty TTK road guide only knows it as 'famous for hosiery products' and it never occurs to my bucket-listing friends, who go fashion hunting in New York or Paris, to stop for shopping in the original 'Banian City' where export surplus showrooms line the streets—and they have chic names like Homme & Femme or Tee Totaller—interspersed with low-budget business lodges, which I guess is Tiruppur in a nutshell.

An epic cyclone hits town in the afternoon—which is odd, since the area is known to be extremely arid, its river a mere trickle of sluggish textile factory goo. The deluge brings everything to a standstill as 47 mm of rainfall in an hour turns streets into interconnected jacuzzis, fells over 100 electricity poles and uproots 200 trees. Luckily the main street features several congenial dives that I can seek refuge in and jolly staff plies me not only with beer, but treat me to complimentary snacks too—which seems to be the hallmark of home-grown bar culture. For every bottle I order, I get fruit salad, handfuls of peanuts and a namkeen platter with puffed rice in large enough quantities to constitute a fulfilling meal.

Suddenly I feel at home, which is quite different from the vibe I got when I stepped off the train that morning. For a fraction of a second I felt almost like Mr Mishra asking myself what I could possibly expect to experience by way of excitement, perhaps I too should simply move on—the smallness of the station made me suspect this was going to be the back of the beyond of the boondocks. But before the question took on an existentialistically defeatist overtone, I spotted a restaurant, Junior Kuppanna, right behind the station, whose reputation for serving authentic Kongu food I had come across. The spacious eatery was empty but clean, a smiling and polite waiter invited me to sit, the kitchen turned out to be ready to feed me even at that early hour despite me being the only guest.

I ate a soulfully rustic mutton pallipalayam—a dry-fry item named after the tiny town Pallipalayam from whence the recipe originates—which is possibly one of the most unique Indian non-veg dishes as it's cooked without oil, instead, relying on the meat juice seeping out from chunky love-me-tender-love-me-true-mutton, seasoned with chillies, diced coconut, shallots, onions and garlic. I just love having dinner in the morning. Further thrills are caused by the simple fact that here in Kongu Nadu, unlike everywhere else, meat isn't necessarily marinated but cooked as is—preserving its meatiness—and it seems as if all ingredients have more texture, and are more natural.

Besides, India's sweetest coconuts grow in Kongu Nadu, around the town of Pollachi, and they do their usual trick of balancing the spicing. In the first minutes of my Tiruppur sojourn, I gobbled up the pallipalayam along with a stack of Erode-style dosas that are fluffy like appams from the top but crisp-fried underneath, and afterwards I just had to order the fêted egg preparation kalakki—a poached omelette with a silky smooth inner core. I decide to stay on and eat my way through town.

The original Senior Kuppanna was founded over sixty years ago in Erode, another smallish place some 50 km away, distinguished as the world's turmeric capital, the largest producer and trader of the GI-tagged spice since Vedic days. Hence nicknamed 'Yellow City'. From there, Senior Kuppanna spread its tempting tentacles by specialising in Kongu non-veg favourites to thirty-plus branches that by logic all carry the name Junior Kuppanna. But while foodaholics go gaga over Pondicherry's flamboyant Creole-cookery served up in stylish *maisons*, and scorching Chettinadian non-veg which may appear to resemble Kongunadian food but uses way more chillies, and the meaty biryanis of Dindigul and the legendary biryanis of Ambur that are said to follow the personal cookbook of the Nawab of Arcot, comparatively few hedonists are familiar with the cuisine of Kongu, despite it having deep roots in the Sangam age. By the way, Kongu Nadu isn't officially a place—not a district or a state, but it has always had its own identity as a heartland of sorts in Tamil Nadu.

Apart from Tiruppur and Erode, the region also encompasses the coffee-growing district of Salem, the ancient capital Karur, Pollachi that links Tamil Nadu across a mountain pass with Kerala's Palakkad and the heavily industrialised Coimbatore, renowned for its heavy-duty wet-grinders. Intriguingly enough, archaeologists have found traces of foodstuffs corresponding to modern eating habits during excavations—remains of rice, pulses and millets—hinting that culinary culture has remained intact since forever. The many kinds of millets that are still eaten today—like ragi, bajra and jowar—make for robust food,

Coconut is very important in Kongu Nadu.

rooted in the soil so to speak, as already in the Sangam age these were staples. So we may say that Kongu Nadu's discreet food is genuinely time-tested.

Kongu has always been arid, hence farming methods developed with mixed cultivation so as not to drain the soil of its nutrients, and the main crops are such that thrive on less water. Irrigation channels from thousands of years ago are still in use. Textual sources too list indigenous ingredients that thrive in the dry climate. These comprise, for example, sesame (*Sesamum indicum*) and its oil, known here as gingelly, sought after since Harappan days and exported to the ancient Greeks as it happens to be one of the first cooking oils produced by humans. Sesame seeds are also popular, though coconut is evidently the #1 ingredient—it stars in pretty much every meal in one avatar or the other. Also, as mentioned, plenty of pungent turmeric grows in the area without which curry would hardly look like itself. India produces and consumes almost all the turmeric in the world. Turmeric is very good for health as it can prevent infectious diseases and hence it is frequently tagged as a panacea, an all-healing super-food, and interestingly, the early Buddhists used it to colour their robes. But in Kongu Nadu, the rhizome is treated in atypical ways, such as grated fresh and then roasted, before it's ground and used in cooking.

Edible heritage apart, I spend time and money on bargain shopping in India's top garment manufacturing hub. In an average year, Tiruppur exports about Rs 275 billion worth of knitwear or half of India's total and a fair part of that ends up as surplus—which makes it the perfect shopping destination for anybody wishing to renew one's wardrobe. I mean, why fly to foreign fashion capitals to dress up, when everything is made right here anyway? At any point of time, garment importers from scores of countries are shopping about in the thousands of manufacturing units that employ half a million labourers to produce knitwear, innerwear and sportswear for the likes of Yankee brand Ralph Lauren, classic Levi's, trendy Scandinavian H&M, dowdy Marks & Spencer of the UK and youthful international fashion house Diesel. So when not eating, I browse factory outlets, export reject godowns and cut-rate fashion emporiums where couture can be bought for a pittance.

After shopping and feeling well-dressed, I get hungry again and head for Kongu Mess, a promising name that shows up on my GPS. When I get to the location, nobody's heard of any mess or Kongu specialities to be eaten so to cut a long story short, I end up at Junior Kuppanna again. With tempting options bearing names like 'naadu chicken gravy' and 'leg piece fry' and 'boneless chukka' and 'brain fry' and 'mutton kola urundal 5pcs' and 'kaadai roast' which isn't a roasted wok (like one might think) but quail...I wish I could order everything but eventually settle down to do justice to a mesmerisingly sublime atavistic mutton curry or so-called kuzhambu that has a delicately lingering tinge of freshly-ground black pepper. I eat it with veechu parathas that turn out not to be at all like the Kerala parathas I've been having lots of lately, but eggishly-egging translucent versions of rumali rotis folded like a postal letter. Except they have no stamp.

The next day I'm determined to find more unusual food and discuss my mission with people who look at me kind of strangely, as if I'm David Bowie in his Ziggy Stardust phase, asking me: 'You want north Indian?'

'No, no, I want Kongu.'

'Go to A2B,' someone suggests, referring to the chain which is like the McDonald's of Tam-Brahm quick meals.

Could it be that they are unaware of their culinary heritage? Or is it the usual reason: Homely isn't eaten out?

Indeed, there's much inventive cookery going on in Tiruppur and I see advertisements for 'chocolate chicken' which appears to be grilled chicken stuffed with chocolate, 'dozza' which I understand to be dosa with pizza topping, and 'disco parathas' that I presume are best inserted into a CD-player. I eventually spot the promisingly named Tiruppur Mess, which should be able to dish up a feast. It's a cavernous hall that could have seated my entire family tree, but there are only a couple of aged plastic chairs and grubby tables in view. When I ask for the menu, the chef who is dressed in sooty boxers and rubber flipflops, but with no shirt, replies, 'Fried rice.'

'Anything else?'

He stares at me as if I'm being a troublesome customer, then says, 'Fried noodles.'

I clarify: 'As this is Tiruppur Mess, I'd prefer Tiruppur food.'

He shakes his head; 'There's no Tiruppur food.'

I don't think it meaningful to argue with that since we're anyway not on the same wavelength, or ever going to be Facebook buddies and he's barely dressed. I personally like to wear clothes when I visit restaurants, especially in towns famous for their garment manufacturing, and it's a nice touch if staff wear them too.

Instead, I hunt for what supposedly is the oldest and most reliable local biryani joint, but the area I mapped it to turns out to be another endless stretch of fancy garment surplus outlets and nobody has heard of any biryani. It also pours again, so the only thing I can think of is Junior Kuppanna and when I enter the eatery this time, I'm feeling I might as well move in and apply for a job as their in-house food quality inspector. I dine on pepper-fried brains and on top of it I order the mildly coconutty chicken biryani; it's made with *al dente* muscular jungle fowl rather than softly spineless broiler. I'm quite taken by it—and not at all surprised when I learn that according to *The Times of India*, online food delivery company Swiggy's statistics show that biryani is Tamil Nadu's most popular order.

In the end, my Kongu food adventure turns out to be exclusively centred around Junior Kuppanna, where I have breakfasts, lunches and dinners. On the other hand, I don't mind it at all—the menu has so many items that I don't eat the same dish twice. For as the oft-repeated foodie saying goes: A good restaurant is a good restaurant is a good restaurant. Or was it Shakespeare who said, 'A biryani by any other name would smell as good?'

❖

Coming to Puducherry, on the Tamil Nadu coast, is like nibbling off the yummiest plates of Europe's best restaurants, but hotted up to match Asian sensibilities—think Parisian fine dining, but tastier, less inhibited spicing, more daring creativity, veritable bliss for lovers of fusion. And what fusion!

Pondicherry, as it was known back in the day, was founded by Frenchmen in 1674. The reason why they built their colonial city here and not on the west coast where all the precious spices could be found, is said to be that the fashion-conscious foreigners were more interested in trading cloth and textiles—which, as we just learnt in Tiruppur, parts of Tamil Nadu remain prominent for. Besides, it was a cosmopolitan coast which already had a Danish settlement 100 km south at Tranquebar, while the English competition was comfortably distant, 130 km north at Fort Saint George (which grew into Chennai). They were all welcomed by Tamilian kings—only the Swedes were chased out (by the French) when they tried to colonise Porto Novo in 1733, no more than 50 km away it was too close for comfort. When the French moved out almost three centuries later, in 1954, they left an occidental *esprit* behind: Street names are still prefaced with Rue, the leafy avenues are lined with plenty of mansions called 'Maison Something or the Other' and policemen wear red pillboxy caps. (I verily feel like I'm inside a Tintin comic.)[20]

Partly, this is thanks to the modern Puducherrian insight that with an economy increasingly dependent on tourism, there's a need to preserve architectural monuments—or less tourists will come—but also partly because of the culinary entrepreneurship that inhabits those preserved buildings, basically making the bar-hangers and restaurant-goers provide for their upkeep. Even new constructions are built to blend in, I notice, as I check into Palais de Mahé on 239, Rue de Bussy. It looks like it might have been there since colonial days, but is in fact, a new addition to the city scene. The sophisticated rooms have all mod cons required for a posh stay, at the same time, every detail down to the wrought-iron door keys bespeaks of tradition-mindedness.

The gourmet fare at the hotel's airy roof terrace is as flawless as it gets. Chef N. Kathir excels at Kerala cuisine, such as prawns in mango-seasoned curry or kokum-marinated fish grilled in banana leaf wraps that preserves the aromas of the juicy flesh (the way he says it's done in Mahe, yes, that other ex-enclave in the previous chapter). But even sublimer is his

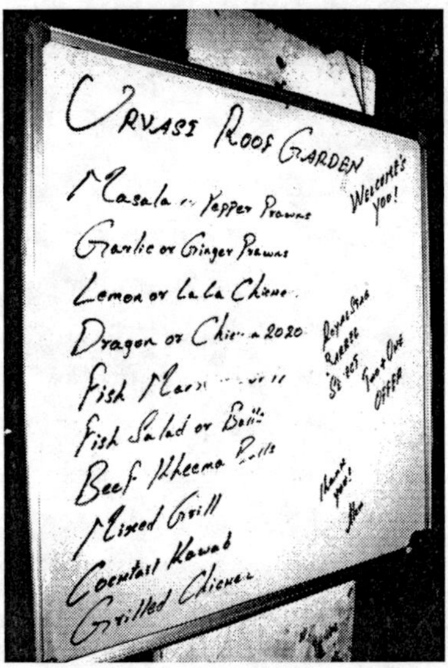

My favourite Pondicherry bar menu.

Indian *haute cuisine*, or what he calls 'progressive'. Dishes to die for include the garlic-marinated medium-rare steak in a peppery gravy served alongside taro root wedges tempered with mustard seeds and a touch of chilli; next I'm totally floored by a fennel-and-lime-crusted kingfish fillet accompanied by a Spanish-influenced roasted paprika sauce—based on the highly complex *salsa romesco* of Catalonia—and crisp-fried julienned veggies; finally I reach nirvana when I bite into grilled curry-marinated tiger prawns with traditional lemon rice (what a masterstroke!) and stir-fried buttery babycorn. Spice levels are heady without overpowering the natural flavours of other ingredients.

Between meals, the town is perfect for a Proustian stroll to build up more of an appetite. I turn the corner into the charming Rue Romain Rolland, named after a long-ago winner of the Nobel Prize for Literature. It is lined by a library, a theatre with an antiquated Pathe-Cine-movie hall sign still intact over the gate, and various other rendezvouses suitable for judicious flaneurs such as La Maison Rose, a café-cum-cocktail bar that is a sibling of Chennai's legendary bistro Amethyst, which also houses an arty bookshop. Afterwards I reward myself with a refreshing banana lassi at the 24/7-open Le Café, housed in the former harbour office with marvellous ocean views.

Puducherry is a pizza-lovers' paradise where authenticity and affordability combine into heavenly hogging. I drop into a random place serving wood-fired pizzas, which also offers cocktails in any size; three sozzled girls at the next table down a pitcher of Bacardi. I make do with a pint and since we're on the coast I order a seafood pizza—topped with generous chunks of fish, sliced black olives, chopped veggies and smothered in a rich layer of cheese. Eating, I observe a girl entering in burqa, dashing into the restroom, coming out in jeans and tank top, and ordering a drink. It's very à la Puducherry or, as Francophones might interject, *ooh là-là*.

However, one needs to pick one's eating options with circumspection, as the scene changes rapidly—yesterday's talk of the town which was top-ranked in guidebooks may be gone... or gone down the drain. For example, a charming courtyard restaurant in Rue Labourdonnais with tables set in pillared verandas attracted me on earlier visits for its grub and gets fine write-ups in all travel handbooks. Now, the owner appears dodgy when I ask for a bottle of red, which eventually arrives, decanted in a teapot. The wine is chilled, which suggests that the bottle was opened long ago and kept refrigerated. Rather than the expensive dry Shiraz I am paying for, they seem to have mixed dregs from different half-drunk flagons of cheap port. When I request to inspect the label, the Frenchman treats me like I'm some kind of second-rate Grimod de la Reynière and evades the question.[21] The meal that hits the table after an inordinate wait, despite the fact that I'm the only customer, is like what a Michelin star might appear like if it turned into a black hole. The meat is as chewy as Charlie Chaplin's shoes and the butter knife I get to carve it with doesn't cut through the leathery slab. The proprietor shrugs when I complain and mutters in a Gallic dialect something that sounds suspiciously like 'up yours', but which hopefully is just his way of wishing me *bon appétit*.

When I need a time-out to digest, I pop into the Bengali poet-guru Aurobindo's former ashram for silent meditation or explore the exhilarating museum-turned-home of poet Bharathiyar who wrote:

Poets in the Tamil land
Made a heady mixture in glee
Of wine, fire, wind and sky
And passed on that potion to me

...or I study the more action-packed Police Museum with its collection of old-worldly uniforms and weapons, and after that I end up at the Puducherry Museum housed in a colonial merchant's eighteenth-century villa. The latter displays a whimsical jumble of things left behind including rotting pianos and a *pousse-pousse* type of car powered by two people who ran behind pushing it. People like me will be most interested in the mock-up of a dining room including special wine cabinets, at the sight of which one easily conjures up the milieu in which Franco-Tamil cuisines fused into Creole, once the French bachelors married Tamil wives. Although milder than regular Tamilian cooking, here *à la Français* grub was spiced up with pepper and made golden by turmeric, with light coconut milk instead of heavy cream, and curry leaves replaced Mediterranean herbs.

After days in the European parts, I shift to the Tamil quarters and check into the pleasant Maison Perumal (58, Perumal Koil Street), a 130-year-old merchant's mansion that's often talked of as Puducherry's finest place to stay boutique style. In its courtyards, artists exhibit their work and the cheerful chef COUGARBABU, a born and bred Puducherrian who writes his name in block letters, puts together an elaborate sampling menu of house specials. Entrées consist of intriguing Tamilian 'falafels' that are called vazhapoo vada and made of mashed banana flowers served with a coconut dip, khuzipaniyaram (dhal with delicious spongy rice balls), karuvepillai varutha meen—fleshy and sweetish mahi-mahi (Hawaiian dolphin) fillets baked in leaves with a sweet-and-sour sauce of jaggery, chilli and tamarind; era podithooval (shrimp sautéed with 'gunpowder' mixture) and parlameen kuzhambu (a hot and sour bluefish curry)—altogether taking the art of cookery to celestial levels.

To make life perfect, Puducherry also happens to have an evolved drinking scene: bars are a dime a dozen and cheaper than anywhere else in the world. Rock-bottom options include a surplus of popular dives such as the friendly Poudou-Poudou (31, Rue Labourdonnais) which combines cheap booze and decent seafood, De Bussy Permit Room (81, Lal Bahadur Shastry Street) offering luxurious tandoori snacks to go with frothy mugs, and last but not least, the Amnivasam Factory Price Retail Outlet Budget Bar (corner of Montorsier and Ellaiamankol Streets) that is perhaps the most cost-efficient of all the city's drinking dens for an ice-cold beer. But my favourite roost is Dhanalakshmi Urvasi Roof Garden (59, Rangapillai Street), on the upper floor of a mansion with a balcony that overlooks the street, making it perfect for people-watching. Despite a certain seediness, it's an easy-going haunt, with uncles in loincloths sipping hard drinks, a bunch of youths chanting 'Happy birthday to Thambi', and a squirrel tries to jump into my beer mug when I'm distracted by the delectable sides such as the 'prawn-fish munch' which is exactly what it sounds like: A hearty mix of fish and prawns fried with spices and veggies.

As I board the train at Puducherry's congenially tiny station, I'm already missing everything about the town.

❖

The journey north towards Telangana goes through arid countryside, which has a rugged beauty, but the entire stretch also happens to be the home of classy non-veg and at virtually all stations one gets hygienically packed biryani-in-a-box. Being a certified glutton, I have one for lunch (a juicy chicken-leg biryani with spicy veggie gravy) and craving more, I buy another for dinner.

Moreover, the train halts at Guntur which is supposedly the true home of Andhra cuisine, and I regret not having scheduled a proper stopover. Then for an hour, the train doesn't budge and I calculate whether to risk running out to shop for more grub. As it eventually rolls again, a vendor hops on to peddle crispy bite-sized samosas served with those revered flaming-hot thin, long, deeply red chillies, so providentially I do get my mouthful of Guntur. Andhraites grow about half of the chillies in the country, with Guntur being the epicentre of chilli-farming.

Getting off the train at Hyderabad's Deccan station at the onset of the holy fasting month, topmost on my list of tourist attractions to check out is the city's GI-tagged (since 2012) ghee-soaked, hard-stirred until ultra-smooth, slow-cooked on wood-fire for twelve hours, meat-wheat paste-like porridge or potage…and which is more commonly simply known as haleem. It ranks as Hyderabad's top contribution to the world's breakfast tables. The singularly filling and nutritious dish has its roots in Central Asia or possibly Iran, but reached its zenith here where it powers the citizens during their austere month of fasting. Apparently, 3,500 goats are cooked nightly and with any luck some of them are positively destined for my tummy.

I check into a lodge where the receptionist proclaims that temperatures average 50°C and sells me an overpriced mosquito-infested so-called AC room. The museum-worthy cooling-machine burps icily and then electricity collapses. Through the night, my perspiration is distilled on my skin into greasy patches until I can't take it anymore. I have a bucket rinse and head out into the dawn. The receptionist was right, the city is suffering from an unprecedented heat wave that, according to the morning papers, is expected to kill off thousands of chickens. Is it the usual greenhouse effect or has the world turned into a tandoor? My guesstimate's as good as yours, but one thing's for sure—soon people may need to only put chicken in a pot of rice outdoors, and hey presto, there's a hot-hot biryani!

My survival chances seem bleak, but I tell myself I'm not a chicken. Instead, I slither like a sweaty beanbag down the road towards the old town where I right away spot the 1980s' Irani canteen Nayaab (Nayapul Road). As luck has it, it's open early and fully non-veg. From a courteous waiter I order the cholesterol-lover's all-time favourite bheja fry, a velvety brain pulp seasoned with a highly agreeable masala—the ideal morning meal for thinking humans. Mopping it up with soft naan, I relish every morsel like a zombie that tastes IQ for the first time.

Down the road, the Charminar circle has been pedestrianised to make it easier for tourists to appreciate the medieval monument. But most of it is covered in ugly scaffolding, because part of it has collapsed, so I can't really take selfies with it in the background. Nevertheless, Hyderabad is gracefully ramshackle with its stately buildings crumbling and bricks tumbling, from once-splendid arcades, to litter the pavements. The countrywide smoking ban doesn't seem to have taken effect either; fag butts crunch underfoot as people happily puff everywhere like it's the first morning after many Arabian nights. A helmet and gas mask might have come in handy, I ponder, as I explore Hyderabadi culture.

I've never been to Pakistan but this feels about as close as I will ever get—everywhere, merchants advertise Pakistani garments and, when I stop for lunch, I sample Pakistani curry at a hyped restaurant near Madina Circle. It's one of the swankier 1990s' joints, its AC-hall crowded with ladies in burqas surrounded by shopping bags, tucking into biryani after biryani. In case you've ever wondered what Pakistani food's like, I can tell you that according to their chef it's vividly phlegm-green and their 'Mutton Pakistani' is a mixture of salt, caramel colour, possibly nuclear waste, and microscopic pieces of something goatish, but only the health ministry of Pakistan would be capable of determining what animal protein it really is. Unable to finish the portion, I don't even consider asking for a doggy bag. Then again, the philosophy behind this book is that I sample dodgy stuff so you can avoid eating dogs, say, by mistake.

But everything else I devour in this town that is ranked as *the* culinary Mecca of India, adds up to a sheer epicurean pilgrimage. Which is why UNESCO included Hyderabad in its list of 'gastronomic metros'. One out of ten Hyderabadis earn their bread and butter from the city's 150,000 food outlets (if you include pushcarts or so-called bandis). The rest love eating—obviously—and every morning in the newspapers I come across alarmist reports devoted to the mounting obesity cataclysm, with helpful fat-burning hacks thrown in.

The oldest heritage snack stop on my tour, Munshi Naan, dates back to 1851 and is a fifteen-minute walk from the Charminar in a street known as Purani Haveli, after the one-time mansion of the Nizam. It's basically a corner shop tandoor that bakes 'char koni naan', squarish thick breads, rich and oily, soft on the inside but with a crisp outer layer. The business is run by fifth-generation descendants of the original munshi, the Nizam's letter-writer, who set it up.

Indeed, much of Hyderabad's cookbook is linked to the Nizams (who ruled the town until Indian independence) but its deeper heredity is actually found in the elitist Mughal 'high cuisine' of Delhi, further traceable to luxurious Persian, elegant Turkish, classic Afghan and rich Arab origins. Muslims from across the world migrated to the Deccan about half a millennia ago or so. But they also combine in them a curious southern accent in the form of great vegetarian dishes prepared with ingredients like coconut, eggplants, peanuts, sesame, tamarind, those extra-deadly Andhranese chillies and, sometimes, even crushed pearls. One of the veggie hits is mirchi ka salan, consisting of whole but rather mild chillies cooked in thickly nutty, gingery gravy. Thanks to its pickle-like character it keeps so well that it is a preferred traveller's lunchbox. Even the meaty biryanis are dramatically spiced up by distinctly un-Mughal ingredients (as against the classic Mughal biryani that packs in slightly gentler aromas, such as saffron). The tamarind sourness that balances out the profusion of chillies, supposedly perks up the appetite at the same time as it improves digestion. But why eat too many chillies in the first place? Well, they believe that chillies are better than air-conditioning or ice-cream, because to eat the heat is to beat the heat...

The ultimate in local fine-dining is the loaded Hyderabadi biryanis, of which more than forty varieties exist (including vegetarian) and that generally have roots in Persian *pilaus*. One of the numerous permutations is made with a complete goat and the animal becomes the vessel that the meal is served in, as it is jam-packed with dry-fruit-enriched chicken-egg pullao. But other than that radically rare dish, everybody has their preferred versions, debating differences between, say, Shah Ghouse Café's branches or the Paradise chain. Personally, I fall for the welcoming 1930s' Grand Hotel (Bank Street) which isn't particularly grand and has no rooms or branches; but their dining hall with its high ceiling appeals to me as does the

A 'bad' Andhra offer one can resist.

splendid mutton biryani. As I am eating, I think of how novelist E.M. Forster loved Hyderabadi food and wrote two books based on his Indian experiences—his greatest novel *A Passage to India* (set in the 1910s) and the lesser-known but equally engrossing non-fiction *The Hill of Devi* (about a sojourn in the 1920s). While his friend Somerset Maugham obsessed about Hinduism, Forster was drawn to Islamic culture which of course included lots of non-veg. Perhaps, I speculate, he tried the biryani cooked up here at Grand?

In *The Hill of Devi*, Forster described journeying to Hyderabad in November 1921 (and even if it was in the winter his train reminded him of 'a stewpan') to spend a month with his 'greatest Indian friend' Dr Syed Ross Masood, a founding father of the city's Osmania University and who was 'fantastically generous, incredibly hospitable...a connoisseur; he loved good books.' They had last met up in Patna ten years earlier (a town that Forster fictionalised in *A Passage to India*) but knew each other from long before; Forster had been Masood's tutor in England. And in turn, Masood tweaked the novelist's mind as Forster wrote in his essay collection *Two Cheers for Democracy*: 'Until I met him, India was a vague jumble of rajahs, sahibs, babus and elephants, and I was not interested in such a jumble; who could be? He made everything real and exciting as soon as he began to talk, and seventeen years later when I wrote *A Passage to India* I dedicated it to him out of gratitude as well as out of love, for it would never have been written without him.' Indeed, Dr Masood was immortalised in that very novel as Dr Aziz (essayed by Victor Bannerjee in the Oscar-winning movie) whose predicament is central to the narrative.

Sightseeing with Masood, Forster found Hyderabad full of 'beautiful things to look at, interesting people to talk to, delicious food,' and after *A Passage to India* became a bestseller he made a 'substantial donation' towards the building of an Urdu Hall just 2 km from the Grand Hotel where I'm swilling down my biryani. Masood passed away in 1937, ending their friendship thus, yet, Forster returned to India for a last trip in 1945, barely months after World War II had ended. He may on that final visit have seen the hall he sponsored which until today houses an archive and a library dedicated to Urdu literature. He doesn't mention it in his writings but he described that out of modern architecture in India, 'the chief example I saw was the great new university at Hyderabad' which 'attempts to blend two styles of architecture which occur in the Hyderabad state—one style being Mohammedan, and the other derived from the famous Buddhist caves of Ajanta.'

By the time I finish my biryani I'm 100 per cent sure (without a shred of evidence but feeling it both in my bones and belly) that Forster too must have eaten similar biryani. 'I have been in my life three times to Hyderabad, some of my happiest Indian days were spent there,' wrote Forster after this last visit to town, and he speaks of discovering the pleasure of buffet dinners: 'Long tables are loaded with Indian food, and sometimes one table is labelled "vegetarian" and the other "non-vegetarian". You help yourself, or are helped. I take away pleasant memories of these buffet dinners, memories of Indians moving elegantly through well-filled rooms, with well-filled plates in their hands, and miraculously conveying food to their mouths in the folds of a chapatti.'

Forster would surely have gone for the biryanis. But before I leave town I learn of a newer novelty, yet another unique biryani variety has taken the city by storm: it's the customary dish of Yemenites, *mandi*, brought by soldiers who migrated here centuries ago to work as royal bodyguards. Their former suburb of military barracks is known as Barkas and its Arab-descendants are estimated to about 100,000 in all. But their eating habits were never talked about until foodies noticed the sweetness of their version of haleem, that evolved from a primeval Arab staple by the name of *tharid*—don't be shocked but rumour has it that sugar is combined with fatty meat in this heartbreakingly rich dish! Also, thanks to the fact that many Indians have worked in the Emirates or done the Haj (and returned feeling sentimental), the Saudi *laham mandi* became a rage in the 2010s.

It may be that 'authentic *mandi*' is advertised on hoardings across town, yet it's rumoured that many spice it up with typically Indian masalas to make it inauthentic, basically turning it into normal Hyderabadi biryani. Therefore, after some excruciating bargaining, I take a rickshaw to Barkas. Passing the Taj Falaknuma Palace, I get off at the humble suburb that at first glance looks rough with smallish pukka houses and even smaller industries. Maybe it's meant to resemble a village in Yemen. People are friendly enough and across from a burial ground the tombstone engraver greets me in Arabic as I ask for directions.

He points me down Mandi Road, named after its illustrious culinary offering. I stop at one out of the thirty or so eateries, the Mataam al-Arabi which supposedly fired up the Arab food trend and sits in a, from all appearances, recently-built complex symptomatic of how once-simple canteens are upgrading thanks to their rising fame in epicurean circles. It's decorated with cannons outside to establish the owner's warrior ancestry, but the dining hall is almost unfurnished save for carpets on the floors.

After kicking off my shoes, I sit on the carpet at a low table to study the colourful menu which is a masterpiece of simplicity and tempting non-veg at rates to suit all pockets from full goat with all the trimmings (to be shared by twenty-five diners) to elementary, cheap mutton soup. I focus on the *laham mandi* that I came for. As I wait, I worry that I'll get enough to feed a joint-family, but the waiter sensibly refrains from stacking the silver platter that's about as wide as the length of my forearm, for which I'm graciously charged half the menu rate.

The elongated rice grains are beautifully separated in a master class of social distancing, scented with saffron, fried onion, and cashews, and a crusty mutton slab sits on top, breaking apart on mere touch—and it's stunningly succulent. Regarding the cooking method, it seems that lightly spiced rice is garnished with dry fruits and then topped by a wire mesh upon which the mutton pieces rest gently; an Arabic version of the classic dum-pukht (which is basically what *laham mandi* is).[22] A dish with its roots in a very old world, it's slow-cooked in a sealed vessel until the meat juices permeate the rice. As a contrast to its subtlety, it comes with chilli-enhanced fresh tomato chutney of the kind one gets complimentary helpings of in northern Africa.

Another nice touch is the desserts selection that includes Bahraini halwa, the Hyderabadi 'cult' dish qubani ka meetha of syrup-boiled apricots in thick cream, and teeth-curlingly sweet baklava sourced from a genuine Turkish pastry chef, no less, oh, so delicious with its nuttiness, honey, and piquant spices wrapped up in crisp-baked flaky-buttery filo dough. I hesitate to leave, because I could easily lie down on the carpeted floor and go on stuffing myself forever. But work beckons—with my next meal in the next town down.

❖

Somehow, Goa had been filed away at the back of my mind as the quintessential hedonist hotspot with its hippies, who still hope that the Beatles will reunite for one last gig in Anjuna with George Harrison playing the Ouija board and John Lennon as the spirit in the bottle. Culture in Goa seemed, at the most, to be about its use as a backdrop by filmmakers—as the perfect hideaway for Matt Damon in the Hollywood blockbuster thriller *Bourne Supremacy* (but the action hero's enchanting Goan bungalow was erected specially for the film and demolished immediately afterwards so there's no point trying to rent it).

Simply a place for letting loose and getting tight, eating on its beaches where shack-chefs innovate permutations of British, French, German, Iranian, Israeli, Italian, Japanese, Mexican, Russian, Swedish and Thai cuisines, and whatever else the tourists' palates crave, to the sound of pot-smoking karaoke artists crooning reggae hits long forgotten in the rest of the world.

Nowhere else in India has restaurant culture aligned itself so perfectly with what tourists need, which can be a welcome change if one has been travelling for too long and is getting tired of the predictable urban multicuisine. Many of the Goan food outlets, whether fancy or humble, rank among Asia's best.

But maybe this is how it should be, considering that Goan cuisine itself is born out of a fusion of colonial influences and local food habits, in particular that of the Saraswath community. The chillies, that are part of nearly all Indian dishes, were brought here by the colonisers (as were tomatoes and potatoes and many other good things) along with the methods for baking leavened bread—Goa's famous pav.

Even their most world-conquering dish bears witness to this, the venerated vinegary vindaloo: Hot-and-sour overnight-marinated pork curry starring a rainbow of spices such as cardamom pods, sticks of cinnamon, several cloves, ground coriander, cumin seeds, roasted fenugreek, much garlic, fresh ginger of course, mustard seeds, big onions, a spoonful of peppercorns, often also some sugar or jaggery, turmeric for sure and heavy-handed usage of those red chillies introduced by the Portuguese to India. It is derived from a Portuguese original, namely *carne de vinho e alhos* or wine and garlic-stewed meat, a name that after a few fennies too many, will sound like vindaloo.

Tourists and restaurateurs apart, in the last two decades it seems that a mysterious migratory trend has made plenty of litterateurs and other intellectuals move in—and Goa has seen literary festivals where one might spot one of my heroes, Amitav Ghosh, who bought a mansion in the picture-perfect bucolic interiors of Goa. As have many other writers that I enjoy reading like Sudhir Kakar and Sunil Khilnani, apparently…and so I was getting mental images of 1800s Berlin or *fin-de-siècle* Paris to where artists from all over the world were pulled…or the Carmel to Big Sur stretch of Californian coast that attracted Robert Heinlein, Henry Miller and even, for a bit, the perpetual hitchhiker Jack Kerouac, who wrote the documentary novel *Big Sur* (1962) about his stay—and of course Big Sur is something of a hub in 'Steinbeck Country' considering John Steinbeck even wrote a novel set in the fish-packing plants at Cannery Row. And being on California's coast, the analogy isn't too much of a stretch.

As much as Goa attracts outsiders, the Goans themselves are attracted to the world and will be found in the Indian diasporas from Africa to New York; rumour has it that there are more Goans in Europe and north America than in Goa itself. Yet few visitors are aware that one such 'expat', Abbe Faria who was born in Candolim in 1755, developed a method for *hipnotismo scientifico* way back before hypnotism was officially invented and became so famous in Paris, of all places, that

Abbe Faria's birth home in Candolim before
he became globally famous.

Alexandre Dumas based a character on him in his swashbuckling bestseller, *The Count of Monte Cristo* (1845).

The celebrated travel writer Norman Lewis, who came to Goa when it was still a colony, wrote in his book *The World The World* that descendants of Abbe Faria's disciples, 'a club of Goanese [*sic*] hypnotists held regular meetings and practised his techniques on each other.' But that apart, 'Goa offered little in the way of entertainment. Night-clubs were banned, the cinema showed Western films only when a minimum audience of fifty could be rounded up. Otherwise there was snake-charming.' Nevertheless, the who's who of travel writing passed through. Shortly after Goa's liberation, Graham Greene, then in his late fifties, partied energetically in 1963 at all-night bashes for two weeks, predicting that here 'are great beaches waiting for great hotels.' But in those days even the venerable Mandovi Hotel in Panjim town wasn't good enough for him to stay at, so he preferred to have long fenny-boosted evening conversations as a house guest of local writer Maria Couto (who subsequently authored her first book on Greene).

This reminds me of how some years ago, on a beach holiday, I was browsing at the Literati bookshop—in a century-old bungalow which has a bookcase devoted to Goan writing. There I bumped into Booker-winner Kiran Desai and her then boyfriend Nobel laureate Orhan Pamuk, who had rented a home across the road. Autograph hunters love this charming shop because Literati has over the years hosted events with everybody who is anybody and…well, myself.

At Literati, I learn that Goa has always been a literary hub. The state's multicultural traditions run deep, as is proven by the fact that Goan literature is written in Konkani, Marathi, Portuguese and English too—its most well-known English writer being memoirist Maria Couto, who during her lifetime captured, in her very personal way, the past and present of Goa as well as the 'composite identity' of Goans who she saw as Indians but deeply European at the same time. Picking up the charming anthology *Ferry Crossings*, I read some of the finest Goan writing, compiled by the renowned Goa-based poet Manohar Shetty. It includes the Jnanpith-awarded Damodar Mauzo whose Konkani novel *Karmelin* won the Sahitya Akademi award in 1983—and who happens to be one of the nicest writers I've ever met—and excerpts from Victor Rangel-Ribeiro's *Tivolem* which is one of those novels that seem to encompass an entire universe between the covers.

Dropping in at some literary event in the state's cultural complex Kala Academy, as luck would have it, I run into the afore-mentioned Amitav Ghosh who invites me home for a party. He explains that he'd been visiting Goa for decades, until he found a crumbling mansion which he bought and restored. One wing was in such a state of disrepair that it had to be almost fully rebuilt. Ghosh's study, which naturally interests me the most, impresses with its large writing desk and a luxurious range of hidebound Egyptian notebooks that apparently contain the hand-written first drafts of all his novels. For Ghosh, one of the pleasures of Goa is that it's such a literary place—he likes to entertain other writers at tremendously enjoyable dinner parties.

At the party, apart from chatting about Graham Greene's and Umberto Eco's visits with Ghosh's neighbour Maria Couto, I enjoy bar-hanging with the humour columnist Cecil Pinto, a distinguished connoisseur of caju (i.e. cashew fenny, also spelled as feni or in Portuguese fenim). He's brought the most exquisite village-distilled brews from his collection to Ghosh's party, where he takes it upon himself to teach the noble art of imbibing caju to guests ranging from the lowly yours truly to Nobel Laureates such as Orhan Pamuk whom I had celebrity-spotted already at Literati. Despite rumours that the Turkish intellectual might, too, be pondering a long-term home in Goa, he sniffed sceptically at the homemade booze which had been poured out of a recycled Smirnoff-bottle.

Being slightly tipsy, I tried to help Pamuk by pointing out that caju becomes sublime as soon as one gets drunk enough—only later did it occur to me that any Nobel laureate sticking his nose into a glass of the potent brew might worry more about potential brain-damage than its rather extreme bouquet. The fact that fenny is a GI-tagged product and the pride of Goa neither tickled his tastebuds nor his intellect. Other foreign writers have taken more interest in the eminent beverage, such as Alexander Frater who wrote (in *Chasing the Monsoon*) that in a small village, he found a country liquor shop selling 'fenny distilled from the crown of the palm, the drink of the monsoon. A single tiny room with a barred window, it contained three men who told me the strength of fenny was such that it could only be comfortably taken in cool weather. I tried some. It was very strong with a kind of curious cheesy aftertaste.'

Fenny, like vindaloo, is an outcome of the colonial

presence—the colonials planted cashews in India and when their imported wine ran out, Jesuit monks who observed how locals made booze from coconut trees found that in similar manner cashew fruits could be distilled into potent liquor. As for myself, fenny has always made me think of tequila—it can actually be drunk similarly with salt and lime—and an interesting new trend in distilling is embodied by Maya Pistola Agavepura which (due to GI-tagging rules) may not be called tequila, but is 100 per cent tequila in all other aspects except, well, that it's made in India. There's also caffeinated gin with beans from the Western Ghats, which is perfect for those who snooze from too much booze.

Goa, where you must have a Limca with your fenny (or the other way around).

When I ask Pinto what he thinks of all these literary migrants flocking to his native place, he frankly states, 'That Goa is becoming a hub for writers, is evident. But regarding your question of Goa benefiting from writers moving here, now that is a complicated matter. Writers, like people, come in different types. When a writer like Amitav Ghosh comes here, he enhances our literary environment through his interactions. There are other writers, on the other hand, who have portrayed a totally bizarre image of Goa to the world. This type we could do without.'

I make a mental note to write respectfully about Goa in this book. As if my fascination for the coastal enclave let out the genie from a bottle (of caju), I wake up with a thunderstorm in my tender and coconut-green head. Waiting for it to cure itself, I head to Old Goa, the eastern capital of Portugal founded in 1510 to manage their trade with East Asia. There the mandatory hours of basilica-beholding, cathedral-canvassing, monastery-measuring, and ruin-reconnoitring includes the stunning Sé Cathedral built in 1562 by Dominicans, the baroque Basilica de Bom Jesus which holds the miraculous body of Saint Francis Xavier (d. 1552) on display inside an ornamental circa 1690 glass coffin gifted by the sixth grand duke of Tuscany, and half a dozen other monuments. Somerset Maugham noted that in 'the cathedral they were holding a service, the organ was playing and in the organ loft there was a small choir of natives singing with a harshness in which somehow the Catholic chants acquired a mysteriously heathen, Indian character.'

Of the once bustling town with bazaars full of silk shops, porcelain sellers, goldsmiths and jewellers, taverns and brothels, nothing else remains. But I'd heard about a small hotel located within ten minutes' walk from the UNESCO World Heritage site on a quiet hillock.

Tucked away in the jungle, Hotel Champakali turns out to be the perfect base camp for me and fulfils the picture of a hidden gem. It's so secret that it wasn't until hours before I was to arrive that I was told, via an anonymous phone call, how to find my way.

'Drive towards the Church of Our Lady of the Mount,' the voice whispered.

'Is there a sign?' I asked.

'No.'

Once I eventually reach Champakali, it is totally worth the trouble. The ultra-luxury B&B feels both small and big. It consists of two whitish mansions that look like the Riviera abode of faded rock stars, encircled by trees—banyan, teak, banana, guava and as expected, flowering champak, or magnolia. Each has three bedrooms filled with antique furniture and knickknacks. I'm the only guest in my mansion; a family is renting the other one next-door.

Utterly ambrosial repasts are dished up in gazebos facing the expansive gardens and the Carambolim Lake, known for its superb fishing, is visible in the distance. For starters, I'm treated to a smoked aubergine soup, cold, probably the most unique thing I ever had—can't even find it in my *Larousse Gastronomique*. The pureed potage with fresh yoghurt is scented with herbs that coat my tongue like a minor key aromatic symphony. It's followed by a plate of fish fillet cooked in banana leaf, grilled vegetables and lemon rice. Again, it's subtle, oh, so subtle, because of which I request the waiter to give my compliments to the chef. He turns out to be a Frenchman called Mathieu and suddenly the eclectic fare makes sense.

Mathieu serves me a complimentary off-menu tasting—a clam soup which he has cooked exclusively for the neighbouring family next-door: Garlicky white wine broth with a salty sea aroma of clams. The dessert is *serradura*, a type of poor-man's pudding that has become exceedingly trendy in Portugal's former colonies, including in parts of China. I'm not a dessert person but this one I could have taken umpteen helpings of.

I spend the following days exploring my surroundings.

Wanting to approach Old Goa from the riverside, like the

visitors did in hoary yore, I stride downhill to where its gate still stands. Known as the Viceroy's Arch it has a statue of Vasco da Gama atop (erected to commemorate the centenary of his arrival in India). As I snap my snaps, I notice that the Mandovi ferry to Divar Island is about to leave from the jetty next to the arch. On an impulse, I jump aboard. Once I make landfall on Divar, instead of taking the ferry back I follow the ribbon straight road cutting across mangrove marshes, curious about where it might lead.

I spot none of the crocodiles that are supposed to live hereabouts, but see a huge snake sleeping on the road. Very easy-going Goan snake...and after a leisurely stroll, I reach a small village of extraordinarily pretty bungalows, where numerous bars greet me. I pick one that isn't haunted by rustic gamblers but might offer victuals instead, Rock Inn, which despite its name turns out not to be a trendy disco-bistro filled with holidaying fashionistas nibbling on overpriced finger foods, but obviously named thus because it lies sheltered by a strange rock. A black-and-white Hindi flick plays on the TV. The cavernous interiors resemble a warehouse, with beer boxes stacked along the walls, and when I ask the bare-chested and barefoot uncle if there are snacks, he rattles off all manner of scrambled eggs, burji and omelettes.

Since I didn't come this far to eat eggs, I ask, 'Seafood?'

'There's fresh snapper and prawns. Rawa fried.'

'Can I have snapper without rawa, just tawa?'

'No.'

'Please?'

'Maybe prawns,' he says and asks his wife, who mans the kitchen, to fry me a plate. Within minutes, heavenly smells waft through the hall and platters of amazingly juicy-crunchy seafood arrive to accompany my chilled beers. There seems to be a rule of thumb in Goa—find any village bar and no matter how unpromising it looks, it'll invariably serve up a feast. Come to think of it, I've never had as good bar snacks as during my travels in India. Authenticity is ensured by the fact that no tourist ever stumbles into a drinking den like Rock Inn. Instead, more semi-nude uncles drift in for pre-noon fenny pegs, 90 ml or 180 ml size appears the norm at this early hour, so once I've had my six-pack for the day I down a big peg, decamp before I fall asleep among the other drunks and revert to reality.

Crossing back on the ferry in a moderately inebriated state, I am in a position to better appreciate how Old Goa would have seemed to visitors arriving by the river and the churches-to-sightsee appears to have doubled in my absence. I stagger uphill through the archway where Vasco da Gama's statue now scrutinises me extra fiercely with his four eyes, arrive at the square where inquisition victims were flogged which makes me really genuinely guilty for being tipsy, and then I drop into each church to do penance, thinking that if I am ever crucified, I must remember to carry nail polish. In case the nails are rusty.

When I get hungry after seeing each cathedral twice—once with the left eye, once with the right—I make a detour into nearby Panjim, the biggest city of the state a short bus ride away, yet enchanting with winding lanes lined with bungalows that have red-tiled roofs. I gorge on nicely spicy mussels at Ritz, the seafood joint which is like a crammed tunnel of fishy love—squeeze in, squeeze down, eat-pay-go. Next, I digest in peace at Godinho's, founded in 1938 and more laidback than Ritz in case one wants to nurse a drink and read newspapers. Indeed, Godinho's is old enough for that connoisseur of seedy bars, Graham Greene, to have guzzled in it. This is pure conjecture, but in the *Sunday Times* (1964), Greene complained about the cheap 'raw Indian gins and whiskies' and their possible health hazards but seems to have missed the candy-sweet Port wines that Goans adapted from their colonisers. Since he would presumably have dined at Mandovi Hotel around the corner—one of the few proper hotels in those days—this would have been the logical place for aperitifs and nightcaps.

As a freelance journalist in Goa, it is probable that he was scouting out settings for a novel, like he usually did whenever he travelled wherever, but decided otherwise—maybe because the hard liquor was too hard or Indian culture too complex—and I can almost hear him sigh, as I sip my fenny, the way Catholics do when they think of Mary. Bloody, that is. Maria Couto later asked why he hadn't written about India to which Greene replied, 'I think India rather frightened me by its size. I have enjoyed myself very much during two weeks in Goa, but to write about India in a novel I would have had to live there over a considerable period of time and I think I was daunted by the problems.'

If one doesn't see a problem with it, there are certainly worse ways to waste weeks than bumming in Goa, over-eating and imbibing lethal levels of rustic tipple, but my marathon-length bender invariably feels unwholesome, thanks to manifold hangovers relieving and replacing one another in a succession of mitigating and palliating manoeuvres, until such a point that one is surprised every morning where one wakes up. This has as much to do with my own priorities as with Goa—about 10 per cent of my days consist of healthy tourism, 90 per cent is spent on hunting things to eat and drink excessively.

The beverage part of my diet is, as always, very straightforward: Zero in on any downmarket bar to sample unbranded beverages, such as that infamous cashew fenny, a decent vintage of which can give the costliest of artisanal tequilas a run for their money. I take it as a compliment when I order a caju with a slice of chonok—a sublime fish often cooked in seedy watering holes—and a scruffy bartender, who until then acted indifferent, stops whatever he's doing, stares at me for three seconds, before he asks: 'Sir, are you Goan?'

My tummy which (perhaps due to the plenitude of fishy bar snacks) has been producing gallons of loose motions, 'Goan gas-tricks', is much improved on the last day, most likely thanks to the underestimated medical properties of fenny that has not only killed many of my brain cells but also all the bacteria in my gut. The train is to leave from Vasco-da-Gama station at 3 p.m. and I decide to have my ultimate final marine meal in the vicinity. For those who haven't been to this town named after the eponymous coloniser, suffice it to say that the port town where the railway line ends and begins is a transport hub, with none too many tourist attractions. In fact, none. Except perhaps for a singular restaurant that has something of a pan-Goan reputation. Avoiding the quick meal joints immediately opposite the station, I peregrinate until, down a side street leading away from the municipal square, I spot Anantashram, that's neither posh nor dingy, but normal-looking and crowded with Goans. Not another tourist in sight, but their evocative slogan beckons with a language I can understand: 'Simply Good Food, Booze & Friendly Ambience.'

The menu includes the usual multicuisine to keep the timid happy, but I browse to the Goan section covering two thrilling pages. A special thali turns out to be something of a seafood encyclopaedia. From left to right my platter is filled with small bowls brimful of prawn kishmur (a fried shrimp salad), tisryo (spicy clams), kingfish curry, crab xec-xec (curried crab), fried kingfish (coated in semolina), bhangda uddamethi (mackerel curry with fenugreek seeds), and a sardine preparation the name of which I don't remember. The delicate aromas range from tomatoish to exceedingly coconutty.

On the side, I order a plate of pan-fried prawns, expecting standard shrimps. Instead I get a bunch of massive crustaceans tossed in a distinctly sweet and vinegary Goan masala. Demolishing that meal, I am reminded of the eminent Samanth Subramanian's travelogue *Following Fish*, in one chapter of which he trawls Mumbai's back lanes for the most authentic 'lunch home'. These are traditional eateries harking back to the industrial revolution of the late nineteenth century when cotton mills dotted the cityscape and workers needed homely but affordable lunches. They evolved with time into modern restaurants, mostly, but Subramanian tracks down the last one in Girgaon, curiously enough also named Anantashram. 'Anantashram aimed to be strictly dedicated to the act of feeding. Lunch ended not at a fixed time but when the kitchen ran out of food, and many customers sat on a bench facing the wall, ate without a flicker of an expression, and left within a quarter of an hour.' There, Subramanian has a fish thali with distinctly Goan aromas.

I wonder if Anantashram might be the name of a chain, a thalassic edition of the omnipresent Udupi 'vegetarian hotels'. But no, from what I gather this particular Anantashram that I am hogging at was born in 1970—making it much younger than its Mumbai counterpart—as a fish shack by a man named Anant, who cooked fish-curry-rice priced at Rs 0.75 per portion. As the shack's reputation grew, it was deemed necessary to open a 'fine dining' version.

Watching the people that I share my table with devour their food, I can't help but accost them—it turns out they're from Margao, a town 25 km away, and ride up on scooters at least once a week to eat here. According to them, it's the topmost in Goa in terms of value, quality and everything else. Unexpectedly, hence the best Goan food isn't found in big Panjim or on the beaches, but in the humdrum heart of a town that lacks other draws. What do you need tourist attractions for when you have Anantashram?

V

The Mahatma's Maharashtra
(Western India)

'Scarcely an American who comes to India goes away without seeing me.'

—Mahatma Gandhi to
The Hindu newspaper (1927)

Watson's Hotel where Mark Twain stayed on the top floor.

I wake up at Chhatrapati Shivaji station in Mumbai, a British-designed building that just has to be one of India's oddest UNESCO World Heritage monuments—I mean, a railway station?—and it's still in use, as lively as ever. If tourists could eat buildings with their selfie-cameras it would have been gobbled up long ago. However, right outside one can instead chew on the commuters' comfort bite, the city's beloved vada-pav to which the snack stalls around the station building are largely committed.

Although vada-pav is technically rather un-Indian—Portuguese-origin bread, filling of Latin American potatoes and chillies make it sound more like Hispanic tapas—the Internet considers this carb-rich energy-booster to be the soul of Mumbai and in 2023 it was ranked, by an online gourmet platform, as the #13 best sandwich of the world, way above any American cheesesteaks or lox-bagels. The snacky meal even rules the Indian skies as every self-respecting airline has vada-pav (though not at streetfood rates) on the menu.

Born in 1966 as a labourer's quick meal, the blobby chickpea batter-coated fritter of masalafied potato mash known as batata-vada, is stuffed in a Goan-style crusty but soft-hearted pav-bun, then tarted up with green coriander chutney and red-hot chillies.

As simple as it sounds the art of perfecting vada-pav takes eons to master. And hence one can only sample the real deal in the streets of Mumbai, where it rules the fast-food scene—or as that city's celebrated chronicler, Suketu Mehta, writes in *Maximum City,* it's 'the lunch of the *chawl* dwellers, the cart pullers, the street urchins; the clerks, the cops, and the gangsters'. According to newspaper articles, that may exaggerate matters, millions of vada-pav are eaten in town daily by everybody from regular workers to the greatest of Bollywood greats, which means basically anybody who doesn't go for the health-conscious option of getting their homely lunches brought by the city's ubiquitous dabbawallas.[23]

Now, the dabbawallas are another unparalleled food phenomenon. They predate modern restaurants, having gone into business in the 1880s, well before it was possible to get vada-pav or any other fast-food in town. The dabbawallas provided the fastest way to get lunch at work and until today their ingenious delivery chain process whizzes home-cooked meals (tiffin box lunches that wives prepare for their office-going husbands) from up to 70 km away without hardly ever mixing up the thousands of deliveries. The 5,000-man strong army are recognised by the *Guinness Book of World Records* for having been in operation for over a century with 99.99983 per cent accuracy.

Anyway, before the advent of vada-pav which the station area is justly famous for, the Victoria Terminus, as it used to be called, was the setting for Mulk Raj Anand's seminal 1940s working-class novel *Coolie*. As poet Adil Jussawalla, who used to be Anand's neighbour, reminisced in his essay 'The Reader as Tourist': 'With a few minor changes, the place Mulk described, the scene he drew, remains the same.' The nowadays highly offensive word 'coolie', a term used by British colonials for low-skilled day-labourers, indentured semi-slaves and porters who carried head-loads, is believed to derive from the hard-working *koli* fisherfolks. They conduct small-scale or 'artisanal' fishing, one could say, and are, I learn to my surprise, the original inhabitants of Mumbai—it is in fact after this aboriginal tribe that the upmarket Colaba is named, a corruption of the word *koliwada* or 'settlement of the *koli* caste fishermen'. Their name is also evident in the yummy prawns koliwada, that are coated in atomic-hot batter and fried village-style. From what I've read there are about half a million who live in *koli* fishing villages around Mumbai and supply daily catch to over one hundred fish markets, and another estimated half a million people are dependent on the fish trade.

Despite its glitzy bar scene, Colaba is also backpackerland and as usual I check into one of the many ex-hippie lodges, one of those that still dot the lanes in the shadow of the historic Taj Mahal Hotel, a bit like the seeker character in *The Razor's Edge* whose cruise ship docked for a few days in Bombay, and after having 'supper in a native eating-house' found that 'the coloured, noisy crowds, the smell of the East, acrid and aromatic, enchanted me' so, on an impulse, he decided to stay on and 'walked slowly back to the native quarter and looked about for a hotel. I found one after a while and took a room. I had the clothes I stood up in, some loose cash, my passport, and my letter of credit. I felt so free, I laughed out loud.'

Maugham of course didn't stay in 'the native quarter' but at the Yacht Club and narrates in *A Writer's Notebook* that while having lunch with a maharaja, he's asked if he knows the difference between the Yacht Club and the Bengal Club:

> *'No,' said I innocently.*
>
> *'In the Bengal Club at Calcutta they don't allow dogs or Indians, but in the Yacht Club at Bombay they don't mind dogs; it's only Indians they don't allow.'*

I couldn't for the life of me think of an answer to that then, and I haven't thought of one since.

The old Taj is where the spiritual Beatle, George Harrison, hard rock group Led Zeppelin and wealthier European authors on tour put up, like Graham Greene (who found inspiration for his novel *The Comedians* while staying there) and Alberto Moravia, and Italian film director Pier Paolo Pasolini who described it in *Scent of India* as 'riddled from one side to the other by corridors and high saloons (like seeing the inside of an enormous musical instrument)'. But it is way too expensive for me. Coincidentally, when E.M. Forster spent time in town in the early 1920s, he too shunned the Taj and preferred the downmarket Green's Hotel—located next-door to the Taj which it, in fact, predated. Apart from finding Green's affordable and less pompous, and not overtly sophisticated, Forster seems to have enjoyed the fact that it was louder and wilder, its clientele a mix of sailors, single ladies and gay gents, bohemian musicians, artists and writers (it was also a haunt of the afore-mentioned Mulk Raj Anand, for example).

Being notoriously mean, V.S. Naipaul too checked into the Green's and rather than spending on an airy sea-facing room picked a cheaper cockroach-infested one at the back, all the while complaining about how his travel agency-appointed guide, sent to receive him from the harbour, Apollo Bunder barely metres away, kept trying to strike a deal with him about 'cheej'. Naipaul of course knew no Hindi, so didn't understand that *chiz* means 'things' and that the 'shabby' Goan wanted to sell him bootlegged booze in lieu of the whiskey that the customs had confiscated. In his inimitable manner Naipaul heard what he wanted to—'cheese', he declared, 'was a delicacy in India. Imports were restricted, and the Indians had not yet learned how to make cheese.'

Naipaul's days were spent trying to find hygienic food and he genuinely despised his own choice of hotel: 'The bathrooms and lavatories are foul; the slimy woodwork has rotted away as a result of this daily drenching; the concrete walls are green and black with slime. You cannot complain that the hotel is dirty. No Indian will agree with you. Four sweepers are in daily attendance, and it is enough in India that the sweepers attend. They are not required to clean.'

Eventually, Green's was annexed by the Taj and, as it kept expanding, in the early 1970s, the modern high-rise extension was built in its place. Alexander Frater, who was *Chasing the Monsoon* (as the title of his book goes), had a better budget than Forster or Naipaul (or me), so he checked into the Taj to get a ringside view of the rains from the twentieth-floor bar. When it wasn't raining, the posh travel writer strolled around the Gateway of India, 'feeling the feathery touch of child beggars on my arms. I gave coins to one, who dashed off and handed them to a haggard, lank-haired crone squatting on the pavement nearby, suckling a baby. Her breast, though, was round and full and I realized she must still be in her twenties. Everything is relative, though in India relativity is geared to medieval expectations.'

Lunch box transportation is very important in Mumbai.

Heading further off than Frater did on his walks, I see fishing boats in a *koli* village, still located within walking distance from Colaba in the heart of the city. Here, ladies dry shrimp on the sidewalk between bus stops, and I instantaneously find myself in Salman Rushdie's *Midnight's Children*, 'follow Colaba Causeway to its tip—past cheap clothes shops and Irani restaurants and the second-rate flats of teachers, journalists and clerks—and you'll find them, trapped between the naval base and the sea.' Eulogising these aboriginals of Mumbai, Rushdie writes one of the most evocative sentences in his collected prose: 'They caught pomfret and crabs, and made fish-lovers of us all.'

Of interest to the literary tourist is the Sir J.J. School of Art, north of the Chhatrapati Shivaji station, as it happens to be the birthplace of Rudyard Kipling (whose father ran the school) who pipped Rabindranath Tagore by six years to become the first Indian-born Nobel laureate in 1907. The spot where the Kiplings lived is marked with a plaque, but the original shack in which he was born had been torn down by the time Kipling returned to work in India as a young man. This used to be the city's outskirts, dotted with palm groves and 'Rudy' rhymed his remembrances of the idyllic city in 'To the City of Bombay' (1896):

Mother of Cities to me
For I was born in her gate,
Between the palms and the sea,
Where the world-end steamers wait.

His two India novels *Jungle Book* and *Kim* capture how the country may have appeared at the end of the nineteenth century. The former is set in the forests of Seoni in easternmost Madhya Pradesh while the latter is a virtual travelogue tracing the Grand Trunk Road through north India.

The arts school is more or less across the street from another landmark: Mahatma Jyotiba Phule Mandai which was then called Crawford Market and where Kipling's father was in charge of decorations such as the artwork above the gates. The senior Kipling liked the town for being a 'cockney sort of place' that was very un-Indian. In his autobiography, *Something of Myself* written at the age of seventy, junior Kipling sentimentally recalled his first memory in life being 'early morning walks to the Bombay fruit market with my *ayah* and later with my sister in her perambulator, and of our returns with our purchases piled high on the bows of it.'

In his *India Impressions*, artist Walter Crane who came in the winter of 1906-7, noted how Crawford Market, 'has a rather English Gothic look, but inside the scene is entirely oriental, crowded with natives in all sorts of colours, moving among fish, fruit, grain, and provisions of all kinds, buying and selling amid a clamour of tongues—a busy scene of colour and variety, in a symphony of smells, dominated by that of the smoke of joss-sticks kept burning at some of the stalls as well as a suspicion of opium, which pervades all the native quarters in Indian cities.' But in Rohinton Mistry's novel *Such a Long Journey*, the market is depicted as charmless and nauseatingly menacing, 'a dirty, smelly, overcrowded place where the floors were slippery with animal ooze and vegetable waste, where the cavernous hall of meat was dark and forbidding, with huge, wicked-looking meat hooks hanging from the ceiling...' Sounds like he was trying to write a horror movie script, but in this oft-quoted passage Crawford Market represents the chaos of Mumbai. Unlike Mistry and his protagonist, I heroically poke my nose into stalls that sell almost everything edible from everywhere, finding imported pâté in a tin, cubes of meaty stock, and other ingredients to take home.

Crawford Market's bas-relief
decorations by Kipling Sr.

The insanely intense but colourfully cosmopolitan Mumbai of Saadat Hasan Manto lies a forty-five-minute walk north at Byculla. Spending a decade in town, before Partition drove him to Pakistan, Manto lived on Clare Road in the same building from where the weekly journal which he edited was published, and regularly ate at the semi-rundown canteen Sarvi (a prominent non-veg destination) where the house specialty is kainchi kebabs washed down with strong, milky half-glasses of 'cutting-chai'. Manto described the squalor of Byculla unflinchingly, 'an extremely dirty neighbourhood dotted with garbage heaps that served as an open toilet.' Nandita Das's 2018 film *Manto* was, on the other hand, mostly shot in the fancy and breezy Marine Lines, whereas the actual Byculla stood in for Pakistan where Manto died from cirrhosis of the liver in a mental asylum in 1955. Byculla market is described somewhat more appetisingly than Mistry's take on downtown's Crawford Market, by Kiran Nagarkar in his cult novel *Ravan & Eddie*: 'The vendors sat on raised platforms with stack upon stack of brinjals, cabbages, spinach, potatoes, onions, beans, pumpkins, melons, bananas, carrots, green beans and cucumbers on either side of them. But there was life under the platforms too, where the reserve stock was kept. Ravan was transfixed by a dwarf at eye level who was burrowing in a hole underneath. No, not a dwarf but a man on his haunches whose duck feet paddled him in and out of the dungeon. On his way out he brought forth an oversized, tumescent jackfruit in his hands.'

Another important spot is The Wayside—known in colonial days as 'A modern English Inn' when it was owned by an English lady—which became like a second home to poet Arun Kolatkar and other intellectuals. I still recall its red-and-white chequered tablecloths from my first visits in the 1990s that transported one to some time-warped utopia. In the 2000s, it lost its hipness and was reduced, last I saw it, to a hole-in-the-wall bakery counter.

Up the road, the disintegrating 1860s' cast-iron edifice of Watson's Hotel is sometimes named as the Indian film industry's birthplace; it's also where Richard Burton translated the *Kamasutra* that became notorious in English and Kipling stayed on visits to his birthplace; and Mark Twain—of *Huckleberry Finn* fame—rented a top-floor suite in the 1890s. Twain never set any fiction in India, but wrote on Mumbai in his travelogue *Following the Equator* something that I always have felt acutely about Indian cities: 'I seem to have a kaleidoscope at my eye;

and I hear the clash of the glass bits as the splendid figures change, and fall apart, and flash into new forms, figure after figure, and with the birth of each new form I feel my skin crinkle and my nerve-web tingle with a new thrill of wonder and delight.' The hotel closed in 1960 and the abandoned heritage structure is forlornly awaiting restoration.

At around the same time that Twain sat sipping tea on his balcony at Watson's, a young British-educated barrister, Mohandas Gandhi, tried to find work in Bombay where he wished to settle down. In 1891, he rented a small place in Girgaon from where he could walk to the High Court by the Maidan. The lack of job opportunities caused him to move to South Africa. Back again in 1902, Gandhi tried to set up a legal practice in Aga Khan's Buildings, near the High Court in what colloquially used to be known as the English Bazaar because of its businesses stocking foreign imports (now, it's the rather downmarket Nagindas Master Road). The cramped city affected his family's health so he shifted to a 'fine bungalow' at an unknown address in Santa Cruz from where he used to take the train to Churchgate station (built in the mid-1890s and so a spanking new building at the time), frequently being the only passenger in the commodious first-class compartment. But again Africa beckoned, where he got thrown off trains by racist conductors, and the rest is history.

In 1915, when the Mahatma-to-be landed at Apollo Bunder, at the cusp of becoming the best-known person in the world, he was interviewed by both *The Bombay Chronicle* and *The Times of India*. On return visits to town, such as 1924 after his first Pune jail stint, he recuperated in a borrowed house at Juhu Beach, walking by the ocean. After a wartime incarceration, he stayed in Juhu again in 1944; when the hosts learnt that he'd never seen a movie, they arranged a private screening of the then running B-flick *Mission to Moscow* (by the director of the classic *Casablanca*) and a mythological extravaganza called *Ram Rajiya* by Vijay Bhatt. Gandhi disliked both and didn't accept cinema with its half-clad heroines as a valid art form according to the book *Mahatma Gandhi in Cinema* by Narendra Kaushik; on his posthumously launched website www.mkgandhi.org, he goes on record—in an article titled *Gandhi on and in cinema* by Akul Tripathi—to state, 'I have never been to a cinema. But even to an outsider, the evil that it has done and is doing is patent. The good, if it has done any at all, remains to be proved.'

And it wasn't just Bollywood, but he, in fact, felt ambivalent about the whole city or as he said in 1921, 'Bombay is beautiful, not for its big buildings for most of them hide squalid poverty and dirt, not for its wealth for most of it is derived from the blood of the masses, but for its world-renowned generosity. The Parsis set the tone, and Bombay has ever lived up to her reputation. Bombay's charity has covered a multitude of her sins.'

It has also always been a city of poetry. Its gritty downtown fostered poets like Dom Moraes about whom many strange stories are told (for example, that he stepped out to buy cigarettes one day and then his wife never saw him again) and Namdeo Dhasal who lived near the Opera House, around the corner from Kamathipura, which has the reputation of being a red-light district. Writing his third book on India, *A Million Mutinies Now*, Naipaul visited the poet 'in the brothel area, among criminals and prostitutes...Namdeo's great originality was that he had written naturally, using words and expressions that Dalits and no one else used. In his first book of poems he had written, specifically, in the language of the Bombay brothel area. That had caused the sensation; he had been praised and condemned.'

Rather than reading Naipaul, I'd recommend *The Book of Chocolate Saints*—loosely based on the life of Dom Moraes—by Jeet Thayil that captures the once-vibrant poetry scene of the late 1900s, when city-based writers still remembered a scandalous 1960s visit by the American beats Allen Ginsberg and Peter Orlovsky. The foreign guests who were basically bumming around like the pre-hippie vagrants they frankly speaking were, on a round-the-globe trip from Paris to North Africa, and via India through Southeast Asia, landed like an alien invasion from a distant solar system. In 1962, the outwardly cool as a cucumber Ginsberg, who kept to vegetarian food in India, wrote to fellow author Gregory Corso about the cheap fare: 'Hardly been diarrhetic here even as much as Paris and I've really eaten the worst. Maybe I'm immune, immunised by Peru, Mexico, Tangier. But ritzy restaurants are cheaper than Tangier even. Bombay has great food all over...come here and have a ball in the greatest, weirdest nation of history.' Ginsberg also tried to convince Jack Kerouac and William Burroughs to join him, but only Gary Snyder turned up for that ball.

Back in the day, these poets habitually met up in so-called Irani joints that, despite the exotic nomenclature, rarely are run by migrants from Tehran. The first were set up around the year 1900 by Parsis, a small but influential community after whom many important streets are named and who, like Gandhi said, 'set the tone' for the city—including its eating-out-scene, it should be pointed out.

Fearing persecution for their Zoroastrian beliefs, they had originally fled from Persia when it was conquered by Muslims in the seventh century, to India's west coast where they found a safe haven. They moved to Bombay around the time it became British in the 1660s, to set up businesses and prospered thanks to their 'western' sensibilities. They ran, for example, many provision stores where the British preferred to shop. A second wave came when famine struck Persia in 1871 and the newcomers were experts at running lodging houses, refreshment rooms and tea stalls. Bombay's population of Zoroastrians peaked at 59,813 during the first half of the 1900s. They were renowned for their lavish hospitality and grand parties to celebrate all manner of occasions, so when they got into the food business, it was a win-win situation—the perhaps most notable outcome of which is the Taj Mahal Hotel that houses several iconic restaurants.

Being westernised, their cafés have a manifestly Mediterranean feel—one might be in Cairo or Istanbul if it wasn't for the food which combines Middle Eastern recipes with Indian spices. To fit in, they gave up beef but are still big on non-taboo meats like chicken and mutton, while their take on Western dishes, omelettes with chillies, pepper, garlic and onions, is notably spicier than in France whence the dish originated. This cultural adaptability, with menus that suited both Indians and foreigners alike, resulted in Parsi eateries kick-starting the restaurant industry. From having had barely any before 1900, save for the odd disreputable tavern catering to travellers, by mid-twentieth century, the city was home to hundreds of Irani cafés. While the original Parsis who have lived in India for more than a thousand years are called Zoroastrians, the later migrants are identified as Persians or Iranis. Hence the name Irani café.

However, in today's age of Punjabification of the food scene only about twenty remain, 'too inexpensively lovely to survive in modern Mumbai' to quote Suketu Mehta. Their cheap buttered buns had such thick crusts that they had to be soaked in chai, food suited for long discussions and hence an imperative part of art, music, and literature, nurturing generations of thinkers—for example I once spotted the living legend of Indian poetry, Adil Jussawalla, at the 1940s Irani café Stadium next to Churchgate Station.

These establishments are definitely worth visiting before they disappear, as they might well do with changing customer preferences in this epoch of cocktail lounges with App-based menus. One of the last to have retained its ambience largely untouched is the 1930s' vintage Cafe Military in Nagindas Master Road steps away from Flora Fountain, where Rushdie has been seen on visits to town and Arun Kolatkar, who didn't own a telephone, could be reached on Thursdays after his previous haunt, Wayside Inn, shut down—so that people knew where to find him. The airy restaurant takes one back to a time when real estate wasn't so expensive that tables had to be cramped together in boxy, low-ceilinged mini-halls. Here one could even dance between the tables, if it was permitted.

The name—Military—hints at the availability of non-veg, traditionally the diet for the warrior caste, *kshatriyas*, and the origin of 'military hotels' is believed to be found in the army messes that the Maratha forces set up across their domains. The concept of meat boosting physical strength and belligerence seems fairly universal, especially compared to how vegetarianism is such a non-violent activity. Here, one can still enjoy the unfashionable but classic atmosphere down to the spindly-legged black wooden chairs, panelled walls with big mirrors, odd notifications posted here and there, and linger for hours and write (or read), while sampling Parsi specials including breathtaking dhansak—imagine dhal boosted with juicy chicken—or freshly-cooked brain served whole, washed down with ice-cold London pilsner (despite its name a very local brew) or raspberry soda (which is only found in such olden places).[24] One cannot but love the café tables with yellow tablecloths, and the seediness lies in minor details such as the cheap plastic plates and pre-modern restroom.

Whenever I'm in Mumbai, I spend the full week at Cafe Military, reading and chatting, thinking and drinking. There I enjoy beering with Sidharth Bhatia, expert on Mumbai's cultural past with books on Bollywood noir and Indian rock to his credit. One day, he tells me all about how he showed his literary hero, the late H.R.F. Keating (1926-2011), around town—ironically in the 1980s, ages after Keating's award-winning first Bombay crime novel *A Perfect Murder* was published (in 1964). It is an interesting fact that the British detective novelist had written several novels about Inspector Ganesh V. Ghote without actually setting foot in the city that serves as an evocative tropical backdrop for his plots. He apparently picked the locale by flipping randomly through an atlas.

A Perfect Murder won both the Gold Dagger in the UK and the Edgar Allan Poe Award in the US, and was being made into a motion picture by Ismail Merchant, which is why Keating found himself in India—to do a cameo in it. The film also starred Naseeruddin Shah in the lead role.

'As I recall,' says Bhatia, 'he had a very striking beard, like George Bernard Shaw, and he appeared gentle, mournful but with a twinkle in his eye. He had this habit of blending in silently while moving about and I found him very pleasant.'

We try to reconstruct what else Keating experienced in town. Exactly how they came to meet is hard to say for Bhatia so many years later, but he suspects that somebody gave Keating his phone number because he's very much a Bombay boy, born in the mid-1950s at Hotel Astoria where his father—an avid reader of crime fiction (literature that his son went on to be deeply besotted by)—was a manager. Bhatia joined the *Free Press Journal* which had its offices in Dalal Street, so he was obviously a perfect cicerone for the foreign writer who wanted to be shown around downtown. Which is the favour that Keating asked of him.

Bhatia, being a fan, was happy to help. He's always felt that Mumbai is the perfect setting for detective novels, with its glamorous super-rich contrasting with the extremely poor, and once-sleazy areas like Colaba, with bars catering to sailors and cheap hotels full of hippies. 'This is a city made to be written about, but it has had no strong tradition of detective literature. It took Harry Keating to do it. Inspector Ghote is a superb character and in the absence of competition Keating did a fine job.'

To my question of how Keating managed to write about the city before he came here, Bhatia says, 'I understand that he studied Indian newspapers in the British Library, and I think he laid his hands on a police manual. He was also helped by a British adman who used to live here in the 1960s.'

Later, Bhatia takes me around the Kala Ghoda district where he and Keating walked all those years ago. He's knowledgeable about the buildings, the streets and which shops have been there for ages. 'I've always felt that the soul of the city is here. Kala Ghoda is a prime spot to set a murder mystery,' he says.

❖

'I have been a cook all my life. I began experimenting with my diet in my student days in London,' said Gandhi as he lectured residents at the Sevagram ashram in 1935. He had just relocated to the India of villages—a paradigm shift about which he felt strongly: 'Now we have embarked on a mission the like of which we had not undertaken before.' Then, eventually, he got to the point he wished to make that day regarding village reforms: 'Let us not, like most of them, cook anyhow, eat anyhow, live anyhow. Let us show them the ideal diet.' He proposed that his followers completely do away with spices and instead eat natural raw food, such as salad, while teaching the villagers to do the same—because boiling vegetables killed their vitamins. Exactly like the ancient Ayurvedic tradition, he believed in food's medicinal values.

Apart from the fact that uncooked food was practically unheard of in that era, it's interesting how Gandhi talked about vitamins. Their role in preventing illness and building health had been proposed by a Polish chemist only in the 1910s and it took much longer for vitamin researchers to win Nobel prizes. Already in the 1920s, Gandhi wrote, 'Vitamin means the vital essence. Chemists cannot detect it by analysis. But health experts have been able to feel its absence.'

Yet I can't envisage everybody salivating in joyful zeal as they listened to Gandhi that day. No masala in the curry? Uncooked food? I visualise jaws dropping and eyes popping. I suspect he wasn't entirely on to the medical benefits of certain seasonings like ginger, garlic, cardamom and turmeric, and so he went a bit overboard, but then a pioneer would probably need to do that.

This reminds me of how, about twenty-five years ago, on a train from Delhi to Kanyakumari, I broke journey midway. I had heard that Gandhi founded his ashram at Sevagram for the precise reason that it was located geographically in the centre of India, and so it seemed appropriate to take a break. The railway station was empty and I was the sole passenger alighting. The only things moving in the quiet heat were dry leaves rustling before a feeble breeze. Outside, stood a lone cycle rickshaw. No hotel in sight. It was an even more unassuming village in the 1930s when Gandhi moved in and he was particular about not making it any more assuming than it was, instructing his helpers that to build his hut 'as little expense as possible should be incurred'.

I approached the rickshaw-puller and not being conversant in Marathi, I showed him a banknote with Gandhi on it. He knew who I had come for and cycled me to the ashram where he directed me to enter. I was planning to look into the museum, then carry on to the nearest town, Nagpur, to spend the night, but before I could do so an elderly ashramite spotted me carrying my luggage, told me to follow and we passed Gandhi's simple hut made of eco-friendly materials like clay, a pipal tree planted by 'Bapu' as per a small sign (he preferred not to be called Mahatma) and we reached the guesthouse where political leaders like Jawaharlal Nehru used to stay when they wished to consult with him. I was shown a roomy room where I could stay for as long as I liked. The cot was of 1930s vintage, so every visiting celebrity must have slept in it back in those days, and there were no mod-cons. But the rent was extremely cheap, so I had no complaints. I was instructed to make myself comfortable and then join the others for supper. It was the strangest thing I had ever experienced as a frequent traveller—they didn't ask me who I was, how long I planned to stay: I was simply made to feel at home.

This 'village of service' turned into a laboratory for Gandhi as it attracted all manner of creative engineers and assorted experts who researched ecological living, devising everything from lanterns that burned vegetable waste oil instead of fossil fuel to potties that automatically segregated what was evacuated from the bowels into fertiliser and manure. Important people who arrived at the station were picked up by what Gandhi jokingly called his 'Oxford'—a broken Ford car pulled by oxen.

And then there was the alimentary mission. Despite his

asceticism and frequent fasting, Gandhi was by no means against food. He was merely keen on making the most of a precious resource. For example, later in that first year at Sevagram—1935—he advocated the daily consumption of soybeans which are more nutritious than meat and have marvellous health benefits. In a series of articles in his journal *Harijan*, he described them as what today would be called a 'super-food'; in fact, in the first half the twentieth century, soybeans were a fairly ignored foodstuff in the West and only rose to prominence as a 'vegan meat' quite recently, so clearly Gandhi saw something that many others missed.

He also introduced novelties to the village such as sugarcane cultivation and bee-keeping, which suggests that sweet teeth weren't frowned upon. Under his leadership, the ashram produced marmalades from seasonal fruits and peanut butter, and bread was made from home-ground, coarse, unsifted wheat in order to keep it fibre-rich. Gandhi even developed his own coffee substitute (he was against caffeine and other stimulants) from dark-roasted wheat. Generally, the fare seems to have been akin to what we'd encounter in the finest amongst urban India's new-fangled organic stores today.

After a bath, I headed for the dining hut. Meals were strictly timed (dinner at 5.30 p.m. as I recall) and the sun hung low on the horizon as I walked towards the hut. Food was had together, as Gandhi usually kept an eye on how much everyone ate—it was his belief that most don't know what's healthy for them and so ate themselves sick, or as he had written in a series of articles on health in 1913: 'All will agree that out of every 100,000 persons 99,999 eat merely to please their palate, even if they fall ill in consequence. Some take a laxative every day in order to be able to eat well, or some powder to aid digestion....some die of thoughtless overeating.'

Humans compared unfavourably to cows in this regard: 'Cattle do not eat for the satisfaction of the palate, nor do they eat like gluttons. They eat when they are hungry—and just enough to satisfy that hunger. They do not cook their food. They take their portion from that which Nature proffers to them. Then, is man born to pander to his palate?' He also pointed out, in a characteristically humoristic remark, that 'we have turned our stomach into a commode and we carry this commode with us wherever we go.'

On another occasion, he emphasised, 'Instead of using the body as a temple of God we use it as a vehicle for indulgences, and are not ashamed to run to medical men for help in our effort to increase them and abuse the earthly tabernacle.'

Therefore, it's not surprising that I wasn't asked for any preferences, but simply served chapattis, a boiled vegetable hotchpotch featuring home-grown beetroots, and a modest salad of raw, plain veggies. The only spice I could make out was salt. Basic but kind of interesting—and it reflected the Gandhian ideals of having food as if it were a medicine 'to keep the body going.' Apart from prayers before food, there was strictly no talking according to ashram rules, 'Silence is obligatory at meals. It is uncivil and a form of violence to criticize while eating any badly cooked item of the food. Such criticism should be conveyed to the manager in writing after the meal.'

Later, as I'm looking up minutes by visitors back in the day, I find that the menu has not changed significantly. During his lifetime, Gandhian cookery was considered truly spaced out as gastronomic experiences go: 'Steaming hell-brew served up in a great bucket' reads one contemporary Englishman's description of the 'ashramatic' menu, related in Ramachandra Guha's biography of Verrier Elwin, *Savaging the Civilized*. Elwin spent a month with Gandhi in 1931 and even jotted down a poem titled 'Thoughts of a Gourmet on being Confronted with an Ashram Meal': 'O food inedible, we eat thee/ O drink incredible, we greet thee./ Meal indigestible, we bless thee.'

Another foreigner wondered, after being fed the same mush of pumpkins cooked in spinach day after day, whether he might possibly look forward to trying something different for lunch.

Gandhi asked, 'You do not like vegetables?'

'It's just that I don't like the taste of the same vegetables three days in a row.'

Gandhi pondered this and suggested, 'Try adding plenty of salt and lime.'

A more articulate and rationalistic critique was framed in 1915 by Gandhi's own son Harilal, then twenty-six years of age, and who'd later go on to take a very different path from his father's. A letter of his suggests that Gandhi was not, for example, always into salty food: 'I cannot believe that a salt-free diet or abstinence from ghee or milk indicates strength of character and morality. If one decides to refrain from consuming such foods as a result of thoughtful consideration, the abstinence could be beneficial. It is seen that such abstinence and asceticism is possible only after one has attained a certain state. By insisting on salt-free diet and on specific abstinences, at the Phoenix institution [Gandhi's ashram in South Africa], you are trying to cultivate self-denial.'

The Bengal-born author Nirad Chaudhuri, in his autobiographical tome *Thy Hand, Great Anarch!*, described Gandhi's visit to Kolkata thus: 'Putting up Gandhi did not present a difficult problem; feeding him did. Mahatma Gandhi's dietary prescriptions were not only rigid and numerous, but also odd.' A list of the vegetables that Gandhi approved of 'was formidably long and representative of the ecology of Bengal. Of course, he did not eat the full range of vegetables at one meal or even on one single day, but he or his secretary in charge might demand one or other of them on a particular day or for a particular meal in order to test the resources and loyalty of his host.'

For modern holidaymakers, the ashram in Sevagram might not compare with a beach resort in Bali, but I actually considered staying on for some days, thinking that I'd shed many kilograms of excess flab and trot home nimble as a goat. Thanks to the light and early meal, I slept well, except for the occasional mosquitoes that I didn't dare to swat so as not to break any non-violence regulations. Anyway, the wake-up call was at 4 a.m. for prayers, just as when Gandhi was still around, so going early to bed turned out to be a sensible strategy. Next, I was told to spend my morning weeding a patch of grass behind the latrines. Following a simple 6 a.m. breakfast, there was mandatory spinning for two hours—a calming exercise akin to meditation.

The author as tourist at the Mahatma's ashram in Sevagram.

Today, as we're used to health pages in newspapers, and every magazine with some instinct as to what sells carries cover stories on wellness and the latest dietary fads, we may note that in this field, too, Gandhi was a forerunner, devoting much space in the journals he published to health. His biggest bestseller during his lifetime wasn't the autobiographical *The Story of My Experiments with Truth*, but a booklet called *A Guide to Health* which was full of interesting cooking instructions. It was constantly reprinted and translated into many languages in India and abroad. Other titles by him that might fascinate modern readers include *The Moral Basis for Vegetarianism* and *Diet and Diet Reform*. Gandhian nutritional principles, were I to attempt to sum them up after reading all that he wrote on the subject, are based on the notion that everybody must know how to cook their own food or even better not cook at all but eat it raw—which in turn, calls for simplicity and the avoidance of complex culinary methodology, something that's increasingly catching on nowadays and is perhaps best reflected in those mix-your-own salad bars that dot many cities in conventionally non-veg territories like California and Scandinavia.

Secondly, by wholesome eating, one eliminates the need for going to doctors and pill-popping—again, a fairly obvious idea to us, but we may recall how not so long ago everybody (including myself) happily wolfed down oily-spicy gravies without thinking of the physical consequences. Or as Gandhi put it: 'I believe that man has little need to drug himself. 999 cases out of a thousand can be brought round by means of a well-regulated diet...' Gandhi's own awakening in this regard happened, as he described it, during his English student days when he, out of financial necessity, learnt how to prepare his own food. Also, there were important social considerations as he found his first English friends among the members of the London Vegetarian Society.

Vegetarianism was a philosophical idea for this movement (in the 1800s when 'isms', whether political, spiritual or otherwise, were the in-thing) and the restaurants backed by the movement were more of public clubs where the young Gandhi found a platform for his personal ideological development—as well as plenty of literature that argued for the benefits of a meatless diet. 'I saw that the writers on vegetarianism had examined the question very minutely, attacking it in its religious, scientific, practical and medical aspects.' Prior to this, for the young Gandhi vegetarianism had been a habit more than a conscious choice—after all he came from India's most vegetarian state, Gujarat.

Boldly, he clarified to his new English friends that 'Indian vegetarians and meat-eaters are quite different from English vegetarians and meat-eaters. Indian meat-eaters, unlike English meat-eaters, do not believe that they will die without meat. So far as my knowledge goes, they (the Indian meat-eaters) do not consider meat a necessity of life but a mere luxury. If they can get their roti, as bread is generally called there, they get on very well without their meat. But look at our English meat-eater; he thinks that he *must* have his meat. Bread simply helps him to eat meat, while the Indian meat-eater thinks that meat will help him to eat his bread.'

Once he found his feet among like-minded folks, the movement proved as edifying an experience as studying law. 'Vegetarianism was then a new cult in England, and likewise for me, because, as we have seen, I had gone there a convinced meat-eater, and was intellectually converted to vegetarianism later. Full of the neophyte's zeal for vegetarianism, I decided to start a vegetarian club in my locality, Bayswater. I invited Sir Edwin Arnold, who lived there, to be Vice-President,' he notes in one of his autobiographies. Sir Arnold was, apart from a confirmed Indophile, also editor of *The Daily Telegraph* and so a useful contact. Soon, Gandhi was reporting on Indian food culture in journals such as *The Vegetarian*. 'Diet cure or hygiene is a comparatively recent discovery in England. In India we have been practising this from time out of mind,' he wrote as cockily as only a twenty-one-year-old can do.

It should be pointed out that this juvenile journalistic experience laid the foundation for his lifelong interest in print media as a tool for spreading ideas. In an article published in England in 1891, he pointed out that 'attributing the Hindu weakness to vegetarianism is simply based on a fallacy', and later, that same year, he wrote that 'it is a pity that so little should be known of the foods of India in England. We have not to go very far to seek the cause. Almost all Englishmen who go to India keep up their own way of living. They not only insist on having the things they had in England, but will also have them cooked in the same way. It is not for me here to go into the why and wherefore of all these incidents. One would have thought that they would look into the habits of the people, if only out of curiosity, but they have done nothing of the kind...'

Having encountered all manner of health theories, he would for the rest of his life go on bravely experimenting with food—diets such as fasting, vital foods, raw foods, no-starch (essentially a precursor of what was to evolve into the even more specialised gluten-free diet of today), milkless (a precursor of lactose-free), sugarless and pickle-free eating, and fruitarianism—as much as he experimented with truth. Now and then projects had to be abandoned as they caused depression, headaches, dysentery and discomfort to such a degree that he could barely stand on his feet. Chewing on hard, uncooked grains broke his teeth. He was well aware of his own folly and once even burst out, 'But what a sacrifice of time and trouble to achieve what is after all a selfish end, which falls short of the highest! Life seems too short for these things.' His son Harilal certainly doubted his fads and questioned these in letters to the Mahatma: 'If my own experience or experiment of being a fruitarian for only twenty days has any validity, I speak with experience—I have also observed this characteristic among those who were fruitarians for six months—that people eat fruits and nuts far in excess to even those who overeat roti and dhal. Therefore, indigestion is bound to happen. Under such circumstances I see no benefits in adopting a fruit diet.'

Nevertheless, despite occasional doubts and criticism from kin and acolytes, Gandhi developed over the years a plan which, according to him, would be the best for mankind. Free from external beauty perhaps, compared to the cuteness of pre-plated *nouvelle cuisine* (only the austere portion sizes do remind one of that nineties food fad), unadorned by sumptuous seasonings and maximised masalas, it was the most functional eating strategy imaginable—and it is, naturally, vegetarian fare rich in fruit. 'A comparison with other animals reveals that our body structure most closely resembles that of fruit-eating animals, that is, the apes. The diet of the apes is fresh and dry fruit. Their teeth and stomach are similar to ours.' The target, as per his calculations, was to cut down ingredients and dishes—one itemised sample menu from 1935 that he planned for village workers contained the following: Wheat flour baked into chapattis, tomatoes, red gourd, soybeans, coconuts, linseed oil, milk, tamarind and salt, and then some jaggery and wood apple combined into a 'delicious chutney'.

Already in 1929, he had described how a scientific ahimsa cuisine can 'reduce the dietetic himsa that one commits.' He pointed out: 'Dieticians are of opinion that the inclusion of a small quantity of raw vegetables like cucumber, vegetable marrow, pumpkin, gourd, etc., in one's menu is more beneficial to health than the eating of large quantities of the same cooked.

But the digestions of most people are very often so impaired through a surfeit of cooked fare that one should not be surprised if at first they fail to do justice to raw greens, though I can say from personal experience that no harmful effect need follow if a tola or two of raw greens are taken with each meal provided one masticates them thoroughly.' Gandhi's own food intake, for much of his adult life, consisted of fixed quantities of grains like sprouted wheat, grated veggies, 40 g of fat and a similar measure of sugar or honey, and fruit. In 1934, he gave instructions to supporters who wished to host him on his tours, 'Fried things and sweets must be strictly eschewed. Ghee ought to be most sparingly used. More than one green vegetable simply boiled would be regarded as unnecessary. Expensive fruit should be always avoided.'

For any gourmand this may sound off-putting, especially in a hedonistic panegyric like this book of mine, but experts will agree that a certain frugality might actually heighten the eating experience almost à la molecular gastronomy. In fact, what Gandhi advocated would nowadays—when most of us are BP-afflicted diabetics—be considered a preferable fare and, for ethical reasons, food ought anyway to be grown in the vicinity entailing a minimal carbon footprint for its transportation. This emphasis on fresh home-grown ingredients is embraced by chefs who see the ridiculous in, say, flying salmon from Norway to Goa where there's so much fish available. Above all, the way he explored the relationship between eating and health in an age when the concept of 'health food' was unknown to most, unlike today when we know that food habits can kill or cure, gave me plenty of—what else—food for thought. Or to quote Gandhi after one of his communal dietary adventures, 'The experiment is not an easy thing nor does it yield magical results. It requires patience, perseverance and caution. Each one has to find his or her own balance of the different ingredients. Almost every one of us has experienced a clearer brain power and refreshing calmness of spirit.'

❖

Under the Ellis Bridge in Ahmedabad, a man is selling half a vacuum cleaner. I'd heard that Gujaratis are shrewd businessmen and this one ought to have an interesting marketing strategy if he comes here every Sunday to sell pieces that lack either hose or engine or both.

Despite its chronic dustiness, because of which vacuum cleaners may be treasured possessions, the city has plenty that might appeal to the semi-professional tourist: Museums for textiles and antiques, assorted Islamic monuments, and not one, but two of Mahatma Gandhi's abodes. The more visited is the

Ahmedabad: Gandhi's room and belongings at Kochrab Ashram, which was his first home when he returned to India from Africa.

Gandhi Smarak Sangrahalaya by the Sabarmati riverfront which is a major sight. The older, at Kochrab, is a surprisingly neat and quiet edifice, where I'm the only tourist when I explore it.

Gandhi first came to Ahmedabad in 1887 to take the entrance test to Bombay University. In those days, there was no railway from Rajkot to Ahmedabad, so he had to go by bullock cart, and it was his first visit to a big city. Ahmedabad had over 100,000 inhabitants then—he was impressed by the grandeur of everything, but unfortunately didn't do well in the test. He came 404th and scored a mere 89 out of 200 in English.

More well-documented is Gandhi's later and longer stay at Sabarmati Ashram, which he established as his permanent base in 1917, conveniently next-door to the Sabarmati Jail, which Gandhi jokingly referred to as the ashram branch (apart from Gandhi's occasional imprisonments, the jail housed many of his sympathisers too). He would go on to spend about thirteen years at the ashram and this is also where he began writing *The Story of My Experiments with Truth*. It was from here that the Salt March marched—quite symbolically—in the month of March in 1930, to break the Salt Law (a tax that had made Indian cooking prohibitively expensive especially for the poor). Gandhi vowed not to live again in the ashram unless India became independent—after which he returned to Ahmedabad now and then, never for long. Some 200 families descended from the original ashramites still inhabited the premises until the 2020s.

Many of the whitewashed buildings date from Gandhi's days—including the frugal Hriday Kunj where he lived. He is said to have slept mostly on the veranda out in front while inside, I view his spectacles, sandals, some spinning yarn and other belongings. The main museum-cum-memorial building—that holds a massive amount of important correspondence and photographs—was designed by world-renowned Goan-origin architect Charles Correa as one of his first big projects, inaugurated by Jawaharlal Nehru in 1963. Afterwards, Correa became known as one of the greatest thinkers in the field of city-planning—he believed in organic architecture and just a few years before he passed away, I had the opportunity to chat with him.

He pointed out that cities should not have highly fixed infrastructure (like metros unfortunately and increasingly do) because they must remain dynamic enough to adapt to people's needs. I thought it was a brilliant observation that countered the idea of how we always end up adjusting to where we live, rather than the other way around, so it has stayed with me up to now and…ah, well, I'll stop rambling and return to my narrative…so after I cover the important sights, I still have a Sunday left and decide to hang out in my hotel—House of M.G.,which in itself counts as among the city's finest sights. Located at the edge of the old town near Lal Darwaza, it is a 1924 mansion with labyrinthine corridors, museum-like halls and terraces worth a meander—dotted as they are with old-style wooden swings and nooks and crannies where one can feel at peace. By the way, the initials 'M.G.' do not stand for Mahatma Gandhi, but for the erstwhile owner Mangaldas Girdhardas, a textile baron who was Gandhi's contemporary.

At its acclaimed roof terrace 'renowned as one of the best—if not the best—restaurants in Gujarat' (according to *The Penguin Food Guide to India* by Charmaine O'Brien), I sample Gujarat's priciest thali which gives visitors the state on a platter, including tons of snacky fried gram flour starters or farsan that are so fundamental to the Gujarati diet, followed by fluffy lentil-and-rice cakes called dhoklas, crunchy kachoris, spicy chaats and invigorating salads, topped by unlimited helpings of mains or shaaks that change daily. That day, these included bateka (a potato curry), kadhi (besan balls in yoghurt curry), fansi (beans preparation), turiya patra (gourd with colocasia leaves), mag nimogar dhal (dry lentil preparation), a couple of different rustic breads, ghee-laced khichdi and dhal (cooked with cane sugar giving the standard lentil stew a luxurious taste), alongside freshly-churned buttermilk, lemon-honey-ginger juice as well as several sweetmeats and homemade fig ice-cream. *Wah!* The lightly-curried and jaggery-sweetened dhal can be a bit of a culture-shock for someone sampling Gujarati food for the first time, but it is said that Gujaratis love eating, so to fit in I polish off everything served on my silver platter.

House of M.G. sits just around the corner from the old town and it would seem a pity not to explore the area with its shops that spill out merchandise into the roads and snack stalls tempting passers-by with intriguing street-foods ranging from cheesy pineapple sandwiches to massive ice-lollies in every colour of the rainbow. Although I know plenty of scary tales about 'Delhi-belly' nobody I know has complained of 'Ahmedabad-abdomen' so in the junk-food alley adjacent to the Teen Darwaza gate, I have kebabs so luscious that I order two more plates (to counterbalance the pure-veg fare at my pure-veg hotel). It was after licking clean the plates of meaty juices that I came across the weekly flea market—by following the trail of Sunday shoppers drifting towards the Sabarmati riverfront by the Ellis Bridge. They all knew something that isn't mentioned in the tourist guidebooks. On the riverbank, traders had set up makeshift counters or laid out tarpaulins for their wares almost all the way to the next bridge downriver.

There are many great flea markets in India—such as Mumbai's 'Chor Bazaar' and Anjuna beach in Goa—but the one in Ahmedabad is the largest of its kind. In fact, it's bigger than the flea markets I've seen in New York, Shanghai, Copenhagen,

Harare and Reykjavik put together and the ultimate place to procure a second-hand treadmill or vintage radio set, a broken laptop or rusty nail, padlocks without keys or keys missing locks, live animals like goats and chicks, a handmade kebab grill (obviously with rather few takers in this vegetarian state), cheap crockery and pottery, empty liquor bottles (remember, Gujarat is a dry state), books for kids and adults and ultra-low-cost garments or machine parts, all in a brutal jumble that gives the refuse of a megacity one last chance to reincarnate as the property of new owners. It's a thought-provoking contrast to the sophisticated selection of period knickknacks that decorates my hotel's corridors.

The customers, too, are an intriguing mix of teenagers and geriatrics on weekend outings, peasants and townspeople, and jhola-carrying arts students foraging for stuff to incorporate into installations of 'found art'. Once I'm done browsing, I ask the broken-vacuum-cleaner-seller who buys them.

'Nobody.'

'Then why sell?'

'Why not?'

Well, ain't that true? Instead, I buy a remote control—there are different models on sale at his stall, handheld units that have been long separated from whatever they were meant to steer. I'm not exactly sure what I can do with it except that it's definitely lighter to carry home than half a vacuum cleaner.

VI

Regal Repasts and Partaking of the Past
(Royal India)

'India is full of such wonders, but she can't give them to me.'

—E.M. Forster in a letter from 1913
(after visiting Ujjain)

Painted haveli in Churu.

A 180-m-tall colossus shimmers on the horizon. A bespoke desert mirage?

No, it's the Alila Bishangarh. Superimposed on a 230-year-old warrior fort standing on a dramatic granite hillock, the hotel appears to guard a remote valley in the Aravalli range, in the heart of Rajasthan. Architecturally, it blends the Jaipuri with Mughal and a dash of cinematic Disneyland. As the bucolic road winds closer, it suddenly turns up to my left, then I glimpse it to the right again, as if it were tracking my approach—its strategic importance becoming quite obvious in a region crisscrossed by trade routes of eternal antiquity.

In the chilled-out arrival lounge away from the desert heat there's no reception counter, no A&D register to fill out. I get a glimpse into the future of hospitality as a staffer takes a shot of my ID with his cellphone and a laptop-wielding lady hands me a printout of my leisure plan including meals, cocktails, massages and excursions. There's nothing for me to do but flip the switch into pause mode. In my three decades of reviewing hospitality ventures for travel publications, I've never ever flowed so smoothly into place—like champagne poured into a flute—and before I know it, I'm set as a curd.

The fort is a maze in which it is really easy to lose one's way.

But that's how it is with traditional structures; one can't expect too many straight corridors, one must just adjust and relax. I'm staying in a suite that's been shaped to fit within the two-and-a-half-metre-thick, towering walls—due to constructional constraints most suites have different layouts, like pieces of a jigsaw puzzle. Mine has a circular bedroom within a south-facing watchtower from where I keep an eye on green parakeets somersaulting in the breeze. The handy hotel handbook catalogues, apart from the usual in-room meal menus, policies regarding environmental efforts (waste minimisation, energy conservation, anti-global warming) and social sustainability (such as employing villagers or growing veggies with recycled water). I almost expect to find Greenpeace sailing in the tub when I prepare to have a bath.

There's an overall localised sensibility which is easy to appreciate. The rooftop restaurant serves the robust cuisine of the Bishangarh hamlet and the Shekhawati region, where the cooking is done like hunters of yore used to, with meats buried in hot sandpits, simmering in their own juices and fats (quite a practical idea in waterless deserts), the way brave heroes have always slow-roasted whatever mammal their arrows hit. Hunting may these days only be done illegally, but the shikar preparations remain in fashion for nostalgic reasons and illustrate, some believe, how dum-pukht was born. It all conspires to make one feel that one is really in a special place—and not in any run-of-the-mill luxury hotel whose chefs are cluster-bombing diners with multicuisine.[25] The first morning, for breakfast, I order genial millet parathas, tomato-chilli sabzi, and buttermilk, all of which reflects a typical farmer's morning meal cobbled together from rural staples. It is almost too good to be true, but it is true.

As for daytime activities, guests are taken to visit the village silversmith, then a lady who weaves carpets by hand, next a potter, and a farmer's wife named Daya cooks me a wholesome lunch with local vegetables and bakes ghee-enriched millet flatbreads over wood-fire in her courtyard. Much of the food has been grown in a patch behind the house. In the evening, I cool down in the castle's war room which is now a bar room with a cigar lounge in a turret. There, I am served an alluring snack menu that the barman calls 'Indian tapas': Pickle-powered watermelon *sashimi*, tofu cooked in chai, hummus of mashed green peas powdered with wasabi and flax seeds served with khakra crisps. Talk about thinking…no, eating out of the box.

It took Rahul Kapur and his two co-owners ten years of work to set it all up. Kapur tells me, over a cuppa at the airy infinity poolside Mediterranean café, 'There was no access road to the fort when we took it over, so we had to climb up to the ruin that was inhabited by a million bats. We found it very intriguing so we thought let's do something. But how do you take construction materials up a hill like that?'

I shrug. *No idea.*

'I became the proud owner of twenty-two donkeys. But once I had loaded them, I stood down here and tried to push them up there,' he says with a laugh.

Donkeys aren't cooperative animals or so I've heard, but I decide not to say, 'I could have told you so.'

'So, I had to hire four donkey drivers!'

Clearly, Kapur wanted to avoid damaging the existing structure or the cliff it rested on, so the property was handcrafted painstakingly with limited use of heavy machinery. He converted the ruined parts into common areas and added three floors of modern rooms on top. It's hard to imagine the complexities of putting in elevators within the rambling structure and incorporating knolls of bedrock into the design.

'We tried to make the new parts look like they were already there from before. To keep the ethos of the place, we used local stone rather than imported marble.'

'Must have still cost a bomb?'

'More than money, our hearts and souls went into this.'

Alila Bishangarh blends new hotel with old bastions almost seamlessly.

On my first trip into Rajasthan way back in 1991, I recall ending up in a nondescript township called Bundi, where one hundred years earlier Rudyard Kipling is believed to have got the idea for his novel *Kim*. Although he held Rajputs in high esteem in a general sense, Kipling had his doubts about Bundi which he ranked as the worst place he'd ever been to:

'There is no order to sell fishing-hooks, or to supply an Englishman with milk, or to change currency notes for him. He must only deal with the Durbar for whatever he requires; and wherever he goes he must be accompanied by at least two armed men. They will tell him nothing, for they know or affect to know nothing of the city. They will do nothing except shout at the little innocents who joyfully run after the stranger and demand *pice*, but there they are, and there they will stay till he leaves the city, accompanying him to the gate, and waiting there a little to see that he is fairly off and away. Englishmen are not encouraged in Boondi.'

I tried my best to walk in Kipling's footsteps but instead of encountering 'little innocents' a bunch of nasty children threw camel turds at me. In spite of this, I decided to linger, having chanced upon Braj Bushanjee—former prime-ministerial mansion, or haveli, now a lodge run by descendants of the minister. As I was served a lightly-spiced vegetarian thali on the rooftop, the proprietor explained that he mainly received busloads of European tour groups. I got a quirky room that hadn't been modernised much. Entering the bathroom, I smashed my head into the low doorframe. I saw stars. Each and every time.

I continued my onward journey with a potato-lumpy head full of bumps. But the stay became an eye-opener. Rajasthan has always been India's #1 inbound tourist destination, but it was only really in the post-liberalisation economy that its many grand heritage structures became hospitality hotspots. Take for example Rohetgarh—founded in 1622 and about an hour's drive from Jodhpur. It's one of the world's loveliest outback lodges. It appears that Rao Jodha, the builder of Jodhpur, had a brother, Dalpat Singh, who became the Thakur of Rohet. His clan has been, from then on, among the prominent breeders of Marwari battle horses—which are considered as important to the Rajput's self-image as the electric guitar is to a rock star's career. Those purebred Marwari horses are actually still there in a stable, waiting to take hotel guests on a safari or a picnic. For true horse-lovers, there's even one room with a panoramic window opening into the stable so that you and the horses can keep an eye on each other.

After independence, the noblemen had to look for other job options outside feudal careers and so the then Thakur of Rohet village, Manvendra Singhji Rathore, became a history teacher at Mayo College in Ajmer. In the 1980s, he met a twenty-something English writer who was desperately looking for a quiet room in which to sit and write, something that seemed not to be readily available at the time, so being hospitable, Singhji put him up for a couple of months. The writer was Bruce Chatwin and the book he wrote, *The Songlines*.

I later checked for further details in Nicholas Shakespeare's biography, in which Rohetgarh is described as a 'writer's paradise' for Chatwin who wrote long letters home praising his marvellous accommodation (and host). Towards the end of the 1980s, at the cusp of liberalisation, the pioneering Thakur decided to open up his home as a hotel and one of the first guests was William Dalrymple, who promptly checked into Chatwin's room (suite #15 if you must know) 'where, in a desperate bid for inspiration, I started the manuscript [of *City of Djinns*] at the desk where Bruce Chatwin wrote *The Songlines*.' Other writers who have worked in the same suite include Simon Winchester and Patrick French.

I can understand why, as writers are superstitious people. But as I don't particularly want this book to sound like its written by one of them, I prefer to stay in a different room. Despite the fact that the family now runs three hotels with a total of fifty-one rooms, their hallmark remains homeliness. The staff is hired mainly from the village, some have worked at the fort for decades, advancing their careers from room boys to chefs. The late Thakurani wrote two cookbooks about the family's kitchen and her daughter-in-law carries on the tradition of good food—there's even a demo kitchen for tourists who want to learn how to prepare heirloom dishes and house specials. I get to sample the robust fare favoured for centuries such as dhal-baati, essentially another hunters' dish of sand-roasted and ghee-drizzled bread balls, eaten with Rajasthani dhal and with it comes an exceedingly succulent laal-maas—literally, 'red meat' in a thick hot gravy made redder by a generous amount of chillies from the Jodhpur region.

Converting palaces and havelis into hotels has become something of a noble hobby—and is probably the best way to preserve these properties for the future. Eminent examples include the majestic fourteenth-century Neemrana fort, considered a path-breaking restoration project, and Jodhpur's super-chilled-out ultra-boutique Raas Haveli which impressed me with its organic design: The moment I floated into its oasis of calm in an otherwise manic city, I sincerely hoped that some form of discernment radiated from my puffy and desert-grime-covered face. The transition, as I passed the unobtrusive reception and entered into the yard where various antique structures serve as chic restaurant, spa block and heritage suites respectively, was absolutely stunning. The high walls dampen the outside noise and a cool Lou Reed song, later followed by Edith Piaf, played discreetly from ambient speakers spread across the 1.5-acre property. I wondered if I'd hear Nirvana next or simply hit nirvana.

I lifted my gaze and right above me, almost so close that I felt I could reach out and touch it, was the high cliff on which Rao Jodha planted the strikingly massive Mehrangarh citadel in 1459, one of Asia's genuinely iconic edifices and every guest room has a view of it. Rooms are all utterly ultramodern, again a stark contrast to the outside world. The floors and beds are all black hand-polished terrazzo, the walls are made of hand-cut rosy sandstone slabs, the balcony is equipped with an ingenious sliding sandstone jaali screen. Interestingly, the fancy furniture dotting the property isn't imported but made for the hotel from salvaged teakwood by a Jodhpur-based carpenter. But when the hotel proprietors bought this haveli, which used to be the city residence of the Thakurs of Ras village, it was a debris-covered ruin that practically had to be excavated.

It's a long, winding road to Churu town, 200 km north of Jaipur. There are an estimated 2,000 painted havelis spread across dusty Shekhawati towns like Ramgarh, Jhunjhunu, Mandawa and Nawalgarh, but most are locked up as the owners, well-heeled trading families that constructed them as proof of their worldly success, have settled in metros across the world.

Malji ka Kamra was built by an enormously prosperous merchant to entertain noble guests such as the Maharaja of Bikaner, who frequently made an overnight halt here on his way to imperial Delhi. But at the turn of the millennium, all that remained was a looted, squatted ruin, and that's when two brothers who own petrol pumps pooled together money with a friend and bought the mansion in 2004. They restored it over a period of six years.

The chambers where visitors slept then, are now enchanting guestrooms, which carry the original, albeit timeworn, frescoes from the 1920s. I check into suite #205 where the vaulted ceilings are entirely covered in curious paintings depicting VIPs and city scenes. Staying here is like living in an Indian version of the Sistine Chapel, and I highly recommend it as perhaps the most eccentric bedroom in Asia.

The mansion's exterior is an equally overwhelming sight, a humongous marzipan wedding cake painted pistachio green with ornamental details in sugar-icing-white. The three tiers are decorated with 3D-figures of Indians and colonials, turbaned soldiers and buxom madams.

The hotel luckily employs a historian, Lal Singh Shekhawat, who guides me through alleys to all the evocatively painted havelis dating from the region's heydays, 1840-1940. Only one seems to be inhabited, the Tola Ram Kothari Haveli from the 1870s; others are semi-abandoned and crumbling—soon perhaps lost for good. Another is used as a cut-rate garment shop, but we can still make out some faint artwork here and there.

The intriguing wall decorations around town depict everything from signs of progress like trains (such as on the 1850s' Lohia Haveli's wall) to hybrid-culture in the form of angels in saris (the circa 1925 Banthia Haveli), and even Bollywood stars (the 1940s' Bacchawat Haveli). Shekhawat tells me, 'The images provide a key to an understanding of the traditional pattern of social life.' He calls the fresco paintings 'gleeful'—like the crazy one, for example, which shows Jesus puffing away on a cigarillo.

Detail of Jesus smoking a cigarillo found at a painted haveli at Churu.

Narayan Balan, one of the brothers who owns Malji ka Kamra, later takes me out on a drive in the desert along with bottles of chilled white wine. A youngish chap, he wishes to put Churu on the map, saying, 'Whenever one travels outside and mentions that one is from Churu, people ask: "Where?"'

He's constantly searching for interesting desert picnic spots, so the next morning we eat millet chapattis and rustic chutneys at a caravanserai, which may perhaps have been part of the fabled Silk Road ages ago and must have hosted numerous travellers before me, but now the only company we have are hoopoes and partridges. As we eat, Balan tells me the moving story of how his grandfather, Pemaram, used to work as a gardener at the Malji ka Kamra mansion in the 1930s. When it was ready to be opened in 2012, the brothers were satisfied by the sight of the former gardener being able to enjoy a cup of tea on the grand veranda of his former workplace.

Back in the day, however, the maharaja would be entertained by dancing girls to enticing musical accompaniment in the colonnaded ballroom, where fancily-clad servants refuelled wine cups and topped up trays of spicy snacks. It is now converted into a restaurant where I sample my way through a limited but exquisite menu of homely fare. On my table, there's gatta curry with those distinctive lumps of chickpea flour in yoghurt gravy and again I get to hog on laal-maas, the state's signature dish of mutton cooked in red chillies. But what intrigues me most is something that the waiter simply introduces as 'desert beans'.

'Desert beans?' I echo.

He nods, yes, I heard it right. I've never eaten anything quite like it before. It is sourish, presumably from the raw mango powder, but has an earthy, deeply natural aroma, and ghee adds a rich touch to it. The stringy beans have been cooked in yoghurt with cashews and raisins. Checking the menu card later, I see that the name is 'kairsangri' which is described as dried beans and berries. Indeed, Churu district consists of a largely semi-desert landscape with sparse vegetation and tall sand dunes, so nothing much grows here except for millets, chickpeas, lentils, and anything that has deep roots and sustains on a minimum of water, which in turn mirrors the food eaten hereabouts.

One day, as I sit down to have tea at Vijaykumar Chaiwala, a celebrated stall in the Churu market that has served the citizenry thick buffalo-milk tea for the last sixty years, I ask around regarding the mysterious desert beans and am informed that they are called sangri and grow on a shrub known as khejri. 'In English, it is acacia.'

Wah! I knew that acacia yields a material used to make glue, but to eat acacia? Was I being fed gluey twigs? That's a new one. He patiently explains that these are actually hardy bushes related to the pea family, that bear fruit in the form of bean pods once a year, which are harvested and then dried, so that in the arid climate they can be stored for six years. This, I think, must be the ultimate foodstuff. Growing where nothing else grows, can be kept in anticipation of famines, keeps for days without refrigeration and is delicious. No wonder then that it is a household dish.

I ask if they're available in the market.

The tea vendor points out a nearby shop outside of which there are sacks of brownish, thin thingies like shrivelled seaweed. Because of the desiccation process, 5 kg of fresh beans becomes one when dehydrated, and as I step closer, the shopkeeper explains that 50 g is enough to cook a meal for a family of four. After thorough washing, they should be soaked overnight in buttermilk together with a spoonful of the equally costly, tangy desert berries, 'kair', until soft. The precious stuff is then fried in butter with the standard vegetable masala—though experts make their own esoteric blends that may include pungent asafoetida and aamchur or powdered unripe sun-dried green mangoes for tanginess and raisins or nuts for a hint of sweetness—and then yoghurt is added to create the creamy gravy. Sounds simple, so I stuff my suitcase with desert beans and berries to last me years—which makes the long trip totally worth it. I am not at all sure when I might be back again, but I suppose the answer is: When I run out of desert beans.

❖

In Ujjain, the temple town of central India, I'm reminded each night of the city's sacredness when the phone in my hotel room rings promptly at 1.30 a.m. When I complain at the reception, I'm informed that the telephone system is programmed to give an automatic wakeup call so that guests don't miss the early *puja* at the Mahakaleshwar temple. I explain to the receptionist that as a non-Hindu I don't really need to wake up before dawn. He says he'll have it fixed. But the next morning, at 1.30 a.m. sharp, the phone disturbs my sleep again. Must be God's will. And, suitably, God works like clockwork here.

Hours later, I'm yawning as I digest breakfast. Food in Ujjain tends to be invigoratingly vegetarian so I do feel both saintly and salubrious after a plate of crunchy poha—parboiled, flattened and savoury rice flakes that powers the people in these parts—available pretty much everywhere and cheaply too. At the stall I picked, I paid about Rs 10 for a satisfying morning meal of poha and chai. Burping spicily, I amble on the shoulder of a dusty road on the outskirts of Ujjain whose 2500-plus years makes it as antique as Rome. It was once the seat of Emperor Ashoka and then in the fifth century CE, the Guptas ruled Ujjain, ushering in a Golden Age of Civilisation, of theatre and arts and many other things. It's always been a centre for learning, while the town's astrologers are, even today, relied upon by Bollywood celebrities as well as political leaders.

Here I am, searching for one of the most intriguing extant constructions, a Jantar-Mantar on the bank of the sacred Shipra River. Out of the five that were built, this is the oldest and the only one that remains in use. The one in Delhi is a sightseeing attraction visited mostly by tourists—such as me on my very first day in India. I am inevitably nostalgic about that encounter, back in the early 1990s, when I was younger and more stupid. I'd landed at the Indira Gandhi airport that very morning, a greenhorn backpacker, suitably clueless, and it was hot—the summer was peaking, the monsoon, weeks away. Later, I read a scholarly paper on the stereotypical tourist experience of India, about how travellers 'experience a degree of cultural confusion when they arrive' and so I was, as far as I understand in hindsight, being a 'neophobic' shocked by the newness of everything and what would have been needed was 'intercultural adaptation' which should 'be applied to a travel-culinary scenario' or something like that. Whatever...I was about to shrug it off and forgive my younger self when I read that 'those travellers that exhibit neophylic tendencies, consider the experience of new or strange culinary fare to be exciting.' Clearly, I had a lot to learn.

Unpacking that academic argot, I basically understood that the way to deal with culture shock is to find something agreeable to eat or drink. And so it happened that I found myself drifting like a rudderless spacecraft in Connaught Place (as Rajiv Chowk used to be called back then) where everything seemed vast, regal and too imposing to get my head around. A bit like getting whacked with a 1000-page history book when one would have preferred the cartoon version—it took me a long time to appreciate that some of the vintage shops and dining halls are historically important and date back, incredibly enough, to the founding times of New Delhi. Touts chased me in circles, shoe polishers threw greenish snot globs on my sneakers, ear cleaners cleaned me out—in that defeated mood, I slunk into United Coffee House, the timeless café-cum-bar with its 1940s' faux-rococo décor. I ordered cheering beer and chased it down with their old-fashioned 'cona' of calming coffee (it comes in a type of laboratory flask that contains an uncommonly potent decoction). I then scurried down Sansad Marg, determined to sightsee myself out of the funk. There I stumbled upon something soothing—cool geometrical structures in red sandstone, sharp shapes that had clarity, focus and oozed mathematical precision. I instantly liked what I saw. It was fenced in, too, so the touts didn't chase me beyond the ticket booth. Inside the park, people lay on the lawns in a post-lunch stupor.

Jantar Mantar, Delhi.

I too lay down on the grass, full of admiration, but had no clue what I was looking at. Or how these massive structures had been built, by whom, or why. I was slightly stupefied by the flabbergasting samrat-yantra, a huge triangular thing which appeared to pierce the sky. As I recall, there was a stone panel next to it that attempted to explain everything. This, it said, was an instrument consisting of a gnomon (I was lost already there), the hypotenuse of which was aligned with the earth's axis (uh?), its quadrants were parallel to the equator...and by now, I was ready to faint only partly because of the summery heat in Delhi. This made me fathom—and correctly so—that it would take me years to digest India.

But the closer I looked, the more fascinated I became with these curves aimed at the heavens, like skateboard ramps built for a race of giants. One of the structures had the shape of a small Roman amphitheatre, with an intricate clockwork type system of stone slats inside, obviously for calculating...the exact time for the end of the world or...I wondered as I wandered in a state of hypnosis from one monument to the next for a good part of that afternoon, until the day cooled down... but where was I? Oh, yes, over the years I strengthened my intellect with plenty of Indian and Coorgi while studying the other monuments in the series of Jantar-Mantar observatories.

Finding the observatory in Ujjain after a lengthy suburban expedition, I'm greeted by a peon-cum-gardener-cum-self-appointed-guide, who offers to show me the finer points of these colossal shining marble constructions. Able to simplify so that even I can follow, he proudly enumerates the intricacies of things with tricky names such as shanku-yantra and nadi-valay-yantra, and I keep nodding, initially as clueless as on my first arrival in India. But then, at the massive samrat-yantra, which actually is, as it turns out, a gigantic sundial, I'm hit by a sense of déjà-vu followed by insight, as my guide points out how the dial's shadow creeps across the curved graded quadrants. I actually see it clocking minutes with twenty-second accuracy. The thing still works—but why not?—like clockwork.

Another instrument records the varying length of days: December has the shortest, the longest are in June. When the sun hits its noontime zenith, the shadow of the instrument magically disappears—again, this happens right as I stand watching it. It's a tropical phenomenon that has to do with the fact that Ujjain is situated on the Tropic of Cancer.

Kaliadeh Palace, where E.M. Forster went on a pilgrimage in Ujjain.

The resident observer, who turns up for duty a little later, tells me that the 'transit instrument' or bhitti-yantra (a high wall with esoteric markings on it), remains indispensable for computing the annual panchang or 'Astronomical Ephemeris of Geocentric Places of Planets', a booklet of tables forecasting the timings for celestial moves and shakes for the entire year which every scientifically minded astrologist refers to. Astonishingly, from his office one can buy mint copies of the first printed panchang—published in 1942—at the original cover price of Rs 10, making it an antiquarian treasure and a perfect carry-back souvenir. In it, I read that 'for centuries Ujjain has been enjoying the astronomical importance of being the Greenwich of India' and the zero meridian simply happens to be here, which goes to explain why this particular site was chosen for the first Jantar-Mantar.

If one considers that they were built when nobody even owned a wristwatch and before computer aided design (in an interesting turn of events, the Jantar-Mantars are now being studied with the help of 3D software), the levels of precision are doubly impressive. I contact Susmita Mohanty, an ex-NASA spaceship designer I happen to know, and she tells me, 'I find the Jantar-Mantar cluster remarkable for its modernist geometrical forms. Sawai Jai Singh-II must have been quite a renaissance man to leave behind such an avant-garde astronomical legacy.' To put things in perspective, she likens the construction of Jai Singh's five astronomical observatories across India, which may have taken altogether about thirteen years to build, to the same time it took to create the modern International Space Station (ISS). Whereas the ISS, because of the complexity and cost of a project to build a 417 tons heavy something over 400 km out there in space, required the cooperation of sixteen nations, by contrast, she says, the Jantar-Mantar 'was commissioned and built 300 years ago by a single empire that needed no one else to share the financial, construction and operational burden.'

You may at this point wonder what a culinary tourist can get to eat on the International Space Station and if it is open for visitors. The going rate, if one can get a ticket (as its crew capacity is limited) is in the range of fifty to ninety million dollars depending on the itinerary. But on the other hand, one gets to eat radiation-sterilised space-food such as steaks and freeze-dried hamburgers with fries out of vacuum-sealed pouches heated in special food-warmers. Condiments are available as pastes—primarily ketchup, mayonnaise and mustard, and even salt and pepper is served in semi-liquid form to avoid having stray grains floating about in a hazardous manner.

If the act of masticating such semi-synthetic comestibles, pabulum and victuals in space sounds dull, it's a vast improvement on the earliest spaceflights when all food was like pre-cooked baby food—viscous substances eaten cold, straight out of repurposed toothpaste-tubes—or freeze-dried bite-sized food concentrates such as bacon-and-egg squares, barbecued beef titbits, turkey morsels, strawberry lozenges, cheese cubes and cereal nibbles, some of which had to be reconstituted with water.

The instant breakfast drink Tang, an orange juice substitute available as a powder in supermarkets, wasn't (contrary to popular belief) developed for use on space trips—it was invented in 1957, before people took off into space—but came in handy when manned space flights became common in the 1960s, as fresh juice was impossible to squeeze in weightlessness. It was drunk on the moon in 1969, for example, because no champagne was allowed in space. Fizz makes astronauts bloat so they might not fit into their spacesuits. Caffeinists generally make do with freeze-dried, powder-based and recycled-urine-mixed coffee with dehydrated cream. Not satisfied with this solution, Italian astronauts got the company Lavazza to design an 'ISSpresso' machine to be used onboard the International Space Station, into which one basically inserts one's own urine (after its been purified) to be rewarded with a shot of espresso. A friend of mine, who aspired to be the first Swede in space, backed out of the space race when he learnt that he was going to, if not literally then at least figuratively, pee into his own mouth every day. Unfortunately for him, there's no way of avoiding drinking urine as the monthly water requirement of long-term stays in space is about 400 litres per person, hugely expensive to transport up there, and there are few water sources outside the earth's atmosphere. Though according to a post on NASA's website space pee is 'much cleaner than anything you'll ever get out of any tap in the United States.'

Once, visiting NASA in Houston, I picked up space food samples at their souvenir stall including a dried ice-cream bar which basically was like munching on a perfumed soap bar! I thought of peeing on it to get an authentic space experience, but couldn't bring myself to do so. Nevertheless, scientific evaluations of, for example, underwater crews have shown that ice-cream and other dairy products are #4 on the list of things that are most missed, after family, sex and creative activities. Further down the top-ten-list came booze.

As technologies develop, making it possible to expand the dietary range, culinary ethnicity nowadays plays an increasingly important role in keeping astronauts happy—which is psychologically important during longer space sojourns. There are therefore tortillas and even pullao on space menus, though for technical reasons spicing is moderated as the waste material can cause trouble, supposing that the pump-action potties fail. The largest selection is naturally Russian, considering how they basically monopolise transport to and from space, so expect goulash, jellied fish, mashed potatoes and meaty borscht.

Due to the travel restrictions on earth in the early 2020s, private space tourism got a boost with tycoons such as Richard Branson (of Virgin Atlantic fame), Jeff Bezos (of online-retailer Amazon), the ubiquitous Elon Musk launching their own designer rockets for commercial spaceflights bringing holiday-goers into the sky, and just as I was writing this three businessmen popped up to the ISS, spent a fortnight onboard, and popped back down to earth in what was termed 'a landmark mission for the commercial sector'. The only problem noticed was that during the first SpaceX flights, the suction stool malfunctioned and the passengers had to poop in their pants, euphemistically known as 'the undergarment option' and, of course, tourists cannot expect private plunge pools or hot showers in space. So I think I'll stay on earth.

But I digress again...now, all five Jantar-Mantars were built ages ago by Sawai Jai Singh-II, a governor and nobleman posted in Ujjain during the Mughal era and something of a Leonardo da Vinci one might say or, in Kipling's words, 'the Solomon of Rajputana...[who] led armies, and when fighting was over, turned to literature; he intrigued desperately and successfully, but found time to gain a deep insight into astronomy, and, by what remains above ground now, we can tell that whatsoever his eyes desired, he kept not from him.' An expert on Arabic, Greek and other astronomical traditions, Jai Singh was aware of large-scale brick and marble instruments built by Timur's grandson Ulugh Beg in Samarqand circa 1428; he apparently also sent a fact-finding team to Europe to check out the then cutting-edge technologies over there. Subsequently Jai Singh invented, or at least designed, many of these instruments.

Probably completed in 1719, when he was about thirty, this Ujjain observatory is the prototype for the four later ones. Apart from Delhi, Jantar-Mantars were erected at Jaipur and two sacred cities—Varanasi (a smaller one) and Mathura (from where it unfortunately disappeared in the 1800s). The one in Ujjain may be the oldest, but the Jaipur observatory is definitely the grandest. Its samrat-yantra sundial is a massive 75 ft high.

Construction began in 1728 and happened at the same time as Jai Singh was building his scientifically planned capital city around it—named Jaipur, after himself.

I understand now a little better how time works in India. All you need is a triangular gnomon 75 ft high, the hypotenuse of which is running parallel to the earth's axis, with its huge quadrants exactly parallel to the equator...hmm, I think as I book a cab for deeper exploration of Ujjain's past. The low-budget 'My Taxi' isn't air-conditioned, but I'm comfortable enough in the backseat, watching the landscape roll by. We're driving via the outskirts of Ujjain on a narrow road winding through villages on the west bank of the Shipra River. With little evidence for my fancy, I'd like to think that this was the very road taken by EM Forster but in a horse-pulled tonga, in the winter of 1912-13.

Forster was by then tinkering with his masterpiece, *A Passage to India*, the final scenes of which are based on his experiences in these parts. The novelist took an interest in all things Indian, so when he learnt that Kalidas had been a court poet of the Guptas, he took the train to Ujjain.

Arriving in this once so cultured city, Forster was told there were no antique structures extant—despite Ujjain, as already noted, being as old as Rome. At the time, Ujjain was under the influence of the progressive Scindia royals, who undertook much modernisation, so that today the city has quaint squares laid out in the early 1900s. The most expansive is centred on a grand clock tower which must have been brand new when Forster came to search for anything that wasn't new.

Making enquiries, he came across rumours of one palace ruin outside town, but the tongawallah tried to palm off every second dilapidated structure along the road as historical enough. Forster insisted that they go on until finally, arriving at the riverside, he caught sight of a rundown mansion on a desert island. He waded across, saw what he believed to be the Gupta court—'the palace that King Vikramaditya built, and adorned with Kalidas', noting to himself that 'ruins are ruins'. And so here I am, a century later, deciphering his travel essay as I'm searching for whatever it was that Forster found. The road takes a dip towards the river and crosses a charming stone bridge (why did Forster wade?) which conceals below it intricate channels and tunnels, inlets and outlets. Later I learn that the waterworks is a cooling system devised by some king who couldn't stand the heat. He apparently sat inside underwater chambers where the air was cold even in the peak of summer. Even air-conditioning seems to have been invented in Ujjain... well, that must be why it was the Golden Age!

On the island stands a handsome red sandstone structure known as Kaliadeh Palace, but with very Islamic-looking cupolas it is certainly less than a thousand years old. It isn't quite a ruin either—one can inspect the high-ceilinged cob-webbed halls provided one removes one's shoes at the entrance, as instructed by the watchman.

For as it turns out, this Islamic-period palace has been converted into a Hindu temple. There aren't any pilgrims, their focus is on the many temples of downtown Ujjain. This remote spot was made into a sacred space, the watchman explains, for the reason that it used to be a haunt of bandits and crooks who came here to indulge in anti-social activities, but after it was consecrated the bad men vamoosed.

The upper storeys are shut, but I do a round of the ground floor, my sweaty socks leaving a snail's trail on the grimy stone surfaces, perhaps wiping out all traces of Forster's footprints...but to paraphrase the philosophers: Art may be long, life surely isn't.

I come to Bhopal and the fasting month is on and I can't help but notice how it affects the city's rhythm—and naturally I worry that I might not get enough to eat but have to starve as the faithful do. When I go out shopping for shoes one morning (because my travel boots are falling apart) I find that few shops in the old town, where I'm staying in a basic lodge, open before noontime.

Even in the middle of the day, the bazaars are relatively empty, making it easy to stroll at leisure (in my bathroom slippers) so instead of shopping, I sightsee my way through Bhopal's mosques (also more or less empty at that hour). Anyway, the handle of my eco-friendly reusable shopping bag has also broken, making it hard to carry back new shoes if I find any. The Moti Masjid or 'Pearl Mosque' is an agreeable structure with reddish sandstone minarets and white domes. It is one of the subcontinent's five historic mosques by that name—the other four being in Agra, Delhi, Karachi and Lahore respectively. In the courtyard, I meet a bearded geriatric who tells me in refined and carefully-worded English, about how a 'lady' erected the mosque. He's speaking of a begum who used to dress as a man in the 1860s, which led Bhopal to be known for its liberated, progressive women.

After drinking buttery lassi in a stall, I spot an open tailoring shop and ask the modern begum inside if she would mind stitching my bag. She fixes it until it is as good as new, but when I dig out my wallet, she waves it away with a 'Welcome to Bhopal.' I find the Bhopalis very likeable.

In the early evening, after sorting out my shoe issue by upgrading from colourful bathroom slippers to new sneakers, I stand outside what is purportedly Asia's largest mosque—the Taj-ul-Masjid—as two cannon shots are heard echoing across town, which is the signal for breaking the fast. Light refreshments, fruits, dates and cold drinks are served from pushcarts and all of a sudden, the city comes alive. It's a completely different picture after dark with the narrow streets chock-a-block with happiness, not to mention meats stewing in pots signalling that something gourmet might be coming my way. Paradoxically, it occurs to me that the one month when food consumption peaks in Muslim quarters is the month of fasting when people feast on an endless banquet of the richest delicacies from sunset to sunrise in order to counterbalance the daytime austerities. And as usual, I have a set of definite targets, names of the hottest tables—one is an alley in the old parts, Chatori Galli and another is a suburban fine dining option in Koh-i-Fiza, where tablecloths can be expected.

I try the latter, thinking it might be easier to handle for a novice. I find the Filfora off Sultania Road, in a backstreet of a Bhopal Development Authority (BDA) suburb. Nice-looking, decidedly upper-crust, with fashionably-dressed kids at one table celebrating a birthday. Strangely, a poster advertises South Indian meals as the waiter emphatically claims that they serve no Bhopali cuisine whatsoever. When I draw his attention to the menu's 'Filfora specials' he argues that the cook is on leave due to his fasting, so no biryani is available. I'm feeling like E.M. Forster when his attempts at sampling non-veg in Madhya Pradesh were thwarted because his aristocratic dining companions generally were strict vegetarians.

I decide to go for Plan B or Chatori Galli. Food-bloggers rave about one particular eatery, Jameel Hotel, which supposedly is *the* place for Bhopali grub. Google maps places Jameel near the bus stand in Hamidia Road, which seems handy as my hotel is around the corner, but it turns out to be completely wrong.

The only way to find it is to ask in every other shop and get pointed deeper and deeper into the glittering night bazaars, jam-packed with burqa-clad ladies, past a trumpet seller and a hat shop for prayer caps that has one shiny red fez for sale, past a Burqa Palace, a handful of Jalebiwallas, more than a few Biscuit Corners, quite a lot of Silk Stores, a couple of Chikan Centres, and then there are shops that sell the glitzy, bead-decked purses that Bhopali artisans are known for, until I reach the very opposite side of town from where I started out, in Ibrahimganj where looming buildings timewarp me back to the Mughal highlife when begums were in charge.

But as the saying goes: Sheekh and ye shall find kebabs. Not far from the Jama Masjid (comparatively smallish mosque in the centre of a roundabout bazaar) I come to a street with lots of bakers who sell sheermal breads and buttery rusk, which is the fabled Chatori Galli.

Jameel Hotel is on the right, with Jameel Chicken Corner to the left. The reddest meat this side of the Red Sea is being grilled right there in the street so I head right. Inside, a waiter plump as a laddu slaps down the menu, which is itself thoroughly smeared in animal fat. Rather than touching it, I naturally order everything mentioned on it. Soon steel bowls of rich mutton korma appear, as does biryani up there among the best in the world, served with the garlicky yoghurt sauce known as burani. The crispy-fried sheekh kebabs on simple wooden sticks arrive by the cartload, along with hot rotis. Hungry families, who must have been fasting all day, keep coming, quickly filling the place to capacity.

My tummy has found a second home. But what about my brain? To feed it, the next morning I take a 45-km ride south of Bhopal in a taxi, to a set of sprawling rock art galleries once occupied by nameless artists who adorned the walls with paintings. The question I suddenly mull is: There's modern art and there's this art, and is there really such a big difference?

Some of the Bhimbetaka Caves' drawings of stick figures make me think of Giacometti's sculptures, other more abstract sketches bring to mind works by Picasso. There are strange mystical geometrical patterns that could be naïvist art. It feels as if I've come to the origins of world art, maybe even of culture, of civilisation, here.

Bhimbetaka is vast. Out of an estimated 750 rock shelters, 400 to 500 are adorned with paintings and fifteen of the best have been made accessible for tourists via walkways and signposting. It is splendid, a Stone Age version of the National Gallery of Modern Art. It is very peaceful too on the weekday I visit. Apart from myself, only a busload of tourists has come to see the UNESCO World Heritage monument and they spend their visit mostly in the car park, complaining about the crappy toilet facilities and looking for Coca-Cola and snack vendors who are thankfully conspicuous by their absence.

Passing under a dramatic cliff I reach the famous 'Zoo Rock' which has over 200 animals painted on it, presenting to us a pre-historic menu of sorts: Deer with stately antlers, bulky buffaloes, colossal elephants, an even more gigantic tandoori chicken, and some dozen other species as if this was a cookbook detailing what our ancestors liked to eat. They all appear to be running helter-skelter across the rock wall, a bit like the mixed grill I often order at Koshy's restaurant in Bengaluru.

After checking out this and that, further down the hillside I come to Rock Shelter #8, shaped like a pocket that I crawl into, almost like a baby returning to the womb in a reversal of the hard labour that was involved when I was born. Squatting in a semi-foetal position I'm able to study several paintings from up-close. Again, here are humans and animals in various poses and I presume I am watching non-vegetarians and their favourite diet. At the next rock, I find a crazy hunting scene depicted—arrows and spears are flying as a gang of hunters chase horned animals, an entire herd done in blood red as if the culinary preference may be labelled 'red meat', reminding me of yesterday's grill in the galli. Other artworks are painted in white, but some artists also used ochre and green. Yet another rock features rows of people dancing and a man beating a drum so huge that I can almost hear the beat 6,000 years later. Is this a successful hunt being celebrated?

I bump into some boys on holiday. One of them shouts to the other in Hindi, 'This surely isn't worth wasting time on. Let's go.' I suppose the caves can seem unimpressive in this age of multiplexes and 3D action movies, but then again, we need to see them for what they are. After the boys leave, the quiet helps me concentrate as I sit in the company of jolly black-faced langur monkeys and strangely colourful lizards. Were these caves a luxury dwelling for some tribal headman? The menu card at cavemen banquets? A religious spot? Some of the cliffs soar like temple spires. Or was it an art school—my favourite theory—because here and there newer paintings have been done on top of older ones, suggesting either recycling or imitation?

Any which way you look at it, it's a great cultural space. The mountain is part of the 1.6 billion-years-old Vindhya Hills, offering charming vistas of a thickly forested, gently undulating countryside. I'm constantly struck by the sounds of nature—birds, animals, wind rustling in the trees, an ambient jungle soundtrack that perfectly accompanies the cave paintings.

As one signboard puts it, this is 'one of the earliest cradles of cognitive human evolution', which probably means that the relics here are the first signs of creatively thinking humans on the planet—showing us the moment when our ancestors stopped being hybrid life forms of worms and lichen, and decided to become people like us instead. It's a thought that humbles me. Although most of the art dates back between 9,000 and 6,000 years, archaeologists think that the site was in use as early as 100,000 BCE, well before the art of painting evolved. The latest artwork is dated to 400 years ago—kings and sword-wielding soldiers—and subsequently the caves were forgotten for centuries, until everything was rediscovered by Indian archaeologists ten years after independence.

I continue further down the face of the hill to a monkey-infested rock that has a huge, red painting of a boar or bison or bull (experts differ), attacking some infinitesimal stick people. If it wasn't for the irony of seeing this after the previous wild hunt scenes, and the post-hunt parties, I'd almost be sorry for those long-ago hunters who suddenly became the hunted!

Well, what comes around, goes around—apparently that's the eternal karmic truth. These rocks tell lots of stories through their paintings, stories from a time long before written language existed. Maybe they're the equivalent of a Stone Age cartoon strip? The sporadic party scenes and dances interpolated into all the action remind me of Bollywood movies. Entertainment, art, religion or a bit of everything? Who can tell?

Heading back towards Bhopal in the late afternoon, I decide to have a look at the eccentric Bharat Bhavan Art Gallery, designed to adorn Bhopal's lakeside by the great architect Charles Correa in 1978. There's modern art in a cavernous hall in various levels, which immediately makes me recall my walk through the Bhimbetaka Caves, and then I find the more tucked-away tribal art gallery, with canvases painted in the traditional manner by Adivasi artists.

And I recognise motifs, artistic expressions, and ideas from the caves. Stick figures are dancing and celebrating...surely, not a coincidence? I realise that the art practised at Bhimbetaka never died out, it merely moved on to being decorations on the walls of village huts, and now, with the recognition being given to Madhya Pradesh's tribal artists, the same school of art has found its way here, to a modern gallery. The passage of art through the ages seems to have come full circle.

VII

Northern Kitchens, Northern Chickens

(The Gangetic Plains)

'Having kept nearly all the English breeds of the fowl alive, having bred and crossed them, and examined their skeletons, it appears to me almost certain that all are the descendants of the wild Indian fowl...'

—*On the Origin of Species*, Charles Darwin

M.G. Marg, Allahabad where Kipling strolled in the evenings.

It's early, but the date merchants are already in position with their pushcarts. Men are offloading bulging jute sacks from small trucks. The spice traders are only beginning to roll up shutters and dust their pickle jars. Counters are being stocked with trays of turmeric roots, nutmeg and dried chillies, and sacks of peppercorn are opened by the roadside. Strangely, the air appears quite smoggy despite the morning hour's freshness, but it takes a bit of time before I realise that my eyes are watering from the dense haze of chilli powder.

This is Khari Baoli, claimed to be Asia's largest spice market, 'the mother of all markets' and the optimal opening to a Delhi snack track. One has got to love how places like this, where one first inhales the spices by way of sampling—like the asafoetida (hing) that catapults its odour to the seventh heaven telling you that it is the A1 quality that is sold here—and then buys them loose at kilogram rates, thrive in an era of malls and online home-delivery services.

Cycle rickshaws are dragged past me, laden with cartons of dry fruits such as exclusive chilgoza pine nuts from Afghanistan or stacks of papadams and fryums going from wholesalers to retailers. Hawkers peddling on the pavements yell, it's like stepping into a medieval saga and after ransacking the condiment shops, I take a turn into Chandni Chowk where, adjacent to the seventeenth-century Fatehpur Mosque's gateway, sits Chainaram's—a sweetmeat maker's outlet founded back in 1901 in Lahore. Like so many others, they shifted shop to this side of the border to cook up their sinful Sindhi sweets in Delhi when the British cashed out and partitioned away parts of India. People tell me their main claim to fame remains the Karachi halwa that some call 'Indian chewing gum', others have dubbed it Bombay halwa due to Pakistaniphobia. Anyhow, a potent vapour of aromas draws me in. Aunties in burqas are stuffing themselves silly on puris with veggie gravy that smells like spice heaven. The hot, ballooning breads look divine and the shop is *the* breakfast joint in the area. But such an oily morning meal would totally fill me up and I need to preserve my appetite as Delhi is world-famous for its snack culture—snacking happens at all times, from morning to evening. Instead I nibble on what I'm told is syrup-glazed wheat, another of the shop's claims to fame, that tastes like boiled candyfloss: Balūshahi.

The centuries-old 'silver square' or 'moonlit market'—okay, since I don't really know how to translate properly from Hindi, let us simply call it Chandni Chowk—extends 1.5 km from here up to the Red Fort, the Lal Qila of the Mughal emperors. It was Asia's premier luxury shopping centre ages before Singapore was invented, lined with smoky Persian-influenced coffee houses where travellers rested by puffing on hookahs (today replaced by sugary chaiwallas). Shopaholics rode on camels from the Far East and the Mediterranean to lay their hands on spices, jewellery and cloth. During the pandemic, the street got a makeover to restore its former glory and is lined with 75,000 businesses (I'm told but can barely believe it) that include bargain garment stores, cheap electronic markets and, most importantly, India's best chaat. Delhi is said to have 300,000 chaatwallas (but judging by the love for snacking I wouldn't be surprised if the actual number is twice as many) and most chaats that are eaten across India, especially those based on boiled chole (chickpeas) were born, according to folklore, at Delhi's court as health food! Others debunk this as myth and maintain that chole was introduced to the diet of Delhi by Partition refugees.

Be that as it may, in the past germs were mysterious beings and harder to fight, and the waters of the Yamuna River weren't considered as pure as the Ganges—hence the royal physician prescribed a diet rich in certain spices, to nuke any germs that may enter the emperor's gut. This actually makes one think of how some modern people dismiss panipuri as 'liquid cholera' but obviously the right spice mix is a germicide. So to avoid unduly irritating the imperial bowel syndrome, the classic chaat masala was born which, I'm told, is a balanced blend of asafoetida, chilli, cumin, mango powder, pepper, rock salt and a pinch of sugar. Soon everybody was munching chaat at all times and feeling too good. Emboldened by these thoughts, I continue 350 m to Tewari Brothers, where I'm offered piping hot kachoris stuffed with pretty much anything that will make your head explode. Actually, the yummy, flaky, tan-coloured pockets of dough are filled with a piquant lentil mixture and served alongside sweet-and-sour tamarind chutney. This well-orchestrated but cacophonous riot of flavours simply has to be the ultimate killer breakfast for chilli champions. And yeah, any germ within me surely kicked the bucket, too!

The old town used to be where tourists went to see the sights but otherwise it was generally not seen as hot enough by urbanites and other moderns. However, since getting themselves a bunch of Metro stations, the bazaars have suddenly turned hot again and guides bring tour groups to enjoy the seventeenth-century ambience. I notice this when I go further down Chandni Chowk to the city's original outlet of the hundred-year-old Haldiram's and meet a Delhi lady who exclaims, 'It's a fully different life we're living! We just had some errands to do around town, me, my daughter and mum, but because the Metro makes travel so easy, we decided to go to Parathewali Galli and eat super-greasy parathas!'

She's in bliss, clearly.

At Haldiram's they're having fresh kulfi ice-cream to digest the parathas with and pick up big bags of those globally beloved, hygienically packaged snacks for a cocktail party on the weekend. Since I've just had a fiery bite, I sample over-sweet confections that balance out the kachoris.

Passing the Town Hall built in 1863 after the colonising Brits had deposed the last Mughal and many other buildings even older than it, I turn right into that much talked about twisting 'alley of paratha-makers' which is a 100 per cent vegetarian party zone dating back to the 1800s, but whether dishes are exactly the same as then, I can't tell. Parathewali Galli is mentioned in most handbooks so flocking to the first grubby paratha shop are a bunch of white tourists in cowboy hats on a food tour—it is a very different scene from a century ago, in colonial India, when freedom fighters like Bhagat Singh (who was executed in 1931, aged twenty-three) allegedly got together at these hole-in-the-wall-joints where, those days, Englishmen would not be seen dead. Or alive, even—allegedly, that is. These parathas fuelled the fight for Indian independence back in the day and it is quite expected that history would have been written here, as already then the paratha alley was a century old—dating back to Mughal times.

The next is crowded with students who have taken the Metro from the university area. The third is empty and feels cleaner, so I sit down at Gaya Prasad Shivcharan's which appears to be the oldest extant, founded in 1872. Their parathas are thin, crispy and freshly fried with twenty-five different fillings from cauliflower to bananas, but I choose the customary peas paratha that is served with five scrumptious vegetable sides including lip-smacking carrot pickles. It's not your usual flaky paratha, but a massive oil-cooked rock-hard biscuit—like biting into a 78 rpm record so it doesn't feel too wholesome considering my already troublesome cholesterol levels, but at least it is freshly cooked.

Ace lifestyle blogger Mayank Austen Soofi of www.thedelhiwalla.com fame told me once, when I asked about the must-eats in town, 'Try not to miss Old & Famous Jalebiwala.' On his food blog he elaborates: 'Thick and juicy, its food porn at its best. Jalebis, the golden-coloured rings of deep-fried maida batter, soaked in sugar syrup, fill the mouth with a warm liquid of such excessive sweetness that modesty blushes in shame. The diabetic may find joy in just looking at its preparation.'

So after a lassi—a genuinely ancient Indian health beverage and with rock salt it is said to be good for digestion—from a corner kiosk, I carry on towards the Old & Famous Jalebiwala. I've been told that one can buy confectionery of a thousand varieties along the chowk, but the topmost have always been the Persian-origin spiral-shaped jalebis that are cooked in pure ghee over smoky charcoal. This sweet arrived in India, according to sugary mythology, in the baggage of Ibn Battuta in the 1330s—he travelled with a confectioner from Yemen—and after further tweaking in India it may then have gone back with Battuta to the Mediterranean where, in Italy, it gave birth to the signature candy of Naples, the *strufoli*. Whether the Moroccan glutton actually was involved in its globalisation or not, we cannot tell. Many years later this Old & Famous Jalebiwala was opened in 1884 in its honour by Mr Nemchand and today his direct descendant sits behind the counter, unsettlingly looking exactly like a younger edition of Hollywood superstar Vin Diesel. He insists, 'Eating jalebis is the perfect antidote to the heat, so buy at least one hundred grams.'

Having boosted my energy levels with the sugar shock that the jalebis produce, I ponder should I carry on yonder or which way to go next—the tiny shop has one other item on its two-dish-menu, namely samosas. These too are a Middle Eastern import, but one that was well established on menus already before Battuta came to India—and perhaps it should be added that the migratory Moroccan didn't set foot in Old Delhi as it was only built later. In those days they also had no potatoes to stuff them with, so he hogged potato-less samosas in what is now the southern suburbs around Begumpur mosque, nearby which he stayed. Hence, to try his favourite samosas one must look for snack stalls outside the Qutb Minar Metro stop and request them to remove any potatoes from them. So I skip Jalebiwala's samosas as I still have other potentially gut-wrenching and stroke-inducing meals to digest.

To rest one's tummy, one may head a little further up the street to sightsee Delhi's divine buildings: A sanctuary of Jainism where sick birds find refugee; a prominent Sikh gurdwara; a church erected in 1814 when the English settled here; and the emblematic Red Fort that ranks as one of the main tourist attractions in the country. But since I am more of a food pilgrim with a restless tummy, I opt to head south on Dariba Kalan from the corner of the jalebi shop. It has traditionally been the street of jewellers and one still finds glimmering ornaments along the winding bazaar, but above all it is fun to observe what short eats patrons pick from the pushcarts that stand here and there. It's evidently true by now that Delhi people are snacking everywhere and always.

These bustling parts may appear a trifle tricky to find one's bearings in, yet Old Delhi has a clearly planned nature. The palatial fort of the Mughals symbolises its brain, Chandni Chowk its spine, its side streets are the ribs, the spice market its tummy (or primary gastric malaise depending on one's tolerance levels) and the main mosque is the city's beating heart that has a capacity to hold an astonishing 25,000 devotees. On his last visit to India, in the 1940s, E.M. Forster made it a point to come here after landing in town and 'stood on the high platform of the Great Mosque, one of the noblest buildings in India and the world. Profound thankfulness filled me. The sky was now intensely blue, the kites circled round and round the pearl-gray domes and the red frontispiece of sandstone, sounds drifted up from Delhi city, the pavement struck warm through the soles of my socks; I was back in the country I loved, after an absence of twenty-five years.' The jewellers' bazaar which I follow leads me straight to that great mosque.

Dhabas at Main Bazaar, Delhi, offer both veg and non-veg options.

As much as Chandni Chowk is a vegetarian street, bearing the stamp of the strict Marwari trading community, by the mosque one has transited into the carnivore club, to feast on the cheapest kebabs in the city.

Tourists flock to Karim's which grew from a pushcart kitchen outside the mosque into a destination listed in all guidebooks for its meats swimming in grease and their dining halls, surrounding a grimy courtyard, that have a distinctly oriental charm. The foundational dish on their menu, dating back to those pushcart days, was the meaty potato stew known as aloo gosht.

To tell the truth, I prefer the more low-key neighbour Yaseen Hotel (on the corner immediately south of the mosque) where they don't charge tourist rates and the gravies with fresh flatbreads are less likely to cause cardiac arrests. Their signboard—'good taste, cheap and best, hygienic environment'—says all that needs to be said. Coincidentally, the area features prominently in Booker-winner Arundhati Roy's *The Ministry of Utmost Happiness*, the sequel to her two decades older global bestseller *The God of Small Things*. When I met her for coffee in Delhi, I asked about how come so much of the novel is set in Old Delhi.

'I actually have a place there.'

'Near the big mosque?'

'Yes, a rented small room, so I've been there for many years. You sometimes feel under siege. It was not that I went there because I was going to write about it, but because I went there it became very much part it. I go there, wander around late at night.'

'All those rabid street dogs, they don't chase you?'

'Not at all. Humans are rabid, dogs are okay.' She has adopted two of them. At one point as we're chatting away, one of her dogs climbs all over me. I'm more accustomed to dogs barking the moment they see me but, puzzlingly, this one wants to lick my face.

Arundhati Roy with her adopted dog at home in Delhi.

Arundhati laughs. 'She's flirting with you. They are both street dogs. She was born outside a drain. Then her mother was hit by a car. That other one I found tied to a lamppost, cruelly.'

'Do your dogs have names?'

'Yeah, her name is Begum Filthy Jaan and this one is Maati K. Lal. That means "beloved of the earth". Both Lal and Jaan mean beloved.'

'So they make up your family?'

'Yes.'

'They're very well behaved to be street dogs.'

'Street dogs are more civilised than other dogs. They're the best. I'm also a bit of a street dog.' A little later, she tells me something I can relate to very much, about life in India as a writer, 'It is a very anarchic, unformatted world that I live in. To me, if anything, it is an overload of every kind of stimulus.

I suppose I'm not closed off in some family thing. There's a porous border between me and the world and lots of things come and go. That's the way I live. There are so many *brilliant* people doing things around me *all* the time, like even just in the process of making this book—if I want someone who's an *insane*...who's actually not a human being, but a printing machine, I lean this way. If I want someone who is skulking around the city taking pictures, I lean that way. One is just surrounded by unorthodox brilliance all the time. And that's my real inspiration. If I want really *badly* behaved dogs I have them too.' She laughs and hugs one of her dogs that is barking, presumably impatient with our talking.

I'm reminded of her words as I dogtrot in the winding bazaars, building up appetite for my umpteenth breakfast, or perhaps I should call it a light brunch by now, that awaits behind the mosque in Chawri Bazaar. This is another artery of the vintage town, where hardware wholesalers have been running shops since the nineteenth century. But hardware is not all there is to Chawri Bazaar, there's also interesting 'software' at the famed Shyam Sweets. It is more of a big kiosk with stainless steel tables abutting the street, making it the perfect place to hang and people-watch (until other foodaholics come and claim one's table). The jolly proprietor, Anil Aggarwal, proudly informs me, 'My grandfather's grandpa's grandfather started this business in 1910.'

Their bedmi aloo, oily hard-puffed lentil-filled breads like edible gold bars served with rich chilli-red and piquant potato curry and veggies pickled Delhi-style, go perfectly with a cooling lassi that has a mild scent of roses. Potato and roses, spicy and sweet, deadly and lively, male and female, yin and yang, East and West, Hollywood and Bollywood, happy go lucky—it's all there in a quick meal.

Next I drag my tummy up Ballimaran, a meandering alley which eventually leads to a memorial in honour of the poet Mirza Ghalib—in fact, this was once his house but now all that is left of his haveli is a portion of its courtyard, the rest having been encroached upon by anybody and everybody. As William Dalrymple laments in *City of Djinns*, 'The *haveli* was a world within a world, self-contained and totally hidden from the view of the casual passer-by. Now, however, while many of the great gatehouses survive, they are hollow fanfares announcing nothing.' There's a collection of objects that give an idea what life in Delhi may have looked like two centuries ago, when Ghalib skulked about popping kachoris and kebabs into his lyrical mouth in these streets. After having snapped my mandatory selfies, I carry on down the ever-narrower alley until I suddenly emerge right next to my final stop for the day: ninety-year-old, barely one-square-metre small Ashok Chaat Corner. Their yogurt-based snacks, such as dahi-vada of savoury, spongy balls (or 'bhalle' that are of course deep-fried) smothered with spiced-up yoghurt, are the best way imaginable to offset a daylong junk-food orgy.

As I bolt down the last cooling vada, it occurs to me that while chaat may be the Indian equivalent to Mediterranean *meze*, there's a great difference. The short-eats of southern Europe are something you dig into over a leisurely evening of nice wines or cold beers, over hours and hours, but chaat can only be eaten methodically and in moderation, in short bursts. Typically cooked in plenitudes of oil and exceedingly spicy, chaat might have killed Mughal germs but it also takes its own toll on the gastric system as well as causing superfluous cardiovascular problems, which differentiates it from the Mediterranean snacks that can be enjoyed to one's heart's delight.

But the occasional encounter with Old Delhi's junk-food is

great for the mind, stomach and wallet. And happily, when I feel the time has come to purge my belly, Ashok Chaat Corner is within walking distance of my lodge—a choice haunt among backpacker flophouses, around the corner from the Main Bazaar. The art deco hotel used to be called Airlines back in the day, but despite its name it primarily catered to passengers from the New Delhi Railway Station diagonally across the road. It's still a great place to stay and drifting into town again decades after first landing in India, I feel a comforting nostalgia as I, for old time's sake, book a room there. The basic lodge I stayed at in 1991 on my first visits (and where the manager memorably plied me with pegs of Bagpiper after all my valuables had been stolen on a trainride) is long gone and the bazaar's lodges have become fancier overall so I end up shelling out more than expected at the renovated Airlines where ACs have replaced fans, but unlike the good old days of shared baths and squat potties, I get a clean attached bathroom with modern commode, bum-shower, shampoo on the house, the works.

By and large the Main Bazaar, or Paharganj as it is also called, has remained more or less the same—a travellers' hub where all manner of neo-hippie firangis converge: Spanish punks with tattooed foreheads, Danish druggies with colourless eyes, Israelis whose hands and fingers seem to clutch invisible Kalashnikovs, American preachers with pierced nipples and tank-sized Russian ladies shopping in bulk, to smuggle and sell garments and trinkets back home, thereby earning their airfare.

Small bookshops like Jacksons sweep up the literature left behind by tourists, so it's a great spot to pick up foreign editions at bargain rates. As a film buff I enjoy spotting locations where *Holy Smoke!* (starring Kate Winslet) as well as the award-winning surprise hit *Dev D.* (starring Kalki Koechlin) were shot—the latter was incidentally filmed in Arakashan Road, a couple of blocks north of the Main Bazaar. In the more recent *Paharganj*, a Spanish tourist is trying to find a dead lover in the bazaar area's underground universe of sleaze, drugs, sex and many other things that I personally haven't encountered here in real life.

The bazaar was born as a royal grain market situated outside the city's south-western gate—where customs duties were collected by the rulers. When the New Delhi Station was built in the 1920s, the area was slowly overtaken by cheap lodging and boarding houses, and the old produce market expanded to encompass garment stalls and cloth merchants. The advent of foreign tourism (with the hippies of the 1960s) also means that Main Bazaar has turned into an international hippie bubble and it is your best bet in Delhi to grab some affordable, cosmopolitan grub: German bakes, Israeli hummus, Japanese or Korean delicacies, Nepalese or Thai curries, Uzbek uh—whatever they eat in Uzbekistan. Food and beer come cheaper than anywhere else in town.

At last count, the bazaar and its alleys had some 400-500 small hotels and an even larger number of food outlets. I used to eat at the classier yet budget-level Metropolis Tourist Home (1634, Main Bazaar), which began as an unassuming travellers' dhaba two years after the station had been inaugurated in 1928. Over time, it grew into the bazaar's first proper hotel, until recently run by the founder's grandson—though on my latest visit in 2023 it was shuttered down, hopefully just awaiting a much-needed renovation. It featured one of the cosiest imaginable rooftop bars with a mixture of retro-food, such as the only known Soviet gourmet dish Chicken à la Kiev, that somehow found its way to India (from Tashkent, they say) not to mention terrific wood-fired pizzas that helped one dream oneself away to Italy for an evening without having to fly all the way there. And to tell you the truth, the pizzas in Rome weren't half as good as the ones served here.

I must admit that I always have trouble convincing my writerly Delhi friends to join me for a night of fun in the bazaar, as their wives presume that they're going to end up indulging in immoral illegalities. Only goes to show that Delhi wives don't trust their husbands too much. And it is true that intellectuals generally don't want to set foot in the area: V.S. Naipaul who toured Delhi chaperoned by Khushwant Singh enjoyed the ruins of older Delhis like Tughlakabad, where they picnicked on bacon-and-egg sandwiches, and he stayed as a paying guest in the newer parts—far from the bazaars. But perhaps they're not to be blamed as even the handbook *Rough Guide* warns of 'police raids on budget hotels' in the bazaar. *Lonely Planet* states that 'Paharganj—with its seedy reputation for drugs and dodgy characters—isn't everyone's cup of chai' and all tourist websites and every travel expert online issue dire admonitions such as 'tourists are advised to avoid the area' because it is 'noisy, filthy, and full of touts' not to mention 'high amount of crime, poverty, drugs, sexual assaults and scams.' The 'lodgings are popular with some Western tourists seeking easy access to cheap and widely-available drugs, and the large number of sex parlours and brothels involved in the sex trade' with links to 'gambling and other illicit activity, resulting in death of tourists.' I may be myopic, but the only parts of all this that I notice are the shops that sell paraphernalia for pot smokers, chillums designed in Italy and rolling paper with exotic Latin American scents. Of the eating options, the above guidebooks dismiss all those catering to international backpackers because 'it's a shame to dine in Paharganj, even if that's where your hotel is. Most of the restaurants on the Main Bazaar are geared to unadventurous foreign tastebuds, offering poor imitations of Western, Israeli, Japanese, and even Thai dishes, or sloppy, insipid versions of Indian curries for foreigners who can't handle chilli.'

Survival is an understandable concern and it is true that many end up at least with 'Delhi-belly', the city's trademark sickness caused by over-exposure to spices and the richness of ghee. Strictly speaking, let me tell you that Delhi-belly wasn't invented in the Main Bazaar, but down the road in tony Connaught Place where, during World War II, foreign soldiers kept boozing until their bellies gave away and they ended up spending much of the war topping up the latrines.

According to studies, 60 per cent of international travellers who visit developing countries experience stomach upsets, so one should perhaps not be shocked if shit happens. Sometimes it isn't even a bug that causes it, but the fact that their tummies are unused to extreme spice levels and the rich ghee content that oils the intestine into a waterchute amusement park for amoebae, thereby switching off the basic digestive functionality of one's intestines. Luckily, in case one develops an urgent need to see a latrine, one can take the Metro from the Ashram Marg station (at the western end of the bazaar) to the Sulabh International Museum of Toilets, which lends perspective to toilet-related matters.

Over my years of travel, I've seen many illustrious restrooms—the one where the Beatles peed after beer-binging in Liverpool, another at a bar in New York in which poet Dylan Thomas' bladder exploded (leading to his premature demise later that same night), a protected monument in Texas on which hard-rocker Ozzy Osbourne urinated and for which he was arrested, and other similarly famous or infamous celebrity privies. But I've never before laid eyes on such a potty collection documenting 4,500 years of scatological technology, a feat that earned this museum a listing in *Time* magazine as one of the world's ten weirdest museums, alongside another darling of mine, Boston's Museum of Bad Art.

At the museum one can see the throne of the French king Louis XVI to whom Tipu Sultan sent an ambassador and which has an inbuilt bed pan so that he could defecate and host courtly dinners at the same time, study Indus Valley civilisation sewerage systems (yes, India invented the first WCs in the world), Roman emperors' golden chamber pots and other exhibits including samples of toilet humour as well as poopy poetry. Established in 1992 by

Dr Bindeshwar Pathak, a social activist and founder of the Sulabh Sanitation and Social Reform Movement, the museum is the perfect sightseeing site when one's gastric system is up to dirty tricks.

❖

Returning to Chandigarh after many decades, I have a really simple plan. I'm looking for Mr Singh *and* for a tandoori chicken. You'd think it ought to have been easy—isn't every second person in town named Singh and doesn't he eat tandoori chicken for breakfast, lunch, tiffin and dinner? But I'm in search of a particular Mr Singh.

In my nostalgic mood, I roam the Rock Garden—a misnomer as it is only partly made of rocks—and where I remember last having seen Mr Singh. The forty-acre surreal artwork is made of broken bangles, empty bottles, oil drums, plates and teacups, tubelights and other recycled debris of modernity, shaped into fantastic birds, monkeys, humans, houses, bridges, winding cobbled paths, waterfalls powered by rainwater harvesting, palaces of discarded rubble...like a caricature of the well-planned city of Chandigarh outside, but I see no gilt-edged roasted chicken flapping its wings. There's great junk food in the vicinity, enticing chaat sold from almost hygienic pushcarts by the entrance gate, but it's veg throughout—not even a masala omelette to raise my cholesterol levels.

Chandigarh Rock Garden built of broken teacups, saucers, etc.

The creator of the Rock Garden, Nek Chand Saini, initiated his art project in the early 1960s when he was turning forty and it was still a work in progress when I visited—probably making it one of the world's grandest works of art. Compare those six decades to the four years that Michelangelo took to paint the celebrated ceiling of the Sistine Chapel! But there's no sign of that specific Mr Singh in the garden as far as I can tell.

By and large, Chandigarh feels much the same as when I visited it first in 1991. In the three decades that have passed, it hasn't, unlike most other cities, become more congested—like the arteries of cholesterol junkies like me. The wide roads that back then used to be empty save for the sporadic squeaky-creaky cycle rickshaw, a scattering of rattling Ambassadors and as I recall an overcrowded scooter with father, mother, granny and kids riding pillion, still easily accommodate traffic. It was once a futuristic city, but now that we live in that future, it has turned into the probably most liveable metro in South Asia. My friends in Delhi keep moving to Chandigarh to improve their health—mental as well as physical.

I chatted once with an Indian architect who complained about Chandigarh. He was a traditionalist and felt that cities of yore were built to match the climate, the culture and above all the lifestyles. Winding, narrow, shady streets work better than wide avenues drenched in sunshine. Open courtyards that facilitated natural air circulation were better than modern airtight glass-façade office complexes that drain precious energy to run their air-conditioning systems.

When I first came here I too found Chandigarh's design puzzling—until I met that particular Mr Singh. I was in my twenties and changing buses in town, on the way from Dharamsala to Delhi, which necessitated an overnight stay since the monsoon had rained on my backpack on the roof of the bus and everything was soaked. As I dried myself in the station canteen an elderly, bespectacled, turban-clad Sikh sat down at my table. 'I'm Mr Singh,' he said. I suspected he might be a tout, but he was a tad too polite and didn't want to sell me a handmade oriental carpet or a houseboat in Kashmir.

It transpired that post-retirement, Mr Singh had taken it upon himself to be the unofficial tourist ambassador of Chandigarh and so he offered me a map and showed me, on it, how the city had been built to reflect the human body—not unlike the Walled City of Delhi, in fact, but this was a much more futuristic take, an ambitious post-independence project to invent a new kind of Indian city. And by the look of it, it was quite obviously designed by a European architect influenced by cubism. The government buildings to the north, in Sector 1, were obviously the brain, the commercial centre where we sat in the Sector 17 bus station encircled by restaurants was the gastric system, the central parks with their flower gardens were the lungs and the roads its arteries. A city as a living organism? *Where was its soul then?*

'Let me take you to the Rock Garden,' said Mr Singh with a gentle smile, and after suggesting a homely guesthouse, he showed me the way to that marvellous tourist attraction.

Leaving town, I forgot all about Singh until years later, when I met another senior tourist and as we shared a tandoori chicken—reputed to be the original recipe—at the anachronistic Moti Mahal in Delhi, we compared notes on places we had gone to. When I mentioned the innovative layout of Chandigarh, he told me of one of the trippiest experiences of India—and I interrupted, 'Yeah, I've been to the Rock Garden.'

But he protested, 'No, the man who collects tourists.' His encounter with Mr Singh, way back in the 1980s, led to them spending days together and eating so much tandoori chicken that he could only cackle at the memory now. Singh wasn't merely an unlicensed tourist guide, my friend explained, but a 'bona fide tourist collector' whose ambition was to meet and greet every single foreigner passing through town, welcome them heartily and make them feel at home according the Sikh tradition of hospitality and cultural tolerance.

So this time, when I land up in Chandigarh again after decades, I want to thank Singh for that map that opened up the city for me. I hope to find him and then ask where to get a perfect tandoori chicken, partly to make up for that chicken I once ate in Patna—as described in the beginning of this book—that caused me ignoble tummy troubles years ago. So I spend an afternoon stalking about the bus station which has grown and is jam-packed with Singhs, but none of them is the right Mr Singh. Hence, I turn to Anthony Bourdain's immortal words, 'Checking off my list of things to do in the Punjab, I gotta score some animal protein. It's time. I've been going all Morrissey for like two days now, and frankly, that's enough. I need chicken. When we're talking [Punjab] must-haves, tandoori chicken is just that.'

It looks like I have to procure my own chicken and so to make it as genuine as possible I try to figure out which might be the oldest kitchen in this modern town—or at least one that was already in existence in the times of Mr Singh. There turns out to be one obvious choice, the somewhat forlorn Ghazal

Punjab's national bird, tandoori chicken.

in the Sector 17-C market. In those days, I recall the entire market square was totally un-happening—not a soul used to be seen—but today, it beats the most cosmopolitan plazas with all the bright fast-food joints of the world at your greasy fingertips and bars where mixologists pour genteel cocktails down your throat. When I find it, Ghazal is a refreshing return to the past with its gloomy lighting, clunky tables and old-fashioned deep sofas that scream: 'Let's go back to pre-1991, pre-liberalisation!'

When the 'murgh' joins me at the table, it thankfully isn't one of those modern deep-red food-colour-spray-painted ones, but crispy turmeric and Kashmiri chilli orangish. Don't misunderstand me—it's a normal, traditional tandoori chicken and one can probably sample a similar fiery fowl in many places, including at Old Delhi's hallowed Moti Mahal. But in this world of escalating complexity, when everything must be fashionably fusion and gastronomically molecular, it is increasingly rare to come across classic honest-to-goodness simplicity. Munching on that hapless hen, it occurs to me how its species of poltroonish pea-brains conquered the world not once, but twice.

Its first ancestor on our planet was a wild jungli murgh (wild fowl) living millennia ago in what is now West Bengal and Bangladesh. After a couple of aeons, these were domesticated by the Harappans 4,300 years ago if not earlier, approximately in the area that is now Punjab, which might explain the Punjabi obsession with chicken. Offbeat scholars claim it happened millennia earlier in China or southeastern Asia, but even then their chickens were likely to have been imported from India—probably via Southeast Asia where Vietnamese archaeologists have found a bronze statue of a chicken dating back to 1,000 BCE. This implies chicken were domesticated around the same time in many parts of Asia.

The Harappans are however credited with building the first tandoor, or at least prototypes for top-loaded clay ovens four-five millennia back in which bread could be baked and meat roasted, though thousands of years before that Mesopotamians supposedly preceded them by using pit ovens known in Babylonian as *timuru* (which we now pronounce as tandoor). Anyway, without going too deep into who invented what and when, it is clear that the Harappans were the first to eat something similar to what's on my plate at Ghazal because once you have a chicken in one hand, and a tandoor in the other, combining the two in the correct manner is just a matter of practice. At least one thing is for sure that the tandoor is emblematic of Punjabi cuisine and since Indian restaurants across the world have their roots in the Punjabi dhabas, tandoori cooking is therefore perceived as virtually synonymous with Indian food. And this is how it happened.

From India, the flightless birds somehow spread westwards, most likely via Persian intermediaries, reaching southern Europe on a happy day in the seventh century BCE (which we know because chickens appear on Greek vases and feature as a delicacy at symposiums) and then onwards to northern Europe in order to become rather common among the Celts and Germans, ruling the non-veg roost about the year 0 when the Roman Empire invaded territories further and further north, which coincidentally is the date from when Europeans count years—but maybe not exactly for that specific reason. To the Americas, chicken migrated as late as five centuries ago, brought across the Atlantic Sea by none other than Columbus himself in 1493, and for all that I know it may well be how the state of Kentucky got its name, from the eponymous fried chicken. About one in every three chickens living on our planet ends up 'Kentucky-fried' while another third is either curried or tandooried.

During the previous century, this prehistoric invasion was followed by a modern conquest when actual tandoori cooking as we know it was developed back in pre-Partition Peshawar, now across the border in Pakistan and some 800 km from the Ghazal in Chandigarh. It conquered New Delhi through the Moti Mahal, owned by a Partition refugee whose food-stall had gained so much fame for its chicken dishes that he upgraded, became the post-Partition foodie rage in the 1950s, the place to be seen at, and it is still a great trip into the past. Curiously, prior to this momentous development there apparently weren't any tandoors in Delhi. In fact, there were hardly any grillable chickens either, only hardy hens, as the soft-fleshed broiler—bred for grilling purposes in the USA since the 1920s—only became available at dhabas after independent India's Second Five Year Plan highlighted the need for industrial-scale poultry production (according to an article in *The Economic Times*).

I'm reliably informed that no radical changes have been made to the Moti Mahal menu card since about 1947 except for adding butter chicken to it—invented in the 1950s, it's essentially a way to use up chicken leftovers by cooking them in creamy tomatoish gravy (the cornerstone of a true Delhiwallah's diet). So even if the tandoori chicken may have Harappan pedigree, it received its modern form at that particular outlet. Moti Mahal was also, in fact, the only proper restaurant in the old parts of Delhi thereby creating something of a template for the archetypal evolved dhaba (and it gained international fame because the then prime minister, Jawaharlal Nehru, took important foreign guests there).

The first tandoor oven outside Asia was installed at Veeraswamy's, which coincidentally is the oldest surviving London-based Indian restaurant (from 1926), and according to food columnist and gastronome extraordinaire Vir Sanghvi the tandoori chicken only showed up on US menus in the 1960s. The original Moti Mahal of today is a somewhat bedraggled shadow of its former self, but it has plenty of branches and wherever one goes—whether San Francisco or Melbourne or anywhere in between—there'll be a piping hot tandoori chicken not far out of reach, connecting us moderns to the Harappan past.

Burping my way out of Sector 17, I think that even if the Rock Garden is still under construction, growing more incredible by the year, and I failed to locate Mr Singh, at least Chandigarh—in other respects—appears to retain its soul in a place like Ghazal, and its heart still belongs to Punjab's beloved national bird: Tandoori chicken.

❖

During a week in Allahabad (now Prayagraj), I do what everyone else goes there to do and visit the Sangam, where the Ganges and Yamuna meet, for holy boating. Then I roam the old town's knotted-up bazaars to shop for snacks and sweets. But the place I am constantly gravitating back to is the Civil Lines. More specifically, its main street, M.G. Marg. It is hard to put one's finger on what's so special, but, on some level, it gives me the odd sensation of having a walk-on part in an E.M. Forster television adaptation, except that M.G. Marg was called Canning Road in those days.

It's a set waiting for the costume drama to begin. Many a paan stall is named Sophiya Laurence Beetle Shop after the bustily bosomy European cine-star of the 1950s, Sophia Loren, who must have been all the rage in the looming cinema buildings that line the street, adding a touch of cosmopolitan elegance. Unlike so many other towns that are busy turning themselves into Singapore-replicas, Allahabad helps tourists imagine the past—as if time left it behind and forgot about coming back to wind its clock up.

Oodles of charisma ooze out of the Indian Coffee House (founded in 1957), where I reboot with a stack of keema omelettes washed down with roohafza, that early 1900s sweet beverage of pre-Coca-colonised India. The café sports sprightly waiters in antediluvian uniforms, uncles crowd tables, hunch over chipped cups, debating in paan-scented Hindi. This would have been where the stalwarts of modern Indian literature sat and made literary history. Allahabad was then known as the

Indian Coffee House, founded in 1957, where stalwarts of modern Indian literature used to meet.

Oxford of India whose Civil Lines was a hub of bookishness, embellished by bards like Firaq Gorakhpuri, who lectured at the university; his bungalow on 8/4 Bank Road was a gathering place for poetry-loving students (such as my late father-in-law) and novelists such as Premchand.

And not to forget Rudyard Kipling, who in the late 1800s, found his first high-profile job at the then principal newspaper of colonial India, *The Pioneer*—'India's greatest and most important paper'. It was in India that he honed his writing craft. For example, the newspaper started a special weekly edition which would print fiction, amongst other things. 'Would I edit it, additional to ordinary work? Would I not?' In *Something of Myself,* he described how he churned out 'soldier tales, Indian tales, and tales of the opposite sex.' Thus he made his 'own experiments in the weights, colours, perfumes, and attributes of words in relation to other words, either as read aloud so that they may hold the ear, or, scattered over the page, draw the eye. There is no line of my verse or prose which has not been mouthed till the tongue has made all smooth, and memory, after many recitals, has mechanically skipped the grosser superfluities.'

The Wheeler's chain of railway bookstalls was founded in Allahabad and they introduced the novel idea of paperbacks with their cheap editions of, well, what else but Kipling, long before the rest of the world bought paperbacks en masse (in the 1940s post-war era when cheaper printing became a necessity). Basically, Kipling popularised the format by upgrading what used to be known as 'dime novels' to encompass good fiction. The main Wheeler's Bookshop (of 1966 vintage) is still found on 19, M.G. Marg and they published many of Kipling's earliest books, both story collections and travelogues of India, including *Plain Tales from the Hills* that lampooned the imperial high-society of Shimla. It is believed that it was Kipling's idea to have stalls at all Indian stations to peddle his books.

An entire galli devoted to snacks in the bazaars of Allahabad.

After a few days, I find the house in which Kipling lived just before moving away from India, and where he—in a handful of frenzied months—penned his celebrated Indian stories. The English family who lived there provided Kipling with 'the Blue Room for his study and the guest room with the big four-poster bed, bath and east veranda'. Today, due to karmic interference its houses a printing press known as the Belvedere Printing Works (56A/13, Moti Lal Nehru Road). The proprietor tells me that he focuses on spiritual pamphlets and what were Kipling's rooms then are now part of an adjacent orphanage where nobody seems to know that a world-renowned children's writer, author of *The Jungle Book* and a Nobel winner, stayed in it. Every morning young 'Ruddy' ate his breakfast on its veranda and I picture him planning, plotting his stories there, in the throes of manic inspiration, before sailing off to embark on his international literary career.

In his travel collection *From Sea to Sea*, Kipling describes the scene as he is about to leave Allahabad for good: 'The Copper-smith sang in the garden and the early wasp hummed low down by the door-handle, and they prophesied of the hot weather to come.' And he wasn't the only literary star around, because the poet Harivansh Rai Bachchan also lived in the same compound at the time when his son Amitabh was a toddler (before he grew up to be the shiniest and biggest Bollywood star ever). Another city poet is Arvind Krishna Mehrotra who, although he lives in a different part of town, in an ode about childhood games reminisces, 'Our tomahawks are butter knives, our crow/ Feathers are real, and riding out from behind/ Plaza Talkies we ambush the cowboys of Civil Lines.'

Which brings me back to the main streets of the former English cantonment. Mofussil charm reveals itself as I loiter about in town. Splendid art deco structures, odd bungalows and equally antique upper-class uncles and aunties dressed in dated fashions hog daintily in fine-diners that haven't changed since the mid-1900s. The chicest, El Chico from 1964, has a completely retro menu of delicacies forgotten by the rest of the world but still au courant here: Russian salad drenched in rich mayo dressing (a memory of those Cold War-decades when India was one of the few non-communist lands with a reach behind the Iron Curtain), soul-stirring 'cottage cheese cutlets' (never has paneer melted in my mouth like this) that I follow up with a hillock of mutton roast plated with butter-sautéed beans and cauliflower. Tea is served in a reassuring pewter pot set. The other guests consist of a geriatric Anglo-Indian taking his greying spinster daughter out for their habitual lunch, a bunch of paunchy men in white kurtas—contractors closing a shady deal—and two families out-bragging each other about their most recent European holidays.

'Was Amsterdam in Germany or in Switzerland?'

'No, sweaty, you're mixing it up with Brussels, where they have the tulips.'

To experience prehistoric grocery shopping, I drop in at Beni Prasad Laxmi Narayan, a congested store in a graceful mercantile arcade from 1934 (which Arvind Krishna Mehrotra told me is a must-see). For my next meal, I step into a servery that advertises itself as over-six-decades-old and my initial reaction is to gasp at its stuccoed ceilings, plaster-of-Paris medallions on all-white walls, and wooden furnishings with red upholstery. It's all classy classic. A certain romantic Frenchness is added by how couples rent the upstairs family compartment, spend fifteen minutes perhaps doing some family planning activities, and hurriedly climb down the steps zipping flies and buttoning up gowns and covering their faces. However, it turns out there's nothing edible available except for mixed-veg curry made with rotten veggies, mouldy papadam and undercooked, doughy chapattis—I usually digest anything, but this is a mortally deadly funerary feast for suicidal omnivores with no sense of what's good for them.

For once, I cannot finish my meal and instead, after sufficient recovery time spent in one of M.G. Marg's characteristic dive bars disinfecting my bowels with vodka, I splurge at the smart Tepso's Jade Garden where muzak wails softly.

It gets crowded with aunties who order Chicken Tikka Masala, that most British version of Indian dishes—a humbug makhani murgh or butter chicken imitation created by Bangladeshi migrant chefs trying their hand at Punjabi cookery, tweaking it to suit palates in London (or Glasgow, if you listen to a Scotsman). The story goes that they made it from leftover chicken kebabs boiled in sweetish canned tomato soup. Whatever the case, 'CTM' recipes in their quintessential Britishness invariably include tins of chopped tomatoes, spoonfuls of cream, glow-in-the-dark radioactive food colouring, yoghurt-marinated chicken, moderate spicing and sugar. It is estimated that Britons devour twenty-three million portions of CTM per year at the approximately 15,000 outlets that have it on their menu.

At Tepso's I rather prefer the cheese-baked fish in white sauce, a sinful dish if there ever was one, made not with frozen fish but freshly-caught North Indian river sole from the Ganges, assures the waiter, and the cheesy crust is honest-to-goodness Amul, finely shredded.[26]

M.G. Marg isn't really built for serious pubbing, but whenever I crave a sunset double-pint along with pre-dinner snacks, I head for the tourist bungalow next to the noisy bus station. For pub grub, the food is decent as evidenced by retired uncles whiling away afternoons sipping beer and nibbling on chicken cutlets. And if I'm still peckish late at night, there are gourmet chefs with pushcarts everywhere, attracting custom for their litti-chokha, whole-wheat dumplings stuffed with mustard oil-and cumin-seasoned roasted chickpea or lentil flour, then baked in cow dung ash which imparts a unique flavoursomeness, rinsed in a cup of melted butter before eaten piping hot with chokha, charred eggplant-cum-boiled potato puree. It is a dish that has quite likely been prevalent in these parts since two or three millennia by now and it tastes as great today as when perhaps Buddha himself—who once toured in the area—would have eaten it.

It is perhaps appropriate that Civil Lines has retained its nomenclature instead of being renamed, because civil is what it is, and if you read between the lines you'll get food of the sort that's hardly imaginable anymore in this epoch of global sameness: Allahabad's flavours of pre-liberalised India remind one of a young country that had just gained independence under a prime minister who—naturally—was born in Allahabad. M.G. Marg remains a living museum of food sophistication from a hallowed history before global junk food machine-gunned its way into our tummies.

VIII

Where Teatime is Anytime
(The East)

'Come, oh come, ye tea-thirsty restless ones—the kettle boils, bubbles and sings, musically.'

—Rabindranath Tagore,
winner of the Nobel Prize for Literature in 1913

Friendly bartendresses running a bar in Bhutan.

'Welcome to Bihar,' says the student who wants to shake my hand as soon as the train rolls into Patna Junction, the modern incarnation of Pataliputra, the once-upon-a-time headquarters of Mauryan civilisation. 'I hope you'll come back again.'

I wouldn't know. Bihar seems nice but people persistently warned me before this trip: 'Don't expect to come back alive from Bihar,' they said. Don't expect any roads, they went on gleefully adding, 'Don't expect electricity.' So, despite the warm welcome by the student on his way to his 'native place' by the Nepalese border, I am wondering how unwise it might turn out to be a vagabond hereabouts. I can't help but notice how the platform behind the student resembles a freshly-ploughed potato-field.

Nevertheless, I've always had a soft corner in my heart, and a rough spot in my tummy, for Patna, perhaps more for its literary importance than its occasionally deadly foods. Patna is, in a manner, where this book, started with *that* tandoori chicken which I can never forget, but it holds more stories than that. To the north of town, in Motihari, a house is identified by a concrete sign on the roadside as George Orwell's birthplace. His father was an opium-tax collector in the Opium Department, a strange British-run government-owned industry devoted to peddling narcotics (which would have landed Orwell's dad in jail had he been alive today). And so young Orwell spent his first years around here. In adulthood, he worked as a colonial police officer in another remote area—erstwhile Burma, which falls outside the scope of this book. His novel *Nineteen Eighty-Four* coined the expression 'Big Brother is watching you' and perhaps it was inspired by the Soviet Union, but apparently it can also be read (alongside his *Animal Farm*) as a fictive history of Myanmar.

Patna is furthermore the model for E.M. Forster's fictional Chandrapore—a city on the Ganges where the 'very wood seems made of mud, the inhabitants of mud moving. So abased, so monotonous is everything that meets the eye, that when the Ganges comes down it might be expected to wash the excrescence back into the soil. Houses do fall, people are drowned and left rotting, but the general outline of the town persists, swelling here, shrinking there, like some low but indestructible form of life' he wrote—after touristing in town for some two weeks—and it is here, where much of the action in *A Passage to India* (written 1912-24) ostensibly takes place.

Except for those pivotal picnic passages in the spooky Barabar caves about 100 km to the south, which he visited in January 1913 and fictionalised as the Marabar Caves, and that literary scholars have been speculating over for nearly a century.[27] Forster was frequently enough quoted as saying, 'When asked what happened there, I don't know.' He visited the caves in a disturbed state of mind and spent much time sobbing in Patna, where his friend Dr Masood (the novel's Dr Aziz) at the time was teaching, which is reflected—or perhaps repressed—in the fictional scene. And which prompted him to write the novel *Maurice*, upon his return to England, although it was only to be published posthumously.[28]

The director of the sumptuous silverscreen spectacle, David Lean, rejected the real caves as not mystical enough. He worked on the screenplay in New Delhi using elements of Karnataka-born writer Santha Rama Rau's stage adaptation and set the film in Karnataka instead of North India, shooting mostly in and around Bengaluru's surrounding rocky landscapes and enigmatic crags. There, a decade before, the wild west-style Hindi blockbuster *Sholay* had been filmed and, at the time when it was still called Bangalore, the town had a fair amount of milieus suitable for a colonial period cinematic extravaganza—some of the recognisable shooting locations include the city's palace and the old Bangalore Club.

The table of fare of the novel's over-the-top picnic remains another mystery save for one man tippling and another smoking a fag, apart from which there is just a fleetingly referenced porridge dish (khichdi?). One may only speculate what Forster's characters ate during their last meal before the culture clash—one colonial-era Indian menu devised for English people I study for reference, in a musty autobiography, mentions hilariously named fusion fare such as cutlets, that are not meat slices as Britons might expect, but potato patties. To further befuddle the English, such veg cutlets are also called chops which as per the dictionary means 'small piece of meat on a bone, usually cut from a sheep or pig'. Or take *hotche-potche* soup. I've no idea what that might be but hazard a guess it is rasam which, after an unknown 'Madrasi cook' added chicken and rice to make it soupy, came to be better known as the colonial Mulligatawny Soup. Then they were served *cotholathe mouthong* (presumably genuine mutton cutlets this time) with *poulay* (most likely a chicken pullao) and *cocks turky* (roasted chicken legs?), and *maccaroning* (hmm...curried pasta?). However, what really takes my cake is a menu of Rice Dumplings with Doll Curry and

Cock-Nut Sauce—it took me a while to decipher it as your standard idli-sambar with coconut chutney!

Of what he encountered on Indian menus, Forster was (as already noted in Hyderabad) into biryani which may have resembled aforesaid *poulay*. And jackfruits were 'extraordinary' according to him. But although the picnic in the novel was hosted by Aziz, the friendly Muslim, vegetarian fare was obviously served as a Brahmin cook is mentioned and one of the characters, Professor Godbole would only eat 'vegetables and rice if cooked by a Brahman; but not meat, not cakes lest they contained eggs, and he would not allow anyone else to eat beef: a slice of beef upon a distant plate would wreck his happiness.' And I'm reminded of how, when Forster lived in Madhya Pradesh, he got tired of the vegetarian spreads—this picnic perhaps mirrors that frustration?

Patna also inspired the city of Brahmpur in *A Suitable Boy*, the 1990s' hit novel by Vikram Seth, but Mira Nair's TV-series based on it shunned Patna just like Lean's movie did decades earlier, and it was primarily canned in Lucknow which was deemed a more suitable backdrop. Despite how it has inspired great novels, Patna isn't a glossy town like Paris, or Rome. Clouds of dust hover over the streets. Hogs dig into piles of garbage—this simply isn't the hottest destination you will read about in award-winning travelogues. Most people, in fact, tell you that it would have been a better option to come here in the days of the Buddha, who wasn't born in Bihar (his birthplace is believed to be Lumbini in Nepal) and didn't die here (he died in Uttar Pradesh). But he did spend much of his life here, roaming around an area covering 180,000 square kilometres or twice the size of present-day Bihar.

It seems to have been an interesting time, but no trains in India run that slow that they can arrive late by 2,500 years. Yet trying to forget the present, I check out the chief attraction at the museum, apparently nicknamed Jadu Ghar ('magic castle'), on Buddha Road which is a life-sized statue of a well-developed woman known as the Didarganj Yakshi, dating from those times. The museum collection also has statues of Buddha. He was so respected in Pataliputra—filled with good people who were 'the most distinguished in all India' according to the ancient Greek geographer Strabo—that one of the sixty-four gates in the city wall was named after him. Perhaps he even strode down Buddha Road, maybe he met and preached to the voluptuous model, I muse in the garden outside the museum. Maybe she ran a tavern in town?

As a matter of fact, Buddhist jataka tales contain India's earliest food-writing—if one may term it so—giving a fair idea of what foodstuffs were on offer to travellers. Bihar itself is named for the many viharas (monasteries) that once existed in the state, both centres of learning as well as safe accommodation where one might break journey for the night and be provided a wholesome dinner. Many monasteries were virtual food plants with sugar mills and oil presses. K.T. Achaya, who studied the matter of Buddhist cuisine, mentions chickpeas and various other pulses, condiments such as black mustard seeds and asafoetida, fruits (bananas and grapes), and also sugarcane which remains a major crop in Bihar. Dishes in Buddhist texts that sound tempting include barley-honey balls—laddus?—and staples such as wild rice khichdi and honey-flavoured kanji. A monk who sailed from China to the Nalanda monastery described a menu of rice with peas and boiled barley—the latter being eaten already since Vedic times. Many kinds of flatbreads were part of the diet, salad and fruit, and—hold your breath—non-veg.

Pigeon meat was familiar fare, fish was also considered

permitted food, perhaps braised in fruit juice like some Asiatic Buddhists still cook them. At one modern monastery inhabited by monks from Cambodia, the chatty disciples I met were cooking what looked like pigeon, squeezing some esoteric fruit juice onto it, but it turned out to be a chicken curry. Some monks, during the Buddha's lifetime, brewed a potent beverage known as Pigeon's Liquor (not made out of pigeon's poop, as you might think, but it was a fortified palm wine thus named due to its somewhat murky greyish colour). This practice stopped in 520 BCE when the Buddha found an old monk lying drunk outside a monastery. Non-veg was also flavoured with lime juice—limes were special fruits for Buddhists and are even depicted in the cave paintings of Ajantha, and it was Indian monks who introduced limes to China in the fourth century CE.

Before achieving enlightenment and after having starved for weeks, the Buddha is said to have eaten a traditional Bihari rice pudding which opened his eyes to the futility of extreme asceticism. And thereafter his diet was quite typical of any Indian—rice and dhal, occasionally non-veg items such as fish and eggs, as well as sweet items. He is even quoted as describing what to him counted as soulfood, 'I recommend food made out of rice, barley, wheat, all kinds of beans, ghee, oil of sesame, honey, sugarcane, sugar, and other seasonal foods which are full of soul qualities…' Such foods were considered rich in merits, virtue, wisdom and they warded off evils. He urged people to embrace moderation and self-control, not to lust too much after delicacies that were bad for karma, as all craving was back in those days before consumerism became our modern religion. Statistical experts have concluded, after studying the meals described in Buddhist literature, that he was 40 per cent vegan, 54 per cent vegetarian and only every twentieth meal he had was non-veg. In fact, the menu consisted of whatever the monks were given in their alms bowls, whether veg or non-veg, and to this day one sees monks in Southeast Asia walking from door to door, between restaurants in the mornings, to collect their daily meal.

Most intriguingly, the Buddha is believed to have spent time in the company of cannibals as he, in the *Lankavatara Sutra*, discussed the problems of cannibalism faced by a king whose 'excessive fondness for meat, his greed to be served with it, stimulated his taste for it to the highest degree so that he ate human flesh.' This of course alienated a ruler from his kinsmen if they suspected that he might cook them. 'In consequence he had to renounce his throne and dominion and to suffer great calamities because of his passion for meat,' said the Buddha as he advocated the benefits of vegetarianism. Though this was of little use as the monarch's rebelling subjects killed him in the end.

If the Buddha has living descendants, it is reasonable to assume that they can be encountered in present-day Patna's restaurants.

❖

On the train east, at most stations, they sell the sinful luchi-sabzi of starchy cholesterol-rich puffed breads dunked in greasy gravy that Bengalis love so much, which tells me that the train is entering West Bengal. Hawkers come on-board to peddle milky mishti-doi, date palm jaggery-sweetened curd in clay pots that are perfect to cool one's intellectual turmoil.

As far as I have counted, there are in all 7,325 stations in India, each of which is likely to be a theatrical display of energising sweets and quick bites often with some regional specialities up their sleeve. I've only visited about 500 of those, so I'm left with this nagging feeling that there's lots left for me to explore in terms of railway food. And it's an absolute fact that food, for some reason, tastes better on tours—like the unexpectedly delicious fish curry I once had in the canteen at Jamshedpur station, the robust Tamil biryani sold on the platform at Khatpadi Junction, Kerala's banana fritters, the chikki peanut candy at Lonavla, the unbelievably smooth dhoklas at Gujarati stations, the aloo tikkis of Uttar Pradesh and choles of Punjab...and not to forget the crunchy Maddur-vada at the eponymous train stop between Bengaluru and Mysuru, which coincidentally was invented by a man peddling snacks on the platform one day when the train wasn't as delayed as it usually was. He suddenly had to cook up a quicker fast-food than his normal offerings (hence he made the vada flatter to fry it faster). Basically, while other tourists take the train to see the world, I do it to eat the world. Or its most intriguing bits.

Finally, I stretch my legs in Kolkata's railway station where India is camping out on the floor, a human tsunami trying to flood the right train in the poorly signposted, cavernous halls that are full of traffic-jammed porters struggling with overloaded carts. I decide to break journey for a week or two.

Eventually every travelling booklover reaches Kolkata where there's so much culture—and where East and West cohabited as Britons built their great eastern metropolis of which Kipling rhymed:

Me the Sea-captain loved, the River built,
Wealth sought and Kings adventured life to hold.
Hail, England! I am Asia—Power on silt,
Death in my hands, but Gold!

Although the Nobel-awardee-to-be was quite dismissive of the 'city of dreadful night' as he liked to call it, Bengali literary sentiment spawned distinguished authors such as Bibhutibhushan Bandhopadhyay who wrote *Song of the Road* that was filmed by Satyajit Ray, Bankimchandra Chatterjee whose 'Vande Mataram' is the poem of the nation, Rabindranath Tagore who bagged that coveted Nobel Prize, besides so many others. The city houses the National Library that stores copies of everything published in India—it's apt that such an institution is here, since publishing in this country in the modern sense really started in the city, with journals first in English such as the scandalous *Hickey's Gazette*, but soon enough they were also printed in Bengali. The earliest printers were in the Chitpur neighbourhood where I still hear the churning of presses that use movable types as I poke along Chitpur Road.

The one condition that always afflicts me in Kolkata, is a profound regret over the fact that I wasn't born a Bengali. Numerous novels, short stories and poems have been translated, but the bulk of Bengali literature is and will remain appreciable only to those who can read the language properly—its nuances, its rhythms and its Aeolian cadences. Hence, being a non-Bengali-speaker in Kolkata is like being a vegetarian in a seafood hotel. My vocabulary consists of about three Bengali words, adda, bhetki, and, uh, vodka. With that, I could only write a really short haiku in the language.

While writing his *The City of Dreadful Night*, Kipling stayed at the Great Eastern Hotel (which later housed prominent communists such as Ho Chi Minh and Nikita Khrushchev) and although he loved the hotel—'Fancy sitting down seventy strong to *tâble d'hôte* and with a deafening clatter of knives and forks! Fancy finding a real bar whence drinks may be obtained!'—for some private reason he was never quite able to digest the city, but rather loved to hate 'Calcutta, which, I was to see, still persisted in being a city...I had formally cursed it one year ago.' His top tip for fellow travellers went: 'One must begin to smoke at five in the morning—which is neither night nor day—on coming across the Howrah Bridge, for it is better to get a headache from honest nicotine than to be poisoned by evil smells.'[29] For whatever reason and ever since, foreigners like to portray the city unfavourably, such as its poverty that shapes the narrative in *The City of Joy* by Dominique Lapierre. As I am trying to get my head around this, I come across the following lines by a local author: 'But to deny the undisputed rule of filth and astounding tardiness in Kolkata is to be in denial about what's unpleasant but real,' writes Inderjit Hazra as he does seem to grant the city's critics a point. 'Despite its colonial architectures, Kolkata everywhere, in all its wetness and rust and ooze, seems like a city built, or in the process of being built, on the remains of another city that someone left behind.'

Rather than ponder such bleakness, it is far better to get oneself invited to an adda, the impromptu ideating salons or vociferous tea party discussions among close friends, that blend gossip and jokes with artistic, political or scientific debates, and that take place at homes or in cafés so beloved among the talkative Bengalis, and that always include tea or coffee, and some gorgeous savouries, sweets and perhaps even fried fish. An adda can happen in any corner if the right quantity of patrons can be gathered. If there's no adda, one can always head to the university area's Coffee House in Bankim Chatterjee Street and launch one's own. The café founded in the 1940s is a Kolkata institution and is in fact housed in the historic Albert Hall (from 1876) which has been the venue of many important talks, including by Mahatma Gandhi. It was at one of these tables that Satyajit Ray scripted his *Pather Panchali*, based on Bandhopadhyay's aforementioned novel *Song of the Road*, that gave him worldwide fame, but he wasn't the only filmy regular—they all hung out here: Ritwik Ghatak, Mrinal Sen, Utpal Dutt and Aparna Sen. Towards the end of his life, Allen Ginsberg spoke passionately about 1960s' Calcutta, 'We poets—Sunil Ganguly, Shakti Chatterjee, and others—met a lot in the coffee houses. Peter [Orlovsky] and I were excited by the idea of there being a whole gang of poets like there were in New York and San Francisco, who were friends, and that we could communicate across the Pacific Ocean, and that East could meet West…' Indeed, West did meet East and so when Ginsberg flew to Bangkok in May 1963, his travel companion Orlovsky stayed behind as he had fallen in love with a Bengali musician.

In the more genteel Park Street, on the other hand, I spot litterateur Amit Chaudhuri having his solitary adda, sipping daintily on a cup of what looks like Earl Grey with low-calorie sweeteners and low-fat milk at Flury's, the 1920s' Park Street tearoom fashionable for its scones and parfaits. This is apparently where Chaudhuri goes when he is slumming according to his book *Calcutta: Two Years in the City*. Although the poet's preferred haunts are the city's exclusive clubs and fully air-conditioned five-star-hotels, he does ask himself 'thinking about this book which I had taken upon myself to write: How would it start?' So after a cuppa at Flury's, he crossed the road and ventured into the somewhat less posh Free School Street: 'Earlier, I would have denied this place its existence, would have seen it but shut it out, would have looked at it as a stubborn aberration…' But on that afternoon he studied it for as long as it took to walk the 650 metres to Sudder Street and back to Flury's, while observing the poor wash their pots and pans in gutter mud, homeless people 'bored, doing nothing' and handed out Rs 50 to an ailing child labourer. This is perhaps the best description I've read of the city's elite viewing their less fortunate fellow city-dwellers.

Whereas streetsy chai-drinking is an all-day affair, high tea in orthodox circumstances is served at 4 p.m. in the finer salons of the Taj Bengal or Great Eastern where éclairs and croissants adorn the spreads, and trendy newer places like Karma Kettle celebrates colonial nostalgia with their 'Gora Sahib High Tea' of chicken roulades, tea-cakes and scones, yet in Kolkata's streets, teatime is anytime if one patronises the chaiwallas who pour milky brew into earthen cups.

There's a lot to be said about tea, the beverage that mankind associates with India. It is one of the two main British contributions to Indian food culture, the other being sliced white sandwich bread which can be stuffed with spiced up veggies, dipped in batter and deep-fried into something that no Englishman would recognise as a sandwich, just like chai is remote from the sedate English Breakfast teas. Technically speaking, tea-drinking was 'invented' according to calculations in the 2730s BCE in China's south-westerly mountains bordering North-east India. And although China remains the #1 producer, a huge share of what the planet consumes comes from Assam's thousands of tea gardens while the most exclusive varieties grow in northern Bengal's hilly Darjeeling district, with Kolkata being the industry's primary trading hub. One Assamese tea estate is movie star Julie Christie's birthplace.

Before the plantation industry commenced circa 1840, the beverage was nigh on unknown here—except by some medievals who traded with China and Assamese tribals in the remotest North-east who plucked wild-growing tea off certain trees (*Camellia sinensis var. Assamica*) which must have spread across the mountains and taken root here by themselves. This slow growth of tea culture is astonishing, considering that there were overland trade routes from China to Assam operational already by the second century BCE—well before the Silk Road opened for traffic. Incredibly enough, only in the years after independence did tea gradually metamorphose from a symbol of colonial snootiness to a national drink when the Tea Board started promoting it as an important Made in India product. Nowadays, all tourist guidebooks and travel documentaries feature, as a characteristic character, the ubiquitous chaiwallah who is boiling (rather than brewing) his maximum spicy and high-punch sweetish concoction, encountered on railway platforms, in bus stations, street-corners, yes, everywhere.[30]

Connoisseurs say good tea is like champagne, to which no Old Monk rum needs to be added, making tea-sipping every bit as exciting as wining-dining-shining in Bordeaux. At least I suppose the Hollywood actress Vivien Leigh may have thought so—as she was born in Darjeeling in the winter of 1913, she

Potential adda in Kolkata.

must have smelled the spring flush as a toddler before her cavalry officer father was transferred to Bengaluru. She then went to school in another tea-planting district, in the southern Nilgiri Hills where she acted in amateur theatre productions. Even after her cinematic career took off in the 1930s, with *Gone with the Wind* turning into an award-winning box-office hit, she went on reminiscing about a masala dosa that she had eaten with her chai in India.

When I'm not busy swilling tea and exploring intellectual life, I drink in the headiness of age-old 'Calcutta' at the 1950s' eastern-European style Broadway beer hall (27A, Ganesh Chandra Avenue) where one might expect Karl Marx to make a meteoric entrance at any moment to snap one's tankard away. Auxiliary peckishness is cured by the mutton kathi rolls that are something of a heritage dish, having been invented at Nizam's near the market a century ago, in about 1930. Also, there are any number of kachoris, puchkas, bhelpuris and jhaalmuris and other dubious but dependably tempting street snacks that I obviously can't resist, with each street vendor (the city has about 130,000 of them) adding his own twist to the mixes that usually contain some cooked but cooled veggies, chillies and onions, puffed rice and crunchy-fried noodles ('sev'), various reddish and greenish spicy chutneys and suchlike tasting both cool, hot, sour and sweet at the same time, then perhaps coriander that gives a soapy tinge, black salt which adds a somewhat farty scent and the chaat masala without which nothing would be anything. Kolkata is like a peckish poem…or at least, I get uncommonly verbose when I try to briefly outline my eating experiences.

Across the road from the hippies' beloved lassi stall in Sudder Street, Tagore composed 'The Awakening of the Waterfall' that inaugurated his poetic career, standing on a balcony (in his brother's house) which was still there thirty years ago. This time, I find that the balcony is walled in and the building turned into a hotel called Plaza. So much for literary heritage buildings in the city of literature. Soon enough it'll all be gone, like the Sudder Street relic Fairlawn Hotel, in which it was possible to be transported back to the Raj and imagine oneself as an extra in some period TV serial. Fairlawn was purchased by a luxury hospitality group recently and will probably be reopened as a boutique inn with a flashy bistro.

Uptown, Tagore's birthplace Jorasanko (Dwarkanath Tagore Lane), where he also breathed his last, has been preserved as a museum, and his deathbed stands in the room where, before dying, he wrote somewhat morbidly, 'O my day-break sparrow/In my last moments of sleepiness/While there is still some darkness/Here you are tapping on my window-slats/ Asking for news/And then dancing and twittering.'

As a food tourist in his house, I am frankly speaking most touched by the kitchen where one can see a rather—from a modern point of view—primitive stove, upon which I imagine that the womenfolk prepared his sugary jasmine tea and his meals. He usually wanted Bengali food for lunch (mutton curry without chillies but tinged with sugar), followed by Western for dinner with soupy starters, meaty or fishy mains, and pudding for dessert. But he was against fusing the two—and all was eaten with imported cutlery, according to a story I heard from another museum visitor who seemed to know a lot about Bengali food culture. Coincidentally, Tagore's niece Prajñasundari Devi wrote one of the earliest Bengali cookbooks in 1902 and not many know that the bard coined a slogan to market tea—apart from inventing several desserts such as modified jalebis to tantalise the Bengalis' collective sweet tooth.

This obviously makes me hungry for Bengali specialities so

I head off, rather impatiently and not too far, to Siddeshwari Ashram in Mirza Ghalib Street (near Janbazaar) to have lunch at the no-frills and very business-like 'pice hotel'—one of the last such remaining, and known by that name because once upon a time food items could be bought for one paisa. The idea was that instead of ordering a full meal, money-minded customers could pick as many items as they could afford. Today, of course there aren't any paisa coins in circulation and dishes are pricier at Rs 100-200, but well worth it as their chingri is the biggest, freshest, juiciest estuary prawn I've ever sank my teeth into, virtually lobster-sized, and fried in a creamy gravy tempered with the typical five-spice blend 'paanch phoron'.

Earlier, the town was full of similar canteens to feed labourers who migrated here in search of work. Even this one existed in Tagore's days so he, being a foodie, may have ordered home-delivery or, perhaps, even sat at one of the marble-topped tables to sample its fare along with his culinary clubbers.

Another, about half-as-historic place but one that I love, is the all-women-run Suruchi (89 Elliot Road) where the divine bhetki tastes truly motherly. The perch-like fish is robed in a banana leaf that traps the aroma of the yellowish mustard paste and other spices during the cooking process. The one pungent note peculiar to Bengal's fishy dishes is 'shorshey tel', I think that may be how it is to be spelled, the local mustard oil that is a must and adds an unusual sharpness like a winding guitar solo in a 1970s' heavy metal tune. Apparently, it is because they view fish to be a vegetable of sorts, albeit one that swims and thinks, that the Bengalis have such evolved intellects and always were pioneers of modern literature. It is said that only every seventeenth Bengali is a vegetarian, the other sixteen love fish—including heads, brains and all.

One more experience of literary interest is the Park Street

cemetery. There's something about its decay that makes it utterly realistic. No plasticky Disney makeup covers its scars, everything is the real deal. The caretakers nap inside the cool crypts of towering tombs that constantly remind of exotic ways to die—the descriptions range from monsoon melancholia to choking on pineapples. It's hard to find anything comparable outside New Orleans's voodoo walks that take one to horror-movie spooky cemeteries, or Paris where everybody who is anybody, from Jim Morrison to Chopin, take final rest at Père-Lachaise, or London's supposedly occult graveyard at Highgate which has an interestingly swinging party crowd (provided that there's an afterlife) including Karl Marx whose tomb has been bombed several times, one alleged vampire who is said not to rest peacefully, not to forget *The Hitchhiker's Guide to the Galaxy* author Douglas Adams, plus music industry phenomena such as Malcolm McLaren (of Sex Pistols fame) and George Michael (of Wham!).

The Park Street cemetery's fame with film buffs has grown after the 2010 Bengali movie *Gorosthaney Sabdhan* based on Ray's story (translated into English as 'The Secret of the Cemetery') turned out to be a box-office success. And the literati are keen on exploring the necropolis of which Rudyard Kipling wrote in one of the more hallucinatory chapters of *City of Dreadful Night*: 'The eye is ready to swear that it is as old as Herculaneum and Pompeii. The tombs are small houses. It is as though we walked down the streets of a town, so tall are they and so closely do they stand—a town shrivelled by fire, and scarred by frost and siege. Men must have been afraid of their friends rising up before the due time that they weighted them with such cruel mounds of masonry.'

As for myself, I bite into a clove of garlic as I enter the cemetery, well aware of the rumours of haunting, how visitors experience spells of breathlessness and dizziness due to weird shapes peeking over their shoulders in their selfies. One tomb is claimed to occasionally bleed, sadly not when I'm visiting. I'm mesmerised instead by the eloquently inscribed tombstones,

A poet lies buried at the Park Street cemetery entrance.

which read like poetry about British times. Already at the entrance, visitors are greeted by the plaque commemorating Henry Louis Vivian Derozio (1809-1831), who according to Kipling was the 'poet of the race' and who influenced a generation of Bengali writers with his passion for everything Indian:

My native land hath heavenliest bowers
Where Houris ruby-cheeked might dwell,
And they are gemmed with buds and flowers
Sweeter than lip or lute may tell.

The most monumental grave belongs to philologist William Jones (1746-1794), a scholar who proposed a world-shattering theory about the relationship between the tongues of India and Europe. This developed into the idea of Indo-European languages, meaning that whether one is a Bengali-speaker or Englishman, what you say has a common source.

Overall, there are more than 1,600 graves, a phantasmagorical assemblage of towering obelisks and pyramids, cryptic cenotaphs and vaults, sarcophagus and catafalques, urns and cairns, occasionally bearing elements of Indo-Saracen architecture's distinct domes amidst Gothic and Greco-Roman designs. It correctly says on an enthusiastic notice board at the entrance that there is 'perhaps no other (non-church) exclusive colonial cemetery of this variety and dimension anywhere else in the world!'

Kipling was particularly drawn to the tomb of one Lucia Palk, 'hot-blooded young writers did duel with smallswords in the Fort ditch for the honour of piloting her through a minuet at the Calcutta theatre or the Punch House.' Unfortunately, 'Lucia fell sick, and the doctor—he who went home after seven years with five lakhs and a half, and a corner of this vast graveyard to his account—said that it was a *pukka* or putrid fever, and the system required strengthening. So they fed Lucia on hot curries, and mulled wine worked up with spirits and fortified with spices, for nearly a week; at the end of which time she closed her eyes,' he jotted in *City of Dreadful Night*. Subsequently, Paul Theroux exploited the boneyard in his Orientalist detective pulp *A Dead Hand*, while William Dalrymple's *White Mughals* drew on characters buried here such as 'Hindoo Stuart', an Irishman who tried to convince memsahibs to don saris ('the most alluring dress in the world') and who rests eternally in a mock Hindu temple.

Maybe the saddest grave is that of Rose Aylmer (1780-1800), who came to India as a teenaged beauty queen and died from enjoying those aforementioned pineapples—in excess. One of her admirers was the cavalier litterateur Walter Savage Landor, a close friend of Charles Dickens whose son Walter is also buried in Calcutta. Dickens junior wanted to become a writer too, but Dickens senior insisted junior take up a military career in India where he promptly died. Landor is best remembered for an elegy to his great love:

Rose Aylmer, whom these wakeful eyes
May weep, but never see,
A night of memories and of sighs
I consecrate to thee.

Booklovers will recall how Amit and Lata, the lovebirds of Vikram Seth's bombastic bestseller *A Suitable Boy*, initiate their infatuation in the graveyard, quoting to each other lines from Landor: 'Amit paused, "Ah, lovely poem, lovely poem," he said, looking delightedly at Lata.' I spend a good hour reading inscriptions about many other prematurely dead Britons who'd be long forgotten but for the memorials preserved here. I've heard it said that two monsoons used to be the lifetime of any foreigner in Kolkata—and the same went for Mumbai and Shillong too—and if not killed by malarial illness, men often succumbed to addictions. The death of one Englishman, for instance, was brought about through 'an inordinate use of the hokkah' though most others simply ate and drank themselves to death.

A chatty Anglo-Indian aunty stops to tell me of how her own ancestors 'came out' back in the day and tore up their British passports when India gained independence. According to her, Anglo-Indians are the finest race that spawned the likes of

Bombay-born 1950s' popstar Tony Brent (who used his music business fortune to open a chain of tiffin joints in Australia), Madras-born Engelbert Humperdinck who had Indian blood (through his mother) topped UK charts in 1967 with nostalgic singles like 'The Last Waltz' as memories of the Raj were fading fast, and Lucknow-born super idol Cliff Richard. The latter's dad was a caterer for the Indian Railways and did his bit to popularise the Anglo-Indian traveller's favourite 'railway mutton curry'.

'Have you heard of him? We used to get his singles before anybody else. He grew up in Howrah because his dad worked for the railways.'

So many stars were born within the community, but 'our race has degenerated through intermarriage'. The constantly scornful Naipaul, in town when the community was at its most vibrant, looked down his nose at Anglo-Indian culture—'those sad bands, those sad Anglo-Indian girls at the microphone, and the air full of dated slang. "Oh, just bung your coat down there."'

At first the expression 'Anglo-Indian' used to refer to Brits residing in India, while those today known as Anglo-Indians would've been labelled Eurasians then. So for example in the 1800s Kipling proudly called himself Anglo-Indian as he thumped his chest—'we who were Anglo-Indians separated ourselves a little from the crowd'—but in the 1900s, the longer colonials stayed on, they became all too happy to mingle and hence the generation of Anglo-Indians that followed had an Indian parent, almost always on the mothers side. This spawned badmouthing to such a malicious degree that even Kipling, fluent in Hindustani as he was, was rumoured to be 'eight annas to the rupee' or what Kipling himself termed 'hyphenated white male' or half-caste. There were a variety of levels to this—

country-bred (educated in India but not born in the country) being slightly less pejorative than country-born (born in India) and so that gradually, as the aunty explained to me, people had less and less of English blood and manners in them. Yet, from an Indian point of view, they were seen as not Indian enough, leaving them in an escalating limbo after 1947. And everybody who was anybody migrated to other former colonies such as Australia fifty years ago anyway. 'Few today have blue eyes and pale skin, and most don't know proper English but make a livelihood begging outside churches,' she laments. After the lady takes my leave, I wonder for a second if she was real or if I had encountered a spectre.

Here then dwell the ghosts of what was Britain in India, in the gloomy necropolis that remains a calming counterpoint to the glitzy tap-dancing highlife of jolly Park Street outside its looming walls, where shady men proposition me—'anything?'—that I gently refuse. They remind me of that bawdy passage in *Calcutta Chromosome*, when Amitav Ghosh's protagonist found such offers 'irresistible. All I had was five rupees but that was enough. He led me down one of those tiny alleys around Free School Street, just around the corner from the Armenian school, where William Thackeray was born. We went up a dark, stinking staircase that looked like it led to the anus of the earth. But then we got to the top and suddenly there was this great sunburst of light and noise and voices and music: it was like walking into a fairground—a huge room, with little curtained cubicles all around it, and vendors selling paan and tea, and all these women sitting on chairs lined up against the wall, with flowers around their wrists. I never looked back; I was hooked. I loved them; I loved everything about them, even the way they laughed behind my back when I was running down the stairs, afterwards, my pants half-unbuttoned.'

That fictional character got syphilis, so as I'm writing non-fiction I studiously avoid such offers. After giving the well-dressed and courteous Anglo-Indian beggars what coins I have in my pocket, I head to Mocambo's, the heavy doors of which preserve an almost sepia-tinted universe within, coincidentally on the same side of the road as the house in which eighteenth-century novelist Thackeray was born (watch out for a plaque on the wall). His dad was a bureaucrat in the East India Company and he was shipped back to England at a tender age. Barely a toddler, Thackeray grew up on Indian food because his aunties in England were addicted to curry—he even published a poem on cooking curry (in *Punch* magazine in 1846 at a time when he was already a celebrated author, so he used a pen name) rhyming:

> *...beef, mutton, rabbit, if you wish*
> *Lobsters, or prawns, or any kind of fish*
> *Are fit to make A CURRY.*

Two years later, a funny wordplay of chillies versus chilling comprise the comical highpoint in his most famous novel *Vanity Fair*, in which Becky falls for a curry-lover and in order to impress the wealthy Anglo-Indian, ladles in curry by the spoonful—only to suffer from its heat. 'She thought a chili was something cool, as its name imported, and was served with some. "How fresh and green they look," she said, and put one into her mouth. It was hotter than the curry; flesh and blood could bear it no longer. She laid down her fork. "Water, for Heaven's sake, water!" she cried.' She might have fared better if she had sampled Mocambo's interpretations of Continental cuisine. Luckily, the fine-diner has remained much the same for seven decades and even if the food they serve isn't the same that Thackeray loved, many of the dishes on offer are pure Anglo-

Indian heritage of the type sometimes labelled 'club food', that go on attracting tummy-tourists like me and puts it firmly on all must-eat lists.

As I relax in the company of my seventh beer, I imagine how in classical Calcutta, the city of too many joys, Anglo-Indians enjoyed a jovial fare of 'pale ale and hot curries, heavy tiffin, and numerous cheroots,' as mentioned by diarists of the time. Dishes in their cookbooks bore intriguingly rhyming names such as ding-ding, dol-dol and pish-pash. The latter is described in one dictionary as 'slop of rice-soup with small pieces of meat in it, much used in the Anglo-Indian nursery' and the name is variously attributed to Persian, Old English, or simply babytalk. All this would presumably be washed down with heady punch cocktails, another Anglo-Indian invention that enriched the world's party scene. 'A bowl of punch was the planter's most companionable drink' it was said and its nomenclature is linked to Hindi 'paanch' due to the five ingredients that went into it—originally half a pint of coconut arrack but nowadays more typically rum (preferably distilled from Indian sugarcane) mixed with cane sugar, lime juice or some other souring agent, and two other ingredients that may vary but generally spice up the mix. A proper punch would contain a choice of cardamom, cinnamon or cloves, or nutmeg. Others added rose water, milk, egg yolks, beer or even tea to soften the blow.

Instances of being punch-drunk were first recorded in 1630s' India, but the classic rum punch was concocted in 1654 after rum production began in the West Indies, and it became a common cocktail in London's harbour areas in the 1670s, even if the word 'cocktail' hadn't yet been coined—making punch the grandmother of all cocktails. It was considered healthier than getting drunk on hard liquor and its ingredients protected sailors against scurvy, and before long it invaded the coffeehouses of

London, too. Today any fruity booze mix is termed punch, but in the 'punch houses' that were set up across India's more westernised parts, from Goa to Bombay and Madras to Calcutta, the Indianised version, sometimes referred to as khimad, was a hot concoction based on orange juice and country liquor served in shot glasses.

Speaking of mixology's Indian roots, Kolkata cuisine is a veritable kedgeree of foreign influences—from those aforementioned Anglo-Indians to exotic Armenians, to enterprising Jews and Parsis, and last but not least the Chinese, who all came here dreaming of making themselves fortunes but in the process joined hands to turn Kolkata into the world's premium food city.

During my sojourn, I go to New Market several times to eat the addictive vanilla fudge from Nahoum's, their pizza puffs and fishy short eats, rum balls and cheese straws. Founded in 1902, the bakery is the last vestige of the Jewish community that once lived hereabouts, but there are so few Jews left today that Nahoum's doesn't cater especially to that community anymore. They've stopped preparing their own salty Jewish plaited cheese, even if people still enjoy their cheese pastries. Luckily, around the corner, two shops still sell a particular kind of Portuguese cheese named after the colonial settlement of Bandel, a short distance upriver. As it is smoked and dried it keeps long enough without refrigeration for me to stuff my bags with it as a souvenir.

Eventually, as I prepare to take off again, I'm quietly wondering what might constitute a final memorable meal and get a brainwave: Kolkata supposedly has the only Chinatown in India and I vaguely know where it is. I haven't really breakfasted yet, so why not go Chinese for a change? Maybe pick up a pair of handmade boots, too, because rumour has it that there

New Market—and Nahoum's, the last Jewish bakery in Kolkata.

are excellent shoemakers in Chinatown and with the amount of walking I've been doing, I use up shoes at a mad pace as I write this book.

I hop into a cab. Half an hour later I'm in Christopher Road, the main street in Tangra. Not much of a street, more of a meandering lane lined with tanneries and eating-houses. Many are shut this early as it turns out—a bunch of students tell me so—that their primary fame is as dirt-cheap bars mostly open at night, after six o'clock. Some showcase crooners, but don't expect Shanghai jazz here, the musical fare is more Tollywood. Until about 1950, the area was infamous for its opium dens. Post-independence they all shut down and boozing took over.

As I walk, I see a Chinese cemetery dating back to 1900, a Formosa Inn for those who wish to stay overnight, and a Kali temple which is getting its gates painted red ahead of some Chinese festival. Next to it, I chance upon one of the few early riser eateries—aptly named Sunshine—where the morning menu consists of wonton and shingara chow. Chinese samosas? Stuffed with instant noodles, perhaps? (A dish that I think impossible to imagine until I learn that it is rather trendy in parts of India! Culinary experimenting knows no limits. Just the other day, I read that enterprising persons had cooked up Maggi-noodle-milkshakes and Fanta-Maggi-floats). I pick the wonton and get a huge plate of meaty dumplings very similar to Tibetan momos, served with fiery sauce and the main difference is the accompanying steamy egg drop broth. Stomach satisfyingly full, I continue my exploration and find a seller of paper lanterns—oddly enough a young Bengali lad—and a soy sauce factory founded in 1954, apparently using traditional slow fermentation methods. According to my GPS, there's a Lao-tzu temple in one of the winding alleys, but I don't find it. One can furthermore buy economy-size bags of MSG—that essential cornerstone of Chinese cookery, which is why eating Chinese can be so addictive and nauseating at the same time—but there's unfortunately not a single shoe shop in sight.

Labourers from the Canton area started migrating to Bengal in the late eighteenth century and a first settlement came up in Kolkata around Tiretta Bazaar (in the centre of town). However, Chinese Buddhists had been travelling to Bengal for at least 1,500 years before that, so Bengalis and Chinese weren't exactly strangers to one another. Until modern times, the Chinese population was large enough to warrant a printed Mandarin newspaper and Chinatown was a lively place with authentic eateries catering to the community. But one chap I speak with estimates that after the 1990s, that saw a lot of migration, only 200 families remain—doing a rapid headcount I figure here must be more outlets selling noodles in Kolkata than there are Chinese descendants. Many relocated to Canada and I only spot about a dozen elderly Chinese during my walk. Two aunties who look like they might belong to the T'ang dynasty or thereabouts, purely agewise if not otherwise, are charmingly clad in flowery silk pyjamas of the kind that must have been very fashionable in mainland China before the 1949 revolution. It is because of that revolution and the fact that today's China isn't the China of their ancestors, that few of them consider moving there an option.

Getting ready for lunch, after a morning's peregrination, I pass a mom-and-pop-style eatery simply called Chung (47, South Tangra), where ladies sit stuffing crab claws. I try to get some, but am told that the crabs are being cooked on order specially for a get-together. Instead, I'm given a generous plate of fried noodles with shrimp, a chowmein variety that in its Tangra translation of the Cantonese *cháau-mihn* uses Indian standard ingredients like chillies and garlic. Canton, as Guangzhou used to be called, is considered the food capital of China and there's even an ancient proverb that goes: The Cantonese eat everything with legs except a table, and everything with wings except an airplane. So when food at Tangra is labelled as 'Can' it obviously doesn't stand for Canada, the new homeland of Indian-born Chinese, but implies Indianised avatars of this celebrated cuisine. Much like in the US where Chinese eateries avoid idiosyncratic delicacies like duck's feet and stir-fried dogs. Americans prefer Americanised Cantonese—like 'American chopsuey'. In China itself, I only found it at restaurants near foreign embassies and its closest relative is the Toisanese *tsap-seui*, which means 'miscellaneous leftovers' or what poor farmers cooked for themselves out of whatever no buyer wanted to purchase from them.

A radio plays distorted Chinese pop. Soon the clan arrives to feast, filling two banquet tables loaded with off-menu specials. Some are indeed visiting from Canada, as if to prove what I've just been told, bringing fancy gifts like iPhones. The MSG-overdosed Canadian-Chinese kids horse about doing cartwheels as they simultaneously update their Facebook pages with fresh selfies, while their Indo-Chinese cousins are silent in wide-eyed wonderment.

Others worth trying are Kimfa (9, South Tangra), considered a pioneering legend and well-liked by the Chinese themselves for genial fare, and Beijing (77/1, Christopher Road), whose fine dining is all the rage with Bengalis (even the author Amitav Ghosh was spotted there when he was working on his big novel trilogy that was partly set in China). Beijing is at the forefront of what is labelled as 'Tangra Chinese' which makes it a point to cater to Bengali tastebuds in particular with extra-spicy, extra-oily, manchurianised starchy gravies, with extra food colouring to make dishes such as chilly chicken vividly neon-red, and an unusually extensive vegetarian selection in which veggies are cooked way softer than their lightly stir-fried Chinese counterparts would be. To just pick one anomaly off the menu there's a highly Tangrafied take on Peking duck: 'Pieces, medium spicy in gravy' the waiter enlightens me. Either they take radical shortcuts or he's unaware of the original's complexity: How the alluring duck first is force-fattened for six weeks, then pumped full of air and dry-roasted on a hook until its fatty skin achieves perfect crispness, before it is served thinly sliced without ever setting a duck's foot in any gravy, so it is rather bland but goes well with palm-sized wheat pancakes and a piquant fermented hoisin-style dip-sauce on the side.[31]

In fact, many of India's commonly eaten off-mainland staples are not really available in mainland China itself, such as gobi manchurian, as cauliflower isn't eaten much in China—in the 1600s, when an independent tribal state called Manchuria actually existed (and whose cuisine is known as Manchu), the European vegetable had only travelled as far east as to India, hence the dish is not only a geographical malapropism but an anachronism too. Or for that matter, take Bengaluru's beloved instant-noodle cheese-paneer dosa—truth is, the Chinese aren't that much into dairy products so the closest to paneer one tastes in China is the nutritious but non-dairy tofu. Unsurprisingly, the chilli-garlicky manchurian cooking was invented by a Kolkata-born Chinese chef (naturally)—Nelson Wang who used it to popularise his restaurant in Mumbai in the 1970s. It has been enthusiastically welcomed everywhere in India as a domesticated form of Chinese food. For example my cosmopolitan hometown Bengaluru's unofficial national vegetable among barflies is the Andhra-style extra-spicy gobi manchurian. So who am I to complain, because after MSG-modified food and too many beers to rinse the MSG-taste out of my mouth, Tangra with its oozing black gutters looks decidedly less grimy and I summon the courage to knock on the gates of a fortress-like tannery where hides are still tanned the traditional way in soaking pits.

A polite lady informs me in Chenglish that they make no shoes. 'You must go to Pen Ching Stli. All sooo-sops are there.'

It sounds like she's telling me to cross the border to China itself, so I get her to spell it out: 'Bentinck Street.'

Aha! That's the street east of Dalhousie Square (BBD Bagh) where those who arrived in the wake of the British sea trade with the port-city of Canton (when opium was shipped from here to pay for tea bought there) set up shops in the 1800s. The area even has an Old China Bazaar said to date back a century further, to 1757, where chinaware was sold.

Worried that I'll find no shoes there either, I stop the taxi just before Bentinck Street, outside Chung Wah on 13A, BCR Avenue, which is a sight to behold for anybody interested in Indo-Chinese fusion food history. In fact, foodies kept mentioning it as *the* landmark when they heard of my plan to go to Kolkata and luckily I remember now that I had made a mental note to check it out. As I step in, I am bowled over by how it retains an effortlessly retro vibe with its all-red interiors, and its private booths popular with secret lovers having tiffs over tumblers of Old Monk. The man at the next table doesn't even remove his motorcycle helmet to down his quota of seven pegs before he shoots off into Kolkata's traffic jams.

Allegedly inaugurated by Mr Wah some 140 years ago when this was a bustling Chinese neighbourhood, I'm told by the bartender who is probably making this up to keep me happy, it's no longer Chinese-run. The menu, DTP printouts in plastic pockets in case one's Daredevil beer spills, offers hybrid delicacies such as chicken tandoori chilly, Chung's special fish-manchurian masala and I half expect to be offered tandooried noodles—but it doesn't get that radical.

Fortified thus, I find that Bentinck Street indeed has about a dozen shoe shops. Some are run by dignified Chinese gentlemen and I buy nice boots—at about one third of what similar footwear might cost in branded chain stores. A little later, at dinnertime, I reach Tiretta Bazaar (famous for its Chinese breakfasts sold from pushcarts at sunrise) and take a right turn into Sun Yat Sen Street, named in honour of the father of the modern Chinese nation, where I ferret out more grub. To begin with, Tangra's Sing Cheung sauce factory turns out to have an outlet on the parallel road which is known as Lu Shun Sarani (named after writer Lu Hsün who is considered the greatest socialist realist by the Chinese communists). The secret of cooking Chinese—apart from MSG which adds killer thrills to eating—is the right sauce. The selection is magnificent, ranging from stir-fry and momo sauces to Schezwan hot sauce in anything from 210 ml bottles to 2.5 kg jerry cans. I go silly and fill my jhola with oyster sauce, wasabi paste and dried shitake mushrooms at highly affordable rates.

Next to it, I spot a picturesque Chinese church, the Sea Ip, which dates from 1905 and I continue eating in Tung Nam (24, Chattawala Galli), at whose eight tables local Chinese are dining and the menu seems totally authentic, as does the pork in hamei sauce. It's quite similar to the simple canteens I've been to in China and Taiwan, with tiny low stools so that many can squeeze in at a table. It even has the mandatory screen to ward off evil at the entrance.

Other gems include D'Lay, Pou Hing, and Eau Chew—the latter opened in the 1920s and is the oldest Chinese family-run eatery in India—and according to tradition its owner invented the Schezwan sauce, and it remains a truly authentic place to sample the times when Kolkata was a melting pot of cultures, by which I end the day. Somehow I manage to pig-out there too—a second round of dinner—call me a monstrous glutton if you will.

❖

Next day, my train trudges northeast. Outside, dreamy sun-bleached landscapes of almost black-and-white paddy fields and lotus ponds look straight out of the Satyajit Ray's *Pather Panchali*. Early afternoon, a eunuch startles me by fondling my behind and I wake up from my slumber to the song of a wandering baul minstrel who provides musical teatime entertainment—as in Kolkata teatime is anytime on regional trains—while vendors peddle nimbu cha, lime tea with a hint of chaat masala. The route through north Bengal that crosses to the North-eastern states has always been great for shopping, as lots of goods are smuggled in from neighbouring China. A man sells colourful shoulder-bags and I buy a few more jholas to organise my gastronomic souvenirs.

A freshly-cooked dinner proves that the best timepass on trains is eating, as it has always been, but there are differences between now and the previous millennium—nobody's smoking after dinner and the pantry crew isn't accommodating enough to supply optional quarts of cheap booze from pocket-stashes any longer. Everything has become wholesome, including the quantity-conscious meals of 'Rice (150 gms), Chapatti (04 nos.), Dhal (150 gms) and Mix Veg. (100 gms)'.

Because the train is late by too many hours, the next morning I take it easy and order breakfast in bed from the efficient waiters in bright orange uniforms, double-egg omelette with bread slices and the ubiquitous sauce that pretends to be ketchup, and liberal quantities of the Assamese national beverage of laal sah, sugary red tea without milk but served with lime.

Later the waiters tempt passengers with piping hot biryani as the lunch hour approaches. I crawl down from my upper berth to grab a window seat. A cloying scent of the Brahmaputra River, mixed with the zesty burps of passengers who stuffed themselves silly with egg biryani, lingers until the final station, Guwahati. I round off the trip with a rickshaw ride to Hotel Bellevue where, while relishing a grand view over the river, I reward myself suitably—namely with chilled beer aplenty plus their world-famous Club Sandwich, that was probably introduced to these parts during World War II to soothe battle-fatigued American soldiers.

❖

'Is it original or duplicate?' asks a tourist in Hindi. We're both staring at a lonesome rhinoceros in Guwahati's Zoo and Botanical Gardens. I glance briefly at the young man and roll my head sideways. He may have a valid point. The rhino doesn't look authentic. It is brooding, walking in rectangles, grunting like a German philosopher or caricatured cartoon character—one of those shape-shifters stuck in mid-transformation, somewhere between a big pig and an amphibious army tank.

The zoo is a mysterious place. Half the animals roam outside the cages: I bump into monkeys, antelopes, deer and pelicans that stake claim to the walking paths. Luckily the zoo's tiger, lion and leopard all remain safely incarcerated. How safely? The other day, says my taxi driver casually, a reporter tried to photograph the tigers and stuck his camera inside the bars, whereupon one hungry tiger ate up the camera as well as the hand holding it. I make a mental note not to repeat the same mistake.

Earlier, the only option for Assamese food was Paradise, an old place showcasing fishy thalis but things have changed. After the zoo, I head to the Upper Assam specialty restaurant Khorikaa in G.S. Road, a short taxi ride away. The main differences between Upper (or eastern) and Lower (western) Assamese cuisine appears to be that the Upper has a hint of Southeast Asian influences, the Lower shares certain Bengali elements (such as the love for mustard-flavoured fish curries that I found on every single menu I sampled in Goalpara, about 157 km downriver, west of Guwahati).

There's no rhino, antelope, monkey, snake or pelican on the menu, no Wuhan-influenced bat soups or barbecued pangolins (even if the northeast is one of the near extinct creature's rare habitats), or other endangered species on the menu. But they do cook plenty of other unusual non-veg items such as duck and pigeon, not to forget fish in many sizes and shapes including preparations with medicinal herbs, something of an Assamese hallmark. Moreover, there's a range of original—not duplicate—vegetarian options: banana flower fry; leafy slightly bitter stir-fries known as xaak (which appears to be how they pronounce saag here); lip-smacking pitikas of mushy vegetable mashes, of potatoes, eggplants or fermented bamboo shoot, redolent with mustard oil and the heady juice of raw onions. Oil is very sparingly used, mostly only for the sake of the exquisite aroma that the mustard oil imbues. The menu card also contains health advice: 'The food you eat can be either the safest and most powerful form of medicine or the slowest form of poison.'

Waiting for my lunch, I explore the pickle platter that includes something called kharoli, a thick paste of fermented mustard seeds mixed with (again) that heavenly mustard oil and a very unique ingredient, namely water treated with khar or banana tree ashes! (This is actually, as one tribal lady explained to me when I visited her kitchen, made by burning the trunk of a banana tree to ashes which are then mixed with water that is strained through a special filter made of cane. The resulting liquid is stored in bottles and used while cooking to give dishes an alkaline flavour—hence it is never added to recipes with sour ingredients such as tomatoes, as the two would be in conflict with one another and might cause a minor culinary war.) A quintessential Assamese side, kharoli turns out to be utterly delicious—the very opposite of overdone and over-the-top. The name of the restaurant itself refers to the wooden skewer or the khorikaa on which dishes are barbequed, such as the smoked pork that melts in the mouth. I also sample a specialty of lightly lemony ginger-garlic marinated pork chunks that are slow-cooked in a hollow tube of bamboo, sunga, which tenderises the meat beautifully. And then I get some petite mowa fish roasted in a banana leaf called patotdiya, eaten with bones, eyes and all. Besides, I cannot resist ordering a plate of lightly fried lean duck which I'm told is special festive food in the Upper Assam district of Lakhimpur where everybody apparently rears their own ducks for this purpose.

To go with this, I have a platter that comes with vegetarian items such as the leafy green xaak and delicately sweetish mashed pumpkin with dhal. The Assamese don't eat roti, except once or twice a year I'm told, but rice is eaten thrice a day.

'Let me guess: Breakfast, lunch and dinner?'

'Yes, you guessed correctly,' says the waiter proudly.

Rice overdose apart, it's a feast to die for. The piggy lard content gives me at least one extra spare tyre circumambulating my waist as if my tummy was a sacred temple, but on the whole the grub isn't as unhealthy as one might assume. Much of it is steamed, boiled or grilled, low on oil and not over-spiced, yet ambrosial.

Another establishment, which like Khorikaa is frequently mentioned when the discussion is about where to have the best food, is Mising Kitchen on Hengrabari Road. It's the most specialised mess in town, serving the rare cuisine of the half-a-million-strong Mising tribe. Like other eateries in town it is a bright cafeteria-style mess and as I step in at lunchtime, full of young tribals having a good time.

The Mising being a largely riverside tribe of possibly northern Chinese riverine origin, their menu tempts with a full page of fishy delicacies. Confused about what to order, especially as I see others tuck into soulful mutton and pork thalis with gusto, kneading the rice and rich gravies into tight mouthfuls before stuffing themselves, I go for the all-inclusive Mising fish thali. Apart from many kinds of dhal and vegetables, it comes with three types of Brahmaputra fish—a mashed fish dish which is another pitika-variety, a delicate fish roasted in a banana leaf, and a catfish ari cooked as a sour fish tenga, i.e.

a thin tart curry. Although tomatoes, lemons and mangosteen are more common souring agents, in this case they've used wild elephant apple!

After lunch, I inspect the comprehensively traffic-jammed G.S. Road that sports several elegant hotels and connects Guwahati with Assam's modern capital Dispur (7 km away). This primary thoroughfare is something of a high street featuring shopping malls, glamorously trendy bistros, even discos and one cool rock club. I spend a weekend drifting up and down the street that is also crammed with momo stalls and snack carts at any of which one may sample a fresh catch of fish and prawns from the Brahmaputra.

I peek into its many side streets—in one, Panjabari Road, I find a barn with a large farmers' market, Bhipanan Khetra, of the kind that is all the rage the world over but is rarer in India. Counters stock fresh produce such as organic vegetables and interesting varieties of rice, there's also a food court and a supermarket that sells exotic ingredients. I load up.

Late that night, I fall for the rock club Café Hendrix. I can almost imagine myself being on the Lower East Side, except that the band showcased isn't some fledgling New York underground newcomer, but an Assamese hard rock outfit that plays an intriguing heavy metal version of The Beatles' 'Come Together'. It goes well with the pork roast and the latest fad beer Simba which, with its slogan 'Roar for More', has invaded all bars along the street, giving the older brands a run for the fun. But it doesn't win me over. I feel too conservative to embrace their lager which is potable if a bit fruity and not nearly bitter enough for me, while its stronger sibling is like gunk that's already been drunk and puked up by somebody else. This may explain why so many gents openly irrigate walls, bushes and lampposts along G.S. Road in full public view.

Nevertheless, the G.S. Road bars are civilised and welcoming. Even the seediest, the name of which I initially mistook as Slime of Lice (seeing the board the next morning in broad daylight, I reread it as Slice of Lime), has friendly staff and serves sublime smoked pork. It's the best pork in the world—to have with beer—even if its fattiness makes me not want to calculate the cardiac hazards.

Returning to the initial question, about duplicate or original, I think Guwahati is peerless when it comes to thrilling eating.

❖

Halfway between Guwahati and Shillong, as the taxi stops for a tea break at Nongpoh, stalls peddling atom-bomb-hot bamboo shoot pickles herald the pleasures ahead. The golden stuff is sold in recycled jars that leak spiced-up oil into my luggage, so that for the rest of my trip I walk around smelling of fermented bamboo.

It's raining in Shillong—these are the legendary rains of the Khasi Hills that pushed colonialists to borderline insanity: A wall of cement-grey cosmic piddle rattles gutters; bullet-sized raindrops ricochet off the pavement and up my legs. Months of this, day after day of wearing mouldy socks that never dried, drove the Britons to deadly alcoholism. Nails rusted and furniture fell apart. Books rotted. Suicide was their only quick fix. While he was *Chasing the Monsoon* all the way to Meghalaya, Alexander Frater stayed at the colonial era Hotel Pinewood and visited the 'old British graveyard. A number of tombstones bore the faint, weathered legend, "Died by His Own Hand".' In the hilly landscape south of Shillong, he finally chased down his monsoon: 'A fountain of dense black cloud came spiralling over the hills, then rose steeply into the sky. It formed a kind of tent, apex high overhead, sides unrolling right to the ground. It was very dark inside but I could just discern, trooping towards us, an armada of shadowy, galleon-like vessels with undersides festooned with writhing cables of water.' But like so often it is with us travel writers, he realises then that the end of a journey never matches the way you took to reach it: 'I felt little of the excitement I had known when the burst arrived in the south. Those had been occasions for public jubilation. This was a routine matiné performance at Cherrapunji, awesome certainly but exhilarating only to earnest collectors of meteorological records; such specialists would now be watching, incredulous, as their gauges foamed like champagne glasses.'

On the other hand, according to his 'Shillonger Chithi', poet laureate Rabindranath Tagore always 'rushed to the cool heights of the hills called Shillong' whenever it got too hot down in Kolkata. This was where he got plenty of time to write and rest from his globetrotting. 'The mountain ranges with their mantle of clouds seemed to beckon weary travellers to take refuge in the deep shade of woods on their hill sides.'

When I'm not roaming in the intense maze of the women-dominated Iewduh market with its banana brokers, fresh fishmongers, honey hawkers, pickle peddlers, swine slaughterers, and tea traders, my sightseeing happens at tables laden with mysterious dishes mildly tinged with ginger, garlic, onions and pinches of chilli without ever being overspiced. I figure that warm food assuages the bone-chilling rains and luckily the town is dotted with numerous intriguing eateries. Each seems to be named 'Ja & Sha' which sounds like the name of a rap band, but I soon learn that 'ja' simply means rice—the red rice of Meghalaya particularly appreciated amongst gourmets and which is uncannily healthy. The side dishes are assumed, but include—generally—at least one pork item. And 'sha' means tea—often had just like in Assam as red tea without milk. By and large, these places have no menus, but the 'national dish' is jadoh, translating roughly as 'pork sparepart pullao of short-grain red rice cooked in pig's blood' and it is usually flavoured with ginger—as almost everything is—and turmeric. It is best eaten with a helping of the paranormally pungent tungryumbai (fermented soybeans stewed with pork) and some dohneiong (a pork curry with black sesame seed paste). These canteens are characteristically dark, cavernous and crammed with low bench seating arranged as if one is sitting inside a bus, with long narrow tables in-between benches and if one by mistake looks up from one's meal the unappetising view is of the next customer's dandruff, which certainly helps to retain focus on that which matters. As I search for mouthfuls of what is traditional, people inevitably direct me to such workers' canteens, always adding disclaimers to dissuade me: 'It will not be comfortable.'

Yet, even if the eateries are sheds patched together from flattened mustard oil tins, they're efficiently run by dignified Khasi ladies identified as 'Kongs' who ensure homely quality and reasonable hygiene. These places go on existing, anachronistically, despite how tribal cuisine has taken centerfield in posher places—its time-tested simplicity and wholesomeness is what attracts customers, perhaps combined with nostalgia for the olden days.

Earlier, as I recall from my first visit in the 1990s, all fancy places in Shillong focused on Chinese but with a pinch of turmeric stirred into almost everything to make it taste less alien, and back in those days, eating out meant pseudo-Chinese instant noodles with ketchup. One of the town's restaurants offered an incongruous 'Chinese thali' consisting of what to outsiders may sound weird pairings but that are locally immensely popular, namely 'veg fried rice, veg noodles, veg manchurian, chilli potato' that somehow was wedged in between your regular full meals and small eats. The only remotely restaurant-like place for Khasi meals, in those days, was the enthusiastically christened Trattoria Dukan Jadoh (now, simply the Trattoria) in Police Bazaar, the main drag. It isn't as classy as the Italianised moniker suggests, but brighter than average jadoh stalls, with polished stone tables and photographic depictions of dishes pasted on the walls. The ebullient proprietor, seeing that I'm a tourist in need of guidance, plates me a gustatory pork thali sampler of all the available dishes—including dohshain or pork meatballs (very yummy), the pretty spectacular semi-veg dohkhleh or boiled and finely-chopped pig's brain salad (mildly-wildly delicate as is the veggie base seasoned with a drop of mustard oil), pork chutney (spicy-dicey) and curried pork—which is a lot of pork for one man. But then I do love pigging out.

Walking about during the next one week, I notice that things have changed and I see many more eating-places advertising ethnic Khasi dishes while shops sell tribal specialities of dried pork and smoked beef—patriotic citizens rave about new eateries such as You & I Arts Café (in VIP Road) that serves back-to-basics meals consisting of native potatoes that customers peel themselves to eat with raw jungle greens, or they drive an hour out of town to the roadside servery Wah Kynshi Khasi Food, run by young ladies who prepare homely lunches for famished travellers. Certain restaurants also offer the foods of the Jaintias, Nagas, Mizos and Manipuris—to pick a few other North-easterly tribes off the magiristic map—so clearly regional pride is reflected in this new-fangled interest in rustic cookery, as in the rest of the world where global is giving way to local. Besides, the tribal foods of the North-east all share a reputation for being fresh, natural, nutritious, organic, unadulterated, well-balanced, and hence essentially the best diet imaginable. Its seems North-easterners as a rule use more herbs than the rest of India's chefs put together but avoid artificial tastemakers, and dishes are typically smoked or cooked with a minimum of oil and salt. The recipes rely a lot on fermentation; they ferment fish that are made into pungent chutneys that set my brain and intestines on fire. Despite overdosing on pork my BP is happy and I love every bite.

Pork is an important ingredient of tribal food in Shillong.

The full extent of North-eastern gastronomic glory is revealed at Phunga, spread across three cosy rooms in a charming bungalow in Laitumkrah Main Road, a bubbly student area a short walk from the town's cathedral. The restaurant is smartly decorated with cane handicrafts and indigenous objets d'art, rough-hewn woodwork and bamboo furniture, and has a stage for showcasing rock bands in the main dining hall. The word phunga apparently means 'kitchen hearth', which is where locals get together after a hard day's work not only to eat, but also to sing and tell stories. Their eclectic recipes encompass all of the North-east—from Khasi staples to Assamese samples (herby and fishy), Arunachali (with treats such as fermented bamboo shoots), Mizo (very healthy stews made out of natural roots and shoots, leaves and stems, low on salt and oil), Naga (famous for the world's hottest chillies known as bhoot jholokia raja mirchi) and Tripuri (that mysteriously merges tribal simplicity with a touch of Bengali-influenced masala sophistication), but there's a special emphasis on the foods of Manipur.

With such a vast menu, all dishes aren't readily available daily and everything I ask for takes a good long time to prepare. I wonder if they might serve that famous Naga delicacy, roast dog, but as I don't find it on the menu I don't dare to ask but go for smoked fish instead.[32] The unhurried *maître d'hôtel* returns half an hour after having taken my order only to let me know that the smoked fish is not on the menu today, suggesting I order something else. Traditional 'slow food' as a reaction against the fast-food chains in town, has apparently been trending in Shillong and this particular kitchen takes that slowness to its very extremes and beyond.

I go with the flow and let him talk me into trying a shitake mushroom dish with sprouted peas and their special off-the-menu caviar gravy, which sounds like it could be terribly pricey. I obviously must have their thali as well—the jungle chicken and wild duck combos tempt me, but in the end I go for a fish thali. A good three-quarters of an hour later, the food is ready and it's so worth the wait. The thali, for example, contains many exquisite preparations—curried, fried, fermented, dried, and mashed fish, all in all twelve bowls on one plate, and the caviar gravy is...well, not possible to describe but has to be experienced. And it must have been my cheapest gourmet experience ever.

Due to an unfortunate combination of circumstances, Meghalaya, where booze once flowed freely and seedy bars was the name of the game, has become restrictive. It is hard to get a beer in the city except at the luxury hotels where a bottle costs more than a budget room. The only proper dive to survive is the quaintly named Sweety, which has a family cafeteria downstairs and a quite lovely boozer upstairs where gents converge from 1 p.m. onwards (which is the permitted hour for having one's first drink in Meghalaya). Friendly service, functioning loos and Sino-Tibetan snacks makes it the perfect watering hole before the daily archery games in the adjacent Polo Grounds.

However, duty calls me on my mobile phone, as is its wont, just like nature does now and then in order to disrupt every enjoyable beer binge, so I say goodbye to the Sweety Cafeteria, hog the last of the porky momos and ask for the bill. There will be momos in Bhutan, too, or as Anthony Bourdain reported from his trip to Thimphu: 'If I'm not on camera, chances are I'm somewhere eating these bad boys: momos. Plump, flavourful, often quite spicy dumplings, filled with meat, cheese, or veg.'

One curious thought after eating my way across much of India, and considering how all this spice is crammed into one's gastrics to perform their gas tricks, is that 500 years ago there was not a single chilli in the Old World, not until after explorers sailed across to America and subsequently spread the plant across Asia—where the chilli found the climate as agreeable as Asians found its Scoville index. Very soon, it grew everywhere and these days it is hard to imagine Indian or even Asian food without this essential ingredient.

❖

The Drukair plane deftly skirts an assortment of mountains before it slides down a narrow valley in the Himalayas and hits the bull's-eye: Bhutan's microscopic international airport. The only thing I can remember from that intensely scary moment is how fortunate it felt that the national carrier of Bhutan isn't misspelled as Drunkair on my ticket. For your information, I double-checked. No 'n'. Waiting to disembark from the plane that is packed with authors going to a litfest in Thimphu, some of my colleagues spot a red carpet on the airfield. I do a spontaneous high-five with myself, only to see it being rolled up as soon as the VIPs in first class have stepped out.

Everything is surreal. Bhutan is one of the eco-friendliest countries on earth and merely opening one's mouth to breathe is said to be nutritious. It helps that cigarettes have been banned since 2010. I've heard that the fines for smoking on the sly equal some two months' salary. Therefore, I left my party pack at home, but those who can't live without their poison pay a hefty 200 per cent customs surcharge and must apply for smoking permits to get their stashes back.

Penalties settled, we're en route to the festival's opening ceremony at the India House in Thimphu, which was built in the 1960s and represents the first permanent diplomatic connection between Bhutan and the outside world. That was also when the country's first road was built—from Thimphu to India. Prior to that, the capital was a cluster of houses surrounding a monastery, peasants bartered between villages, transporting goods on yaks along mountain paths, which suggests a certain leisurely manner that didn't involve bitcoins and mobile wallets and scanning potentially phishing-afflicted barcodes.

From then on, Bhutan underwent what may seem like a contradiction in terms, but it actually was a consciously abrupt yet gentle progress—the first foreign tourists came in the

1970s about the same time when the concept of GNH (Gross National Happiness) was established as an unconventional gauge of sustainable growth, the adrenaline-heightening airport was inaugurated in the 1980s, TV came in 1999, democracy in 2008, iPhone7 in 2016 and rather expectedly, in 2021 during the peaking COVID-19 pandemic, it was one of the first countries in the world to provide the vaccine to virtually all eligible citizens...but there are still no traffic lights and barely any vehicular traffic to speak of. This litfest that I've come to speak at is another sign of the opening up of Bhutan. The queen mother Ashi Dorji Wangmo Wangchuck, its founder-patron, emphasises in her inaugural speech how much the meetings with inspiring authors have enriched life for the Bhutanese people including herself.

I later learn that Her Majesty grew up in a village without books. She says, 'After dinner we gathered around the hearth and my grandparents told stories. I try to keep the same oral history-telling alive by telling my grandchildren the stories that my grandparents told me. It wasn't until I went to India to study that I saw a book for the first time in my life.' Now she's writing her third book, chronicling her grandson who is an intelligent toddler. At almost every session, I see her seated on a throne right in front of the stage, listening keenly—so when I do my talkshow it makes me extremely nervous because at first she frowns when I wisecrack. As I do it again and again, and the hundreds of citizen in the auditorium get the joke and merriment spreads, she looks confused, then hesitant as she hears them guffaw unanimously and finally, when Her Majesty too giggles, I feel a certain triumph at having added a spot of laughter to the happiest country on earth. It's like they say, the hardest jobs on earth are being an ice-cream vendor among Eskimos or opening a refrigerator shop in Alaska...or having to prove that one is funny in Bhutan, where everybody is happy sixteen hours per day.

Made in Bhutan, happiest chips in the world.

Occasionally, I suspect that people here worship writers. One of the first things I did was to visit the National Library, a gorgeous building modelled on monasteries. Apparently, people circle it clockwise due to the fact that its enormous collection of religious books—by the likes of Guru Rimpoche (a.k.a. Padmasambhava) and other Buddhist prophets—bestows one with top-class karma. At the entrance, it says that a previous queen of Bhutan founded the library in 1967, and I discern a pattern: The queens here take books seriously.

Mita Kapur, an old friend and literary personality who founded the Crime Writers Festival in New Delhi and is my literary agent for this book, also manages the festival in Bhutan. She says to me, 'I am nuts about this festival, I love it, I love Bhutan, I love its people. The festival reflects shared cultural threads between Bhutan and India, and since we've kept it small, it lends itself to a lot of interaction between readers and writers.'

Small is a relative word as the festival saw 10,000 footfalls every year before the pandemic. Considering that Thimphu's entire population is no more than 91,000, it is a respectable figure. 'There has also been a fivefold increase in the number of books being published in Bhutan and now writers experiment with new genres as well. Book sales have gone up, there are book clubs in schools—it's just so satisfying to see many more people reading and writing,' points out Kapur.

She mentions that authors usually spend their evenings at the Druk Hotel's bar, so that's where I head as my literary duties at the festival are over. Dating back to the 1970s as the first 'international' hotel, it's endowed with the city's nicest drinking den. Moreover, as Kapur predicted, I do spend the night in the company of jolly colleagues—a chicklit novelist, a webzine editor and a children's writer, along with reporters looking for either scoops, scandals or bottles of Druk beer which they—as so many of us—misread as 'Drunk beer'.

A high for me as a travel writer is bumping into Pico Iyer who is a living legend that I used to read as a young vagabond in Nepal, where his *Video Night in Kathmandu* (1988) was a must-read at the time. After his lecture on *The Art of Stillness* at the festival, he confesses to me, 'I felt really embarrassed to be talking about stillness here in Bhutan, because Bhutan is really the model of sanity, quiet and health that the rest of us aspire to. Landing here, the first thing I saw was a sign that said, "Faster, spells disaster."' Bhutan, he points out, could be the paradigm for the rest of the world where everything is going faster and faster and social media has replaced social interactions. He doesn't own a mobile phone, which has—or so he feels—made his days longer and given him more time to read.

Despite his rosy nostalgia, which I envy, Iyer observes that Bhutan is changing. 'Physically, Thimphu is unrecognisable to me, coming back after decades. When I went to the Druk Hotel and back to the Swiss Bakery, what I principally remember from 1988, I lost all sense of orientation—I didn't know where I was. I thought, well, it is less idyllic seeming for me than it was, but development probably means a richer and happier life for people here. We visitors have to be careful about the wishes we project—the fact that we want places to remain beautiful for our camera lenses. But when I talk to people, they sound very similar to the people I was talking to back then.'

I ask him what else he has been up to in Thimphu. 'I visited four or five temples. And have you tried the hamburgers at Cloud 9?'

All the authors rave about those burgers, but I am sorry to say that because my mission has always been to go native in the widest sense, I can't review them as I only eat and drink what is genuinely Bhutanese. Like most tourists to Bhutan, all I knew about its cuisine was that chillies are the most eaten vegetables, for unlike elsewhere in the world, here chilli isn't considered a spice. The national dish emadatsi, for example, is 250 g chillies cooked with a smaller quantity of cottage cheese (serves two). Therefore, I do realise that I might not have any intestines left at the end of this book, people warned me of bum burns, that my undies might turn into ashes if I fart... but as Shakespeare once pointed out, 'it is the baseness of thy fear that makes thee strangle thy propriety.' And so (as I believe that in his day the word 'propriety' meant true nature), I fearlessly proceed according to my true nature, avoiding the dining options suggested in the guidebooks and instead sneak into all the cook shacks where I check what Bhutanese customers eat, order the same, and if it means overdosing on chillies, then...well, so be it.

Helpful people who felt I was heading for disaster tried

to steer me towards other more easily digestible thrills of Thimphu. For such a small town it offers a surprising array of cuisines ranging from Indian to Far Eastern, Mediterranean and even Mexican, to American-style bagel cafés.

I ignore all these and, at the northern end of the main street Norzin Lam, I find an eatery called Apy's. The lady running it explains that she hails from the town of Phuentsholing, so she'll cook a south Bhutanese meal. She asks which meat I prefer and says she'll make a datsi of it (with cheese and chillies), and also serve the local lentil curry, fresh salad and the staple maaso (red rice).

In case the food turns out insufficiently spicy, she takes out homemade pickles—one with mangoes from her own garden in Phuentsholing, another with cocktail-cherry-sized chillies grown in Sikkim. While she's in the kitchen, for my entertainment, her uncle connects a video call on his smartphone to Phuentsholing and I get to wave to all their relatives back home and tell them how happy I am to be in Bhutan—they are excited that foreigners eat at Apy's and ask me how I like it. I do a thumbs up and to prove how much fun I'm having, I pop one of the innocuous-looking Sikkimese chillies into my mouth. It's oh, so juicy, and I swallow it only to suffer a thousand deaths as it releases its bombastic fury. Hot burps shoot up my throat. Throughout the video call, puffs of chilli smoke erupt from my mouth and every other word I speak is an oral volcano. How do the Bhutanese handle this? Later, reading local novelist Chador Wangmo, I realise that toddlers are fed chillies as soon as they open their eyes (or mouths). '"Dechzangmo, come, eat your breakfast!" my mother yelled…It was red rice with beef emadatsi. My mother's special dish always had me licking my fingers. She cooked small chunks of dry beef with a lot of green Indian chillies and datsi,' opens the fifth chapter of Wangmo's novel *La Ama: A Mother's Call.*

Spicy enough to nuke curry-hardened tummies, Bhutanese food also differs from Indian (and Chinese for that matter), in its cautious approach to oil. In fact, it can be made without any oil at all—emadatsi, for example, is chillies basically boiled with water and cheese for ten minutes. Other varieties have fall-in-love-with names such as kewadatsi, which is like a potato-au-gratin and quite mild; saagdatsi of stir-fried greens; and several types of meat datsi—usually either sikam (pork) or shakam (beef)—and then there's shamudatsi which is cheesy chillies with mushrooms.

Regarding this 'shamu' phenomenon, Bhutan has at least one hundred species of edible wild mushrooms (and 250 inedible ones, so one must choose wisely) among which the finest varieties include matsutake and chanterelles. I am a total cheese and mushroom fanatic—even my writing, as you may have noticed, combines cheesiness with a mushy mentality—and as soon as I get into the habit of ordering shamudatsi, in which the mushrooms cushion the chillies as it were, I'm at ease in Thimphu.

My best meal is a total chance experience at the Dorji Trotzey that a random man points me to. The eatery is otherwise impossible to find as it is hidden in a back alley and not at all aimed at tourists. Kind of cool in a Bhutanese way: Low benches and tables, lunch menu comprising staples written on a whiteboard and as they run out, the names are removed from it. I have shamudatsi again (mushrooms stir-fried in you-know-what sauce), pork ribs with chilli, and shakam paa—after datsi, paa is the second most common dish, usually involving sun-dried chewy meat such as beef, pork or weird intestines. Refreshing jaju (riverweed soup), unlimited chilli pickles and a cooling whey beverage are complimentary, as is the Himalayan red rice.

After returning home I try to recreate the shamudatsi. It appeared so simple, but turned out to be trickier in one's own kitchen. I experiment with different cheeses and mushrooms, including yak's cheese and dried mushrooms imported from the Himalayas, but it isn't anything like it was in Bhutan. The only thing that tastes about right is the pickles I brought with me—homemade shakam ezzay and fishy ayzey.

As a matter of fact, genuine Bhutanese food is next to impossible to get outside the country's borders. I've heard of one joint called Ema Datsi in New York and I've had emadatsi in certain Tibetan settlements in south India. That's about it.

Yet what I sampled in Bhutan was always perfect, once my tastebuds had been sufficiently adjusted...meaning, numbed. This left me wondering whether Bhutan might become the next secret gourmet pilgrimage destination. The combination of exclusivity—ain't easy to get there—and accessibility, once you do get there, good cheap food can be had everywhere. In one word? Yum-yum-yum. Anything to add? Yum.

Before I forget, one must also try all the different beers that are brewed in the hills from the purest mountain waters. On a surprisingly sunny monsoon day, I'm walking about with my shirt soaked and I can't tell whether it is the natural perspiration shooting out through the pores on my back, or the emadatsi I had for lunch clawing its way out of my body, or a bit of both. My life instantly takes a turn for the better when I spot a handful of downmarket bars north of the Chubachhu Roundabout. They are...how should I put it...the most beautiful things I have ever seen. Not only because I'm thirsty, but the row of tumbledown houses look incredibly inviting—wooden structures with about two drinking dens each, wall to wall. Each of them stares back at me as if they have been waiting a truly long time for my arrival.

It's a mind-altering moment.

We fall in love. It helps that the first I step into (no obvious name on the outside) is run by a couple of ladies and now and then a Buddhist monk drops in to down a can of super-strong beer. For me it takes a six-pack to get accustomed to the yeastiness of Red Panda—a fresh beer which is apparently unfiltered and brewed without preservatives—but by and large, my philosophy is that anything that is drinkable is probably drinkable. I sit quietly, meditate and read Bhutanese newspapers, acting Buddhistic.

When a drizzle cools the air outside, I move on to the next sensation that turns out to be another bar—it may be too early to have more beer, but I must get indoors since it starts pouring. This bar (again, no name on the outside) is in an alley by Clock Tower Square in the centre of town and looks like it could date back 500 years, but from a purely scientific perspective, I know it can't be older than from the 1960s—when Thimphu was built. A princess-like girl with sharp features mans the bar, while lads sleep on mattresses on the floor, and one aunty sips on her grog. They seem all to be part of a family living in the bar. I order a Druk, a soothing lager type of beer made from pure Himalayan spring-water, and something of the country's flagship alcohol.

From there on it is downhill. To clarify, I mean that I walk down towards the weekend market by the river running through town, which is known to be a haven of vice. Not that shoppers notice the supposed drug and flesh trade (I certainly don't) as it is one of the tidiest markets in South Asia. Nevertheless, it appears to be a good idea to sample momos at a shady bar in a dilapidated corner building, which has a menu hanging on the outside wall, suggesting the by far cheapest rates in town. It's the first bar that has a name, so as I'm downgrading to the city's supposed underworld haunts, it feels as if I'm upgrading as I step into Rignam Bar.

For the third time in a row, here's yet another of the finest dives of the world. I could easily write a novel about it. There's a rack of intriguing bottles on a wall behind the glass counter, a variety of interesting snacks, and some four tables. At one, a girl of about ten sits and chops green chillies. She turns out to be the bartender—I kid you not—and she calls out to her daddy who is a bald wrestler-type operating the kitchen, to steam me a plate of momos. She then brings me a sample of the strongest beer of the country, brewed by Kinjore Breweries that specialise on extra-strong beers. Their Thunder 15,000 has a slogan claiming 'Happiness for All' and is way ahead of all the others in punch. Their momos are extra-salty and hyper-chillified, as if made to keep one thirsty for more. So, I have another Thunder 15,000 to verify that the quality is consistent.

Other bar nibbles I encounter in town, as I go on scientifically exploring the scene, include fried yak skin chips and what looks like a sausage but turns out to be black pudding. It is so spicy that it's inedible. When I try to slip my plate to a stray dog that drifts in, pretending to be a customer, the stern lady who runs the bar admonishes me that I must not share the food with non-paying quadrupeds. She pours a mug of water on the dog that until then has been leisurely gobbling leftovers under the tables and I'm forced to eat up the unpalatable pudding alone—and it doesn't help that the only accompaniment is volcano-hot chilli sauce. More drink is needed to wash it down and luckily the bars in Bhutan are well stocked not only with ales and stouts, but grainy lagers brewed from rice and sweet wines fermented from peaches.

An interesting story I hear about the many practical uses of alcohol in Bhutan—though I'm not sure how factual it is—goes that until 1970 when the country got its own currency, taxes were collected in kind. It could be farm produce such as dried meat or rice wine, the latter being a smoky, potent cousin of sake distilled from various types of fermented grains. Because meat, as one might expect, got infested with maggots when stored for too long in the treasury, booze was preferable. This caused another problem, as taxmen were frequently found dead drunk in the royal vault. The unavoidable decision was that Bhutan must begin using money and hence the local currency Ngultrum was born, and still today, 10 Ngultrum (which equals Rs 10 or $0.13) buys me a cup of booze in dive bars.

According to drinking etiquette, it might be good to know that whenever you've had enough of whatever you've had, rotate your hand before your mouth clockwise murmuring, '*me zhu, me zhu*' and they'll put you either in a taxi or in an ambulance depending on your physical condition. If you are sober enough to walk out on your own legs, say '*kardrinchhey*' and pay your bill. If you find that you must spell out the Bhutanese word letter by letter, or cannot find your legs anywhere nearby, then revert to the previous alternative and ask for the nearest hospital by saying, '*Menkhang ga tey in na*?' And all will end well.

The End?

Acknowledgements

No book is just a book, to paraphrase an old saying, and especially in the case of a travel memoir like this, lots of people and places obviously contributed to it finding its shape. First of all, I would like to extend my heartfelt thanks to all—whether named or nameless—chefs, barkeepers and hoteliers who enriched my travels beyond the imaginable.

So many really nice real humans populated this book's path but probably more than by anybody else, it has been virtually co-authored by my constant companion, fellow foodie and wonderful wife Anjum Hasan, who taught me how to cook and eat like an Indian, to like chilly chicken, chilly pakoras, chilly pancakes, chilly pickles, chilly chillies...until I got completely chilled out. Spice is nice! Adds love to life and life to love.

The phenomenal foodie Mita Kapur and her hospitable husband Rahul frequently crossed my path during the 2010s when I wrote this book, so it owes a lot to their seemingly limitless *joie de vivre*—you'd not be reading this without the two of them and the beers Rahul would hand me whenever Mita, who eventually became my literary agent, graciously looked the other way.

Moreover, I thank all the collegial writers I've encountered over my travels in India—novelists, poets and others too numerous to mention but who all shared their precious time—

as well as fellow booklovers, who offered ideas and suggestions, often over too many beers.

And last but not least, it must be acknowledged that Indian culinary culture is great—no, let me rephrase that: overwhelming—and so to make it possible to fit so much of it into this book I sincerely thank, for their feedback and suggestions on various things to add or cut or simply understand better (in alphabetical order) Aditi De, Aditi Sengupta, Amit Dixit, Amitav Ghosh, Amrita Dutta, Anders Mathlein, Anders Paulrud, Ann Ighe, Avtar Singh, Basav Biradar, Dave Besseling, Ishita Chatterji, James Brunner, Jan Ekholm, Johan Lindskog, Johan Mikaelsson, Jonas Eklöf, Kareena Gianani, Lakshmi Sankaran, Michael Dwyer, Mukund Padmanabhan, Nandini Nair, Neha Dara, Nina Solomin, Paul Fernandes, Per Styregård, Pradeep Sebastian, Ramachandra Guha, Renuka Chatterjee, Robin Walsh, Sanjukta Sharma, Shreevatsa Nevatia, Soity Banerjee, Stellan 'the Kitchen Obelisk' Wahlström, Vaishna Roy, Veena Venugopal and Vineetha Mokkil. Anything great that I've written in this book is thanks to them, while all that appears flawed is obviously my own errata, not theirs, because I am not as intelligent as they are.

As I'm still trying to digest India, let this book—which may be a big leap for a gluttonous bibliophile like me but hopefully less painful than a sprained foot (or upset tummy) for its readers—be a first tiny step towards my optimal and ultimate karmic enlightenment.

Notes

1 Note to readers: In this book the word hotel doesn't necessarily imply a place where one sleeps, but rather where one can eat or buy (or 'parcel') food that isn't home-cooked. The places where one gets rooms are usually called lodges, guesthouses or boarding houses—at least in my budget range. In recent times, some of these have rebranded themselves as hotels to be more in tune with globalisation, but as one travels across India one still comes across hotels where, if you ask for a room rather than food, they'll think you illiterate. So for example, Kamat Hotels, which is a restaurant chain dating back to the 1950s, does not usually let you stay overnight unless it is explicitly stated that rooming facility is available.

2 This was not the first time that Bengaluru was lampooned in an international bestseller. One of the first occasions that comes to mind is 'the military station of Bundlegunge, in the Madras division of our Indian empire' in *Vanity Fair* (1848) by the Kolkata-born William Thackeray, where we encounter, amongst others, a caricature of a British colonel: 'Time has dealt kindly with that stout officer, as it does ordinarily with men who have good stomachs and good tempers and are not perplexed over much by fatigue of the brain. The Colonel plays a good knife and fork at tiffin and resumes those weapons with great success at dinner. He smokes his hookah after both meals and puffs as quietly while his wife scolds him as he did under the fire of the French at Waterloo.'

3 IPA incidentally translates as Indian Pale Ale and the story goes that it was brewed stronger so that it would survive the transportation from England to India. In modern England, IPA generally denotes a very strong beer but earlier IPA was medium-strong; it has been brewed in England for more than 200 years and hence predates Indian beer manufacturing.

4 The bar bill was eventually written off as 'irrecoverable' in 1899. Interestingly, Churchill later confessed in his memoir, *My Early Life*, about his youthful habits when he was living in Bengaluru, that he 'liked wine, both red and white, and especially champagne; and on very special occasions I could even drink a small glass of brandy.' After his hasty departure, when Churchill swapped his army career for a journalistic one (to cover some war or the other), he didn't carry more luggage than he could lift onto the train and hence Churchill's library with his scribbled opinions on the margins of the pages ended up in Bengaluru's second-hand bookshops (where lucky collectors may come across them occasionally even today).

5 The dubious but oft-repeated quote from Pliny's encyclopaedic work reads: 'This ant excavates gold from holes, in a country in the north of India, the inhabitants of which are known as the Dardæ. It has the colour of a cat, and is in size as large as an Egyptian wolf. This gold, which it extracts in the winter, is taken by the Indians during the heats of summer, while the ants are compelled, by the excessive warmth, to hide themselves in their holes. Still, however, on being aroused by catching the scent of the Indians, they sally forth, and frequently tear them to pieces, though provided with the swiftest camels for the purpose of flight; so great is their fleetness, combined with their ferocity and their passion for gold!' This would suggest that Pliny did not at all refer to Kolar, which is situated in the deep south and where camels are rare, but that rather these mines (if at all they existed) must have been in the north in the regions between erstwhile Hindustan and the Tibetan plateau. Scholars have suggested that this references the Punjabi river Sutlej's banks.

6 Food conundrums run like red threads through Narayan's writings and in his autobiography he describes the hatred that the Lutheran Mission School teachers displayed against Hindu students: 'Among the non-Christians in our class I was the only Brahmin boy, and received special attention; the whole class would turn in my direction when the teacher said that Brahmins claiming to be vegetarians ate fish and meat in secret, in a sneaky way, and were responsible for the soaring price of those commodities.' It was not just vegetarianism that bothered, for even when a Malgudian goes to north India in a rare geospatial shift, as in *Waiting for the Mahatma*, he finds himself starved: 'He yearned for coffee, his favourite, like a true South Indian, but coffee could not be had here.' When he is longing for something to eat, he is told: 'You can't expect all our South Indian stuff,' and then instructed matter-of-factly that he would have to learn to eat chappati, and vegetable and curd and fruit, and 'not ask for rice or sambar.' As he works his way through the meals, he 'longed for the taste of the pungent South Indian food and its sauces and vegetables, but he suppressed the thought.' This might be an echo of Narayan's troubles to find homely food abroad where most Indian restaurants serve Punjabi food.

7 The vada is 100 per cent indigenous and was mentioned in sutras in the centuries BCE. Known to foreign tourists as curried donuts, 'vadē' are scientifically defined by food scholar Achaya as a 'disc with a hole in the centre, soft and elastic inside and crispy brown on the outside' and is, obviously, my top candidate for the UNESCO world heritage list. The oldest known Indian snack, the vada is also the likely ancestor of that quintessentially Newyorkish bagel. It must have travelled from India to the eastern Mediterranean along with the people previously labelled as gypsies who left Rajasthan around 1,000 years ago to adopt Europe's roads as their home. Interestingly, a traditional breakfast dish of theirs is the iconic Turkish *simit* consisting of savoury-crispy bread rings sprinkled with sesame seeds and estimated

to have become popular 500 years ago. And as its Latin name indicates, *Sesamum indicum* had its origins in India. Other proto-bagels can be found in Kashmir, where the 'desi donut' called czochworu (also topped with sesame seeds) is eaten. Even the westernmost provinces of China have varieties of vada– suggesting that vadai are as global as they are round, so there is nothing unusual about them being the origin of bagels. In medieval Italy, those Mediterranean bread rings became a Jewish staple that subsequently through migration turned into a popular street-food in Germany, which is where it eventually came to be known as bagel (from *bent* in German). It travelled to America in the nineteenth century and then even beyond earth on space missions—as comfort food for Jewish astronauts, bagels have been approved as suitable space grub.

8 In *The Man-Eater of Malgudi*, a brass food container found in a dead man's room is examined despite the fact that the man obviously had his head smashed with a blunt instrument and his tiffin box was unopened—and once opened the 'smell of stale food hit the ceiling—a strong-smelling, overspiced chicken pulav, brown and unattractive and stuffed up to the lid.' In *Waiting for the Mahatma* a character gets pukey at the sheer mention of chicken crying out, 'Chicken! Chicken! Oh! I can't stand the thought of it!'

9 In the Malnad area of Karnataka the name 'doddamane' was traditionally a generic term for stately bungalows or small palaces owned by a particular district's biggest landlord; they often doubled as administrative centres where village meetings were held.

10 The fact that Malgudi has no palace is the main difference between the fictional city and R.K. Narayan's hometown. Another intriguing detail regarding the books, now that we are analysing their veracity, is that they form a loose autobiographical arch should one read them with that in mind: *Swami and Friends* is on Narayan's childhood, *The Bachelor of Arts* is about his student years up to his marriage, *The English Teacher* deals with his early

working life and the premature death of his wife (he himself tells us so in his autobiography) while in other novels, he uses his experience of writing for cinema, his attempts at launching a periodical and so on.

11 Apparently, the fictional Raju's real name was Keshav. A trivia footnote for the cultural tourist: the Metropole has hosted every literary celebrity that has set foot in Mysuru, from Somerset Maugham…to myself. Author of *The Sheltering Sky*, Paul Bowles, noted that 'in places like the bar of the Hotel Metropole at Mysore, or at the North Coorg Club of Mercara, one may still come across vestiges of the old colonial life'. This hotel is also where cult director Alejandro Jodorowsky stayed during the shooting of his film *Tusk*, a psychedelic feminist version of *The Jungle Book*, in nearby jungles. It was originally the maharaja's guesthouse for foreign visitors while the century-old heritage hotel Lalitha Mahal—allegedly modelled on Saint Paul's Cathedral in London—was the guest accommodation for viceroys, royalty and state guests.

12 Incidentally, the more urban locations of the TV series *Malgudi Days* seem to be recognisable as places in Mysuru. In one episode I spot, for example, what is now the Green Hotel (part of Premier Studios from 1954 to 1989). The regal century-old building has a Malgudi café, staffed by Dalit women, and there I find myself drinking the nicest *café au lait* in town. I suspect that Narayan, who was fussy about coffee and constantly chasing the perfect blend, may have enjoyed a sip of it too.

13 In case you wonder, like I did, what all this GI-tagging is about, it's a Geographical Indication that suggests that something belongs somewhere—for example whiskey must be Scotch where it is distilled laboriously (never mind that India consumes more Scotch than Scotland has produced since whiskey was invented in 1494). It seems parmesan is only real if the cheese is from the vicinity of Parma in Italy (even if high-quality parmesan is produced near Puducherry in Tamil Nadu). And champagne

that is not made in France is nothing but bubbly white wine. The decision is finalised by the World Trade Organization in Switzerland which, considering how many GI-tagged products originate in Mysuru, perhaps ought to shift its headquarters here.

14 If any reader is desperate to sample a dosa similar to what the author would have eaten, try Dasaprakash Paradise's 'dose dhamaka' platter—across the road from the R.K. Narayan Museum—where he used to go. Furthermore, in his autobiography, he notes regarding his dosa habit that during morning walks down Vani Vilas Road, he 'was trapped by the frying smell emanating from a little restaurant tucked away in a lane off the main road, where I ate a *dosai*, washed it down with coffee, and, lighting a cigarette, resumed my walk. I was careful with money, never spending more than a rupee a day. All morning I wandered. At every turn I found a character fit to go into a story.' It is hard to pinpoint this 'little restaurant', but in the same area today, between Agrahara Circle and the palace, one finds a Brahmins Dosa Point and a 'branch' of the branch-less Mylari Hotel. Take your pick.

15 Interestingly, potato, without which any dosa would be rather slim, is not native to the country, but was introduced by Englishmen and officially first enjoyed at a gala dinner in colonial Calcutta. Ditto tomatoes and chillies and capsicums that nowadays form the basis of so many Indian dishes, not to mention cashew nuts, corn and fruits ranging from papaya to pineapples. Whether curried like the bhaji that is served with puris, sautéed with cumin into a main course such as aloo jeera, or simply tandooried, or stuffed into parathas, samosas and dosas, potatoes have become more than a cornerstone of Indian cuisines, especially in Bengal where the per capita consumption—in the form of poshto and shukto or added to biryanis—is second only to that of Ireland.

16 For those unaware, idlis are not merely dull 'rice cakes' as often referred to scornfully in English. In the south, the disk-shaped delicacy holds a status akin to the tandoori chicken in the north.

Even if it is suspected by scholars to be an Indonesian or Arabian import, according to Achaya, idlis were first mentioned in the oldest literary work in Kannada, *Vaddaradhane*, in about 930 CE; here, a monk begging for alms receives an idli from a kind lady. So whether idlis came from the East or the West, the ingenious fermented low-calorie high-nutrition rice roundels, if we may call them so, have been adorning plates hereabouts for more than a 1,000 years.

17 In his travelogue *The Gentleman in the Parlour: A Record of a Journey from Rangoon to Haiphong*, Maugham describes seeing his Indian chef 'nimbly shin up a tree in the compound and shake down the fruit he needed for some sauce. Like many another artist his personality was more interesting than his work; his cooking was neither good nor varied, one day he gave me trifle for my dinner and the next cabinet pudding; they are the staple sweets of the East,' Maugham infers before adding that his 'own knowledge of these matters is small, but I made so bold as to teach my Telegu [*sic*] how to make a corned beef hash. I trusted that after he left me he would pass on the precious recipe to other cooks and that eventually one more dish would be added to the scanty repertory of Anglo-Eastern cuisine.'

18 I obviously tried cooking rum-rasam at home by mixing Old Monk with takeaway thali leftovers, but it tasted like hand-sanitiser boiled with those pink things they put in urinals. French fusion is perhaps an acquired taste?

19 Amazingly, the low-profile is one of India's greatest culinary exports popular from China to Europe. In Portugal *canja de galinha* is a traditional chicken soup thickened with rice gruel. In Hong Kong, restaurants such as Trusty Congee King even get listed in Michelin-guides for their slow-stewed seafood-flavoured gourmet permutations of kanji.

20 I feel slightly bad about my Swedish fellow countrymen once having tried to colonise India. However, a small consolation is that it was an utter failure and lasted only for a month—

September 1733 to be precise. A Swedish ship disembarked some twenty sailors and despite being badly afflicted by scabies and scurvy they managed to build a shop at the place which became known as Parangipettai ('foreign market'). Between them, they had fifteen firearms and were unable to protect themselves when the French attacked with the assistance of British troops a few weeks later. Subsequently, Porto Novo also harboured Dutch traders. The adjacent Danish settlement at Tranquebar lasted longer—from the 1620s, the Danes clung on for centuries until they sold their fort in 1845.

21 The son of a pork butcher, Grimod de la Reynière published the *Almanacs des gourmands* from 1803 onwards, a calendar for gluttons who loved eating excessively, ranking restaurants and other food outlets in post-revolution Paris where the former private chefs of executed noblemen were in the process of giving birth to the French food scene; hence he has been labelled the first restaurant reviewer in culinary history.

22 The dum-pukht, known as dumb-poked in English or, in the language of Persia, *dampukht* (meaning 'slow-baked') became a staple in 1784 when a Nawab in Lucknow noticed that day or night his labourers ate tastier food than he himself. He sent his cooks to learn from the construction workers' wives, who buried a potful of rice and meat under coals for hours at end, thus uplifting their practical dum-pukht to an elaborate dish fit for kings by using the finest basmati rice, mutton and the most aromatic spices such as cardamom, cinnamon, mace and saffron. Unless that's an apocryphal story (since food critics believe the dum-pukht legend originated at a Delhi restaurant in 1998), it triggered a biryani revolution in India that spread to the eastern and southern regions too—reflecting local preferences such as the addition of potatoes in Kolkata or sour tomatoes in Chennai.

23 Even if vada-pav is sold at stalls in my hometown Bengaluru, they're not at all the same as what Mehta describes: 'The crispy batter, the mouthful of sweet-soft pav tempering the heat of

the chutney, the spices of the vada mixture—dark with garam masala and studded with whole cloves of garlic that look like cashews—get masticated into a good mouthful, a good mouthfeel.' However, people aren't as purist as I make them sound, because there's plenty of innovation in the field, to the extent that there nowadays are weird permutations like Schezwan vada-pav that may have been created to counter the foreign hand's attempt at cornering the vada-pav market with their McAloo Tikki®™ burgers.

24 The colour of raspberry soda is like an angry traffic light, but it gives a heritage high. These raspberry pops date way back to when Ardheshir & Sons soda factory was founded in 1884 (making it two years senior to Coca-Cola of the US) and their Pune plant still produces purely 'desi' sodas.

25 Interestingly, similar cooking methods are practised by the Romani communities in Europe among whom pigs and sheep roasted in hay-lined pits is a festive dish. As discussed in a previous footnote, they are believed to have reached Europe from Rajasthan some thousand years ago and were earlier referred to as gypsies, who may well have brought along this technique as a memory of an otherwise forgotten home.

26 Actually, in genuine Continental culinary art, fish is hardly ever topped with cheese nowadays (even though the ancient Romans may have done so), unlike in this wonderful Indian version of 'Conti'. But it tastes really good. Other dishes that Indian chefs have adopted creatively from Europeans include cutlets and chops that in their 'desified' versions are more often vegetarian than not, as is the chutney sandwich, whereas European sandwiches generally contain a slice of meat. In the other direction, Indian cookery has improved European eating habits in fundamental ways for example by showing how to make vegetarian food tastier in the form of veg curries. As we saw in Chapter V, Mahatma Gandhi was pleased to encounter theoretical vegetarianism among the 'isms' of the nineteeth-

century England when he moved there in 1888, but despite that it wasn't an evolved gastronomic art and Indian restaurants were rare (it is another matter that London, last I went, had six named after Gandhi). Regarding Indian influences, in certain cases such as with the vegetarian khichdi, the English turned it into non-vegetarian kedgeree in the 1790s and theirs is rather like a fish biryani–which was their interpretation of the Mughal way of eating khichdi. South Indian rasam became Mulligatawny Soup in its English avatar (believed to be a mispronunciation of the Tamil word *milagu-tannir,* 'black pepper water'), re-engineered with the addition of chicken, that on fancier menu cards was renamed as *potage de Madras*. The earliest mention of the soup is from 1784 when a Britisher imprisoned by Tipu Sultan lamented being fed more kanji and rasam than he could stomach: 'In vain our hard fate we repine, In vain our fortunes we rail; On Mullighy-tawny we dine, On Conjee, in Bangalore jail.' Although the colonials took to rasam, it was popular to make fun of—such as in this poem called 'The Police-Wallah's Little Dinner': 'First we had Mulligatawny soup,/ Which made us all perspire,/ For the cook, that obstinate nincompoop,/ Had flavoured it hot as fire.' Anglo-Indian fusion had already spread across the empire by then and entered the culinary vocabulary, although curry was spelled *currey* as in *Receipt To Make a Currey the Indian Way* by Hannah Glasse (1758). It is sometimes mentioned that the 1390s' book, *The Forme of Cury* by an English royal cook, is the first curry cookbook in English, but as it was written well before colonial days, it would seem unlikely—rather it is referring to health food, how the right diet can 'cure'. That stereotypical catchphrase for the diversity of Indian gravy items was first referenced in English in 1681, but even seventy years earlier Edward Terry had documented his foodie adventures in India that included lovely non-veg without specifying whether they were curries or not. The spicy relish *piccalilli*, known since the 1750s, is essentially a British version of Indian pickle, Worcestershire sauce was born out of a hilariously failed attempt to recreate a Bengali curry in Worcester, near Birmingham, at a time when restaurants in London were adding curries to their menus in the mid-1700s. Their insatiable craving for curried food became increasingly common when Englishmen retired from colonial service. A first full-fledged Indian-owned restaurant serving Mughal curries, the pioneering Hindostanee Coffee House opened, it is said by a gentleman from Patna, in about 1809 in London replete with bamboo recliners and hookahs. The compound 'curry powder' was coined the next year to denote 'a condiment consisting of several pungent ground spices' and perhaps unsurprisingly, by 1845, the curious Anglo-Indo-Italic dish 'curried macaroni' rewrote the pages of food history as India became an increasingly important colony—even Queen Victoria hired two fulltime Indian cooks to prepare curry *every* day for her luncheons. In spite of the fact that English food has traditionally been considered to be bland and dull, they did in their own bumbling way popularise Indian gastronomy. Perhaps it is because of this that culinary experts suggest western origins for various Indian gravies such as 'ishtoo'; the Mughal's classic slow-stewed meat with ghee and onions. But it's difficult to determine whether stew is a British version of curry or ishtoo is an Indian modified stew; anybody who wishes to pass judgement on the matter can pay a visit to the last Mughal's chef's descendants at Karim's in Delhi, and order their signature ishtoo, known as aloo gosht. Current curry houses have their roots in the Punjabi dhabas, whose owners migrated with the exodus that followed upon Indian independence. These post-Partition migrants set up affordable canteens across England, which is how the Hindi word tikka found its way into English dictionaries (in 1955) as an 'Indian dish of marinated meat cooked on a skewer'. Thus, what may have initially been perceived as *ethnic* food gained the status of a national dish once it was married with that legendary canned tomato soup, giving birth to Chicken Tikka Masala. Another similarly Anglicised dish which appears to be a product of a second wave of South Asian UK-bound migration following Bangladeshi independence, is Balti, that's actually a traditional Lahori chicken dish, woked in a *karahi* pan nicknamed 'balti' in which it is also served. It may be noted that during this process of Anglicising subcontinental foods, restaurant names too changed from stereotypical nomenclature such as Maharaja to things like Balti Brassiere that, in a purely geographical sense, disconnect their menu from its origins. Indeed, distinctly Indo-British dishes such as 'Birmingham Balti' (first attested in 1977) are considered part of British heritage worthy of GI-tagging.

27 To be precise, the fictional Chandrapore is based on Bankipur, the colonial parts of Patna. A guidebook from the time notes that the 'modern city contains nothing of much interest to the traveller, except a building called the Gola, which was built for a granary in 1783, but has never been used for that purpose,' but inside of which 'there is a most wonderful echo, the best place to hear which is in the middle of the building. As a whispering gallery there is perhaps no such building in the world. The faintest whisper at one end is heard most distinctly at the other.' This may well have inspired the sound phenomena that spooked the memsahib at Barabar.

28 The only time I went to Barabar (in 1992) I too found them unnerving—a fat man tried to kidnap me and another man had his throat slit—so understandably I haven't gone back. In the decades since, I have decoded Forster's novel as the story of...ah, well, I'll write about it in due time, but it is basically about cultural misinterpretation when somebody clueless goes where they misunderstand everything without realising that they haven't understood anything. It is a common phenomenon among tourists—sometimes causing the ecstasy that tourists feel in India, at other times the disappointment they come away with—but this delusional aspect of tourism has not yet been named by psychiatrists. But maybe *A Passage to India* is a book for India rather than about India, 'probably the best novel ever

written about the country by an Englishman,' to quote literature professor Harish Trivedi, 'an enduring literary monument of the 200 years of British rule in India. It preserves for us human feelings and attitudes from that fraught period as only literature can.'

29 'Where can a man get food? Calcutta is not rich in respect of dainty accommodation. You can stay your stomach at Peliti's or Bonsard's,' Kipling advises travellers, 'but in Lal Bazaar, not far from "The Sailors' Coffeerooms," a board gives bold advertisement that "officers and seamen can find good quarters." In evidence a row of neat officers and seamen are sitting on a bench by the "hotel" door smoking,' he says and describes the boozy '*tâble d'hôte*. The fare is substantial and the regulation "peg"—every house has its own depth of peg if you will refrain from stopping Ganymede—something to wonder at. Three fingers and a trifle over seems to be the use of the officers and seamen who are talking so quietly in the doorway.'

30 In China, where tea may also be said to be (as in India) the national drink, it is drunk without milk or sweeteners, very light—except in former colony Hong Kong where it is had the English way. The Chinese swill cup after cup and the tea houses tend to provide unlimited refills, whereas in India it is common to share the cup 'by-two' (in Bengaluru parlance) or 'cutting-chai' (in Mumbai) so for obvious reasons there's no free refill policy. The Chinese tea habit dates much further back, presumably to the T'ang dynasty, at which time it became known as *cha* which is the origin of the word chai.

31 So-called 'Sino-Indian' cuisines can be broadly divided into four main styles, of which the original is the Bengali from Tangra. The other three consist of the Mumbai-style notable for Chinese bhelpuri, chicken lollipops and anything called manchurian, and the North Indian Chinjabi, a Punjabified version with its chili potatoes, chilly paneer skewers, Schezwan naans and of course tandoori momos, and last but not least the even more chillifed

Andhranese with its chilly chicken that is extremely popular in south India alongside the increasingly common Schezwan dosa. There are many other localised variations such as the Gujarati noodle-topped pizzas and dhokla manchurian while Instagrammers experiment with dishes such as 'chocolate manchurian'. As to how domesticated it has become, it's instructive to consider that 37 per cent of restaurants in India have 'Chinese' items on the menu while in a major city like Mumbai the figure jumps up to 53 per cent.

32 Regarding the potentially contentious issue of eating certain non-veg items deemed to be pets, the Chinese who are famous for their dog dishes, domesticated canines tens of thousands of years ago. But when I was living in China a decade ago, I only heard rumours of their so-called 'chow dogs' that were especially fattened for culinary use (tasted like chicken, I was told), never able to find these at restaurants. More recently, while travelling in Vietnam and Cambodia, I learnt that the once popular dog meat had virtually vanished from menus due to protest from European animal right's groups (which hurts tourism) and could only be had in rural backwoods villages or was sold discreetly in the form of dog salami in the big cities where I managed to score a portion—it is a rather gamey meat, by the way, although others compare it to chicken or mutton. Maybe they ate different dogs. It is true that my Viking ancestors also enjoyed canine barbecue before getting Christianised and like them I try my best to shrug off any Biblical dictates that claim hounds to be taboo, as the actual wording (*Leviticus 11:27*) goes that 'four-footed animals that walk on their paws are unclean; whoever touches their carcasses will be unclean until evening'. This suggests to me that dogs may be enjoyed for dinner after sunset. It is a little known fact that the explorer James Cook found roast puppy a delicious festive food. These Polynesian *kuri*-dogs resembling foxes with long bodies and short legs, were according to Cook one of the tastiest dishes 'next to an English lamb' (as retold by Anne Salmond in

The Trial of the Cannibal Dog: Captain Cook in the South Seas) served on Tahiti in 1769, so he got a doggy bag to bring along (or at least live dogs that provided fresh meat at sea) on his onward journeys, that ended a decade later in 1779, when Hawaiians cooked Cook. Previously, he had already lost crew members to cannibals who used to roast their feet, hands, heads, hearts and lungs. So the famous dog-meat market at Dimapur, the capital of the Nagas, suggests itself as a place all semi-professional foodies ought to sample at least once in their lifetimes. I'll go there in my next book if readers like this book. If not, then not.